NetWare® Power Tools® for Windows™

Charles G. Rose

BANTAM BOOKS

NEW YORK • TORONTO • LONDON • SYDNEY • AUCKLAND

NetWare® Power Tools® for Windows™
A Bantam Book / June 1993

ISBN 0-553-37039-1

Published simultaneously in the United States and Canada

Bantam Books are published by Bantam Books, a division of Bantam Doubleday Dell Publishing
Group, Inc. Its trademark, consisting of the words "Bantam Books" and the portrayal of a rooster,
is Registered in U.S. Patent and Trademark Office and in other countries. Marca Registrada,
Bantam Books, Inc., 1540 Broadway, New York, New York 10036.

PRINTED IN THE UNITED STATES OF AMERICA

0 9 8 7 6 5 4 3 2 1

Contents

To Lauren

ACKNOWLEDGMENTS

This book would not have been possible without the help of a number of people who deserve both recognition and my sincerest thanks.

First, I would like to thank Bill LeBlond, author of *Windows 3.1 Power Tools,* for an exceptional editing job. Bill consistently went above and beyond the call of duty, providing corrections, suggestions, and comments. His efforts are appreciated and have helped shape the book into what it is. Thanks also to Bill for providing Oriel, which you'll find on the enclosed diskette. Bill's company, the LeBlond Group, developed Oriel.

Brett Warthen, from Infinite Technologies, is due a great deal of applause for his job as technical editor. Brett's comprehensive NetWare/Windows experience was apparent from the start, and his generous comments about the book were an aid to every chapter. Thanks also to Brett for compiling Appendix B (Netware/Windows Troubleshooting Tips) and Appendix C (PC Memory Architecture Overview), and for providing copies of ExpressIt! for Windows and IQueue!, which are on the disk included with this book.

Many thanks go to Claudette Moore, an exceptional literary agent, for helping me land this project in the first place. Congratulations to Claudette and her husband on the birth of their son, John Paul.

I would also like to thank the people at Bantam, especially Kenzi Sugihara, who is in charge of the electronic publishing group; Nancy Sugihara, who did the internal design of the book; and Ron Petrusha, who led this project. I appreciate Ron's vision, patience, and thoughtful leadership throughout the project. Congratulations also to Ron, who was promoted while the book was being written.

Also many thanks to those who put in many long hours to get this manuscript through its final stages, such as Michelle Neil, Sarah Weaver, Bridget Leahy, and Mark Heffernan. I appreciate all of your hard work.

In addition, I send a thank-you to Amy King for designing one of the most stunning covers I've ever seen.

I appreciate the people at Novell, such as Starla Barrier, Ron Thomas, Ken Lowrie, Cheryl Seeman, Kristin Burkland, and Willie Tejada, who were always helpful in getting me the information and resources I needed, and those at Microsoft and Borland who readily answered my questions.

The shareware authors who let us include their software in the book deserve a special thank-you. Hopefully, the book can serve to further this growing method of software distribution. In particular, I would like to acknowledge the people at Automated Design Systems for letting us include their software in the book, with special thanks to Ruth Rainey for her help in facilitating the process.

I am also grateful to the following companies for providing copies of their software for use while writing the book: Microsoft Corporation, Novell Inc., Borland International, Aldus, Word Perfect Corporation, and Delrina Technology.

I would also like to thank my cats, Bud and Muse, for their companionship and consultation on this project; usually one or the other was in my lap while the book was being written. Thanks to Bud for filling me in on Windows 3.1 topics like OLE and DDE and thanks to Muse for his continued NetWare guidance.

Finally, I would like to thank my wife, Lauren. Without her constant support and encouragement, the project would not have been possible, or fun. I appreciate her patience, companionship, humor, and love, but most of all, I appreciate her being my best friend.

PREFACE

On the road ahead, Windows and NetWare can be seen for miles. In every trade journal, on every store shelf, on every desktop, Microsoft Windows is the most popular graphic user interface there is—and it's here to stay. No matter how much IBM and Microsoft bicker, the fact is that Windows will be around for a long time, whether it's under the Microsoft "New Technology" or under IBM's new OS/2.

Novell's NetWare was written in 1983 by several Brigham Young University graduates and has since become the world's most popular network operating system, boasting a user base of over five million. In fact, LAN technology is considered the fastest-growing segment of the computer industry.

The fusion of these two technologies provides the computing industry with a powerful combination, which so far has been met with excitement, fanfare, confusion, and frustration. Frustration results because Microsoft seems unwilling to make it easy for people to use a competitor's operating system. Now, Microsoft doesn't prevent one from using Windows on NetWare, but they don't go out of their way to explain how to do it either. The fact is, both NetWare and Windows are on millions of desktops, but in many cases, they're not on speaking terms. The industry is literally crying out for information on how to get the two products to work together successfully. Trade journals reported that at a recent conference, the most popular topic by far was one addressing Windows' problems running on networks—specifically, NetWare.

No matter how large these two giants are, if you don't know how to make their products work together, you may begin looking for other solutions. Therefore the time is right to help remove the barriers and make these two roads unite into one.

This book provides the tools you need to understand the interaction of NetWare and Windows and to successfully integrate them on the network. Furthermore, you will learn how to set up applications to run smoothly under Windows on the network and how to configure and troubleshoot the NetWare/Windows installation. You'll find the two disks included with this book brimming with NetWare/Windows software, not just written for NetWare or for Windows; this software was written specifically to run under Windows **and** to take advantage of the resources of NetWare. Finally, you'll learn how to write NetWare-aware applications that run under Windows.

Audience

The audience for the book covers a broad spectrum, including anyone either contemplating or currently mixing Windows with NetWare. This includes:

- The network supervisor who needs to install Windows on the LAN and get it working within the current environment.

- The LAN administrator who needs to install networked applications in Windows.

- The consultant whose client has a LAN, wants to add Windows, and needs advice on how to smooth the transition.

- The developer who's interested in the market for Windows and wants to find out what's involved in integrating Windows and NetWare applications.

- The MIS staff member who wants to write a Windows utility to find all of the users on the LAN rather than having to drop to DOS every time.

- The analyst who wants to know what's involved in making the two products work successfully together, or wonders why Word Perfect isn't working right under Windows on the LAN.

- The power user who is continually looking for utilities for the Windows desktop, especially those that are network-oriented.

In all, the average user will be aware of NetWare and Windows, probably somewhat proficient in either, and interested in integrating the other.

Chapter Summary

This book has been written in a flexible format. You can read it cover-to-cover or use it like a survival guide, where you pick and choose those sections that are most relevant to your needs; other sections can be read when the fires have been put out. The focus is to provide practical, useful, productivity-oriented information in the form of direct, hands-on suggestions and valuable utilities.

The first two chapters lay a foundation for the user unfamiliar with either NetWare or Windows, and provide basic information that will be necessary for later chapters. Experienced users may browse the first two chapters as a refresher.

Chapter 1: NetWare Basics

The initial chapter provides user-level information about NetWare, including discussions of NetWare's history, local area network (LAN) concepts, network topology, servers and workstations, hardware and software elements, NetWare 2.x and 3.x, drive mappings, search paths, file sharing, security, trustee assignments, printing, and a thorough explanation of NetWare command-line and menu-based utilities.

Chapter 2: Windows Basics

This chapter provides introductory information about Windows, including Windows history, elements of the Windows environment, memory management, device independence, multitasking, the Windows utilities, Protected mode, and so on.

Chapters 3 through 9 break out the hoses for the real fire-fighting, beginning with installing Windows on NetWare. Next, the reader is led through the general aspects involved in setting up applications, followed by a software package-specific discussion.

Once things are up and running, the reader is shown ways of optimizing and tweaking performance out of Windows, a resource-intensive environment. The last section covers the inevitable troubleshooting any supervisor or LAN administrator will be faced with when supporting this combination.

Chapter 3: Network-Specific Windows Facilities

This chapter looks at the network-specific features of Windows in general as well as several applications included with Windows that allow you to access network features. These applications include Control Panel, Print Manager, File Manager, Program Manager, and the NetWare popup window in NETWARE.DRV.

Chapter 4: Planning for Windows

This chapter provides an overview of the concepts surrounding the NetWare/Windows installation as well as some "food for thought" before installing Windows on NetWare. Concepts like performance, drive mappings, rights and security, user communications, file sharing, printing, global versus private configurations, and virus security will be discussed.

Chapter 5: Setting Up Windows on NetWare

This chapter will address the issues involved in installing Windows on the LAN, including discussions of hardware setup, NetWare shell setup and configuration, and installation placement of Windows (on the local hard drive or server). This discussion will discover the Windows parameter files which may need adjustment, the basics of mapping drives and managing security, setting up NetWare printers for use under Windows, setting up diskless workstations, and configuring the appropriate Novell-specific utilities.

Chapter 6: Setting Up Applications

There are some special considerations for installing both non-Windows (DOS-based) applications as well as Windows applications on NetWare. This chapter will explore what's involved in setting up both types of applications. In addition, techniques for setting up an application that will allow it to take better advantage of the network will receive attention. For example, details will be given about how to set up directory structures for multi-user operation, and how to set up icons for documents so you can double-click on the icon to load both the document and application used to create it (as you do on the Apple Macintosh).

Chapter 7: Specific Application Setup on NetWare

This chapter will examine the installation options, configuration details, and optional parameters for several popular Windows applications like WordPerfect for Windows, Microsoft Word, Microsoft Excel, PageMaker, Ventura, and Delrina Technology's PerForm PRO. Specific setup information about certain applications—from a networked perspective—will be presented. You will see how to assign rights, map drives, and configure applications for NetWare with Windows running on it. In addition, the discussion will cover specific ways of using network resources and facilities, and ways of troubleshooting your applications once they are set up.

Chapter 8: Optimizing Windows on NetWare

This chapter begins with a definition of what performance means and a discussion of the various types of performance optimization that can be done. Also covered will be what "adequate performance" means for a given situation and user type. Specific ways you can improve the performance of Windows on the network, in DOS sessions, on the hard disk, at the printer, and in memory, will be presented.

Chapter 9: Troubleshooting Windows on NetWare

This chapter provides help for those having trouble running Windows on NetWare. It is organized into a Problem/Solution format and covers a wide variety of topics, including installation problems, printing problems, application-specific problems, serial port problems, speed problems, freezing, machine locking up, applications not being found, out-of-memory errors, Unrecoverable Application Errors, and General Protection Fault errors.

Chapters 10 and 11 cover the tools that are provided on the disks, Automated Design's Net TOOLS and a host of other NetWare/Windows software.

Chapter 10: NetWare/Windows Software

This chapter provides a full discussion of each of the applications and utilities on the NetWare Power Tools for Windows diskettes included with this book. Apart from a few brief comments, the documentation is provided by the software vendor. The following software, which is included with the disk accompanying this book, is discussed in detail:

- NetScan, a network virus scanner, by McAfee Associates.
- Network Application Installer (NAI), an automated, Windows-based network application installation utility, by Aleph Systems.
- While You Were Out, a networked Windows phone message-taking system, by Caliente International.
- WSEND, a Windows SEND utility, by Steve Goulet/ GDG Systems.
- WSUPER, a Windows utility that lets you switch NetWare supervisor equivalence on and off as needed, by Wolfgang Schreiber.

- SHOWDOTS, a Windows utility that lets you change the NetWare shell's Show Dots parameter, by Wolfgang Schreiber.

- Express-It! for Windows, a Windows-based Email system, by Infinite Technologies.

- IQueue!, a Windows-based NetWare print queue/print capture utility, by Infinite Technologies.

One disk also includes an Install program created with Oriel for Windows, a powerful batch language processor that is used to help you install the utilities on the disk.

Chapter 11: Net Tools by Automated Design Systems

Automated Design Systems was one of the first providers of Windows-based software for NetWare. Net Tools (formerly Windows Workstation) has been improved and revised for several years and is now at version 4.1. The current version provides a robust Applications Manager, a network security module, a flexible network script language, a network print manager, and a network applications metering utility. This chapter includes all of the Automated Design documentation for the software included with this book. All but the print manager and metering software are included.

Chapters 12 and 13 provide a deeper insight into Windows on NetWare for those who would venture further. Object Linking and Embedding (OLE) is discussed thoroughly, and a full discussion of Microsoft's Windows for Workgroups is provided.

Chapter 12: Object Linking and Embedding

This chapter begins with an explanation of OLE, then provides you with some exercises so that you can become comfortable with the concepts of linking and embedding. Although OLE can be easy to visualize, it can be difficult to conceptualize exactly how to do it until you've tried it a few times—that is, actually linked and embedded a few times yourself. Once you've tried it and can see how it works, you can decide how you'd like to use it.

Chapter 13: Windows for Workgroups

In late October 1992, Microsoft released Windows for Workgroups, a bold step toward integrating Windows and networking. Microsoft enhanced this release of Windows by adding several significant networking features, which will be explained in this chapter. In addition, you will be walked through the installation and configuration of Windows for Workgroups.

There also will be a detailed discussion of the networking enhancements that have been made to existing utilities, including the Windows Control Panel, Print Manager, File Manager, and Clipboard viewer which has been renamed to ClipBook Viewer. Also, Windows for Workgroups' new applications like Microsoft

Mail and Schedule+, will be discussed as well as the three new accessories: Chat, Net Watcher, and Win Meter. The icons for these new applications and accessories can be found in Program Manager's Main and Accessories group windows as shown in Figures 13.1 and 13.2.

The final chapter introduces the reader to the concept of creating NetWare/Windows applications in Visual Basic and C, and provides three complete Windows applications with source code.

Chapter 14: Programming NetWare on Windows

This chapter will explore the concepts involved in programming NetWare applications under Windows, and will talk about how you can accomplish this with or without the use of Novell's function call libraries.

Developing for NetWare under Windows is much different (and more difficult) than developing for NetWare under DOS. Therefore, we'll start by briefly showing you the basics of how to program for NetWare under DOS and progress from there to Windows. Along the way, we'll point out how NetWare programming concepts differ under the two environments.

After showing you the ropes, we'll roll up our sleeves and get down to some actual coding examples. First, we will use Visual Basic as a programming platform to show how you can write NetWare-aware applications using this platform. The application you'll create will show your privileges for the current directory. Next, you will see how to create a Windows IPX chat utility (in C) that lets several users on the LAN chat together at the same time. Finally, we'll develop a client-server database application using the Sequenced Packet Exchange (SPX) protocol. To do this, we will use the Borland C++ environment to show how you can have a Windows front-end application interface to a back-end DOS-based server on the LAN. The source and executable code for all three of the example programs discussed in this chapter are included on the NetWare Power Tools for Windows diskettes that come with this book.

The **Appendices** provide additional information that you may find useful, including installation details for the software included with the book, Windows troubleshooting tips, a discussion of PC memory architecture, and a list of resources for further information on NetWare/Windows integration.

Appendix A: Installing the NetWare Power Tools for Windows Software

You will find two diskettes included with this book. One disk contains the Net Tools software from Automated Design Systems. The other disk contains Windows applications and utilities written specifically for NetWare. You can find out how to install the software on the Net Tools disk by turning to Chapter 11. This section will explain how to install the software on the other diskette. To make installation easier, we have included a Windows scripting environment called Oriel, which is a graphics-based batch language for Windows developed by the LeBlond Group, authors of *Windows 3.1 Power Tools*.

Appendix B: Windows versus NetWare Troubleshooting Tips

This appendix provides a list of troubleshooting tips for NetWare and Windows compiled by Brett Warthen, the technical editor of this book. These tips, provided in addition to those in Chapter 9, are meant as more of a "quick reference" to help get you up and running.

Appendix C: PC Memory Architecture Overview

This appendix provides a discussion of the different types of memory in the IBM PC. There's conventional memory, upper memory, expanded memory, extended memory, and the high memory area, to name a few. Plus, there are acronyms like UMB (Upper Memory Block), EMS (Expanded Memory Specification), XMS (eXtended Memory Specification), HMA (High Memory Area), VCPI (Virtual Control Program Interface), and DPMI (DOS Protected Mode Interface), which confuse matters even further. In this appendix, Brett Warthen explains the PC Memory Architecture as well as popular memory management techniques and standards.

Appendix D: NetWare/Windows Resources

Once you've been through the book, you may want to turn to other sources for further information, such as on-line services, books, and publications. This appendix provides a list of places you can look for further information.

Appendix E: NetWare Shell History File

This appendix follows the evolution of the NetWare shell from version 3.01 to the most recent version as of this writing (3.31). Problems encountered along the way, and solutions to those problems, are highlighted. The text for this appendix was provided by Novell and is used with permission.

NetWare®
Power Tools®
for Windows™

1 NetWare Basics

In the beginning, there were mainframes. And mainframes were good. But mainframes were expensive and unwieldy. Then there were minicomputers. Finally, there were LANs (Local Area Networks) . . . and NetWare.

The first chapter of this book explains the basics of NetWare, and Chapter 2 presents the basics of Windows. Seasoned professionals, depending on their knowledge of NetWare and Windows, may skip chapter 1 or 2, both of which are provided to bring the user up to speed on the concepts to be discussed throughout the remainder of the book.

Chapter 1 provides a perspective of NetWare's place in the evolving model of network computing, and reviews the elements of the NetWare operating system, such as directories and drive mapping, security, and printing. The chapter concludes with a concentrated discussion of the specifics of the NetWare user environment, including command-line and menu-driven utilities.

In the Beginning . . .

Before plunging into the specifics of NetWare, it's important to gain a perspective on Local Area Networks in general, and the role they play in the evolution of how we work with computers.

Mainframes are built around a centralized model where all of the processing is done at the mainframe itself. "Dumb terminals" are strung from the mainframe so that users can access it. However, all of the "thinking" is generally done at the mainframe, not at the individual terminals. This also is usually the case with minicomputers, whose terminals are similarly strung from a central computer.

NetWare was built around the emerging technology of microcomputers. In fact, when NetWare was first written, the authors were unsure as to the ultimate success of CP/M or DOS. The DOS version of NetWare was written second; therefore, as you might have guessed, the CP/M version suffered a shorter life.

3

The first servers were disk-based, rather than file-based servers. They responded to requests based on head and cylinder information rather than individual file names. NetWare's architects soon realized that this approach compromised security and omitted the potential for file-management capabilities.

Later versions of NetWare incorporated a higher level approach, using file management instead. With the new scheme, security could be implemented, as well as better synchronization (file-locking), management, and performance.

Evolution of NetWare

NetWare has matured over the years since its first version was released in early 1983. Originally a disk-serving operating system that ran on proprietary hardware based on the Motorola MC68000 microprocessor, NetWare was ported to the IBM PC platform soon after it became available from IBM.

In 1985, Novell introduced Advanced NetWare 1.0 which increased the functionality of the operating system. Version 1.2, released in 1985, was the first protected-mode operating system for the Intel 80286 processor. In 1986 Novell released version 2.0 of Advanced NetWare which brought improved performance based on the Intel 286 processor and internetworking (which meant that up to four different networks could be connected to a single file server).

In 1987 Novell released System Fault Tolerant (SFT) NetWare. This new system greatly improved the reliability and network management capabilities of the NetWare operating system. Novell's new FCONSOLE utility, resource accounting, and improved security allowed network administrators to gain more control over the network and to determine when and how access to the network would be provided. Also, the value-added process (VAP) application interface provided a method for applications to run in the server and take advantage of operating system resources for the first time.

In December of 1988, Novell shipped NetWare 2.15 and NetWare for Macintosh, which added support for the Apple Macintosh to NetWare. Now Macintosh computers could be connected to NetWare servers and transparently access the resources on the network.

NetWare 386 version 3.0, a full 32-bit version of NetWare that took specific advantage of the capabilities of the Intel 80386 and 80486 microprocessors, was shipped in September of 1989. Also, significant improvements in security, performance, and flexibility were made and new protocol support and a superior distributed application environment were introduced. NetWare 386 version 3.1, shipped in June of 1990, included performance enhancements and overall improvements in system reliability, network administration, and the third-party development platform (the NetWare Loadable Module or NLM).

In 1991, Novell consolidated its 80826-based product lines (SFT, Advanced, and ELS NetWare) into one operating system: NetWare 2.2. Novell is positioning NetWare 2.2 as a "workgroup" operating system, supporting from five to 100 users per server. That same year, Novell introduced NetWare 3.11, the first network operating system to support DOS, Macintosh, OS/2, Windows, and UNIX file and print services.

Next for Novell is NetWare 4.0, a major leap forward in network technology. As of this writing, NetWare 4.0 is only in beta release, but the shipping version is scheduled for release in 1993.

Workgroup and Network Computing

Since the file server was created, the network industry has continued to expand the definition of a server. Although file services continue to play a vital role, other services such as printing, backup, and even resource directory services are becoming important. As the industry has matured, so have the terms used to describe it. You may hear many different terms used to describe NetWare: file server operating system, network operating system, workgroup connectivity, enterprise-wide connectivity, and so on. It may be helpful to define several of these terms and distinguish among them.

First, all modern versions of NetWare qualify as file server operating systems, which act as servers on a file level, as opposed to earlier implementations of NetWare and other operating systems that provided resources at the disk level. With a file server operating system, a workstation can ask for a file to be opened, deleted, and so on, whereas on a disk server operating system, the workstations ask the server to seek a particular track on the disk and read or write a certain number of sectors.

It is important to distinguish "workgroup" connectivity from "enterprise-wide" connectivity. Workgroup connectivity refers to a relatively small group of people, possibly comprising a small company, school, or group. NetWare 2.2 is considered a "workgroup" operating system because it is suitable for groups of five to 100 users. Enterprise-wide operating systems are robust enough to service an entire corporation or large school because they have the performance and flexibility to work well in larger environments. For example, NetWare 3.11 handles up to 250 users (there's a special version that will handle 1000 concurrent users) as opposed to the NetWare 2.2 limit of 100.

In either case, for the discussion in this chapter and for the remainder of the book, the text will apply equally to all current versions of NetWare 2.x and NetWare 3.x. Any differences between NetWare 2.x and NetWare 3.x will be pointed out.

Elements of the LAN

Before we can talk about specifics of NetWare, such as how to log in or print, you should have a basic understanding of the underlying elements of a local area network.

Cabling

The one element of the LAN that physically forms the "network" is the cabling between personal computers which allows them to "talk" to one another and to the file server. There are several different types of cabling and several different ways it can be arranged between computers.

The cabling types include coaxial, twisted pair (shielded and unshielded), and fiber optic. The cable type you use will depend on several factors including cost, speed, the type of network adapters you will be using, and your need for connectivity with other types of computers. For example, fiber optic cabling is the fastest cable type, but is also the most expensive.

The cabling that you use will be arranged in a certain order called the cable "topology." There are several cable topologies used for local area networks; the most popular ones are Bus, Star, and Token Ring.

The Bus topology is used for Ethernet networks and consists of a long line of cable that is terminated at both ends with resistors. Nodes are connected to the cable at certain intervals. As of today, quite a few different cabling types are available for Ethernet, including coaxial ("thin net"), unshielded twisted pair, and thicker types of cabling. Ethernet is relatively fast (generally 10 megabits per second) and moderately expensive.

The Star topology is used for Arcnet networks and consists of a central node with cables branching out directly to other nodes in a star formation. Often nodes can be replaced with hubs to form a "tree" structure. Generally coaxial cable is used for Arcnet networks. Arcnet is relatively slow and is inexpensive.

The Token Ring cabling system is the topology of choice for many companies that have mainframes and/or IBM equipment to interface to. Token Ring, an IBM-dominated topology, consists of a circle or ring of cable where nodes reside. A software "token" is passed from node to node and determines which node's "turn" it is to communicate. Token Ring can be relatively fast or slow depending on the cabling type and network adapters (4 megabits per second or 16 megabits per second) and is expensive.

Network Adapters

We discussed the different cable types and topologies above, and also mentioned the different adapter types you may purchase (Ethernet, Arcnet, and Token Ring), how they relate to cabling, and why one is chosen over another.

You will need one network adapter for each workstation and server on your network. Two or more network adapters may be placed in the server if it will be used to route packets between two different networks.

Also, bus bandwidth (as we will mention below) is a factor when choosing network adapters. The old 8-bit boards provide a common, albeit slow means of accessing the network. The 16-bit network adapters, which provide a much needed gain in performance, are commonly available now and are not much more expensive. Several companies have begun shipping 32-bit bus-mastering boards that promise great leaps in performance (one 32-bit board manufacturer claims 33 MB per second transfer rate in burst mode).

Each increase in bandwidth also means an increase in price. Keep in mind, too, that no matter how fast the interface between the adapter and the PC is, the speed will never exceed the limits of the topology. For example, many Arcnet implementations will only provide one megabit per second throughput.

Workstation Hardware and Software

In order for each personal computer to access the file server, it must have an interface card to allow it to communicate over the network cabling. There are many different types of cards with characteristics such as bus bandwidth (8-bit, 16-bit, and 32-bit), topology (Ethernet, Arcnet, Token Ring), and cabling method (coax, twisted pair, "thick Ethernet," and so on). Each of these characteristics helps determine both the speed of the card as well as the hardware environments in which it will work.

In addition to adding a network card to a personal computer, we need to add network software. This software talks to the network card, exchanging messages with the file server over the network cabling, and also communicates with DOS at the local computer. Collectively called the "shell," this local software is generally composed of two Terminate-and-Stay-Resident (TSR) files that are loaded prior to logging into the file server. They serve to mediate and interpret between DOS and the network interface hardware.

For instance, when you do a "DIR" command on the local workstation to list the contents of a network directory, the shell intercepts that command and sends a directory request through the network interface card out over the network cabling to the file server.

When the file server responds with the contents of the network directory (or the first part of the directory), the result comes back over the wire into the network card where the local shell software converts the message from the file server into a form DOS can understand. Then, DOS displays the directory to the user. The directory display looks no different to the user than a local C: drive directory listing. This "transparency" is an important goal of local area networking.

Chapter 3 discusses the need to have current versions of the NetWare shell files in order for Windows to run properly on your workstation.

File Servers

In addition to cabling and workstation hardware/software, you also need one or more file servers. Through the network software, the server provides other workstations on the network with access to network services, including the ability to run shared applications, exchange data, and share peripheral devices—for example printers and modems. In short, the server is the one entity that ties the whole network together. To perform adequately the server should be a very capable machine—that is, it should have a fast processor, lots of RAM, and a fast hard drive with a large capacity.

File servers perform a variety of functions:

• Store Files. Servers store files that are shared by network users. The network software that runs on them allows several people at once to read from or write to certain files, and helps to arbitrate the sharing process (this is done in tandem with the network software running locally on the workstations).

- Manage Print Queues/Printers. When several users want to use a printer that is connected to a file server, there must be some mechanism to allow documents to be "queued up" and printed one after the other on a first-come, first-served basis. The file server performs this task. More recently, software has become available to let workstations double as print servers. Within Windows, you can control which file server and to which print queue you want your printed documents sent.

- Route Packets. A network may be composed of several different types of cabling systems. For instance, a file server may act as a router if you place two network cards in the server and connect different types of cable to each card. These cable types could be of the same or different topology. In this case, the server has the added task of routing information back and forth between the various heterogenous or homogenous topologies.

There are many other services provided by the file server, such as security, messaging, accounting, and others, but as you can see, the server performs a multitude of functions. And, with Value-Added Processes under NetWare 2.x and NetWare Loadable Modules (NLMs) under NetWare 3.x, third-party software vendors can provide additional value-added services that run on the file server.

NetWare User Environment

If you are relatively unfamiliar with NetWare or if you need a review, there are several important concepts you must understand before embarking on NetWare/Windows integration. As a user, the following material will give you a perspective that may keep you from becoming confused when you no longer have a command-line environment to work with. As a supervisor, it is imperative that you learn the implications of drive mapping, directory rights, user management, and so on.

This section will cover the basics of NetWare from the user's perspective, then proceed to issues relevant to the NetWare administrator.

Drive Mapping and Search Paths

One of the basic elements you learn when you begin using DOS is the disk drive; for example A: is the first floppy disk drive on the PC and C: is the first hard disk drive. You also learn the way DOS organizes a directory structure. It is essentially a tree, a hierarchy of directories, starting at the root directory which may contain other directories and subdirectories. This structure allows you and software applications to organize files in logical ways. Otherwise, you might have thousands of files stored in one area which makes them difficult to locate and to manage.

Software written to run under DOS relies on these drive letters and basic disk organization to function. So, when Novell wrote their shell software, they had to make it compatible with DOS. That is, Novell needed to make the file server's hard drives appear to the user and the application program like a regular DOS drive.

NETWARE VOLUMES

Under NetWare 2.x a server's hard drive, or a part of a hard drive, is called a volume. The first volume is always called SYS: and it contains the system directories and files plus any other directories you care to add. Other volumes, by default, are called VOL1:, VOL2:, and so on. But the network administrator can set them up with any name. For example, a 500 MB drive can be named SYS: or the first half can be named SYS: and the second half, VOL1:.

Under NetWare 3.x the same rules apply, but you may combine several hard drives under one volume name—the first two hard drives (a 500 MB and a 125 MB drive, for instance) can be combined and collectively called SYS: (a 625 MB volume, in this case). The operating system takes care of the details.

In either case, this basic storage unit, the volume, is seen by DOS as a drive letter, as though it were a hard drive installed in the local workstation. This translation is one of the primary services offered by the NetWare shell.

The NetWare shell portrays a server volume to DOS by simply using another drive letter—for example, F:. This is done through a process known as mapping. In this case, drive F: is "mapped" to the volume SYS: and you can refer to both directories and files on the SYS: volume by using the F: drive letter. For example, assuming you are connected to the network, and drive F: is mapped to the SYS: volume, you can perform nearly any DOS command (except CHKDSK, for instance) on the drive and it will appear like a local drive. You can search directories, copy files to/from the drive, run applications, and so on.

In fact, when you first load the NetWare shell files, the shells find the closest server, create a logical "attachment," and map the next available drive letter on your PC to the SYS: volume on that server. The next available drive letter is determined by the DOS-based LASTDRIVE= statement in your CONFIG.SYS file. The default value for the DOS LASTDRIVE= statement is E:. Therefore, NetWare usually shows you drive F:. See your DOS manual for more details on using the LASTDRIVE= statement.

Mapping a drive letter of your PC to the SYS: volume serves a key purpose. The root directory of the SYS: volume contains a NetWare program named LOGIN.EXE. By switching to the mapped drive and typing **LOGIN,** you can run the LOGIN.EXE program and log on to the network. NetWare will prompt you for a name and password before allowing you to log on. You must log on to the network before you can use network-based services.

LOGGING ON

Logging on to the network is a process by which you supply your login name and password, and the network makes its resources available to you. This process of giving you resources is usually maintained by the network administrator in a file called the "login script." The login script is composed of two parts: the global login script that everyone executes and a private version that is unique to each user. Each component is a text file that contains a list of instructions to the file server to do each time a user logs on.

Networks can be configured to use either the global or private login scripts, or a combination of both (the global script is executed to allocate resources common to all users, then the private login script is executed which performs setup tasks private to each user). One of the most important things the login script does is to map network server volumes to your local workstation's drive letters.

THE MAP COMMAND

MAP.EXE is the command-line program used in NetWare to assign logical drive letters to file server volumes and directories. If you were to type "map" at the DOS command line when logged in, you might see something like:

```
Drive  A:    maps to a local disk.
Drive  B:    maps to a local disk.
Drive  C:    maps to a local disk.
Drive  D:    maps to a local disk.
Drive  E:    maps to a local disk.
Drive  F:  = ROSE_286\SYS:    \
Drive  G:  = ROSE_286\VOL1:   \DATA

SEARCH1:   = Z:. [ROSE_286\SYS:   \PUBLIC]
SEARCH2:   = Y:. [ROSE_286\SYS:   \DOS]
SEARCH3:   = X:. [ROSE_286\SYS:   \UTILS]
SEARCH4:   = C:\
SEARCH5:   = C:\UTIL
SEARCH6:   = C:\QEMM
```

In this case, Drives A through E are local drives. Notice that the MAP command reminds you of this. Drive F: is mapped to the SYS: volume on the server named ROSE_286. Similarly, drive G: is mapped to the \DATA directory of the VOL1 volume of the same server.

If you wanted to map drive H: to the \USER\CHARLES directory on volume VOL2 on server ROSE_286, you would type the following line for the DOS prompt (once you were logged in):

```
MAP H:=ROSE_286/VOL2:\USER\CHARLES
```

Note that you specify the server first, a forward slash ('/'), the volume name, a colon (':'), then the full DOS path. If you do not specify the server (and the forward slash) then the current server is assumed. Similarly, if you specify just the DOS path, the current server and volume (that your default drive is mapped to) is assumed.

FAKE ROOTS

Although they sound like some sort of deceptive genealogy, fake roots are a phenomenon that came about because of the way Windows handles drive mappings. By default, when you map a drive to a network directory, say the PUBLIC directory on the SYS volume, NetWare actually maps the drive in such a way that the root directory of the drive points to the root of the volume. The current directory on the drive is then set to the requested directory.

For example, with F: mapped to SYS:PUBLIC, a user can issue the DOS command "CD \," or change directories to the parent directory in the Windows File Manager, to change directories to the root directory of the volume.

"Fake roots" in NetWare provide a way for the root directory of a mapped drive to actually point to a network directory. For example, issuing the NetWare command MAP ROOT F:=SYS:PUBLIC creates a logical F: drive that sees its root directory as the files and subdirectories in SYS:PUBLIC.

Many people see the option of mapping fake roots as providing additional system security. For nonexperienced users, this may be the case. However, experienced users can easily create their own drive mappings. Instead, think of fake roots as an option of convenience and an aid in simplifying the user's view of the network.

Fake roots are also needed in Windows 3.0 to keep File Manager from continually showing you the root of the volume and to keep the Setup program from scanning the volume multiple times when automatically setting applications for you. These problems have been fixed in Windows 3.1. Nevertheless, the NetWare Driver for both Windows 3.1 and Windows for Workgroups includes a MAP ROOT feature which can be very convenient. Please see Chapters 5 and 6 for further information about fake roots and the "MAP ROOT" command.

SEARCH PATHS

When you are at the DOS command line and type a command, such as "MAP", DOS searches for a program called MAP.COM, MAP.EXE, or MAP.BAT, and runs the program. It first looks in your default directory, then uses the "DOS search path" to try to find it. The search path is a list of directories where DOS looks to find the program file. The list of directories to search is determined by the PATH= statement in your AUTOEXEC.BAT file. If DOS does not find the program you are trying to run, you get a "Bad Command or Filename" error.

NetWare offers a similar feature known as search paths. The MAP command offers the facilities needed to manage your search paths.

When you are attached to one or several file servers, you can have many different search paths. If you look at the map listing above, the output of the MAP listing first gives local drives, then network drives, finally network search drives. These are listed as:

```
SEARCH1:   = Z:.  [ROSE_286\SYS:   \PUBLIC]
SEARCH2:   = Y:.  [ROSE_286\SYS:   \DOS]
SEARCH3:   = X:.  [ROSE_286\SYS:   \UTILS]
SEARCH4:   = C:\
SEARCH5:   = C:\UTIL
SEARCH6:   = C:\QEMM
```

Like logical drives, search paths are identified by drive letters working backward from the letter Z. For example, in the above listing, the first three drives are mapped to directories on the SYS: volume on server ROSE_286. The final three drives are local to that workstation.

The first three drive letters in this PATH statement have a period "." after them. This signifies the current directory at that drive letter. Notice also that the final three directories have no server or volume name, indicating these directories are local to the workstation.

The search paths defined by NetWare are added to the beginning of your DOS search path. For example, if you type PATH at the DOS prompt, you would see "PATH=Z:.;Y:.;X:.;C:\;C:\UTIL;C:\QEMM."

NetWare search path entries are always added to the DOS path in a format such as "Z:.," so that whatever directory is current on that drive is the one that is in the path. By changing the current directory on the search drive, you effectively change the current path. We'll use this to our advantage later when configuring Windows applications.

Based on this search path mapping, if you did type "MAP" at the command line, DOS would first search for the command in the current directory, then it would search SYS:PUBLIC on server ROSE_286 where it would find MAP.EXE and run it. The SYS:PUBLIC search drive is usually the first in the sequence of search paths because it contains NetWare's user utilities and is, therefore, used most often.

When mapping search drives, it is always important to use the "INS" (for insert) parameter to add entries to the path, rather than overwriting existing entries. For example, the NetWare command MAP INS S1:=SYS:PUBLIC maps a drive to the SYS:PUBLIC directory of the default file server, and adds an entry for this drive mapping to the current DOS path as the first entry. By contrast, MAP S1:=SYS:PUBLIC also maps a drive; however, it will replace the entry that is currently listed first in the path when added to the current DOS path, which is rarely desired.

Flagging Files/File Attributes

In DOS, there are four possible attributes a given file can have: archive, read-only, hidden, and system. NetWare adds several additional file attributes, including:

Shareable
Transactional
Indexed
Read Audit
Write Audit

The shareable attribute under NetWare is commonly misunderstood. This attribute allows more than one user to access the same file at the same time. However, many users and vendors wrongly believe that files to be shared by multiple users (like a database file) need to be flagged "shareable." This is not always true and, in some cases, doing so can actually cause file corruption problems.

Any program designed to run in a networking environment should make provisions for using DOS file and record locking conventions when working with files. Do not flag files shareable read-write except as a last resort.

Sometimes flagging files shareable read-only can serve a useful purpose. In DOS, you may be using a BUFFERS= statement in your CONFIG.SYS file to allocate disk buffers that DOS uses to buffer reads and writes to files on your local drives. These buffers are not used for file i/o to network drives. Instead, separate buffers are allocated when the network shell is loaded to serve as cache buffers for network file i/o. By default, NetWare allocates five 512 byte buffers (the CACHE BUFFERS = statement in NET.CFG/SHELL.CFG controls how many buffers are allocated).

These buffers must be used sparingly by the shell, as this could cause problems for multi-user file access. Only files opened for exclusive access (allowing no other workstation to access these files at the same time) or files that have been flagged shareable read-only will be cached in these local buffers. It's a good idea to flag Windows executables (EXEs) and dynamic link libraries (DLLs) shareable read-only to take advantage of this caching.

> **CAUTION:** Some versions of the NetWare shell, most notably v3.22, have bugs that can lead to cache buffer and possibly file corruption. For these shells, a setting of CACHE BUFFERS = 0 in the NET.CFG or SHELL.CFG file is recommended. These problems appear to have been fixed in NETX v3.26, which is a prerequisite for running Windows 3.1.

Security

When many users have access to shared disk space, there must be some means of regulating who has access to what information. NetWare takes care of this with a variety of security features.

DIRECTORY TRUSTEE ASSIGNMENTS

As we discussed above, DOS lets you organize files by subdirectory. Novell's security is partially based on this same system—that is, specific rights to a directory can be granted only to specific users.

These rights include the ability to do a "DIR" listing on the directory, read files from the directory, write to files in the directory, and so on. By granting a combination of these rights to specific users, the network supervisor can customize network security. For instance, when NetWare is installed, users can search the directory of the SYS:PUBLIC directory area and read the files there. They cannot, however, delete files, make other subdirectories, or modify the files in that area.

The administrator may also set up other directory areas in the same manner for those circumstances where users should only "look but not touch." For server-based user directories, however, supervisors generally grant all rights to the user who owns that area. For example, the user Charles has the right to create, delete, read, write, and otherwise manipulate files in SYS:USER\CHARLES.

RIGHTS CAN BE GRANTED TO USERS OR GROUPS

Trustee rights may be granted to users either individually or as a group. For example, the supervisor may assign rights (Directory Scan and File Read) to a specific directory area (SYS:APPS\LOTUS) to a certain user (Mark). Or, the supervisor may assign those rights to a group of users (the group ACCOUNTING, for example).

The ability to assign rights to a group, then add or remove users from a certain group helps the supervisor save a lot of time rather than assigning each user's directory rights separately. With this scheme, the supervisor can assign all of the basic "global" rights to user groups, then assign rights that are specific to a certain user to that user only.

WHAT ARE YOUR RIGHTS?

There are two different sets of directory rights, depending on whether you are using NetWare 2.15 and versions below, NetWare 2.x, or NetWare 3.x. For NetWare 2.15 and versions below, the rights are:

(R)	Read	Lets you read the contents of a file. (requires Open rights to be useful)
(W)	Write	Lets you write to a file. (requires Open or Create rights to be useful)
(C)	Create	Lets you create files.
(O)	Open	Lets you open an existing file.
(D)	Delete	Lets you delete files and remove subdirectories.
(M)	Modify	Lets you change file status flags or rename files.
(S)	Search	Lets you scan the directory for files (DIR command).
(P)	Parental	Allows you to create directories, and assign trustee rights for this directory to others.

For NetWare 2.2 the rights are:

(R)	Read	Lets you read the contents of a file.
(W)	Write	Lets you modify a file.
(C)	Create	Lets you create subdirectories and files.
(E)	Erase	Lets you erase files and remove subdirectories.
(M)	Modify	Lets you change the file status flags (see "Flagging Files/File Attributes" earlier in this chapter) and rename files.
(S)	Scan	Lets you scan the directory for files (using the DOS DIR command).
(A)	Access	Lets you change the access control (you can give or take away rights to a directory area).

For NetWare 3.x, the rights available are:

(R)	Read	Lets you read the contents of a file.
(W)	Write	Lets you modify a file.
(C)	Create	Lets you create subdirectories and files.
(E)	Erase	Lets you erase files and remove subdirectories.
(M)	Modify	Lets you change the file status flags (see "Flagging Files/File Attributes" earlier in this chapter) and rename files.
(F)	File Scan	Lets you scan the directory for files (DIR command)—this right may also apply to a file, in which case it would determine whether the file would show up in the directory display or not.
(A)	Access	Lets you change the access control (you can give or take away rights to a directory area).
(S)	Supervisor	Grants the user Supervisor rights to a particular file or directory.

The Bindery

Every NetWare file server contains a small database called the "Bindery" that is composed of two (NetWare 2.x) or three (NetWare 3.x) hidden files in the SYS:SYSTEM directory. The Bindery contains information about "objects" in the system, such as users, groups, and print queues.

For each user, several different properties of information are stored, including the user's full name, account restrictions, and so on. This type of information is available through the SYSCON utility. If you're not familiar with SYSCON, it will be discussed later in the chapter.

As a user, you won't need to worry much about the Bindery, although it may help you to know it's there. As a supervisor, the Bindery is a vital piece of NetWare to understand. You will inevitably be using different utilities that manipulate the Bindery in a number of ways to manage the users on your network. When you need to add, delete, or modify any aspect of a user's account, the Bindery will most likely be involved. Several of the command-line utilities that manipulate the Bindery as well as the powerful menu-based utilities provided with NetWare that allow you to manage users on the network will be covered later in this chapter.

Printing

Aside from file sharing, printing is one of the chief benefits of having a network. Networks provide a means for multiple users to share a common printer. It is important, however, that you understand the process, especially if you are a network supervisor. For users, things should be as simple as entering the "Print" command from within an application. Unfortunately, things rarely seem to work exactly as you wish they did.

FILE SERVER OR PRINT SERVER—WHERE WILL YOU PRINT?

In the DOS world, printers are connected to the local computer using either a parallel or a serial port. Aside from the possible MODE command for serial port hookups, very little is required to get printing.

When the LAN is setup, the installers must decide where the network printers will be attached—they still need to be connected to PCs. There are three choices available:

File Server	This is the most traditional way of connecting a network printer and involves connecting a printer (either through a parallel or serial connection) to the file server. You can fill all parallel and serial ports with printers, if you so desire.
	The advantage of this method is its ease and simplicity of setup. The disadvantage is that the printers generally must be geographically located near the file server.
Workstation	You may also attach printers to local workstations—the only hitch is you must run software that talks to the file server to get the print jobs, then print them on the local printer.
	This process can slow down the local computer; if the local computer hangs or freezes up, the print server is incapacitated.
Workstation (Ded.)	Computers may also be dedicated print servers, meaning they do not double as a workstation. These PCs sit all day doing nothing but servicing a queue and printing jobs on the printers that are locally attached.

PRINT REDIRECTION

When the bulk of software companies write their software, it is assumed that printing is done to a local printer port, usually LPT1, LPT2, or LPT3. More sophisticated programs can address the serial ports directly as well. However, the problem is that the LAN software vendor has the challenge of making the software look like DOS to applications, as was the case with the DOS drive/network drive situation discussed above.

That's exactly what NetWare does. Local LPT ports can be rerouted ("captured" in NetWare parlance) to a network print queue where they will be serviced by a print server (which, remember, is either the file server or a local workstation). This way, the application thinks it's printing normally to a local printer and the output is actually going to a network printer.

Actually, many newer or "network-aware" applications can take advantage of network services in what's called the NetWare Application Program Interface (or API) to print directly to a NetWare print queue without going through the print redirection. The LPT port capture process is only needed for those applications that print to local LPT ports (which, at this time, is the majority of applications).

NETWARE PRINT UTILITIES

Novell provides several utilities, some menu-based and some command-line-based, that assist the user and the supervisor in the printing process. The following utilities are available:

PConsole	Controls NetWare print queues, and lets you create, delete, change, and view the contents of print queues. You can also add queue users (those that can print to the queue—add jobs), queue operators (those that can remove print jobs or change them), and queue servers (those that "service" the print queue—remove jobs from the queue and print them).
PrintCon	Manages print job configurations, which are essentially combinations of printing parameters (such as which file server to print to, which form to use, how many copies to print, and so on). You can use these print job configurations when printing individual files or when capturing from a local LPT port.
PrintDef	Lets you specify drivers for certain printers in use on the LAN. NetWare comes with printer drivers for a variety of printers. You can define specific print devices and forms which can then be used in other utilities, such as PrintCon. Print devices let you define the forms, page length and width for certain print jobs.
	You can use forms if you need to stop and mount different types of paper (like preprinted checks, address labels, etc.) at the printer before printing a certain job.
PStat	Shows the status of network printers.
Capture	Lets you redirect LPT ports to network print queues.
EndCap	Turns off the capture process manually (so that what is sent to a local LPT port goes to the printer physically attached to that LPT port).
NPrint	Lets you print a specified file to a network printer.

Command-Line Utilities

As a user on a Novell network, chances are you will need to use one or more of the NetWare command-line utilities. Although many users are sheltered from the NetWare command-line environment by a menu system, there still may be cases when you need to use these utilities.

NetWare comes with two basic types of utilities: menu and command-line. The command-line utilities are executed by typing the name of the utility at the DOS command-line. Menu utilities are more elaborate and have multiple functions—they present the user with a menu of choices to execute. Whereas a command-line utility like MAP will map a drive for you, a menu-based utility like FILER will show you the contents of directories, change directories, remove or create directories, and so on.

The following sections will give you a feel for what command-line utilities are available to you, their command syntax, and what you can do with them. For more details on these commands, see your NetWare documentation.

ALLOW

This command-line utility lets you list or change the Inherited Rights Mask for a directory or file, but it only works on NetWare 3.x. The syntax for this command is:

```
ALLOW [path [TO INHERIT] [rightslist]]
```

Use one or more of the following letters—for example, S for Supervisor, in place of rightslist above.

ALL	(C)reate
(N)othing	(E)rase
(S)upervisor	(M)odify
(R)ead	(F)ile Scan
(W)rite	(A)ccess Control

ATOTAL

This is a Supervisor-only utility that totals the use of accounting services on your network. You must have accounting services installed to use this utility. The command syntax is:

```
ATOTAL
```

ATTACH

This connects the user to an additional file server while remaining logged into the current one. The syntax for this command is:

```
ATTACH [fileserver[/name]]
```

Replace fileserver with the server you want to attach to and replace name with the user name you want to log in as. If you don't specify the user name, you will be prompted for it. Once you've attached to another file server, you can map drives to its volumes, print to its queues, and access other services.

BINDFIX AND BINDREST

These two utilities are available to the Supervisor to fix the file server's bindery if it becomes corrupted in any way. When run, BindFix makes a copy of the bindery files and leaves them in the SYS:SYSTEM directory. BindRest is used to restore these files should that be necessary. The command syntaxes are:

```
BINDFIX
BINDREST
```

CAPTURE

Capture is one of the most popular command-line utilities for users. It is used to reroute local printer output to a network print queue. Although there are many possible options, most of the defaults should work fine for you. The command syntax is:

```
CAPTURE
```

/SHow	Show the status of the local LPT ports.
/Job=jobname	Use a predefined print job configuration (use PrintDef and PrintCon to create these).
/Server=fileserve	Specify which printer to send the output to.
/Queue=queuename	Specify which queue to send the output to.
/Local=n	Specify which local LPT port (1, 2, or 3) to redirect to the network print queue.
/Form=form or n	Specify (by name or form number) which form to use—if the form specified is different from the one currently at the print server, the user will be prompted (at the print server) to change to the proper form.
/CReate=path	Redirect the printer output to a file rather than to a network print queue.
/Copies=n (1–99)	Number of copies to print.
/TImeout=n	The timeout interval to flush the print buffers to the network print queue.
/Keep	Don't delete the print queue file when done printing.
/Tabs=n (1–18)	How many spaces to substitute for a tab character.
/No Tabs	Do not perform tab substitution (this is used for binary files).
/Banner=bannername	Specifies the banner to be used in the print job.
/NAMe=name	Specifies the user from whom the job is coming.
/No Banner	Disables banner printing.
/FormFeed	Turns on automatic form feeds.

/No FormFeed	Turns off automatic form feeds.
/AUtoendcap	Automatically flush the buffer when the LPT port is closed.
/No Autoend	Don't do any automatic flushing—the user will have to manually flush the buffer to the printer with the ENDCAP.EXE utility.
/NOTIfy	Notify the user (with a SEND-type message) when the job is done.
/No NOTIfy	Don't perform job notification.
/DOmain=domain	Specify a domain (used with Novell's NetWare Name Service product).

CASTOFF

This blocks SEND-type messages coming from other users. You would use this if you were running an application and don't want to be disturbed or if you were running an unattended program and don't want it stopped by a message. If you type "CASTOFF ALL," you will prevent all users plus the system console from sending you messages. The command syntaxes are:

```
CASTOFF
CASTOFF ALL
```

CASTON

This command-line utility enables the station to receive SEND-type messages, and its syntax is:

```
CASTON
```

CHKDIR

This shows the user information about a directory and a volume, and requires NetWare 3.x. The command syntax is:

```
CHKDIR [path]
```

CHKVOL

This utility displays information about a file server volume. Its command syntax is:

```
CHKVOL [path]
```

DOSGEN

A Supervisor's utility, it sets up a file that diskless workstations use to perform a remote boot to access the file server. The command syntax is:

```
DOSGEN
```

ENDCAP

This ends the capture of one or more local LPT ports. If there is data in a print queue, it will be sent to the printer—or you can specify that the data be deleted. The commands are:

```
ENDCAP [/CANCEL]
ENDCAP [/CANCEL] [/LOCAL=N]
ENDCAP [/CANCEL] [/ALL]
```

The /CANCEL switch deletes any information in the print queue. The /LOCAL switch lets you specify which local LPT port you wish to end the capture for. /ALL specifies that you want to ENDCAP all LPT ports.

FLAG

This lets the user view or change file attributes in a given directory. (The menu-based utility Filer can perform these functions as well.)

```
FLAG [path [TO INHERIT] flaglist]]
```

(A)rchive Needed	(R)ead (A)udit
E(x)ecute Only	(W)rite (A)udit
(R)ead (O)nly	(C)opy (I)nhibit
(S)hareable	(D)elete (I)nhibit
(H)idden	(R)ename (I)nhibit
(SY)stem	ALL
(T)ransactional	(N)ormal
(P)urge	(SUB)directory

You may insert a /C after the command for a continuous display—otherwise the display pauses every screenful of information.

Note that some of these flags either serve no purpose in current NetWare versions (reserved for future use), or are of limited use in the DOS/Windows environment.

FLAGDIR

Directories have attributes somewhat similar to the attributes you can see and modify with FLAG. FLAGDIR lets you view and change the attributes of directories. The command syntax is:

```
FLAGDIR [path [flaglist...]]
```

where flaglist is one or more of the following (use first letter or abbreviation):

(N)ormal	(D)elete (I)nhibit
(H)idden	(R)ename (I)nhibit

(SY)stem   HELP

(P)urge

You may insert a /C after the command for a continuous display—otherwise the display pauses every screenful of information.

GRANT

This is used to give trustee rights to users or groups for a certain directory or file. Its command syntax is:

```
GRANT rightslist... [FOR path] to [USER | GROUP] name /option
```

Use one or more of the following letters—for example, use S for Supervisor—in place of rightslist above:

ALL	(C)reate
(N)othing	(E)rase
(S)upervisor	(M)odify
(R)ead	(F)ile Scan
(W)rite	(A)ccess Control

Replace path with a directory or file where you want the rights assigned.

The identifiers USER and GROUP are optional unless there's a group and a user with the same name.

Replace option with either /S for subdirectories or /F for files.

HELP

This invokes the FOLIO Infobase help system, a hypertext database of information on NetWare.

HELP   You receive general system help.

HELP command   You receive help on that command.

LISTDIR

This lists the subdirectories in your default directory, the Inherited Rights Mask of each subdirectory, the effective rights of each subdirectory, and the creation date of each subdirectory or subsequent subdirectories. The command syntax is:

```
LISTDIR [path] [option...]
```

where option is:

/R)ights	Lists the Inherited Rights Mask.
/E)ffective rights	Lists effective rights for a directory.

/D)ate or /T)ime	Shows creation date of directories.
/S)ubdirectories	Show all subdirectories of a directory.
/A)ll	Turn on all options.

LOGIN

This logs you into a file server and runs your login script. Its command syntax is:

```
LOGIN [/option] [fileserver/[name]] [script_parameters]
```

Replace fileserver with the name of a file server you want to login to. Replace name with your username.

Replace script_parameters with the LOGIN parameters that you set in your login script. You can pass parameters to the Login script in this way.

The /option possibilities are:

/S)cript	Overrides the default system and user login scripts and runs a login script you specify immediately following the switch. Use with /No Attach.
/N)o Attach	Allows you to invoke a particular login script without logging out of current servers and attaching to a server.
/C)lear screen	Clears the screen immediately after you enter your password.

LOGOUT

This logs you out of one or more file servers to which you are attached. Its command syntax is:

```
LOGOUT [fileserver]
```

You can specify a file server to logout of by specifying the server name after the LOGOUT command. If you don't specify a server to log out of, you are logged out of all attached servers.

MAP

Map is one of the most popular command-line utilities and is used to attach DOS drive letters to NetWare file server volumes. The various command syntaxes are:

To view settings:

```
MAP [drive:]
```

To create or change mappings:

```
MAP path
MAP drive := [drive: | path]
MAP [option] drive
```

To map a drive to a fake root directory:

```
MAP ROOT drive := [drive: | path]
```

Replace drive with the drive letter you want to assign to the NetWare volume. Replace path with the NetWare path you want the drive mapped to (i.e. SYS:DATA, \DATA, ROSE_286/SYS:DATA, and so on). Replace option with:

INS)ert	Changes search drive mappings.
DEL)ete	Deletes a drive mapping.
REM)ove	Deletes a drive mapping.
N)ext	Used to map the next available drive to a specified path.

MENU

This is Novell's character-based menuing system. See Novell documentation for further details.

NCOPY

This performs a copy at the file server rather than sending the data to and from the local workstation. Also, NCOPY preserves file attributes and sparse files, and is generally considered more reliable. Its syntax is:

```
NCOPY [path] [[TO] path] [option]
```

The options are:

/s	Copy subdirectories.
/s/e	Copy subdirectories, including empty directories.
/f	Copy sparse files.
/i	Inform when nonDOS file information will be lost.
/c	Copy only DOS information.
/a	Copy files with archive bit set.
/m	Copy files with archive bit set, clear the bit.
/v	Verify with a read after every write.
/h (/?)	Display usage message.

NDIR

An enhanced "network DIR" command, NDIR shows you Novell's extended information about files and lets you browse files and directories in a wide variety of ways. The following command-line options are available for NDIR:

usage:	NDIR [path] [/option...]
path:	[path] [filename] [,filename, ...] (up to 16 in chain)

options:	[format], [flag], [sortspec], [restriction], [FO] (files only), [DO] (directories only), [SUBdirectories], [Continuous], [HELP]
format:	DATES, RIGHTS, MACintosh
flag:	[NOT] RO, S, A, X, H, SY, T, I, RA, WA
sortspec:	[REVerse] SORT [OWner], [SIze], [UPdate], [CReate] [ACcess], [ARchive], [UNsorted]
restriction:	OWner <operator> <name> SIze <operator> <number> UPdate <operator> <date> CReate <operator> <date> ACcess <operator> <date> ARchive <operator> <date>
operator:	[NOT] LEss than, GReater than, EQual to, BEFore, AFTer

To search filenames equivalent to any of the capitalized KEYWORD options shown above, the filename must be preceded by a drive letter or path.

NPRINT

The syntax for this command-line utility, which prints a specified file to a network print queue, is:

```
NPRINT path [option...]
```

The options are:

/Job=jobname	Use a predefined print job configuration (use PrintDef and PrintCon to create these).
/Server=fileserver	Specify which printer to send the output to.
/Queue=queuename	Specify which queue to send the output to.
/Form=form or n	Specify (by name or form number) which form to use. If the form specified is different from the one currently at the print server, the user will be prompted (at the print server) to change to the proper form.
/Copies=n (1–99)	Number of copies to print.
/Tabs=n (1–18)	How many spaces to substitute for a tab character.
/No Tabs	Do not perform tab substitution (this is used for binary files).
/Banner=bannername	Specifies the banner to be used in the print job.
/NAMe=name	Specifies the user the job is coming from.
/No Banner	Disables banner printing.

`/FormFeed`	Turns on automatic form feeds.
`/No FormFeed`	Turns off automatic form feeds.
`/NOTIfy`	Notifies the user (with a SEND-type message) when the job is done.
`/No NOTIfy`	Don't perform job notification.
`/DOmain=domain`	Specify a domain (used with Novell's NetWare Name Service product).
`/Delete`	Deletes the file after it's printed.
`/PrintServer=`	Selects NetWare Print Server on which to print the file.

NVER

This lists the current version numbers for the network shell, the file server operating system, and other relevant software. Its syntax is:

```
NVER
```

A sample output appears below:

```
NETWARE VERSION UTILITY, VERSION 3.12
IPX Version: 3.10
SPX Version: 3.10
LAN Driver:  NetWare NE1000  v3.02EC (900831) V1.00
     IRQ = 2, I/O Base = 300h, no DMA or RAM
Shell:       V3.26 Rev. A
DOS:         MSDOS V5.00 on IBM_PC
FileServer: ROSE_286
Novell NonDed NetWare V2.2(10) Rev. A (02/11/91)
```

PAUDIT

An accounting utility, PAUDIT lets you view the system accounting records, but you must have accounting installed (through Syscon) on your server before the accounting system will function. The command syntax is:

```
PAUDIT [/c]
```

The /c will allow continuous scrolling of output; otherwise, a screenful of information will be shown at one time.

This is a utility that is placed in the SYS:SYSTEM directory and by default is only available to the system Supervisor.

PSC (PRINT SERVER COMMAND)

PSC controls print servers and network printers; its command syntax is:

```
PSC PS [=]printserver P [=]printernumber flaglist
```

where printserver is the name of the NetWare print server, and printernumber is the number of the printer.

Flaglist can contain any of the following flags:

STATus	Displays the status of the print server.
FormFeed	Performs a form feed at the print server.
PAUse	Pauses a certain print server/printer.
MOunt Form=n	Equivalent to a file server mount form command, it prompts the print server operator to insert the appropriate form paper (new form type is specified in n, such as "MO=3" would prompt the operator to insert form type 3 into the printer).
ABort [Keep]	Abort a print job and optionally Keep the spool file rather than deleting it (which is the default action).
STOp [Keep]	Stop a print server and optionally Keep the spool file being printed.
Start	Restart a print server after it has been STOpped.
Mark [character]	
PRIvate	Specifies a print server as being private.
SHAred	Specifies a public print server.

PURGE

This permanently deletes previously erased files. The command syntax is:

```
PURGE [filename | path] [/ALL]
```

REMOVE

This deletes a user or group from the trustee list of a file or directory. This can be used instead of Revoke when you want to remove someone's specific rights to a directory or file (Revoke could be used to delete certain individual rights to a particular directory or file). The syntax is:

```
REMOVE [USER|GROUP] name [[FROM] path] [option..]
```

The options can be:

-SUBdirectories	Include this option to remove trustee rights from all subdirectories of the path specified.
-Files	Include this option to remove trustee rights from files. If you use this option with the - SUBdirectories option, you can remove the rights from all files in the directory specified and all subdirectories under it.

RENDIR

The command syntax for this utility, which renames a directory, is:

```
RENDIR path [TO] directoryname
```

REVOKE

This deletes specific trustee rights from a user or group in a file or directory, and can be used instead of Remove. The command syntax is:

```
REVOKE rightslist...[FOR path] FROM [USER|GROUP] name [option..]
```

For rightslist, use one or more of the following letters; for example, use S for Supervisor in place of rightslist above.

ALL	(C)reate
(N)othing	(E)rase
(S)upervisor	(M)odify
(R)ead	(F)ile Scan
(W)rite	(A)ccess Control

The options can be:

-SUBdirectories   Include this option to revoke trustee rights from all subdirectories of the path specified.

-Files   Include this option to revoke trustee rights from files. If you use this option with the -SUBdirectories option, you can revoke rights from all files in the directory specified and all subdirectories under it.

RIGHTS

This displays your effective rights to a certain directory area or file. Its syntax is:

```
RIGHTS [path]
```

A sample of the output from rights is shown below:

```
ROSE_286\SYS:PUBLIC
```

Your Effective Rights for this directory are [RWCEMFA]:

May Read from File.	(R)
May Write to File.	(W)
May Create Subdirectories and Files.	(C)
May Erase Subdirectories and Files.	(E)
May Modify File Status Flags.	(M)
May Scan for Files.	(F)
May Change Access Control.	(A)

You have ALL RIGHTS to this directory area.

SECURITY

A Supervisor's utility, Security is used to show where there may be holes in the security of a particular file server. The syntax is:

```
SECURITY [/c]
```

Use the /c switch if you don't want to view a page of text at a time.

Below is a sample output:

```
SECURITY EVALUATION UTILITY, Version 2.23
User GUEST
  Has no login script
  Account has not been used for more than 3 weeks
    Last Login: Tuesday  April 7, 1992  3:00 pm
  Does not require a password
  No Full Name specified
Group EVERYONE
  No Full Name specified
User SUPERVISOR
  Does not require a password
  No Full Name specified
```

In this case, Security has shown several possible holes in the security of a file server. Situations like no password, no login script, no full name, or old accounts are shown to the supervisor.

SEND

This sends a one-line message to another user on the network. The command syntax is:

```
SEND "message" [TO] [[USER | GROUP] [server/] name [,
server/] name ...]
                  [server/] CONSOLE
                  [server/] EVERYBODY
                  [STATION] [server/] n[,n...]
```

Use the CONSOLE keyword to send a message to the file server console.

Use EVERYBODY instead of a user's name to broadcast the SEND message to all stations on the network.

Use STATION to send to a certain network station.

Otherwise, the keywords USER and GROUP can be used, specifying a user or group name to send the message to.

SETPASS

This allows users to change their passwords. Passwords can contain up to 127 characters. The syntax is:

```
SETPASS [fileserver] [/username]
```

SETPASS will prompt the user for the old password and the new one to change to. SETPASS will optionally synchronize (change) passwords on other file servers for you (if you use the same password on all of the servers you log in to).

SETTTS

This sets the logical and physical lock thresholds for the Transaction Tracking System (you can read about TTS in the NetWare Concepts manual from Novell). The syntax is:

```
SETTTS [logical level [physical level]]
```

SLIST

This lists the known file servers on your network and their Network and Node addresses. The command syntax is:

```
SLIST [/C]
```

Use the /C option for a continuous listing (otherwise, the display will pause for every screen page).

SMODE

This lets you view or modify the way a program will use search drives when it looks for data files. The syntax is:

```
SMODE [path [mode] [/SUB]
```

See Novell's Utilities Reference manual for further information.

SYSTIME

Use this utility to view the default file server's date and time. When you run Systime, you automatically synchronize your local workstation's time and date to that of the default file server. The command syntax is:

```
SYSTIME
```

TLIST

This displays the trustee list of a directory or (in NetWare 3.x) a file. The command syntax is:

```
TLIST [path [ USERS | GROUPS ] ] [/C]
```

Path is the directory path specifying the directory or file you want to see the trustee rights for.

You can specify GROUPS or USERS after the path to limit the search to only include GROUP trustee assignments and/or USER trustee assignments.

As with most command-line utilities that produce long lists of information, you can use the /C parameter to specify a non-stop, continuous list.

USERLIST

This lists the users currently logged into the file server. Your station is marked with an asterisk in the display. The displayed information includes the user's name, connection number, and login time. The syntax is:

```
USERLIST [fileserver/][name] [/A] [/O] [/C]
```

where fileserver/ is the name of a file server you want to explicitly examine, and name is a user you specifically want to view.

/A lets you view the full network address of each user; /O shows you the object type for each connection; and /C produces a continuous display.

VERSION

This displays the version number for a specified executable file. Its syntax is:

```
VERSION [path]
```

WHOAMI

This displays the current logged in name and user information. The syntax is:

```
WHOAMI [fileserver] [option...]
```

Fileserver lets you specify which server to query for user information.
Options include:

/S	Security	View security equivalences.
/G	Groups	View groups you belong to.
/R	Rights	View effective rights.
/O	Object	View object supervisor information and the users and groups being supervised.
/W	Workgroup	View workgroup manager information.
/SY	System	View general system information.
/A	All	View all of the above information.
/C	Continuously scrolling display.	

WSUPDATE

This lets you update old local workstation files with more recent versions from the network. The command syntax is:

```
WSUPDATE [source path] [destination drive:destination
filename] /option
```

See Novell's Utilities Reference manual for further information.

Menu-based Utilities

In addition to the command-line utilities, Novell has provided several more complex, menu-based utilities that let the system administrator manage the NetWare LAN. While space does not permit a detailed explanation of each utility, a brief summary will be provided.

COLORPAL

This sets the color palette for the other menu-based utilities.

DSPACE

This menu-based utility lets the supervisor control maximum disk space usage for a file server volume or (on NetWare 3.x) a directory.

FCONSOLE

A file server console utility, FConsole provides a wealth of information and statistics about a file server. In addition, several control facilities are available to manipulate active user connections and even to bring down the file server.

The File Server Console utility acts as a remote console (although not quite as literally as the RCONSOLE utility in NetWare 3.x). In it, the user can gather performance and usage statistics about the file server and perform control functions, such as enabling or disabling login and even bringing the file server down.

FILER

The Filer utility acts as a front-end to many DOS-based commands. With filer, users can get information about the current directory (which includes security, creation, and attribute information), and view the contents of a particular directory. Users can change directories, copy files, and gather information about volumes on a particular server.

MAKEUSER

Since the task of creating large numbers of users one-by-one in Syscon can be tedious for the system administrator, Novell created MakeUser to provide a more automated means of creating user accounts. MakeUser lets the supervisor type in one line of information for each user to be created, and it takes the steps necessary to create the user accounts.

NBACKUP

This is a backup management program to handle file archives.

NWSETUP

This is a tutorial-type utility to introduce supervisors to the task of creating users, login scripts, and generally configuring the LAN setup.

PCONSOLE

PConsole is a console to the print queues. With this utility, the supervisor can view and modify the activity on a print queue and create or delete queues. Also, queue properties, such as the servers, operators, and users, may be changed.

PRINTCON

This allows print job configuration files to be created and changed.

PRINTDEF

This lets the supervisor define which printers and forms will be used on the LAN.

PSERVER

This loads the print server software on the file server and establishes printing services for the LAN.

RCONSOLE

This is a remote console facility to control the file server console of a NetWare 3.x network.

RPRINTER

This connects or disconnects a remote printer from the file server.

SALVAGE

This retrieves files (undeletes them) after they were erased.

SESSION

Similar to Filer, session acts as a front end to your drive mappings, group memberships, and user information. Users can manage normal and search drives, send messages to individual users or groups of users, change the default drive, and inspect logged in users.

SYSCON

This SYStem CONfiguration utility lets the network administrator configure user accounts and configure them for varying levels of security. Parameters like passwords, user names, groups the user belongs to, personal login scripts, and trustee assignments can all be assigned to a particular user.

Also, group management can be performed (such as creating or deleting groups, and changing who belongs to a particular group). Finally, several global changes can be made to the network, such as the system-wide login script and default user security parameters that specify options like the minimum size for a user password.

SYSCON is an invaluable tool for network administrators and users may run SYSCON to find out (and modify) different aspects of their own user account.

USERDEF

This allows a supervisor or workgroup manager to perform bulk user management tasks such as creating multiple users, login scripts, home directories, security, disk space restrictions, and print job configurations.

VOLINFO

The VOLINFO utility provides information on disk volumes mounted on a file server. The utility shows disk usage (total and remaining space) and directory slot usage (a directory slot is where the information about a file is kept).

CHAPTER

2 Windows Basics

Chapter 1 explored the concepts surrounding networking with Novell's NetWare. However, the focus of this book is to illustrate how to use Windows and NetWare together. Networking is concerned with connecting you with others and sharing information; Windows is involved with presenting that information to you in a clear, flexible, and powerful way. If a picture is worth a thousand words, then Windows provides you with several thousand of them.

In this chapter the concept of a windowed desktop environment, specifically Microsoft Windows, will be introduced, the elements of the Windows environment will be identified, and the concepts surrounding Windows and their effects on you will be mapped out. We'll address the major Windows utilities, like the Program Manager, the File Manager, the Print Manager, and the Control Panel. The basic history of Windows will also be covered so you will be able to see the evolution from version to version and make sure you are taking advantage of all the environment can do for you. In addition, there will be a discussion of running DOS applications under Windows and how to use all of the keyboard and mouse commands that are common to Windows applications.

Finally, you will see what some of the often confusing acronyms like OLE and DDE mean and how you can use them within your Windows applications.

This chapter is intended as a practical introduction to the Windows environment. Although it can't cover all of the details of Windows, perhaps it can inspire you to learn more by spending time trying out different parts of Windows and by referring to the *Microsoft Windows User's Guide* (and third-party books). If you are already familiar with Windows, you may wish to skip this chapter and proceed directly to Chapter 3 which will familiarize you with the NetWare-specific features of Windows.

Why Windows?

If you follow the trade press, you may hear a lot of discussion about the merits of a graphical user interface, or GUI (pronounced 'gooey') as opposed to a character-based user interface (like DOS). The press often assumes that you know what a GUI is and may take for granted that you know the relative benefits from using one.

This section will begin with a discussion of the merits of a visual user interface, then proceed to identify the specific elements of the Windows user interface, and how they can help you.

Visual Presentation

If you trace the evolution of software in the PC-compatible world over the last few years, you will see an evolution from character-based systems to visual, graphical user interface-based systems. This may be a reflection of the industry. As businesses automate more and more of their tasks, the pace of incoming information quickens dramatically. To accommodate this influx of information, software developers have attempted to present the material in more meaningful ways. The visual/GUI approach is one of those ways.

INFORMATION DESIGN/LAYOUT

People respond to visual, graphic presentations more than they do to dull, monotonous heaps of data. Even in our most basic print media, like newspapers, magazines, or books, readers respond immediately—positively or negatively—to the way the printed material is laid out. If it's all crammed together in a monotonous way, it will be difficult to read and the reader may get bored or frustrated with it. However, if the printed matter is neatly arranged and well laid out, the reader will be able to enjoy the material more, it will be more accessible, and the reader may even find the material more fun to read.

The basic job of visual software is to somehow organize information so that it can be dealt with in an orderly way. To this end, the Windows GUI is modeled after the way we think and work; there are real-life symbols like buttons, knobs, switches, check boxes, and other gadgets that let us not only run an application but also interact with it. The idea is that if a software environment can model the way we think and work more closely, then we can be far more productive when using it.

COMMON USER INTERFACE

One of the major problems with software is the cost of retraining when a group of users decides to adopt a new application. Suddenly, staff must be trained for the new software. The Windows GUI provides at least a partial solution to this problem by providing common methods for performing similar tasks. These methods are essentially the same from one application to the next.

The idea is simple. If the software sticks to standard methods of doing certain things, like opening a file, printing a file, cutting and pasting information, then applications that conform to the standard are much easier to use. Users don't need to be retrained. If you already know how to open a file in one application, you know how to do it in all of the others.

To this end, Microsoft has published a suggested specification for developers to comply with when programming Windows applications. This specification defines how many common tasks will work and how they will look to the user. This greatly simplifies matters for users.

This commonality not only helps users learn and use applications more quickly and easily, but it also helps applications work better together. For instance, most Windows applications have a cut and paste facility that uses the Windows clipboard (a common/shared data area). This means that you can cut text from one Windows application and paste it into just about any other Windows application.

Although the previous two examples do show the advantages of a graphical user interface (visual presentation and a common user interface), they are by no means complete. There are several other advantages to Windows that help complete the picture:

Device Independence. One other advantage to the Windows environment is its device-independent architecture. What this means is that it works essentially the same for a wide range of hardware. An office may have EGA, VGA, and Super-VGA monitors, and they will all be running Windows and whatever Windows applications they have. You could have a Microsoft mouse or a mouse from one of several other vendors, and the mouse should work the same way under Windows.

This feature allows Windows to be shared by a wider variety of users, and sharing is what the NetWare/Windows connection is all about.

Multitasking. Another example of Windows working as you do is multitasking. When working, we rarely perform just one task at a time. Most people are involved in a number of tasks simultaneously: for example, talking on the phone while scheduling a meeting, preparing a report, and so on. Windows accommodates this multitasking nature by letting you run many applications at once. You can flip between applications by using the Alt-Tab key combination, by pressing the mouse button while the mouse pointer is on the window of the other application, or by pressing Control-Esc (which gives you a menu of active tasks), and selecting the task you want to focus on.

Windows runs on top of a single-tasking operating system, DOS. To get around this problem, it takes control of the processor in your machine and doles out its resources to applications that need it.

In most cases, the user is in control of which application gets the processor. Windows usually "gives the processor" to an application based on events that you control. When you switch to a new application, Windows creates an "event," signaling the new application that it now has the "focus," meaning it has the attention of the processor. The application is also responsible for releasing the processor when it's done using it.

Windows keeps track of events through a "messaging system." It sends messages to applications for a wide range of "events," such as your switching to a new application, moving the mouse, or typing on the keyboard. In this way, Windows lets you run several applications at once and thus, lets you accomplish more in a shorter period of time.

Memory Management

The Windows environment requires memory in which to run. In addition, the DOS windows and the Windows applications also require memory. There are several memory-related issues you should be aware of. Memory requirements in general, the HIMEM.SYS driver, the SmartDrive disk cache, and the Windows Swap Files will be discussed in this section.

MEMORY

When the IBM PC was first introduced, there was only one type of memory available: conventional. This was the random-access memory (up to 640K) that the IBM PC could address. Then came the Expanded Memory Specification (EMS) which let the PC access megabytes worth of memory. This was accomplished by swapping 16K "pages" of memory in and out of a block of memory between the address space from 640K to 1 MB.

Finally, the release of the Intel 80286 processor let the new PC address up to 16 MB of memory and the eXtended Memory Specification was created to let applications access this XMS RAM. All three types of memory can be used by Windows. Chapter 5 contains a fuller discussion of memory.

Windows running in 386 Enhanced mode works well with at least 4 MB of RAM in the workstation. It is recommended, however, that you use 8 MB of RAM in the workstation for the best performance. This will allow Windows more "breathing room" to manage multiple applications and all of the resources Windows makes available to the user. Standard (286) mode users should have 2 MB of RAM, but 4 MB is preferred.

HIMEM.SYS

HIMEM.SYS is an extended memory device driver that is included with Windows. It allows Windows to access the DOS High Memory Area (HMA) on your 286- or 386-based PC, giving you access to RAM above 1 MB. It also coordinates memory access so that no two applications access the same memory simultaneously.

SMARTDRIVE

Windows includes a disk-caching program called SmartDrive. This utility uses memory to store the most recently accessed parts of your disk. You can speed disk access both inside and outside of Windows by using SmartDrive. Chapter 5 includes a discussion of SmartDrive.

SWAP FILES

When Windows runs out of memory, or needs to make more space available to applications, it swaps some of the information in RAM to disk. This information is written to a swap file. Swap files can be temporary, meaning that they are created and deleted each time you run Windows, or they can be permanent, meaning that they stay on your hard disk all of the time. Chapter 5 includes a detailed discussion of Swap Files.

Elements of the Windows Interface

The following list examines the elements of the Windows interface and how they affect you:

- Window. The window, the basic organizational unit in Windows, is simply a rectangular box in which an application communicates with you, the user. Windows can contain text, graphics, or other windows to further subdivide and organize the information presented to you.

- Application Menu. In most applications, a menu bar will appear across the top of the Window, just below the caption bar (which states the name of the application). Even the menus have been standardized so that on most applications, the first menu on the left is the File menu. That's part of Microsoft's set of standards for the Windows user interface. If you click on the File menu (or press Alt-F), the File menu will display its options.

  These options have also been standardized. Usually you will see New, Open file, Save, and Save As as standard File menu options. Also, the look of the Open file window will be very similar among applications, usually changing only to accommodate specific features of an application.

- System Menu. Most windows have a small square box in the upper left corner that has a horizontal bar in the middle of it. If you click on this box (or press Alt-Space), a menu drops down. This is the System Menu, which is also common to most every Windows application. The system menu lets you perform many of the tasks that you can do with the mouse, such as making the window a different size by expanding it to fill the screen or minimizing it to a small icon, or moving the window to a different location on the screen, or closing a window. You can also close a window by double-clicking on the System Menu box.

- Dialog Box. Many times applications need a means of communicating with the user, such as to request the name of the file the user wants to open. Rather than printing the question and answer right on the current window, Windows applications often use another window to request the name of file to open. This 'window' pops up over top of the application's window and is called a dialog box. This dialog box is simply a means for the application to communicate with the user. It may contain places to enter text or it may have other methods for soliciting user interaction, such as buttons, list boxes, check boxes, or other such "controls" which will be discussed very shortly.

- Maximize/Minimize Buttons. On most Windows you will see a set of arrows in the upper right corner. The arrow that points up is the maximize button—pressing this will expand the window to fill the entire screen. Once you've done this, the maximize arrow turns into an arrow that points up and down. Pressing this will return the window to its former size.

  The arrow pointing down is the minimize button; this will reduce the window to a small icon (about 1 inch square) at the bottom of the screen. This is useful to get the application out of the way without unloading it from memory. It's sort of on "stand-by."

- Sizing Borders. You can also size a window manually by using the System menu, which we discussed above, or by using the mouse. If you move the mouse around the border of a window, you'll notice that the cursor (the arrow that moves around) changes shape, from an arrow to other objects. Windows uses the arrow to indicate a change in modes.

  You'll see an hourglass instead of the arrow whenever a Windows application is busy doing something. This indicates that you need to wait for a procedure to complete before doing anything else.

  For now, we're concerned with the shapes the cursor takes on when we move the arrow around the border of the window. When you are on one of the borders and not near a corner, the cursor becomes a left-right cursor or an up-down cursor, depending on where you are. Pressing and holding the left mouse button lets you "size" the window however you want it.

  When you position the mouse cursor over a corner, you see the cursor change to a diagonal set of arrows. Now if you press the left mouse button, you will be able to change two sides of the window at once.

- Window Caption. You can also move the window by positioning the mouse cursor over the window caption bar and holding down the left button. This lets you drag the window around the screen and position it where you want.

- Scroll Bars. Scroll bars are a handy tool that you will see in several situations. In each case, the scroll bar is used to let you see a different part of a set of information than is currently shown on the screen. It's a way of saying, "I've got a lot of stuff to show you, but I only have room in this window to display a smaller amount; which part do you want to see?"

  You can work with a scroll bar in one of several ways. You can position the mouse cursor over the bar, hold down the left button, and drag the scroll bar left and right or up and down, depending on whether the scroll bar is horizontal or vertical.

  Or, you can click on one of the arrows at each end of the scroll bar—this moves the information over by "one line" (in quotes because it may be text displayed but it also may be graphics). Finally, you can click between the arrow and the scroll bar, which moves the information over by "one page."

- Help Screens (F1). Another common, and comforting, aspect to Windows is a powerful help system. The F1 key is almost always reserved for help in a Windows application. Also, there are two different kinds of help: general and context-sensitive.

If you are anywhere in an application, you can press F1 and receive help. You can search the help text for keywords or walk through a layered table of contents. Another useful aspect of Windows help is that it's all connected using the principles of "hypertext." This means that if you're reading about one topic and several words are highlighted, you can click on those words and jump to a broader discussion of them. When you're finished, you can jump back and continue reading from where you left off.

Context-sensitive help is also available. It lets you get help on what you are specifically working on at the time. For instance, if you are entering information into a particular field in an application, you can often get help specifically on that field. The help is specific, or sensitive, to the current working context.

- Controls. Controls are buttons, check boxes, edit controls, and listboxes that let you interact with an application. As mentioned previously, controls let you work with an application in ways that are more like we think—they can even make using an application more fun. The best way to learn about the different controls an application may use is to try them, since a great deal of Windows training comes from simply using Windows.

Windows Version History

If you're thinking that tracing the history of Windows is about as interesting as watching grass grow, you may not be alone. However, it's good to know how things got to where they are today, what the differences are between the versions (in case you and the people you work with are using different versions), and what are the specific advantages of the most recent versions of Windows. You might even find it interesting!

Windows Version 1.0

This was the first version of Windows, shipped in November 1985 following its announcement two years earlier. It provided a basic GUI for DOS users. Tiled windows were the only type available. They can be moved and their size can be changed, but they cannot overlap another window. Also, the first Windows mini-applications, like Windows Write, Paintbrush, Clipboard, and so on were made available.

Version 1.0 essentially laid Windows on the table for the public. It provided a new way of looking at things for PC users, but something which was already familiar to Apple Macintosh users (just how familiar may be debated by the courts for some time).

Some of the problems with version 1.0 included a lack of hardware (many users didn't have the monitor, RAM, or mouse to support the demands of this new environment), few available applications, and a general lack of functionality—it simply didn't do a great deal.

Windows Version 2.0

Nearly two years later, in 1987, Microsoft launched Windows 2.0. The new version featured a new look with overlapping windows (rather than just tiled) and support for Expanded Memory (EMS). Supporting EMS allowed users to run quite a few more applications at once than was possible before.

In 1988, Version 2.1 (also called Windows/286) appeared with improved functionality, but was still somewhat slow performance-wise and needed better memory management. Version 2.11 introduced the HIMEM.SYS driver which let people running real-mode applications (real mode is the nonprotected or 8086 mode of the Intel 80×86 processor) use the High Memory Area (the first 64 KB of memory above the 1 MB line).

Windows/386

This version of Windows began to pick up the pace of Windows development by taking advantage of the Intel 80386 processor. Windows/386 v2.1 was designed specifically for the Intel 386 processor and was the first version of Windows to support multitasking not only of Windows applications but also of DOS applications. This was done by taking advantage of the Intel 386 processor's innate ability to create separate virtual DOS machines. Each of these virtual machines provided the equivalent of a separate DOS session. By placing both Windows and Windows applications in one virtual machine and each DOS application in its own separate virtual machine, both DOS and Windows applications could peacefully coexist on the same system. This meant that you could simultaneously run not only multiple Windows applications, but also multiple DOS applications and switch back and forth among them.

Still, Windows was not being purchased for its own merits. In fact, it was usually purchased to do desktop publishing with PageMaker or to do other work with a specific application written for Windows.

Windows 3.0

Windows 3.0, announced in May of 1990, came out with one of the largest and most expensive fanfares ever given to a software product. Windows 3.0 quickly became one of the most popular software products ever.

Windows/286 and Windows/386 were effectively merged into one single product—a product that would run on and exploit the capabilities of an XT, a 286, or 386, or even the new 486 machines. Windows now ran in one of three modes: real mode (XT-mode, basically), standard mode (took specific advantage of the 286 chip and required at least a 286), and enhanced mode (took advantage of the 386 chip and required at least a 386).

As a result of Microsoft's use of design consultants when overhauling Windows for the 3.0 version, all sorts of new visually appealing elements were infused into the product. Shading and color were used to give the product a three-dimensional look—for example, buttons now had a 3-D, beveled appearance. Other desktop elements were also shaded to give them more depth and make them "pop off" the screen.

The user interface was also improved. For example, a new Program Manager was shipped that used icons to represent applications, much like the desktop of the Apple Macintosh. Further, proportional fonts were added to give text a less rigid look, something far more pleasing to the eye and much better for desktop publishing and other "printed-matter" applications. This also greatly improved Windows' ability to provide applications with "what-you-see-is-what-you-get" or WYSIWYG display.

Finally, and perhaps most important, Windows 3.0 provided the first glimpse of network functionality. Windows 3.0 lets you connect to file servers and network printers directly from Windows. You'll see exactly how to do this in upcoming chapters.

Windows 3.1

In the spring of 1992, Microsoft released Windows 3.1, an upgrade with many improvements over Windows 3.0. Among these improvements was a 20 percent increase in overall speed, a much-needed and appreciated enhancement. The sections that follow outline some other significant improvements in Windows 3.1

ERROR RECOVERY

Windows 3.1 dealt with errors much better than Windows 3.0. While Windows 3.0 was great with all of these new features, it crashed a lot. Users grew weary of the frequent Unrecoverable Application Errors (UAEs). UAEs occurred for a variety of reasons, such as an application mistakenly writing to an area of memory that belonged either to Windows or another application. A fatal error caused by a single application (including a DOS application window) could bring the entire system down, often causing you to lose work in other applications you had running at the same time. Often, your only recourse was to reboot your machine.

Windows 3.1 is more robust; that is, it is better able to protect itself from the fatal errors caused by a single application. When a Windows or DOS application causes an error that would be fatal to the system, Windows 3.1 generally responds by shutting the application down while the rest of the system continues to operate. In addition, in the event an application (including a DOS window) stops responding to the system, Windows 3.1 gives you the option of closing that specific application, without affecting other applications running on the system.

If a Windows 3.1 application (including a DOS window) is such that it has "fallen and it can't get up," you may press the Control-Alt-Delete keys simultaneously to reboot and close only that virtual DOS window, not the entire PC. Windows will offer you a choice of pressing Control-Alt-Delete again to reboot the entire PC or pressing the Enter key to just reset the failed application window.

TRUETYPE

Windows 3.0 provided only a limited set of internal fonts. If you selected a font supported by your printer that was not included in the Windows 3.0 internal font set, Windows would display the closest internal font it had. For this reason, there was often a disparity between your printed output and your screen display. In addition, the fonts provided by Windows were of the prebuilt, bitmapped variety and were only designed to be displayed in a discrete number of point sizes. If you selected a point size for which a prebuilt bitmap was not available, Windows 3.0 would attempt to simulate the appearance of the font by adding or deleting pixels. Often, this resulted in poorly displayed fonts with jagged outlines. In addition, Windows' internal bitmap fonts would not print on laser printers. These gaping holes in Windows internal font technology created a market for Windows font managers like Adobe Type Manager (ATM) and Facelift from Bitstream, which provided scalable-outline fonts (fonts that could be scaled to virtually any size) for both printing and screen display.

Windows 3.1 marked the debut of a new font technology known as TrueType which was developed by Apple and Microsoft together. TrueType fonts are scalable fonts, which means they are not fixed to a certain point size. TrueType fonts also include "hints" which improve the font's displayed and printed appearance.

TrueType fonts bring Windows much closer to WYSIWYG by using the same font for both printing and screen display. TrueType fonts work well for a number of reasons, and they are convenient because users don't need to purchase soft or cartridge fonts for their printers to match Windows internal font set. TrueType fonts work on a wide variety of printers.

OBJECT LINKING AND EMBEDDING

Another new technology to come along with Windows 3.1 is Object Linking and Embedding, or OLE. OLE represents a quantum leap in the way users think about applications. It lets you place (embed) objects from one application (like a drawing, a spreadsheet, or a graph) into a master document (like a word processing document).

Not only can you embed (place) an object into a document, but you can also link it. Linking means that the drawing, spreadsheet, graph, or whatever object is immediately updated in the master document whenever the original is updated. For example, imagine you have embedded a financial spreadsheet from Excel in Word for Windows. You realize that a figure, which is relied on by dozens of formulas, is wrong. Rather than recalculating the spreadsheet and importing it again, or worse yet, retyping it, you start Excel, open the appropriate spreadsheet, and insert the correct figure. As soon as you make the change to the spreadsheet in Excel and save it, the document in Word is immediately updated with the correct information.

The implications of OLE are tremendous, especially for an office environment. Users can build a group report by letting one user work on the spreadsheet while another is working on the drawing, and yet another is working on the body of the report.

Also, users can keep "official" copies of certain objects (like spreadsheets, charts, and so on) that they can use to embed into their documents. That way, everyone is working from the same base and workers are allowed to specialize on those objects for which they are responsible.

MULTIMEDIA AND PEN WINDOWS

Microsoft realizes that as computing power becomes more affordable, users will welcome multimedia support like stereo sound, full-motion video, enhanced graphics, and CD-ROM storage. Windows 3.1 includes built-in "extensions" which lay the groundwork for the integration of multimedia devices. For instance, drivers for Creative Labs' SoundBlaster cards are directly provided with Windows 3.1 (as well as drivers for the Adlib sound cards and others). Windows 3.1 even comes with digitized sounds so that Windows will chime, beep, buzz, or play a chorus of "Ta-Da!" when Windows comes up.

In addition to multimedia support, a special version of Windows 3.1 supports pen-based computing. It has been estimated that pen-based computers (those with no keyboard, just a light pen or stylus) will become much more popular in the future. By then, Windows should support handwriting recognition, among other features.

ENHANCED FILE MANAGER

The Windows' File Manager application has been improved dramatically for Windows 3.1. It supports the new Windows 3.1 "drag-and-drop" interface which lets you click on a file and, while holding down the left mouse button, literally "drag" the file to other directories, to Program Manager groups, or to the Print Manager to be printed. This "drag-and-drop" interface may become more popular in the future as other applications take more advantage of it. Also, File Manager doesn't build the entire directory structure each time you start the program (it used to take a LONG time just to get started each time you ran File Manager).

IMPROVED NETWORK SUPPORT

Finally, Windows 3.1 boasts improved network support. As you will see in coming chapters, Windows 3.1 is MUCH easier to install on a LAN than Windows 3.0 was. In addition, Windows now remembers and restores drive and printer mappings when you start it. With Windows 3.0, you had to perform this task manually each time you entered Windows. Finally, more control is built into individual user desktops, which the system administrator can use to grant or restrict access to system facilities.

Windows for Workgroups

In the fall of 1992, Microsoft released Windows for Workgroups (WFW) which is really composed of two distinct pieces. The first is Microsoft's debut into the

DOS-based peer-to-peer networking arena. The software lets users connect PCs together and form a small network, similar in function to Novell's NetWare Lite or Artisoft's LANtastic.

The second piece of WFW is an enhanced version of Windows specifically for networks. WFW contains enhanced File and Print manager functions that really begin to tap the power of the network. You'll see these in action later in the book.

The Future

With Windows-NT coming (or already here by the time you read this) the Windows future looks promising. Windows-NT promises the performance and flexibility of 32-bit computing coupled with enhanced memory management, a new filing system, and improved network functionality. The future looks bright for Windows!

Windows Utilities

If you are new to the Windows environment, you owe it to yourself to take some time to get familiar with Windows. The best way to learn is to sit down and "play" with Windows for a while. Run several of the applications included with Windows and experiment. Using Windows generally takes very little time to learn (especially compared to DOS) and many find it fun to use.

The sections that follow take a brief look at some of the major applications included with Windows that you may want to explore.

Program Manager

Program Manager (Figure 2.1) is the application you will probably become most familiar with in your experience with Windows. It is started when you first run Windows, and displays each application available to you in iconic form. If you simply double-click on an icon, that application will be started.

File Manager

File Manager (Figure 2.2) organizes the files on your hard disk or network drive and presents them using the graphic power of Windows. File Manager lets you perform most of the file manipulation functions you can do at the DOS command line, except that you perform those functions using menus, buttons, and the mouse.

Control Panel

The Windows Control Panel (Figures 2.3 and 2.4) provides you with the ability to configure many different aspects of your Windows environment. For example, you may change your printer setup, modify communications port parameters, or select a new background wallpaper for the Windows desktop.

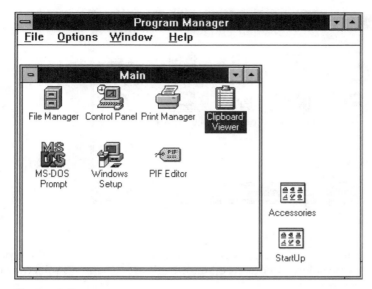

Figure 2.1 Program Manager.

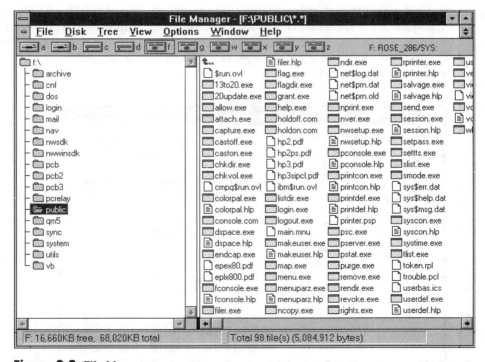

Figure 2.2 File Manager.

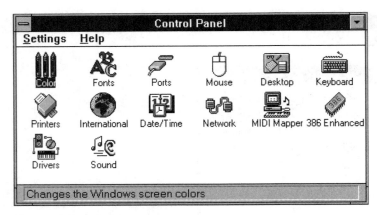

Figure 2.3 Control Panel.

The Network icon lets you modify parameters that are specific to the type of network you have installed—in our case, that's NetWare. Chapter 3 will cover this Control Panel feature in detail.

Print Manager

Print Manager (Figure 2.5) organizes the jobs that you send to printers in Windows applications. It acts as a print spooler, which copies printer output to disk files, then sends the disk files to the printer ports in the background. This is convenient because you can print a job, then get back to work without having to wait for the entire job to finish printing.

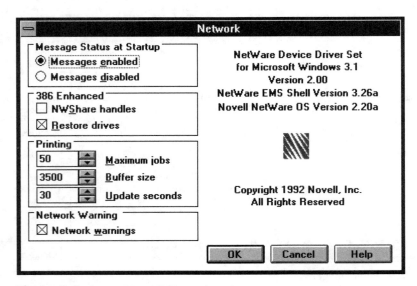

Figure 2.4 Control Panel, Network options.

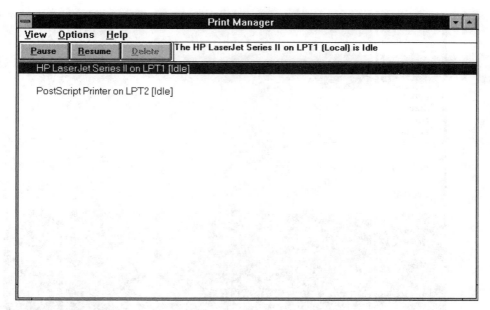

Figure 2.5 Print Manager.

Running DOS Applications

While you may be excited by Windows and all the new Windows applications
(fondly referred to as "WinApps"), you may nevertheless be saying "What about
my DOS applications?" Well, not only does Windows run your DOS applications,
it will let you run several at the same time. In fact, the multitasking properties of
Windows 3.1 are better than any previous version of Windows. You will learn about
customizing and fine-tuning your DOS applications in a later chapter, but for now,
let's examine some of the options your DOS applications have when running.

Multitasking: Exclusive/Background

There are two separate options that you may want to turn on or off, depending on
the DOS application and your personal preference. These are the Exclusive and
Background prompts. If you start a DOS window (double-click on MS-DOS in the
Main group in the Program Manager), you can press Alt+Space to look at the
system menu for the DOS window (see Figure 2.6). The options discussed here
can be found under the "Settings" option. When you select this option, Windows
displays the dialog box in Figure 2.7.

BACKGROUND

As you can see in Figure 2.7, there's a check box in the Settings window called
"Background," which serves a special purpose for DOS applications. Normally,

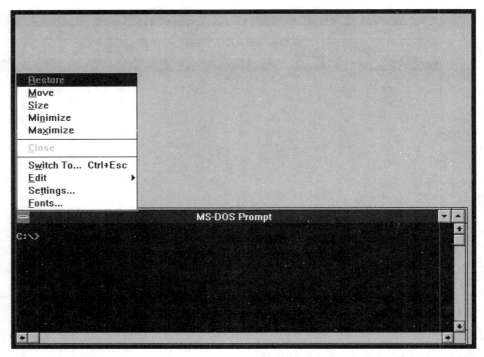

Figure 2.6 DOS window and system menu.

when you switch away from a DOS application, Windows suspends further activity in that application. In fact, only when you return to the application does the process continue. In most cases, this does not cause a problem. However, if you happen to be downloading a file using a communications program, or copying a 10 MB file from one disk to another, interrupting the application may cause the process to terminate. To help prevent this, you can turn on the Background check

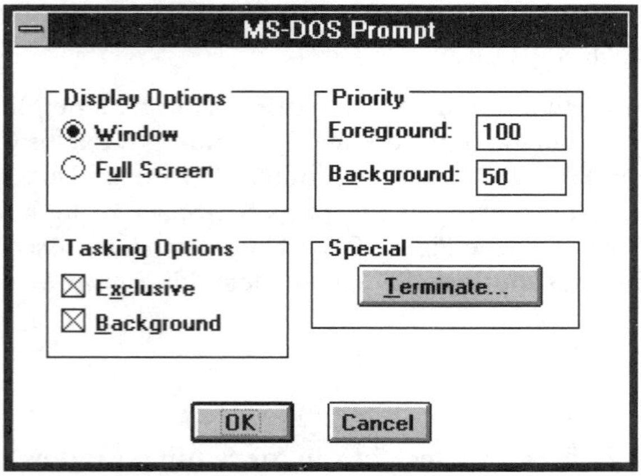

Figure 2.7 Settings box for a DOS window.

box. With this setting, the DOS application will continue to run in the background when you switch to another application.

PRIORITY

In Figure 2.7, the priority box contains values for foreground and background. These values represent the amount of processor attention this DOS window will receive when it is running in the foreground (when it has the "focus," when it is the currently selected application), and when it is running in the background. Note that by default, the foreground priority setting is 100 whereas the background setting is only 50. Therefore, when this DOS window is running in the background, it will only receive half as much processor time as it would when it's running in the foreground.

Specifics concerning these values will be covered later. For now, just realize that you have the choice. If this window is chugging away in the background, that means it will be taking some of the processor's attention, thereby slowing down other tasks.

EXCLUSIVE

When the exclusive box is checked, the window will get all of the processor's attention, to the exclusion of others. You may want to think of this setting as the "spoiled child" flag for a window.

Full Screen versus Window

A little known fact is that you can switch a DOS application between a full-screen display and a windowed display by using the ALT+ENTER key sequence. Alternatively, you can use the Window and Full Screen radio buttons in the System Menu (Figure 2.7) to control this function. Full-screen display means the application looks as it would under DOS—it occupies the whole screen. Window means the characters are shrunk a little and the entire screen is put into a window. The advantage of the full screen is it's easier to read and it may be a little faster at times. The advantage of the windowed approach is you can see other windows, allowing you to refer to their contents and switch to them easily.

PIF Files

As we progress in our discussion of installing and fine-tuning Windows, you'll learn about the Program Information File or PIF, which lets you customize different DOS application windows. You can set how much memory a DOS session may use, whether it runs as a windowed or full-screen display, and other attributes. There's even an application that comes with Windows, the PIF Editor, that you use to create PIFs. Don't worry too much about PIFs for now, as they are covered in more detail in Chapter 6.

Command-Line Parameters

The purpose of this section is to make you aware of the command-line parameters available when you start Windows. Instead of simply typing "win," you can type **win** followed by a space and a parameter that controls the operation of Windows. The sections that follow detail these parameters and what they do.

/3 Parameter

This starts Windows in 386 Enhanced mode. Usually Windows auto-detects the mode it can startup in and it picks the best mode. You can try to force Windows into 386 Enhanced mode by using this switch. However, if you aren't using at least a 386 chip or don't have enough memory, Windows still won't start in Enhanced mode.

/S Parameter

This starts Windows in standard mode, following the same idea as with /3. It requires at least a 286 chip in the PC.

/B Parameter

This creates the BOOTLOG.TXT file that records system messages that get generated during system startup (boot). It can be useful when troubleshooting your system for software/hardware conflicts during the Windows installation/troubleshooting phase.

/D: Parameter (F, S, V, X)

You've installed Windows and everything's a go. You proudly step up to the keyboard and type "win," smirking as you hit the Enter key with confidence. The screen blanks out and the PC locks up, or simply returns back to the command line.

This scenario is familiar to many with software or hardware conflicts in Windows. The following command-line switches can be used when troubleshooting Windows startup. These parameters will be covered in more depth later in the book, however, so you don't need to dwell too much on the specifics here.

:F   Turns off 32-bit disk access. Equivalent to SYSTEM.INI file setting: 32BitDiskAccess=FALSE.

:S   Specifies that Windows should not use ROM address space between F000:0000 and 1 MB for a break point. Equivalent to SYSTEM.INI file setting: SystemROMBreakPoint=FALSE.

:V   Specifies that the ROM routine will handle interrupts from the hard disk controller. Equivalent to SYSTEM.INI file setting: VirtualHDIRQ=FALSE.

:X   Excludes all of the adapter area from the range of memory that Windows scans to find unused space. Equivalent to SYSTEM.INI file setting: EMMExclude=A000FFFF.

Keyboard Commands

There are several windows keyboard commands that you should be aware of; they may help you navigate Windows more efficiently. The sections that follow explain what these keyboard commands are and how to use them.

Ctrl+Esc

This key sequence (Figure 2.8) brings up the Windows Task Manager. (You can also bring up the Task Manager by double-clicking the left mouse button on the background [the grey area, or on your wallpaper if you have it installed] of your Windows desktop.) The Task Manager lets you choose which running task you want to switch to (just double-click on the task name).

Alt+Tab

While the Ctrl-Esc key lets you choose from a menu of available tasks, the Alt-Tab sequence lets you switch between currently active tasks. Conveniently, Windows remembers the last task you were using. Therefore, if you have two favorites (a word processor in Windows and a DOS spreadsheet program for instance), you can press Alt-Tab to switch back and forth between them.

Alt+Enter

When you're in a DOS window, you can use this key sequence to quickly switch between a full-screen display and one where the entire DOS screen fits into a window on your Windows desktop.

Figure 2.8 Windows Task Manager.

Alt+Space

If you are using the keyboard and don't have your hand on the mouse, you can press Alt-Space if you need to bring up the System Menu for a particular Window. The System Menu is shown earlier in Figure 2.6.

Alt+F4

This is the default "Close Window" key sequence. Rather than double-clicking on the System Menu box or clicking on it and selecting "Close," you can use Alt-F4 if you need to close the window and/or exit the application in a hurry.

Alt+Accelerator

The designers of Microsoft Windows wanted to make the wonderful world of the mouse available to all users, but they also wanted to accommodate those who prefer the keyboard. In fact, if you take the time, you will find that you can pretty much get around Windows without a mouse. (You'll also find, however, that there are several areas where it's just easier to use the mouse.)

To aid keyboard users in getting around Windows, Microsoft has implemented the use of Accelerators. An accelerator is simply a hot-key substitute for a button or a menu entry. To use an Accelerator, hold down ALT, then press the appropriate key. The file menu, for example, almost always has an accelerator associated with it. Pressing Alt+F pulls down the file menu. Then select the item you want and press Enter. You can also shorten your keystrokes if there are accelerators in the menu—press the key for the letter that's underlined to jump right to the item (for Open, press O, for instance).

Accelerators are often available for buttons as well. If you see a button with a letter underlined (like Save) press the letter while holding down Alt (Alt+S, in this case). It will have the same effect as if you had clicked on the button with the mouse.

3 Network-Specific Windows Facilities

Microsoft built networking features into Windows 3.0 and has expanded those features for version 3.1. Actually, many networking companies, such as Novell, wrote a large part of the code specific to their network. As a result, there seems to have been a "cooperative effort" in placing this new network functionality into Windows. This chapter will examine this functionality and those aspects of Windows that deal directly with the network.

Windows' network-specific facilities interact with the network by making calls to the network operating system directly, rather than writing to DOS. These calls are passed to the network by means of a special Windows driver. The driver used is specific to the type of network you are using. Normally, these network drivers have a .DRV extension and are stored in your \WINDOWS \ SYSTEM directory. For example, if you are running Windows with Novell NetWare, the NETWARE.DRV driver is used.

Generally, Windows network drivers allow you to do such things as modify drive mappings, change print capture settings (you can set the individual parameters, such as tab size or timeout, and you can set the network queue to which the job goes), or alter network-specific options, such as whether you will receive "SEND" messages from other stations.

This chapter will focus on the network-specific features of Windows in general, as well as several applications included with Windows that allow you to access network features. These applications include:

- Control Panel
- Print Manager
- File Manager

- Program Manager
- NetWare popup window in NETWARE.DRV

> **Note:** The sections that follow will take you on a tour of the various commands and dialog boxes that allow you to access the features of the network from within Windows. However, the commands and dialog boxes featured in this chapter are specific to Novell NetWare. If you are running on a different type of network, the commands and dialog boxes you see may be different.

Control Panel

The Windows Control Panel (see Figure 3.1) allows you to modify your Windows operating environment while on-line, rather than changing .INI files in an editor. Icons are provided that let you modify system colors, fonts, ports, mouse, desktop, and several other types of settings. The settings that are specific to networking, however, are accessed by using the Network, Printers, and 386 Enhanced icons.

The Network Icon

The Network icon gives you access to the dialog box in Figure 3.2. This dialog box, probably the most network-specific aspect of Windows, lets you change settings specific to your type of network.

Since we are working with NetWare, all of the parameters controlled by the dialog box in Figure 3.2 are specific to NetWare. If we were running LAN Manager or Vines, the parameters would be specific to those environments.

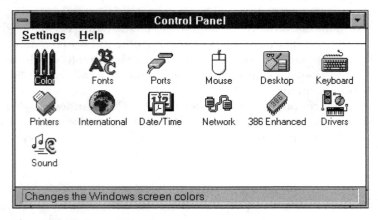

Figure 3.1 Control Panel.

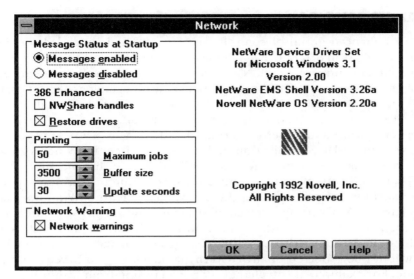

Figure 3.2 Control Panel, Network settings.

THE MESSAGE STATUS AT STARTUP SETTING

The two options in the Message Status group, "Messages enabled" and "Messages disabled" (Figure 3.3), dictate how your workstation will handle incoming messages from other users or the file server console. In DOS, these messages normally are displayed on the last line in reverse video with the message "CTRL-ENTER to Clear" on the right side of the line. However, in Windows these messages are displayed in a small window that pops up in the middle of your screen. The options in this group control whether you want to receive these messages or not, much like the operation of the CASTON and CASTOFF utilities in NetWare. The controls are radio buttons; only one can be selected. The default for this control is for messages to be enabled.

▶ **Tip:** To display incoming messages in a small popup window, the NetWare driver relies on a utility named NWPOPUP.EXE, which can be found in your \WINDOWS directory. When you install the NetWare driver for Windows (see Chapter 5) a reference to this utility is automatically added to the LOAD= statement in your WIN.INI file. This loads the utility on Windows startup so that incoming messages can be received.

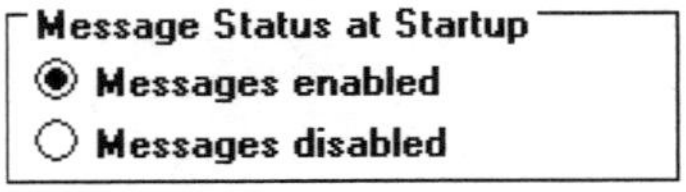

```
┌ Message Status at Startup ──────────┐
│ ◉ Messages enabled                  │
│ ○ Messages disabled                 │
└─────────────────────────────────────┘
```

Figure 3.3 Message Status at Startup box.

386 ENHANCED SETTINGS

The 386 Enhanced group of controls (see Figure 3.4) is intended for those running Windows in 386 Enhanced mode. The controls are check boxes so you can turn either control on or off. NWShare handles indicates that you want each of your DOS sessions to share a common pool of drive mappings—if you change drive F: to point to SYS:DATA in one DOS session, drive F: should point to SYS:DATA in another. The default for this control is off.

The NWShare handles setting primarily affects your DOS applications. When you start a DOS application in 386 Enhanced mode, Windows opens a DOS virtual machine and loads the application into that machine. (Windows itself, and your Windows applications, continue to run in a separate virtual machine.) Upon opening the new virtual machine, Windows passes it the current NetWare environment settings—logical drive connections, print queue connections, and so on. However, if NWShare handles is set to off (the default), any drive-mapping changes you make from within Windows will not be reflected in any DOS virtual machine you have running at the time. For example, if you change a drive mapping from within Windows (see "Network Connections" later), your DOS applications will continue to think that mapping is still available. If the application attempts to access a file in the directory referenced by the now defunct mapping, an error message will result.

To avoid this problem, you can turn on the NWShare handles check box. With this setting, all drive mappings are stored in a common pool of drive mappings maintained by Windows, and all virtual machines get their drive mappings from this pool. In addition, when you make a change to a drive mapping, all virtual machines running on the system (including those running DOS applications) are informed of the change. Furthermore, the change is noted regardless of whether the change is made from within the virtual machine in which Windows is running or from another virtual machine in which a DOS application is running. (A surprising number of DOS applications will allow you to change a NetWare drive mapping.) For example, if you change drive F: to point to SYS:DATA from a DOS session (or from within Windows), your other DOS and Windows applications will immediately be informed of the change.

At startup, Windows comes up recognizing your NetWare drive connections. Furthermore, any drive connections you create or change while in Windows are maintained once you leave the program. Upon leaving Windows, if you want to have your NetWare drive connections restored to the way they were before you started Windows, you can turn on the "Restore drives" check box. The default setting for this check box is off.

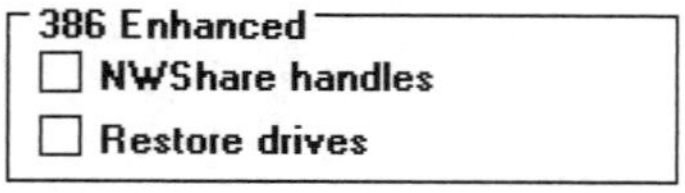

```
┌ 386 Enhanced ─────────────────┐
│  ☐ NWShare handles             │
│  ☐ Restore drives              │
└────────────────────────────────┘
```

Figure 3.4 386 Enhanced box.

> **Note:** The terms 'on' and 'off' have been used to mean that a particular check box is checked or not checked. NWShare handles and Restore Drives (as you will learn in Chapter 5) can be specified in the [NetWare] section of SYSTEM.INI and are generally set using 'True' and 'False' rather than 'on' and 'off.'

THE PRINT SETTINGS

There are three parameters in the Printing box (see Figure 3.5): "Max jobs," "Buffer size," and "Update seconds." They control how Print Manager handles several of its network-specific printing options.

- Max jobs — This parameter controls how many print jobs you can see in the Print Manager queue. Possible values range from 1 to 250. The default for this parameter is 50.

- Buffer size — Buffer size sets the maximum buffer size for a print job. Measured in bytes, it ranges from 3,500 to 30,000, with 3,500 as the default. Increasing this setting may help print speed at the cost of memory.

- Update seconds — The Update seconds parameter determines the time interval (in seconds) for Print Manager to update the Print Manager queue. Possible values range from 1 to 65. The default for this parameter is 30.

THE NETWORK WARNING SETTING

The Network Warning option (see Figure 3.6), if enabled, warns you about network problems, such as if the network is not running, or if the wrong network is running. It will also report shell version conflicts. Novell recommends that you leave this box checked (on) so that you will be notified of any problems. One reason you might not want this box checked is if you are not using the network (if, for example, you decide to run Windows off the network). In that case you can deselect this box. The default for this option is on.

```
┌ Printing ──────────────────
│  ┌────┐ ▲
│  │ 50 │ ▼  Maximum jobs
│  └────┘
│  ┌────┐ ▲
│  │3500│ ▼  Buffer size
│  └────┘
│  ┌────┐ ▲
│  │ 30 │ ▼  Update seconds
│  └────┘
```

Figure 3.5 Printing options.

```
┌ Network Warning ───────────
│  ☒ Network warnings
└────────────────────────────
```

Figure 3.6 Network Warning setting.

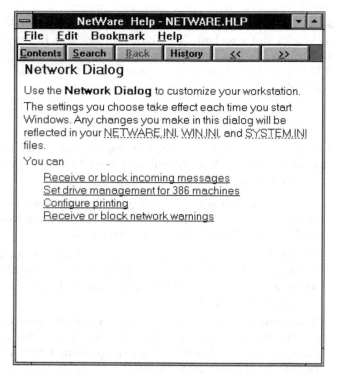

Figure 3.7 Network Dialog help window.

In addition to the four sets of controls available to you, there is on-line help available by pressing the F1 key or clicking on the Help button (see Figure 3.7).

Press the Cancel button to abort any changes and return to the Control Panel screen. Press the OK button to save any changes you made. If you made changes, then close the Window (by pressing ALT+F4 or Close from the system menu, or double-clicking on the system menu bar), you will get a window asking you if you want to save your changes (Figure 3.8).

Also, if you made any changes to the "NWShare handles" or "Restore drives" parameters, when you press OK to save your changes, you will get a message similar to the one Figure 3.9 informing you that "Share Handles" and "Restore drive" changes will take effect the next time you start Windows. This is because these

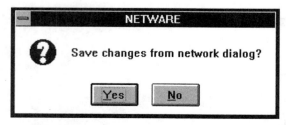

Figure 3.8 Save Changes message box.

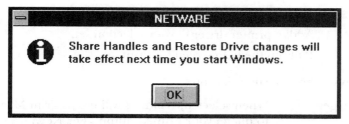

Figure 3.9 Share Handles and Restore Drive message box.

options update your SYSTEM.INI file in the [NetWare] section. Changes to SYSTEM.INI or WIN.INI do not take effect until Windows loads again.

If you want to see how your changes to the Network dialog box are having an effect, look at the [NetWare] section of SYSTEM.INI and the NETWARE.INI file (the initialization file for the NetWare driver).

The Printers Icon

The Printers icon in the Control Panel gives you access to the dialog box in Figure 3.10. (You can access this same dialog box by selecting the Option|Printers Setup command in Print Manager.) This dialog box lets you set parameters for printing while in Windows. You have several buttons that you can select to perform the following functions:

- Cancel   Abort the window and return to the Control Panel.
- Connect   Assign a printer driver to a particular printer port and optionally connect that printer port to a network printer (similar to Novell's CAPTURE command)—this choice, the meat and potatoes of network functionality in the Printers tool, will receive special concentration.
- Setup   Allows you to configure the driver for a particular printer, choosing options such as print resolution, fonts, paper size, printer memory, and so on.

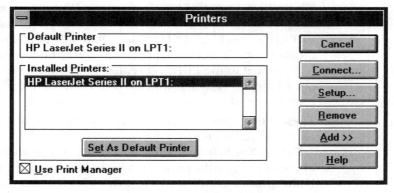

Figure 3.10 Control Panel, Printers dialog box.

- Remove   Removes a printer driver from your selection set.
- Add   Adds a printer driver to your selection set.
- Help   Pulls up the help screen for Printers.

Additionally, two other selections let you:

Use Print Manager   When selected, Windows will use its Print Manager to queue your printed output. For NetWare users, this step is redundant since NetWare keeps print queues for all network printers. Generally, it is recommended that this selection be turned off for network printing.

Set as Default Printer   Makes the printer you choose the default for your Windows applications.

Since the Connect button gives you access to a dialog box that has network functionality associated with it, that is where we will focus our attention. When you select this button, the connect dialog box in Figure 3.11 is displayed. This lets you assign a printer driver to a port—for example, you might assign an HP LaserJet to LPT1. Let's go through the options available to you in this dialog box.

In the upper left corner, the current driver you are assigning to a port is displayed. In this example, we are "Connect"–ing the LaserJet Series II to a port. The following options are used to configure that printer:

- Ports   This list shows the available ports to which you can assign your printer; in our case, the Laserjet Series II is selected. LPT1-LPT3 and COM1-COM4 are provided for parallel and serial printer interfaces. In our case, we'll select LPT1.

      EPT is for an IBM Personal PagePrinter and requires a special controller to work.

      FILE prints your documents to a file rather than to a printer port.

      LPT1.DOS and LPT2.DOS are suggested for those having problems printing on the network. With these selections, Windows uses DOS services to print to a file called LPT1.DOS or LPT2.DOS. Since DOS will not allow a filename with the prefix identical to a device, the file output is redirected to the LPT port (either LPT1 for LPT1.DOS or LPT2 for LPT2.DOS), which is then redirected to a LAN print queue (if you have your LPT port redirected).

- Timeouts   These settings are relevant only when you have Print Manager activated for use.

      Device Not Selected controls how many seconds Print Manager will give the printer to respond to a print request. If the printer is not ready to print after 15 seconds, a

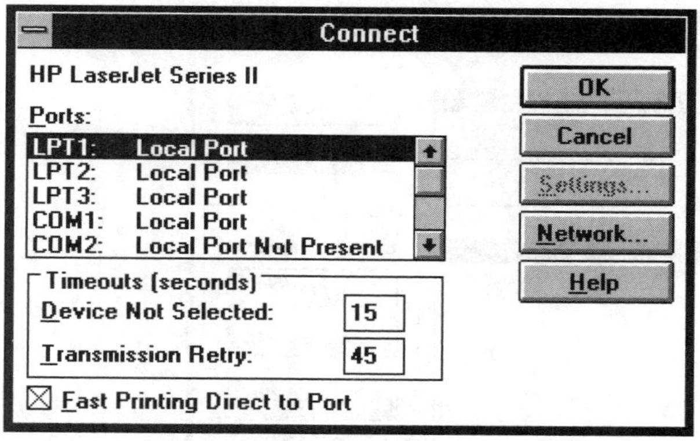

Figure 3.11 Connect dialog box.

message will appear indicating the printer is off-line. The default for this value is 15 seconds.

Transmission Retry controls how many seconds Print Manager should wait before informing you the printer cannot accept any more characters. The default for this value is 45 seconds, which gives most printers ample time to print the information in their buffer and signal Print Manager to send more data. If the printer takes longer than 45 seconds to print the contents of the buffer, Print Manager will generate an error message.

• Fast Printing Direct to Port — Controls the method Windows uses to print documents. By default this option is selected and Windows prints documents by manipulating the printer port directly. If you clear this option (turn it off), Windows will use MS-DOS calls to print. If you are using software that prints using DOS calls, or are having trouble printing, you may need to clear this option.

In addition to these three groups of settings you can make in the Connect dialog box, there are several buttons you can choose from, including: OK, Cancel, Network, Settings, and Help. OK saves your selections and returns to the Printers dialog box. Cancel aborts your changes and returns to the Printers dialog box. Settings lets you change the COM port parameters for COM ports 1–4. Settings such as baud rate, parity, and stop bits can be changed. Help provides you with context-sensitive help for this window.

The Network button, however, is the primary reason for our exploring the connect dialog box in such detail. It is this button that allows you to redirect a printer port to a network print queue.

When you click on the Network button, the "Network–Printer Connections" window in Figure 3.12 is displayed. Let's look at each button available in this window.

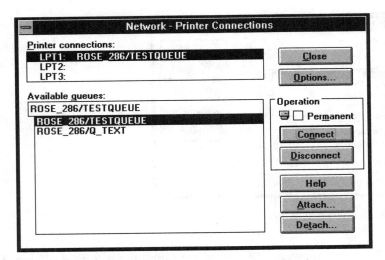

Figure 3.12 The "Network–Printer Connections" dialog box with LPT1 mapped to ROSE_286/TESTQUEUE.

- Close   Closes the window and returns to the Connect window (Figure 3.11).

- Options   Opens the dialog box in Figure 3.13 which lets you change the CAPTURE characteristics for an LPT port, like the number of copies to print, the timeout count, whether to print a banner, and so on.

- Permanent   Allows you to make printer attachments permanent. (Windows attempts to establish the connection each time you start the program.)

- Connect   Attaches an LPT port to a File Server/Print Queue combination.

- Disconnect   Detaches an LPT port from a File server/Print queue combination and returns it to Local status.

- Help   Provides help on this window and will explain how to map printers using this tool.

- Attach   Attach to other file servers (to increase the list of queues you can map to).

- Detach   Remove file server attachments.

If you are familiar with the NetWare CAPTURE utility, you know it accepts various parameters that let you set different characteristics for the capturing of printed output to an LPT port—for example, number of copies, banner printing, and so on. To set these same characteristics for an LPT port from within Windows, you use the Options button in the Network–Printer Connections dialog box (Figure 3.12). When you select this button, the Printer Options dialog box in Figure 3.13 is displayed. The settings you make in this dialog box apply to the currently selected LPT port in the Printer Connections dialog box (Figure 3.12).

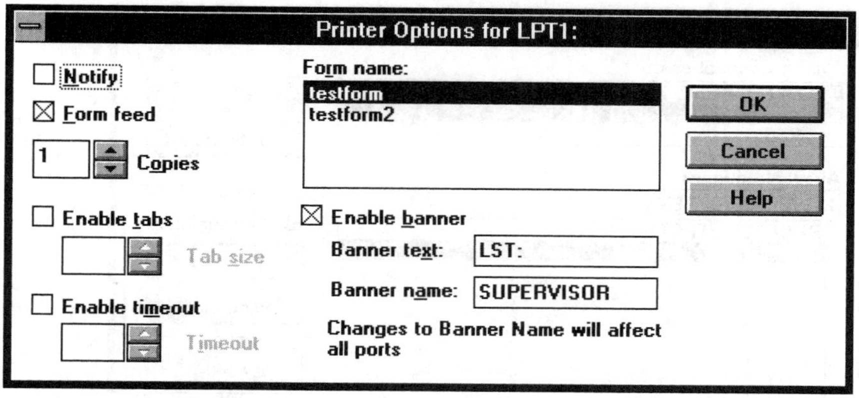

Figure 3.13 Setting Printer Options for LPT1.

The Notify option alerts the user that a job has been completed. The Form feed option adds a form feed at the end of a print job. The Copies option lets you set the number of copies. Enable tabs translates tab characters into the number of spaces specified in the "Tab size" window. Enable timeout, if turned on, waits the number of seconds specified in the Timeout box to flush the print buffer to the network print queue. The form name box lets you select a form by name, and the Enable banner option lets you turn banner printing on or off. If turned on, the banner text and name can both be defined.

All of these options (except for Banner Name which is global) are specific to each LPT port. For example, you can have LPT1 print one copy while LPT2 prints three copies.

To map an LPT port to a specific network print queue, first click on an LPT port (LPT1, LPT2, or LPT3) in the Printer Connections list box. Then select a server/queue combination from the Available queues list box. (In our example, we've selected LPT2 and ROSE_286/Q_TEXT). When you're ready, press the Connect button and the port will be mapped.

You can also click on a port and select the Permanent box to make the LPT port assignment permanent. Then, Windows will attempt to connect to the port each time you start the program. (For example, in Figure 3.14 LPT1 and LPT2 are mapped to network queues and are made permanent.)

As with permanent drive mappings, printer assignments are recorded in the [Network] section of WIN.INI. For example, Figure 3.15 shows what the [Network] section looks like after making the printer connections described above. Notice that LPT1 is mapped to ROSE_286/TESTQUEUE. The next line, LPT1-OP-TIONS, is a summary of the choices you made in the Options window; these are saved for each LPT port.

You have the option of attaching to and detaching from file servers while in the dialog box in Figure 3.15. To detach from a server you are attached to, press the Detach button. You will then see the window in Figure 3.16 with a message pertaining to the loss of all drive, queue, and path mappings to that server if you detach from it. You must choose the server you want to detach from by clicking

Network - Printer Connections
Printer connections:
LPT1: ROSE_286/TESTQUEUE
LPT2: ROSE_286/Q_TEXT
LPT3:
Available queues:
ROSE_286/Q_TEXT
ROSE_286/TESTQUEUE
ROSE_286/Q_TEXT
Close
Options...
Operation
Permanent
Connect
Disconnect
Help
Attach...
Detach...

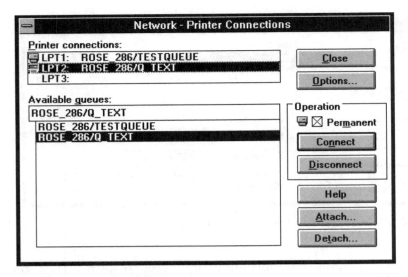

Figure 3.14 The Network–Printer Connections dialog box with LPT2 now mapped to ROSE_286/Q_TEXT, and LPT1 and LPT2 designated as Permanent printer mappings.

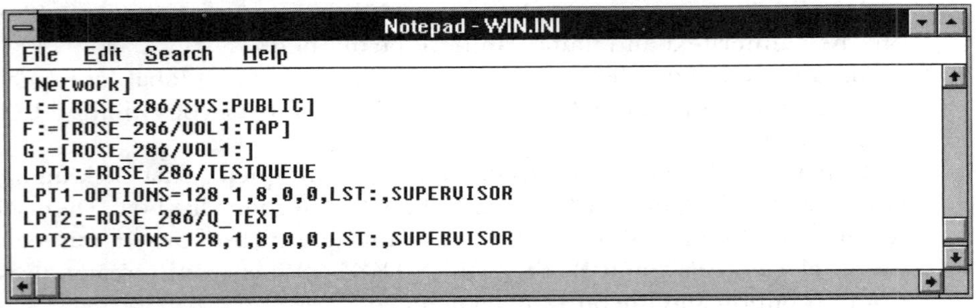

Notepad - WIN.INI
File Edit Search Help
[Network]
I:=[ROSE_286/SYS:PUBLIC]
F:=[ROSE_286/VOL1:TAP]
G:=[ROSE_286/VOL1:]
LPT1:=ROSE_286/TESTQUEUE
LPT1-OPTIONS=128,1,8,0,0,LST:,SUPERVISOR
LPT2:=ROSE_286/Q_TEXT
LPT2-OPTIONS=128,1,8,0,0,LST:,SUPERVISOR

Figure 3.15 Printer connections are stored in WIN.INI as well.

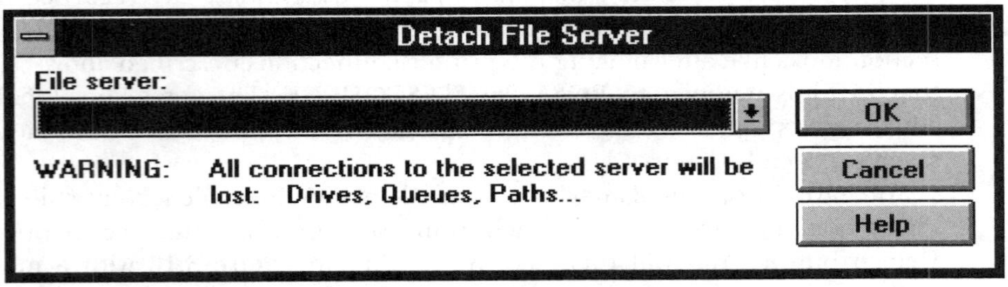

Detach File Server
File server:
WARNING: All connections to the selected server will be lost: Drives, Queues, Paths...
OK
Cancel
Help

Figure 3.16 Detach File Server window.

on the down arrow by the "File Server:" prompt. Then you can cancel the operation by pressing the Cancel button, or you can go ahead and detach by pressing "OK." You should choose this option cautiously because of possible side effects, such as losing drive mappings, print queue connections, and so on.

You may attach to a server by choosing the Attach button. From the displayed window, as shown in Figure 3.17, you can choose the name of the file server to which you want to attach. Click the down arrow by the file server name prompt and choose the server you want. Then you will be prompted for the user name and password under which you want to log in.

The buttons in the Network–Printer Connections window, as in many others in Windows, are smart—they will be shaded if they do not apply. For instance, the Attach button will not work if there are no more file servers you can attach to and Detach won't work if you are not attached to any servers.

Choose Close from the Network–Printer Connections window to save your server/queue path and return to the Connect dialog box (Figure 3.11).

Now you need to assign that server/queue to an LPT port. (You can only redirect LPT ports to a network queue.) Therefore, choose which port you want to redirect to the server/queue combination you've just selected.

The Network–Printer Connections window (Figure 3.12) lets you "capture" a local LPT port to a network queue. Data sent to that (captured) LPT port will be redirected to the file server/queue pair you chose. That's all fine and good, but we still need to assign that port to a printer. Realize that printer/port selection is independent of port/queue capturing. Let's complete the printer configuration process by assigning our sample queue ROSE_286/TESTQUEUE to the LaserJet Series II:

1. Press the Close button from the "Network–Printer Connections" window. This will show the Connect window, as shown again in Figure 3.18, which is the one you use to assign or "connect" a printer port to a printer.

   Notice (in Figure 3.18) that LPT1 is no longer listed as a "Local Port" like LPT2 and LPT3 are. Instead, it is listed as being captured to "ROSE_286/TESTQUEUE" (the mapping of LPT2 to ROSE_286/QTEXT in Figure 3.14 has been removed to simplify matters).

2. The only thing left to do is to assign our printer, in this case the LaserJet Series II, to LPT1. You know the LaserJet Series II is the current printer because its name appears in the upper left corner of Figure 3.18. Therefore,

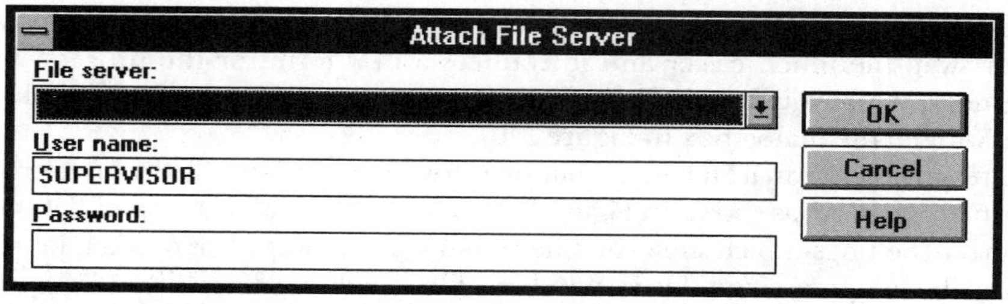

Figure 3.17 Attach File Server window.

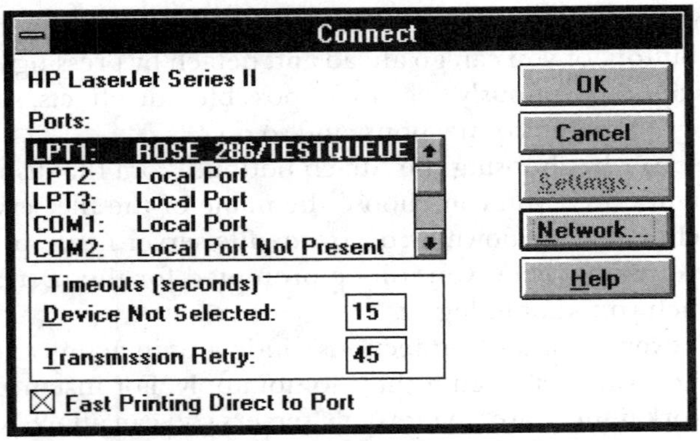

```
┌─────────────────────────────────────────────────┐
│ ═                   Connect                       │
├─────────────────────────────────────────────────┤
│ HP LaserJet Series II                ┌─────────┐ │
│                                      │   OK    │ │
│ Ports:                               └─────────┘ │
│ ┌─────────────────────────────┬─┐   ┌─────────┐ │
│ │LPT1:   ROSE_286/TESTQUEUE   │▲│   │ Cancel  │ │
│ │LPT2:   Local Port           │ │   └─────────┘ │
│ │LPT3:   Local Port           │ │   ┌─────────┐ │
│ │COM1:   Local Port           │ │   │Settings…│ │
│ │COM2:   Local Port Not Present│▼│   └─────────┘ │
│ ┌─Timeouts (seconds)──────────────┐ ┌─────────┐ │
│ │                                 │ │Network… │ │
│ │ Device Not Selected:    │ 15 │  │ └─────────┘ │
│ │                                 │ ┌─────────┐ │
│ │ Transmission Retry:     │ 45 │  │ │  Help   │ │
│ └─────────────────────────────────┘ └─────────┘ │
│ ☒ Fast Printing Direct to Port                   │
└─────────────────────────────────────────────────┘
```

Figure 3.18 Connect window, showing LPT1 now mapped to ROSE_286/TESTQUEUE.

choose LPT1 and press OK (or double-click on LPT1) to assign the Series II to LPT1, the same port that has been routed to ROSE_286/TESTQUEUE.

The Printers window will then reappear, showing you that the printer you were Connecting a port to (a Series II in this case) is now running on LPT1.

That's it for network printer selection. If you have any other printers you want to define, you can choose the Add button from the Printers window (Figure 3.10) to select other drivers, or you can choose another printer driver and Connect it to another port (and maybe connect that port to a network server/queue pair).

The 386 Enhanced Icon

There isn't a great deal of network-specific functionality added in 386 Enhanced mode, but there is one aspect worth mentioning: the Windows swap file. Installation of the swap file will be discussed in detail in Chapter 5, which contains an explanation on how to install Windows on NetWare. For now, let's go through the process of installing a temporary swap file on a network drive. Be aware that the temporary swap file on the network is a point of controversy and may not be (and often is not) right for your network. However, this example is offered to show you the steps involved in managing a swap file wherever it may reside, and whether it is temporary or permanent.

In Windows 3.0, the swap file was created by a utility called SWAPFILE.EXE that you ran under Windows in real mode. Windows 3.1 makes the process of managing your swap file much easier and introduces a new term for the process: Virtual Memory. When you double-click on the 386 Enhanced icon in the Control Panel, you will see the dialog box in Figure 3.19.

Pressing the "Virtual Memory…" button will reveal a window called, not surprisingly, "Virtual Memory" as shown in Figure 3.20. This window has a group of fields called "Current Settings" which show you where your current swap file is residing (as in what drive; the temporary swap file is stored in a file called WIN386.SWP and is stored, by default, in your Windows directory), how big it is (in kilobytes), and what type it is

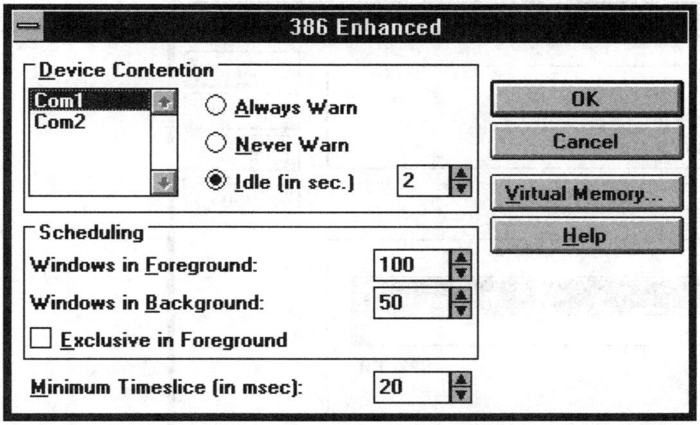

Figure 3.19 386 Enhanced window.

(Temporary or Permanent). It also sports four buttons: OK, Cancel, Change, and Help. OK, as usual, saves your work; Cancel aborts any changes; and Help gets you context-sensitive help. The Change button lets you modify your swap file.

Temporary swap files are created whenever Windows loads and are deleted when one exits Windows. Permanent swap files stay on the disk indefinitely (until modified with this utility or deleted through other means). You cannot create Permanent swap files on the LAN because Windows needs to control the disk hardware directly for a Permanent swap file. Refer to Chapter 5 for discussion of the issues involved in deciding whether to use a permanent or temporary swap file, and where to store it.

Let's go through the steps involved in creating a temporary swap file on the LAN. Although it is generally recommended that you create a permanent swap file on the local hard disk, you may not have enough disk space or you may be running from a diskless PC. Here are the steps involved in creating a temporary swap file:

1. Press the Change button. The utility will search for local hard drives and return the first candidate for a swap file. In this case (Figure 3.21), it found the D: drive, with 882K free. This is not enough for a permanent swap file (which generally consumes between 1 and 2.5 times the workstation's physical memory), so we must look to another drive, a network drive.

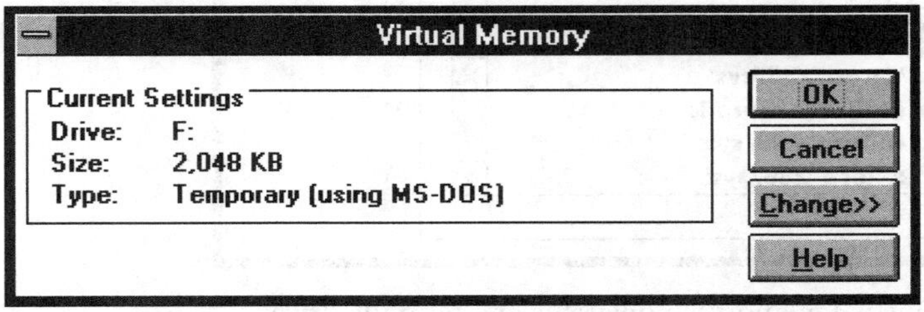

Figure 3.20 Virtual Memory window.

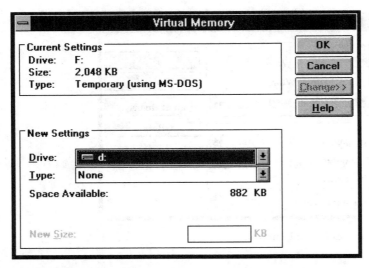

Figure 3.21 Virtual memory window, expanded to show new settings.

2. Open the drop-down listbox labeled "Drive." Note the drives available to you (Figure 3.22). Also, note that Windows only shows you the drives you're currently mapped to. Although there could be a ROSE2_286 server with 10 gigabytes out there, if it is not mapped as a drive, it won't appear in this list. Also, ROSE_286 could have other drives; however, if they are not mapped, you can't assign a swap file to them. In this case, the author chose drive F: for the temporary swap file.

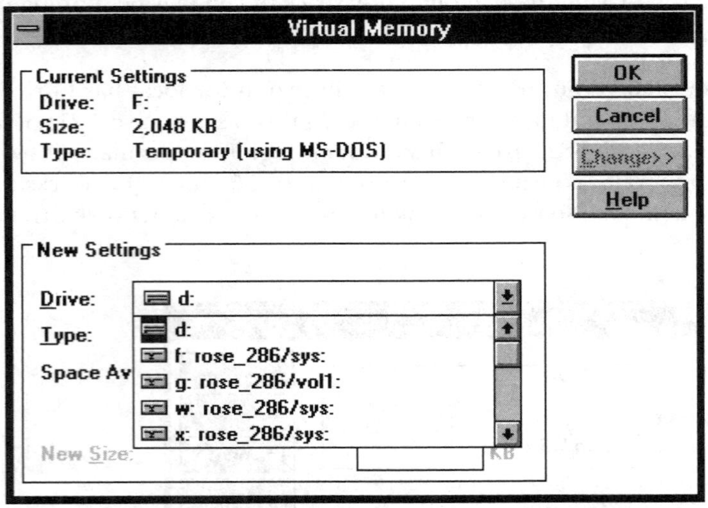

Figure 3.22 Virtual memory window, showing swap file drive choices.

Notice that "Temporary" is chosen for you automatically as the swap file type in the "Type" drop-down listbox. That's the only type you could have here (other than None). Notice also that several new fields have now been filled in at the bottom of the window (Figure 3.23): Space Available, Recommended Maximum Size, and Maximum Size. These indicate the following:

- Space Available   Shows how much space you have left on the drive.

- Recommended   Usually half of the Space Available figure or 2.5 times
  Maximum Size   physical memory. In this case, space available is 10,988 KB and the recommended size is 5,494.

- New Size   Defaults to the recommended size, but it is an editable field. You can click on the field and change it to what you would like. For our example, we changed the 2,084 KB to 5.4 megabytes for illustration, but you will likely need more space in a swap file.

3. Enter the size of the swap file you would like in the New Size field and press OK. You will receive a confirmation message (Figure 3.24) asking you to confirm the new setting.

After you confirm the dialog box in Figure 3.24, another dialog box will be displayed explaining that the new swap file cannot take effect until you restart Windows (Figure 3.25). This dialog box gives you the option of restarting windows right away, or continuing with the current swap file until you decide to exit Windows and restart it. Choose whichever option seems most appropriate for you (if you have no swap file and need one right away, restart Windows). If you chose Continue, you will be returned to the 386 Enhanced window where you can press OK to return to the Control Panel.

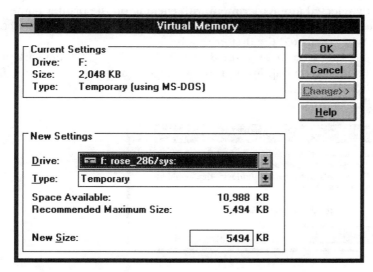

Figure 3.23 Virtual memory window, New Settings section expanded.

Figure 3.24 Virtual memory change confirmation
message box.

Print Manager

The Print Manager in Windows 3.1 has been given more network functionality than
its Windows 3.0 predecessor. In order for Print Manager to run, however, the "Use
Print Manager" box must be checked in the Printers utility in the Control Panel.

Print Manager's icon is located right next to the Control Panel in the Main
group in Program Manager. When you double-click on Print Manager's icon to
start the program, the window in Figure 3.26 is displayed, showing print jobs
waiting for the printers you've installed for Windows.

Screen Display

As mentioned, the first thing you will notice when you start Print Manager is a
listing of the names of printers you've installed for Windows (and what the printer
is connected to, a local printer port or a network server/print queue). Beneath
each printer name will appear a list of jobs waiting for that printer. The text box
next to the Pause, Delete, and Resume buttons shows you the status of the printer
or the currently selected job. Experiment with clicking on the printer name line
and the queue job lines to see what appears in this box. The rest of this section
will assume you have selected the first print job.

In our case, we captured LPT1 to the ROSE_286/TESTQUEUE network print
queue, so that's what shows up in the Print Manager status box. Notice the first
text line in this box says:

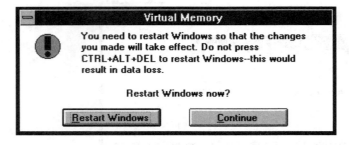

Figure 3.25 Virtual memory change, restart or continue
message box.

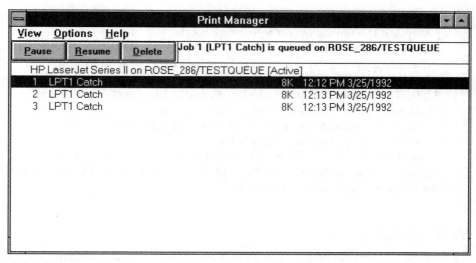

Figure 3.26 Print Manager main window.

```
Job 1 (LPT1 Catch) is queued on ROSE_286/TESTQUEUE
```

This tells us that the selected job (#1) is queued up (as opposed to paused, inactive, or some other status).

The name line for each installed printer shows you its status. (Remember, Windows organizes the print queues by printers, which are connected to certain ports, which may then be connected to print queues—Novell utilities often list information by queue.) In our example, it displays:

```
HP LaserJet Series II on ROSE_286/TESTQUEUE [Active]
```

The printer driver is listed first, followed by the port (in this case ROSE_286/TESTQUEUE; it would be LPT1 if this port was not captured to the network queue). Following that is the status of the printer, Active, which means the printer is on-line.

QUEUE ENTRIES

Following the printer name line is a list of the print jobs the local workstation has sent to the queue for that printer. (For a complete listing of queue jobs, see the View-Selected Net Queue option below in the Menu Options section.) They are listed as:

```
Sequence#     Banner Name     File Size     Time     Date
```

Note that the sequence number is not Novell's job # but simply a way of numbering the jobs that are stacked up at the queue.

On-Screen Options

There are three buttons in the Print Manager window that let you modify the status of a print job. These are strategically placed right along side of the job status. You can Pause, Resume, or Delete a job by using these buttons. You must first select a job (place the cursor over a job and press the left button) before using one of these buttons, or Windows will assume you want to operate on the first job listed.

Pausing a job will cause a hand to be placed over the sequence number and the job status line will display that "Job x (LPT1 catch) is paused on ..." (See Figure 3.27). The job will not print until it is resumed by pressing the Resume button which will remove the pause status and make it revert to an active job.

The Delete button will remove the job selected from the queue. Of course, you must have the appropriate rights before you can delete a print job.

To show you how the Print Manager display compares to PCONSOLE, look at Figure 3.28 which shows a PCONSOLE queue display for TESTQUEUE. Notice the fields displayed are quite similar.

Menu Options

There are several menu choices in Print Manager that affect network operations. We will start with the options associated with the View menu shown in Figure 3.29.

The Selected Net Queue option lets you see all of the print jobs in the currently selected network queue that were submitted by anyone on the LAN. Remember that the default listing of jobs in the Print Manager window shows only those submitted by the local workstation—it will not reflect jobs placed in the queue by other workstations. Figure 3.30 shows the window that appears when you select this option; note that it shows jobs printed by the Supervisor (the login account we used in our examples above) and user Guest. The job submitted by Guest did not appear on our local print listing in the main window of Print Manager.

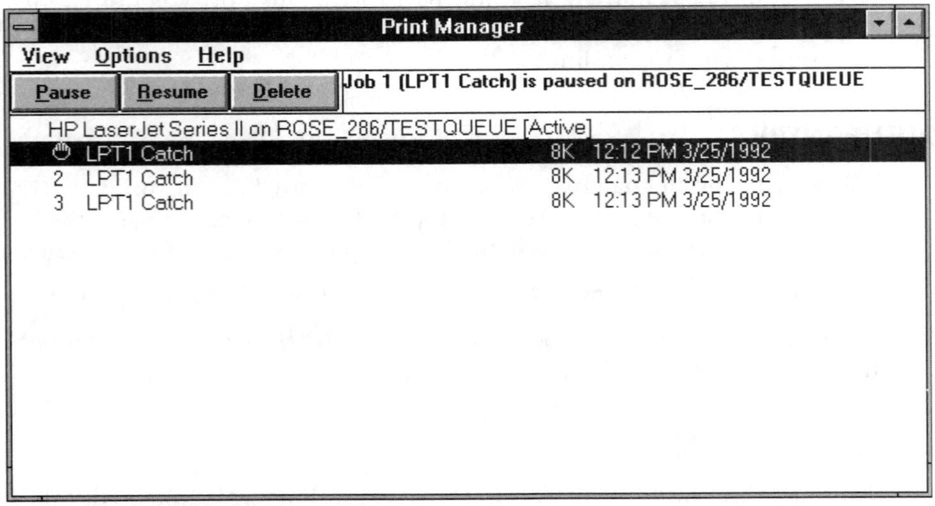

Figure 3.27 Print Manager window with paused job.

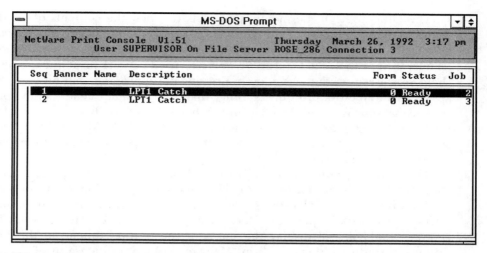

Figure 3.28 PCONSOLE queue job listing.

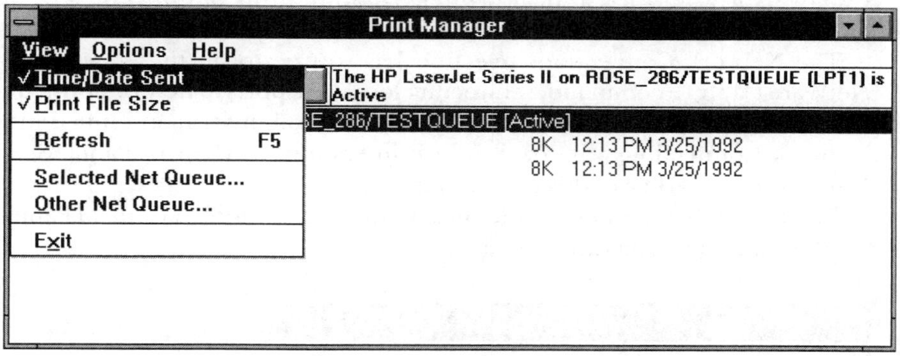

Figure 3.29 Print Manager View menu.

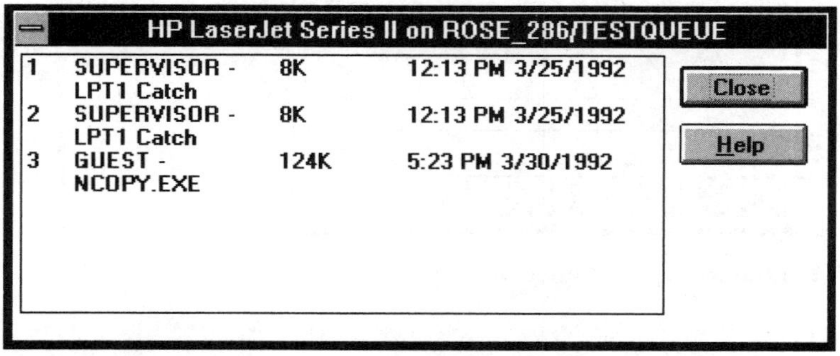

Figure 3.30 Print Manager—Selected Net Queue dialog box.

The Other Net Queue menu option lets you view the contents of another network queue, similar to the way you can view other queues with Novell's PCONSOLE command. When you choose this option, you will see a window similar in appearance to Figure 3.31. You can view a network print queue, receive help, or close and exit the window by pressing the appropriate button.

To view a network print queue other than your default queue (i.e. the print queue that your Windows default printer is being routed to), type the name of the queue in the Network Queue box (using the FILE_SERVER_NAME/QUEUE_NAME method) and press View. In Figure 3.32, the author typed the name of the queue we've been using and pressed View.

The Options menu, shown in Figure 3.33, provides several other options for network printing. For example, the Network Settings Option gives you access to the window titled "Network Options" in Figure 3.34 that has two Options: "Update Network Display" and "Print Net Jobs Direct." Update Network Display, if enabled, will display the status of the network queue in the Print Manager window. Otherwise, Print Manager will ignore the status of network queues. Print Net Jobs Direct, if enabled, will allow Print Manager to send network print jobs directly to the network print queue. If this setting is turned off, Print Manager will store the job on the disk, then send it to the LPT port, exactly as it would for a local printer. Disabling this option will slow performance considerably. Both of these Network Settings options default to on.

The Network Connections selection lets you perform the equivalent of the NetWare Capture command, redirecting local LPT ports to network print queues. The window displayed by this command is identical in form and function to the Network Connections window in the Printers tool in Control Panel. See "The Printers Icon" earlier in this chapter for details.

The Printer Setup option is identical to the Printers tool in Control Panel—the windows and functions are the same.

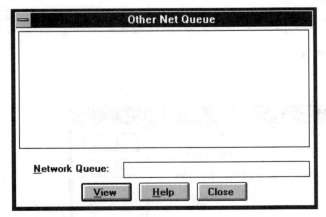

Figure 3.31 Print Manager—Other Net Queue dialog box.

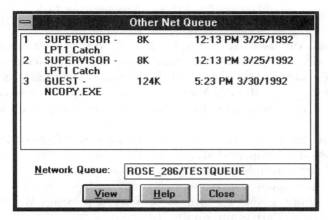

Figure 3.32 Print Manager—Other Net Queue dialog box showing queue listing.

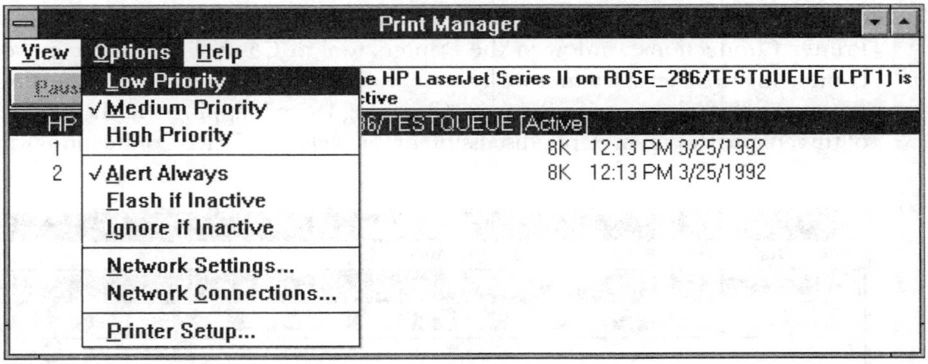

Figure 3.33 Print Manager Options menu.

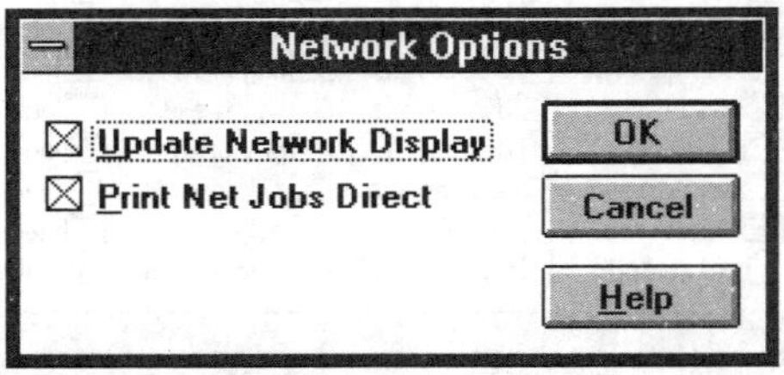

Figure 3.34 Network Options window.

File Manager

File Manager provides the user with a graphic front-end for file manipulation. The latest File Manager provides a multiple-document interface (MDI) with split windows for the directory tree and the directory's contents. Note the drive icons near the top of the File Manager screen in Figure 3.35—Windows detects which drives are floppy, hard, and network, and provides an appropriate icon.

In Figure 3.35 we're looking at drive F: which is mapped to ROSE_286/SYS:—note the "F:ROSE_286/SYS:" displayed near the upper right corner to the right of the drive icons. We are currently examining the PUBLIC directory.

File Manager has been updated in Windows 3.1 to provide several network-specific features in addition to those already present in previous Windows releases. These new features are found on the Disk menu.

Network Connections

The Network Connections option from the Disk menu provides a method for changing drive mappings. When you select this option, the window in Figure 3.36 is displayed. The "Network–Drive Connections" window is similar to the Network–Printer Connections window in the Printers tool in Control Panel, except you are connecting drive letters to network server/volume pairs rather than connecting LPT ports to server/queue pairs. Refer to "Changing Drive Mappings" in the next section of this chapter for an in-depth discussion of the Network–Drive Connections window.

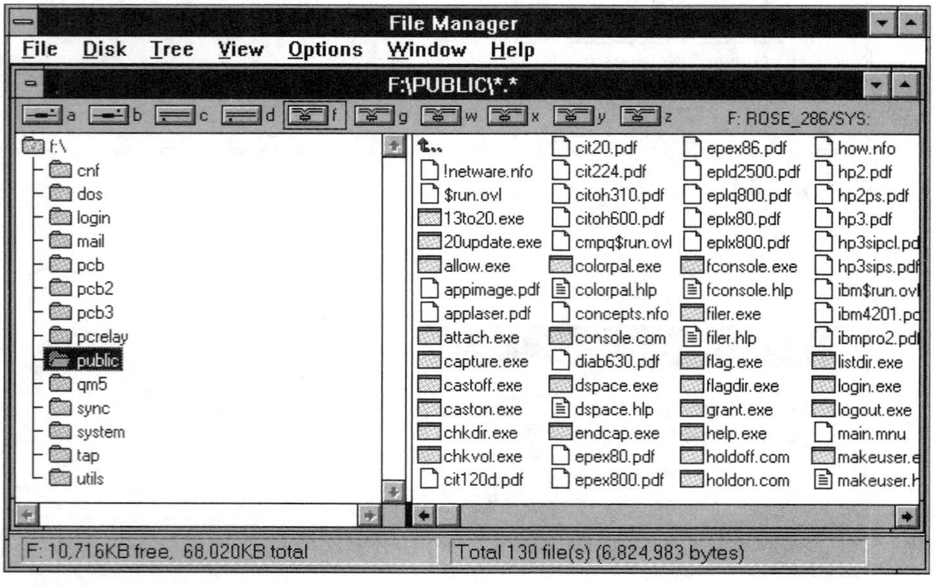

Figure 3.35 File Manager main window.

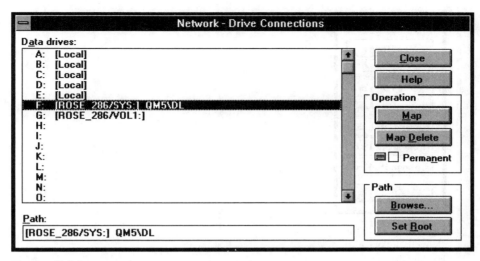

Figure 3.36 Network–Drive Connections window.

The Hidden Powers of NETWARE.DRV

There is a powerful force that, for many, lies dormant deep within Novell's network driver for Windows, NETWARE.DRV. This force will make the Windows/NetWare connection seamless, and will offer you more flexibility in managing your NetWare environment in Windows than you may have thought possible. What makes all of this possible? Novell engineers programmed a very helpful set of tools into NETWARE.DRV, although very few people know about this as yet.

Actually, it's no mystery why so few are aware of this set of tools: You have to specifically activate the set through what is, as of this writing, still an undocumented process. Simply edit your NETWARE.INI file (if you don't have one, create one; it lives in your \WINDOWS directory with the other .INI files). You should have this text in the file:

```
[Options]
NetWareHotKey=1
```

You'll learn more about setting up the NETWARE.INI file in Chapters 5–8, but for now let's enable this feature for you. Once you have added these two lines to your NETWARE.INI file (if you already have an [Options] section in your NETWARE.INI, simply add the "NetWareHotKey=1" line to that section), save NETWARE.INI, exit Windows completely, and restart Windows. This gives Windows a chance to reread the NETWARE.INI file and pick up the change.

Now that you're back in Windows, press the F6 function key. You should see a small popup window of buttons appear on your display that looks similar to Figure 3.37. To remove the NetWare popup window from your screen, you can press ESC or click on the Close button.

Figure 3.37 The "Novell NetWare" Hotkey Popup Window.

Once the hidden NetWare popup window has been unlocked, you can press F6 to activate it from within most any Windows application. The NetWare popup window lets you perform the following functions:

Change drive mappings, including:

• Delete drive mappings.

• Insert drive mappings.

• Map drives as a 'root.'

• Make permanent drive mappings. (These will automatically be remapped next time you run Windows.)

• Attach/Detach file servers.

Change printer assignments, including:

• Capture network print queues to local LPT ports.

• End the capture of any local LPT port.

• Set the options for any LPT port capture (number of copies, tab expansion, form feed, capture timeout, banner text, banner name, form name, and notify user when complete).

• Attach/Detach file servers.

• Attach to another file server.

• Detach from a file server.

• Change your "permanent connections"—those that Windows uses again when it reloads (for example, drive mappings and printer assignments can be made permanent so that every time you run Windows, drive F: is mapped to SYS:DOS and LPT1 is captured to SERVER1/QUEUE_A).

• Change or disable the NetWare popup window hotkey. (You can use F1 through F12 to activate the NetWare popup window.)

The main advantage to using the NetWare popup window is that it gives you direct access to the same NetWare dialog boxes accessible from File Manager, Print Manager, and Control Panel, thereby allowing you to manage your network connection without accessing these utilities. This section will demonstrate how to use the NetWare popup window to help you take better advantage of the Windows/NetWare connection.

Changing Drive Mappings

If you press the "Map Drives" button from the main "Novell NetWare" menu, you will see a window similar to Figure 3.38. Notice that this is the same window displayed when you select the Disk Network Connections command from within File Manager (see Figure 3.36).

The Network–Drive Connections window can be viewed as a Windows version of the MAP command-line NetWare utility. This window lists your drive mappings and lets you modify those mappings to meet your needs.

You'll notice in Figure 3.38 that the first five drives, A through E, are labeled "[Local]." This means they are either local drives (like floppy drive A: or hard drive C:), or they are reserved for a local disk drive. Also in Figure 3.38, drive F: is mapped to the \QM5\DL directory on the SYS: volume of the ROSE_286 server. Drive G is mapped to the root of the VOL1 volume of that same server. You can scroll through this listing of drive mappings which can include up to 26 mappings, A: through Z:.

The buttons in the "Network–Drive Connections" window are organized by function: The first two provide basic window operations; the next two perform the actual map assignment or removal and can optionally make a mapping permanent (more on this soon). Finally, the last two buttons help define and manipulate the

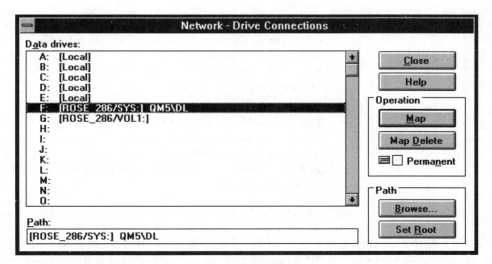

Figure 3.38 The "Network–Drive Connections" window.

path for your drive mapping. (The path for a drive mapping is defined in the one-line edit window at the bottom of Figure 3.38.) Let's look at each of these buttons more closely:

- **Close**
Closes the window and returns to the main menu (Figure 3.37).

- **Help**
Opens the NETWARE.HLP file in the standard Windows Help facility providing an explanation of how to map drives using this tool.

- **Map**
Lets you create a drive mapping. To map a drive, type the path to be mapped to a drive into the Path box at the bottom of the window, then click on a drive (to map the path to) in the Data drives listbox, and press the Map button. What you're doing is separately selecting a drive and a path—the Map button simply joins the two together.

- **Map Delete**
Deletes an existing drive mapping. To do this, click on a drive and press the Map Delete button. You will be asked if you're sure about this; if you say you are, the drive mapping will be removed.

- **Permanent**
Makes a drive mapping permanent. Windows will attempt to make the connection each time you start the program. To make a drive mapping permanent, choose a drive letter that is mapped to a network path (like F: or G: in Figure 3.38), then turn on the Permanent check box. With this setting, Windows will remember that drive mapping the next time you start the program and it will be remapped for you, even if the mapping was not there when you started Windows. We'll walk through an example of how to do this shortly.

- **Browse**
Pressing this button opens a window that lets you graphically choose the server, volume, and directory you would like to map a drive to (see Figure 3.39). Your choice is recorded in the Path text box at the bottom of the Network–Drive Connections window (Figure 3.38).

- **Set Root**
This button makes the drive mapping that appears in the Path at the bottom of the Network–Drive Connections window a "fake" root (it essentially puts brackets around it). Selecting this button is the equivalent of entering a "MAP ROOT" statement at the DOS prompt. More on this below in our walk-through.

Let's walk through a short session in which we will change the mapping of drive F. Since we're not sure which directory we want, we'll first use the "Browse" feature. To begin, select drive F from the Data drives listbox of the Network–Drive Connections window. Its mapping is displayed in the Path textbox. Next, select

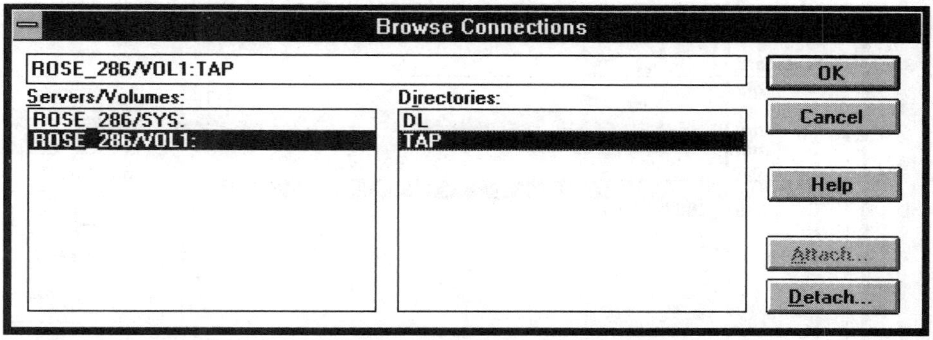

Figure 3.39 "Browse Connections" Window called from Figure 3.37.

the Browse button which brings up the "Browse Connections" window (Figure 3.39). This window lists the file servers we're logged into on the left and the volumes available on each of those servers on the right. In this case, we're logged into ROSE_286, which has two volumes available: SYS and VOL1.

We decide we want the VOL1 volume, so we click on it. This lists the two directories on that volume, DL and TAP. We select the TAP directory, which is recorded in the text box at the top of the Browse Connections window.

If we decided we wanted to look at the drives on another server, we could press the "Attach" button (or if we wanted to release one of our server connections we could press the "Detach" button).

To confirm the selection, we press the OK button. The "Browse Connections" window is closed, returning us to the "Network–Drive Connections" window. Now the path we've selected appears in the path textbox (at the bottom of the window) and reads ROSE_286/VOL1:TAP. (If we had decided we didn't want the path to be changed, we could have pressed "Cancel" to exit the Browse window without changing the path.)

Now we decide we want to map drive F: to the new path, ROSE_286/VOL1:TAP, so we press the Map button. The "Remap Network Device?" message appears (Figure 3.40) asking us if we really want to remove the current mapping of drive F: in favor of the new path. When you select OK, the mapping for drive F is changed to the new path as shown in Figure 3.41.

Figure 3.40 The "Remap Network Device?" Message Box.

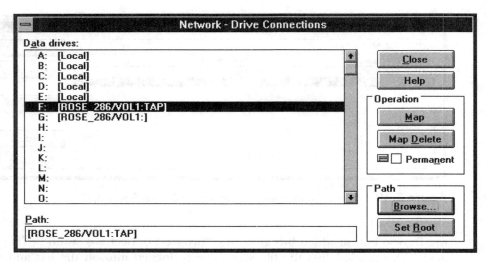

Figure 3.41 The "Network–Drive Connections" window with drive F remapped.

Note that drive F: is mapped as a root drive (appears in brackets). By default, paths selected with the Browse feature are set up as root drives. A root drive is a drive that is mapped to a certain directory, but DOS thinks it's at the root. So, in the case of drive F:, if you typed "CD \" at drive F:, you would still be at the \TAP directory—it would have become the root. This feature is not only convenient but also necessary, because some Windows utilities automatically back up to the root each time they look at the contents of a drive. (We'll explain mapping root drives in more detail later in the book.)

As you might imagine, you aren't limited to mapping drives solely by using the Browse button. Instead, you can simply type the path for the drive mapping straight into the Path textbox. For example, you might type **sys:public** into the Path textbox, choose a drive like I, then press the Map button. Figure 3.42 shows the results of doing this.

When you create a drive mapping for SYS:PUBLIC using the method just described, the PUBLIC directory will not be considered as a root directory (it is shown outside of the right-hand bracket, as seen in Figure 3.43). This may cause problems with certain Windows applications, like File Manager, that always look for files and directories starting at the root of a disk. Since the PUBLIC directory will not be considered as a root directory, the contents of the root directory of the server volume will be displayed, rather than the contents of the PUBLIC directory, when you click on the drive I icon in File Manager. By comparison, notice that the mapping for drive F, which is mapped to the TAP directory, is enclosed entirely in brackets. This means that the TAP directory will be considered as a root directory by all DOS and Windows applications, including File Manager. Therefore, when you click on the drive F icon in File Manager, only the contents of the TAP directory will be displayed.

If you want to turn the drive I mapping into a root mapping, select the mapping containing drive I, then press the "Set Root" button. A message asking if you are sure you want to make this a "root" (Figure 3.43) is displayed. When you select OK, brackets are placed around the path for the mapping.

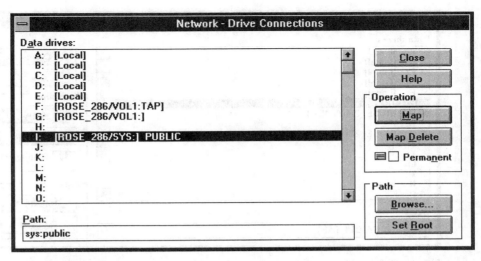

Figure 3.42 Network–Drive Connections window, having just assigned non-root drive I: to SYS:PUBLIC.

You can also use the Map button to remap the drive as a root. To do this, select the mapping for drive I. Next, edit the Path textbox and move the right bracket to include the PUBLIC directory within the brackets. Finally, press the MAP button. (Figure 3.44 shows drive I: mapped as a root.)

Now that we've mapped several drives, let's make them permanent. Making a drive permanent saves its mapping to the [Network] section of WIN.INI. Every time Windows loads, those permanent drives get mapped so you can count on them being there every time you run Windows.

To make a drive permanent, simply click on the drive mapping in the Data drives listbox, then click on the Permanent box. A small drive icon will appear next to the drive letter to show that the drive has been mapped permanently as shown in Figure 3.44.

As mentioned, when you create, change, or make permanent a NetWare drive mapping, the NetWare driver records the new setting in the [Network] section of the WIN.INI file. For example, if you look at WIN.INI after creating the permanent drive mappings described in the preceding paragraphs, the [Network] section might look something like Figure 3.45.

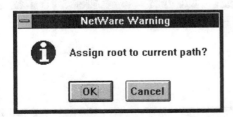

Figure 3.43 "Assign root to current path?" Message Box.

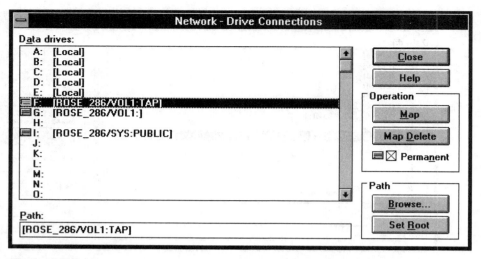

Figure 3.44 Drives F, G, I have been assigned Permanent status and drive I: has been designated as a root drive.

Changing Printer Assignments

The NetWare driver provides the same flexibility in changing printer assignments as it does with drive mappings. You can change printer assignments by using the MAP Printers button in the NetWare popup window. In the same way the "Map Drives" button corresponds to NetWare's MAP command-line utility, the "Map Printers" button is like a Windows version of CAPTURE and ENDCAP. This button gives you access to dialog boxes that capture and end the capture of LPT ports, make permanent printer attachments, and attach and detach from file servers—much as you can with the Map Drives button.

See the discussion earlier in this chapter about the Control Panel's Printers icon for a thorough explanation of how to change printer assignments.

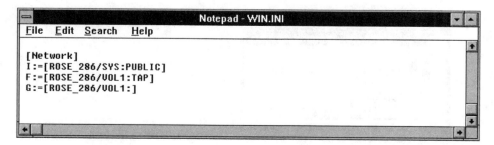

Figure 3.45 The NetWare driver records your drive mappings in the WIN.INI file.

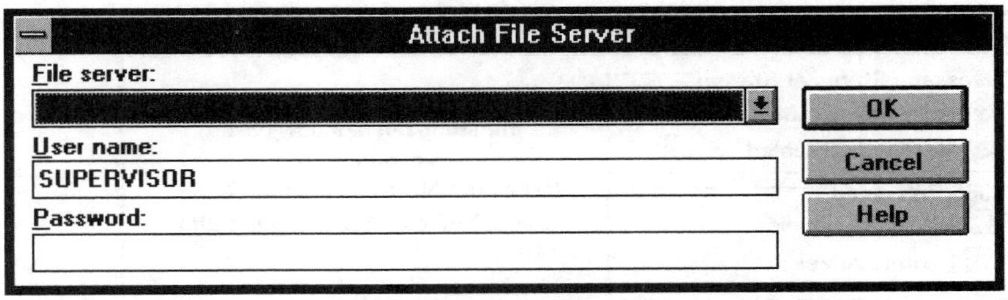

Figure 3.46 Attach File Server dialog box.

Attaching to Other File Servers

Another feature of the NetWare/Windows popup is the "Attach File Server" window that is displayed when you press the "Attach Server" button (Figure 3.46). This window lets you specify a file server, user name, and password to attach to a file server. The File Server selection is a listbox; if you press the down arrow, it will list all of the file servers on your internetwork that you are not currently logged into. You can then choose the server you would like to log into.

Detaching from a File Server

The NetWare driver also lets you detach from a file server. To do this, select the Detach Server button from the NetWare popup window (Figure 3.37). When you select this button, the Detach File Server window in Figure 3.47 is displayed.

Using the Detach File Server dialog box is very simple—you simply choose the server you want to detach from and select OK. You can see a list of attached servers by opening the File server drop-down box.

Network Options

The "Network Options" button in the NetWare popup window (Figure 3.37) displays the "Network" window (Figure 3.48). This is the same window you get when you select the Network icon from the Control Panel. For a full explanation of this window, see the Control Panel discussion earlier in this chapter.

Figure 3.47 Detach File Server dialog box.

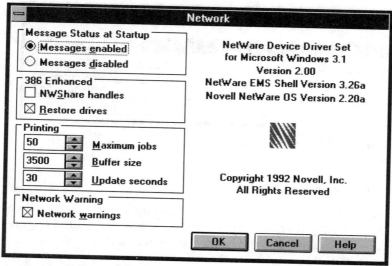

Figure 3.48 The Network window.

In general, this window gives you information about the driver versions you are using and lets you make several global NetWare settings, such as whether you want to receive SEND-type messages, to restore your original drives, to share drive assignments between DOS sessions, to set how many print jobs you can handle, to specify the buffer size for printing, to set the default printer update (in seconds), and finally, whether you want to receive network warnings or not.

Permanent Connections

If you press the "Permanent List" button in the NetWare popup window (Figure 3.37), you will be presented with a list of the permanent connections you have specified for drives and printers as shown in Figure 3.49. This window simply lets you view those connections. You can delete a permanent connection by clicking on it and pressing the Delete button. The connections listed in the [Network] section of WIN.INI will be updated accordingly.

> **Note:** This dialog box is unique to the NetWare popup window—it cannot be accessed from any other Windows application (i.e. Control Panel, File Manager, Print Manager).

Change Hotkey

The last option in the NetWare popup window (other than Close which removes the window from the screen) is "Change Hotkey." This option lets you modify the

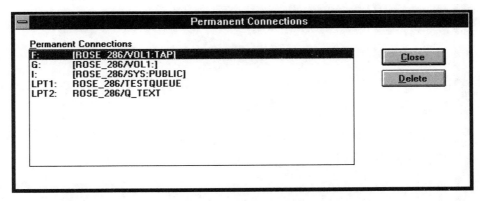

Figure 3.49 "Permanent Connections" shows what's saved in WIN.INI.

function key that is used to bring up this tool. When you select this option, the "Reconfigure Hotkey" window in Figure 3.50 is displayed. The default key is F6. To change the active hotkey, simply choose from F1-F12. If you want to disable the hotkey, you can click on the "Disable Hotkey" box.

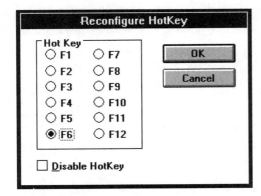

Figure 3.50 The Reconfigure HotKey window.

4 Planning for Windows

Before plunging into installing Windows on your network, let's examine several of the issues you will face. Among these are: differences between networked DOS and networked Windows, setting up applications to be shared effectively, printing under Windows in a NetWare environment, virus scanning, security, and backup and archive management.

This chapter is intended to provide an overview of these concepts and some food for thought before installing Windows on NetWare. If you are already familiar with these concepts, or are a seasoned integrator, you may want to skip ahead to Chapter 5—Installing Windows on NetWare—and get right to the heart of the matter. If you decide to do this, you can always come back and review this chapter at your leisure.

The first issue to be examined is the difference between managing a network running Windows and managing a network running DOS (and primarily character-based applications). The most obvious difference is the look and feel, but you should also be aware of performance differences, differences in configuration, and potential areas of conflict where you may spend time troubleshooting. In addition, elements such as drive mappings, rights and security, and user communications should be considered. It's important that you think about these points before going ahead with installing Windows on the network (which we cover in the next chapter). In Chapter 6, we'll address setting up applications on the network.

Apart from file sharing, printing is the most popular function of a LAN. Printing under Windows has its differences from the DOS world, and you need to be aware of how you will print (or, if you are a system manager, how your users will print).

The chapter includes discussion of global configurations versus user-specific setup, how to capture local LPT ports to the network in Windows, and how to configure those settings for other users. In addition, setting up Windows applications to print on the network and whether to use Print Manager or Novell's PRINTCON utility will be covered. Finally, an explanation of the differences between the NetWare PRINTDEF and PRINTCON utilities, and how they can be useful to you under Windows will be given.

Another issue that may confront you as a system manager or as a user is virus security. At this point, if you haven't already been affected by a virus, someone you know may have been. We will discuss preventive measures you can take, including using the virus scanning software included with this book to ensure a safe, virus-free environment. See Chapter 10 for details on this software.

Finally, we will discuss backup and archive, and the necessity for it on your network when using Windows.

What's Different About Running Windows on NetWare?

Look and Feel

The first thing you will notice when running Windows on your NetWare network is simply the look and feel. Windows is different from DOS, and it may take a while longer to do the same things you normally do in DOS on NetWare. For instance, you may be familiar with several NetWare command-line utilities and use them often under DOS. In fact, typing the appropriate command-lines to map a drive or connect to a printer may have become almost automatic. On the other hand, performing the same operation with the Windows graphical user interface may require a few more steps (not to mention learning a new interface), but it's best, and perhaps faster, in the long run to learn how to use the Windows interface, rather than shelling to the DOS prompt every time you want to perform a NetWare operation.

Rather than invoking a DOS window and running MAP every time you want to map a drive, there are several other ways of mapping a drive under Windows. The fastest is the NetWare popup tool that comes included with the NetWare driver for Windows 3.1, NETWARE.DRV. See Chapter 3 for a full discussion of how to make use of this powerful tool. With it, you can map drives, capture LPT ports to network print queues, attach to and detach from other file servers, change your global NetWare/Windows options, and maintain a permanent list of drive mappings and captured LPT ports.

Instead of running Windows like DOS, it may pay to take the time to learn how to use the facilities in Windows. This will ease things considerably if you learn to take advantage of the resources the Windows environment provides.

Windows 2.x and even Windows 3.0 did not have much network support; you may have been forced to rely on DOS-based utilities to work with the network. But, with Windows 3.1, and to an even greater extent in Windows for Workgroups (discussed in detail in Chapter 13), you are now able to interact with the network without having to switch to a DOS box for most tasks.

Performance

Another difference you will notice right away when using Windows on a network versus using only DOS on a network is performance. Although Windows can be configured to maximize its performance on a LAN, it will likely be slower than a pure DOS environment. This is true because Windows is busy performing far more tasks than DOS is responsible for, such as providing a graphic user interface, multitasking Windows and DOS applications, and generally handling input from a myriad of sources.

You or your system administrator may attack this problem with higher performance hardware, so the impact of Windows' slowdown may be lessened or even removed. Also, upgrading to Windows 3.1 provides a noticeable performance increase over Windows 3.0. Because performance is so important, we have devoted all of Chapter 8 to optimizing Windows on NetWare.

Configuration

In a stand-alone environment, applications are configured for one user. For each application, there is usually only one configuration file, and the system generally has a menu tailored to only one individual. On a network, however, there is a wide array of users, each with a wide (and different) array of needs.

Although you may be used to multiple configurations on a DOS-based network, the situation can become even more complex under Windows. There are several different strategies for installing Windows on the network, but there will very likely be a global Windows area where users share read-only files and a personal area for each user (which may be in a directory on the file server or on a local hard drive). There will be both global configuration files that affect all or groups of users, and there will be individual, local configuration files (usually .INI files in Windows applications). You may want to refer to Chapter 6, which covers installing Windows applications on NetWare.

Troubleshooting

Any time you have a situation where there is more that can go wrong, often more will go wrong. Try not to be pessimistic, but you can only anticipate so much. Although the goal of Windows is to provide a simpler, more flexible front-end to the user, it is not as simple to set up for the system administrator.

Perhaps the first step is simply to be aware of the complexities involved in setting up Windows. This necessitates doing more planning than you might otherwise do. Often, if you can visualize how you are performing an installation, the process will go more smoothly; if you have problems, they can be corrected much easier. You may wish to sit down and physically draw the directory structures for the applications you will be installing (Windows included). Include the directory rights for each user. Chapters 5 and 6 cover the steps you will go through when planning for and installing Windows on NetWare.

Chapter 9 has been devoted to troubleshooting problems with Windows on NetWare. You may also find the troubleshooting tips section in Appendix B quite helpful during your installation/configuration phase.

Effectively Installing Shared Applications

If you are involved in installing Windows applications on NetWare, you should be aware of the elements you must consider when planning the installation: drive mappings, user security/file and directory rights and privileges, and the communications strategy between users, if any.

Drive Mappings

When you configure an application for NetWare, you will usually need to map a search drive for the executable files of an application. You will also need to map a different drive for a user's private files.

You have several different methods of configuring drives for applications when working with Windows on NetWare. First, you can map the drives before starting Windows and not change those mappings once in Windows.

This is a straightforward approach—you do just what you would normally do in DOS. When you set up an application in Program Manager, you may want to specify a "Working Directory" which will become the default directory when the application is run (you'll learn more about this in Chapter 6). This approach depends on certain drives being consistently mapped to certain server/volume/directory combinations.

For instance, if drive G: is mapped to SERVER1/SYS:APPS\123 and the Lotus 1-2-3 icon in Program Manager specifies that its working directory is G:\APPS\123, then that drive must be mapped before the application is run.

Another approach is to use the [Network] section of WIN.INI to set the network drives when you enter Windows. These are called "Permanent Connections" and are discussed in Chapter 3. With this approach, you can let Windows map the drives you will depend on for you—when Windows is first loaded. Windows reads the [Network] section in WIN.INI on startup and maps the drives you have specified there.

A final word about mapping drives: Decide ahead of time whether you will allow Windows to share drive mappings between Windows and DOS sessions. You can control drive mappings so that if a user in a DOS session changes drive G: to SYS:DOS, for example, then drive G: is changed in any other DOS or Windows session. Or, you can keep the change isolated so that no other DOS or Windows session is affected—the choice is yours. Most users opt to keep things separate. You'll find out more about this option in the next two chapters on installing Windows. Also, you may want to refer back to Chapter 3, which covers drive mapping options in Control Panel and the NetWare popup window.

Rights and Security

Rights and security are a necessary part of any LAN environment; one based on Windows is no exception. Whenever planning a Windows installation, you should always consider what rights to give to what users, and which directories will be affected. With NetWare 2.x you can limit a user's access to any directory on the network; with NetWare 3.x and above you can limit access to directories and/or individual files.

You should also be aware of file flags such as Shareable and Read-Only, especially because the majority of the common, shared Windows system files on the network are usually flagged Shareable Read-Only, so that any number of users can simultaneously read but not write to them.

Keep in mind that certain rights affect a user's ability to perform certain functions in Windows. For instance, the File Scan right is necessary to see the files in an Open window when trying to open a file. If you grant the File Scan right but not the Read right, the file cannot be opened. Also, some applications try to open files as read-write, so even if the user does not intend to do any writing, the open may fail unless the user has the Write privilege.

In short, it helps to plan in advance which rights you will assign to which users (or groups of users), and how that will affect their access to certain Windows applications or the Windows environment as a whole. You may want to examine Chapter 5 which covers rights, security, and file flags when installing Windows.

User Communications

As groupware becomes more prevalent, software is becoming better at tying users together and helping them communicate more. With most applications, however, the office intercom is quicker, simpler, and more useful. If you have an idea for user interaction on a project, you may want to plan in advance how they will communicate.

Office Email, groupware, and even chat utilities can help to organize and enhance user communications. A chat utility and the source code for it appear in the disk that comes with this book. You may want to experiment with it to see if you enjoy chatting with other users on the network. See Chapter 14 for operating instructions and the full source code to this utility.

You may even want to invent a system whereby certain users work on tasks in particular areas. For instance, you can keep a master copy of a document on drive M: and rough drafts on drive L: (these drives would be mapped to a common directory area where all users had access)—it's truly up to your imagination.

You could give all users read-only access to the master document area so they could get updates, but only give write access to the user who was responsible for maintaining the master copy. It can help to smooth a project along to have a system thought out in advance that will help users coordinate on projects.

Printing Under Windows on NetWare

Aside from sharing files, one of the great advantages of networks is printer sharing. This section will explore what's involved in taking advantage of NetWare printers and print queues while using Windows.

Managing Network Printer Configurations 101

Like drive mapping, printer assignments can be configured in a variety of ways. With drive mappings you consider not only how users had drive mappings set up as a group (to use a certain application for example, you may want to set drive G: to point to a certain area), but also how the drive mappings were set up for individuals. In a similar manner, if you are responsible for configuring the Windows setup on the network, you must consider what choices users will have when printing through Windows on the network. Windows 3.1 is far more flexible regarding network printer connections than Windows 3.0 was, but you must sift through the choices to decide how you will configure the network printers.

With Windows 3.1 you can attach network printers to LPT ports directly through the Control Panel/Printers series of menus (or through the NetWare driver's hotkey popup utility) discussed in Chapter 3. Users will then be able to choose from those preconfigured network printers in their applications.

It is generally better if the system administrator preconfigures the printer/network queue settings and leaves it to the user to simply choose which printer to use in a particular application. It is too easy for a user to pick a Postscript driver for a network queue that uses an HP LaserJet printer, often because network print queue names are cryptic and don't always reflect the type of printer that is servicing the queue. See Chapter 5 for information on installing Windows printers on NetWare.

For users that require more printing flexibility, I-Queue! Windows from Infinite Technologies helps isolate the user from this awkward configuration process. With I-Queue!, the network administrator defines the appropriate print driver for use with different network print queues. When a user selects that print queue with I-Queue!, the correct Windows print driver is loaded automatically. A 30-day trial version of I-Queue! Windows is included on the diskette accompanying this book.

Mapping Local LPT Ports in and out of Windows

With Windows 3.0 it was generally considered best to use CAPTURE to map LPT ports to network queues before running Windows. With Windows 3.1 you have the flexibility to choose whether you will perform this from DOS or take advantage of the "Permanent Connections" feature of the NetWare network driver (NETWARE.DRV).

The Netware driver will read the [Network] section in WIN.INI and map the printer ports specified there. See Chapter 3 for a full discussion of this mechanism.

The choice of configuration will depend on the environment, but using CAPTURE before running Windows involves using the login script or batch files to configure a user's available printers. Using the WIN.INI approach involves configuring each user's WIN.INI. In some circumstances, such as where each user has a local hard drive, it may become too cumbersome for the network administrator to edit each user's local WIN.INI file individually. This can be done when installing, however. See Chapter 5 on Windows installation on NetWare.

Setting Up Windows Applications versus DOS-based Apps

One challenging task of the network administrator is anticipating the types of applications users will need to use in the Windows environment. Not only accommodating the new applications, but also integrating them into the established environment can often be a challenge, especially when some applications are DOS-based and others are Windows-based.

Configuring printing options for DOS-based applications versus Windows-based applications poses a certain type of challenge. DOS-based applications generally come in two flavors: those that are network-aware and those that are not. The network-aware applications, like Word Perfect 5.1 (for DOS), can print directly to network print queues without sending information through an LPT port.

Other DOS applications still send information directly to LPT ports only. For these applications, system managers will have to make sure that the LPT ports are captured to the appropriate network print queues. However, these captured LPT ports in DOS will need to be coordinated with those in Windows.

For example, in a certain environment, LPT1 is mapped to HP_QUEUE which has an HP LaserJet attached, and LPT2 is mapped to PS_QUEUE which has a PostScript printer attached. If you are aware of the way the queues are mapped, then DOS-based applications that need to print to the HP will send their output to LPT1 and PostScript output to LPT2. In Windows, the HP driver would be configured to send to LPT1 (which will be attached to HP_QUEUE) and the PostScript driver will be configured to LPT2 (attached to PS_QUEUE).

The difficulty comes in when you have more than three printers from which to choose because you can only premap three LPT ports. One way to handle the problem in DOS is to have batch files for the applications that capture the appropriate LPT ports before running an application, then remap those ports back to the way they were when the application terminates.

In either case, anticipating and planning to overcome these types of situations will help the system manager enormously when the time comes to install, configure, then support Windows on NetWare.

Managing with Print Manager versus PCONSOLE

If you are used to NetWare in the DOS world, you may have been using a third-party print manager or you may be using the PCONSOLE utility that comes with NetWare. PCONSOLE lets you view network print queues, add, delete, or change jobs, and change the security of the queue (who can print to the queue, who can service the queue, and who can "operate" or manage the queue). It's important that you understand the differences between Print Manager and the PCONSOLE utility.

Within Windows, the Print Manager (if it's turned on in the Control Panel/Printers window) handles jobs before they are sent to the printer port (or network print queue if the port is captured). One decision you will need to make if you are a system manager is whether to use the Print Manager on NetWare. Within Windows 3.1, there is no real equivalent of PCONSOLE, although third-party utilities do fulfill this role; therefore, you will not be able to substitute PCONSOLE for Print Manager.

In fact, many system administrators remove Print Manager simply because NetWare already does the print queuing for you. Now that print jobs are usually sent to network printers, there is no need to use yet another queuing step (because it would go from the application to Print Manager to the network queue to the printer). You may want to consider disabling Print Manager for users that print to the network.

PRINTDEF and PRINTCON

NetWare gives users the ability to print using predefined forms and print devices. The forms specify the length and width of a page, and the print device defines escape sequences for different tasks the printer can perform (like font changes, reset, and so on).

The PRINTDEF utility is used to manage these predefined forms and print devices (the print devices are stored in .PDF files in SYS:PUBLIC).

The PRINTCON utility lets you define "print job configurations" which are predefined CAPTURE settings. Rather than set each CAPTURE flag (like copies, tabs, form feeds, and so on) individually, a user or system manager can define a list of print configurations for different printing tasks, then call CAPTURE with the "/Job" parameter set to the appropriate print configuration name.

Neither PRINTDEF or PRINTCON have an equivalent in Windows 3.1, so you will need to go to DOS to use these utilities. Windows also does not support print job configurations, so the CAPTURE utility will have to be run (with the /Job parameter) before running Windows if you want to use print job configurations. There is a facility, however, to set many of the same parameters in the [Network] section of WIN.INI (for a full discussion of this topic, see Chapter 3).

RPRINTER and Windows

If you're already running Novell NetWare, you've probably grown accustomed to running the RPRINTER utility on some of your workstations. RPRINTER allows printers attached to network workstations to be shared as network printers.

Unfortunately, current versions of RPRINTER have proven to be quite unreliable when on workstations running Windows, particularly in 386 Enhanced mode.

For the best results running RPRINTER on a workstation running Windows, it is suggested that you run Windows in standard mode (WIN /S). You may also want to try increasing the SPX timeout values specified in your NET.CFG file by adding the following statements:

```
SPX ABORT TIMEOUT = 4000
SPX LISTEN TIMEOUT = 2500
```

You will be best served by investigating third-party print server solutions if remote printing capabilities are required on your network.

Many newer printers, like the HP LaserJet IIIsi and LaserJet IV, have optional features that support connecting the printer directly to the network cabling. These options generally provide the fastest network printing. Additionally, devices like the Castelle LanPress and Intel NetPort are small devices that connect into your network cabling and provide parallel and/or serial ports for connecting printers. For software alternatives, there are Printer Assist from Fresh Technologies, LANSpool from Intel, and PS-Print from Brightwork.

Virus Scanning and Security

The Virus Threat

Security is one of the top issues for system administrators. As software viruses become more prevalent, it becomes increasingly important to be aware of how they are spread and what can be done to detect and eliminate the virus.

This book comes with what is generally considered some of the best virus-scanning software available: McAfee's NetScan. There is also a new Windows version of McAfee's virus-scanning software that is included with the book (see Chapter 10).

Aside from regular network scanning, good LAN security can help minimize virus infection and spread. Limiting a user's rights to only those areas on the system where the person needs access and, if possible, granting read-only rights to those areas, will help keep the virus from spreading. Generally, if a virus can't write itself to another file or disk, it can't spread.

Because so many aspects of the operating system are hidden from the user by Windows, it can be easier at times to contract a virus in this environment than under DOS alone. This is because the DOS user is often closer to the operating system and more aware of what's going on. Although this is no guarantee, there are hundreds of viruses preying on today's PCs. You should anticipate the need for security and have a means of removing viruses from your system.

Security

Novell provides a utility called SECURITY in the SYS:SYSTEM directory. If you are a system administrator, you should consider running this utility on a regular basis to test the security of your network. The utility can point out holes that you may not have seen (users without passwords, completely unprotected areas, and so on). Especially as modern networks increase in size, it becomes more difficult to detect security breaches without some automated tools. You may also want to start with the SECURITY utility from Novell and move on to a third-party utility.

Backup and Archive

Windows is a computer-resource-intensive operating environment. It requires a high-resolution monitor, a fast computer, a fast hard disk, a mouse, lots of memory, and so on. Because of all of the resources (bitmapped graphics, sounds, fonts, and so on) in Windows applications, Windows takes a great deal of hard disk space to run. And, as multi-media becomes more popular, Windows will require even more hard disk space.

This requirement will undoubtedly impact your backup routine. If you are a system manager, you will need to consider the implications of a network based on Windows and whether you have the hard disk space not only to run Windows, but also to back up the data associated with it.

Although it's often an unpopular task, the importance of regular system backups cannot be over-stressed. The system manager should also consider an archive system where files not used for a certain period of time (like a year or more) can be archived to tape, optical disk, or some other less costly storage method.

Many of the leading backup and archive hardware vendors have begun to incorporate Windows front-ends into their backup and archive software, so you may not even have to leave the Windows environment to perform this task.

5 Setting Up Windows on NetWare

It's important to lay a good foundation for your NetWare/Windows installation. That foundation begins with installing and configuring your NetWare hardware and NetWare and Windows software properly.

This chapter will address the issues involved in installing Windows on the LAN, including discussions of hardware setup, NetWare shell setup and configuration, and choice of location to install Windows (on the local hard drive or server). It will also cover the Windows parameter files, which may need adjustment, the basics of mapping drives and managing security, setting up NetWare printers for use under Windows, setting up diskless workstations, and configuring the appropriate Novell-specific utilities.

General Hardware Considerations

Before delving into software installation, it's wise to ensure you've got the hardware installed correctly. To run Windows, whether locally or on the server, you will need the following hardware:

Real Mode - an 8086/8088-based PC with 640K of conventional memory. (Real Mode is only relevant to those of you using Windows version 3.0—this mode is not available in Windows 3.1.)

Standard Mode - an 80286-based (or higher) PC and one megabyte or more of memory (640K conventional, 256K extended).

Enhanced Mode - an 80386-based (or higher) PC and two megabytes or more of memory (640K conventional, 1024K extended). This is purely a minimum configuration. It is recommended that you have at least 4MB of RAM—8MB would be better for optimal performance.

In addition, you must know how your network interface card (NIC) is configured. Interrupts 2, 9, or higher have been known to cause conflicts within Windows 3.0, 386 Enhanced Mode, although a Novell-supplied driver, VPICDA.386, exists that you can use to try to ease those conflicts. Although this problem has been fixed in Windows 3.1 (in fact Novell highly recommends that you DO NOT use VPICDA.386 with Windows 3.1), it is suggested that you not use interrupts 2 or 9 on your NIC. Standard Mode users should be concerned about IPX conflicts. (See the TBMI discussion later in this chapter for further details.)

If you have configured your NIC with an I/O address of 2E0h, you may want to change that, as it will conflict with the Windows 3.0 Setup program. Windows may think you have a particular display adapter when you do not.

Additionally, if your network adapter maps RAM memory for its use, you should write down the RAM address range used by the adapter. Later you will learn how to exclude that range of memory from use by Windows. Otherwise, a conflict may develop when Windows attempts to use that range of memory for its own purposes.

You will want to note the configuration of your network adapter, no matter how it is set up, to be aware of these and other precautions to be covered later.

NetWare Shells

The next step you must take when installing Windows onto NetWare is to determine whether you have set up your NetWare shells correctly and whether they are of a high enough revision level to support Windows. In case you are unaware of what the shell is, the "shell" is a collection of (generally two) Terminate-and-Stay-Resident (TSR) files that allow your workstation to talk to the file server.

Shell Types and Versions

There are two main families of NetWare shells: the original Internetwork Packet Exchange (IPX)/Sequenced Packet Exchange (SPX) shell family and the newer Open Data-Link Interface (ODI) shell family. Both families will work with Windows and both will allow you to talk to NetWare. The distinction is the IPX/SPX shells will only talk to NetWare because IPX/SPX is the native protocol running on NetWare LANs.

The ODI shells allow you to have "dual protocol stacks," which essentially means the shell can talk to more than one type of network entity at the same time. For example, with the ODI shells you can have a Unix server and a NetWare server on the same LAN and talk to both of them.

The files in the original IPX/SPX shell set are as follows:

IPX.COM

This file implements the IPX/SPX protocol. If it were loaded by itself, you could talk to another workstation that had IPX loaded but that's about it. You need the DOS portion of the shell to translate DOS services into NetWare services and communicate with the file server. This file takes up between 15KB and 25KB, depending on your network adapter and configuration options.

This file is specific to your particular network adapter. Typing "IPX /i" will tell you how your IPX.COM is currently configured.

You configure IPX.COM to your network adapter by using the WSGEN utility under NetWare 2.2 or 3.1x. (Use SHGEN for prior versions of NetWare. Note that Windows is not supported on NetWare versions prior to v2.1.) See your Novell installation documentation for details about shell generation and configuration.

NETx.COM

This is the NetWare workstation shell portion that provides the services you need to interact with the file server. It uses IPX/SPX as the communications protocol, so IPX.COM must be loaded first.

This version of the shell is loaded into conventional memory and occupies approximately 40K of space.

The x in NETx means that there are several different versions of the NetWare shell. Earlier versions had a number associated with each DOS version with which you ran the shell. For instance, NET3.COM was run under DOS 3.x, NET4.COM under DOS 4, and so on. Now there is a NETX.COM that runs with DOS versions 3–5.

If you are currently running a DOS version-specific NetWare shell, you will need to upgrade to the current NETX version for proper support of the Windows environment. Newer versions of NETX may use an EXE file extension rather than a COM extension. Since DOS will execute COM files before EXE files, you may need to delete NETX.COM before installing an updated NETX.EXE in order for the new version to be used.

This file is considered generic and non-specific to any LAN adapter hardware.

EMSNETx.EXE

Similar to NETx.COM, except this program is automatically loaded into expanded memory, thereby making more conventional memory available. The expanded memory must be compliant with the LIM/EMS 4.0 specification (which sometimes requires additional hardware and always requires additional software). The naming convention used with the file is similar to NETx.

This file occupies approximately 7K of conventional memory and 64K of expanded memory.

There is a performance penalty associated with this file because of the memory paging associated with expanded memory. You should weigh the benefits gained from less memory consumption with the decreased performance. The XMSNET shell (see below) is slightly faster than EMSNET.

Note: The Windows 3.1 NETWORKS.WRI indicates that EMSNETX is not supported with Windows 3.1, so use it at your own risk.

XMSNETx.EXE

The bulk of this shell file is automatically loaded into extended memory. It uses approximately 6K of conventional memory and 64K of extended memory.

You must have a 80286-based (or higher) PC to use this shell and an extended memory driver that is compatible with version 2.0 or higher of the Microsoft XMS 2.0 specification, such as HIMEM.SYS. XMSNETx uses the same naming convention as NETx.

This shell is somewhat faster than EMSNETx but slower than NETx. Again, you must weigh the pros and cons of memory savings versus a slight performance penalty.

XMSNETX uses a 64KB region of XMS memory, known as the high memory area (HMA), which is the first 64KB of extended memory. If you are running MS-DOS 5.0 with DOS=HIGH in your CONFIG.SYS file (or DR-DOS 6.0 with HIDOS=ON in your CONFIG.SYS file and the /B=FFFF parameter on your DEVICE=EMM386.SYS statement), then you should be aware that DOS is using this same 64KB block of memory, and will not allow XMSNETX to load into this region.

In practice, you will get better performance and memory savings by letting DOS use this high memory area, and by using the DOS LOADHIGH (or DR-DOS HILOAD) command to load NETX into upper memory. (Upper memory is the region of memory between 640KB and 1MB. 386 memory managers, like EMM386, remap extended memory into unused areas of this memory region for loading programs high.)

You must have a NETX shell that is v3.26 or higher for compatibility with Windows 3.1. In general, it is recommended that you try to acquire the latest revision of the NetWare shell from on-line sources such as the Novell forums on CompuServe, RoseNet Online, or other services (see the appendices for on-line resource information).

BNETX.EXE

BNETX.EXE is a special version of NETX that implements a burst mode technology for communicating with NetWare 3.11 file servers running PBURST.NLM. Whenever a workstation submits a file read or write request to the file server that is larger than 512 bytes, BNETX and PBURST implement a faster algorithm for transferring data between the workstation and file server.

The standard NETX requires that these requests be sent one packet at a time (packet sizes can range from 512 bytes to 4KB), and after each packet, NetWare waits for an acknowledgement that the previous packet was received before sending the next one. BNETX and burst mode technology allow multiple packets to be sent and sequences the acknowledgments, thereby permitting faster network performance in some environments.

You should note that the initial release of BNETX, v3.26, is not compatible with Windows 3.1 (results range from system lockups to a gradual slowing of performance until it becomes unacceptable). v3.31 of BNETX was the first release to correct this incompatibility with Windows 3.1.

BNETX requires approximately 5KB more memory than NETX, plus additional memory depending on the number of packet burst buffers (PB BUFFERS) allocated in the NET.CFG file. Each PB BUFFER is the size of your configured network packet size, which varies based on topology and other considerations beyond the scope of this book. For more information on packet burst technology, an excellent article on this topic was printed in the March 1992 issue of *NetWare Application Notes*. You can subscribe to this publication or order individual back issues by calling 1 (800) 453-1267, Ext. 5380, or by writing:

Novell Research Order Desk
122 East 1700 South
C251 Provo, Utah 84606

The files in the ODI shell set are as follows:

LSL.COM

This file comprises the Link Support Layer. The LSL enables the workstation to communicate over several protocols. LSL's memory consumption depends upon the number and size of buffers and the memory pool you specify, although the default size is about 4K of conventional memory. With a typical dual protocol stack, such as IPX/SPX and TCP/IP, this file takes up approximately 40K.

driver.COM

This file conforms to the Multiple Link Interface Driver (MLID) specification and is specific to your make and model of network adapter. The name of the file corresponds to the adapter; for example, NE1000.COM for a Novell NE1000 board, 3C501.COM for a 3Com 3C501 board, and so on. This file occupies approximately 4K of conventional memory.

IPXODI.COM

This file implements the IPX/SPX protocol stack and occupies approximately 16K of conventional memory.

If the shell is loaded with the /D switch, the Diagnostic Responder is not loaded and the shell will occupy approximately 8K of conventional memory (the Diagnostic Responder answers queries for diagnostic-type information about your workstation). Further, using the /A switch loads only IPX (and not SPX or the Diagnostic Responder), thus saving an additional 4K and making the total memory consumption 4K of conventional memory.

When using the optional command-line parameters to conserve memory, be aware that you may be running application software that uses SPX or the diagnostic responder. In particular, Novell's RCONSOLE and RPRINTER programs use SPX. The diagnostic responder is used by programs that record system configuration information, like Network HQ from Magee Enterprises, and diagnostic utilities, like TxD from Thomas Conrad Corporation.

NETx.COM

Same as the NETx.COM from the original IPX/SPX shell set (see discussion above).

The ODI shell version requirements are as follows: LSL v1.21 and IPXODI v1.20. The version of your MLID (driver.COM) file will vary depending on the manufacturer. NETX v3.26 or higher is required for proper Windows 3.1 support, as with the standard IPX drivers.

Loading Shells into High Memory

You may load the NetWare shells into the DOS upper-memory area (the 384K space located directly above 640K), if desired, to conserve the amount of conventional memory used by the shells. DOS versions prior to 5.0 could not utilize the memory space between 640K and 1024K, so utilities like 386Max by Qualitas and QEMM by Quarterdeck were used to load TSRs into that region of memory (although you must have a 386-based PC to use these utilities).

If you have DOS version 5.0 running on a 386 PC, and you want to load the NetWare shells into high memory, perform the following steps:

1. Make sure your CONFIG.SYS file contains a device= line for an extended memory manager like HIMEM.SYS—for example,

   ```
   DEVICE = C:\DOS\HIMEM.SYS
   ```

2. You must also load an upper-memory driver like EMM386.EXE which is included with DOS 5.0. You can do this by including a line similar to the following in your CONFIG.SYS file:

   ```
   DEVICE=EMM386.EXE /X=xxxx-xxxx
   ```

   where /X=xxxx-xxxx is an optional parameter specifying a range of memory that EMM386 should not overwrite. EMM386 will not automatically detect the shared memory areas used by many network adapters, so it may be necessary to include this parameter to exclude your network adapter's shared memory area. As an example, if you have a network card configured to use a 16KB buffer at segment D000h, this would be denoted as /X=D000-D3FF.

3. Your CONFIG.SYS file should include the line "dos=umb" to allow DOS to maintain a link between conventional memory and the upper-memory area. The line "dos=high,umb" loads DOS into the upper-memory area to conserve even more conventional memory.

4. Finally, you should use the internal DOS command "loadhigh" in your AUTOEXEC.BAT file to load the NetWare shell components into the DOS upper-memory area.

Your CONFIG.SYS should look like:

```
device=HIMEM.SYS
device=EMM386.EXE

dos=umb
or
dos=high,umb
```

Your AUTOEXEC.BAT or NETWORK.BAT should contain the lines:

```
loadhigh IPX
loadhigh NETX
```

To load the NetWare shells into the upper-memory area with QEMM, perform the following steps:

1. Ensure that QEMM's driver, QEMM386.SYS, is loaded early in your CONFIG.SYS.

2. Use the LOADHIGH command to load the shell components high.

Your CONFIG.SYS should look like:

```
device=QEMM386.SYS and whatever arguments you need to use
```

Your AUTOEXEC.BAT or NETWORK.BAT should contain the lines:

```
loadhigh IPX
loadhigh NETX
```

When running QEMM in stealth mode with Windows, Windows will search for the following files at enhanced-mode initialization time: WINHIRAM.VXD and WINSTLTH.VXD in the root directory of the boot drive. If you are using remote boot, then Windows will not be able to load in enhanced mode and, unfortunately, many versions of QEMM will not be able to report why.

In the CONFIG.SYS file, on the QEMM386.SYS command line, add the phrase "VXDDIR=path" where path contains the two .VXD files—for example, "VXDDIR=F:\DOS." It's an undocumented "feature" of QEMM.

DR-DOS 6.0 from Novell (formerly Digital Research) also allows you to load the NetWare shells into high memory, according to the following steps:

1. First, you must have an 80386-based (or higher) PC.

2. You must load an upper-memory driver in your CONFIG.SYS file, like EMM386.SYS which is included with DR-DOS 6.0.

3. Use the internal DR-DOS command "HILOAD" to load the NetWare shell components into the DOS upper-memory area.

Your CONFIG.SYS should contain the following statement:

```
DEVICE=EMM386.EXE /E=xxxx-xxxx
```

where /E=xxxx-xxxx is an optional parameter specifying a range of memory that EMM386 should not overwrite. EMM386 will not automatically detect the shared memory areas used by many network adapters, so it may be necessary to include this parameter to exclude your network adapter's shared memory area. As an example, if you have a network card configured to use a 16KB buffer at segment D000h, this would be denoted as /E=D000-D3FF.

Your AUTOEXEC.BAT should contain the following statements:

```
HILOAD IPX
HILOAD NETX
```

Configuring Your NetWare Shell for Windows

Now that you've chosen the correct shell and know the version is right for Windows, there are several configurable parameters you can change that affect the shell's performance under Windows. When the NETX shell file loads, it looks for a file called NET.CFG or SHELL.CFG. Since NET.CFG is the newer name for this file, you should place all options documented for the SHELL.CFG file in the NET.CFG file to avoid confusion.

These files contain parameters that let you configure the default settings for the shell. For example, you can include parameters that set to which file server the shell defaults, how many buffers the shell uses for certain tasks, and so on. You can also use these files to specify various settings for Windows. The settings described below will work in either SHELL.CFG or NET.CFG.

DOTS

The first parameter that pertains to Windows involves how the NetWare shell handles the "." and ".." directory entries. When you execute the DIR command in DOS against a local drive (in any directory other than the root), you see a listing for "." and ".." before any other entries. These entries represent the current and previous directories respectively.

Windows uses these directory entries in certain dialog boxes when loading or saving files. You may double-click on the ".." to move one directory up, toward the root. When using certain programs, NetWare will not usually show ".." as a directory entry. Modify (or create, if necessary) your NET.CFG file by adding the following line:

```
SHOW DOTS = ON
```

Next time you load the NetWare shell, the "." and ".." entries will show in Windows file open/save dialog boxes. If you are using MS-DOS (as opposed to DR-DOS), the DOS DIR command will still not show the "." and ".." entries, even though you have specified SHOW DOTS=ON in your NET.CFG file. However, they will be displayed in Windows applications.

If you are running a NetWare 2.1x version, before making the SHOW DOTS = ON setting, you should update your MAKEUSER and BINDFIX utilities that were included with NetWare. The dots can confuse these utility programs; under certain situations, these programs can accidentally delete your entire SYS volume. This problem does not exist in NetWare 2.2 or any of the NetWare 3.x versions.

FILE HANDLES

The NetWare shell, by default, reserves 40 files per workstation. Microsoft recommends increasing that number to a minimum of 60 open files by setting "FILES = 60" in your CONFIG.SYS file. However, this setting only pertains to the number of files that can be opened simultaneously on any of your local drives.

To open more than 40 files simultaneously on the network, you need to update your NET.CFG with a "FILE HANDLES =" statement, such as "FILE HANDLES = 60."

The values of "FILES =" and "FILE HANDLES =" are independent; the total of these values cannot exceed 254 with current NetWare shell revisions.

NETBIOS PARAMETERS

Sometimes, NetBIOS applications can have specific timing requirements for NetBIOS broadcasts (such as with 3270 terminal emulation software). The following settings can be used in SHELL.CFG or NET.CFG if a NetBIOS session hangs:

```
NETBIOS BROADCAST COUNT = 5
NETBIOS BROADCAST DELAY = 10
```

Installing Windows on a Novell LAN

When preparing to install Windows on NetWare, you must decide where certain portions of Windows will reside. There are essentially two significant portions of Windows: the system files and the user initialization files.

The system files are common to all users and can be stored in a central facility. The user initialization files are specific to each user, and contain information about the user's workstation, such as its display type, keyboard, printers, and so on.

Refer to Table 5.1 for a list of options with their evaluations to decide which option to use.

The following sections will describe each scenario in detail and list the steps for installing each option.

Stand-alone Configuration

The Stand-alone configuration option involves loading an individual user's hard drives with Windows. The installation procedure is nearly identical for non-LAN installations in that the user specifies the local hard drive (such as C:) to be the destination for Windows. The only thing you need to be aware of is the network driver.

It is generally best if you have the NetWare shell files loaded before you start the installation; that way, Windows will detect a network installation and select the Novell driver for you. If you don't have the shell files loaded or if, for any reason, the Novell driver is not selected, you will need to perform this step manually. In addition to the memory requirements described above in "General Hardware Considerations," you should be aware that you must have at least DOS version 3.1 or later, a monitor that is supported by Windows (most are), and a Windows-supported mouse (again, most are supported).

Here are the steps involved in a local installation (you may want to read them over completely before actually starting your installation, so that you know what to expect):

1. Place the Windows Disk 1 in the drive you want to install from. Type the drive letter, a colon, and press Enter (for example, A: then <Enter>).

2. Type "setup" and press Enter. The screen in Figure 5.1 will appear.

3. If you press the Enter key, you will be shown the screen in Figure 5.2, which gives you the choice of a custom setup—more flexibility but also more time-consuming—or the express setup—quicker but with fewer options. It is recommended that system administrators choose option C (Custom Setup) for the most flexibility.

4. Once you choose the Express or Custom setup option, the Windows Setup program asks you where you want to install Windows. In the screen shown in Figure 5.3, the user has chosen to let Setup place the files for Windows 3.1 in C:\WIN31.

5. Next, Setup will do a hardware determination to try to find out what kind of hardware you have. Setup will display its findings in the next screen, shown in Figure 5.4. Pay particular attention to what Windows recommends you use for a network driver. Make sure it says it's a Novell driver. If it's not Novell, or if it has not been selected at all, you should select the Novell driver yourself.

   If you need to change the Network driver, use the arrow keys to move the cursor to the Network line and press the Enter key. You will be shown a screen like the one in Figure 5.5. Use the up and down arrow keys to select the Novell NetWare

Configuration	Advantages	Disadvantages
Stand-alone: All Windows files reside on the local hard disk	Fast file access. Minimal network traffic. User can operate Windows even when LAN is down.	Requires approximately 12 MB of disk space (6.3 MB for Windows 3.0). Greatest administrative overhead of any option.
Server-based: Windows system files on file server, user files on local hard drive.	Only 200K local hard disk space needed. Less administrative overhead.	Increased network traffic. Windows unusable when LAN is down.
Diskless workstation: All files on Server	Less hardware expense: no local hard or floppy drives. Increased network security. Increased administrative control.	Increased network traffic. No permanent swapfile.

Table 5.1 Possible Windows Network Configurations.

```
Windows Setup

Welcome to Setup.

The Setup program for Windows 3.1 prepares Windows
to run on your computer.

   • To learn more about Windows Setup before continuing, press F1.

   • To set up Windows now, press ENTER.

   • To quit Setup without installing Windows, press F3.




ENTER=Continue  F3=Exit  F1=Help
```

Figure 5.1 SETUP's main screen.

driver that corresponds to the shell version (NETX.EXE, EMSNETX.EXE, or XMSNETX.EXE) you have installed. Preferably, you will have the latest version of the shell (version 3.31 as of this writing) so you will select the line in Figure 5.5 that says "shell versions 3.26 and above." If you do not have the most recent version of the NetWare shell, you may not be able to take advantage of Windows-specific features that have been included in the shell.

If you don't know which shell version you have installed, press the F3 key to exit Setup. You can then type the name of the shell followed by the letter 'I'. For instance, if you were using NETX.EXE, you would type "NETX I"

```
Windows Setup

Windows provides two Setup methods:

Express Setup (Recommended)
Express Setup relies on Setup to make decisions,
so setting up Windows is quick and easy.

   To use Express Setup, press ENTER.


Custom Setup
Custom Setup is for experienced computer users who
want to control how Windows is set up. To use this Setup method,
you should know how to use a mouse with Windows.

   To use Custom Setup, press C.

For details about both Setup methods, press F1.



ENTER=Express Setup  C=Custom Setup  F1=Help  F3=Exit
```

Figure 5.2 SETUP Express versus Custom screen.

```
Windows Setup

  Setup has found a previous version of Microsoft Windows on your hard
  disk in the path shown below. It is recommended that you upgrade this
  previous version to Windows version 3.1.

     • To upgrade, press ENTER.

  If necessary, you can keep your older version of Windows and add
  Windows version 3.1 to your system. Press the BACKSPACE key to erase
  the path shown, and then type a new path for version 3.1.

     • When the correct path for Windows 3.1 is shown below, press ENTER.

   C:\WIN31

  Note: if you set up Windows version 3.1 in a new directory instead of
  upgrading, you will not maintain any of your desktop settings or any
  Program Manager groups and icons you set up. Also, you must make sure
  that only version 3.1 is listed in PATH in your AUTOEXEC.BAT file.


  ENTER=Continue  F1=Help  F3=Exit
```

Figure 5.3 SETUP prompt for the installation path.

and the version number would be displayed. Then type Setup again and follow the prompts back to the NetWare Driver Choice screen.

6. At this stage, Windows will load and the graphical portion of the installation will ensue. You will have the opportunity to choose printers. For now, choose the printers you know you will be printing on, whether they're local or network printers. We will get them printing on the LAN later on.

7. You will also be prompted to install the applications located on the hard drives to which you have access. (This includes network drives.) If you respond positively to the prompt, Windows will scan your hard drives for applications

```
Windows Setup

  Setup has determined that your system includes the following hardware
  and software components. If your computer or network appears on the
  Hardware Compatibility List with an asterisk, press F1 for Help.

        Computer:         MS-DOS System
        Display:          VGA
        Mouse:            Microsoft, or IBM PS/2
        Keyboard:         Enhanced 101 or 102 key US and Non US keyboards
        Keyboard Layout:  US
        Language:         English (American)
        Network:          Novell NetWare (shell versions 3.26 and above)

        No Changes:       The above list matches my computer.

  If all the items in the list are correct, press ENTER to indicate
  "No Changes." If you want to change any item in the list, press the
  UP or DOWN ARROW key to move the highlight to the item you want to
  change. Then press ENTER to see alternatives for that item.


  ENTER=Continue  F1=Help  F3=Exit
```

Figure 5.4 Hardware Determination screen.

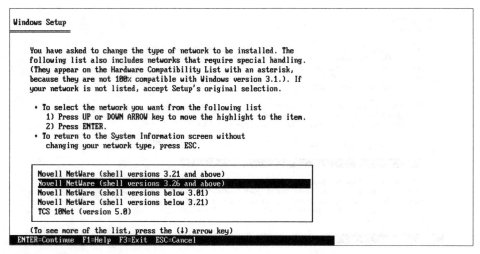

Figure 5.5 Network Driver Choice screen.

and create icons for those applications in a Program Manager group window. Often this saves you the trouble of having to setup each application individually.

However, electing to install applications while connected to a Novell LAN may cause problems. With a LAN, drives F, G, and H, for example, may all point to the SYS: volume. When Windows searches these drives, it will start from the root and tag any application it finds, once for each drive letter.

To prevent this, you can use the MAP ROOT option of the MAP command prior to running Setup. For example, the command "MAP ROOT F:=SYS:APPS" creates a fake root at the F:\APPS directory. When Windows searches drive F:, it would think the root of the drive begins at F:\APPS and search no lower than that.

If you haven't used the MAP ROOT command yet, you can cancel the drive search procedure and run it again later. To execute this later, run the Windows Setup program from Program Manager and choose "Options, Set Up Applications."

That's all you do for the local installation! If you are installing using this method, you can skip the next two sections and go directly to the discussion about swap files.

Server-based Configuration

INSTALLING WINDOWS 3.0

There are two basic methods you can use to set up a server-based Windows installation.

The first method is the official one recommended by Microsoft. This procedure involves copying the contents of each distribution diskette to a directory on the file server and decompressing each file. Then the Windows Setup program can be run, using the /N parameter—for example, SETUP /N to set up individual users.

> **Note:** The files on the Windows distribution disks are compressed. Microsoft uses a dollar sign ($) to indicate a compressed file, so MYF-ILE.SYS becomes MYFILE.SY$ in its compressed form.

Running Setup with the /N parameter copies several personal files to a user's directory (either to the user's local hard drive or to another directory on the file server). The advantage of this method is its straightforwardness and simplicity. The disadvantage is that there are some third-party device drivers available with Windows (for displays, for instance) that cannot be used with Setup when you use the /N parameter.

The second method involves making a master copy of a Windows setup, then placing hardware-specific files in subdirectories, one subdirectory for each hardware setup. For example, you could have a directory for a VGA computer, a directory for a Super VGA computer, and so on. Advantages of this method are that you only need to copy some files to set up a new user, and you standardize on the hardware configurations you are willing to support.

Keep in mind that in both scenarios we're sharing the common Windows files on the server and keeping the users' private, user-specific files on either a local hard drive or a local network directory. Both options rely on pooling all of the Windows files in a particular network directory, then performing the Windows Setup program from there.

Let's discuss the first option, the one suggested by Microsoft. The steps involved in this process are as follows:

1. Load the NetWare shell files and create a Windows directory on the file server, such as SYS:WINDOWS. Map a drive letter to it, like W:, so your path to the Windows directory will be W:\WINDOWS (although you can choose any drive letter you want). Make that directory current by typing "W: <ENTER>" and "CD \WINDOWS."

2. Copy all of the files from the distribution diskettes to your new Windows directory (W:\WINDOWS, for example). Since the files on the Windows installation disks are compressed, they need to be decompressed before you can install them. To do this, create a batch file to expand the files. The syntax used in this step assumes you will be copying files from the A: drive to our sample W:\WINDOWS directory.

At the DOS prompt, type:

```
copy con expall.bat
```

(this will create a batch file called expall.bat)

```
%1
for %%i in (*.*) do %2\expand %%i %2\%%i
rename %2\*.sy$ *.sys
attrib %2\*.* +r
```

Press the F6 key or CTRL-Z, then <Enter>; this writes our batch file to the disk.

3. Place the Windows Installation Disk 2 in the A drive and type:

```
copy a:expand.exe w:\windows
```

Now you have Windows' decompression program on your hard drive.

4. Now place the Windows Installation Disk 1 in the A drive and type:

```
expall a: w:\windows
```

All of the files on the disk will be decompressed and copied to the LAN. Repeat this step for each Windows installation disk you have. Even though the files have been decompressed, they will still bear their original, compressed names (such as *.SY$, rather than *.SYS). The Windows Setup program will rename these files to their proper extensions as it copies them to your local directory.

5. Type "setup /n" from the W:\WINDOWS directory. Tell Setup you want the files put on the local drive (such as C:\WINDOWS). It will then place all of your personal Windows files on the local drive. It will not prompt you for any disks since they all reside in W:\WINDOWS. Please refer to the Stand-alone Configuration discussion for additional detail.

When the installation is complete, you will want to make the network Windows directory a search drive so that Windows can find its shared files. You can do this by typing "MAP INS S1:=SYS:WINDOWS." If you have a personal directory on the network, you can also map a search path to it by typing "MAP INS S1:=SYS:directoryName" where directoryName is the path to your personal Windows directory. Typing this after the first map statement will make the SYS:directoryName path first, followed by the path to SYS:WINDOWS. If your personal Windows directory is local, Windows will attempt to update the PATH statement in your AUTOEXEC.BAT file to include your local Windows directory, so you will not need the second MAP statement.

To access Windows, go to your local hard disk directory where you placed your local drives, and type "win."

Note: The Expand program is being run singly against each file on each Windows Installation diskette. This is done because the Expand program will stop if it comes to an uncompressed file (such as SETUP.EXE). Therefore, you cannot reliably type "expand a:*.* w:\windows" to decompress the files on the Windows program disks.

INSTALLING WINDOWS 3.1

Microsoft simplified the installation process tremendously from Windows 3.0, especially for server-based installations. All you do to create the shared Windows directory on the server is use the /A switch when running SETUP—for example, SETUP /A. Windows will prompt you for the directory name in which you want to install Windows. Then you will be prompted for the disks one by one. The files they contain will be copied to the file server and decompressed. This process creates the directory containing all of the files from the installation disks (approximately 12MB) on the server.

To install an individual user's copy of Windows on the user's local hard drive, make the new shared Windows directory on the server (the one you created in the previous paragraph) current—type this from the user's workstation. Then type SETUP /N and Windows will prompt you for a place to put the user's workstation-specific Windows files.

DISKLESS WORKSTATION CONFIGURATION

The diskless workstation setup is identical to the Server-based configuration, except in this option: You don't have a local hard drive on which to put your personal Windows files. Instead, these will be stored in a personal directory on the LAN, such as SYS:USER\CGR\WINDOWS.

If you are running Windows 3.0, perform all of the steps in "Installing Windows 3.0" above. If you are running Windows 3.1, perform the first step under "Installing Windows 3.1" above. Then perform the following steps:

1. Type "setup /n" from the network directory containing all of the files from the Windows installation disks. When prompted, tell Setup where you want your personal directory—for example, F:\USER\CGR\WINDOWS. It will then place all of your personal Windows files in this directory. As in the Server-based installation, it will not prompt you for any disks since they all reside in W:\WINDOWS. Please refer to the Stand-alone Configuration discussion on drive searches above.

2. When the installation is complete, you will want to make the main Windows directory a search drive so that Windows can find its shared files. You can do this by typing "MAP INS S1:=SYS:WINDOWS," assuming the main Windows directory is SYS:WINDOWS. You may have difficulty starting Windows if you do not make your personal LAN directory for Windows part of your search path. To do this, type "MAP INS S1:=SYS:\USER\CGR\WINDOWS," assuming your personal Windows files are stored in SYS:\USER\CGR\WINDOWS.

3. To start Windows, go to your personal Windows LAN directory where you placed your local drives, and type "win."

Table 5.2 shows the files copied to the user's personal directory (for either the Diskless Workstation or Server-based configuration options).

Note that the *.SYS files and EMM386.EXE do not need to remain in the user's directory on the server, and can be deleted—these files are usually stored on the boot device.

Also, if you are running MS-DOS 5.0 and EMM386.EXE on a diskless workstation, be sure that in your CONFIG.SYS file, you include a "/y=d:\path\EMM386.EXE" parameter on the "device=EMM386.EXE" statement, where d:\path\EMM386.EXE is a valid path for locating a copy of EMM386.EXE when Windows 3.1 is loading. This is necessary for Windows to load a virtual device driver for EMM386.EXE that virtualizes upper memory for DOS boxes under Windows.

Customizing Workstation Installation

The following section covers several advanced customization options you may want to take advantage of during your Windows installation on the network. These options will let you customize the setup procedure, create custom group windows, copy additional files automatically during Windows installation, and cripple the functionality of Program Manager so that users don't have access to certain functions.

File	Description
WIN.INI	Windows' preferences configuration text file
SYSTEM.INI	Windows' system configuration text file
PROGMAN.INI	Program Manager configuration text file
CONTROL.INI	Control Panel configuration text file
WIN.COM	Windows Startup program
SMARTDRV.SYS	The SmartDrive disk-caching device driver
RAMDRIVE.SYS	The RAMDrive RAM disk device driver
EMM386.EXE	386-based expanded memory manager (EMM386.SYS in Windows 3.0)
WINVER.EXE	Used by Setup to determine the Windows version
MAIN.GRP	Main group file
ACCESSOR.GRP	Accessories group file
GAMES.GRP	Games group file
_DEFAULT.PIF	Default program information file (PIF)
HIMEM.SYS	XMS extended memory driver (This file is only copied for diskless workstations; it is copied to root on local hard drive installations in Windows 3.0. Windows 3.1 copies this file to your personal Windows directory and attempts to update your CONFIG.SYS file to contain HIMEM.SYS.)
MOUSE.SYS	Microsoft Mouse driver (copied only if you have an MS-compatible mouse)

Table 5.2 Files in the Personal Windows Directory.

Using an Automatic Install File (.AIF) for Workstation Setup

When installing Windows you can use the /H (Hands off) parameter to pass Setup the name of a system settings file. This ASCII text file essentially answers Setup's questions about the hardware and software setup, so that the users don't have to be involved. This gives you, the administrator, tremendous freedom to configure certain types of Windows installations. Further, it can make it very easy to add new Windows users on the LAN.

Windows 3.1 comes with a sample system settings file called SETUP.AIF that you can use as a model or modify as you like. Because Microsoft chose to call it SETUP.AIF, we'll refer to it that way from now on. The following paragraphs document the sections in the SETUP.AIF file.

THE [SYSINFO] SECTION

When you run Setup without the /H parameter, you are shown a list of system settings that Setup arrives at after performing its hardware determination (see Figure 5.4). When you perform a custom configuration using the SETUP.AIF file, you have the option of showing the user this screen or not. If you want users to see the system settings screen, include the following line in your SETUP.AIF file:

```
[sysinfo]
showsysinfo=yes
```

If you do not want this screen shown (because it may slow you down on a large, multistation installation), simply leave this line out (the default is 'no') or substitute 'no' at the end of the line.

THE [CONFIGURATION] SECTION

This section lets you specify the actual system settings that Setup would normally arrive at through its hardware determination. This way you can "force" a setting a certain way whether Setup detected something else or not. For example, you can specify a Novell NetWare shell of 3.26 or higher, even though the machine you are setting up on only has version 3.21 of the shell.

The following list illustrates each option for the [configuration] section that you can modify. These options correspond to the system settings screen shown in Figure 5.4. In many cases, you'll be asked to model an entry in the SETUP.INF file. You'll find a copy of this file in the shared Windows directory on the server.

- machine   Machine profile string from the [machine] section of SETUP.INF—for example, machine = ibm_compatible.

- display   Display profile string from the [display] section in SETUP.INF—for example, display = svga.

- mouse   Mouse profile string from the [pointing.device] section in SETUP.INF—for example, mouse = ps2mouse.

- network   Network profile string from the [network] section of SETUP.INF followed by a slash and the appropriate version number from one of the [xxxx.versions] sections in SETUP.INF—for example, network = Novell/00032100.

- keyboard   Keyboard profile string from the [keyboard.types] section of SETUP.INF—for example, keyboard = t4s0enha.

- language   Language profile string from the [language] section of SETUP.INF—for example, language = usa.

- kblayout   Keyboard layout profile string from the [keyboard.tables] section of SETUP.INF—for example, kblayout = nodll.

THE [WINDIR] SECTION

This section lets you specify the target directory where Windows will be installed. Simply follow the [windir] sections line with the path where you want Windows installed. If the specified directory does not exist, Windows will prompt the user if the creation of this directory is wanted. If you do not include this section, the user will be prompted for a target Windows directory.

```
[windir]
F:\USER\CHARLES\WINDOWS
```

THE [USERINFO] SECTION

The [userinfo] section lets you specify registration information for a given user. You may follow the [userinfo] line with up to two lines of information. The first line provides the user's name and is required if this section is included in your SETUP.AIF file. The second line, which supplies a company name, is optional. Each line may contain up to 30 characters. If you need to have blank spaces between the words on a line, enclose the line in double quotation marks (" ").

```
[userinfo]
Charles
"Rose's Uranium 2-Go, Inc."
```

THE [DONTINSTALL] SECTION

When you want to exclude certain components of Windows, the [dontinstall] section is one you should add to SETUP.AIF. This section can contain the following options:

```
[dontinstall]
accessories
readmes
```

```
games
screensavers
bitmaps
```

THE [OPTIONS] SECTION

The [options] section lets you select how Setup handles the application setup portion of the installation. You can also control whether the Windows tutorial is run at the end of Setup. There are three keywords you can specify (each on its own line) in the [options] section: *setupapps, autosetupapps,* and *tutorial.*

If you specify *setupapps,* the user will be prompted to select certain applications to setup. The *autosetupapps* keyword will cause Setup to scan the user's hard disk and set up all applications with a .EXE, .PIF, .COM, or .BAT extension. The *tutorial* keyword can be specified to run the tutorial at the end of Setup.

If you don't specify the [options] section, no applications will be set up and the tutorial will not be run. It is not recommended that you use *autosetupapps* because it will set up each and every application on the user's hard drive; this may result in massive group files and bewildered users.

```
[options]
setupapps
autosetupapps
tutorial
```

THE [PRINTERS] SECTION

You can shield users from the complexities of printer setup by specifying the [printers] section. Here you can specify printer drivers to load and the ports to connect them to. Each line in the [printers] section should contain the name of the printer and a port assignment, separated by a comma. The printer names come from the [io.device] section of CONTROL.INF. If you need a list of port names, consult the [ports] section of WIN.INI (WIN.SRC on the file server). If the printer name contains blank spaces, make sure to surround the name with double quotation marks (" ").

```
[printers]
"HP LaserJet Series II,"LPT1:
```

If this section is omitted, no printers will be installed.

THE [ENDINSTALL] SECTION

The final section, fittingly named [endinstall], lets you control how Setup finishes. You can control whether Setup updates the AUTOEXEC.BAT and CONFIG.SYS files, restarts windows, exits to DOS, or reboots when the Setup program is done. To control AUTOEXEC and CONFIG updates, the *configfiles* line can be set to one of two choices: save or modify. If you set *configfiles* to *modify,* Setup will try to change the user's AUTOEXEC.BAT and CONFIG.SYS files. If you specify *save,* however,

Setup will leave the original files alone and save its recommendations to AU-TOEXEC.WIN and CONFIG.WIN.

To control how Setup ends, you can set the *endopt* to *exit, restart,* or *reboot.* The *exit* option will exit to DOS after performing the install; *restart* quits then restarts Windows; and *reboot* will force a warm boot. If you are installing on a network with the /N switch, the *reboot* option is ignored.

If the [endinstall] section is not included, Setup will try to modify CONFIG.SYS and AUTOEXEC.BAT. If *endopt* is not included, Setup will show the user a dialog box from which to choose a procedure.

```
[endinstall]
configfiles = save
endopt = exit
```

Customizing Group Windows

Setting up Windows on a multitude of workstations can be an arduous process. Often, the more setup tasks that you can automate, the better. One area that demands a great deal of installation attention is applications, which are setup in groups on the Program Manager desktop. This section will describe how you can automate many of the tasks that are usually done by hand, such as creating new group windows and adding new applications to groups. Also, we will discuss how you can setup one group file and let it be shared by all or some of your users. That way, if you want to make a change to a particular group for everyone, you only have to do it once.

ADDING NEW GROUP WINDOWS

The [new.groups] and [progman.groups] sections of SETUP.INF can be used to direct Setup to create new Program Manager group windows. The [prog-man.groups] section is used when you are installing a new copy of Windows 3.1 and [new.groups] is used when you are upgrading from any Windows version prior to 3.1. The defaults for these sections look something like the following:

```
[new.groups]
group7=Main,1
group1=Startup
group2=Accessories
group6=Games

[progman.groups]
group3=Main,1
group4=Accessories
group5=Games
group1=StartUp
```

The *groupx* identifier to the left of the equal sign is used later in SETUP.INF (covered in the next section) to define which applications are part of each group. The name to the right of the equal sign defines the name of the group and the 1 next to Main tells Program Manager to open that group window on the desktop when Windows is run.

To define your own groups, simply add more lines using the same format. For example, if you wanted to add an electronic mail group and an Excel group, you might modify your SETUP.INF to look like the following:

```
[new.groups]
group7=Main,1
group1=Startup
group2=Accessories
group6=Games
group8=Email
group9=Excel

[progman.groups]
group3=Main,1
group4=Accessories
group5=Games
group1=StartUp
group8=Email
group9=Excel
```

Adding these two entries to each section will cause Setup to create two new groups every time users install Windows for the first time or upgrade from previous versions.

ADDING APPLICATIONS TO GROUPS

With the SETUP.INF file, you have the flexibility of directing Setup to place new applications in a user's group files in the Program Manager desktop. The last section described how to add new groups to a user's desktop during installation—now let's discuss how to add applications to them. It's actually quite simple. Look at the entries in the [new.groups] and [progman.groups] sections above. Remember that each of the *groupx* identifiers corresponds to a section in SETUP.INF. For example, the [group3] section of SETUP.INF looks like the following:

```
[group3]
"File Manager",      WINFILE.EXE
"Control Panel",     CONTROL.EXE
"Print Manager",     PRINTMAN.EXE
"Clipboard Viewer",  CLIPBRD.EXE
"MSDOS Prompt",      DOSPRMPT.PIF, PROGMAN.EXE, 9
"Windows Setup",     SETUP.EXE
"PIF Editor",        PIFEDIT.EXE
"Read Me",           README.WRI,,,
readme
```

> **Note:** The "Read Me" line has a fifth prompt, *readme*, which is used internally by Windows.

Each line is composed of several fields. The following list shows you what each field is:

- Description — The name you want to appear beneath the icon (must appear in quotes).

- Filename — The name of the executable filename. It must reside in the Windows directory, or include a full path to where the file resides.

- Icon File — The name of the file to use to get an icon from (for instance, PROGMAN.EXE is used to get icon #9 for the MS-DOS prompt above).

- Icon Number — The number of the icon to use—in the case above, ninth icon from PROGMAN.EXE is used for the MS-DOS Prompt.

Now that you know the format for the lines in the [groupx] sections in SETUP.INF, you can create your own. To follow our example from the last section which creates our own Email and Excel groups, let's add some applications to those groups. To do so, add the following lines to your SETUP.INF:

```
[group8]
"ZMail", f:\apps\zmail\zmail.exe
"DOS Mail Package", mail.pif, mailicon.exe, 5

[group9]
"Excel", f:\apps\excel\excel.exe
```

The first line in the [group8] section specifies the "Zmail" application and lists the full path of where to find zmail.exe. The second line shows how to specify a DOS-based application. Setup will associate mail.pif with the "DOS Mail Package" description; it will use the fifth icon from mailicon.exe. Finally, we specified a title and path to the Excel application.

SHARING GROUP FILES

One way to manage some of the frustration from organizing one set of group files for each user is to use one set of group files for all users, or for groups of users. The way to do this is to modify each user's PROGMAN.INI file. The [Groups] section in PROGMAN.INI tells windows where to find each of the group files. You can change the path for these group files to a shared directory. However, you will probably want to flag these group files shareable read-only to prevent overwrite and file contention problems. A possible [Groups] section is shown below:

```
[Groups]
Group1=F:\SHARED\MAIN0.GRP
Group2=F:\SHARED\ACCESSOR0.GRP
Group3=F:\SHARED\GAMES0.GRP
Group4=F:\SHARED\STARTUP0.GRP
```

This way, you can share each of the groups among as many users as you like. The 0 in the filenames above (i.e MAIN0.GRP) is a suggestion—for example, if you had an administrative set of users that you wanted to have certain groups, you could end their group names with 0, and the other users could have their group names end with 1.

Copying Additional Files Automatically During Installation

You can direct Setup to copy more files to the user's personal Windows directory than it normally would. This can be useful if you have any custom files that you want automatically distributed to users when Windows is installed on their workstation. To do this, you will first need to copy the custom files into the shared directory on the server. Next, modify the SETUP.INF file, load SETUP.INF into an editor, and locate the [net] section. You can add a line in this section for each file you want copied to a user's personal Windows directory. The line might look like the following:

```
4:ROSEAPP.PIF,"Charles' Special PIF File"
```

The number represents the disk ROSEAPP.PIF resides on. Since you will be installing from the network, this number is irrelevant. Following the filename is an optional description of the file. If you want a file to be loaded from a floppy drive instead of being taken from the shared Windows directory, locate the [disks] section in SETUP.PIF and add a line similar to the following:

```
4=A:,ROSEAPP.PIF,"Charles' Special PIF File"
```

This way, Windows will look for ROSEAPP.PIF on the A: drive during the installation.

Added Security Through Modifying PROGMAN.INI

Windows 3.1 includes a new feature that is proving useful to network administrators—the ability to restrict access to certain functions in Program Manager. To modify a user's access to Program Manager, all you have to do is modify that user's PROGMAN.INI file (located in that individual's Windows directory). The PROGMAN.INI contains sections that define which groups are present on the desktop as well as some information (such as screen coordinates that tell Windows where to put the Program Manager window the next time Windows is run, and so on). The new feature is the [restrictions] section which can contain five keywords that let you limit certain functions in Program Manager.

Simply changing the [restrictions] section is not enough to guarantee security, because a user aware of the [restrictions] section could simply edit PROGMAN.INI and remove the section. You need to restrict the user's access to PROGMAN.INI in order to ensure that PROGMAN.INI stays the same. If you are using NetWare 3.11, you can use the GRANT command (or SYSCON) to give the user limited rights to this file by typing "GRANT users_name R F FOR PROGMAN.INI," assuming PROGMAN.INI is in the current directory. This will give the user read and file scan access to PROGMAN.INI which will prevent any modification of the file.

You should only restrict access this far if you want to prevent users from changing their desktop at all; Windows is unable to save any changes to PROGMAN.INI once the GRANT command has been executed. In NetWare 2.2, you can only restrict access to the directory (rather than the file) level, so this option is not available.

The following sections describe each of the keywords in the [restrictions] section and their functions.

THE NORUN KEYWORD

You can use the [NoRun] keyword to disable the Run... command in the File menu. It will appear grayed out on the menu. The result is that users will not be able to use the Run menu command to start other applications. (They still, however, could choose New and set up their own icon to an application of their choosing—for more strict security, see the NoFileMenu below.) You can turn this option on by setting its value to 1 (shown below). The default setting for this keyword is 0 which turns on the File; Run menu selection.

```
[restrictions]
NoRun=1
```

THE NOCLOSE KEYWORD

The [NoClose] keyword prevents the user from closing the Program Manager, either by pressing the ALT+F4 key combination, by double-clicking on the system menu box, or by choosing File; Exit from the menu. The Exit menu item will appear grayed out in the menu. To turn this option on, set NoClose to 1. The default setting is 0 which turns on the File; Exit menu selection.

```
[restrictions]
NoClose=1
```

THE NOSAVESETTINGS KEYWORD

To ensure that the Program Manager desktop appears on the screen the exact same way each time, set the [NoSaveSettings] keyword to 1. This will prevent the user from saving personal preference settings, such as the arrangement of the Program Manager windows and icons on the desktop, colors, and so on. It also has the result of graying the Options; Save Settings menu item. This setting overrides the value of the SaveSettings keyword in the [settings] section of PROGMAN.INI. To prevent the user's personal settings from being saved each time the user exits Windows or uses the Save Settings menu item, set this item to 1. The default setting is 0, which allows users to save their settings.

```
[restrictions]
NoSaveSettings=1
```

THE NOFILEMENU KEYWORD

The [NoFileMenu] keyword removes the entire File menu from Program Manager. As a result, users can only run applications that have been set up in a group—for example, they can run File Manager, Print Manager, Excel (if you have it set up as an icon in a group), and so on. Also, users will be prevented from exiting Program Manager by using the File; Exit menu command. However, if the NoClose keyword is set to 0, they will be able to exit Program Manager by using the ALT+F4 key combination or by double-clicking on the system menu box. Turn this option on by setting NoFileMenu to 1. The default setting is 0 which makes the File menu available (but subject to the restrictions of other keywords in this section, like NoRun and NoClose).

```
[restrictions]
NoFileMenu
```

THE EDITLEVEL KEYWORD

The last keyword, [EditLevel], is not an option you turn on or off. Instead, you set it to a value (a level) between 0 and 4. The following list describes how each level works.

- 0   (Default) Lets the user make any modifications to Program Manager. These changes can be saved if NoSaveSettings is equal to 0.

- 1   Prevents the user from renaming, deleting, or creating Program Manager groups.

- 2   Includes all level 1 restrictions, plus the user cannot remove or create program items.

- 3   Includes all level 2 restrictions, plus the user cannot change the command line for any program items, such as icons.

- 4   Includes all level 3 restrictions, plus the user cannot change any information for existing program items. This information includes the description, working directory, icon, or any other information available from the File; Properties menu.

Other Notes

Be aware that Windows will attempt to modify your AUTOEXEC.BAT and CONFIG.SYS files, although it gives you the choice of actually modifying these files. It's worth giving each of these files a final check before relying on them. For example, make sure that memory management drivers are being loaded before other programs that need access to extended or expanded memory.

Swap Files

Several different types of "swap files" can come into play when we talk about how Windows operates. Most commonly this term refers to the swap files that Windows uses as "virtual memory" when running in 386 Enhanced mode. This allows an application running under Windows to see more memory available than is physically installed on the system. Windows uses the swap files behind the scenes in order to move data in and out of actual RAM memory.

Additionally, other types of swap files may be created, including standard and real mode application swap files that are used for swapping DOS programs in and out of memory, and print spool files from Windows Print Manager. When printing in a network environment, it is wise to turn off Windows print spooling, as this spooling is already being performed by NetWare at the file server.

In 386 Enhanced mode, Windows can use either a permanent or temporary swap file. Permanent swap files are created once and are used each time Windows loads. Temporary swap files are created dynamically and deleted each time Windows runs.

Permanent swap files cannot be created on network drives because Windows uses low-level disk access through BIOS routines to speed swapping performance. Permanent swap files must be contiguous blocks on your local hard drive; such low-level access is not possible through NetWare or other network operating systems.

Permanent Swap File

When you install Windows 3.1 on a machine capable of running in 386 Enhanced mode, a permanent swap file is created automatically. Under Windows 3.0, a permanent swap file must be created by the SWAPFILE.EXE program (found in the \WINDOWS\SYSTEM directory). You can run this program by exiting Windows to DOS and, from the \WINDOWS\SYSTEM directory, typing "win /r swapfile"—the "/r" tells Windows to run in Real Mode, which SWAPFILE.EXE needs.

Nothing should be running in memory except Windows, which is running in real mode when you start SWAPFILE.EXE. This includes the Novell network shell and any other TSRs. An often overlooked TSR is NWPOPUP.EXE (the NetWare Windows message utility) which is loaded from WIN.INI. To temporarily remove NWPOPUP.EXE from Windows memory, comment out the LOAD=NWPOPUP.EXE statement in WIN.INI (by placing a semi-colon in front of the line). Then run SWAPFILE by typing "win /r swapfile" from the \WINDOWS\SYSTEM directory. Finally, un-comment the LOAD=NWPOPUP.EXE line in WIN.INI.

In Windows 3.1, you can use the 386 Enhanced icon in the Control Panel (which is covered in detail in Chapter 3) to change the size and location of your permanent swap file. You can also use this icon to delete a permanent swap file and create a temporary one.

This point bears mentioning again: If you are using Enhanced mode Windows and want to create a Permanent swap file, you will need to create it on a local hard drive. Permanent swap files cannot be created on a NetWare drive.

Temporary Swap File

Temporary swap files are created and deleted each time Windows runs in Enhanced mode. If you choose not to use a Permanent swap file or you prefer to store your swap file on the network (or you have a diskless machine and have no choice), you have the freedom of deciding where the temporary swap file will be created. Temporary swap files are automatically deleted when you quit Windows without rebooting.

Temporary files default to the location of the Windows startup files unless explicitly told otherwise. You should set the "PagingDrive=d" parameter in your SYSTEM.INI file, where d is the driver letter on which temporary swap files should be created.

The "PagingDrive=" statement creates swap files in the root of the specified drive, which can be quite inconvenient in the network environment. For Windows 3.1, it is also possible to use a "PagingFile=d:\path\filename" statement in SYSTEM.INI which specifies the path and filename to be used for the temporary swap file.

Be aware that placing swap files on the network server will increase traffic and reduce server performance. If temporary swap files are used on the network, Windows load time will increase significantly when using NetWare 2.x. This extra slowdown is caused by Windows requesting swap file space from the file server. When allocating this space, NetWare 2.x file servers prefill the file with null data, and physically write this information out to disk. By contrast, NetWare 3.x file servers utilize a "sparse file allocation" strategy, where the space is marked as allocated, but no data is physically written out to disk until data actually exists.

Application Swap Files

Application swap files are created by Windows only when operating in Real or Standard modes. When you switch from a particular application, Windows moves some or all of its memory to a disk file. This gives you more working memory and allows you to have more applications loaded at the same time.

These application swap files are hidden files with a ~WOAxxxx.TMP name, where WOA means Windows Old Applications. You can specify where these files get placed with the "Swapdisk" parameter in the SYSTEM.INI file. If this parameter is not set, the default location is where your Windows startup files are stored.

You will run into the same types of problems with Application swap files as you did with temporary ones. If you have workstations with hard drive space, you might want to use them for swapping to reduce network traffic load. Also, if you can choose between several local drives, pick the quickest drive for better performance. You should have at least 512K on the drive you choose; however, the more space you have, the more Windows can free up to let you load more applications at once.

Among other things, the DOS TEMP environment variable controls where Windows writes the Application swap files, so you can direct them where you want. See the discussion below on the SwapDisk parameter (in the section on SYSTEM.INI settings) for further information about how TEMP works.

Use caution when putting application swap files on network drives to ensure that no two users are pointing to the same swap path; this can cause disastrous consequences.

You may wish to use a RAM disk for optimizing swap file operations, although you will need at least 2MB of RAM space and have a RAM disk driver that doesn't conflict with any of your memory managers. Since the application swap files are used when switching between DOS applications, the decision to use a RAM disk boils down to whether your configuration is better served by having RAM available to Windows applications (which can use up to 16MB of installed RAM in standard mode), or by the speed of using a RAM disk when toggling between DOS applications. The choice is yours.

SmartDrive

SmartDrive is a disk-caching program that comes with Windows. Because it was written by Microsoft, it was written to be Windows-aware. SmartDrive can be useful in improving the speed of local drives by caching their data. SmartDrive will not cache network drives, however. In fact, it is not safe for use with files available for multi-user access. This is no great loss, however; Novell file servers already cache files stored on the network.

If you decide to use SmartDrive, or any other cache program, you should experiment with different memory settings, remembering the RAM you need for Standard (256K extended) and Enhanced (1MB extended) modes.

SmartDrive is added as a line to your CONFIG.SYS file as follows:

```
device = c:\windows\SMARTDRIVE.SYS 512 256
```

SmartDrive needs a memory management driver to be installed in order to work properly. A memory management device driver like HIMEM.SYS, or a third-party memory manager like Quarterdeck's QEMM386.SYS or Qualitas' 386MAX.SYS will work fine. The first number (after SMARTDRIVE.SYS) is the amount of extended memory, in kilobytes, that SmartDrive normally uses. The second number is the "minimum cache size" to which Windows adjusts SmartDrive whenever it runs. It reclaims this memory for its own use (in Enhanced or Standard modes; in Real mode it reclaims this memory as needed).

With Windows 3.1, Microsoft began shipping SmartDrive 4.0 which has been changed to SMARTDRV.EXE and is called from AUTOEXEC.BAT. Its default sizes are as follows:

Extended Memory Up to	Outside Windows	Inside Windows
1 MB	All Extended	0 - No caching
2 MB	1 MB	256K
4 MB	1 MB	512K
6 MB	2 MB	1 MB
Above 6 MB	2 MB	2 MB

You should also investigate other cache programs, both commercial and shareware, because many have been shown to be faster than SmartDrive.

Windows Files and Their Purpose

The following lists describe the NetWare files included with Windows and their functions. The first list describes the NetWare/Windows files that are supplied by Novell:

IPX.COM
: This file is generated using the WSGEN or SHGEN utilities, depending on your version of NetWare. Generated from the IPX.OBJ file, it is configured for your specific network adapter. The file is part of the Novell shell and consumes 15KB to 25KB of conventional memory, depending on your network adapter and other configuration options. (A recent version of the IPX.OBJ file is shipped with Windows 3.1.)

TBMI.COM
: This stands for Task-Switched Buffer Manager; it handles IPX/SPX virtualization for non-Windows programs. It is discussed in more detail below in the section on TBMI.

TASKID.COM
: This works in conjunction with TBMI.COM. TBMI is loaded prior to loading Windows and TASKID is loaded once for each DOS shell invoked under Windows. Note that TBMI.COM and TASKID.COM are for Windows 3.0 real and standard modes only.

TBMI2.COM
: TBMI2.COM is a version of the Task-Switched Buffer Manager Interface (TBMI) that is used with Windows 3.1 in standard mode.

VPICDA.386
: VPICDA.386 is necessary for Windows 3.0 in 386 Enhanced mode only, when running a network adapter using interrupt 2, 9, or higher. The VPICDA.386 driver replaces the virtual programmable interrupt controller device driver built into Windows 3.0. To install this device, edit SYSTEM.INI replacing "device=*vpicd" with "device=vpicda.386" under the [386Enh] section header.

NETWARE.PIF
: This is a sample Program Information File (PIF) for NetWare utilities. You can use PIF files to optimize the operation of NetWare utilities and, in general, ensure a smoother operation. We will discuss PIF files in more detail in the next chapter.

NetWare Utilities

The latest versions of NetWare contain Windows-aware versions of the NetWare utilities stored on the PUBLIC directory, but older NetWare versions may need to have several of these updated. See the appendices for a list of sizes and dates for files like MAP, LOGIN, GRANT, BINDFIX, and others to determine if you need to update these files.

The following NetWare/Windows files are supplied by Microsoft with Windows:

NETWARE.DRV

The NetWare driver for Windows. Windows uses this driver to run the Network Printer Browse, File Manager Connect Net Drive, and the NetWare Utilities dialog boxes. NETWARE.DRV also provides protected mode API translation so that programmers can access NetWare API services.

VNETWARE.386

Enhanced mode virtual NetWare driver. This driver virtualizes the NetWare shell file NETx.COM in Enhanced mode.

VIPX.386

Enhanced mode virtual NetWare driver. This driver virtualizes the NetWare shell file IPX.COM. See the discussion below about TBMI versus VIPX.

NETWARE.HLP

NetWare help file. It is used in Windows and is viewable from the network sections of the Control Panel and the File Manager, among others.

NETWARE.INI

NetWare utilities configuration file. Under Windows 3.0, this file lists the utilities that will be displayed in the Network Utility list from the Network option of the Control Panel. You may add internal or external utility programs to this list. See "NETWARE.INI" below. Under Windows 3.1, this file contains default parameters used by NetWare running under Windows.

NWPOPUP.EXE

NWPOPUP intercepts NetWare broadcast messages and displays them in a Window when received. It is set up by the Windows Setup program to load automatically by placing the line "load=NWPOPUP.EXE" in WIN.INI.

Task-Switched Buffer Manager (TBMI) versus VIPX

VIPX.386 is a virtual device driver for Enhanced mode that virtualizes (or synchronizes) incoming or outgoing packets with the virtual machine associated with them. This prevents IPX from getting confused when you have two DOS sessions that use IPX/SPX running simultaneously—it doesn't know which DOS session to route the packets to.

If you are running in Enhanced mode with either Windows 3.0 or 3.1, load VIPX support by including "VIPX.386" in the "network=" statement under the [386Enh] section header.

If you are running in standard or real mode, you will need to use the Task-switched Buffer Manager Interface (TBMI) for IPX/SPX. TBMI performs functions similar to VIPX, only for real and standard modes. There is no need for running TBMI if your applications do not communicate directly with IPX or SPX, but go through the NetWare shell interface. If you are not sure whether your applications make direct calls to IPX, it is a good idea to load the TBMI interface to be on the safe side. Applications that use IPX/SPX communications directly and require TBMI or TBMI2 include NetWare 3.x's RCONSOLE utility, and the chat program included on the diskette accompanying this book.

For Windows 3.0 in standard or real mode, you use TBMI.COM., which is a DOS TSR that should be loaded before Windows. TBMI.COM depends on TASKID.COM to be loaded in every Windows DOS session. TASKID tells TBMI what the task number is for the currently running DOS session. That way, TBMI can help IPX figure out how network packets should be properly routed.

For Windows 3.1 standard mode, TBMI2.COM is used in place of TBMI.COM. TBMI2.COM supports the DOS 5 "task switcher API" implemented originally by DOS 5's DOSSHELL program, and by Windows 3.1 standard mode. TBMI2 is able to track the different tasks under Windows without the need for a TASKID program.

Setting Up NetWare Parameter Files

Most programs have configurable options of some sort. In the DOS world, these options can be handled in several ways. Users may select their favorite options from a setup program or they may set certain options from within an application. In either case, the application must save that custom environment of settings somewhere. In the DOS world, there are about as many ways of saving program configuration information as there are programs.

However, with Windows, Microsoft has attempted to standardize these configuration/option files with their .INI (assumably for INItialization) file format. There are several default .INI files that are created when Windows is installed, such as WIN.INI, SYSTEM.INI, CONTROL.INI, PROGMAN.INI, and of special significance to NetWare users, NETWARE.INI. All are ASCII text files that can be edited easily with Notepad.

We will discuss these .INI files in detail below, but first it's important to understand the structure of these files. One nice thing for the system administrator responsible for editing these files is that the structure for each .INI file is the same. The .INI file is organized into blocks of parameter settings grouped under common headings, as in:

```
[Section Name]
Parameter1=Value1
Parameter2=Value2
ParameterX=ValueY
```

```
[Another Section]
YetAnotherParam=YAV1
AreWeDone=True
```

Parameters can be of several types: an integer, a Boolean value, a string, or a quoted string. An integer is a non-decimal number that can be positive or negative. A Boolean is a True/False indicator that is used to turn a particular option on or off. Possible values for Boolean parameters are True, False, Yes, No, On, Off, 1, or 0. A string is simply a phrase made up of letters that apply to the parameter, such as Parameter1=MyOperator. A quoted string simply has quotes on either side as in DriverDescription="A really powerful driver."

If you edit an .INI file, use an editor that does not insert any extra formatting characters, like TABs or other ASCII codes that would confuse Windows. When in doubt, use the Notepad or the SysEdit utility.

SysEdit comes with Windows, but does not appear on the Program Manager as an icon when you start Windows, unless you put it there. You can run SysEdit from Program Manager by selecting 'Run' from the File menu and entering "system\sysedit.exe," or you can set up SysEdit as an icon on your desktop.

To setup SysEdit as an icon, choose New from the Program Manager 'File' menu and choose "Program Item." Enter "SysEdit" as the description of the program and enter "system\sysedit.exe" as the program name. Press OK and SysEdit should be installed on your desktop.

When you run SysEdit, it loads your CONFIG.SYS, AUTOEXEC.BAT, SYSTEM.INI, and WIN.INI files each into its own window. You can edit any of the files as needed.

The SYSTEM.INI file is critical to Windows operation, especially on a LAN, so let's start with it.

SYSTEM.INI

The SYSTEM.INI file determines how the hardware in your system is configured to work with Windows. In addition, it specifies the device drivers Windows will use to work with your particular hardware. You might think of SYSTEM.INI as a kind of extended, run-time CONFIG.SYS for Windows.

SYSTEM.INI is composed of several sections:

`[boot]`	Device drivers and Windows modules.
`[boot.description]`	Stores the names of the devices in use.
`[keyboard]`	Keyboard-specific parameters.
`[NonWindowsApp]`	Parameters used by Windows to run non-Windows applications.
`[standard]`	Parameters used by Windows for Standard mode.
`[386Enh]`	Parameters used by Windows for 386 Enhanced mode.

[NetWare]   A special section for those running NetWare, it defines how drive mappings are handled under Windows and whether they are restored when you exit Windows.

In the following section, you will see those settings in SYSTEM.INI that are specific to those running Windows on NetWare. For complete information on all of the settings in SYSTEM.INI, consult the SYSINI.TXT, SYSINI2.TXT, and SYS-INI3.TXT files that come with Windows 3.0 or the SYSINI.WRI file that ships with Windows 3.1. You also may want to look at Microsoft's Windows Resource Kit for more detailed information.

[NETWARE] SECTION

This is a special section that is used only when users are running Windows under NetWare. The following two parameters can be specified:

```
RestoreDrives=<Boolean>
```

While in Windows, you may wish to create, delete, or change certain drive mappings. This parameter controls whether your original drive mappings (those that were set before you ran Windows) will be restored when you exit Windows. The default setting is True, meaning the mappings will be restored to their former glory.

```
NWShareHandles=<Boolean>
```

While in 386 Enhanced mode, Windows opens a virtual machine (VM) for each DOS session you have. These sessions can share a common set of drive mappings or each one can have its own. The default setting, False, keeps each session's drive mappings separate. You may change the setting to True so that when you map drive F: to SYS:SYSTEM, drive F: will be mapped to SYS:SYSTEM in all other DOS sessions.

Setting NWShareHandles=TRUE can produce some unexpected results. For example, if you change directories on a drive in one session, it is immediately changed in all other sessions, which may not be appreciated by some applications.

The only situation where it makes sense to set NWShareHandles=TRUE is when running on NetWare 2.x networks experiencing a memory shortage in dynamic memory pool (DMP) 1. To view DMP 1 usage, select the Statistics/Summary options from the NetWare FCONSOLE utility, and observe the peak and maximum settings for the amount of memory in this pool. Each drive mapping consumes 16 bytes of DMP 1 memory, so opening multiple DOS boxes and changing directories on network drives will allocate additional drive mappings and consume DMP 1 memory. It is advisable to minimize the number of drive mappings that you perform on your network when running in the NetWare 2.x environment.

[BOOT] SECTION

The setting

```
network.drv=<filename>
```

defines which LAN driver will be used. The drivers are for network operating systems rather than individual network adapter boards. For example, NetWare users will have network.drv=netware.drv in this section.

[NONWINDOWSAPP] SECTION

The setting

```
NetAsynchSwitching= <or 1>
```

indicates whether Windows will allow you to switch away from an application (running in real mode or standard mode) after it has made an asynchronous NetBIOS call. The default value is 0 and specifies that such task-switching is not allowed. Switching from some applications that make these calls might cause your system to fail. Once Windows detects an asynchronous NetBIOS call, it will not allow switching from the application even if no more of these calls are made. Set this value to 1 if you are sure the applications you use will not receive network messages while you are switched away from them.

```
SwapDisk=<drive-colon-directory>
```

This parameter, when set, defines where your application swap files will be placed for real or standard mode. If this parameter is not defined, then the default location is the directory pointed to by the TEMP environment variable. If no TEMP environment variable exists, application swap files are placed in the Windows directory.

On some diskless workstations, you may not be able to start Windows unless this parameter is set or you have the TEMP environment variable set to a valid directory for which you have rights.

[STANDARD] SECTION

The parameter

```
Int28Filter=<number>
```

specifies the percentage of INT28h interrupts, generated when the system is idle, that are made visible to software loaded before Windows. Windows will reflect every nth interrupt, where n is the value of this setting. Increasing this value might improve Windows' performance, but may interfere with some memory-resident software, such as a network. Set this value to 0 to prevent INT28h interrupts. Note that setting this value too low will add to system overhead that might interfere with communications applications. The default is 10.

Programs like print servers often use Int 28h interrupts (the DOS idle interrupt) to perform background processing. For increased background printing performance, it may be desirable to configure a lower non-zero value for this parameter to pass more Int 28h calls to the background printing process.

The parameter

```
NetHeapSize=<Kilobytes>
```

specifies the size (in kilobytes) of the buffer pool that standardmode Windows allocates in conventional memory for transferring data over a network. Some networks require a larger buffer than the default. Increasing this value will diminish the amount of memory available to applications. If no network software is running, this setting will be ignored and no memory will be allocated. The default is 8 (kilobytes).

NETBIOS applications, such as Lotus Notes, may require larger NetHeapSize values. It is not uncommon to require 32 or 64KB values for this parameter when running applications that perform extensive NETBIOS communication.

[386ENH] SECTION

The parameter

```
AllVMsExclusive=<Boolean>
```

makes all applications run in exclusive mode with a full screen. This setting overrides any PIF settings you may have set up. You may want to set this option to TRUE if you are having problems with TSRs or network software that is incompatible with Windows. The default is False.

```
COM1Base=address
COM2Base=address (etc...up to COM4)
```

These entries specify the base I/O address for the serial port adapter you are using. The default for these fields are COM3Base=3E8h, and the port address values read from the BIOS data area for COM1, COM2, and COM4.

COM4 is often configured for I/O base address 2E8h, which can cause conflicts with Arcnet cards configured for the Arcnet default base I/O address of 2E0h. If you originally run the Windows install on a PC with COM4, and copy this SYSTEM.INI to a workstation running Arcnet at 2E0h, you may encounter problems.

```
COM1Irq=#
COM2Irq=# (etc)
```

These entries specify which interrupt line is used by the device on the specified serial port. The defaults for ISA and EISA machines are COM1Irq=4, COM2Irq=3, COM3Irq=4, and COM4Irq=3. For MCA machines, the values are the same except COM3Irq=3.

If you have a network adapter installed using IRQ 4 or IRQ 3, you may need to ensure that no COM port is configured to use the same interrupt (whether this is a problem depends on your network card's drivers). To disable a COM port, use COM1Irq=1.

The Device= option specifies which virtual devices are being used with Windows in 386 Enhanced mode. You can specify the option in one of two ways: by using either the name of a specific virtual device file, or an asterisk (*) followed immediately by the device name.

```
Device=<filename-or-*devicename>
```

The latter case refers to a virtual device that is in the WIN386.EXE file. Synonyms for Device= are Display=, EBIOS=, Keyboard=, Network=, and Mouse=. Filenames usually include the .386 extension. Multiple device lines are required to run Windows in 386 Enhanced mode. Device settings can be changed through an editor, such as the Notepad, but are generally changed through the Windows Control Panel.

The setting

```
Display=<filename-or-*devicename>
```

specifies the display device that is being used with Windows in 386 Enhanced mode (and is a synonym for Device=).

```
DualDisplay=<Boolean>
```

Normally, when running in 386 Enhanced mode, the memory between B000:0000 and B7FF:000F will be used by the general system, unless a secondary display is detected. If you set this option to TRUE, the memory in this range will be left unused and available for display adapters. If you disable this option, the address range will be available on EGA systems but not under VGA systems, since the VGA display device supports monochrome modes, which use this address space.

The setting

```
EBIOS=<filename-or-*devicename>
```

specifies the extended BIOS device that is being used with Windows in 386 Enhanced mode (and is a synonym for Device=).

The setting

```
EMMExclude=<paragraph range>
```

specifies a memory range that Windows will ignore when it scans to find unused address space in the range A000h through EFFFh. Normally, Windows scans this space and uses the addresses that it thinks are not being used by other software or hardware. Windows does not always exclude the portions of memory that it should, so you may need to use this setting to tell Windows to specifically exclude an address range. This is particularly important on networks because Windows may interfere with a network adapter which maps memory into this range (A000h through EFFFh).

This is probably the single most important setting in this section for network users. If you have not specified an EMMExclude and your network adapter uses memory in the range of A000h through EFFFh, you will undoubtedly have problems with Windows. Check your network adapter documentation for details. If you are having trouble with your network installation, you can always add the line "EMMExclude=A000-EFFF" to exclude everything, then narrow the address range once you determine that Windows works.

```
EMMInclude=<paragraph range>
```

The opposite of EMMExclude, this parameter lets you specify an address range that you want Windows to specifically scan for unused address space, whether Windows detects anything there. Note that EMMInclude takes precedence over

EMMExclude if you specify ranges that overlap. The starting value is rounded down and the ending value is rounded up to a multiple of 16K. For instance, if you set EMMInclude=C800CFFF, you would be directing Windows to scan the addresses C800:0000 through CFFF:000F. You can specify more than one range by including more than one EMMInclude line.

The parameter

```
EMMPageFrame=<paragraph>
```

lets you specify where the 64K page frame will begin if Windows cannot find a suitable page frame on its own. Note that this is the expanded memory page frame that is applicable if Windows is providing expanded memory support for DOS applications, and not a memory manager like EMM386 or QEMM.

```
EMMSize=<Kilobytes>
```

This setting lets you limit Windows' consumption of expanded memory. One possible use is for applications that allocate all available expanded memory. The default is 65,536.

```
FileSysChange=<Boolean>
```

This setting determines whether File Manager will automatically receive messages any time a nonWindows application creates, renames, or deletes a file. If you enable this setting, system performance can suffer dramatically. The default for this setting is on, but if Setup creates a standard SYSTEM.INI file, it will set FileSysChange=off, disabling this setting.

```
InDOSPolling=<boolean>
```

If you set InDOSPolling to True, you will prevent Windows from running other applications when memory-resident software has the InDOS flag set. This can be helpful if you are running memory-resident software that needs to be in a critical section to do operations off an INT21 hook. If you enable this setting, system performance will be degraded slightly. The default is False.

```
INT28Critical=<Boolean>
```

If you set INT28Critical to True, Windows will enter a critical section during an interrupt 28h. Some network virtual devices do internal task-switching on INT28h interrupts. These interrupts might hang some network software, indicating the need for an INT28h critical section. Although the default for this option is True, if you are certain that your network software does not need this option set, you may increase system performance slightly by setting it to False.

The setting

```
MapPhysAddress=<range>
```

specifies an address range (in megabytes) in which the Windows memory manager will preallocate physical pagetable entries and linear address space. This setting can be useful if you are using a DOS device driver (such as an older version of RAMDrive that uses extended memory) that needs contiguous memory.

The parameter

```
MaxPagingFileSize=<Kilobytes>
```

specifies the maximum size (in KB) for a temporary swap file.
The parameter

```
MinTimeSlice=<milliseconds>
```

sets the minimum amount of time a virtual machine will be allowed to run before Windows switches to another virtual machine. If you set this value to a small number, such as 10 milliseconds, it will make multitasking appear smoother, but will diminish the overall system performance. The default is 20 (milliseconds). Apart from editing SYSTEM.INI, you can change the value by clicking on the 386 Enhanced icon in Control Panel.

```
MinUserDiskSpace=<Kilobytes>
```

The MinUserDiskSpace option tells Windows how much disk space (in kilobytes) to leave free when creating a temporary swap file. This setting can be useful if you have a limited amount of space on the drive where the temporary file will be placed. The default is 500KB.

```
NetAsynchFallback=<Boolean>
```

If you set this option to True, Windows will attempt to save a failing NetBIOS request. If an application issues an asynchronous NetBIOS request, Windows will try to allocate space in its global network buffer to receive the data. If the global buffer is full, Windows will normally fail the NetBIOS request. If this setting is enabled, Windows will attempt to save the request by allocating a buffer in local memory, and by preventing any other virtual machines from running until the data is received and the timeout period (specified by the NetAsynchTimeout setting) expires. The default is false.
The setting

```
NetDMASize=<Kilobytes>
```

specifies the DMA buffer size (in kilobytes) for NetBIOS transport software. The buffer size is the greater value of the NetDMASize parameter and the value of DMABufferSize. The default is 32 (KB) on Micro Channel (TM) machines, 0 on nonMicro Channel machines.
The setting

```
NetHeapSize=<Kilobytes>
```

specifies the buffer size (in KB) that Windows in 386 Enhanced mode allocates in conventional memory for transferring data over a network. All values are rounded up to the nearest 4K. The default is 12 (KB).
NETBIOS applications, such as Lotus Notes, may require larger NetHeapSize values. It is not uncommon to require 32 or 64KB values for this parameter when running applications that perform extensive NETBIOS communication.
The setting

```
Network=<filename-or-*devicename
```

specifies the network device driver you are using with Windows in 386 Enhanced mode. This setting is a synonym for Device=. You can also change this setting by using the Windows Setup icon from the Main Group window.

The option

```
Paging=<Boolean>
```

has a default of True. You can disable swapping to temporary swap files by setting this option to False. You might need to do this if disk space were extremely low.

The setting

```
PagingDrive=<drive-letter>
```

tells Windows in which drive to place temporary swap files. If you have a permanent swap file, this setting is ignored.

The setting

```
PagingFile=path-and-filename
```

specifies the path and filename for a temporary swap file that is to be created when Windows is started in 386 Enhanced mode. This setting overrides the PagingDrive setting (Windows 3.1 only).

The setting

```
PSPIncrement=<number>
```

specifies the memory that Windows should reserve (in 16-byte increments) in each successive virtual machine when the UniqueDOSPSP setting is enabled. The setting that will work best for your machine will vary depending on your memory configuration and the applications you are running. Valid values range from 2 through 64, and the default is 2.

The setting

```
ReflectDosInt2A=<Boolean>
```

specifies whether Windows will reflect DOS INT 2Ah signals or consume them. The default (False) tells Windows to consume these signals which makes Windows run more efficiently. Enable this setting if you are running memory-resident software that relies on detecting INT2A messages.

The setting

```
SysVMEMSLimit=<Kilobytes>
```

specifies the amount of expanded memory (in KB) that Windows should be allowed to use. Setting this value to 0 prevents Windows from allocating any expanded memory; setting it to 1 lets Windows use all available expanded memory. The default is 2048 (KB).

```
SysVMEMSLocked=<Boolean>
```

If enabled, this option will prevent Windows from swapping expanded memory to the hard disk. This will improve the performance of a Windows application that uses it, but will slow down the rest of the system. The default is False.

The setting

```
SysVMEMSRequired=<Kilobytes>
```

tells Windows how much memory (KB) must be free to start Windows. It should be 0 (the default), if no Windows application requires expanded memory.

The setting

```
SysVMV86Locked=<Boolean>
```

has the default of False. If you enable this option, the virtual mode memory being used in the system virtual machine will remain locked in memory rather than being swappable out to disk. This process is internal to Windows, so there is no known reason to enable this setting.

```
SysVMXMSLimit=<Kilobytes>
```

Like SysVMEMSLimit, this option sets a cap on the memory the extended memory driver will allocate to DOS device drivers and memory-resident software in the system virtual machine. If you set the value to 1, Windows will give an application all the available extended memory it wants. The default is 2048KB.

```
SysVMXMSLocked=<Boolean>
```

Like SysVMEMSLocked, the default for this setting is False. If you enable this option, it will prevent Windows from swapping XMS memory to disk.

```
SysVMXMSRequired=<Kilobytes>
```

Like SysVMEMSRequired, this option sets the minimum XMS memory to start Windows. The default is 0 (kilobytes).

```
TimerCriticalSection=<milliseconds>
```

If the value is over 0, this item tells Windows to enter a critical section around all timer interrupt code, and specifies the timeout period (in milliseconds). If set, TimerCriticalSection will ensure that one virtual machine at a time will receive timer interrupts which may be required for some networks (try setting this option to 10000 or greater if you are having trouble running Windows with your network adapter). Using this option, however, will slow down system performance and can make overall system performance seem sluggish. The default is 0.

```
TokenRingSearch=<Boolean>
```

If this option is enabled, Windows will look for a token ring network adapter on machines with IBM PC/AT (R) architecture. You can disable this setting if you are not using a token ring card and the search interferes with another device. The default is True.

```
UniqueDOSPSP=<Boolean>
```

This parameter defaults to False, but if enabled, it tells Windows to start every application at a unique address (PSP). This setting may help ensure that applications in different virtual machines all start at different addresses. Some networks may require that you turn this option on.

The setting

```
VirtualHDIrq=<Boolean>
```

instructs Windows, if enabled, to terminate interrupts from the hard disk controller, bypassing the ROM routine that handles these interrupts (the default). Although this speeds system performance, some hard drives might require that this setting be disabled in order to process interrupts correctly. If this setting is disabled, the disk controller's ROM routine handles the interrupts, which will slow overall system performance.

The setting

```
WindowKBRequired=<Kilobytes>
```

specifies how much conventional memory (KB) you must have free to start Windows. The default is 256 (KB).

The setting

```
WindowMemSize=<number-or-Kilobytes>
```

sets the ceiling on conventional memory that RAM Windows can use. The default (-1) tells Windows to use all it needs, but you can enter a value less than 640 if there is not enough memory to run Windows in 386 Enhanced mode.

WIN.INI

Whereas SYSTEM.INI is the initialization file for Windows from a systems perspective, WIN.INI is the initialization file for Windows as an application. WIN.INI contains default settings for Windows, such as which applications get loaded onto the desktop when Windows is loaded, how the desktop looks, what fonts are used, and so on. In addition, Windows-compatible applications may place their default configuration information in their own section in WIN.INI in the format:

```
[WinApp1]
Default1=A
Default2=B
```

WIN.INI is divided into the following sections:

[windows]	Affects several different elements in the Windows environment.
[Desktop]	Controls the appearance and positioning of windows and icons.
[Extensions]	Assigns associations between file extensions and applications.
[intl]	Allows for display of items for countries other than the United States.
[ports]	Available output ports.
[fonts]	Screen fonts loaded by Windows.

[PrinterPorts]	Active and Inactive output devices that have been installed.
[devices]	Active output devices that provide compatibility with Windows 2.x.
[colors]	Defines Windows display colors.

The following sections were added to WIN.INI in Windows 3.1:

[FontSubstitutes]	Lets you map Windows 3.0 font names to Windows 3.0 raster fonts.
[TrueType]	Controls enabling and configuration of TrueType.
[mci extensions]	Defines the Multimedia Player for different types of files.
[Network]	Contains your network permanent connection settings, such as your drive and printer connections. Windows uses this information to restore drive mappings and printer port capturing when it is loaded.
[embedding]	Used for compatibility with Windows 3.0. This section lists objects, the programs that create them, and the format they are in.
[Windows Help]	Controls default main Windows help coordinates, maximized/minimized status, and positioning of the History and Copy dialogs.
[Sounds]	Sounds that are played when certain system events occur.
[Programs]	Lists directories Windows will search in addition to AUTOEXEC.BAT when you open a data file that is associated with an application. These settings only get read when Windows can't find the program in your path.

One of the NetWare-specific aspects of WIN.INI follows the load= statement in the first line of the [windows] section, as in:

```
[windows]
load=nwpopup.exe
```

NWPOPUP.EXE is a program included with Windows that intercepts NetWare broadcast messages and displays them on the Windows desktop. There will be no window or icon on the screen to indicate the presence of this application.

Note that NWPOPUP.EXE must be unloaded to run the Windows 3.0 SwapFile (the program that creates your 386 Enhanced permanent swap file). To disable the program, you can either remove it from the load= line and reload Windows, or you can choose the "Disable Broadcast Messages" option from the Network option on the Windows Control Panel. If you are running Windows 3.1, this is not a concern.

NETWARE.INI

NETWARE.INI is exclusive to those users running on a Novell LAN. The file is created by the Windows driver, NETWARE.DRV, whenever the driver cannot find a current copy of the file. NETWARE.INI is composed of several sections, described below.

THE [MSW30-UTILS] SECTION

Internal utilities are those utilities available to the user through the network driver. They appear on the Network Utilties menu (invoked from the Network icon on the Windows Control Panel). The following section, taken from a sample NETWARE.INI, shows how these are set up:

```
[MSW30Utils]
Attach A File Server=<Attach
Detach A File Server=<Detach
Enable Broadcast Messages=<Messages
Disable Broadcast Messages=<No Messages
System Configuration Utility=SYSCON.PIF
File Server Console Utility=FCONSOLE.PIF
```

The text to the left appears on the Network Utilities menu. The programName syntax means to execute a routine, such as Attach, that is internal to NETWARE.DRV. The equal sign before a program (or Program Information File, PIF) name means the program is external to NETWARE.DRV and Windows should execute that program. In this way, network administrators can set up commonly used external programs that appear on the NetWare Utilities menu.

> **Note:** This section has been removed from Windows 3.1. In Windows 3.1, when you click on the Network icon in Control Panel, you see the Network settings (covered in detail in Chapter 3) rather than the Network Utilities menu.

THE [MSW30-PRTQ] SECTION

NETWARE.INI also controls NetWare environment settings, such as those for printing. The following section in NETWARE.INI performs this task.

```
[MSW30-PrtQ]
MaxJobs=50
MaxBufSize=3500
UpdateSeconds=30
```

MaxJobs controls how many jobs are visible in the Windows Print Manager queue. The range for this setting is 1–250 and the default value is 50.

MaxBufSize configures the size of the buffer (in bytes) that Windows uses to store information about print jobs in the Print Manager queue. The range is 3500–30000 with a default of 3500.

UpdateSeconds defines how often (in seconds) Windows checks and updates the Print Manager queue. The range for the parameter is 1–65 with the default of 30. The update function can also be done manually from the Print Manager menus.

THE [OPTIONS] SECTION

```
[Options]
PermDrive=1
Messages=1
RestoreConnection=1
NetWareHotKey=1
```

The first three options correspond to settings defined using the Network settings dialog box (which is reached through the Network icon in Control Panel). These options are discussed in detail in Chapter 3.

NetWareHotKey activates the NetWare popup window that is part of NETWARE.DRV. For a full discussion of the NetWare popup window, refer to Chapter 3.

Sections other than these may appear in NETWARE.INI and are maintained by other Novell utilities, such as the Novell Workstation Utilities available from Novell.

Mapping Drives

If you have spent much time at the command line on a Novell network, you are most likely familiar with the NetWare MAP command, which allows you to assign a drive letter to a file server, volume, and directory combination, as in:

```
MAP F:=ROSE\SYS:USER\ME
```

In this example, the F: drive will point to the \USER\ME directory on the SYS: volume on file server ROSE.

Problems crop up with NetWare drives under Windows because many Windows applications ignore default directories. Programs like Windows' File Manager reset the default directory to the root of a particular drive. For example, if you made the above drive mapping and invoked File Manager, the F: drive would point to ROSE/SYS:, not ROSE/SYS:USER\ME as you might expect.

Another area where Windows ignores default directories is in the Windows Setup program when it scans your drives looking for Windows applications. The Setup program scans each directory, starting from the root of the drive. If your drive mappings looked something like:

```
Drive   A:     maps to a local disk.
Drive   B:     maps to a local disk.
Drive   C:     maps to a local disk.
Drive   D:     maps to a local disk.
Drive   E:     maps to a local disk.
Drive   F:  = ROSE\SYS:   \
Drive   G:  = ROSE\SYS:   \SYSTEM
Drive   H:  = ROSE\SYS:   \USER\CGR

SEARCH1:    = Z:. [ROSE\SYS:   \PUBLIC]
SEARCH2:    = Y:. [ROSE\SYS:   \MENU]
SEARCH3:    = X:. [ROSE\SYS:   \DOS]
```

then when Windows Setup went to scan your drives for Windows files, the SYS: volume on file server ROSE would get scanned six separate times! Setup would also attempt to install six different copies of any application that it found.

To combat this situation, Novell modified the NetWare shells and the MAP.EXE program to allow you to make a particular drive mapping appear as a root directory to Windows, thus making the directory mapping "stick." Make sure you have the correct versions of MAP.EXE and the NetWare shells.

The concept of mapping a root is simply mapping a drive so that neither you nor any application can back up any further in the directory chain above the mapping. For instance, if you typed:

```
MAP ROOT F:=ROSE\SYS:USER\MOI
```

when you changed to the F: drive and typed "CD \" or "CD ..," you would stay in the same directory, namely \USER\MOI, because DOS would think you were already at the root of the drive.

In a MAP listing, such as:

```
Drive   A:     maps to a local disk.
Drive   B:     maps to a local disk.
Drive   C:     maps to a local disk.
Drive   D:     maps to a local disk.
Drive   E:     maps to a local disk.
Drive   F:  = ROSE\SYS:   \
Drive   G:  = ROSE\SYS:PUBLIC   \

SEARCH1:    = Z:. [ROSE\SYS:   \PUBLIC]
SEARCH2:    = X:. [ROSE\SYS:   \DOS]
SEARCH3:    = Y:. [ROSE\SYS:PUBLIC   \]
```

drive G: and search drive Y: are MAP ROOT drives, and the others are normally MAP'ped drives.

The way you can tell G: and Y: are MAP ROOT drives is the backslash follows the VOLUME:PATH, indicating you're at the root of that drive.

Unfortunately, MAP ROOT drives are not a total panacea. Be careful with applications that expect to access a file with a full drive:directory pathname. For instance, if you have a TEST directory below SYS:PUBLIC and you type "CD

\PUBLIC\TEST" while on drive G (assuming drive G is mapped as shown), you would receive an "Invalid Directory" message. On the other hand, you could type "CD TEST," then you would be at the G:\TEST directory which would really put you at ROSE\SYS:PUBLIC\TEST.

Configuring Directory Rights and File Flags

When you install Windows on NetWare, depending on the degree to which you put Windows on the LAN, you will likely want to place some degree of security on the files. In addition, you will need to flag files depending on their use.

If you chose to use the Server-based or Diskless configurations for Windows, you will have a \WINDOWS directory containing the contents of all of the Windows Setup disks. The rights for the \WINDOWS directory should allow each user with access to Windows the ability to read and open the files in the \WINDOWS directory and to search the directory itself.

Microsoft recommends that this directory be flagged Shareable Read-Only since multiple users may need to read files simultaneously, and since no files in that directory should need to be written to.

For the Server-based installation, most Windows files reside on the server while the user-specific files reside on the local hard drive. Since the local files are not on the server, no specific flags or rights apply.

In the Diskless installation, the user-specific files are placed in a user's private directory. Unless users share accounts, you will generally want to restrict others from a person's private Windows directory. A user should have all rights to his private Windows directory (with the possible exception of creating subdirectories or assigning rights to it).

Setting Up NetWare Print Devices for Windows

Printing can be a sensitive subject if you talk to network managers with Windows running on their LAN. There are several different ways of printing on Novell networks, so each will be discussed separately. Essentially you must have certain capture flags set correctly and your LPT ports must be redirected to NetWare print queues before you can print to the network.

The Capture command is one of the more popular ways to print on the network, whether you are talking about Windows printing or not. Local LPT ports are redirected to a network queue which is in turn serviced by a network printer.

The PrintCon utility can be used to create default Capture settings for users. Table 5.3 shows which settings should be used. (In addition, users can print a file by using the Nprint command.) You would only use the /NFF and /NT switches when printing a file generated from Windows (if you had printed to disk, for instance). Table 5.3 also shows options that should be used for Capture. Suppress

NetWare Print Option	Setting	CAPTURE Switch
Suppress Form Feed	Yes	/NFF
File Contents	Byte Stream	/NT
Enable Timeout	No	/TI=0 or /TI=45
Auto Endcap	No	/NA

Table 5.3 Optional PrintCon and Capture Settings.

Form Feed should be turned on because Windows handles the task of page ejection so NetWare doesn't have to do it.

NetWare will, by default, expand tabs to eight blank spaces. Most files that are printed from Windows are binary. When NetWare receives the ASCII code for a tab, it will print eight codes for a space. This can mangle a bitmapped file. Therefore, for Windows, this setting should be turned off.

Auto Endcap allows the workstation shell to flush the print buffer to the file server every so often. Because Windows can take a long time printing and thus exceed the timeout value, this option should be turned off. If you were to flush a partial bitmapped image to the printer, the result could be, at best, a partial picture at the printer and, at worst, garbage.

Enable Timeout works in tandem with the Auto Endcap setting. The two options (/TI=0 or /TI=45) are used because some DOS applications will not release print jobs properly if you have specified /TI=0.

To print from Windows to a network printer, the port you are printing to must be redirected to a network print queue. You can do this by running the CAPTURE program before you enter Windows or by using Control Panel to perform the CAPTURE for you. See Chapter 3 for details about how to capture LPT ports to NetWare print queues using Control Panel.

If you are running Windows 3.0, be aware that the Control Panel does not specify any particular capture options; therefore, you must set the default options ahead of time using PRINTCON. This has been corrected in Windows 3.1 (see Chapter 3). In addition, Novell has an enhanced version of the Control Panel print device setup utility as a part of the NetWare Windows Workstation Utilities.

6 Setting Up Applications

Once you get Windows installed, you will eventually get bored playing solitaire and changing wallpaper patterns—you will want to install some applications. There are some special considerations for installing both non-Windows (DOS-based) applications as well as Windows applications on NetWare. This chapter will explore what's involved in setting up both types of applications.

In addition, the techniques for setting up an application so it can take better advantage of the network will be discussed. For example, the chapter will cover how to set up directory structures for multiuser operation, and how to set up icons for documents so you can double-click on the icon to load both the document and the application used to create it (as you do on the Apple Macintosh).

DOS Application Considerations

Plunging headfirst into Windows configuration can sometimes be a frightful task for a system administrator. You have countless DOS-based applications that people need to use on a daily basis, and you now have to get them running under Windows. This section will discuss how you can smoothly incorporate DOS-based applications in the Windows environment.

Setting Up a Global Windows Menu

If you are administering a large Windows network (or even a relatively small one), adding a new application can be a hassle if you have to change the menu for each Windows user on the LAN. What you may want to do is set up a global, shared menu that users have on their Windows desktop in addition to a private, shared menu that they have for private applications and data.

Program Manager organizes icons representing applications or data files into groups. When you install Windows, three default groups are created: Main, Accessories, and Games. These groups can be minimized as icons on the Program Manager window or they can be moved or sized as needed.

You can create your own groups and tell Windows where to look for those groups by using the PROGMAN.INI file, which is stored in the default Windows directory. A typical PROGMAN.INI file looks like this:

```
[Settings]
Window=21 14 627 454 1
SaveSettings=0
MinOnRun=1
AutoArrange=0
display.drv=vga.drv
Order= 2 1 7 10 4 9 3 5 6 8

[Groups]
Group1=D:\WINDOWS\TEST.GRP
Group2=D:\WINDOWS\MAIN0.GRP
```

The four lines in the [Settings] section are set when you exit Windows and the "Save changes" box is selected. The Window parameter contains the X and Y coordinates in pixels from the upper left-hand corner of the screen, the horizontal and vertical width of the window, and a boolean flag that determines whether Program Manager should load and display as an icon or a window.

SaveSettings determines whether the "Save changes" box defaults to on when you exit Windows. MinOnRun (if turned on) tells Windows to minimize the Program Manager to an icon when another application is run. AutoArrange specifies whether the icons should be rearranged and aligned each time a window is resized.

The display.drv= line—new for Windows 3.1—shows the display driver you've installed for Windows. The Windows 3.1 version of Program Manager needs this information to operate properly. The contents of this statement may vary from one computer to the next. The Order= statement, also new for Windows 3.1, shows the order of your group windows as of the last time you exited Program Manager to leave Windows. This statement tells Program Manager how to arrange your group windows on startup and which group window was last active.

The icons are distanced according to the "Icon Spacing" parameter in the Control Panel Desktop function. When you set the spacing and choose "Arrange Icons" from Program Manager's Window menu, the icons will be arranged neatly in rows and columns in the group window.

The Groupx= lines in the [Groups] section tell Windows where to find the group files that control each group.

There can also be a [restrictions] section, covered in detail in Chapter 5. You can refer to that chapter for other information about customizing groups, creating your own groups and programs within them, and sharing groups between users.

Rights, Flags, Drive Mappings, and Search Drives

Any time you install an application on NetWare you need to think about several issues: security, "shareability," drive connections, and search paths.

Any time you have a shared system, you are inevitably forced to examine the issue of security: Who gets access to what and to what degree. When you install applications on the LAN, whether they're related to Windows or not, you should always consider what users have which rights to a given application, which is composed of one or more directory areas. Within Windows, the security issues are no different, so you should assign directory rights as you would if Windows were not involved.

You may, however, wish to tailor each user's desktop based on those applications to which they have rights. It would not make a lot of sense to give all users an accounting package icon on their desktop if only two people in the organization could run it. The downside to this approach is that it takes a certain degree of management to configure a Windows desktop for each user.

File flags also become important any time files will be used simultaneously by two or more users. You will want to flag files either Shareable Read-Write or Shareable Read-Only, depending on how they will be used. Consult your application's documentation for details.

Drive Mappings are another issue to consider. Whenever you have multiple users running the same application, it helps, from a management perspective, to have similar drive mappings. If you know every user maps drive L: to Lotus 1-2-3, then you know exactly which drive to refer to when you answer a support call about Lotus. Also, applications often store the path where they expect to access their own overlay files and will look for them in a specific directory, so the drive mappings for an application should be consistent.

Although specific application setup will be covered in the next chapter, you generally should map a common set of drives for all users to access your installed applications. In addition, you may also want to create a user-specific drive mapping for accessing each user's private application data.

You may want to map separate drives for your Windows applications and your DOS applications that run under Windows. If you have drives with fake roots (which were set up for Windows applications), your DOS applications may try to specify full pathnames and be unable to find the proper directory. For instance, if drive F: is MAP ROOTed to SYS:PUBLIC and an application specifies it wants to open "F:\PUBLIC\TEMP.DAT," it will not be able to find the file (because the root of the F drive is now PUBLIC, so it would be looking for F:\PUBLIC\PUBLIC\TEMP.DAT which does not exist). However, if the application had specified "F:\TEMP.DAT" then the file would be found. It's probably best to separate Windows MAP ROOT drives and regular drives for simplicity.

Finally, you should also consider how search paths need to be set up so that your applications will run properly. You may need to add a search drive for each application by using the MAP command. The same caveats about MAP ROOT drives apply to search drives as well.

Printer Setup

Setting up printers for DOS-based applications (running under Windows) is similar to their setup without Windows. You choose the same drivers as you would without Windows, since the DOS-based applications do not use Windows as a mechanism for printing.

For NetWare-aware DOS applications, such as Word Perfect, that print directly to NetWare print queues, using the CAPTURE.EXE mechanism is unnecessary. However, for applications that are not NetWare-aware or for situations where you want to print to an LPT port, you will have to ensure that you have the right capture settings.

It is important to note that if you have CAPTURE turned on for certain ports using values such as suppress form feed, no tabs, and so on, those settings will remain on for your DOS applications. The Novell shell only keeps one set of printer capture settings. If you set the capture flags before loading Windows, then you change them in a DOS session, they are immediately changed for Windows and any other DOS sessions. For example, if you hot-key from a DOS session to a Windows session, the capture settings will be the same as they were when you left the DOS session.

Therefore, you can take one of the following possible routes:

• Set up your DOS-based applications as if you were printing bitmapped graphics. This would mean your application would have to treat the printed documents as Windows would, by taking steps to put in its own form feeds and to do its own tab expansion (exchanging TAB characters for a certain number of spaces).

• Use one LPT port for Windows output and one for DOS output. Granted, you only have three LPT ports to work with, so if you have several LAN printers, this option may be impractical. You can capture one LPT port to PRINTQ _ 0, for instance, with Windows settings and capture another LPT port to PRINTQ _ 0 with settings for printing text.

• Configure a batch file for a DOS application that changes the capture flags before the application is run and returns them to the proper Windows settings after the application exits. This is still not a perfect solution, because you run the risk of the user switching back to a Windows application and printing binary data while the LPT port is capturing using text-based settings. In all, this is not the best option.

• Under Windows 3.1, network print configuration has been improved. See the sections in Chapter 3 regarding the Control Panel Printers selection and the NetWare popup utility, both of which let you specify "permanent" printer mappings—these printer settings are stored in INI files so that your LPT ports are captured to the right network print queues every time you run Windows.

If you only have one port but want the flexibility of printing to multiple print queues, you may want to try modifying the LPT port definitions in the [ports] section in WIN.INI. This can be changed by editing the WIN.INI file or by using the Printers icon in Control Panel (See Chapter 3). You can change the LPT1:= (or LPT2:= or LPT3:=) to LPT1.DOS=, which makes Windows act as if it were printing to a file called LPT1.DOS. But DOS won't let you save a file under the name of a device (LPT1 in this case), so it redirects the output to that device.

Windows uses DOS and ROM BIOS routines to write the output to the printer port rather than to manipulate it directly. Actually, the .DOS could be .ABC, as long as it's three letters. The problem with this solution is that it slows print time because it's using higher-level routines.

This modification might be useful if you have a limited number of LPT ports, but several queues servicing different types of printers. This practice was also prescribed for Windows 3.0 users who had difficulty printing on the network, although the printing problems experienced in Windows 3.0 have largely been eliminated by Windows 3.1.

Creating a Program Information File (PIF)

Windows uses certain default settings for DOS applications. However, in many cases you may want to change those settings, either to get an application running or to improve its performance. You change the settings Windows uses for a DOS application by creating a Program Information File (PIF) for the program. Generally, PIFs are named with a prefix of the program name and a suffix of .PIF. PIFs are stored in the Windows directory by default. However, you can put them anywhere you want, including on the network.

Before we plunge into the specific steps involved in creating PIFs, let's go over some of the things you should know first.

STANDARD (OR REAL) MODE PIFS AND ENHANCED MODE PIFS

The PIF Editor (available from the Main group window in Program Manager, shown in Figure 6.1) allows you to create two different types of PIFs, depending on the Windows mode in which you are running. A shorter PIF is created when you are running in Standard or Real modes, and a more complex PIF is created when you are running in Enhanced mode. If you have some users running in Standard mode and others in Enhanced, you will probably want to create two different sets of PIFs.

Figure 6.1 PIF Editor shown in Program Manager window.

Setting	Effective in Both Standard and Enhanced Modes?
Program Filename	Yes
Window Title	Yes
Optional Parameters	No
Startup Directory	Yes
Video Mode (Text or Graphics)	No
Memory Requirements	No
XMS (Extended) Memory	No
Close Window on Exit	Yes
Reserve Shortcut Keys	No

Table 6.1 Cross-reference of Standard and Enhanced Mode PIF Settings.

However, there are some fields that are cross-compatible. For instance, if you create a PIF in Standard mode and you only specify the program name, title, startup directory, and Close Window on Exit parameters, that PIF will work the same in Standard and Enhanced modes. If you need to set any other parameters, you must create two PIFs. Table 6.1 illustrates the parameters that are effective in both modes.

BATCH FILES AND PIFS

You can execute a PIF file the same as you can an EXE or COM file. For example, you can place a PIF file in a batch file as in:

```
@echo off
c:\mypath\mytsr
c:\mypath\myapp.pif
```

When this batch file is executed, **mytsr** will be loaded and **myapp.pif** will be run. Windows will load the PIF file **myapp** and run it according to the PIF parameters.

REMOVING THE [PIF] SECTION FROM WIN.INI

If you installed Windows into the same directory as an older (or run-time) version of Windows, you will probably have a [pif] section in your WIN.INI file that is obsolete and can cause potential problems with your PIF files. For example, there may be an entry that limits your memory when COMMAND.COM is loaded. It is recommended that you remove this section or comment it out by placing semicolons (;) in front of each line in the section.

ADDING PIF TO THE PROGRAMS= LINE IN WIN.INI

Additionally, if you installed Windows into the same directory as an older (or run-time) version of Windows, the Setup program may not have added 'pif' to the Programs= parameter in WIN.INI. This parameter tells Windows the acceptable file extensions that can be executed. For instance, the line should look like:

```
Programs=com exe bat pif
```

which means Windows will run files with a .COM, .EXE, .BAT, and .PIF extension. If the 'pif' is missing, you will get a "No association exists for this data file" message when you try to run a PIF file from File Manager.

Once you have made this change to WIN.INI, you will need to restart Windows for it to take effect.

SETTING UP A PIF DIRECTORY

It is generally a good idea to create a separate directory for PIF files. You will find that as you add more programs to Windows, you can end up with quite a number of them. So, to separate PIFs from other files, it is often wise to create a PIF directory, like \WINDOWS\PIF. If you do, make sure you add the PIF directory to your search path or MAP a search drive to it so Windows can find your PIFs.

PIF CONFIGURATION

As we discussed, there are two different screens for setting a PIF: one for Standard or Real mode and one for Enhanced mode. See Figure 6.2 for the Standard/Real mode window.

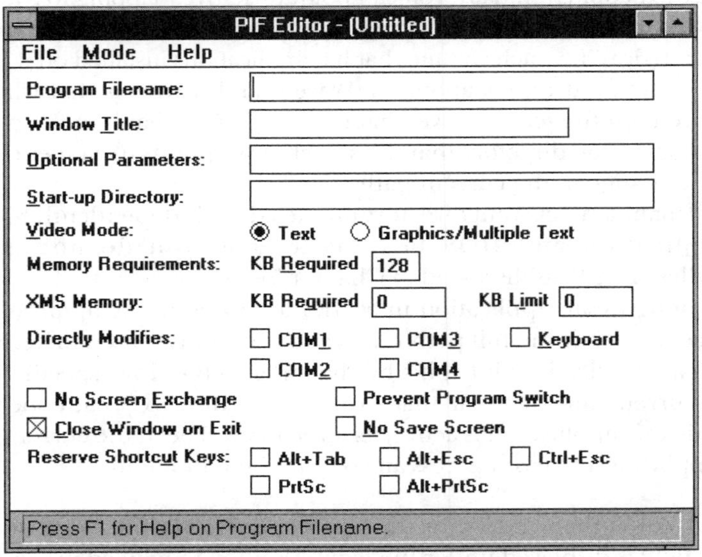

Figure 6.2 Standard/Real mode PIF Editor window.

STANDARD/REAL MODE PIF EDITOR OPTIONS

Program Filename. This specifies the name of the program to run, and is a required field. If you specify a full path, then Windows will look there for the program. If you only specify the program name (i.e. "PROGRAM.EXE"), Windows will search the directories included in your path to find the program. You may specify program names with .EXE or .COM extensions (use COMMAND.COM /E:512 /C batfilename.BAT to start a batch file).

You may want to use an 8-character name for the PIF that is identical to the one you use here, so that you can run the program and have Windows use the associated PIF. For example, if you create a PIF called MYAPP.PIF and place MYAPP.EXE in this field, when you run the program and specify MYAPP.EXE as the program you want to execute, Windows will search for MYAPP.PIF and, if found, it will be run.

If you choose to name a PIF differently from the program filename, you need to specify the full PIF name when you go to run the application. For example, if MYPIF.PIF is used to run MYAPP.EXE, you must run MYAPP by specifying MYPIF.PIF when you use the run command in Program Manager's File menu, or when creating an icon to run the PIF.

Also, defining the location of the program filename can be a difficult issue in a network environment, as you must specify the filename relative to a mapped drive letter. To make matters worse, a number of applications require that their directory be in your search path.

If you're running a lot of applications, you're probably starting to think about what network drive letters you are going to assign to which application, and hoping that you won't run out. However, there is an easier way to handle this. In your system login script, it's a good idea to assign at least one search drive for all users that is used as a utility search drive mapping. Initially, you can point this drive mapping to SYS:PUB-LIC, although this initial directory mapping is not important. (Although you will require one search drive for each volume that has applications installed on it.)

One of the convenient things about NetWare search drives is that whatever directory is current on the search drive, that is the directory that is in the current path. So, by changing the directory that the search drive points to, you effectively make a dynamic change in the current path.

Windows will maintain a current directory on each drive independently for each Windows application and DOS box (as long as you do not specify NWShareHandles=TRUE, as discussed in Chapter 5).

When you configure an application in a PIF file or define the application to Program Manager, specify the full path relative to this utility search drive. When Windows starts an application, it begins by changing to the drive specified, and changing the current directory on that drive to the directory path specified. Therefore, while that application is active, its directory will be in the current path, allowing the application to easily access any required components.

Window Title. When the window for this application is minimized to an icon, the text in this field is displayed under the icon. Also, for Enhanced mode, when the application is in a windowed state (as opposed to full-screen), this field is displayed in the title bar of the window. It is an optional field; if you don't enter anything in this field, Windows will use the name of the program's executable file (minus the extension) as a title.

Optional Parameters. Any parameters you would normally type after the program's name at the DOS command line go in this optional field. For example, if you normally type "PROGRAM /C /NF /PQ /RZ" at the command line, you should put "/C /NF /PQ /RZ" in this field.

If you need to run the program using parameters other than those specified in this field, you can specify them by using the Run option from the File menu in Program Manager or File Manager; Windows will use parameters you supply instead of the ones specified here.

If you simply put a question mark (?) in this field, Windows will prompt you for command-line parameters before it executes the program. In Windows 3.0 (only), this option may not work for batch files, due to a bug in the program.

Note: You can also specify an environment variable in this field. By using an environment variable, you can place a variable name in the PIF and assign it a value by using the set command in the AUTOEXEC.BAT file. When you type the variable name, enclose it in percent signs (%).

This can be useful in a network environment. For example, if you include the statement SET USER="%LOGIN_NAME" in your NetWare system login script, then you could include %USER% in the optional parameters to pass the current user's login identification as a parameter to the application.

Startup Directory. This specifies what directory Windows will change (CD) to before executing your program. Windows will make that directory the default for the application. This parameter is optional, but can be useful in LAN environments where you need to make Windows default to a user's private directory to store data files. In this case, if every user's private directory was mapped to F:, you could place "F:" in this field. It can also be useful for DOS applications that require you to run the application from its own directory in order to read overlay or configuration files.

There is, however, a snag. Setting this parameter may make Windows unable to load a document you have associated with this PIF (see section below on setting up a Macintosh-like interface). For example, you can create a WP.PIF to start Word Perfect for DOS, and you can associate any file with a .WP extension with Word Perfect by adding the line "WP=WP.PIF ^.WP" in the [Extensions] section of WIN.INI. That way, when you double-click on a file with a .WP extension in File Manager, Word Perfect will be used to load up the file. But if you specify a directory in this Startup Directory field, Windows will prevent the document name from being passed to Word Perfect.

If you want the capability to do this type of association, you should leave this field blank and have the PIF call a batch file. It performs a "CD" to change the directory to a default directory before the program is run, but only if a filename is not being passed on the command line.

This could be accomplished with the following simple batch file:

```
IF NOT %1$==$ THEN GOTO CONTINUE
G:
CD \USERS\%USER%\DOCS
:CONTINUE
WP
```

In the preceding example, if a command line parameter is specified (tested with "IF NOT %1$==$"), then the batch file skips over the statements that establish a default directory while using Word Perfect.

Video Mode.   This option is only available in Standard mode and tells Windows how much memory Windows sets aside for video RAM. When you switch away from a program, Windows saves the memory used by the video adapter so that the screen can be restored when you go back to the application.

The memory used to store the application's screen is part of the same memory allocated to the application. Therefore, setting this parameter correctly could mean, at worst saving some memory, and at best ensuring that your application's screen is properly restored. In other words, if you are unsure about whether your application uses graphics mode, set this parameter to Graphics/Multiple Text. Otherwise, you may not be able to switch back to your application.

There are two options for this parameter: Text and Graphics/Multiple Text. Text mode is used for applications that only use text mode to display information. This setting uses less Windows memory and means more memory for your application. One text video page is about 4K of memory (80 columns × 25 lines = 2,000 bytes plus one attribute byte that determines the color of the character for a total of 4,000 bytes).

Graphics/Multiple Text mode should be used when you have an application that uses the graphics mode of your video adapter or when multiple text pages are used to display information (most video adapters can hold up to eight text pages for a total of 32K).

The Graphics/Multiple Text setting takes up more memory but is the safest option if you are unsure of the operation of your application. At worst it will waste some memory.

Although text mode uses less memory, you will not be able to switch away from the application, if your program does use graphics mode or multiple text pages. The only way to get back to Windows would be to quit the application.

Memory Requirements.   The Memory Requirements field tells Windows the *minimum* amount of memory that must be available before it can run the application. In Standard mode, Windows will give the application as much conventional memory as is available when you start the application. This is due to the fact that only one DOS session is possible in Standard mode; all Windows applications are suspended while the DOS session is running in the foreground. In this case, the Memory Requirements field gives Windows a way to determine whether it is practical to start the application. The default value is 128K, but you may change the number if necessary. If your application requires more or less memory, and you are aware of the figure, you may enter it here.

Most application vendors document the minimum amount of memory needed for their application, but the figures given are usually estimates of total system memory required and are rarely the actual figure in kilobytes of the amount of free memory required for the program to run. In other words, you may need to play with this figure a bit to find the right value.

If you run an application and Windows cannot meet the minimum memory requirements of this field, you will get an error message telling you there is not enough memory to run the application.

XMS Memory. This setting tells Windows how much XMS memory to reserve for the application. XMS stands for the Lotus-Intel-Microsoft-AST eXtended Memory Specification standard. Don't let the term XMS confuse you; the usual name for XMS is simply "extended" memory. Some non-windows programs, such as Lotus 1-2-3 version 3.1 use extended memory, although most, at present, do not.

The KB Required and KB Limit fields specify the boundaries for an application's use of extended memory. (You can prevent an application from using any extended memory at all by setting both fields to 0.) KB Required tells Windows the minimum amount of extended memory that must be available before starting the application. Windows will not run the program unless the specified amount of extended memory is available. Placing a value in this field can dramatically increase the time it takes to switch to and from the application. Normally, this field is set to 0 which removes any startup requirement for extended memory.

KB Limit places a cap on the amount of extended memory Windows will let the application have. This option can be useful with applications that try to grab all available extended memory. If you set this option to 0, Windows will not allow the application to have any extended memory. If you set this option to –1, Windows will give the application all available extended memory. Microsoft recommends you do not use this option unless it is absolutely necessary, since it slows down the system dramatically. If you know your application does not use extended memory, you should set both KB Required and KB Limit to 0 which will free up some conventional memory for your application.

Directly Modifies. Some programs require exclusive use of certain system resources, such as communication ports or the keyboard. This option can be used to tell Windows that your application wants to be exclusive about its resource usage. There are two groups of settings for this parameter: communication ports and keyboard.

Turning on the COM1, COM2, COM3, or COM4 check boxes tells Windows that the application needs to use that/those communication ports exclusively. This prevents two applications from trying to use the COM port simultaneously which would generally result in garbled or lost data.

Turning on the keyboard check box tells Windows that the application will assume total control of the keyboard. This means that Windows does not have to "listen" to the keyboard for commands to switch away from the application or other commands. This results in less memory consumption by Windows since it will no longer need to reserve memory for a saved screen.

Selecting any of these options will prevent you from switching away from the application (same effect as turning on the "Prevent Program Switch" option below). To get back to Windows, you will have to quit/exit the application. If you are uncertain about these options, it's probably best not to select them at first. Then if you find they are needed, you can always add them later.

No Screen Exchange.   If you turn on this check box, Windows will not be able to copy information from the application's window onto the Clipboard (using the ALT+Print Screen or Print Screen keys). This will save some memory as a result. The effect is similar to selecting PrtSc and Alt-PrtSc check boxes in the Reserve Shortcut Keys options below. You should know that in Real or Standard modes, Windows cannot send graphics screens to the Clipboard from a DOS session; only text can be copied.

Prevent Program Switch.   This disables the ability to switch away from a program, and saves you a little memory because Windows doesn't have to check for application-switch keystrokes. The effect is similar to selecting any Directly Modifies option or selecting all of the Reserve Shortcut Keys options.

Close Window on Exit.   Closes the application display and returns you to Windows once you have quit the program. If you do not select this option, Windows will leave the window displayed with "Inactive" showing in the title bar.

No Save Screen.   You should use this option only when the application can retain its own screen information and knows when to redraw the screen. When you switch between applications, Windows saves the memory your screen occupies and restores it when you return. You can save some memory by checking the box associated with this option, but do so only if you are sure the application can restore its screen when you switch back to it.

Reserve Shortcut Keys.   Windows normally reserves a list of keys that are active in your DOS applications. These keys allow you to switch to the next or previous application, call up the Task List, or print the screen to the Clipboard. You can turn on the check boxes corresponding to the keys that control these functions to disable Windows' use of these keys while the application is active. You might want to do this if your program used one of these keys for a specific purpose.

For example, if your editor used the Alt+Tab key sequence to configure tab settings, you could reserve this Windows shortcut key. (Normally, this key sequence is used to toggle between applications.) With this key combination reserved, you would be able to use Alt+Tab while the application is running and Windows would not intercept the key combination; you would then be able to set up tabs by using Alt+Tab.

Under both Standard and Enhanced modes Windows 3.1, you can mark PrintScreen as reserved, and Windows will allow you to use the standard PrintScreen functionality, instead of having PrintScreen send the text to the clipboard.

ENHANCED MODE PIF EDITOR OPTIONS

This section describes the Enhanced mode PIF Editor options. Although a few of the fields duplicate those in Standard mode, they are shown here for completeness, so you won't have to flip back to the Standard mode section above. Many of the settings, however, are unique to Enhanced mode, such as Video Memory, EMS Memory, Display Usage, Execution, and all of the Advanced options (shown in the next section). Figure 6.3 shows the Enhanced mode PIF Editor window.

Program Filename. This specifies the name of the program to run, and is a required field. If you specify a full path, then Windows will look there for the program. If you only specify the program name (i.e. "PROGRAM.EXE"), Windows will search the directories included in your path to find the program. You may specify program names with .EXE or .COM extensions (use COMMAND.COM /E:512 /C batfilename.BAT to start a batch file).

You may want to use an eight-character name for the PIF that is identical to the one you use here, so that you can run the program and have Windows use the associated PIF. For example, if you create a PIF called MYAPP.PIF and place MYAPP.EXE in the this field, when you run the program and specify MYAPP.EXE as the program you want to execute, Windows will search for MYAPP.PIF and, if found, it will be run.

If you choose to name a PIF differently from the program filename, you need to specify the full PIF name when you go to run the application. For example, if MYPIF.PIF is used to run MYAPP.EXE, you must run MYAPP by specifying MYPIF.PIF when you use the run command in Program Manager's File menu, or when creating an icon to run the PIF.

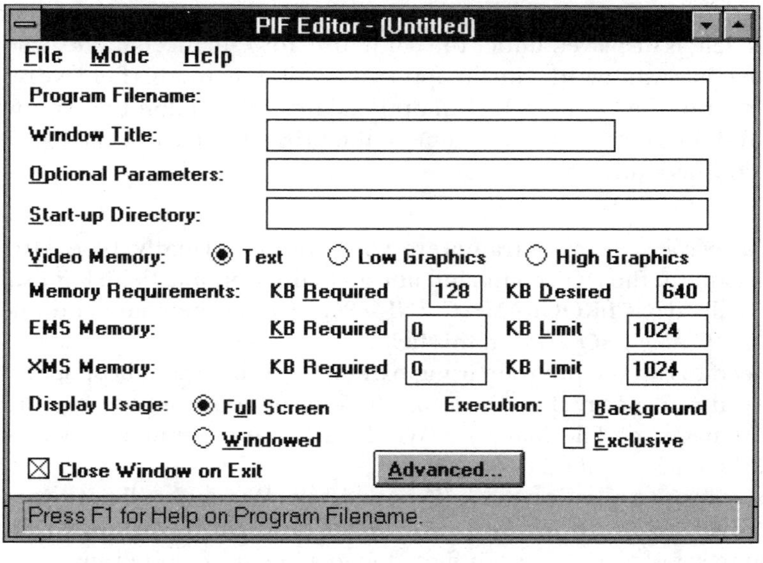

Figure 6.3 Enhanced mode PIF Editor window.

Also, defining the location of the program filename can be a difficult issue in a network environment, as you must specify the filename relative to a mapped drive letter. To make matters worse, a number of applications require that their directory be in your search path.

If you're running a lot of applications, you're probably starting to think about what network drive letters you are going to assign to which application, and hoping that you won't run out. However, there is an easier way to handle this. In your system login script, it's a good idea to assign at least one search drive for all users that is used as a utility search drive mapping. Initially, you can point this drive mapping to SYS:PUBLIC, although this initial directory mapping is not important. (You will require one search drive for each volume that has applications installed on it.)

One of the convenient things about NetWare search drives is that whatever directory is current on the search drive, that is the directory that is in the current path. So, by changing the directory that the search drive points to, you effectively make a dynamic change in the current path.

Windows will maintain a current directory on each drive independently for each Windows application and DOS box (as long as you do not specify NW ShareHandles=TRUE, as discussed in Chapter 5).

When you configure an application in a PIF file or define the application to Program Manager, specify the full path relative to this utility search drive. When Windows starts an application, it begins by changing to the drive specified, and changing the current directory on that drive to the directory path specified. Therefore, while that application is active, its directory will be in the current path, allowing the application to easily access any required components.

Window Title. When the window for this application is minimized to an icon, the text in this field is displayed under the icon. Also, for Enhanced mode, when the application is in a windowed state (as opposed to full-screen), this field is displayed in the title bar of the Window. It is an optional field; if you don't enter anything in this field, Windows will use the name of the program's executable file (minus the extension) as a title.

Optional Parameters. Any parameters you would normally type after the program's name at the DOS command line go in this optional field. For example, if you normally type "PROGRAM /C /NF /PQ /RZ" at the command line, you should put "/C /NF /PQ /RZ" in this field.

If you need to run the program using parameters other than those specified in this field, you can specify them by using the Run option from the File menu in Program Manager or File Manager; Windows will use parameters you supply instead of the ones specified here.

If you simply put a question mark (?) in this field, Windows will prompt you for command-line parameters before it executes the program. In Windows 3.0 (only), this option may not work for batch files, due to a bug in the program.

> **Note:** You can also specify an environment variable in this field. By using an environment variable, you can place a variable name in the PIF and assign it a value by using the set command in the AUTOEXEC.BAT file. When you type the variable name, enclose it in percent signs (%).

This can be useful in a network environment. For example, if you include the statement SET USER="%LOGIN_NAME" in your NetWare system login script, then you could include %USER% in the optional parameters to pass the current user's login identification as a parameter to the application.

Startup Directory.   This specifies what directory Windows will change (CD) to before executing your program. Windows will make that directory the default for the application. This parameter is optional, but can be useful in LAN environments where you need to make Windows default to a user's private directory to store data files. In this case, if every user's private directory was mapped to F:, you could place "F:" in this field. It can also be useful for DOS applications that require you to run the application from its own directory in order to read overlay or configuration files.

There is, however, a snag. Setting this parameter may make Windows unable to load a document you have associated with this PIF (see section below on setting up a Macintosh-like interface). For example, you can create a WP.PIF to start Word Perfect for DOS, and you can associate any file with a .WP extension with Word Perfect by adding the line "WP=WP.PIF ^.WP" in the [Extensions] section of WIN.INI. That way, when you double-click on a file with a .WP extension in File Manager, Word Perfect will be used to load up the file. But if you specify a directory in this Startup Directory field, Windows will prevent the document name from being passed to Word Perfect.

If you want the capability to do this type of association, you should leave this field blank and have the PIF call a batch file. It performs a "CD" to change the directory to a default directory before the program is run, but only if a filename is not being passed on the command line.

This could be accomplished with the following simple batch file:

```
IF NOT %1$==$ THEN GOTO CONTINUE
G:
CD \USERS\%USER%\DOCS
:CONTINUE
WP
```

In the preceding example, if a command line parameter is specified (tested with "IF NOT %1$==$"), then the batch file skips over the statements that establish a default directory while using Word Perfect.

Video Memory.   Since every application uses some type of video display memory, but not all applications use the same kind, Windows provides the three radio buttons—Text, Low Graphics, and High Graphics—that describe the kind of video memory the application uses. Windows will initially reserve the appropriate amount of memory for the setting you select so that it has enough memory to start the application.

Once you are running the application, Windows may allocate or release memory depending on the video mode you are using. If you start the application in Text mode and switch to a graphics mode, Windows will need to allocate more memory. Conversely, if you are in graphics mode and switch to text mode, Windows will release some memory.

If you do switch to a higher-memory video mode from a lower mode, such as Text, Windows may not be able to provide you with enough memory to create the display. In this case, you may get a partially or totally garbled screen. You can prevent this from happening by telling Windows not to release extra video memory once it has been allocated by selecting the Retain Video Memory option described below. Briefly, each setting is most effective under the following circumstances:

- Text   The application will only use text mode (no graphics). This setting requires the least amount of memory (usually less than 16K).

- Low Graphics   The application will only use low-resolution graphics mode, which is CGA for most video adapters (usually requires around 32K).

- High Graphics   The application will use high-resolution graphics modes, such as EGA or VGA (usually requires about 128K). Setting this option and Retain Video Memory will ensure that there's always enough memory to get back to the application after switching away to another. The cost of this security, however, is less memory for other applications.

For some video adapters, Hercules and color graphics adapters (CGAs), there is only one graphics mode, so the Low Graphics and High Graphics options are identical.

Memory Requirements.   This is composed of two fields that specify the minimum and maximum amount of conventional memory used in the application.

KB Required tells Windows the minimum memory requirements to run the application. Windows will give the application as much conventional memory as is available when you start the application, but this field gives Windows a way to determine whether it is even practical to start the application. The default is 128K, but you may change the number if necessary. If your application requires more or less memory, and you are aware of the figure, you may enter it here.

Application vendors generally document memory usage, but the figures given are usually estimates of total system memory required and are rarely the actual figure in kilobytes of the amount of free memory required for the program to run. In other words, you may need to play with this figure a bit to find the right value.

If you run an application and Windows cannot meet the minimum memory requirements of this field, you will get an error message stating that there is not enough memory to run the application. You can set this field to –1 to give the application all available conventional memory.

KB Desired allows you to place a limit on the amount of conventional memory given to the application. The value (and maximum) is 640K, but you may set the value lower to leave more memory for other applications. If you set this value to –1, Windows will give the application as much conventional memory as is available, up to the maximum of 640K.

Display Usage.   This option specifies the screen mode in which the application should be started. Full Screen tells Windows to start the application with a full-screen display rather than a window. Windowed specifies that the application should be started in a window. This option takes up more memory but gives you some flexibility on the display, allowing you to have a DOS application running in a Window on the desktop where you can see other windows as well. Once the application is running, you can toggle between Full Screen and Windowed modes by pressing ALT+Enter.

Execution.   This option controls when the application can run and how it works with other applications. Normally, the execution is suspended when you switch away, and, normally, Windows pre-emptively multitasks DOS applications—allocating each an equal amount of processor time.

Choosing Background allows the application to run while you are using another application (whether it's another DOS application or one that is in Windows). If you do not click on this box, Windows will suspend this application when you switch to another one (and the Background Priority box for this application is ignored, since this application will never run in the background).

Choosing Exclusive will suspend other applications while this application is in the foreground (even if other applications have chosen Background in their PIF file). This option can give the application more memory and processor time.

You have the option of turning Exclusive on for applications that run full-screen or windowed, although Microsoft recommends giving Exclusive applications the full screen to better take advantage of the option. Be aware that Windows will continue to reserve some resources for itself and for running Windows applications.

Close Window on Exit.   This option defaults to on, meaning that Windows will close an application's window and return to Windows when you exit the application. Turn this option off if you want to leave the window on the screen once you leave the application.

ADVANCED PIF OPTIONS

The Advanced button is located at the bottom of the 386 Enhanced mode PIF Editor window, shown in Figure 6.3. When you click on the Advanced button you will be shown a window similar to Figure 6.4. The Advanced options let you define and "fine tune" a DOS application's usage of Windows resources more finely than can be done in the 386 Enhanced options window alone. The options available in the Advanced window are discussed in the sections that follow.

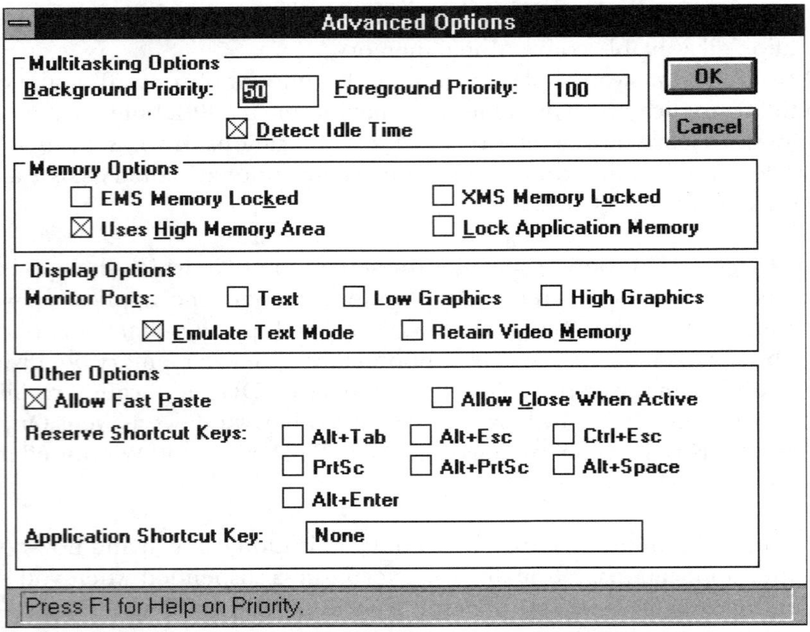

Figure 6.4 Advanced 386 Enhanced Options in the PIF Editor window.

Multitasking Options. These options determine the relative amount of processor time given to the application when it's running in the background and foreground. The value placed in the Background Priority and Foreground Priority fields has a range of 0 to 10,000. The way Windows uses this number is rather interesting. It adds up the combined priorities of the running tasks and splits up processor time for each process based on the ratio of the task's priority value to the combined priority values for all running tasks. For instance, if two tasks were running in the background with priority values of 50 each and a foreground task was running with a priority value of 100, it would be receiving 100/200 or 1/2 of the total processor time.

The Background Priority setting specifies how much relative processor time is given to an application when it's running in the background. This value is only valid when the application's Background option is selected and the foreground application's Exclusive option is not selected. The default is 50.

The Foreground Priority setting specifies how much relative processor time is given to a foreground task. The default value is 100.

The Detect Idle Time setting allows Windows to determine if an application is not doing anything; for example, if it is idle. If this option is selected and Windows believes an application is idle, it will give less processor time to that application. The problem is in determining if the application is idle, because Windows is not always right. In most cases, however, leaving this option selected will speed up overall Windows performance.

If for some reason the application is running extremely slowly, Windows may have judged an active application as idle and is thus denying it most of its processing time. If you determine this to be the case (or to try to determine if it is), you can turn this option off.

Memory Options.   The EMS Memory Locked setting determines whether Windows is allowed to swap expanded memory to the hard disk. Most applications will run well with this option turned on (swapping EMS to disk), although there are two cases in which an application does not work well when this option is turned on. The first case is a Terminate-and-Stay-Resident program, and the second is a device driver that uses expanded memory. In each case, the application's memory must be locked. Turning this option on, however, can slow down the rest of your system and reduce available memory.

The XMS Memory Locked setting is similar to the EMS Memory locked, except it applies to XMS memory. When turned on, the application will be able to take advantage of virtual memory (Windows will swap XMS memory to disk). The same restrictions and performance penalties in the EMS Memory Locked setting apply to this one. This setting has no effect on the high memory area (HMA).

The Uses High Memory Area setting determines whether this application has access to the High Memory Area (HMA) of RAM. If you have XMS (version 2.0 or higher) memory, you can use this setting to allow an application to use its own HMA. If the HMA is available when Windows starts, Windows allows virtual machines to have their own copy of the HMA. In most cases, you can choose this option because each application has its own HMA, which is independent of all the other applications' HMAs. Clear this check box if you have an application that cannot use HMA for some reason.

The Lock Application Memory setting determines whether Windows will swap parts of the application to the hard disk or keep the whole application in memory at all times. If you select this option, your application may run more quickly, but the rest of Windows may slow down somewhat. You may want to use this option sparingly because it consumes more memory, thereby limiting the number of concurrent applications you can have running in Windows simultaneously. The option is provided for applications that fail when extra time is taken to read from and write to the hard disk. Also, this option only applies to conventional memory. Locking EMS and XMS memory is controlled by the EMS Memory Locked and the XMS Memory Locked options.

Display Options/Monitor Ports.   Sometimes applications control video displays by accessing the ports directly rather than using DOS or BIOS routines. If an application does this, Windows might not know how to restore the display once the application has been switched away from.

If the screen is garbled when you return to an application after having switched away from it, you may need to have Windows monitor the video port for a particular graphics mode to determine in what state the video adapter has been left. Most applications, if they require this option at all, will need the High Graphics turned on. All three settings in this section default to off. Briefly, the available settings are as follows:

- Text tells Windows to monitor the video port when the application is in text mode.

- Low Graphics tells Windows to monitor the video port when the application is in low-resolution graphics mode, like CGA.

- High Graphics tells Windows to monitor the video port when the application is in high-resolution graphics mode, like EGA or VGA. Some display adapters, like the IBM VGA, will not be affected by these settings.

Emulate Text Mode.   This option can increase the text display rate for an application. It defaults to on and can be left on for most applications unless text on the display is garbled, the cursor appears in the wrong place, or the application will not run.

Retain Video Memory.   As briefly discussed in the options above, Retain Video Memory tells Windows to hold on to an application's video memory once it has been allocated.

When you tell Windows to run a program, Windows uses the Video Memory option to ensure that enough memory is available to start the application. Once the application gets going, it may switch video modes. If the application starts in High Graphics mode and switches to Text mode, Windows will release the extra memory used by High Graphics mode. However, if you need to switch back to High Graphics mode, Windows must allocate enough memory for that mode. If that memory is no longer available (because another application is using it, for instance) Windows will be unable to bring up the graphics screen.

On the down side, if this option is turned on and you switch from High Graphics to Text mode, no memory will be returned to service. It is instead kept around waiting to be used again. The memory that's saved sits around until needed—it cannot be used by another application.

OTHER OPTIONS

Allow Fast Paste.   This option allows Windows to used the fastest method possible to transfer information from the clipboard to an application during a cut/paste operation. (The default setting for this option is on.) If a program has problems with the fast paste, Windows will, in many cases, detect that it has a problem and use a slower method.

If you are having trouble pasting to an application, try this procedure: If you are in the middle of a paste operation, press ESC to quit the paste. Then exit the application. Run the PIF Editor and turn off this option in the application's PIF and try running the application again.

Allow Close When Active.   This option allows Windows to close the application without your having exited the application first. Normally, this option is turned off. You should select this option only if you are sure the application uses DOS file handles for file operation (rather than FCBs or some other mechanism). If you are unsure, leave this option unselected.

Be aware that this can be a risky option. Closing an application that has not saved or closed its active files could result in partial or complete data loss or damage to the files.

Reserve Shortcut Keys.   Windows normally reserves a list of keys that are active in your DOS applications. These keys allow you to switch to the next or previous application, call up the Task List, or print the screen to the Clipboard. You can turn on the check boxes corresponding to the keys that control these functions to disable Windows' use of these keys while the application is active. You might want to do this if your program used one of these keys for a specific purpose.

For example, if your editor used the Alt+Tab key sequence to configure tab settings, you could reserve this Windows shortcut key. (Normally, this key sequence is used to toggle between applications.)   With this key combination reserved, you would be able to use Alt+Tab while the application is running and Windows would not intercept the key combination; you would then be able to set up tabs by using Alt+Tab.

Under both Standard & Enhanced modes Windows 3.1, you can mark PrintScreen as reserved, and Windows will allow you to use the standard PrintScreen functionality, instead of having PrintScreen send the text to the clipboard.

Also, it is a good idea to select shortcut keys that are less likely to conflict with other applications. Using CTRL+ALT and a letter is a good choice. It may be more convenient and consistent not to define any shortcut keys in the PIF, but instead define them in the Program Manager properties when adding the application to the Program Manager.

Application Shortcut Key.   An Application Shortcut Key lets you switch directly to an application, no matter where you are in Windows. For instance, suppose you have set up a PIF for Novell's PCONSOLE utility, ran the program, then switched to another program. If you had set ALT+P as the application shortcut key for PCONSOLE, you could be printing in another application, hit ALT+P, and immediately check the print queue to which the job was supposed to go. You could also delete the job from the queue, then switch back to the application to print again.

The key combination you specify must have an ALT or CTRL key in it. You cannot specify a key combination that has the ESC, ENTER, TAB, SPACEBAR, PRINT SCREEN, or BACKSPACE keys in it. Be careful what keys you use as an application shortcut key. For instance, suppose you assign ALT+F as the shortcut key for Novell's Filer utility. You then load Filer and switch to, say, the Windows Program Manager. If you hit ALT+F to access the File menu, you will be transported to Novell's Filer. Moral: The Application Shortcut Key supersedes any definition of that key combination in any other application, whether it's a DOS or Windows application, or Windows itself. You should also make sure you have not used the same key combination for more than one application.

To set up a shortcut key:

1. Select the Application Shortcut Key option.

2. Press the key combination you want. Windows will display the combination you pressed in English (for example, ALT+Q).

3. Choose the OK button. If you pressed an invalid key combination, Windows will let you know with a dialog box telling you there's something wrong with the value you chose and it sets the definition to its former value.

To remove a definition, select the Application Shortcut Key option and press SHIFT+BACKSPACE to set the shortcut key to None. This means there is no definition for the Application Shortcut Key for this application. If, while entering a key combination, you press the backspace key, Windows will set the shortcut key definition to its previous value.

PREFERRED PIF SETTINGS FOR NETWARE UTILITIES

Novell recommends the following settings (also shown in Figure 6.5) for PIF files that are created to run NetWare utilities like SYSCON and FILER:

Standard (or Real) Mode Settings:

Program Filename:	Name of NetWare utility .EXE file
Window Title:	User-definable (put what you'd like)
Optional Parameters:	User-definable
Start-up Directory:	User-definable
Video Mode:	Text
Memory Requirements:	
KB Required:	128
XMS Memory:	
KB Required:	0
KB Limit:	0
Directly Modifies:	None
No Screen Exchange:	Unselected
Prevent Program Switch:	Unselected
Close Window on Exit:	Unselected
No Save Screen:	Unselected
Reserve Shortcut Keys:	None

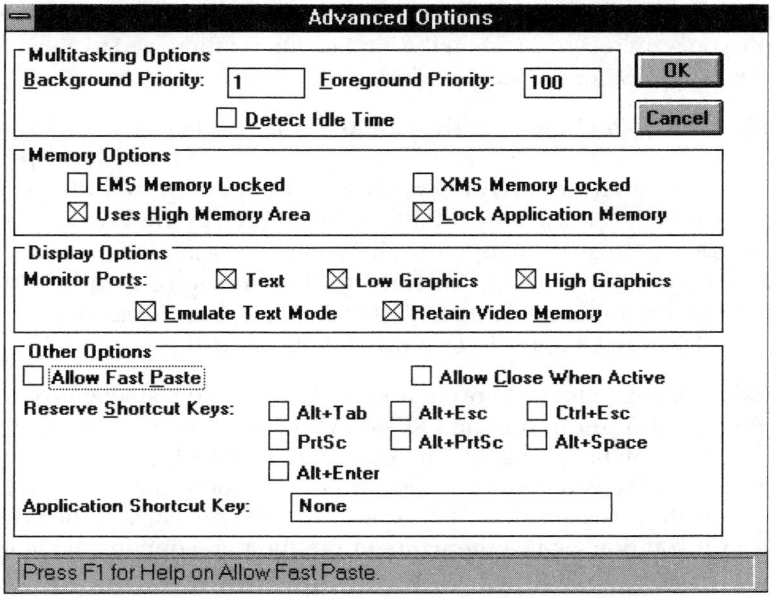

Figure 6.7 Recommended Enhanced Mode Advanced PIF Settings.

Allow Close When Active:	Unselected
Reserve Shortcut Keys:	All unselected
Application Shortcut Key:	None

Assigning Icons to Non-Windows Applications

One of the advantages of the Windows desktop is its functional appearance. Normally, each icon on the desktop represents an application (either Windows or non-Windows) that can be run. When you place a Windows program on the desktop, the default icon for that application appears in the Program Manager. When you install a non-Windows (DOS) application, a standard MS-DOS icon or another icon you've selected appears.

You may wish to change this icon to something more representative of the application. For instance, for Novell utilities, there are icons included on the disk with this book that look like the Novell logo.

To use an icon other than the default, you will need to get the icon from another application, a Windows .EXE file. Windows provides several icons you can use in the Program Manager executable, PROGMAN.EXE.

To add an icon to a non-Windows application, perform the following steps:

1. Click on the Program Manager Group you would like to place the new application in, such as "Main" or "Accessories," or one of your own. Select New from the File menu in the Program Manager and choose "Program Item."

2. You will see a window similar to Figure 6.8. Under Description, type in the name you want to appear when the application is minimized to an icon and for DOS applications when it is windowed in Enhanced mode.

3. Under Command Line, type the path to the file and the executable name (or the name of the PIF file, if there is one). You may wish to specify a path, but be aware that Windows will use that path to find the program in the future. If you specify F:\APPS\WP\WP.EXE as the Program Name, then drive F: must be mapped to the same server and volume all of the time in order for Windows to find it. Also, be aware of difficulties in specifying the full path with MAP ROOT drives. See the section on MAP ROOT drives in Chapter 5 for more details on this.

4. Click on "Change Icon" to bring up the "Change Icon" dialog box, shown in Figure 6.9. You can use the PROGMAN.EXE for several different icons which Microsoft has provided. This is the default .EXE file for non-Windows applications. Or, you can enter the name of a Windows .EXE file you would like to get the icon from in the File Name field. You can click on the Browse... button if you don't know the name of the file that contains the icon you want. You can scroll through the icons by using the horizontal scroll bar in the middle of Figure 6.9. Once you have chosen an icon you like, click on "OK" or double-click on the icon of choice.

5. You will be returned to the Program Item Properties window with the icon showing in the lower left corner (see Figure 6.10). Click on "OK" to save the application's icon in the group you have selected on the Program Manager desktop.

Windows Application Considerations

Setting up Windows applications to run on NetWare is slightly easier than configuring non-Windows applications because they were written to function in the Windows environment. However, you still need to be aware of many of the same elements as you did with DOS-based applications in the discussion above.

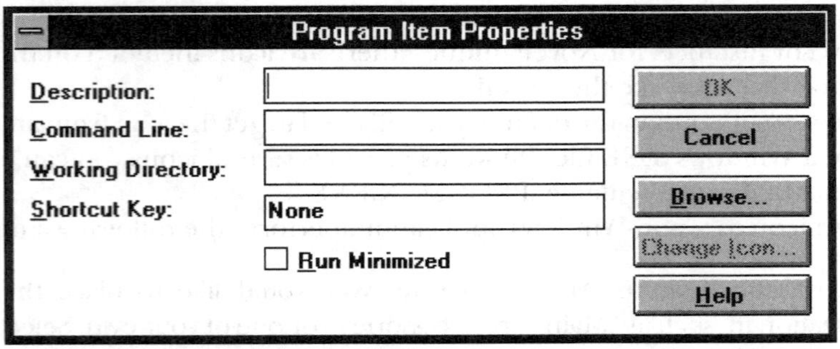

Figure 6.8 Program Item Properties window.

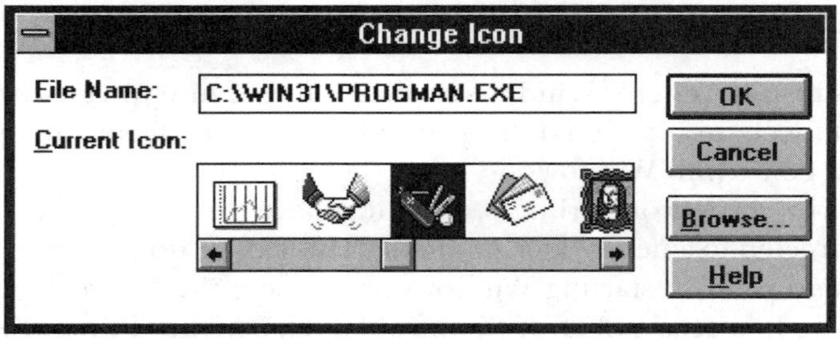

Figure 6.9 Change Icon dialog box.

Rights, Flags, Drive Mappings, and Search Drives

We need to look at the same issues we did above when talking about non-Windows applications: security, "shareability," drive connections, and search paths. Also, you will need to go through the same process in assigning directory privileges that you did with DOS applications. You can use SYSCON to assign these or use the command-line utilities GRANT and REVOKE.

Concerning program privileges, the author suggests that if a user does not have the right to run a particular program, he should not have it on his desktop. This is more practical for smaller systems. On a large network with several hundred workstations, if you give each user an individual desktop file, adding one new program to 400 desktops can be quite burdensome. Therefore, you need to weigh the costs versus the benefits.

When it comes to data files, trustee assignments can be an effective means of controlling file access, especially since you may be able to read files in other users' directories, but not save them. Or, you may not even see the files at all, depending how you set up the Novell rights. (See Chapter 1 if you have any lingering questions about how to set up trustee assignments and which work. Remember that NetWare 2.x versions 2.15 and below, and NetWare 3.x have two different sets of directory privileges.)

File flags work the same for Windows applications as they do for DOS applications: Flag files either Shareable Read-Write or Shareable Read-Only depending on how they will be used. Again, you will want to consult your application's documentation for details.

For Windows applications you should also consider how search paths need to be set up so that your applications will run properly. You may need to add a search drive using the MAP command.

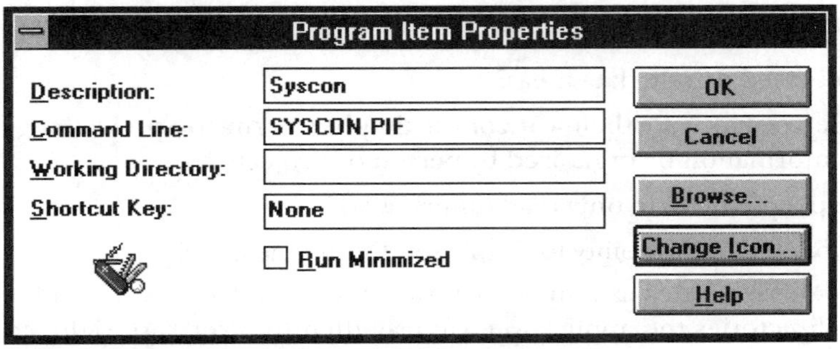

Figure 6.10 Program Item Properties window.

Printer Setup

Printer setup is a little different for Windows applications because you go through the Windows print mechanisms. Generally, you will be choosing from among the printer drivers that come with Windows.

If you want to print to network printers, you must have the LPT port on your local machine redirected to a network print queue. This can be done by using the CAPTURE command prior to starting Windows or by using the Network option on the Printer dialog box accessible from Control Panel. See the "Printer Setup" section under "DOS Application Considerations" as well as Chapter 3 for further information on using Control Panel's Printer icon and the NetWare popup window to capture LPT ports to NetWare print queues.

Changing Icons in Windows Applications

Windows applications usually include a default icon in the .EXE file supplied with the application. When you place this program on the Program Manager desktop, you see this default icon. You may change the icon if you wish using the same procedure supplied in "Changing Icons in DOS Applications" earlier in this chapter.

Enhanced Application Environments for Windows

This section demonstrates how you can enhance application operation under Windows. Discussion will revolve around how you can create a certain directory structure more conducive to multi-user operation, and how you can set up a Macintosh-like desktop where you have icons for data files as well as for programs.

Some "groupware" applications have built-in facilities to help you share files and work with other users on projects. We will discuss ways to get similar benefits by setting up your directories and rights even for applications that are not specifically titled "groupware."

Organizing the Directory Structure for Multi-User Operation

The way you set up and configure Windows applications on your LAN will depend largely on the way people work. Ask yourself the following questions before you begin to structure how an application is set up under Windows:

- Do people need private data areas?
- Do people need to share their work or will they be working on projects together? Will the information be organized by person or project?
- Do some people need to only read other's work?
- Does anyone need the ability to simply send someone a file?

Once you have an idea as to how to answer these questions, you can begin to set up the directories the application will use, then the NetWare rights to limit access to those areas, if necessary.

Generally, you will set up one shared directory for the application's executable files. For data directories, you have three options:

- You can set up a global data area where people can share files.
- You can create separate areas (subdirectories) to organize the global data by project, by application, or by any other logical division.
- You can set up individual data areas.

You may also want a combination of directories. For example, you may want several people to work together on a project in Word Perfect, so you create a shared directory, SYS:GLOBAL\PROJECT_A, where the people can share files and create different parts of a proposal together.

In addition, you may create a directory, SYS:USER\username\WP, to house each user's private Word Perfect files. When the user has completed a document in the private area, it can be copied to the global area for comments and suggestions.

There are several reasons for creating a global data area. It facilitates the exchange and sharing of files, and it provides a central place for a project's data. You must be wary of some of the dangers of shared data directories, however.

You want to make sure that data over-write does not occur. For example, suppose Bob loads up PROJECT.DAT and starts working on it in some application and Jim does the same. Then Bob saves his work and quits, but when Jim saves his work (to the same filename) and quits, Bob's work will be lost.

In many cases, leaving the file flags at their default (non-shareable, read-write) will prevent this from happening because many programs leave a file open while you work on it. If someone else tries to use a file you have open, that user will get an error message saying the file is already in use.

Let's go back over each of the questions just posed and see how we can configure Windows to address each of them.

The first question is: Do people need private data areas? If they do, you can create a directory area, such as SYS:USER\username, where "username" is the name of a user (8 characters or less). You should give the user most rights to this private data area and restrict access to it from others, unless you want to create private data areas only for compartmentalization of files, rather than for security purposes. Further, you can give managers access to employees' private data areas, if required, to create a hierarchy.

You can organize private directory areas by applications, as in SYS:USER\CHARLES\123, SYS:USER\CHARLES\WP, and so on, or you can create them by project where each project directory could contain files from several different applications. Choose whatever offers you the best organization of your files.

To use the directory in an application, you can either make the drive the default directory in the PIF setting for the program, use a batch file if the program is DOS-based and CD to the user's directory before the program is run, or make the user change directories to the private data area once the application is run.

The next question is: Do people need to share their work or will they be working on projects together? Will the information be organized by person or project? Once you know whether users can share files, you need to decide how they will share them. Users can share files by copying them from their private directories to another's directory, or they can use a global directory area to copy them to. In some cases, it may make sense to have users work on files for a certain project in a global area so that the most current files are always there. Organization by person or project simply determines how you will structure subdirectories. It is really up to you which method you choose.

When thinking of how users will share files, you must consider directory rights. Will you let users see each other's private directory areas? If so, you will need to give them the ability to open and read files there.

You may only want them to be able to copy files to another user's directory area. In this case, you must give them the ability to create and write files to another user's directory area. After experimenting a bit, you can get creative in your use of directory rights to set up the scenario that works best for you.

You may also want to use NetWare groups to determine who has what access to which directory areas. This can be especially helpful when organizing users working on a project together.

Another question is: Do some people need to only read other's work? As discussed above, this would require read access to another user's private directory area.

The final question is: Does anyone need the ability to simply send someone a file? This would involve having at least write and create rights to another user's directory area, if that is how you wanted to share files. You could also have users exchange files through a common directory area (another user copies to the common area; you copy it from the common area back to your private area).

The best way to get a feeling for directory areas is to write down how your users work. Diagram the directory structure so you can visualize it better and figure out who needs access to what. That will help you when you start creating directories and assigning rights.

The next chapter will discuss ways you can set up individual applications, such as Word Perfect or Lotus 1-2-3, for networked operation under Windows. You may also want to look over Chapter 4 for some ideas about how users can work together with certain applications.

Setting Up a Macintosh-like Desktop

The Apple Macintosh operating system software has been immensely popular in the last several years largely because of its simplicity. Users see graphic representations of their work and are better able to visualize what they are doing on the computer. Also, documents are given icons, often representing the application that created them. Users then have a better feel for what files are available for them to work with because they can "see" them.

Most people think that in Windows you only have icons for programs. You can set up icons for documents, but it simply takes a step beyond what you have to do on the Mac.

To create an icon for a document:

1. Choose "New" from the File Menu in the Program Manager and select "Program Item."

2. In the "Program Item Properties" dialog box, in the "Description" field, give your document a title, something brief but descriptive that will appear under the icon on the Program Manager desktop.

3. In the "Command Line" field, you have two options:

You can type in the command line you would normally use to load the program and bring up your document, as in "WRITE TEST.WRI" which would normally run Windows Write and immediately load the TEST.WRI document. The advantage of this approach is Program Manager will use the icon associated with Write by default—you don't have to go searching for an appropriate icon.

The alternative to this is to type the name of the document only. So, you would type "TEST.WRI" at the "Command Line" prompt. There is one additional step needed because Windows doesn't know how to execute documents, but it does maintain a list of associations between a file's extension and the program that operates on that file. This list is stored in WIN.INI in the [Extensions] section.

You can use Notepad or SysEdit to edit your WIN.INI and add the extensions and the programs you will be using. For example, the Calendar accessory uses files with a .CAL extension, so the entry in [Extensions] looks like:

```
cal=calendar.exe ^.cal
```

4. Once you've entered your command line, either with or without the application's name, you will want an icon for the document. If you entered the application name, the icon defaults to whatever the application uses. If you didn't enter the name of the program, or if you want to change the icon anyway, click the "Change Icon" button to pop up the "Change Icon" dialog box.

If you entered the name of the document, the "File Name" field will default to PROGMAN.EXE, which contains several icons provided by Microsoft for you to use. You can accept the default icon or you can scan through the available icons by clicking the "View Next" button.

You can associate your document with its application by entering the name of the application in the "File Name" box and by using the horizontal scroll bar to view other icons. If the application is a Windows application, you will be able to associate the application's icon. If your document uses a DOS-based application, you will have to choose an icon from PROGMAN.EXE or some other file (such as an icon library file).

Figure 6.11 shows the Program Item Properties window filled out from the example above and Figure 6.12 shows the result on the Program Manager desktop. If you double-click on the setup.txt icon, Windows runs Notepad for you and loads setup.txt, as shown in Figure 6.13.

Once you are satisfied with the appearance of the icon, click the OK button and return to the Properties dialog box. You can the click OK and save the icon on your desktop.

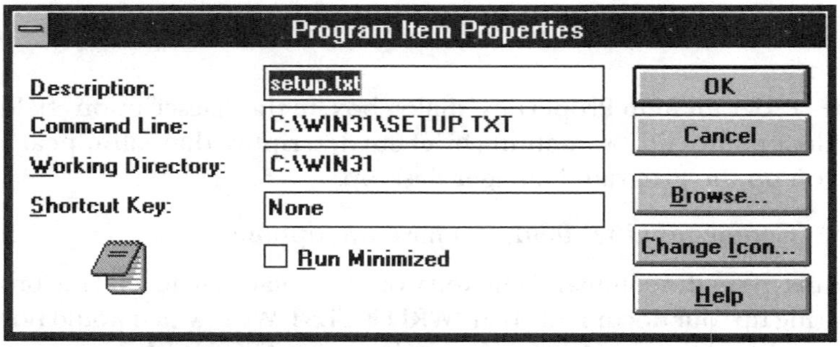

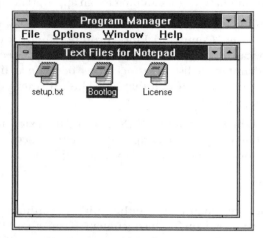

Figure 6.11 Program Item Properties window.

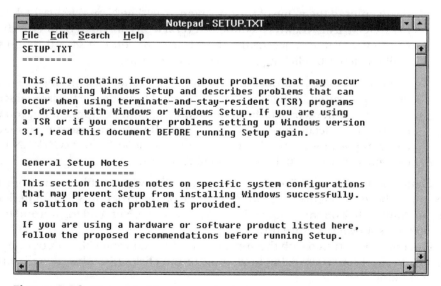

Figure 6.12 Program Manager window with text icons.

Figure 6.13 Notepad with setup.txt loaded.

7 Specific Application Setup on NetWare

In the last chapter, we discussed methods of setting up Windows applications to run smoothly on NetWare and configuration in a general sense. Now let's look at some specific applications that you may be installing on your LAN. This chapter will examine the installation options, configuration details, and optional parameters for several popular Windows applications like WordPerfect for Windows, Microsoft Word, Microsoft Excel, PageMaker, Ventura, and Delrina Technology's PerForm PRO.

This chapter will give you specific setup information about certain applications—from a networked perspective. You will see how to assign rights, map drives, and configure applications for NetWare with Windows running on it. In addition, we will discuss specific ways of making use of network resources and facilities, and examine ways of troubleshooting your applications once they are set up.

Word Processors

In this section we will describe how to set up and configure two very popular Windows word processors, WordPerfect for Windows and Microsoft Word for Windows, on a network.

WordPerfect for Windows

WordPerfect is one of the most popular, if not *the* most popular word processor in the world, and the release of a Windows version in late 1991 prompted a rush of sales nearly as strong as the surge to purchase Windows itself.

WPWIN (WordPerfect for Windows) 5.1 is presented first because many of you may have to integrate it onto the Novell LAN. There are several network-specific features of WPWIN and some that are somewhat confusing from a management perspective, such as the fact that you can use Windows' printer drivers or you can configure WPWIN to use its own WordPerfect drivers and bypass the Windows print mechanism. In addition, you can configure WPWIN to use its old familiar keys or the new Common User Access (CUA)-style keyboard layout.

Let's begin with the installation of WordPerfect for Windows.

INSTALLATION

Installing WordPerfect for Windows is relatively straightforward, but there are a wide array of configuration options and files to set up for a LAN installation. Let's take the installation one step at a time and go through the options you will have.

The first thing you will want to do is use the WordPerfect Install program to copy and configure the files on the installation disks. Let's look at what the install program will do for you as well as what it won't.

WHAT INSTALL DOES DO

The WordPerfect installation program does the following:

- Prompts you for source and target drive names and subdirectories where your files will be initially copied.

- Copies the WordPerfect program files that you specify—Install will prompt you for groups of files and allow you to do a complete installation, or you can leave off some modules, such as the Macro facility if you have limited drive space.

- Modifies your AUTOEXEC.BAT (if you request it) and adds the proper directories to your path.

- Creates the master environment file, WP{WP}.ENV, and the master INI file, WPC_NET.INI. The .ENV file contains your startup command-line options for WordPerfect and the .INI file has settings for where to find .EXE files and paths to other mini-application .INI files.

- Prompts you for printer installation and selection.

- Let's you view the README files for the main WordPerfect program or other modules.

WHAT INSTALL DOES NOT DO

According to WordPerfect documentation, "Install does not ensure that Word-Perfect will work on the network." This means that after Install is run, you will have to go back and do some fiddling with one or more configuration files. In addition, you will have to perform file flagging to make some files shareable and to assign directory rights and privileges for different WordPerfect areas. In summary, Install does not do the following:

- Flag files as read-only. WordPerfect recommends that you do this to ensure that critical files are not overwritten.

- Make the WordPerfect directory accessible to all users. You need to ensure all users have sufficient rights to their own private data areas as well as to the shared WordPerfect directories.

- Adjust each user's login script or AUTOEXEC.BAT files. You, the system administrator, will have to do this to ensure that each user's path statement and/or login script are set properly.

- In addition, the AUTOEXEC.BAT or login script will need to perform printer redirection by using the CAPTURE command for printer ports that will be redirected to network printers.

COPYING THE FILES

So, let's proceed with Install. The first thing to do is (in DOS) place the Install/Program disk in drive A: and type "a:install." This will run a DOS-based installation program that will copy the WordPerfect files from the disk and initially configure WordPerfect for you. The first screen you will see is shown in Figure 7.1.

Press the Enter key to continue. You will be shown the screen in Figure 7.2. Select 'Network,' option 3. Install will ask you by module whether you want to install that particular module. You can choose to install the entire WordPerfect system at this time, or reserve certain modules to install later.

You will also have the opportunity to specify the directory for each part of WordPerfect, such as the program, the graphics files, and so on. Figure 7.3 shows the screen where you specify these directories.

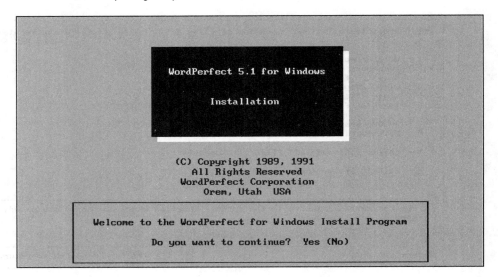

Figure 7.1 WordPerfect for Windows Introductory Install screen.

```
WordPerfect Installation Options                    Installation Problems?
                                                        (800) 228-6076

 ▶ 1 - Basic       Install standard files to default locations, such as c:\wpwin\,
                   c:\wpwin\graphics\, and c:\wpwin\macros\.

   2 - Custom      Install standard files to locations you specify.

   3 - Network     Install standard files to a network drive.  Only a network
                   supervisor should use this option.

   4 - Printer     Install additional or updated WordPerfect printer files.

   5 - Interim     Install Interim Release program files.  Use this option only if
                   you are replacing existing WordPerfect for Windows files.

   6 - Copy        Install every file on a diskette to a location you specify
                   (useful for installing all the Printer .ALL files).

   7 - Language    Install additional WordPerfect Language Modules.

   8 - README      View WordPerfect for Windows README files.


 Selection: 1                                      (F1 for Help; Esc to exit)
```

Figure 7.2 WordPerfect Installation Options screen.

Next, you can choose option 3 (Perform Installation) on the next screen, shown in Figure 7.4. When you choose this option, WordPerfect will try to determine whether you have enough disk space for the installation. The results of this determination are shown in Figure 7.5. Confirm that you want WordPerfect to go ahead with the installation by choosing the 'Yes' option.

WordPerfect then copies its files from the floppy disks to the network. The installation program will prompt you for answers on a few other questions. Figure 7.6 asks whether you want WordPerfect for Windows to conform to the key sequences common to Windows applications (referred to as the Common User Access, or CUA

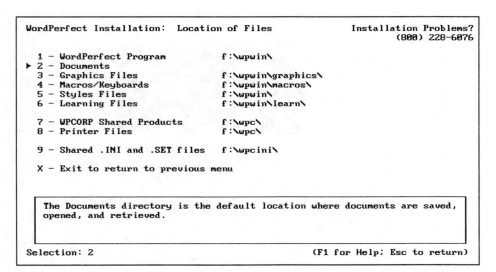

```
WordPerfect Installation:  Location of Files         Installation Problems?
                                                         (800) 228-6076

   1 - WordPerfect Program        f:\wpwin\
 ▶ 2 - Documents
   3 - Graphics Files             f:\wpwin\graphics\
   4 - Macros/Keyboards           f:\wpwin\macros\
   5 - Styles Files               f:\wpwin\
   6 - Learning Files             f:\wpwin\learn\

   7 - WPCORP Shared Products     f:\wpc\
   8 - Printer Files              f:\wpc\

   9 - Shared .INI and .SET files  f:\wpcini\

   X - Exit to return to previous menu


 ┌──────────────────────────────────────────────────────────────────────┐
 │ The Documents directory is the default location where documents are saved, │
 │ opened, and retrieved.                                                 │
 └──────────────────────────────────────────────────────────────────────┘

 Selection: 2                                      (F1 for Help; Esc to return)
```

Figure 7.3 WordPerfect Installation: Location of Files screen.

```
WordPerfect Network Installation                    Installation Problems?
                                                        (800) 228-6076

   1 - Install From              b:\

   2 - Install To

 ▶ 3 - Perform Installation

   4 - Check .ENV Files

   5 - Select Printer(s)

   6 - README

   7 - Exit Install


  ┌──────────────────────────────────────────────────────────────────┐
  │ The Perform Installation option installs all files from the location│
  │ specified in Option 1 to the location specified in Option 2.  You are then│
  │ asked which sets of files you would like to install.               │
  └──────────────────────────────────────────────────────────────────┘

 Selection: 3                              (F1 for Help; Esc to return)
```

Figure 7.4 WordPerfect Network Installation screen.

keystrokes) or the key sequences normally used in Windows 5.1. Although users familiar with WordPerfect 5.1 will be able to move around right away if the latter option is chosen, you may wish to choose the CUA option, in the interest of a common user interface.

Next, the screen shown in Figure 7.7 will appear, and you will be asked to decide whether you want Windows to use the WordPerfect printer drivers or those supplied by Windows. WordPerfect Corp. recommends that you use their printer drivers.

When the installation is done, you will see the Reminder screen shown in Figure 7.8, which reminds you to do several things. These steps will be covered in the post-install configuration discussion later in this chapter.

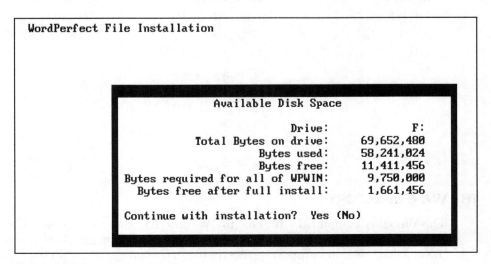

Figure 7.5 WordPerfect File Installation/AvailableDisk Space screen.

```
WordPerfect Keyboard Selection                    Installation Problems?
                                                      (800) 228-6076
 ▶  1 - CUA Keyboard
    2 - DOS WordPerfect 5.1 Keyboard

This option lets you decide whether the keystrokes in WordPerfect for Windows
conform to standard Windows (CUA) keystrokes or to DOS WordPerfect 5.1
keystrokes.  The keyboard you choose will be in effect when you run WordPerfect,
but you can switch to the other keyboard from WordPerfect using the Keyboard
option under Preferences.

CUA Keyboard
    -- Conforms to Windows standards using Common User Access (CUA) keystrokes.
    For example, on the CUA keyboard Alt+F4 will exit the application.
    -- CUA is the default keyboard in WordPerfect for Windows.  The manuals
    use CUA keystrokes.

DOS WP 5.1 Keyboard
    --  Conforms to most of the common DOS WP 5.1 keystrokes.  For example, on
    the DOS WP 5.1 keyboard Alt+F4 will turn on the Select ("Block") feature.

    Important:  One limitation of the DOS WP 5.1 keyboard is that whenever you
    open a dialog box (options for features), the CUA keyboard overrides the
    current keyboard because of the Windows operating environment.
Selection: 1
```

Figure 7.6 WordPerfect Keyboard Selection screen.

Now that WordPerfect for Windows is installed, you can check that the Program Manager group was created correctly (shown in Figure 7.9) and that the application loads (see Figure 7.10) when you double-click on the WordPerfect icon in Program Manager.

Once you've got the initial installation done, you will need to do some configuration. There are three main directories that Install creates by default. Below, we discuss each directory and the configuration files (.INI, .ENV, and .SET) you will have to work with in each of the three directories.

Assuming that you install to drive W, for example, the following directories will be created with the following files:

W:\WPC	W:\WPCINI	W:\WPWIN
FM{FM}.ENV	WPMC_NET.INI	WP{WP}.ENV
SP{SP}.ENV	WPMX_NET.INI	WP{WP}.SET
TH{TH}.ENV	WPTH_NET.INI	
	WPSP_NET.INI	
WPC_NET.INI	WPFM_NET.INI	
	WPMF_NET.INI	
	WPWP_NET.INI	
	WPXXX}.SET	

THE \WPC DIRECTORY

This directory contains the files for the WordPerfect shared programs, like the Spell Checker, Thesaurus, Macro Compiler, and File Manager. It contains the .EXE, .DLL, and other supporting files for the shared programs. In addition, \WPC contains the .ENV files for the shared programs.

```
WordPerfect Printer Selection


   When printing in WordPerfect, you can use either a Windows printer
   driver or a WordPerfect printer driver.

   We recommend that you install a WordPerfect printer driver for each of
   your printers.  If you install a WordPerfect printer driver, that
   driver will be selected when you run WordPerfect for Windows, but you
   can switch to a Windows printer driver at any time.

   These drivers are the same .PRS files used in WordPerfect 5.1 for DOS.

   Do you want to install WordPerfect printer driver(s)?   Yes (No)
```

Figure 7.7 WordPerfect Printer Selection screen.

```
┌─────────────────────────────────────────────────────────────┐
│                           Reminder                            │
└─────────────────────────────────────────────────────────────┘

When the Network installation is complete, you will probably need to make the
following adjustments:

 - Set the WordPerfect program files to read-only status.

 - Make the WordPerfect directory accessible to all network users.

 - Adjust the AUTOEXEC.BAT file, network profile, or login script of
   each workstation.

 - Select a printer port (such as LPT1 or COM1), designate the printer
   as a network printer, and enter the appropriate redirection command(s)
   at the DOS prompt.

For more information on setting up your network, see "Appendix M: Networking
WordPerfect" in the WordPerfect Reference manual.  For information on setting
up your specific network, see the README.NET file on the Shared Program 1
diskette.
                      Press any key to continue
```

Figure 7.8 WordPerfect Install Reminder screen.

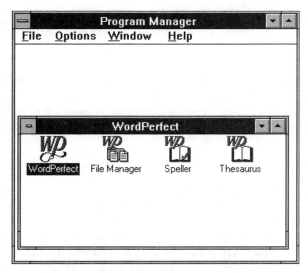

Figure 7.9 WordPerfect for Windows Group in Program Manager.

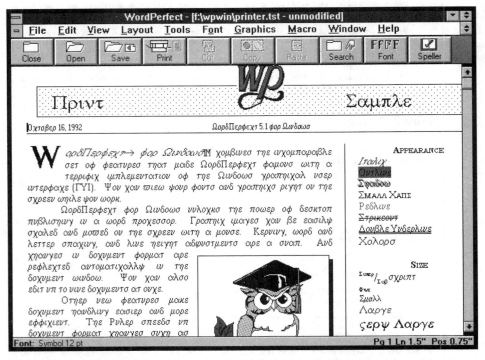

Figure 7.10 WordPerfect for Windows Main Screen with sample document loaded.

An .ENV file is like a command-line file—it contains nothing but command-line parameters that you would normally specify at the command line, but they are instead placed here. The .ENV file for the Spell Checker, SP{SP}.ENV, for instance, gets read whenever the Spell Checker is invoked.

The defaUlt contents of SP{SP}.ENV are:

```
/NT=1
/NI=w:\wpc\
```

which shows that the network (/NT) number is 1, indicating Novell's NetWare. The second parameter (/NI) indicates where WordPerfect should look for the .INI file for this program. The .INI file contains program feature configuration information, such as user preferences.

THE \WPCINI DIRECTORY

This directory contains the .INI files for the main WordPerfect program and all of the supplemental programs. You can create user-specific .INI files as well. It also contains a .SET file for each network user (initials shown above are XXX). SET files contain a user's personal settings for screen colors, printer selection, and startup parameters, such as paper type and size, margins, and so on. There is a master SET file in \WPWIN, but once a user customizes the settings, a personal SET file gets created in \WPCINI.

There is also an initialization (.INI) file for the main WordPerfect program in \WPCINI and each supplemental program. For instance, WPSP_NET.INI contains

```
[Settings]
Language=US
```

which specifies that the language to be used in the Spell Checker is US English.

THE \WPWIN DIRECTORY

This directory contains the main program files for WordPerfect, including the .EXE, .DLL, and other supporting files for the main program. In addition, the GRAPHICS, LEARN, and MACROS directories are subdirectories of \WPWIN that contain the graphics clip art, learning files accompanying the Workbook, and sample macro files respectively. Finally, the master .ENV and .SET files are stored here.

If you modify any of the .INI or .ENV files (you can only change a .SET file through using WordPerfect or by using the NWPSETUP.EXE program), you must use an ASCII text editor like Windows Notepad. If you use WordPerfect to manipulate these files, make sure you save the files as ASCII text files. Otherwise, binary codes are placed in the files which confuses both Windows and WordPerfect.

FLAGS

WordPerfect recommends you flag files in non-personal directories (which would include \WPC, \WPCINI, and \WPWIN) as shareable. In addition, files with the following extensions should be flagged as read-only, so they are not overwritten by over-zealous users on the LAN:

.DLL	.LEX
.DRS	.PRS
.DRV	.THS
.EXE	.UIF
.HLP	

If you do flag .PRS files as read-only, you will not be able to change printer settings, such as adding paper sizes, new fonts, or new printer settings. WordPerfect suggests you may want to give users read-write access to .PRS files on a temporary basis. This would, however, cause an unrealistic amount of management overhead; so, if you trust your users not to muck up their printer settings, you may want to leave the .PRS files read-write.

NETWORK SPECIFIC SETUP INFORMATION

The following has been excerpted from WordPerfect's README.NET file which contains network-specific setup information. Information relevant to NetWare installations has been included.

WordPerfect ® 5.1 for Windows README.NET

ENVIRONMENT FILES

During installation, an environment file is created for each WPCorp product (for example, WP{WP}.ENV for WordPerfect, FM{FM}.ENV for WordPerfect File Manager, SP{SP}.ENV for WordPerfect Speller, and TH{TH}.ENV for WordPerfect Thesaurus). These files allow WordPerfect products to operate in a networked environment. At your request, the Installation Program checks these files (or creates them if they do not exist) to make sure the following startup options are included:

ENVIRONMENT FILE	STARTUP OPTIONS INCLUDED
WP{WP}.ENV	/nt, /ps, /ni, and /wpc
FM{FM}.ENV	/nt and /ni
SP{SP}.ENV	/nt and /ni
TH{TH}.ENV	/nt and /ni

For more information about these startup options, see STARTUP OPTIONS below. The following is an example of how the WP{WP}.ENV file might look after network installation:

/NT=1

/PS=J:\WPCINI

/NI=J:\WPC

/WPC=J:\WPC

The exact network number and pathnames depend on the network you choose and the pathnames you specify for the Shared .INI and .SET files and the WPCorp Shared Products.

THE PATH

If the WP{WP}.ENV file contains the /WPC startup option and a pathname, the path statement (normally located in each user's AUTOEXEC.BAT file) is NOT necessary to run WordPerfect 5.1 for Windows. The Installation Program does not add directories or drive letters to the path. If you decide to have a path statement, the WPCorp Shared Products pathname specified in the /WPC startup option overrides any pathnames you establish for the same purpose in the path statement. See NETWORK SPECIFIC HELPS AND HINTS below for more information about the path.

WPW51US.GRP

The WPCorp Group file contains the WordPerfect 5.1 for Windows and WordPerfect File Manager icons. Each network user must have a group in order to set up the icons. The Installation Program creates the Group file and adds it to the PROGMAN.INI file. If you want all users on the network to use this group file, it must be copied to users' Windows directory. In addition, their PROGMAN.INI file must be edited to include this group.

STARTUP OPTIONS

The /NT, /NI, /PS, and /WPC startup options are necessary for successfully running WordPerfect 5.1 for Windows from your file server. During installation, the Installation Program places all four of these startup options (at your request) in the WP{WP}.ENV file, while only the /ni and /nt options are placed in the environment files for other WPCorp products (see ENVIRONMENT FILES above). The /D and /PI startup options are also useful for running WordPerfect on the network. The following information defines these six startup options in alphabetical order.

NOTE: THE ONLY PLACE YOU MAY USE THE /WPC STARTUP OPTION IS IN THE WP{WP}.ENV FILE (SEE BELOW).

/D

The /D startup option redirects the creation of the user work directory and temporary files to a specified location. Use the following syntax when using this option: WPWIN.EXE /D-DRIVE:\DIRECTORY (for example, WPWIN.EXE /D-C:\TEMP). This startup sequence will force the work directory to be created and subsequent temporary files to be created in the specified directory. You can include this startup option, using the same syntax, in the DOS environment via a SET command. You can also use the /D startup option in the file properties of the WordPerfect 5.1 for Windows icon itself, for example: W:\WPWIN\WPWIN.EXE /D-C:\TEMP.

/NI

The /NI startup option lets you specify the path to the WPC_NET.INI file. The syntax of this startup option is /NIPATH and is processed when the first WPCorp application starts. You can put the startup option on the command line, in the application specific DOS environment variable (for example, "WPWIN" for WP 5.1 for Windows), in the DOS environment variable "WPC," or in the application specific ENV file (for example "WP{WP}.ENV" for WordPerfect 5.1 for Windows).

If you don't specify the /NI startup option, but the /PI startup option is specified, the application searches for the WPC_NET.INI file in the location given in the /PI startup option. If the WPC_NET.INI file is not found in either location, the application will look in the following directories in the listed order:

1. The directory in which the application .EXE file resides.
2. The Windows directory (containing WIN.COM).
3. The directories listed in the DOS PATH environment variable.
4. The directories mapped in a network.

If WordPerfect cannot find the WPC_NET.INI file, it will still run but will not be able to access this file.

/NT

The /NT startup option tells WordPerfect which network you are using (for example, /NT=1 for Novell, /NT=2 for Banyan). Unless you use the /NT startup option, and the corresponding network number or letter, WordPerfect will NOT run as a network version for your network.

NOTE: Appendix M: Networking WordPerfect in your copy of the WordPerfect for Windows Reference Manual may say that the existence of the WP{WP}.ENV file is sufficient for WordPerfect 5.1 for Windows to run as a network version. However, THIS IS NO LONGER THE CASE. You MUST use a /NT startup option in the WordPerfect Environment file for WordPerfect to run as a network version. See IS WORDPERFECT

5.1 FOR WINDOWS SUPPORTED ON YOUR NETWORK above for a listing of the networks that currently support WordPerfect 5.1 for Windows and the corresponding numbers and letters. This list is subject to change. To find out about any changes, call WordPerfect Information Services at 801-225-4777.

/PI

This startup option lets you specify the path to the WPC.INI file, and is OPTIONAL. Use it only if you choose NOT to place the WPC.INI file in users' Windows directory, or if you want to use a different language version of WordPerfect 5.1 for Windows (see below). The syntax for this startup option is /PI-PATH.

NOTE: Before establishing a directory pathname in the /PI startup option, you should make sure that directory exists and that it contains the WPC.INI file.

The /pi and /ni startup options let you install and use multiple languages of the same WPCorp product on one computer. For example, let's suppose that you already have a U.S. English copy of WordPerfect 5.1 for Windows installed on your computer, but you would also like to install the French version of WordPerfect 5.1 for Windows.

Because the U.S. English and French versions are considered separate applications, you would put them in different locations on the file server, each with its own WPC.INI and WPC_NET.INI files. If users ask to use the French version of WordPerfect 5.1 for Windows, you can change the directory pathname in the /pi and /ni startup options, and thereby redirect the program to the "French product" WPC.INI and WPC_NET.INI files containing the locations of the appropriate .INI files and other executable files.

You can easily add the /pi startup option to the WordPerfect environment file using a text editor.

/PS

This startup option provides the directory path where individual personal setup files will be located. The /PS option identifies a common directory that is accessible by each network user to store his or her personal WPXXX}.SET file, where XXX represents the individual user's initials. WordPerfect .SET files are used to define the initial settings that the WordPerfect program will use, such as WordPerfect (nonWindows) printer selections, display attributes, and backup options. See /PS under Startup Options in Appendix M: Networking WordPerfect for more information.

/WPC

The /WPC startup option provides the directory path where the WPCorp Shared Products code is stored. Using this startup option frees you from having to include the Shared Products directory in the path. During installation, the Installation Program places this startup option in the WP{WP}.ENV file. THIS STARTUP OPTION SHOULD NOT BE ANYWHERE ELSE EXCEPT IN THE WP{WP}.ENV FILE. You may still include the Shared Code directory in the path, but the /WPC startup option will override it.

.INI FILES

A .INI file is an ASCII text file that an application uses during initialization. In other words, .INI files tell applications which customized settings to use upon startup. Applications write to .INI files (usually upon closure), recording the changes a user makes in Preferences and elsewhere. Regardless of whether a user makes changes, however, these files always exist.

NOTE: You may need to modify global .INI files. For example, if you want all users to have a default QuickList or Short Menus turned on or standard macros on their menus, you will need to edit the WPC_NET.INI and WPWP_NET.INI files. Since .INI files are ASCII text files, you can easily do so using any text editor.

This section defines each type of .INI file and illustrates the information it contains (for more information, see .INI Files under Appendix M: Networking WordPerfect).

WPC.INI and WPC_NET.INI Files

The user-specific, product-global .INI file (WPC.INI) is created for each user and stores information common to each WPCorp product. The shared-network, product-global .INI file (WPC_NET.INI) is a shared file which means it can be used by any number of network users. It is "product-global" because it stores information common to all of the WPCorp products.

Both files may contain the same information. Here are some examples of the settings:

[Settings]
SuppDictionaryPath=j:\users\kelli\docs
MainDictionaryPath=j:\wpc\DE

[Quicklist]
Backup Files=j:\users\kelli
Documents=j:\users\kelli\docs*.doc

[App Server]
WPWP=w:\wpc\wpwin\wpwin.exe;00600000;WordPerfect

[FileOpen Options]
Show QuickList=Yes

[WPDB]
SculpturedDialogs=Off

[LaunchOpen]
Ami Pro 1.0=WPWIN
and so on

WP??_NET.INI and WP??XXX.INI Files

The settings for each product are stored in either a shared network, productspecific .INI file (WP??_NET.INI), or a user/product specific .INI file (WP??XXX.INI), where ?? identifies the two letter product code (for example, WP=WPWIN, SP=SPWIN, TH=THWIN, MX=MXWIN), and XXX stands for the user's initials.

The two files differ in that the WP??_NET.INI contains default settings for all users, whereas the WP??XXX.INI file contains unique settings for individual users. You can manually place settings in the "master" .INI file (WP??_NET.INI) to establish default settings for each user on the network. These files are stored where the WPC_NET.INI [Ini Paths] specifies. Some examples of settings found in these files are:

WPWPXXX.INI or WPWP_NET.INI
[Settings]
Keyboard=* (for CUA keyboard) or
Keyboard=x:\wpwin\macros\wpdos51.wwk (for DOS 5.1)

[Button Bar]
ATTRIBS=112 (text and left side)
BARNAME=w:\wpwin\macros\wp{wp}.wwb

[LastOpened] (four last opened files)
labels.tst=j:\users\kelli\labels.tst
bottle.pri=j:\users\kelli\bottle.pri
bottle.sec=j:\users\kelli\bottle.sec
test.doc=j:\users\kelli\test.doc

WPSPXXX.INI or WPSP_NET.INI
[Settings]
Language=US
Pos=124,348,552,254

NOVELL

On Novell networks, we suggest that you map a drive to the shared resource where WordPerfect 5.1 for Windows has been installed. This drive letter MUST be used when setting up the file properties. For example, when setting the file properties for the WordPerfect 5.1 for Windows icon, the path might read W:\WPWIN\WPWIN.EXE.

SHARED DIRECTORY SETUP

GRANTING RIGHTS TO THE WPWIN, WPCINI, AND WPC DIRECTORIES

The table below lists the rights that users should have to the WPWIN, WPC, and WPCINI directories. The utility that you will need to grant these rights is listed in the third column.

Network Operating System	WPWIN and WPC	WPCINI	UTILITY
Novell Netware 286	Read, Open Search	All rights but Parental	SYSCON
Novell Netware 386	Read, Filescan	All but Supervisor and Access Control	SYSCON

You should limit users' rights or privileges to the WPWIN directory. For example, users should not be able to create temporary work directories or temporary files in this directory. In handling temporary files and temporary work directories, WordPerfect looks for the following, in the listed order:

1. SET WPWIN=/D-DRIVE:\DIRECTORY NAME
2. SET TEMP environment variable

If the SET WPWIN=/D-DRIVE:\DIRECTORY NAME option exists, WordPerfect creates the temporary files directory and places the temporary files in that directory. If this doesn't exist, then WordPerfect uses the SET TEMP environment variable. If the TEMP directory is not specified, then temporary files are created in the TMP directory. If none of these are specified, then temporary files are created in the current WordPerfect default directory (that is, where WPWIN.EXE is located).

If WordPerfect cannot find one of these two variables and cannot create the temporary work directories and temporary files, it displays a message box that reads: "Unable to create work directory for work files." Choosing OK on this message box displays another message box which reads: "Cannot initialize - The most probable reason is insufficient memory." If you choose OK on this message box, you will return to the Program Manager.

On Novell networks, you can also put the /D startup option in the users' login script. For example:

DOS SET WPWIN="/D-U:\USERS\%LOGIN_NAME" Use SYSCON to edit login scripts.

On Banyan networks, you can put the /D startup option in the group profile. For example: SET WPWIN=/D-C:\TEMP. Use the MANAGE utility to edit group or user profiles.

GRANTING RIGHTS TO WORDPERFECT SUBDIRECTORIES

You should make sure that you give users sufficient access to the directories they need while they work with WordPerfect. The table below lists the rights users may have in these directories.

NOTE: You may want to give users more rights to the printer files directory so they can change Paper Size/Types and Soft Font and Cartridges. If this is the case, see Granting Additional Rights to Printer Files Directory later in this chapter.

Network Operating System	Backup Files	Document Files	Graphic Files	Printer Files	Spread Sheets
Novell Netware 286	All except Parental	All except Parental	Read, Open, Search	Read, Open, Search	All except Parental
Novell Netware 386	All except Supervisor and Access Control	All except Supervisor and Access Control	Read, Filescan	Read, Filescan	All except Supervisor and Access Control

Network Operating System	Macros*/ Keyboards/ Button Bars	Styles	Thesaurus/ Speller/ Hyphenation (Main)	Thesaurus/ Speller/ Hyphenation (Supp)
Novell Netware 286	All except Parental	All except Parental	Read, Open, Search	All except Parental
Novell Netware 386	All except Supervisor and Access Control	All except Supervisor and Access Control	Read, Filescan	All except Supervisor and Access Control

* You should compile all macros that users are going to use before restricting access to the macro directory. If you restrict access before compiling macros, users won't be able to run them.

GRANTING ADDITIONAL RIGHTS TO PRINTER FILES DIRECTORY

Limiting users' access to the printer files directory to READ will not permit them to make permanent changes to Printer Resource (.PRS) Files. These files include Paper/Size/Type and Soft Font/Cartridge information.

To give users access to these files, you need to grant at least the rights listed in the table below. We suggest that you grant these rights on a temporary basis only.

Networking Operating System	Rights/Privileges Required for User Access to Printer Files
Novell Netware 286	Parental
Novell Netware 386	All but Supervisory and Access Control

PRINTING

As with printing from any other Windows application to network printers, you must use the internal control of Windows to redirect local printing of WordPerfect output to network print queues. With the DOS version of WordPerfect, you can specify file servers and print queues in the printer definition. However, the Windows version of WordPerfect follows more of the Windows convention of letting you do the redirection through either the CAPTURE command (before you start Windows) or through the Control Panel.

TROUBLESHOOTING

If you receive the message "Unable to Create Directory for Work Files" when you attempt to start WordPerfect, perform the following steps:

1. Ensure you have sufficient directory rights to create the temporary files in your private directory.

2. Confirm that if the WP{WP}.ENV file uses the /PS option to specify the location of personal setup files, a path is used with drive letters rather than volume names. For instance, /PS=SYS:WPWIN\SETUP is invalid, but /PS=F:\WPWIN\SETUP is fine.

3. Are you using the /D startup option to redirect temporary files? This option is recommended.

4. Try changing the properties in the Program Manager for the WordPerfect for Windows icon, so that the program file is WPWIN.EXE rather than the full path—F:\WPWIN\WPWIN.EXE.

If you receive the message "Access Denied" while changing paper sizes or types, or when selecting a printer, perform the following steps:

1. Make sure you have sufficient directory rights to the directory area containing the printer files.

2. Ensure that the .PRS file you are editing has not been flagged read-only. If it has, you can flag it to read-write, make your selection, then change it back. This way, you can preserve the security of having these files read-only.

3. For NetWare 2.x, make sure you have not run out of directory entries. You can use VOLINFO or CHKVOL to determine the remaining directory

entries for a volume. If the entries are 10 or less, you will have to bring down the file server and increase them. In NetWare 3.x, this is not a consideration since the software automatically adjusts directory entries based on usage/need.

4. WordPerfect suggests trying the following if you still cannot get things going:

- Try using another networked computer.
- Try logging in as another user.
- Try running WordPerfect on a stand-alone machine.
- Try checking file attributes (read-write versus read-only and shareable versus non-shareable).
- Try unloading TSRs that may be conflicting with the operation of Word-Perfect or Windows, particularly if you are having printing problems.
- Try exiting WordPerfect and reloading it.
- Try using the /d startup option—this is documented thoroughly in Appendix P: Startup Options in the WordPerfect for Windows Reference.

WordPerfect has excellent technical support. If you have tried the preceding suggestions without success, WordPerfect's network support numbers are:

Toll-Free	1-800-228-6066
Local Orem, Utah or out of the US	801-226-4777

If you have problems with Install specifically, you can call 1-800-228-6076.

Microsoft Word for Windows

The other dominant Windows word processor is made by the company that wrote Windows, Microsoft. Microsoft Word has been around for some time, sporting DOS, Windows, UNIX, and Apple Macintosh versions.

> **Note:** The installation information below is specific to Word for Windows 2.0.

SERVER INSTALLATION

Word for Windows is installed in a similar fashion to the way Windows 3.1 is installed in that you first create a server directory and copy all of the files from the setup disks. This server directory is shared between users; individual workstation installations are performed to copy several custom files to each user's personal directory—for example, F:\USERS\CHARLES\WINWORD. We will first describe how to create a server installation of Word for Windows, then we'll describe how to perform the workstation install. To install Word for Windows 2.0 on the server, perform the following steps:

1. Start Windows if it's not already running; from the File menu in Program Manager, choose Run.

2. Insert the Disk1—Setup disk in drive A:.

3. Type **a:\setup** and press ENTER.

4. Setup will first ask you for the name of your organization. Type this in and click on the Continue button (your organization name can take up to 50 characters).

5. You will then see the window shown in Figure 7.11 which prompts you to enter the target directory for Word for Windows. Enter the directory where you want the server files to be stored—for example, F:\APPS\WINWORD.

6. You will then be shown the window in Figure 7.12 from which you choose between a Complete Installation, a Custom Installation, or a Server Installation. The Complete Installation copies all of the Word for Windows files to your local directory and the Custom Installation option lets you specify which Word for Windows options to install. However, you must choose the last option, Server Installation, in order to set up a shared, server-based copy of Word for Windows.

7. Setup will now copy the diskette files to your server. When complete, you will see the window shown in Figure 7.13. After you have read the contents of the window, click on the OK button to return to Program Manager.

WORKSTATION INSTALLATION

To install an individual workstation copy of Word for Windows, perform the following steps:

1. Flag the files in the Word for Windows directory (the one you specified in step 5 above) shareable, read-only. You can do this with the MAP command—for example, type "MAP F:\APPS\WINWORD*.* SRW" at the DOS command line.

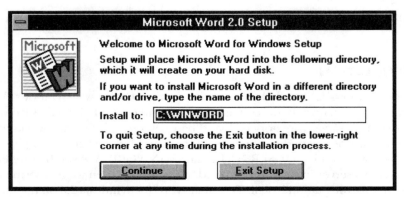

Figure 7.11 Word Setup window, prompting for target directory.

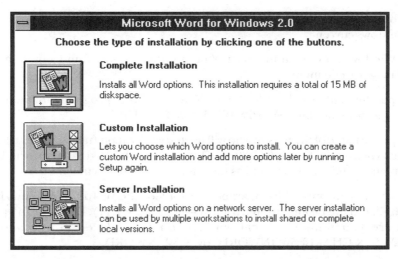

Figure 7.12 Choice of Complete, Custom, or Server installation window.

2. Edit the WIN.INI file for the workstation and locate the [Microsoft Word 2.0] section. Add the line "NovellNet=Yes" to indicate that you are running on a Novell network.

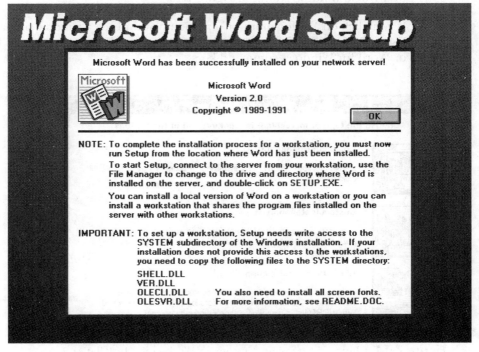

Figure 7.13 Setup completed window.

3. From the workstation, make the directory where you installed Word for Windows current.

4. If Windows is not running, start Windows, then choose Run from Program Manager's File menu.

5. Type the path to the Word for Windows setup program, followed by **setup**—for example, "F:\APPS\WINWORD\SETUP."

6. Type the name of the person who will use the workstation (up to 50 characters), then click on the Continue button. This name can be used as a return address for letters and envelopes, and as the author name for documents.

7. You will be prompted for a target directory for the Word for Windows files (similar to the prompt in step 5 above—see Figure 7.11). Enter the full path where you want the local workstation files placed—for example, "F:\USER\CHARLES\WINWORD" or "C:\WINWORD."

8. Next you will see a window, shown in Figure 7.14, that is similar to the installation choice window in step 6 above (and shown in Figure 7.12), except the Server Installation choice has been replaced by Workstation Installation. Click on this option.

9. Word for Windows provides the capability of emulating Word Perfect keystrokes. You will be given the opportunity to read about this capability in the next window, shown in Figure 7.15.

10. If you click on Yes for more information, you will see a window similar to Figure 7.16, which gives you the chance to use Word Perfect command keys or Word for Windows command keys.

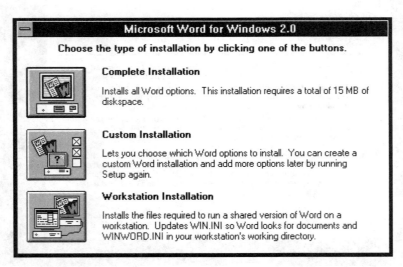

Figure 7.14 Choice of Complete, Custom, or Workstation Installation window.

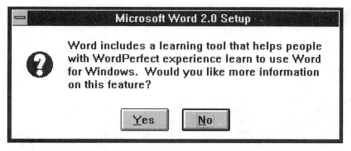

Figure 7.15 WordPerfect Compatibility message box.

11. After you decide about the keys, you will see a window similar to Figure 7.17 which will ask you if you want Setup to modify your AUTOEXEC.BAT file by loading the SHARE utility and placing the Word for Windows directory in your PATH statement.

Once you have chosen whether to let Word for Windows modify your AU-TOEXEC.BAT file, the workstation setup process will be complete and you should see the Word for Windows 2.0 group, opened on your File Manager desktop (shown in Figure 7.18). Double-click on the Microsoft Word icon to load Word. Figure 7.19 shows Word for Windows 2.0 with the README file loaded.

SHARING FILES

Microsoft suggests that you can share files in one of several ways. First, you can flag a file as read-only, so that multiple users can access the same file without worry about locking and over-writes.

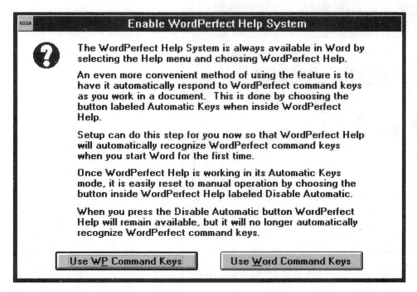

Figure 7.16 WordPerfect versus Word Command Keys window.

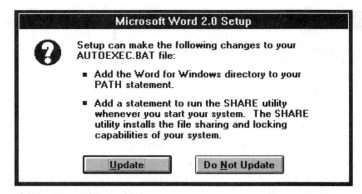

Figure 7.17 AUTOEXEC.BAT File Update/Don't Update window.

Second, a file can be flagged read-write. This allows shared access to the files. The first user to open the file read-write will have access. Subsequent users will only be able to open the file as read-only.

Finally, local and shared files can be linked using DDE. Links can be created between two or more documents and even between other applications, such as Microsoft Excel or any other application that supports DDE. The links allow one document to update others. For further information about Links, see Linking Files in the Word manual.

PRINTING

Printer setup under Word is identical to printer setup under Windows because Word utilizes the Windows print mechanism. If you are printing to a network

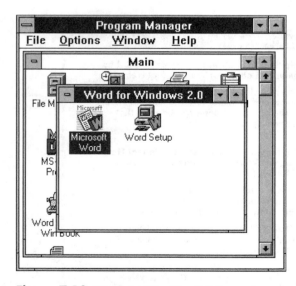

Figure 7.18 Word for Windows 2.0 Group in Program Manager.

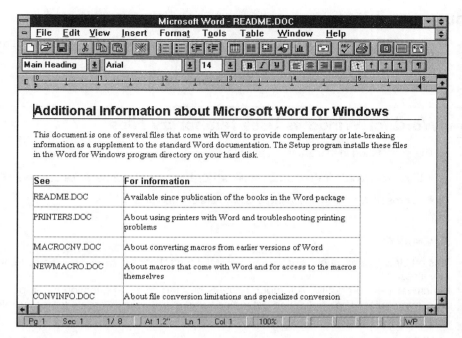

Figure 7.19 Word for Windows 2.0 Main Window.

printer, you will need to redirect printer output from a local LPT port to a network queue. This can be accomplished through the CAPTURE command before starting Windows or through the Control Panel, NetWare Popup (see Chapter 3), or third-party applications. Printer selection can be made through the Windows Control Panel.

OPENING A DOCUMENT AS READ-ONLY

To open a file as read-only in Word, choose File Open and type the name of the file. Choose the Read-Only switch in the File Open dialog box, then choose OK.

To open a document as read-write, perform the same steps as above, but make sure the Read-Only switch is turned off.

SAMPLE SETUP

The following scenario suggests how a local/network setup might be accomplished and how Word works with the files involved:

```
Setup:
```

`F:\USERS\CHA RLES\WINWORD`	Default drive. User's private Word directory.
`C:\WINWORD`	Local Word program with spelling and thesaurus files.
`W:\WINWORD`	Shared Word files on network directory.

TROUBLESHOOTING

The following technical notes were released by Microsoft and show problems and solutions encountered when running Word:

How Word for Windows Uses Temporary Files

The information in this article applies to:

- Microsoft Word for Windows, versions 1.0, 1.1, 1.1a, 2.0, 2.0a, 2.0a-CD, and 2.0b
- Microsoft Windows operating system versions 3.0 and 3.1

SUMMARY

This article explains when, where, and how Microsoft Word for Windows creates temporary files.
Definition: Temporary File. A temporary file is created by an application to temporarily store information. The application determines where and when to create temporary files.

MORE INFORMATION

General Notes: How Word for Windows Handles Files

All Word for Windows files are always stored on disk and referenced during each Word session. Word for Windows sometimes copies portions of a file into memory so that it can access the information more quickly when you copy and paste information or scroll through a document. Word references the location of the information instead of actually accessing the information, which reduces the time Word spends performing these functions. If you copy large portions of a Word document to the Clipboard, Word for Windows maintains an open handle to the file that contains the copied information.

At the MSDOS level, you can use the RENAME command within a directory. If you want to move a file to another directory, you must use the COPY command. The COPY command is slower than the RENAME command because COPY rewrites the entire file to disk, whereas RENAME only changes a few bytes of the file

WHEN AND WHERE WORD FOR WINDOWS CREATES TEMPORARY FILES

1. Record Macro: TEMP Directory

   When you record a macro, Word for Windows creates a temporary file in the TEMP directory. This also occurs when a template is being duplicated because the macros in the template are duplicated through the recording code. The TEMP directory is specified using the SET TEMP command, which is usually located in your AUTOEXEC.BAT file.

"How Word for Windows Uses Temporary Files" is reprinted with permission from Microsoft Corporation. Document Number: Q89247. Publ Date: 23-NOV-1992. Product Name: Microsoft Word for Windows. Product Version: 1.00 1.10 1.10a 2.00 2.00a 2.00a-CD 2.00b. Operating System: WINDOWS.

2. File Save: Same directory as the saved file

When you run the File Save command, the following happens:

- Word builds a new temporary file (named ~DOC####.TMP) using the edited version of the document.

- Once the temporary file is successfully created, Word deletes the previous version of the document.

- Word renames the temporary file to the same name as the previous version of the document.

  NOTE: If Always Create Backup is selected, Word renames the previous version with a .BAK extension instead of deleting it. Word for Windows gains significant performance speed by placing the temporary file in the same directory as the saved file. If Word placed the temporary file elsewhere, it would have to use the MSDOS COPY command to move the temporary file from the other directory to the saved location. By leaving the temporary file in the same directory as the saved document file, Word can use the MSDOS RENAME command to quickly designate the temporary file as the saved document file.

  Word for Windows uses this scheme to protect against system errors. By saving to a temporary file first and then renaming the file to the proper name, Word ensures the integrity of your original file against problems (such as a power failure or lost network connections) that might occur while the file is being written. If Word for Windows wrote directly over the original file or copied the file from another directory, the original file would be more vulnerable to damage.

3. Open a locked file: TEMP directory

When you open a file that is locked, either because it is open in another instance of Word for Windows or because another user on the network has it open, you can make a copy of the file. Word for Windows places this copy in the Windows TEMP directory. If you attach a locked template, Word for Windows automatically makes a copy of the file in the TEMP directory. Note: This copy of a locked file does not automatically update the original owner's file.

4. Autosave: AUTOSAVE directory

The temporary file created when Word for Windows performs an autosave is stored in the AUTOSAVE directory, which is defined in the [Microsoft Word 2.0] section of the Windows WIN.INI file.

5. Embedded Word Objects: TEMP directory

When Word for Windows acts as an object-linking-and-embedding (OLE) server application, the embedded Word objects are stored as temporary files in the TEMP directory.

6. Scratch File: TEMP directory

When Word for Windows runs out of internal RAM, it always creates a single temporary scratch file in the TEMP directory to hold information. This scratch file holds information that is swapped out from the Word for Windows internal file cache, which is allocated from global system memory. The scratch file varies in size from 64K to 3.5MB. You can prevent Word from having to write to the scratch file by allocating more RAM for Word to use internally. You do so by increasing the CACHESIZE setting in the [Microsoft Word 2.0] section of the WIN.INI file. Experimentation is required to find optimal settings for every configuration.

7. Converting files: TEMP directory

The word processing converters supplied with Word for Windows create temporary files in RTF file format, which are read when Word accesses a specific converter.

8. Paste between files: Same directory as source file

When Word copies and pastes between documents, it may create a temporary file in the same directory as the source file, especially if the source file is saved or closed. The temporary file represents the information that was referenced by the Clipboard prior to saving the file. Word for Windows creates this temporary file by renaming the old copy of the file to a temporary filename (~DOC####.TMP).

Additional reference words: 1.00 1.10 1.10a 2.00 2.00a 2.00a-CD 2.00b tmp w4wmemory

How to Use NDIR to Find Multiple WIN.INI Files

The information in this article applies to:

• Microsoft Word for Windows, versions 1.0, 1.1, 1.1a, 2.0, 2.0a, and 2.0a-CD

• Microsoft Windows operating system versions 3.0 and 3.1

SUMMARY

If you have multiple copies of the Microsoft Windows WIN.INI file, you may experience the following problems in Microsoft Word for Windows:

• Added fonts are not displayed as expected.

• Printer driver changes are not reflected in Word for Windows.

• DOC-PATH, DOT-PATH, INI-PATH, or other WIN.INI changes revert to previous settings.

If you are using Novell network software, you can use the Novell NDIR utility to check your user network drives for multiple copies of WIN.INI.

MORE INFORMATION

To use NDIR to check your user network drives for multiple copies of WIN.INI, use the following steps:

1. At the MS-DOS prompt, type "MAP" (without the quotation marks). A list similar to the following should appear:

```
Drive A:=Local Drive
Drive C:=Local Drive
Drive F:= ServerName\Sys:\User\Username
Search1:=Z: [ServerName \sys: \Public f
Search2:=Y: [ServerName \sys: \Apps\Win31|
```

2. From the map list, note the drive letter for any search-mapped drives except the PUBLIC drive, which is usually assigned to Z. Search-mapped drives are named SEARCH1 through SEARCH16.

3. Type the drive letter for one of the search-mapped drives followed by a colon (for example, Y:), then press ENTER.

4. Type "CD\" (without the quotation marks), then press ENTER to move to the root of the search-mapped drive.

5. Type "NDIR Y:\WIN.INI /SUB" (without the quotation marks), then press ENTER.

A list of all copies of the WIN.INI file appears, along with the file attributes and network owner of each file. The owner is the person who created the file, not the person using the file. The owner is frequently the Novell system administrator. If you find more than one WIN.INI file in your user directory, rename the file(s) not located in the WINDOWS directory.

Additional reference words: w4wnovell w4wnetwork 1.00 1.10 1.10a 2.00 2.00a 2.00a-CD 1.x netware

---

"The Directory You Typed Is Invalid..."

The information in this article applies to:

- Microsoft Word for Windows, versions 2.0, 2.0a, and 2.0a-CD

- Microsoft Windows operating system versions 3.0 and 3.1

SUMMARY

The following error message may appear in Microsoft Word for Windows:
The directory you typed is invalid or incomplete. Please type a full path with drive letter; for example "C:\WINWORD." if the following conditions exist:

a. You are installing Word for Windows on a Novell Netware 386 server.
   and
b. You do not have create rights.
   and
c. You are trying to install Word for Windows on a nonexistent directory.

MORE INFORMATION

During Word for Windows Setup, if you specify a nonexistent directory, the following prompt appears:

The specified directory does not exist. Do you want to create the directory?

If you have Novell create rights and you choose the Yes button, Setup creates the directory. (If you are using Novell Netware 286, you must have create and parental rights to create subdirectories.) If you do not have create rights, Setup cannot create the directory and the error message appears.

To successfully run the Word for Windows Setup program, you must have Novell write, create, file scan, or search rights. It is advisable to log on as a supervisor because Setup adds files, writes to files in a number of directories, and creates several subdirectories. For more information on network Setup, refer to the Word for Windows README.DOC file.

Additional reference words: 2.00 2.00a 2.00a-CD w4wnetwork w4wnovell privileges w4werror w4wsetup

Unrecoverable Disk Error on File ~DOC####.TMP

The information in this article applies to:

- Microsoft Word for Windows versions 1.0, 1.1, 1.1a, 2.0, 2.0a, 2.0a-CD, and 2.0b
- Microsoft Windows operating system version 3.0 and 3.1

SUMMARY

In Microsoft Word for Windows, you may receive the following error message if Word cannot locate or read the document's temporary (.TMP) file:

Unrecoverable Disk Error on File ~DOC####.TMP

This error message usually occurs when you are working with a file from a network drive or a floppy disk drive. The error message does not disappear when you choose the Retry or Cancel button.

MORE INFORMATION

Word creates a .TMP file in the current directory. The filename of a .TMP file begins with the tilde character (~) and ends with a .TMP extension. Word accesses this file while you work on your document. If Word cannot access this file, Word will halt, and the error message will be displayed.

FLOPPY DISK DRIVE

If your current directory is a floppy disk drive, this error will occur after you remove the floppy disk where the .TMP file is located. You must put the floppy disk back in the disk drive so that Word can access the .TMP file.

"Error Message: Unrecoverable Disk Error on File ~DOC####.TMP" is reprinted with permission from Microsoft Corporation. Document Number: Q86271. Publ Date: 19-NOV-1992. Product Name: Microsoft Word for Windows. Product Version: 2.00 2.00a 2.00a-CD 2.00b. Operating System: WINDOWS.

To avoid this error message, copy your file from the floppy disk to the hard drive. Open the file in Word from the hard drive; do not open the file from the floppy disk. By working from the hard drive, you ensure that the .TMP file can always be accessed by Word. When you finish working on your document, copy it back to the floppy disk.

NETWORK DRIVE

If your current directory is a network drive, this error will occur if you do not have sufficient user rights in that directory. The message may also occur if your connection to the network drive is disrupted.

You must have create, modify, and delete rights to a network directory if it is the current directory. Word must be allowed to modify and delete the .TMP files it creates; if Word is prevented from completing these actions, the "Unrecoverable Disk Error on File ~DOC####.TMP" error message will appear. See your network administrator to obtain adequate user rights, or move your files to a different directory in which you have adequate rights.

STEPS TO REPRODUCE PROBLEM (Floppy Disk)

1. On a formatted blank floppy disk, create the following two directories:
   A:\DIR1
   A:\DIR2
2. Copy a Word document to A:\DIR1.
3. Launch Word. Open the document copied to A:\DIR1 in step 2.
4. Select a portion of the document. From the Edit menu, choose Copy.
5. Move the insertion point to a different position in the document. From the Edit menu, choose Paste.
6. From the File menu, choose Save.
7. Create a new document, based on the NORMAL.DOT template.
8. Type some text into the document.
9. From the File menu, choose Save. In the File Name box, type "A:\DIR2\TEMP.DOC" (without the quotation marks), and choose the OK button.
10. Select a portion of the document. From the Edit menu, choose Copy.
11. Move the insertion point to a different position in the document. From the Edit menu, choose Paste.
12. From the File menu, choose Save to save TEMP.DOC.

    Additional reference words: 2.00 2.00a w4werror err msg errmsg 2.00b 2.00a-CD

Editing Commands Available When Template Is ReadOnly

If you open a read-only template in Microsoft Word for Windows, the Edit, Rename, Delete, and Set (Set is in Word for Windows version 1.x only) macro options do not appear unavailable (dimmed). If you make changes to any template macros, Word doesn't display an error message to warn that changes cannot be made to the template until you try to save the template.

"Macro Editing Commands Available When Template Is ReadOnly" is reprinted with permission from Microsoft Corporation. Document Number: Q80785. Publ Date: 5-NOV-1992. Product Name: Microsoft Word for Windows. Product Version: 1.00 1.10 1.10a 2.00. Operating System: WINDOWS.

MORE INFORMATION

When using a read-only template, such as one on a network, the options to Rename, Delete, Edit, or Set are available. In Word for Windows version 2.0, the Rename, Delete, and Edit buttons are available in the Tools Macro dialog box when the Show Template Macros option is selected. In Word for Windows version 1.x, the Delete, Rename, and Set buttons are available in the Macro Edit dialog box when the Global Context is selected. However, if you use any of the above buttons to make changes to macros in a read-only template and choose the File Save command, you receive the error following message:

> File is read-only. (version 1.x)

> This file is read-only. (version 2.0)

> The Save As dialog box displays, and you can save the changes to a new filename.
> Additional reference words: 2.00 1.00 1.10 1.10a 1.0 1.1 1.1a w4werror w4wnetwork w4wmacro greyed ghost unavailable

Doc Error in README.DOC: No Shared WINDOWS\SYSTEM Directory

The information in this article applies to:

- Microsoft Word for Windows, versions 2.0, 2.0a, and 2.0a-CD
- Microsoft Windows operating system versions 3.0 and 3.1

SUMMARY

Page 10 of the Microsoft Word for Windows README.DOC file contains the following incorrect statement:

> With a shared version of Windows, the Workstation option of Setup copies some files to the workstation's program directory, and the network administrator should copy other files to the shared SYSTEM directory on the server.

> With a shared copy of Microsoft Windows operating system version 3.0 or 3.1, a WINDOWS\SYSTEM directory is NOT created. The list of files is actually copied to the shared WINDOWS directory. The list of files is correct in the README.DOC.
> Additional reference words: docerr doc err 2.00 2.00a 2.00a-CD

Hidden Temporary Files Left on Hard Drive

SUMMARY

If you do not exit Microsoft Word for Windows version 2.0 properly, hidden temporary files are written to the current directory (the directory of the open Word for Windows file). An improper exit occurs if your system locks up, the power is lost or turned off while Word is active, or you encounter an unrecoverable application error (UAE). Any of these occurrences leave hidden temporary files on your system.

Temporary files have a .DOC extension, and their filename begins with the tilde character (~).

MORE INFORMATION

If you have hidden temporary files on your system, you may notice a loss of disk space. You also cannot delete any directory that contains these hidden files. To display and change the attribute of hidden files from Windows version 3.0 File Manager, choose Include from the View menu, and select the Show Hidden Files check box.

To change file attributes in Windows version 3.1 File Manager, display the hidden files by choosing By File Type from the View menu and selecting the Show Hidden/System Files check box. Select the flagged hidden file. From the File menu, choose Properties, and clear the Hidden check box.

You can also locate these files with the MSDOS ATTRIB command (type "attrib \~*.*/s" at the MSDOS prompt). Clear the hidden attribute using the ATTRIB command. Type "ATTRIB-h {filename.ext}" at the MS-DOS prompt.

NOTE: Temporary files have a file size of 51 bytes. They contain the current user information and a one-directory reference.

Word for Windows stores information about who is currently using a file in its temporary files. This information is useful in a network environment when someone tries to open a file that is already being accessed by another user; Word looks at the temporary file to see who is using the file and returns that information to the second user. You can prevent Word for Windows from creating this hidden temporary file by adding the line "NoOwnerFiles=YES" to the [Microsoft Word 2.0 section of the WIN.INI file with the following steps:

1. From the Tools menu, choose Options.
2. Under Category, select WIN.INI.
3. From the Application box, select Microsoft Word 2.0.
4. In the Option box, type "NoOwnerFiles" (without the quotation marks).
5. In the Setting box, type "Yes" (without the quotation marks).
6. Choose the Set button, then choose the Close button.
7. Exit Word for Windows. Restart the program to activate the change.

The "NoOwnerFiles" setting prevents Word for Windows from attempting to write a temporary owner file when opening a file.

REFERENCE(S)

"Microsoft Word for Windows User's Guide," version 2.0, pages 798–802
Additional reference words: 2.00 crash hang

"Doc Error in README.DOC: No Shared WINDOWS\SYSTEM Directory" is reprinted with permission from Microsoft Corporation. Document Number: Q88542. Publ Date: 28-AUG-1992. Product Name: Microsoft Word for Windows. Product Version: 2.00 2.00a 2.00a-CD. Operating System: WINDOWS.

"WinWord: Hidden Temporary Files Left on Hard Drive" is reprinted with permission from Microsoft Corporation. Document Number: Q78386. Publ Date: 17-JUL-1992. Product Name: Microsoft Word for Windows. Product Version: 2.00. Operating System: WINDOWS.

"Call to Undefined Dynalink" Error with Old Printer Drivers

SUMMARY

If the Microsoft Windows operating system version 3.1 accesses a Windows version 3.0 printer driver, the following error message may be displayed:

Application Error - Call To Undefined Dynalink

You must remove any Windows 3.0 printer drivers and install the appropriate Windows version 3.1 printer driver(s) to correct this problem.

MORE INFORMATION

For instructions on removing an installed printer driver and installing a new printer driver, refer to pages 201–206 and page 214 of the "Microsoft Windows User's Guide" for Windows 3.1.

NOTE: You must remove duplicate printer driver entries from the Installed Printers list. If you do not, you will be unable to install a new Windows 3.1 printer driver from the Windows disks.

NOTE: Be sure to search all drives and directories for outdated printer drivers. This is especially important if you are running Word on a network, where printer drivers may be stored in multiple directories.

For information on other causes of the "Call to Undefined Dynalink" error message, query on the following words in the Microsoft Knowledge Base:

call and undefined and dynalink and shell.dll

REFERENCE(S)

"Microsoft Windows User's Guide," version 3.1, pages 201–206, 214

"Microsoft Windows Resource Kit," version 3.1, pages 426–428

Additional reference words: 2.00 2.0 2.0a 2.00a 3.00 3.10 old w4wprint w4werror win31

File Sharing & Save Format Type Not Available with Annotations

SUMMARY

If you select the Lock File for Annotations option when saving a Microsoft Word for Windows version 2.0 file and another person later attempts access the file and choose Save As from

" 'Call to Undefined Dynalink' Error with Old Printer Drivers" is reprinted with permission from Microsoft Corporation. Document Number: Q85887. Publ Date: 23-JUN-1992. Product Name: Microsoft Word for Windows. Product Version: 2.00 2.00a. Operating System: WINDOWS.

the File menu, the File Sharing and Save File as Type options are unavailable. Steps To Reproduce Problem

1. From the File menu, choose New, and choose the OK button.
2. From the File menu, choose Save As.
3. Name the document, and select a disk or network drive.
4. Choose the File Sharing button. Select the Lock File for Annotations check box, and choose the OK button.
5. Reopen this file on a different computer. Or, from the Tools menu, choose Options, select the User Info category, and change the user's name before reopening the file.
6. From the File menu, choose Save As.

The File Sharing button and the Save File as Type box are unavailable. If you want to save a new version of document, select the whole document choose Copy from the Edit menu, open a new document, and choose Paste from the Edit menu. This procedure makes the File Sharing button available.

Microsoft is researching this problem and will post new information here as it becomes available.

REFERENCE(S)

"Microsoft Word for Windows User's Guide," version 2.0, pages 800–801
Additional reference words: grayed greyed 2.00

Network Message "Another User" When Second User Opens File

SUMMARY

If you attempt to open a Microsoft Word for Windows file that has already been opened by another network user, you receive the message "Another user" if Word for Windows did not create a temporary file when the other network user opened the file.

MORE INFORMATION

If you open a Microsoft Word for Windows file from a network directory, Word writes a hidden temporary file that contains your name. If a second user tries to open the same Word for Windows file, Word detects that the file is in use. Word reads the temporary file and sends a message to the second user containing the name of the first user (in this case, your name).

These temporary files are not created if you enter the "NoOwnerFiles=Yes" setting in the [Microsoft Word 2.0] section of the WIN.INI file. If Word for Windows does not find a temporary file when a second instance of a file is opened, Word sends a generic "Another user" message to the second user.

"File Sharing & Save Format Type Not Available with Annotations" is reprinted with permission from Microsoft Corporation. Document Number: Q80457. Publ Date: 27-FEB-1992. Product Name: Microsoft Word for Windows. Product Version: 2.00. Operating System: WINDOWS.

"Network Message 'Another User' When Second User Opens File" is reprinted with permission from Microsoft Corporation. Document Number: Q78425. Publ Date: 19-NOV-1991. Product Name: Microsoft Word for Windows. Product Version: 2.00. Operating System: WINDOWS.

REFERENCE(S)

"Microsoft Word for Windows User's Guide," version 2.0, pages 800–801, 810
Additional reference words: 2.00 w4werror

Word for Windows Err Msg: Cannot Open Existing NORMAL.DOT

SUMMARY

In Microsoft Word for Windows you may receive the error message:

Cannot open existing NORMAL.DOT.

MORE INFORMATION

There are three possible causes for this problem:

1. There is not enough available memory to open the NORMAL.DOT file. Close all applications you are not currently using. Remove any memory-resident programs loaded.
2. The file NORMAL.DOT may be corrupted. Try renaming NORMAL.DOT and reloading Word for Windows.
3. Another user logged on to the network has the NORMAL.DOT open. Wait until the person closes the document and try to open the file again.

Additional reference words: w4werror 1.00 1.10 1.10a 2.0 2.00

WinWord Err Msg: Cannot Create Work File

SUMMARY

The Word for Windows error message

"Cannot create work file"

occurs if Word cannot create a temporary work file for storing editing changes.
This error can occur for the following reasons:

1. A "SET TEMP=" variable has not been set. Add the command "SET TEMP=C:\" to the AUTOEXEC.BAT on the hard disk.
2. The disk temporary files are written to (where SET TEMP= is set to) is full. Remove unnecessary files to free up hard disk space.
3. If running on a network, verify that the network drive you write temporary files to is connected and that you have write privileges.

"Word for Windows Err Msg: Cannot Open Existing NORMAL.DOT" is reprinted with permission from Microsoft Corporation. Document Number: Q58891. Publ Date: 21-OCT-1991. Product Name: Microsoft Word for Windows. Product Version: 1.00 1.10 1.10A 2.00. Operating System: WINDOWS.

"WinWord Err Msg: Cannot Create Work File" is reprinted with permission from Microsoft Corporation. Document Number: Q58880. Publ Date: 10-DEC-1991. Product Name: Microsoft Word for Windows. Product Version: 1.00 1.10 1.10A 2.00. Operating System: WINDOWS.

Additional reference words: w4werror 1.0 1.1 1.1a 1.00 1.10 1.10a 2.0 2.00

Mixed Orientation Sections Print As Separate Print Jobs

SUMMARY

In Microsoft Word for Windows version 2.0, if you print a document with multiple page sizes or orientations, each section that has a different orientation or size prints as a new job.

MORE INFORMATION

Word for Windows 2.0 supports printing mixed orientation within a document. You can print one page in portrait orientation, the next page in landscape orientation, and so on within one document. However, Microsoft Windows version 3.0 cannot print documents with mixed orientation or page sizes to a single print job. This problem does not occur with Windows version 3.1 printer drivers.

NOTE: The pagination of Word for Windows documents is not affected by multiple print jobs.

The following are results of this behavior:

1. If your printer is configured to print to FILE:, Word prompts for a file name for each page of different orientation.
2. Network jobs may become broken up, causing one job to print in the middle of another or to print with multiple banner pages.

STEPS TO REPRODUCE PROBLEM

1. Create a Word for Windows document containing four sections. In each section, choose the Format Page Setup command, select Size and Orientation, and select Portrait or Landscape Orientation, as follows:

   Section 1: Portrait

   Section 2: Landscape

   Section 3: Portrait

   Section 4: Landscape

2. From the File menu, choose Print. Select 2 copies and Collate Copies. The following is the result on a network that prints a banner with each print job:

   banner page for job 1
       sec 1 portrait

"Mixed Orientation Sections Print As Separate Print Jobs" is reprinted with permission from Microsoft Corporation. Document Number: Q77795. Publ Date: 5-MAY-1992. Product Name: Microsoft Word for Windows. Product Version: 2.00. Operating System: WINDOWS.

banner page for job 2
  sec 2 landscape

banner page for job 3
  sec 3 portrait

banner page for job 4
  sec 4 landscape

This repeats for second copy of document.

3. With the same document, choose Print from the File menu, select 2 copies, and clear the Collate Copies check box. The result on a network that prints a banner with each print job is the following:

banner page for job 1
  sec 1 portrait copy 1
  sec 1 portrait copy 2

banner page for job 2
  sec 2 landscape copy 1
  sec 2 landscape copy 2

banner page for job 3
  sec 3 portrait copy 1
  sec 3 portrait copy 2

banner page for job 4
  sec 4 landscape copy 1
  sec 4 landscape copy 2

Microsoft has confirmed this to be a problem in Word for Windows version 2.0. We are researching this problem and will post new information here as it becomes available.
Additional reference words: w4wprint 2.00

Saving Grammar Settings with WinWord Installed on a Network

SUMMARY

Network users of Microsoft Word for Windows version 2.0 may want to keep the Grammar command files on a network drive to save space on workstation drives. (The GR_AM.LEX file is almost 800K; the GRAMMAR.DLL file is slightly more than 300K.) If the Grammar command files are located on a network drive, some configuration settings may not be maintained as expected. To maintain individual Grammar settings, copy the GRAMMAR.DLL file to the user directory.

MORE INFORMATION

To customize the configuration of the Grammar command, choose Options from the Tools menu, select the Grammar category, and adjust the settings.

There are three basic modes listed in the Use Grammar and Style Rules box: Strictly (All Rules), For Business Writing, and For Casual Writing. You can also select the Show

Readability Statistics after Proofing option. The options you choose are maintained in your personal WINWORD.INI file.

You can access additional settings by choosing the Customize Settings button. Word for Windows maintains these settings in the GRAMMAR.INI file.

WINWORD.INI FILE

The Word for Windows network workstation Setup program is designed to provide each user with a personal directory to which the user has read, write, and create access. Various files, including the user's WINWORD.INI file, are stored in this directory.

The default location of the user's WINWORD.INI file depends on the type of installation you perform for your workstation.

- If you perform a complete or custom installation, the default location of the WINWORD.INI file is your Word for Windows program directory. If you perform a workstation installation, the default location of the WINWORD.INI file is your Word for Windows user directory, which you specify during the installation.

- In either case, the location path is stored in the [Microsoft Word 2.0] section of your WIN.INI file as follows:

    INIpath=ath

To verify this setting, choose Options from the Tools menu, and select WIN.INI from the Category box.

GRAMMAR.INI File

If you choose the Customize Settings button and change any of the settings from their default values, Word for Windows attempts to create a GRAMMAR.INI file to store the new settings. This file is created in the same directory as the GRAMMAR.DLL file.

The default location of the GRAMMAR.DLL file (and GR_AM.LEX) is the WINWORD program directory. If this is a read-only directory, which is common with network installations, the GRAMMAR.INI file cannot be created. Word for Windows maintains any changes in the Customize Grammar Settings dialog box for the current session, but does not warn you that the GRAMMAR.INI file cannot be created to permanently save the changes. When you open a new session of Word for Windows, the default Customize Grammar Settings selections appear; any changes previously made are not maintained.

WORKAROUND

You can copy your GRAMMAR.DLL file to a directory where you have write access; this allows the creation of an individual GRAMMAR.INI file in the same directory. The larger GR_AM.LEX file can remain in the original location. You can specify the new file location by modifying the Grammar path specification in the WIN.INI file with the following steps:

1. From the Tools menu, choose Options.
2. From the Category box, select WIN.INI.

"Saving Grammar Settings with WinWord Installed on a Network" is reprinted with permission from Microsoft Corporation. Document Number: Q79882. Publ Date: 29-APR-1992. Product Name: Microsoft Word for Windows. Product Version: 2.00. Operating System: WINDOWS.

3. From the Startup Options box, select the Grammar entry. The Grammar option displays in the Option box as follows:

Grammar 1033,0

Word displays the current Grammar setting in the Setting box; the default setting is

<programdir>\grammar.dll, <programdir>\gr_am.lex

where "programdir" is the setting for the programdir option shown in the Startup Options box.

4. You can change the location where Word for Windows looks for the GRAMMAR.DLL file by specifying the following new path to the user's directory:

<user_dir>\grammar.dll,<programdir>\gr_am.lex

NOTE: You must copy the GRAMMAR.DLL file from the original location to the newly specified one.

Any subsequent changes you make to the Customize Grammar Settings dialog box causes the creation of a GRAMMAR.INI file to maintain the changes.

Microsoft is researching this problem and will post new information here as it becomes available.

REFERENCE(S)

"Microsoft Word for Windows User's Guide," version 2.0, pages 803–805
Additional reference words: proofing lost hold stick saved reset 2.0 2.00

WinWord Err Msg: This Document Is a Copy of a File...

SUMMARY

If you save a file in Microsoft Word for Windows version 2.0 on a Novell network drive and then save it again, you must have read, write, create, delete, and modify rights for the directory in which you are saving it. If you don't have modify rights, you receive the following error message:

This document is a copy of a file that was being edited by another Word session. Changes may have been saved to the original file. Do you want to save the document using the original name and overwrite other possible changes?

You can choose a Yes, No, Cancel, or Help button. If you choose the Yes button, the file is saved. Note: You do not receive this error message when you save the file for the first time.

The window name at the top of the document indicates that the current document is a copy. For example, after you first save a file, the name is as follows:

F:\USERDIR\THISDOC.DOC (COPY)

After the second save, the name reads as follows:

THISDOC.DOC

If you then choose Open from the File menu, your file does not appear. Word for Windows has saved it as a temporary (.TMP) file, with a name such as ~DOC075F.TMP. The .TMP file is a usable copy of your document. Note: Your directory may contain many .TMP files. You can only tell which file is yours by opening it. You may be able to identify your file by looking at the date and time of the file. You can also use the Find File command to locate your file based on its summary information.

You can check your network rights in a directory by going to the MS-DOS prompt and typing "rights" (without the quotation marks); a list of the current rights appears.

If you open an existing file and save it to a network drive where you do not have modify rights, use the Save As command when you save the file the second time. This prevents any error messages; however, Word for Windows still saves the file as a .TMP file. When you overwrite a file that already exists (for example, "BOO.DOC") using the File Save As command, the following process occurs:

1. BOO.DOC is saved as ~DOCxxxA.TMP. (This is a copy of BOO.DOC).
2. If step 1 is successful, BOO.DOC is renamed ~DOCxxxB.TMP.
3. ~DOCxxxA.TMP is renamed BOO.DOC.

If you do not have modify privileges, Word for Windows cannot rename these files; therefore, Word for Windows stores the documents as .TMP files.

You must have read, write, create, modify, and delete or erase rights in a directory to be able to save a file under all conditions. You may receive a wide variety of error messages when trying to save files if you do not have these five rights.

Additional reference words: 1.00 1.10 1.10a 1.0 1.1 1.1a 2.00 w4werror w4wnetwork w4wnovell

WinWord Err Msg: You Cannot Save While File Is in Use...

SUMMARY

If you need to save a file on a Novell network drive and the file was previously saved in Microsoft Word for Windows version 2.0, you must have modify rights to the directory in which you want to save the file.

MORE INFORMATION

Modify rights allow Novell users to change file attributes and rename files. If you don't have modify rights, you receive the following error message in Word for Windows version 2.0:

You cannot save while the file is in use by another process. Try saving the file with a new name.

After you choose the OK button to exit the dialog box, the Save As dialog box appears. If you type a new filename, Word for Windows saves the file.

"WinWord Err Msg: You Cannot Save While File Is in Use..." is reprinted with permission from Microsoft Corporation. Document Number: Q80626. Publ Date: 9-MAR-1992. Product Name: Microsoft Word for Windows. Product Version: 1.00 1.10 1.10a 2.00. Operating System: WINDOWS.

In Word for Windows version 1.x, the error message is as follows:

Cannot Save File, ~DOCXXXX.TMP is Locked.

NOTE: You do not receive this error message when saving a file for the first time.

You can check a network user's rights in a directory by typing "rights" (without the quotation marks) at the MS-DOS prompt; a list of the current rights appears.

In Word for Windows, when you overwrite a file that already exists using the File Save As command (for example, "BOO.DOC"), the following process occurs:

1. BOO.DOC is saved as ~DOCxxxA.TMP. (This is a copy of BOO.DOC.)
2. If step 1 is successful, BOO.DOC is renamed ~DOCxxxB.TMP.
3. ~DOCxxxA.TMP is renamed BOO.DOC.

If you do not have modify privileges, Word for Windows cannot rename these files.

You must have read, write, create, modify, and delete or erase rights in a directory to be able to save a file under all conditions. You may receive a variety of error messages when trying to save files if you do not have these five rights.

Additional reference words: 1.00 1.10 1.10a 1.0 1.1 1.1a 2.00 w4werror w4wnetwork w4wnovell

---

Spreadsheets: Microsoft Excel

Microsoft Excel has enjoyed a popular following among spreadsheets. The following section covers Excel version 3.0, which sports protection and sharing features for those on a network.

Installation

Excel can be easily installed on the network by running the Setup program on the installation diskette. You must specify a network directory where the files should be placed, such as W:\EXCEL (the window where you will type this is shown in Figure 7.20). You must also select the parts of Excel that you want installed, as shown in Figure 7.21. You should have sufficient rights to the directory when performing the install. Once you are done, run Excel to verify a correct installation (Figure 7.22 shows Excel with a sample spreadsheet loaded).

The Excel setup program creates an EXCEL.INI file in the directory where WIN.INI is stored. As with Word (see the Word installation notes above), you can create personal EXCEL.INI files for individual users.

The EXCEL.INI file contains, among other things, your feature preferences and a recent file list. Excel keeps track of the last few files you loaded and allows you to load them back into memory with a simple click of the mouse rather than the more lengthy File Open process. The full path names of these files are stored in the EXCEL.INI file in the [Recent File List] section.

A sample EXCEL.INI file looks like this:

```
[Microsoft Excel]
Options3=3
```

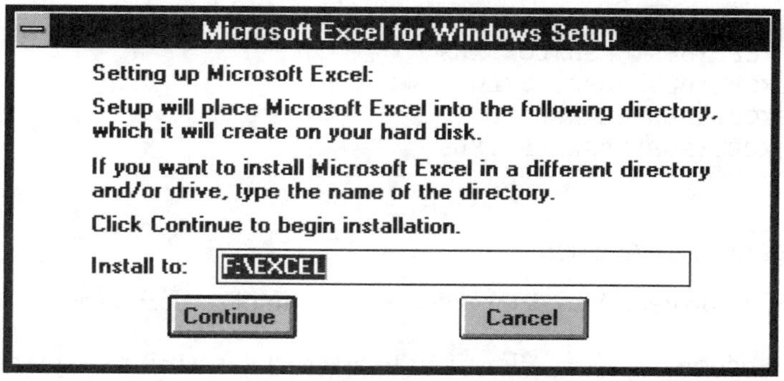

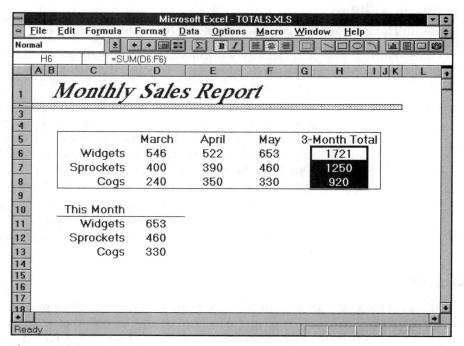

Figure 7.20 Excel Target Directory window.

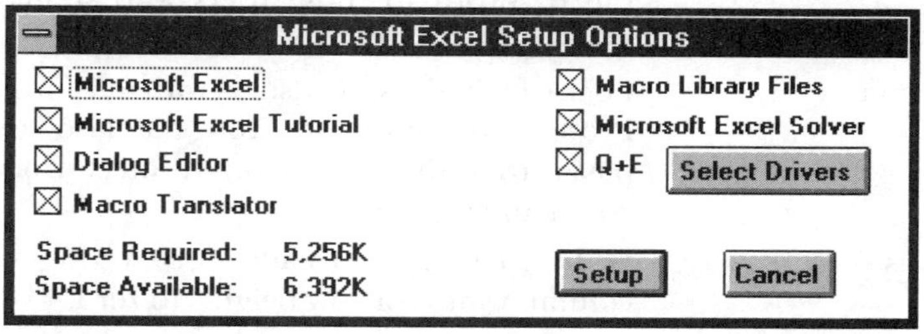

Figure 7.21 Excel Setup Options window.

Figure 7.22 Excel with sample spreadsheet loaded.

```
[Recent File List]
File1=C:\EXCEL\BBS\CASHFLOW.XLS
File2=C:\EXCEL\BBS\BBSFIN.XLW
File3=C:\EXCEL\BBS\BEANAL.XLS
File4=C:\EXCEL\BBS\BBSEXPEN.XLS
```

Document Protection Features

Excel allows you to protect shared spreadsheets in one of several ways:

Password Protection	Allows you to assign a password to a spreadsheet (using the File Save As command). You can allow limited access to the spreadsheet by distributing the password to those users who should have access.
Cell Protection	Lock cells in the spreadsheet with the Format Cell Protection command. You can also assign a password with the Options Protect Document command.
Invisible cells	Hide part of a spreadsheet, setting certain column widths or row heights to zero.

Document Sharing

As with Microsoft Word, Excel has certain file-sharing features built-in.

• Read-Only	You can save a document with read-only access. This will allow any number of users to open the document read-only at one time.
• Read-Write	When you save a document with read-write access, one user can open the document as read-write. Subsequent users will be given a message that the document is read-only. They can still open the document as read-only for simple viewing, if they wish. Once the first user has closed the document, it is then free for another user to open it with read-write access.
• DDE	You can create links between other documents and even between other applications. See Chapter 11 for further details on DDE. Excel 3.0 also supports OLE as a server.

PRINTING

Printer setup under Excel is identical to printer setup under Windows because Excel utilizes the Windows print mechanism. If you are printing to a network printer, you will need to redirect printer output from a local LPT port to a network queue. This can be accomplished through the CAPTURE command before starting Windows or through the Windows Control Panel Printers icon after startup. You can also use the Control Panel to select a particular printer.

TROUBLESHOOTING

The following technical notes were released by Microsoft and show problems and solutions encountered when running Excel:

FastTips for Excel 3.0 for Windows: Installing Q&A

SUMMARY

Microsoft Product Support Services Application Note (Text File)
WE0566: INSTALLING QUESTIONS AND ANSWERS
Revision Date: 8/92 No Disk Included
The following information applies to Microsoft Excel for Windows version 3.0.
INFORMATION PROVIDED IN THIS DOCUMENT AND ANY SOFTWARE THAT MAY ACCOMPANY THIS DOCUMENT (collectively referred to as an Application Note) IS PROVIDED "AS IS" WITHOUT WARRANTY OF ANY KIND, EITHER EXPRESSED OR IMPLIED, INCLUDING BUT NOT LIMITED TO THE IMPLIED WARRANTIES OF MERCHANTABILITY AND/OR FITNESS FOR A PARTICULAR PURPOSE. The user assumes the entire risk as to the accuracy and the use of this Application Note. This Application Note may be copied and distributed subject to the following conditions:

1. All text must be copied without modification and all pages must be included;
2. If software is included, all files on the disk(s) must be copied without modification [the MS-DOS(R) utility DISKCOPY is appropriate for this purpose];
3. All components of this Application Note must be distributed together; and
4. This Application Note may not be distributed for profit.

Copyright 1992 Microsoft Corporation. All Rights Reserved. Microsoft, MS-DOS, and Multiplan are registered trademarks and Windows is a trademark of Microsoft Corporation. dBase is a registered trademark of Ashton-Tate Corporation. Lotus and 1-2-3 are registered trademarks of Lotus Development Corporation. Q+E is a trademark of Pioneer Software Systems Corporation.

1. Q. When I try to install Microsoft Excel version 3.0 for Windows, I receive a message telling me that Microsoft Windows needs to be in standard or in 386 Enhanced mode. How can I correct this problem?

   A. Microsoft Excel version 3.0 for Windows requires that Microsoft Windows version 3.0 be either in standard or in 386 Enhanced mode. To run in either standard or 386 Enhanced mode, the Windows memory manager, HIMEM.SYS, must be present in the CONFIG.SYS file.

To configure your system for proper Windows 3.0 operation, use the following five-step procedure to install HIMEM.SYS:

Step 1. Find HIMEM.SYS on your system's hard disk. (Windows installs this file into the WINDOWS directory; MS-DOS installs this file into the DOS directory.) Once you determine where HIMEM.SYS is located, copy it to the root of your hard drive by typing the following:

copy himem.sys c:\

If you can't locate HIMEM.SYS on your system, please call Microsoft Windows technical support at (206) 637-7098.

Step 2. Start Windows. From the Program Manager File menu, choose Run. In the Command Line dialog box, type "sysedit" (without the quotation marks) to start the Microsoft System Configuration Editor.

Step 3. Four windows, titled CONFIG.SYS, AUTOEXEC.BAT, SYSTEM.INI, and WIN.INI, appear on your screen. Choose the CONFIG.SYS window by clicking the title bar or by choosing CONFIG.SYS from the Window menu.

Step 4. Type the following line at the beginning of the file:

device=c:\himem.sys

Step 5. From the File menu, choose Save. Quit the System Configuration Editor, quit Windows, and reboot your computer. Restart Windows and confirm that Windows 3.0 is running in standard or in 386 Enhanced mode by choosing About Program Manager from the File menu. If Windows is in standard or in 386 Enhanced mode, you now can install Microsoft Excel 3.0. If Windows is still in real mode, please call Microsoft Windows technical support at (206) 637-7098.

2. Q. Is there anything special I need to know about installing Microsoft Excel version 3.0 for Windows on a network?

A. There is a text file called NETWORK.TXT on the Microsoft Excel 3.0 for Windows Setup disk that specifically discusses installing Microsoft Excel 3.0 on a network. To view this file, use the following four steps:

Step 1. Put the Setup disk in drive A.

Step 2. Start Windows by typing "win" (without the quotation marks) and pressing ENTER.

Step 3. From the Program Manager File menu, choose Run. In the Command Line dialog box, type the following:

notepad a:network.txt

Step 4. Press ENTER to start the Microsoft Windows Notepad application and load the NETWORK.TXT file. For more information regarding installing Excel on a network server, please refer to page 701 of the "Microsoft Excel User's Guide" for version 3.0.

3. Q. When I install Microsoft Excel version 3.0 for Windows, I am given the opportunity to select which Excel options I want. What are each of these options and why should I install them?

A. There are seven options you can install during the Microsoft Excel 3.0 for Windows Setup program. The following is an overview of the seven options available:

Option 1. Microsoft Excel: This option installs the minimum files necessary to use Microsoft Excel 3.0. If you are installing Microsoft Excel 3.0 for the first time, you must select this option.

Option 2. Microsoft Excel Tutorial: This option installs a series of online lessons, an excellent way to learn Microsoft Excel 3.0 interactively.

Option 3. Dialog Editor: This option installs an application called the Dialog Editor. You can use the Dialog Editor to create custom dialog boxes for Microsoft Excel 3.0 command macros and custom forms to enter database information.

Option 4. Macro Translator: This option installs the Macro Translation Assistant, a utility that helps you translate your Lotus 1-2-3 (R) and Microsoft Multiplan (R) macros into Microsoft Excel 3.0 macros.

Option 5. Macro Library files: This option installs a set of sample worksheets and add-in macros that offer ideas about combining Microsoft Excel 3.0 features to create powerful worksheets, macros, and models.

Option 6. Microsoft Excel Solver: This option installs Microsoft Excel Solver, an easy-to-use companion application that allows for linear programming capability and complex "what-if" analysis.

Option 7. Q+E: This option installs Q+E (TM), a powerful and easy-to-use database application that allows you to manipulate and update database files from a variety of database systems, including dBASE(R) and Microsoft SQL Server.

For more information on installing Microsoft Excel 3.0, please see page 4 of the "Microsoft Excel User's Guide" for version 3.0.
Additional reference words: 3.00 ivrfax fasttips

Changing the Default Directory for Excel

SUMMARY

This article discusses methods of changing the default directory that Excel starts in. Excel will normally start up with the EXCEL directory active, but you may want to change this default to a specified directory. You can check the current default directory by choosing Open from the File menu after starting the Excel program. The current directory is listed after "Directory is..."

"Changing the Default Directory for Excel" is reprinted with permission from Microsoft Corporation. Document Number: Q74342. Publ Date: 10-JUL-1992. Product Name: Microsoft Windows Excel. Product Version: 2.x 3.00] 2.20 2.21 3.00. Operating System: WINDOWS] OS/2 .

MORE INFORMATION

Method 1

This first method is accomplished by changing the properties of the Excel icon in the Windows 3.0 Program Manager.

1. Verify that the directory containing EXCEL.EXE is in the path statement of your AUTOEXEC.BAT file.
2. From the Program Manager, select the Excel icon and choose Properties from the File menu.
3. Type the path of the desired directory in the Command Line text box, followed by "\excel.exe" (without the quotation marks). For example, type the following:

   c:\user\excel.exe

4. The error message "The specified path is invalid" will appear. Choose OK to bypass this message.

Excel will now start with the specified directory as the default drive and directory. A problem with this method is that the icon will be changed from the standard Excel icon to a DOS icon. To correct this, do the following:

1. Select the icon once again in the Program Manager. From the File menu, choose Properties.
2. Choose the Change Icon button.
3. Type the correct path for the EXCEL.EXE file (for example, c:\excel\excel.exe) and press the ENTER key.

You will see the message "The specified path is invalid" once again. However, you can ignore it at this point and everything will still work properly.

Method 2

The second method is for Excel 3.0 only. The following macro will open Excel in a specified default directory:

A1: DEFAULT_DIR

A2: =DIRECTORY("C:\USER")

A3: =RETURN()

1. Enter the above macro into a macro sheet. Select cell A1. Define this macro as an Auto_Open macro by choosing Define Name from the Formula menu, entering "auto_open" (without the quotation marks) in the Name box, and selecting the Command button. Choose OK.
2. Save the macro as an add-in macro in the XLSTART directory by choosing Save As from the File menu, choosing Options, and selecting AddIn from the list. Choose OK. For the filename, enter the path to the XLSTART directory, followed by the filename (for example, c:\excel\xlstart\defltdir.xla).

Any documents that are saved in the XLSTART directory are automatically opened when the Excel program is started. Because this macro sheet is saved as an add-in macro, it will open as hidden. You are unable to view it, even by choosing the Window

Unhide command. However, the macro will execute because it has been saved as an Auto_Open macro.

Method 3

The third method is for all other versions of Excel. Method 3 creates a macro similar to Method 2 and then saves it as an Auto_Open macro. The macro sheet is hidden so that you do not see it. The macro sheet filename is added to the WIN.INI file so that it is opened each time the Excel program is run.

1. Open a new macro sheet. Choose Save As from the File menu and enter "c:\changedi.xlm" (or any valid path and filename, without the quotation marks) in the File Name box. Choose OK.

2. Enter the following macro into the macro sheet:

   A1: Auto_Open

   A2: =DIRECTORY("C:\USER")

   A3: =NEW()

   A4: =RETURN()

   The =DIRECTORY statement will set the current drive to the path described in the pathname. The =NEW command will open up a blank worksheet.

3. Define the macro as an Auto_Open macro by doing the following:

   a. Select cell A1.

   b. From the Formula menu, choose Define Name.

   c. Choose the Command button.

   d. Choose OK.

4. From the Notepad program, open the WIN.INI file (located in the WINDOWS directory). Scroll down to the [Microsoft Excel ¦ heading and add the following line below the heading:

   open=c:\changedir.xlm

   This causes CHANGEDIR.XLM to open every time the Excel program is started. Note: Method 1 is the simplest method to use, and is recommended. In some cases, perhaps in a network situation or if you do not have Windows 3.0, Method 2 or Method 3 may be preferable.

REFERENCE(S):

"Microsoft Windows User's Guide," version 3.0, pages 89–91

"Microsoft Excel User's Guide," version 3.0, pages 553, 651

"Microsoft Excel Reference Guide," version 2.1, pages 209–211

"Microsoft Excel Functions and Macros," version 2.1, pages 270, 353

Problems with the Excel for Windows Tutorial on a Network

SUMMARY

When using the Excel for Windows Tutorial and Feature Guide does not work properly; the screen flashes, and you are returned to Excel.

MORE INFORMATION

When you start the Tutorial or Feature Guide, Excel tries to save a workspace file to disk so that when you are done with the Tutorial or Feature Guide, you will be at the same place you left off.

This problem occurs when you install Excel in a read-only directory. In a read-only directory, Excel cannot write a workspace. The solution is to set the attributes for the Excel directory to be read/write. For information on setting the attributes of a network directory, consult your network documentation.

Additional reference words: 2.0 2.00 2.01 2.1 2.10 3.0 3.00

"Cannot Access CBT.XLW" Message Running Tutorial on a Network

SUMMARY

If you attempt to run the Microsoft Excel Tutorial from a network, the error message "Cannot Access CBT.XLW" may occur if the network drive that Excel is installed on has read-only privileges.

MORE INFORMATION

The Excel Tutorial will attempt to create a workspace file (CBT.XLW) in the current directory, when the tutorial is started. If the current directory inhibits the writing of the file, you will receive the above message.

WORKAROUNDS

1. Change the current directory before starting the tutorial. This can be done thorough the FILE/OPEN dialog box.
2. Temporarily change the privileges to read, write, and create for the Excel drive or directory until everyone has worked through the Tutorial. Be sure to make a backup of the files because anyone working on the server can make changes to these files.

"Problems with the Excel for Windows Tutorial on a Network" is reprinted with permission from Microsoft Corporation. Document Number: Q26729. Publ Date: 20-FEB-1992. Product Name: Microsoft Windows Excel. Product Version: 2.X 3.00. Operating System: WINDOWS.

"'Cannot Access CBT.XLW' Message Running Tutorial on a Network" is reprinted with permission from Microsoft Corporation. Document Number: Q72838. Publ Date: 20-MAY-1992. Product Name: Microsoft Windows Excel. Product Version: 3.00 4.00. Operating System: WINDOWS.

3. Copy the complete Excel directory to the hard drive of the workstation while using the Tutorial and then erase the directory from the hard drive after the user finishes the Tutorial.

Additional reference words: 3.0 3.00 4.0 4.00

Troubleshooting Unrecoverable Application Errors in Excel

SUMMARY

When running Microsoft Excel under Windows, you may encounter the following error message:
Unrecoverable Application Error–Terminating Current Application. There are many common causes for this error. This article is intended as a guide to troubleshooting the Unrecoverable Application Error (UAE). It lists the common causes of the error and some possible solutions.

MORE INFORMATION

TSRs and other Programs in CONFIG.SYS and AUTOEXEC.BAT

As with any Windows troubleshooting it is best to start with a clean configuration. Remove any programs from these files that are not necessary to boot the computer and run Windows.

Incorrect Memory Manager

Use HIMEM.SYS in your CONFIG.SYS file. Make sure it is the correct version (the file date should be 5/1/90 or later). Replace any expanded memory managers (EMMs) with the Windows copy of EMM386.SYS.

Load= and Run= Lines in the WIN.INI File

These lines run programs in Windows automatically (similar to the AUTOEXEC.BAT file for DOS). Put a semicolon (;) in front of these lines in the WIN.INI file, save the file, and restart Windows. The semicolon disables these lines and nothing will be loaded in Windows except the Program Manager.

High-Resolution Screen Drivers

Some high-resolution screen drivers have been known to cause UAEs from Excel, particularly when using the Preview or Print options on the File menu. Try reinstalling the Windows VGA driver that is provided on your original Windows disks.

Standard Mode

UAEs can be Enhanced-mode specific. Try running Windows in standard mode by typing the following at the command (DOS) prompt:

```
WIN /S
```

This forces you into standard mode.

"Troubleshooting Unrecoverable Application Errors in Excel" is reprinted with permission from Microsoft Corporation. Document Number: Q77720. Publ Date: 16-MAR-1992. Product Name: Microsoft Windows Excel. Product Version: 2.10c 2.10d 3.00. Operating System: WINDOWS.

Soft Fonts

Some soft font packages, utilities, and cartridges have been known to cause UAEs from Excel, particularly when using the Print Preview or Print commands in the File menu. Try disabling or removing the soft fonts from Windows.

Spreadsheets, Macros, or Utilities in the XLSTART Directory

A corrupted spreadsheet or invalid macro sheet that is automatically run when Excel is started may cause a UAE. Either remove all spreadsheets and macros from the XLSTART directory or redefine the XLSTART directory to an empty directory.

Corrupted Installation

If Windows has difficulty reading the Setup disks during installation it is possible that the EXCEL.EXE file will not be completely expanded onto the hard drive. This can be verified by comparing the EXCEL.EXE files size to those in the following table:

File Date	Correct File Size
12/9/90	1254400 Bytes
6/12/91	1268352 Bytes

If your EXCEL.EXE is a different size, try copying your Setup disks into a temporary file on your hard drive and run the Setup program from there.

Excel Directory Is Not in the Path

It is important that Windows knows where to find the proper Excel files. If the Excel directory is not specified in your MS-DOS path variable, Windows may locate and try to use an incorrect file in another directory resulting in a UAE. Note that the Path variable is limited to 128 characters under MS-DOS. To see if Excel is in the path, move to a command (DOS) prompt and type

    path

and press ENTER. Note that if you change your path in an MS-DOS window, that change will not affect Windows overall. It is only changed for that MS-DOS window.

Lost Clusters on the Hard Drive

Exit Windows completely and type the following at the command (DOS) prompt:

    chkdsk /f

This searches for and removes lost clusters from your hard drive. These lost clusters can cause UAEs in Excel and other Windows applications.

Corrupted Spreadsheets

If the UAE only occurs when opening a specific spreadsheet, try copying that sheet to a different disk (hard drive) using MS-DOS. If you still can't open the sheet, it is possible that the sheet is corrupted.

Low Memory, System Resources, or Hard Disk Space

When running Excel, your system should have plenty of memory, system resources, and hard disk space available. Try exiting Windows and restarting it with Excel running only. In addition, select the MS-DOS Prompt icon from inside Windows. While you are at the command (DOS) prompt, check the available disk space by typing the following:

    chkdsk

If the available disk space is below 3 MB, clear some files off of your drive.

Version of DOS

The version of DOS that you use on your machine can be very important. Most IBM clones should be running MS-DOS. True IBM machines ONLY should run IBM PC-DOS. Some clone manufacturer's versions of DOS are specially modified to work on their computer systems. If your machine came with such a version of DOS, run that DOS only. An incorrect version of DOS may cause UAEs in Excel or any other Windows application.

Unsupported Networks

Windows only directly supports certain networks. During the Windows Setup routine, Setup will generate a list of networks from which to choose. If your network is not listed, you may experience problems running Windows on the network. If possible, try not logging on to the network and repeat the steps that cause a UAE on your machine. If it does not occur, then you may have an incompatible network.

Corrupted or Invalid SMARTDRV.SYS

If the SMARTDRV.SYS file that is loaded in your CONFIG.SYS file is corrupted or an old version you may have trouble running Excel and other Windows applications. Make sure that you are using the SMARTDRV.SYS file provided on your Windows disks. To test if SMARTDRV.SYS is causing a problem, simply remove the line from your CONFIG.SYS file and reboot your machine.

Corrupted Printer Driver

If you get UAEs only when you print, your printer driver may be corrupted. Test with another printer driver or reinstall the printer driver that you are using.

ProCollection Font Cartridge Printing in Landscape

The Windows LaserJet II driver has a problem with the ProCollection Font Cartridge that causes a UAE when printing in landscape mode. This has been corrected in later versions of the printer driver. Contact Product Support Services at (206) 454-2030 for an updated driver.

Additional reference words: 2.10c 2.10d 3.00 2.1c 2.1d 3.0 err msg tshoot

Installing Excel Version 3.00 on a Network

SUMMARY

The Setup program for Microsoft Excel version 3.00 will copy some files that are global (that is, the files need to be available for all network users) into the users' private directories. These files need to be removed from the private directories and placed into the shared Excel directory on the network.

Specifically, on a full installation of Excel, there will be two files in the WINDOWS directory and eight files in the WINDOWS\SYSTEM directory. These can easily be identified as they will have a date of 12/9/90 and a time of 12:00 PM.

The installation program will also build a Program Manager group that has four items. If you choose, the group can be constructed for each user; the instructions are included at the end of this article.

"Installing Excel Version 3.00 on a Network" is reprinted with permission from Microsoft Corporation. Document Number: Q68358. Publ Date: 29-MAY-1991. Product Name: Microsoft Windows Excel. Product Version: 3.00. Operating System: WINDOWS.

MORE INFORMATION

The following are descriptions of the three directories that Setup modifies:

The first directory is the one to which you choose to install Microsoft Excel. This is the main directory that holds the supporting files required to run Microsoft Excel. This directory will be referred to as the EXCEL directory.

The second directory installation is the directory that holds Microsoft Windows version 3.00. This directory is the user's private WINDOWS directory. One file that will be contained in this directory is the WIN.COM file that is specific to the user's installation. This directory will be referred to as the WINDOWS directory.

The last directory that installation will modify is the SYSTEM subdirectory of the WINDOWS directory. Microsoft Excel uses this subdirectory to store utilities required for some functions. This directory will be referred to as the WINDOWS\SYSTEM subdirectory.

The following files are placed in the directory (named under the Directory heading) when you install the program (listed under the Put There When You Install heading):

Filename	Directory	Put There When You Install
XLBIG.BMP	WINDOWS	Microsoft Excel
XLCUBES.BMP	WINDOWS	Microsoft Excel
FILEFNS.DLL	WINDOWS\SYSTEM	Microsoft Excel Library Files
DBNMP3.DLL	WINDOWS\SYSTEM	Q+E
QEDBF.DLL	WINDOWS\SYSTEM	Q+E
QESS.DLL	WINDOWS\SYSTEM	Q+E
QETXT.DLL	WINDOWS\SYSTEM	Q+E
QEXLA.DLL	WINDOWS\SYSTEM	Q+E
QEXLS.DLL	WINDOWS\SYSTEM	Q+E
W3DBLIB.DLL	WINDOWS\SYSTEM	Q+E

Once these files have been identified, remove them from the WINDOWS directory and WINDOWS\SYSTEM subdirectory, and place them in the shared EXCEL directory.

It is very important that the EXCEL directory be included on the search path. The search path is a list of drives and directories that the system will search through to find executable files or supporting utilities.

For more information about the search path, please refer to your network documentation and your DOS manual for a discussion on the PATH command.

BUILDING EXCEL 3.00 GROUP FOR EACH USER

To build the Microsoft Excel 3.00 group for each user, do the following:

1. Run the Windows Setup application from the Main Group of Program Manager.
2. From the Options menu, choose Setup Applications.
3. Search the drive to which Excel was installed. (Please refer to page 93 of the "Microsoft Windows User's Guide" for version 3.00 for more information.)

4. A list of applications will appear in the left-hand box. The four that need to be selected are:

- Dialog Editor
- Macro Translator
- Microsoft
- Excel QE

5. Press the Add button and these will appear in the right-hand box.
6. Choose OK and these programs will be added to the Windows Applications group. If no Windows Applications group exists, one will be created.
7. The installation program for Microsoft Excel creates a Program Manager group named Microsoft Excel 3.0. You can either leave these items in the Windows Applications group or create the Excel group and move the program icons as described on pages 87 and 95 in the "Microsoft Windows User's Guide."
8. After making these changes, exit Windows and check the Save Changes checkbox to record the new settings.

REFERENCE(S)

For more information on setting up Excel, see "Microsoft Excel Getting Started."

For more information on setting up an Excel group, see pages 87 and 95 of the "Microsoft Windows User's Guide."

Desktop Publishing

Desktop publishing has become an important consideration for many companies. Whether publishing a newsletter, designing product brochures, or marketing literature, desktop publishing offers an economical alternative to an art department in even the smallest of companies. And, for larger companies, the benefits gained from desktop publishing, such as savings on traditional layout and design services, can be enormous.

Networking is a logical companion to desktop publishing because it fits the way a document is produced. In traditional publishing, a published work is very often composed of different pieces that are created by different people. All of those pieces must eventually be brought together to form the finished product. With networking and desktop publishing, this process can be simplified and the network can promote true teamwork.

For instance, one user can create an ad or story copy using a word processor on one machine while another user can be creating graphs using a spreadsheet or graphics package on another. Also, a third user may be creating the layout in PageMaker or Ventura using rough drafts or dummy text.

When the three people are finished with their work, the person operating the desktop publishing software can update that document with the ad copy from the word processor and the graphs from the graphics package. The desktop publishing package keeps track of the directory and filenames associated with the ad copy and the graphs, so all the art department has to do is get the latest copy and they have a new publication.

PageMaker

Aldus has been producing electronic desktop publishing software for some time now. Starting with the Apple Macintosh, Aldus created PageMaker and later ported a version to the PC.

PageMaker 4.0 was obtained for this book and it runs completely under Windows. You can use the network to distribute aspects of a document, such as text and graphics as described in the example given above.

PRE-INSTALLATION

Before installing PageMaker, you should have at least 5 megabytes of free space on the network and at least 2 megabytes of RAM in any workstation running PageMaker. Actually, if you will be doing any desktop publishing more serious than simple document composition, you should also have more memory.

INSTALLATION

There are three main steps when installing PageMaker on a network:

1. Install PageMaker on the file server.

2. Create user-specific directories and files.

3. Configure WIN.INI and other files.

INSTALLING PAGEMAKER ON THE SERVER

To Install PageMaker on the file server, perform the following steps:

1. Create two directories on the server: \NETALDUS and \PM4. Make sure users can scan the directories and open and read files in those directories.

2. Use the Aldus Setup disk to install PageMaker on the server. When Setup asks where you want to install files that are shared by, or are specific to, Aldus products, enter the path of the NETALDUS directory (example: F:\APPS\NETALDUS).

3. Select and install all of the options in Setup's main window. When Setup asks where you want to install PageMaker (shown in Figure 7.23), specify the directory path where you created PM4, such as F:\APPS\PM4. When Setup asks whether it can modify AUTOEXEC.BAT or CONFIG.SYS, say 'No.'

> **Note:** The PageMaker tutorial was designed for only one user at a time, so it cannot be shared. If you want to use the tutorial, you can copy it to a local drive. To do this, type "XCOPY F:\PM4\TUTORIAL*.* C:\PM4TUTOR /S" to copy all of the tutorial files to a directory called \PM4TUTOR on your C drive.

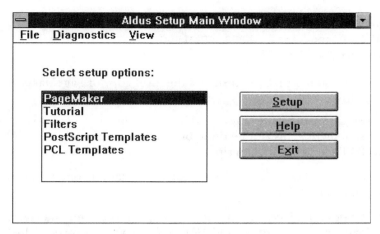

Figure 7.23 PageMaker Setup Main Window.

Also, each workstation running PageMaker on the network needs a copy of ALDUS.INI, ALDENG.UDC, and PM.CNF (created by PageMaker when you start it up and open a publication). These files are not shared.

INSTALLING PAGEMAKER ON A WORKSTATION

Okay, PageMaker is on the file server and shared directories are created. Now you need to setup individual directory areas for users. To do this, proceed as follows:

1. Rename the ALDUS.INI file on the server in the \ALDUS\USENGLSH directory to ALDUSINI.SAV. This file needs to be copied into each user's directory as ALDUS.INI, so a backup copy is made here.

2. Copy the PM4 directory and all subdirectories and files to each workstation (you could do this with a "XCOPY F:\PM4 C:\PM4 /S" DOS command).

3. Copy the NETALDUS directory and all subdirectories and files to each workstation. Rename the local directory to ALDUS.

4. Copy the file ALDUSINI.SAV from the server to each workstation and rename it ALDUS.INI. The file should be in the \ALDUS\USENGLISH directory.

5. Copy ALDENG.UDC to \ALDUS\USENGLISH.

CONFIGURING WIN.INI AND OTHER FILES

Now that you have the files set up, you need to configure a few files. Proceed as follows:

1. Edit the ALDUS.INI file and remove the PM4DEFAULTS entry from the [PageMaker] section.

2. Add a section called [Aldus] to the WIN.INI on each user's workstation. Add the following entries to that section:

```
AldusDirectory=C:\ALDUS
NetAldusDirectory=F:\APPS\NETALDUS
PM4LangDir=USENGLISH
```

This entry assumes that you installed the local copy of PageMaker on the local C: drive.

3. Add the local PM4 and the network NETALDUS directory paths to the user's PATH statement. This can be done by modifying either the local AUTO-EXEC.BAT file or the login script.

4. Make sure that the CONFIG.SYS for each workstation contains at least 30 FILES and 10 BUFFERS.

5. Start Windows and create an Aldus group in Program Manager. Add PageMaker and Table Editor (and Aldus Setup, if you've copied Aldus Setup to the workstation). The result is shown in Figure 7.24. Double-click on the "PageMaker 4.0" icon to start PageMaker (the main PageMaker window is shown in Figure 7.25).

SHARED RESOURCES

PageMaker allows only one person to access a publication at a time and only exclusive access to the 'Master' version of a publication. If you try to open a publication and receive a "File in use" message denying you access, someone else is using the publication. You can open the publication as a copy if you still want to use it—then save the publication under a new name.

The problem with this approach is that you end up with multiple versions of a publication. You would then have to cut and paste any relevant changes to the master publication at some time in the future. It may be best to simply let one user modify the Master publication at one time. You can still edit the elements of the publication, such as word processing and graphics files, then have the user update the master with the newest versions of those files (see the PageMaker manuals about manual versus automatic updating).

Ventura

Ventura Publisher originally was written for the GEM graphical desktop environment. But, when it was seen that Windows was an important graphical environment as well, a new Windows-based edition was created. For several years people would say, "If you are working on a small document or brochure, use PageMaker; if you're working on a long document, use Ventura." PageMaker simplifies layout with many of its features, while Ventura simplifies the process of working with long documents by assigning "tags" to certain bodies of text. If you change the characteristics of a tag, all text that has been assigned that tag will change throughout the entire document. Now, new feature sets in both packages have brought them closer together in what they can do.

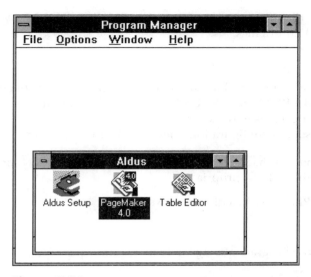

Figure 7.24 Aldus Group in Program Manager.

PRE-INSTALLATION

Before you install Ventura on the LAN, though, there are a few considerations. First, be sure you have at least 2MB of RAM in workstations that will be running Ventura. However, the general rule is the more RAM, the better. Also, make sure that each

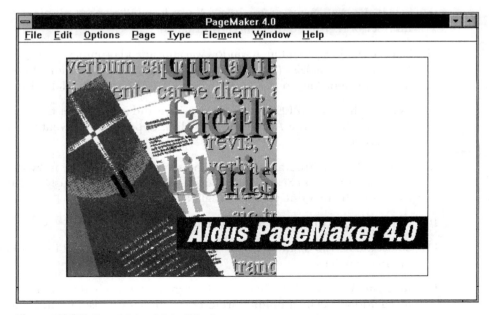

Figure 7.25 PageMaker Main Window.

workstation has a private directory area created (such as F:\USER\CHARLES\VENTURA) to store private Ventura files.

INSTALLATION

First install Ventura as you would on a local hard drive, except specify the network drive you want to use, like W:\APPS\VENTURA. This will copy all of the Ventura files to the LAN and set up a master directory.

Then, to create workstation configurations, perform the following steps:

1. Xerox requires that you have a separate Network Node Kit for each node, so make sure you have the appropriate kits.

2. Insert the EXAMPLES disk in a diskette drive.

3. Start Windows.

4. Select Run from the Program Manager File menu and type

   ```
   A:\UTILITY\SERNSTAL F:
   ```

   where A: is the drive you put the floppy in and F: is the network drive where you want the private Ventura files installed.

   If the network drive is not valid or you don't have sufficient rights to the drive, a dialog box will appear, prompting you to enter a valid network drive. You must enter the drive letter with a colon after it, (as in F:). If the specified drive is valid, you will see the Sernstal window with three menu items: Exit, Add Seats, and About Sernstal.

6. Select the Add Seats menu item. A window will appear, displaying the number of registered users already installed.

7. Select the Add Seat button. A window will appear and prompt you to insert the Network Node Kit Disk (if you purchased multiple copies of Ventura Publisher instead of Node kits, you will need to insert the APPLICATION disk instead).

8. Remove the EXAMPLES disk from the drive and insert either the Network Node Kit disk or the APPLICATION disk, depending on what you have purchased.

9. Select OK. The program will write the serial number to the network disk and display the Add Seats window again, showing the previously registered users and the new one you just installed.

10. Repeat steps 7 through 9 for each additional user.

11. Select the Finished button in the Add Seats window and select Exit from the menu of choices.

12. Run the Ventura Publisher install program for each new user. During installation, specify a unique preferences directory. Also, ensure that the Copy Examples box is not checked.

13. Flag the files in the main network VENTURA directory as shareable read-only (you can do this with the command "FLAG \VENTURA *.* srw" at the DOS prompt).

When complete, you will see a message box similar to that shown in Figure 7.26. Figure 7.27 shows Ventura Publisher in its group in Program Manager.

NETWORK FUNCTIONALITY

If you take the above steps to install Ventura on the network, you will have multiple configurations, meaning that each user will retain individual preferences and settings when each one leaves Ventura.

Also, temporary files will be stored in each user's private directory. These files, created by Ventura when you start the program, are used during the operation of Ventura as overflow and work files that are not stored in memory. They will be deleted when you exit the program.

Ventura's locking scheme revolves around the "chapter." Within Ventura, you work on one chapter at a time which may contain several documents and graphical elements. Multiple chapters are linked together to form a publication.

Chapters are locked exclusively for use by one person at a time. The Save operation detects whether any file within a chapter is being used and, if so, gives you the option to cancel the Save, then store your changes under a different name.

You may, however, use the Browse option to view a chapter in read-only mode. Therefore, multiple users can Browse a chapter simultaneously.

PRINTING

Ventura Publisher Windows Edition uses the Windows mechanism for printing, so you should set up printers as normal under Windows. If you are printing to a network printer, you will need to redirect printer output from a local LPT port to

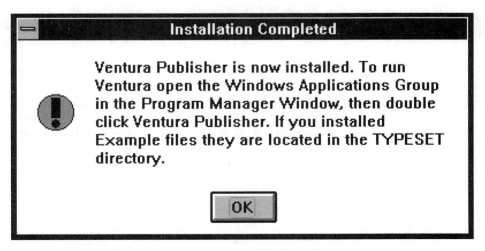

Figure 7.26 Ventura Installation Complete message box.

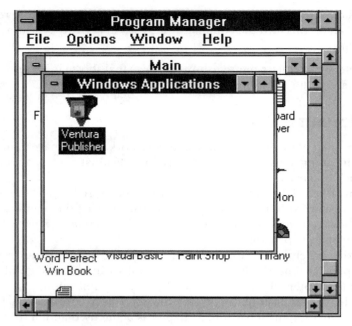

Figure 7.27 Ventura Group in Program Manager.

a network queue. This can be accomplished through the CAPTURE command before starting Windows or through the Control Panel afterward. Printer selection can be made through the Windows Control Panel.

Other Applications

Other than the mainstream applications like word processors and spreadsheets, there is a vast array of "other" applications. This section contains several miscellaneous applications to show you the kinds of packages you can integrate with the network.

PerFORM Pro

Delrina Technology makes a forms package called PerFORM Pro which allows you to design and print paper forms. Once created, the forms can be filled out by customers, employees, and so on. The information on those forms can be filled in electronically and stored in dBASE-compatible .DBF files for later searching and reporting.

Placing PerFORM on the LAN allows you to:

• Centralize the storage and management of PerFORM, including forms design as well as forms entry or "filling."

- Keep one copy of a form as it evolves. This way, those doing the filling will all work from a central, standard form. If the form changes, everyone works from those changes, rather than having multiple copies on local hard drives in various states of evolution.

- Organize access to the functions associated with forms management. With network security you can organize and administrate who can design the forms and who can fill in the forms.

To install PerFORM Pro, make sure Windows is properly installed and take the following steps:

1. Load Windows and make the Program Manager the active window.

2. Place the PerFORM Disk #1 in a diskette drive.

3. You should make sure that the Program Manager (and Dr. Watson, if you have Windows 3.1) is the only running task. You can shut down other tasks conveniently by using the Task Manager (accessible by pressing Control-ESC).

4. From Program Manager, choose the File Run command.

5. Enter "A:\INSTALL" to run the INSTALL program on drive A:, assuming that's where you put the first diskette.

You will be shown the PerFORM installation dialog box (shown in Figure 7.28). Follow the instructions and prompts to complete the PerFORM installation.

Once you have completed the installation, you should be able to see the PerFORM PRO group in Program Manager (shown in Figure 7.29). Figure 7.30 shows PerFORM PRO Designer running with a sample form loaded, and Figure 7.31 shows the PerFORM PRO Filler loaded, filling in the same form.

The install program only updates the WIN.INI of the user running it, so other users will have to run the PFSETUP.EXE program to have WIN.INI updated.

The PFSETUP.EXE file is located in the same directory as the other PerFORM program files. If you installed PerFORM to F:\PERFORM, for example, then choose File Run from the program manager and enter "F:\PERFORM\PFSETUP." PFSETUP updates the user's WIN.INI file with the proper settings.

PERFORM PRO OPERATION ON THE LAN

Before you unleash the masses to use PerFORM, Delrina suggests you perform the following tests to see if it is working properly on the workstation:

1. Start up PerFORM Filler under Windows.

2. Open a form. If possible, open a compressed form with a graphic image, such as your logo, in it.

3. Open a data file.

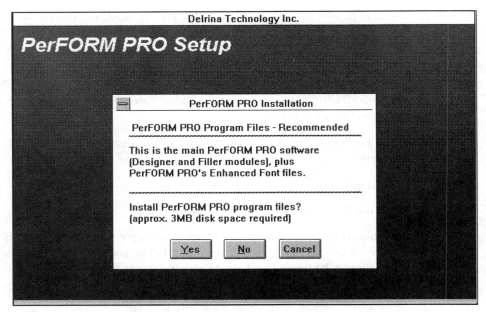

Figure 7.28 PerFORM PRO Installation dialog box.

4. Perform database lookups (if the form includes these in its design).

5. Print a few form records.

6. Perform the above steps on several different workstations. Also, run PerFORM on several workstations at the same time.

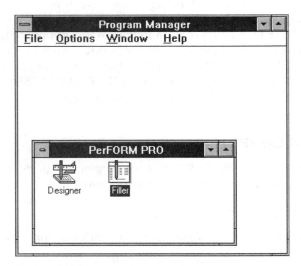

Figure 7.29 PerFORM PRO Group in Program Manager.

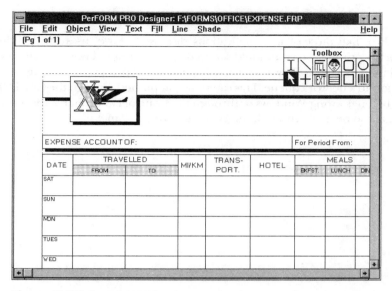

Figure 7.30 PerFORM PRO Designer with expense form loaded.

You also might want to test importing ASCII or dBASE files into a form or exporting to .DBF or ASCII files.

PerFORM gets around the file sharing obstacles by allowing each form filler to create an individual database file. For instance, if three users are filling in the same form, there will be three separate .DBF files created with the filled information. Multiple users cannot add data to the same data file (.FIL files) at one time. If more than one user attempts to open the same file, the following message will be displayed:

```
Access Denied ... Data File could not be opened
```

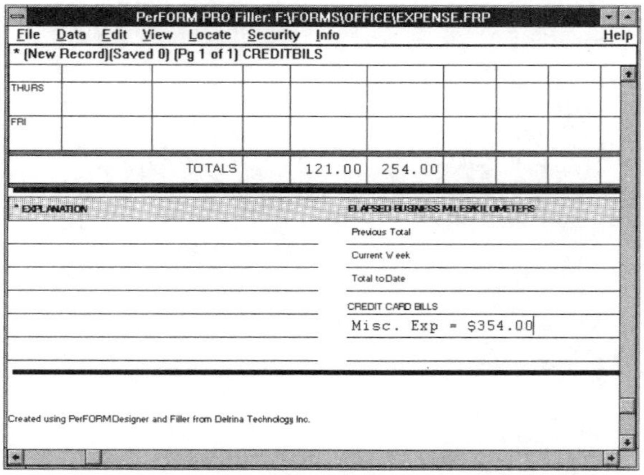

Figure 7.31 PerFORM PRO Filler with expense form loaded.

PRINTING

PerFORM Pro, like most of the applications discussed above, uses the Windows mechanism for printing, so you should set up printers as normal under Windows. If you are printing to a network printer, you will need to redirect printer output from a local LPT port to a network queue. This can be accomplished through the CAPTURE command before starting Windows or through the Control Panel afterwards. Printer selection can also be made through the Windows Control Panel.

8 Optimizing Windows on NetWare

Performance can be an ambiguous word. To some, getting Windows to work on the LAN at all might be considered "high performance," whereas to others, performance might be tweaking the last bit of loading time out of a DOS application.

This chapter will begin with a definition of performance and a discussion of the various types of performance optimization that can be done. The meaning of "adequate performance" for a given situation and user type will also be covered. Then, we will examine specific ways you can improve the performance of Windows on the network, in DOS sessions, on the hard disk, at the printer, and in memory.

What Is Performance?

As stated above, performance can mean various things to various people. We will consider performance to have three facets:

- Speed
- Capacity
- Functionality

Speed determines how quickly Windows or some task in Windows will run. Because Windows puts more of a demand on your hardware than DOS and DOS-based applications do, you need to be aware of the various ways you can speed up different Windows processing tasks. For example, these tasks can include initial loading time of Windows, the time to load an individual application, and overall system response time as you switch from one application to another. After all, you don't want to wait for Windows all day.

Speed will be the primary performance element to consider because it tends to be most important to users. No matter how much capacity or how functional a system is, if it is too slow, users will be frustrated, *especially* when they have been used to a faster system, such as running DOS-based applications.

Capacity allows you to do more of whatever you are doing. For instance, network file server disk space might be one of the capacities that is important to a Windows user. After all, Windows, its applications, and graphics data files can require an inordinately large amount of disk space to store. Also, Windows' capacity for loading multiple applications in memory at one time might be another important capacity for a certain type of user (swap files take up a lot of disk space).

Functionality can mean two different things. The first definition, and the one used for this chapter, is that functionality allows you to do more, period. Better functionality means your desktop environment works better, either through new functions, improved interaction between various elements within Windows, or a combination of improved speed and capacity.

An alternative definition is that something is functional, meaning it simply works (which may be an issue in some cases). We'll address issues pertaining to simply getting things working in Chapter 9.

What Is "Adequate Performance"?

When measuring performance, any system manager or user is faced with the issue of determining how much performance is enough. The answer is that performance is subjective and relative to the profile of the user being considered.

For instance, consider the following types of users and the applications they use. Note what might be appropriate hardware for their particular needs:

	Word Processor	Desktop Publisher	Database Station
Processor	386/16 or 386/25	386/33 or 486/?	386/33 or 486/?
Graphics	VGA	Full-page or SVGA	VGA
Memory	2MB or 4MB	4MB or 8MB	4MB or 8MB
Disk space	20MB	80MB	250MB
Traffic	light	moderate	heavy

In this scenario, the person doing word processing may require a slower computer than someone doing desktop publishing. For the most part, the computer will be accepting keystrokes as the user types new documents. An occasional file save will impact other users only very slightly or not at all. VGA graphics and 2–4MB RAM are probably sufficient. The disk space requirements are fairly low since most of what will be saved will be text documents.

The Traffic column is irrelevant to anyone working from a local hard drive; but to those on a LAN, the traffic load imposed by different users can be important because it affects every other user on the network. System managers and supervisors should consider network loads imposed by various types of users and plan for their traffic on the network. For example, automatic backup options for word processors should not be set so frequently that a storm of file saves causes a network-wide slowdown.

The person doing desktop publishing will require a faster computer since the application will likely demand that the loading and manipulating of large graphics and text files. This user's system needs to be fast enough to load the files quickly and more important, update the display responsively when changes are made to the design or layout of the publication.

The desktop publisher will likely need a Super VGA or a full-page monitor to preview what the publication will look like. The faster processor is required to display all of this material quickly. Also, 4–8MB (or more) of RAM will be required to hold the text and graphics files in memory for manipulation.

In addition, disk space requirements will be higher than they were for word processing because of the combination of several text and graphics files. Graphics files can consume a tremendous amount of space because they are bitmapped (one graphic can consume over 1MB of disk space). Traffic will be higher than for word processing because of the loading and saving of the intermediate text and graphics files that make up a publication.

Finally, a database application will likely require a fast processor to handle the demands normally associated with database manipulation. The more data stored and transactions processed, the greater the hardware demand. In the above example, the database user will likely need a fast processor, VGA graphics, a moderate amount of RAM, and a large quantity of disk space.

The network traffic from a database application depends on the amount of data that will be manipulated throughout the day. If a large number of reports are generated on the database or if update procedures are run at length, then a considerable load could be placed on the LAN. This load is then multiplied by each user running the database application and performing reports, and so on.

Determining the hardware combination that's right for you is not an exact science. The measure of adequate performance usually falls within a range and your goal should be to place somewhere within that range. In addition, meeting the high or low end is often a matter of money.

Beyond Hardware—General Tips for Speeding Up Windows

Once you are convinced that your hardware is sufficient for the job, there are a great many methods in software that can be used to speed up Windows. The rest of this chapter will cover those methods. This first section considers general methods you can use to tune up your Windows environment.

Add More RAM—at Least 4MB

Although this isn't a software method for speeding up Windows, it is the best hardware method available, and is relatively inexpensive.

Windows itself uses about 1MB of RAM, while other major applications use another megabyte at least. If you only have 2MB or less in your machine, Windows will very likely thrash around excessively as it moves temporary files to and from the network or local drive. This may result in running applications twice as slowly as compared to a machine with enough RAM. Adding the needed memory is probably the least expensive hardware upgrade you can make and it results in the best overall improvement in speed.

Use a Disk Cache and/or RAM Drive

This requires memory over and above that specified in the previous section, but can improve performance even further. In fact, using memory where a disk would normally be used can increase performance tremendously. SmartDrive version 4 comes with Windows 3.1 and can be used for disk caching (or one of several third-party disk cache programs can be used).

Also, Windows' RAMdrive program (or one of several third-party RAM drive programs) can be used to speed up Windows' use of temporary files. The TEMP environment variable determines the location in which temporary files are stored and can be set to point to the RAM drive. Later in this chapter we will discuss specifics for setting up a disk cache and a RAM drive.

Note that you cannot cache a network drive—this is already done by the file server. You can, however, cache local drives where you may have a copy of Windows or Windows applications stored.

Close Some Windows

Many Windows applications steal processor time while they are idle and running in the background. They may have background processes running or some other mechanism that grabs an indeterminate amount of your environment's speed. You can test this by loading a few applications in the background and timing a few procedures in your main application. Then time the same procedures with the background applications closed.

Avoid Background DOS Sessions

DOS sessions use processor time when they're running in the background. Of course, DOS applications don't normally run in background unless you've placed the appropriate parameter in the PIF file (see Figure 8.1, Execution: section) for the application (or _DEFAULT.PIF if there is no application-specific PIF). To

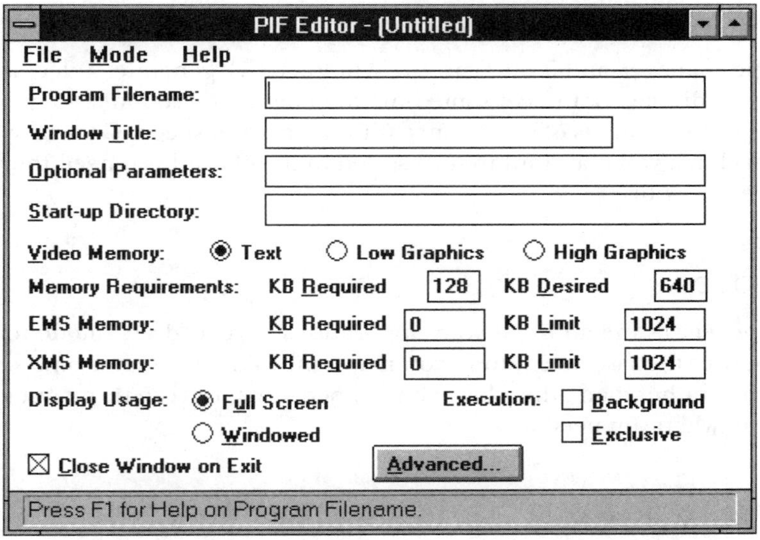

Figure 8.1 PIF Editor window.

check the Background Priority for a running DOS task, pull down the Control menu for the Window (or hit Alt-Space) and select Settings (see Figure 8.2). Check the Tasking Options Background Setting, and the Foreground Priority and Background Priority values. The former will show how much processor time is used while the application is in the foreground and the latter will show time used in the background. You may also want to use the "Detect Idle" PIF setting for background DOS sessions.

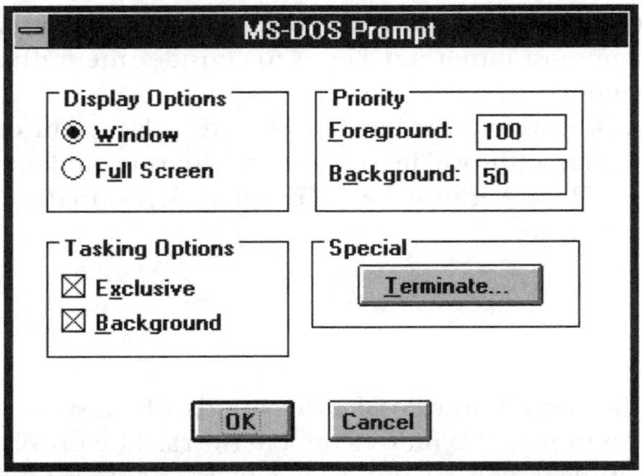

Figure 8.2 Background Tasking Option shown in Settings window.

Avoid Screen Font Scaler Software

Adobe Type Manager and TrueType (in Windows 3.1) generate scaled screen fonts for your display. Both take some time to generate these fonts, so you may want to weigh the benefits of appearance with the costs in speed. Generally, with a slower machine, you may want to turn scaled fonts off until you need them for appearance or layout.

Use Draft Mode

In the same vein as the above, if your applications have a "draft" mode for the screen that uses the fast system font, you may want to use it to save some screen painting time, rather than other slower bitmapped fonts. You can turn draft mode off for layout when you need it.

Maximize Your Window

If Windows must figure out which window is the recipient of mouse events (move, button up, and so on), it takes away some processor cycles. For example, if you have four different Windows on the screen at once, Windows must do a certain amount of processing when you operate the mouse to figure out which window it should tell, "The user just moved the mouse to coordinates 100,25 and pressed the left button." If you maximize your window, Windows doesn't have to worry about where to send those mouse events. This may result in a slight increase in performance (or sometimes not so slight).

Network Tuning

There are several network-specific steps you can take to improve the performance of Windows on the LAN. The most important step is to consider the traffic you will introduce by placing Windows on the network.

If you decide on a network (rather than local hard drive) placement of the Windows system files, realize that traffic will increase as users start up and operate in the Windows environment. This is because the .EXE and .DLL files in the user's personal directory take time to load.

Windows' Swap Files

The swap file is one of the largest hurdles in the minds of most network administrators when they go to install Windows on a network. The problem is that under 386 Enhanced mode, if you are not using a permanent swap file on a local drive, Windows slows down to a crawl when it initially loads because it must create a temporary swap file. However, this is really only an issue for

NetWare 2.x users. NetWare 3.x supports "sparse files" so this is not as significant a performance issue.

The reason a server-based swap file must be **temporary** rather than **permanent** is that NetWare cannot support permanent swap files on a server volume. To optimize its use of the permanent swap file, Windows controls the hard drive in which a permanent swap file resides at a very low level. (You should defragment your disk before creating a permanent swap file because the disk blocks it occupies must be contiguous.)

With temporary swap files, however, Windows does not control the server's hard drive at so low a level; therefore, NetWare can support a temporary swap file. A temporary swap file is created automatically when you start Windows and removed when you exit the program. However, be aware that when Windows creates the temporary swap file, the server, NetWare, allocates the necessary space, but it also zero-fills that space. This is a NetWare operating system security measure. This zero-fill time increases the load time for Windows significantly.

However, this swap file can be very useful if you don't have a lot of memory. Memory gets swapped to the file in a least-recently-used fashion which allows you to use more memory than you might otherwise be able to.

From an administrator's point of view, your basic options are as follows:

1. Use the local hard drive for a permanent swap file. If you have the local hard drive, this is probably the best option for the average setup. You gain the functional benefits of a swap file and the speed of a permanent one.

    This way, you can keep Windows on the LAN and do your management of it there, and still have the benefits of the local hard drive for the swap file. You create the swap file by using the SWAPFILE.EXE in Windows 3.0 or by using the Virtual Memory dialog box in the 386 Enhanced section of the Control Panel in Windows 3.1 (also, see Chapter 5 for details on creating a swap file).

2. Use the network for a temporary swap file. This option offers you the benefits of the swap file, but at the cost of additional network traffic and extended Windows load time. In fact, it could take as long as 30 seconds to a minute to load Windows with this option.

3. Use no swap file at all. This option offers you the benefits of quick loading at the cost of the benefits of a swap file. You can turn swapping off in Windows 3.0 by editing your SYSTEM.INI and changing the Paging= option to False. In Windows 3.1, use the Virtual Memory dialog box in the 386 Enhanced section of Control Panel (also, see Chapter 5 for details on disabling a swap file).

4. Use a RAM drive as a temporary swap file. This option lessens the bite of a temporary swap file by making it fast. The problem with this approach is that if you have enough memory for a swap file (usually 1–2MB), that memory would be better put to use by Windows itself!

Loading the Network Shell into High Memory

When you choose which NetWare NET shell file you want to use, you may want to consider speed. Although the shell files NETX, EMSNETX, and XMSNETX are fairly close in speed, the NETX shell that uses conventional memory is generally considered the faster of the three. This is because it doesn't have to worry about code pages as the EMS shell does, or about protected mode or XMS calls as the XMS shell does.

However, again you must weigh speed over capacity. If you need the conventional memory, you may want to use the EMS or XMS shell, or you may want to load the NETX file into high memory using DOS 5.0 (or later) or a third-party memory manager like QEMM. See Chapter 5 for the steps required to do this.

Since IPX.COM doesn't have EMS or XMS options, your only choice is to load it into the high memory area, if you want to save on conventional memory. Once again, you can do this if you have DOS 5.0 (or later) or a third-party memory manager like QEMM.

Increasing Performance When Using the XMS Shell

Many people set the 32-bit access option on in the Virtual Memory window (under 386 Enhanced from the Control Panel) to increase system performance (Figure 8.3, last option). If you have this option turned on, you can increase overall system performance when using the eXtended Memory Specification (XMS) NetWare shell, XMSNETX.EXE, by setting OverlappedIO to ON in the [386Enh] section of SYSTEM.INI.

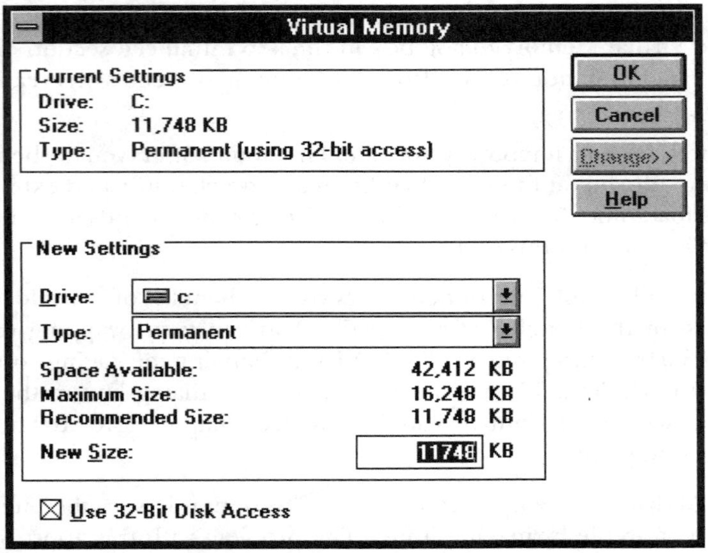

Figure 8.3 Virtual Memory window in the 386 Enhanced section of Control Panel.

Shell Configuration Parameters

For speed improvement, you might consider increasing the CACHE BUFFERS parameter in your NET.CFG file. The default is 5 (512 bytes) buffers that are used by the shell to cache network file read and write requests in local workstation memory. (This is similar to the way BUFFERS= works for files on local drives.) To prevent problems with files that could be accessed by multiple workstations, only two types of files will be cached in these cache buffers:

1. Files open for exclusive access, which cannot be accessed by other workstations on the network while open. Few files other than print queue files are opened in such a manner.

2. Files that are flagged shareable read-only. Flagging executable files and DLLs shareable read-only will allow them to be cached, and could speed up performance when loading applications.

It should be noted that recent v3.2x versions of NETX have had bugs in the cache buffer algorithm that could lead to corrupted files. So, while this problem appears to have been fixed in NETX v3.31, it may still be a good idea to sacrifice the performance gains by disabling CACHE BUFFERS with a CACHE BUFFERS = 0 statement in your NET.CFG file.

In addition to speed, you should ensure that the SHOW DOTS parameter is set to ON, which makes Windows applications show entries for the "." and ".." in File Open dialog boxes.

Also, FILE HANDLES = should be set to whatever value you have in CONFIG.SYS, which should be at least 60, according to Microsoft. See Chapter 5 for a full discussion of the SHOW DOTS and FILE HANDLES parameters.

Adjusting the Size of Data-Transfer Buffers

If you are having trouble running some applications on the network, you may need to adjust the size of the data-transfer buffers in Windows. Edit the SYSTEM.INI file and find the [386Enh] or [standard] section, depending on which Windows mode you are using, and change the NetHeapSize parameter. The default is 12(K) for the 386 Enhanced mode and 8 for Standard mode. Values are specified in kilobytes and are rounded up to the nearest 4K.

Disabling File-Handle Caching

Windows keeps 14 file handles open by default, so 30 users running Windows would require 420 file handles to be open at the server. If this is too many for your server and you do not want to or cannot modify the maximum file handles at the server (because of memory restrictions, for instance), you can change the maximum number of file handles Windows uses.

Edit SYSTEM.INI and change the CachedFileHandles parameter in the [boot] section. The default value is 14 and the minimum is 2. Windows may slow down if you decrease the number, so you must balance the trade-off between functionality and speed.

NetWare 2.x requires that you configure how many simultaneous open files are allowed, and has a limit of 1000 simultaneously open files.

Running Non-Windows Applications

If you are having trouble with a network-specific non-Windows application, you may need to edit the PIF for that application. One trick is to turn on the Exclusive option in the application's PIF (use the PIF editor for this). However, the program may not be running exclusively even when this parameter is turned on in the PIF because Windows is alerted every time a file is manipulated.

Microsoft suggests that you can prevent Windows from being alerted by changing the FileSysChange setting in SYSTEM.INI in the [386Enh] section. Change the parameter to read (or create a new line with the parameter in it if there isn't one there already) "FileSysChange=no."

If you have difficulty running a DOS session under Windows or are running an application that does not need to be exclusive but is still having trouble, you may need to adjust the TimerCriticalSection parameter in SYSTEM.INI. This parameter prevents task-switching for a specified time period (milliseconds), which ensures that only one DOS application at a time receives timer inputs.

To change TimerCriticalSection, edit the [386Enh] section of SYSTEM.INI and specify "TimerCriticalSection=x," where x is the amount of time you want to ensure a task has before it is switched from (a setting of 10,000 would mean that each task is given 10,000 milliseconds or 10 seconds). Setting this number to a high value may slow Windows' overall performance.

Other SYSTEM.INI Settings That Impact Performance

You may want to check these parameters if you are concerned about Windows performance on your network. For full details about the settings, see Chapter 5.

- network.drv (should be network.drv=netware.drv)
- Int28Filter
- AllVMsExclusive
- InDOSPolling
- INT28Critical
- NetAsynchFallback
- ReflectDosInt2A
- TokenRingSearch

DOS Applications

If you don't create a PIF file for a DOS application, Windows will run the application using the settings in a file named _DEFAULT.PIF, the PIF file. This file ships with Windows and is optimized to provide the broadest, safest coverage of DOS applications, which is probably the best way for Microsoft to ship it. However, this file is not optimized for speed (it's set up to handle an ill-behaved EGA application that [in 386 mode] may use EMS and XMS memory).

There are several steps you can take to speed up DOS-based applications. The main way is through the PIF file. As mentioned, if no specific PIF file is created for your application, the _DEFAULT PIF will be used. Therefore, you may decide you want to make a change to the _DEFAULT.PIF file which will affect all programs that don't have their own PIF. Change the settings in _DEFAULT.PIF with caution—you should make a copy of this file before any changes are made.

In this section, we'll show some settings for creating a generic, yet optimal, _DEFAULT.PIF file suitable for running most DOS applications. Obviously, the settings recommended won't work for every DOS application. However, they will work for most. After a review of the settings common to both Standard and 386 Enhanced-mode PIF files, we'll cover those settings specific to Standard-mode PIFs, the settings specific to 386 Enhanced-mode PIFs, and the advanced settings for 386 Enhanced-mode PIFs. Explanations of each setting value will be provided where appropriate. (For detailed information on what each PIF setting does, see Chapter 6.) Figures 8.4, 8.5, and 8.6 show the recommended settings implemented in the Standard and 386 Enhanced-mode PIF Editor windows.

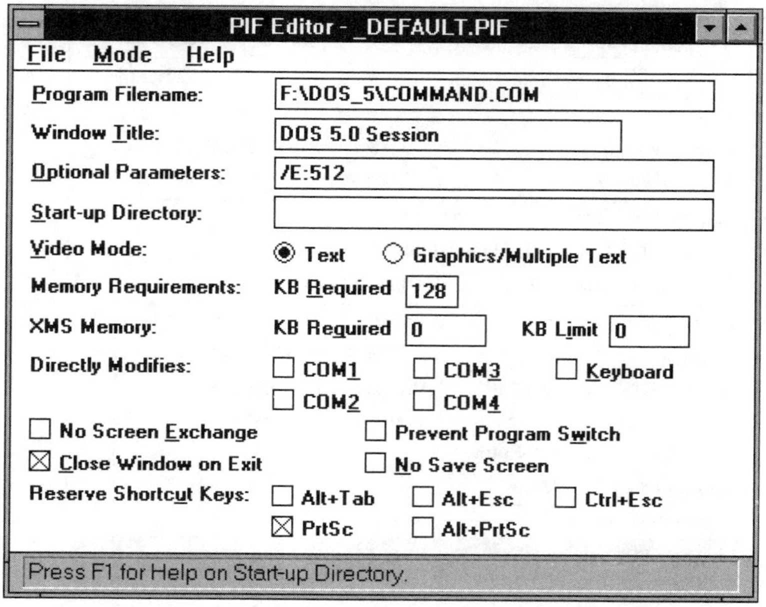

Figure 8.4 Recommended settings for _DEFAULT.PIF in Standard mode.

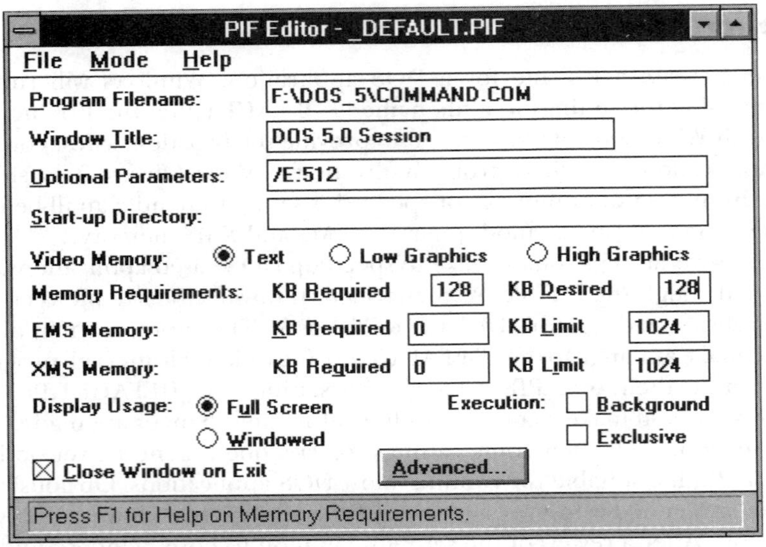

Figure 8.5 Recommended settings for _DEFAULT.PIF in 386 Enhanced mode.

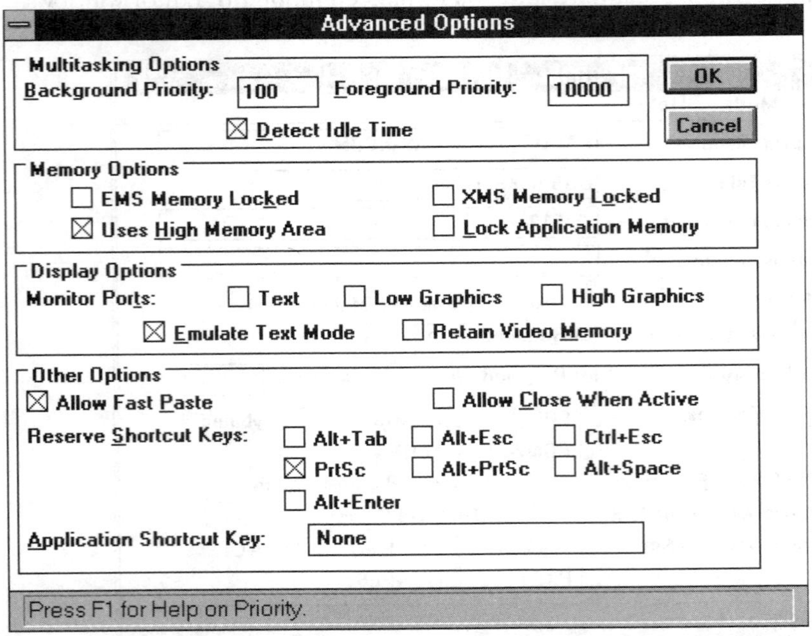

Figure 8.6 Recommended advanced settings for _DEFAULT.PIF in 386 Enhanced mode.

Standard- and Enhanced-mode PIF Editor Parameters

Here are some recommended _DEFAULT.PIF settings that apply to both 386 Enhanced mode and Standard mode.

Program Filename. Place "F:\DOS_5\COMMAND.COM" in this field, assuming F:\DOS_5 is the location of your COMMAND.COM file. Specify the full path to the file.

Window Title. "DOS Session." You may want to place the DOS version number in the string, as in "DOS 5.0 Session," but then you will need to make sure that each person's _DEFAULT.PIF file matches that individual's actual DOS version. This setting is really up to you.

Optional Parameters. /E:512. This reserves 512 bytes for the environment strings.

Start-up Directory. -blank-. If this field is not set, the Program Filename (in this case COMMAND.COM) will be run from the default directory. If you do not place anything in this field, you are assured that any file extension associations will work properly. Associations are entered in your WIN.INI file in the [Extensions] section and allow you to associate document types with the programs that operate on them.

For instance, you might have an association setup in the [Extensions] section of WIN.INI for files with a .WP extension to run WordPerfect. Then, when you click on a .WP file in File Manager, WordPerfect will be run with that file loaded.

Placing a value in the Startup directory field may prevent you from performing this association because Windows makes the Startup directory the default directory before the program is run. Your .WP file in File Manager may be in a different directory and may not be loaded. For PIF files specific to applications, this file extension association may be less of a concern, but you should still be aware of the potential pitfalls.

Standard-mode PIF Editor Parameters

Here are some recommended _DEFAULT.PIF settings that apply to Standard mode.

Video Mode. Text. This minimizes the amount of RAM required to start a DOS session. Also, most DOS sessions are text-based. Further, if the application needs to run in graphics mode, it can, provided there is enough memory left for the display.

Memory Requirements

• *KB Required: 128.* This is the Windows system default and should be sufficient for most DOS windows. If you generally start DOS applications that require much more memory, you may want to increase this figure.

XMS Memory

- *KB Required: 0*. This setting (and the next) is suggested because most DOS applications do not use XMS memory. For those that do, you may want to create application-specific PIF files. If most of your applications use XMS memory, you may want to set this figure to the minimum XMS you estimate is required.

- *KB Limit: 0*. See the explanation above for KB Required.

Directly Modifies. -blank-. This setting should be set off to give you the most freedom in Windows to move from application to application and to use keyboard and serial I/O ports. If you are having problems with device contention, you may need to set one of these options in an application-specific PIF. Since this is the default PIF, it should be off for these settings, in general.

No Screen Exchange. -blank-. For the default settings, you should allow yourself the option of sending screens to the Clipboard. It can be useful in many different situations.

Prevent Program Switch. -blank-. It is suggested for the default settings that this setting be left off.

Close Window on Exit. On. Unless you want to close the window yourself after exiting the application, this option should be turned On.

No Save Screen. -blank-. Leaving this option blank will ensure that your screen will be repainted if you switch away, then back to it.

Reserve Shortcut Keys. PrtSc. Windows defaults to reserving no shortcut keys. In the case of the PrintScreen key this means that when it is hit, Windows redirects the screen contents to the Clipboard rather than to a local printer. If you want DOS to operate as it normally does without Windows, reserve the PrintScreen key.

Enhanced-mode PIF Editor Parameters

Here are some recommended _DEFAULT.PIF settings that apply to 386 Enhanced mode.

Video Memory. Text. This is chosen because most DOS-based applications are text-based and the DOS session starts out as a text application.

Memory Requirements

- *KB Required: 128*. This is the Windows system default and should be sufficient for most DOS windows. If you generally start DOS applications that require much more memory, you may want to increase this figure.

- *KB Desired: 128*. If you generally start DOS applications that require much more memory, you may want to increase this figure.

EMS Memory

- *KB Required: 0.* If you need this type of memory, you should be using an application-specific PIF file, unless nearly all of your applications need some type of extended/expanded memory.

- *KB Limit: 1024.*

XMS Memory

- *KB Required: 0.*

- *KB Limit: 1024*

Display Usage. Full Screen. This is generally a faster setting for the application and it requires slightly less memory than when running in a window. However, the setting is also generally a matter of preference. If you really like most of your DOS sessions in windows then, by all means, set this field to Windowed.

Execution

- *Background: -blank-.*

- *Exclusive: -blank-.* This setting will turn Exclusive mode off for applications by default. Setting an application to Exclusive may interfere with background routines you may have running, like timed application launch programs or screen savers.

Close Window on Exit. On. Unless you want to close the window yourself after exiting the application, this option should be turned On.

Advanced PIF Options

Here are some recommended _DEFAULT.PIF settings that apply to advanced 386 Enhanced mode. Click the Advanced button on the basic 386 Enhanced-mode PIF screen to change the following options.

Multitasking Options

- *Background priority: 100.* This setting is ignored since the Background setting is off, but it could be used if you set it on.

- *Foreground priority: 10,000.* Since the application is running in the foreground and the default is not to have any background tasks, setting this value to 10,000 will guarantee you the fullest attention from the processor. This setting gives you the benefits of leaving the Exclusive flag off yet still having command of most of the processor's time.

- *Detect Idle Time: On.* If the system runs extremely slow for some reason, Windows may have judged an active application as idle, thus denying it most of its processing time. If you determine this to be the case (or to try to determine if it is) you can turn this option off.

Memory Options

- *EMS Memory Locked: -blank-.*

- *XMS Memory Locked: -blank-.*

- *Uses High Memory Area: On.*

- *Lock Application Memory: -blank-.*

Display Options

- *Monitor Ports (c): -blank-.* These settings are required with applications that: write text to the screen in a "misbehaved" manner, write CGA graphics that get garbled when switching to other applications, or use EGA graphics modes. Since most DOS sessions will not use applications with these problems, you should not need these settings on. If you do, you may consider application-specific PIF files.

- *Emulate Text Mode: On.* Generally, applications that display text do so faster with this setting turned on. Windows will now use faster video routines if applications make standard ROM BIOS video calls. Turn this setting off if you receive garbage characters or if the mouse no longer works.

- *Retain Video Memory: -blank-.* This setting is generally best for having the most available memory for other applications.

- *Allow Fast Paste: On.* This lets you paste at the fastest speed possible and is set for performance reasons.

- *Allow Close When Active: -blank-.* This field is left blank for functional reasons. In general, you should not allow Windows to close an application because files may be open that could become damaged or lost if not closed properly.

- *Reserve Shortcut Keys: PrtSc.* Windows defaults to reserving no shortcut keys. In the case of the PrintScreen key this means that when it is hit, Windows redirects the screen contents to the Clipboard rather than to a local printer. If you want DOS to operate as it normally does without Windows, reserve the PrintScreen key.

Application Shortcut

- *Key: None.* The main reason for this recommendation is that you should be careful which keys you want to make Windows sensitive to. For example, if you did use ALT-P, as in the above paragraph, you might be stepping on the toes of the application that is running.

  Let's say you are running an accounting program in a DOS session and the key sequence to print is ALT-P. Let's also say that you have setup a PIF for PCONSOLE and the Shortcut Key is ALT-P (and PCONSOLE is running in another window). When you are in the DOS session window where the accounting program is running and you press ALT-P to print, PCONSOLE will become the current application and you will have effectively locked yourself out of the print function for that accounting package (unless there is some other key sequence that you can use to print).

The moral here is to choose your Application Shortcut Keys very carefully, if at all. One of the problems with the Application Shortcut Keys is that the application must be running at the time. The Application Shortcut Key is simply a task-specific switch key.

There are other easy ways to perform this task. The ALT-TAB key switches among the currently running task (it also remembers the last task you ran; if you hit ALT-TAB, the last task you ran will pop up—you can use it to quickly toggle between applications).

Also, the CTRL-ESC sequence displays the Windows Task List which gives you a menu of the currently running tasks. You can use this as well, rather than setting an Application Shortcut Key.

Finally, you can define a Recorder Macro to run the program. The Recorder gives you more flexibility in how you start the program—you can have it start an application, size the window, and load a favorite file, if you wish. See Chapter 2 for an explanation of the Recorder.

Hard Disk

If you store any part of Windows on your local hard drive, such as Windows system files, Windows applications, or even permanent swap files, you want the operation of the drive to be as fast as possible. There are two techniques you can use to speed up the drive:

• Caching the local hard drive

• Interleave optimization and Defragmentation

Microsoft provides a local disk-caching program with Windows in the form of SmartDrive. With Windows 3.0, SmartDrive was SMARTDRV.SYS, a device driver you placed in your CONFIG.SYS file. Windows 3.1 includes SmartDrive 4.0, which has the following command-line options (this is the screen that is displayed when you type "SMARTDRV /?"):

```
4.0
Installs and configures the SMARTDrive diskcaching
utility.

smartdrv [[/E:elementsize] [/B:buffersize] [drive [+]|[]]
[size] [winsize]]...
```

drive letter	Specifies the letter of the disk drive to cache.
+	Enables write-behind caching for the specified drive.
-	Disables all caching for the specified drive.

size	Specifies the amount of XMS memory (KB) used by the cache.
winsize	Specifies the amount of XMS memory (KB) used in Windows.
/E:element size	Specifies the size of the cache elements (in bytes).
/B:buffer size	Specifies the size of the read buffer.
/C	Writes all write-behind information to the hard disk.
/R	Clears the contents of existing cache and restarts SMARTDrive.
/L	Loads SMARTDrive into low memory.

You can start the SMARTDrive utility by typing smartdrv at the MS-DOS prompt before you start Windows, or by placing a command line in your AUTOEXEC.BAT file. The SMARTDrive command line has the following form:

```
[drive:][path]smartdrv.exe [[drive[+|-]]...] [/E:ElementSize]
[InitCacheSize
[WinCacheSize]] [/B:BufferSize] [/C] [/R] [/L] [/Q] [/S] [/?]
```

Here's what those command-line parameters do:

Use this value	To do this
drive	Specify the letter of the disk drive for which you want to control caching. If you don't specify a drive letter, floppy disk drives are read-cached but not write-cached, hard disk drives are read- and write-cached, and CD-ROM and network drives are ignored. You can specify multiple disk drives.
path	Specify the location of the SMARTDRV.SYS file.
+|-	Enable (+) or disable (-) caching. Use the plus (+) and minus (-) signs to override the default settings. If you specify a drive letter without a plus or minus sign, read-caching is enabled and write-caching is disabled. If you specify a drive letter followed by a plus sign (+), read-and write-caching are enabled. If you specify a drive letter followed by a minus sign (-), read- and write-caching are disabled.
/E:ElementSize	Specify in bytes the amount of the cache SMARTDrive moves at a time. This must be greater than or equal to 1, and a power of 2. The default value is 8K.

InitCacheSize	Specify the size in kilobytes of the cache when SMARTDrive starts (before Windows is running). The size of the disk cache affects SMARTDrive's efficiency. In general, the larger the cache, the less often SMARTDrive needs to read information from the disk, which speeds up your system's performance. If you do not specify an InitCacheSize value, SMARTDrive sets the value according to how much memory your system has (see the table below this list).
WinCacheSize	Limit to what amount (in kilobytes) Windows can reduce the cache size. Windows reduces the size of the cache to recover memory for its own use. Windows and SMARTDrive then cooperate to provide optimum use of your system memory. When you quit Windows, Windows restores the cache to its normal size. The default value depends on how much available memory your system has (see the table below this list). If you specify a value for InitCacheSize that is smaller than the value specified for WinCacheSize, InitCacheSize is set to the same size as WinCacheSize.
/B:BufferSize	Specify the size of the read-ahead buffer. A read-ahead buffer is additional information that SMARTDrive reads when an application reads information from the hard disk. For example, if an application reads 512K of information from a file, SMARTDrive then reads BufferSize amount of information and saves it in memory. The next time the application is to read information from that file, it can read it from memory instead.
	The default size of the read-ahead buffer is 16K. Its value can be any multiple of ElementSize.
/C	Write all cached information from memory to the hard disk. SMARTDrive writes information from memory to the hard disk at times when other disk activity has slowed. You might use this option if you are going to turn off your computer and want to make sure all cached information has been written to the hard disk.
/R	Clear the contents of the existing cache and restart SMARTDrive.
/L	Prevent SMARTDrive from loading into upper memory blocks (UMBs), even if there are UMBs available. You can use this option if you are using MS-DOS version 5.0 or later and UMBs are enabled.

/Q	Prevent the display of SMARTDrive information on your screen.
/S	Display additional information about the status of SMARTDrive.
/?	Display on-line Help about the SMARTDrive command and options.

The following table shows what the default values for InitCacheSize and WinCacheSize will be, depending on the amount of available extended memory your computer has.

Extended Memory	InitCacheSize	WinCacheSize
Up to 1 MB	All extended memory	Zero (no caching)
Up to 2 MB	1 MB	256K
Up to 4 MB	1 MB	512K
Up to 6 MB	2 MB	1 MB
6 MB or more	2 MB	2 MB

Caution: Check that SMARTDrive has completed all write-caching before you turn off your computer. To make sure this has happened, type **smartdrv /c** at the MS-DOS prompt. After all disk activity has stopped, you can safely turn off your computer.

Using Double-Buffering

If your computer has a BIOS that is more than three years old, you probably need to use the double-buffering feature of SMARTDrive. Double-buffering provides compatibility for computers that cannot work with virtual memory. When you run the Windows Setup program, it places a SMARTDrive command line in your CONFIG.SYS file (or AUTOEXEC.BAT in Windows 3.1). If your computer requires double-buffering, this line is required. If your computer does not require double-buffering, you can remove the command line.

To determine if you can remove the SMARTDrive command:

1. In the Main group, choose the MS-DOS Prompt icon.

2. At the MS-DOS prompt, type **smartdrv**, then press ENTER. SMARTDrive displays information about your system.

3. Look at the column labeled "Buffering." If every line in this column reads "no," you can remove the device=smartdrv.exe /double_buffer command line from your CONFIG.SYS file (or AUTOEXEC.BAT in Windows 3.1).

The command line options for the new SMARTDRV.EXE are roughly compatible with the parameters to the old SMARTDRV.SYS; for example, you first specify the size of the cache in kilobytes, then the size the cache will be reduced to when Windows is loaded. For example, the line

```
SMARTDRV 1024 256
```

will load SmartDrive and reserve 1024 bytes for the disk cache. When Windows is loaded, SmartDrive shrinks the cache to 256 bytes and releases the rest for use by Windows.

OLD SMARTDRIVE VERSION CAVEATS

In order to use SmartDrive 3.0 or earlier, you must have an XMS memory driver. You can use HIMEM.SYS by running it from your CONFIG.SYS file or you can use a third-party driver like QEMM or 386MAX.

You must be careful if you are using an old version of SMARTDRV.SYS with an unusual disk partition—for example, one created with third-party disk utility like OnTrack Disk Manager or Storage Dimensions' SpeedStor. With versions of DOS prior to 4.01, SMARTDRV.SYS from Windows 3.0 (not 3.0a) could potentially destroy the FAT table on a disk drive larger that 32MB with one of these partitions so badly that only a low-level format would help.

The following products are known to have problems with SmartDrive in Windows 3.0 (with versions of DOS before 4.01, and disk drives larger than 32MB):

Golden Bow Systems	VFeature Deluxe
Ontrack Computer Systems	Disk Manager
Priam Systems	Innerspace
Storage Dimensions	SpeedStor

Double-Buffering

You can improve the performance of SMARTDRV.SYS (Windows 3.0) by turning off the double-buffering operation that is performed for SCSI and bus-mastering devices. Using the "/B-" option disables double-buffering and improves performance. If you have a SCSI or other bus-mastering device, you should leave double-buffering on because it is required. For some devices, you must turn double-buffering off in order for them to work (such as some Adaptec disk controller boards).

Third-party Disk-Caching Programs

There are alternatives to SmartDrive, such as PC-Kwik from Multisoft Corporation and HyperDisk from HyperWare, Inc., that have been shown in tests to be compatible with Windows and faster than SmartDrive. Make sure that the PC-Kwik version is higher than 3.55 for use with Windows 3.0 and higher.

If you do want to invest in a third-party disk-caching utility, first check to see that it is compatible with Windows. Then you should evaluate the performance benefits over SmartDrive.

Interleave Optimization and Defragmentation

If your hard drive is not set to the correct interleave, you could be suffering a performance penalty and not know it. The disk interleave is a measure of how data is stored on the drive.

In general, when DOS makes requests for data, disk controllers read sectors of data from the hard disk and return that data to DOS. The controller must wait until the CPU has processed the data before it can read the next sector . . . meanwhile, the disk is still spinning around. If the CPU is slow, the sector after the one read first may have already spun half-way around the platter. Now the controller must wait for it to come around again to read it.

To account for this timing problem, sector interleave was created. With this scheme, sectors are spaced apart on the disk. For example, with a 3 to 1 (3:1) interleave, sequential sectors are placed three apart. So, if you were reading sectors sequentially from the hard disk, the first would be 1, the second would be 4, the third would be 7, and so on.

This scheme worked well for slower machines, but as computers are becoming faster, interleaves are becoming smaller because the CPUs can keep up much better. With a 386 computer, you may be able to have a 1:1 interleave on your hard drive—this would mean each sector on the disk is sequential (first sector is sector 1, next is sector 2, and so on). Several utilities can check your disk interleave and determine if it is optimal.

These utilities, such as SpinRite from Gibson Research and Calibrate in the Norton Utilities, can detect and change your interleave to the optimal setting, without your needing to remove any files from the drive. They read data, format part of the disk to the new interleave, and write the data back.

Fragmentation occurs over time with any hard drive. As hard disks are read from and written to over time, files are often stored in seemingly random sectors on the disk. It takes the drive time to seek to one spot and read some of the file, then seek to some other spot and read more of the file, and so on. Defragmentation utilities read all of the parts of a file and write them back in a straight line on the drive, placing the parts of the file in sectors that are contiguous. This can dramatically improve the performance of your hard disk and, therefore, of Windows. Software like the Norton Utilities, PC Tools, and others will perform defragmentation on a drive.

Printing

Windows can be a slow environment in which to print, especially on a network, but with the right optimizations you can vastly improve the time it takes to print a file on the LAN.

> **Note:** If you are having problems printing, see Chapter 9, "Troubleshooting Windows on NetWare," or Chapter 6, "Setting Up Applications."

If you are printing large files, as is often the case with the graphics in Windows, make sure you have sufficient disk space. If you're getting low and ten people are all printing 2MB documents, you could have problems.

The following suggestions should improve your printing performance:

1. Don't use print manager for network printing. Print Manager is Windows' built-in print spooler. NetWare provides print spooling resources as a part of the network, so you don't want to slow down your print job by a factor of two by duplicating the services already provided to you.

   To turn off Print Manager, turn off the "Use Print Manager" option in the Printers dialog box from the Control Panel. Figure 8.7 shows this dialog box.

2. Use 150 dpi setting for text printed on laser printers. If certain users print mostly text, they can improve their printing performance by selecting 150 dpi rather than 300 dpi. Even when printing outlines and boxes, they are usually at least two pixels wide, so 150 dpi will not be as much of a problem. You can change to the 150 dpi setting by changing the Resolution setting in the Printer Setup dialog box, which is available by clicking on the Setup button in the Printers window, shown in Figure 8.7. Figure 8.8 shows a typical driver's Setup dialog box.

3. Get a parallel connection or a fast serial connection. This may seem obvious, but many networks have Postscript or other printers hooked up to a 9600 baud serial connection. Parallel connections can easily get four times the speed of this. If you are stuck with using a serial port, try to get the fastest port speed that you can on the printer. At the print server, you may need to install a buffered UART chip like the 16550AN to get maximum performance.

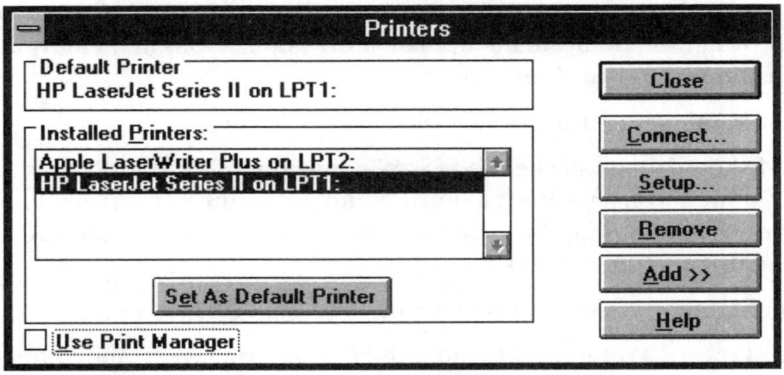

Figure 8.7 Control Panel Printers dialog box.

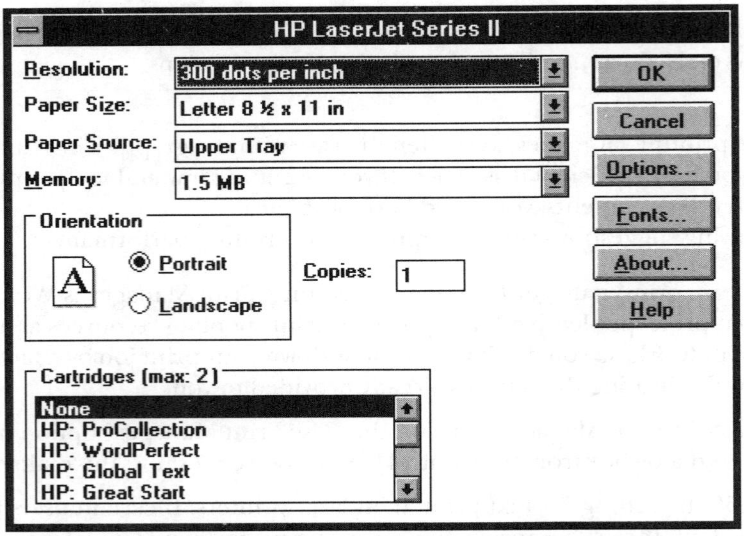

```
┌─────────────────────────────────────────────────────────┐
│ ▬              HP LaserJet Series II                     │
├─────────────────────────────────────────────────────────┤
│ Resolution:   [300 dots per inch        ▼]    ┌───────┐ │
│                                               │  OK   │ │
│ Paper Size:   [Letter 8 ½ x 11 in       ▼]    └───────┘ │
│                                               ┌───────┐ │
│ Paper Source: [Upper Tray               ▼]    │Cancel │ │
│                                               └───────┘ │
│ Memory:       [1.5 MB                   ▼]    ┌───────┐ │
│                                               │Options...│ │
│ ┌─Orientation──────────────┐                  └───────┘ │
│ │       ◉ Portrait   Copies: [1]            ┌───────┐ │
│ │ [A]                                         │Fonts...│ │
│ │       ○ Landscape                           └───────┘ │
│ └──────────────────────────┘                  ┌───────┐ │
│                                               │About..│ │
│                                               └───────┘ │
│                                               ┌───────┐ │
│ ┌─Cartridges (max: 2)──────────┐              │ Help  │ │
│ │ None                      ▲ │              └───────┘ │
│ │ HP: ProCollection          │                         │
│ │ HP: WordPerfect            │                         │
│ │ HP: Global Text            │                         │
│ │ HP: Great Start           ▼ │                         │
│ └──────────────────────────────┘                        │
└─────────────────────────────────────────────────────────┘
```

Figure 8.8 Print Driver Options for the HP LaserJet Series II.

RAM/Graphics Cards

Beyond disk I/O, graphics adapter speeds limit the performance of Windows significantly. For the fastest performance possible you may want to investigate new graphics accelerator cards that are coming on the market. Generally, once you have 4–8MB of RAM, Windows is about as fast as it will get until you start speeding up the graphics adapter.

The following suggestions pertain to RAM and Graphics adapter cards in your workstation:

1. Add lots of fast RAM.

   Windows eats RAM chips for breakfast. The more RAM you have, the better Windows will be able to manipulate the applications you have loaded. Generally 4–16MB of RAM is advisable. As stated above, once you reach a certain limit, you are no longer improving performance; however, you are improving your ability to manipulate more applications in memory at once which improves your functionality.

2. Use a RAM drive for temporary files.

   RAM should generally be used for Windows directly rather than as a RAM drive. But, if you have RAM to burn, Windows on the network, and no hard drives to place a swap file, you can direct your swap file to the RAM drive rather than to the network.

3. Font Scaling can slow graphics throughput somewhat.

   TrueType in Windows 3.1 and Adobe Type Manager (and others) for Windows perform on-the-fly font scaling to your screen to let you see exactly how printed output will look (and to improve the look of your documents on-screen).

These managers take time to calculate what they will display. You may want to turn these off and see how they affect your own setup. If you notice a significant difference, you may consider keeping them turned off until you need to perform layout-related tasks where you would need to see how something looked before it was printed.

4. Turn Monitor Ports setting off in the PIF file.

This setting can slow your graphics throughput as well, so if your programs don't need it, you should turn this setting off for your DOS-based applications. See Chapter 6 for a full discussion of PIF settings, or earlier in this chapter for the best PIF settings for performance.

3. Wallpaper.

Wallpaper can slow down your graphics throughput somewhat because Windows must keep track of it and redraw the wallpaper every time an object is moved. You should experiment with wallpaper on versus off and see if it improves your individual performance.

There are several aspects of Windows that many may consider "frivolous," but that nonetheless add to the charm and character of Windows and make it fun to use. Wallpaper is one such area. You will need to decide whether its presence has enough of an effect on performance to remove it. Generally, the fun and morale-boosting these extras generate are worth more than the slight performance penalty they impose.

5. Graphics accelerators.

As mentioned above, you should investigate faster graphics boards if you are concerned about the graphics throughput under Windows.

9 Troubleshooting Windows on NetWare

The purpose of this chapter is to help you find solutions to any problems you might have running Windows on NetWare. The remainder of the chapter includes discussions of problems followed by an explanation of how to solve each one.

Problem

When shelling to DOS under Word Perfect 5.1 or other DOS-based programs, Windows becomes extremely slow and sluggish, sometimes taking 10–60 seconds to print several characters.

Solution

In general, avoid shelling DOS while running an application in a DOS session. This tends to confuse Windows and its DOS memory management. It is generally best to switch back to the Program Manager and run another DOS session if memory permits.

Problem

There is an error when saving a file in Word Perfect for DOS 5.1. Using 3.02A IPX drivers for Racal-Interlan NI5210 and 3Com 3C507, saving a file under Word Perfect for DOS 5.1 resulted in the error "ERROR:0." Using 3.01E drivers worked okay.

Solution

NETX v3.22 had a bug that sometimes caused corruption in workstation cache buffers. Upgrade to a later version of NETX or set "Cache Buffers = 0" in

SHELL.CFG file. The Cache Buffer "sets how many 512-byte buffers the shell will use for local caching of non-shared, non-transaction tracked file. Increasing the number of cache buffers can speed up the process of sequential read/writes." The default Cache Buffers is 5, so you can experiment with this command and see if you can increase this from 0 to 1, 2, or 3 without any problems.

Problem

There are printing problems. Printing anything with binary data, such as anything that uses Adobe Type Manager or any graphics files from Windows on the network, results in reams of paper with one or two lines of random characters on each page.

Solution

The following steps have been shown to be effective in getting printing to work with Windows on NetWare:

1. In WIN.INI, a section called [ports] looks something like the following:

    ```
    [ports]
    ; A line with [filename].PRN followed by an equal sign
    causes
    ; [filename] to appear in the Control Panel's Printer Con
    figuration dialog
    ; box. A printer connected to [filename] directs its out
    put into this file.
    LPT1:=
    LPT2:=
    LPT3:=
    COM1:=9600,n,8,1
    COM2:=9600,n,8,1
    COM3:=9600,n,8,1
    COM4:=9600,n,8,1
    EPT:=
    FILE:=
    CAS=
    ```

    Add a line that looks like the following:

    ```
    LPT1.DOS=
    and/or
    LPT2.DOS=
      and/or
    LPT3.DOS=
    ```

    depending on the LPT ports you use, and use Control Panel/Printer setup to set your printer ports to the .DOS setting rather than the LPTx:= setting (choose the Configure... submenu rather than the Network... submenu to make this change).

    Changing the LPT1:= (or LPT2:= or LPT3:=) to LPTx.DOS=, makes Windows act as if it were printing to a file called LPT1.DOS. But, DOS won't let you save a file under the name of a device (LPT1 in this case), so it redirects the output to that device.

Windows uses DOS and ROM BIOS routines to write the output to the printer port rather than manipulate it directly. Actually, the .DOS could be .ABC, as long as it's three letters. The problem with this solution is that it slows print time because it's using higher-level routines.

2. Set CAPTURE to use no timeouts (/TI=0), no auto-endcap (/NA), no form feeds (/NFF), and no tab expansion (/NT).

3. Try disabling the Windows Print Manager.

4. PSERVER.NLM v1.21, that shipped with NetWare 3.11, has some bugs in printing large print jobs; you should upgrade to a later version of this utility.

Problem

While printing complex graphics to a laser printer attached to a network print queue through Windows, you get an error message about disk space being full.

Solution

If Print Manager is running, the spool file is probably on your local C: drive—check that you have enough local disk space. If you are printing directly to a network queue, NetWare spools the file on the SYS: volume of the server where the queue is located. Make sure there is enough space on the SYS: volume.

Also, your system administrator may have enabled disk space limitations for your account and you may have exceeded your allotted space. Check with the system administrator about this (if you ARE the system administrator, check SYSCON).

Finally, do a CAPTURE SHOW from DOS and see what the timeout value is for the port you are sending to. Anything less than 30 seconds is likely to cause printing problems with Windows.

Problem

When printing under Windows, the local LPT port keeps changing from being captured to a network print queue to printing locally.

Solution

It is very likely that some application is issuing an ENDCAP which sets the port back to local printing. You can test this by using the Control Panel/Printers utility or the Novell F6 popup utility to check how the printers are mapped before and after you print in a particular application and watch what happens.

Problem

Garbage characters are printed before or after the banner page of a print job.

Solution

If this happens, you are likely running extremely old NetWare drivers, and should update the NETWARE.DRV and VNETWARE.386 files.

Problem

Windows prints an unwanted banner page before each document (LST:NETWARE).

Solution

If this happens, it is likely that you are running extremely old NetWare drivers, and should update the NETWARE.DRV and VNETWARE.386 files.

However, if you are troubleshooting a printing problem and need to be sure of the status of your LPT ports while in Windows, shell to DOS and issue a "Capture SH" command at the DOS prompt. This will present a display similar to the following:

```
LPT1: Capturing data to server ROSE_286 queue TEST_QUEUE.
      User will not be notified after the files are printed.
      Capture Defaults:Enabled   Automatic Endcap:Disabled
      Banner :(None)             Form Feed      :No
      Copies :1                  Tabs           :No conversion
      Form   :0                  Timeout Count :Disabled
LPT2: Capturing Is Not Currently Active.
LPT3: Capturing Is Not Currently Active.
```

This will show you exactly how your three printer ports are being directed and where. In this case, LPT1 is redirected to TEST_QUEUE on server ROSE_286. No banner will be printed. You can change this Banner setting either by using the CAPTURE command and the No Banner (/NB) switch or by using a program that will change the capture settings for you in Windows.

Problem

Upgrading from NetWare 2.15 to 3.x produces printing problems, specifically extraneous characters/pages before or after a print job.

Solution

Make sure you have the most recent version of PSERVER.NLM. You may want to check PS121B.ZIP or other Print Server ZIP files.

Problem

RPRINTER won't work on a Windows workstation, freezes the workstation, or generates seemingly random UAEs in other running applications.

Solution

Currently there is no total solution to this. To run RPRINTER with Windows, you need the 3.22 or later shell and current IPX. You also need to run TBMI before running RPRINTER.

In addition, there is a new PSERVER.VAP and .NLM:

PSV120.ZIP Ver 1.20 PSERVER NLM for NetWare 3.10.
PS121B.ZIP Ver 1.21 PSERVER NLM for NetWare 3.11.
PSV121.ZIP Ver 1.20 PSERVER VAP for NetWare 2.x.

Try adding SPX ABORT TIMEOUT=1500 and IPX RETRY COUNT=100 to your SHELL.CFG file at the machine running PSERVER.EXE and the stations running RPRINTER.

You may also encounter jerky mouse movement when running RPRINTER because it "steals" processing time to print documents. At best there has been mixed luck getting all this to work.

You may want to investigate one of several third-party alternatives to RPRINTER from the following vendors:

Printer Assist from Fresh Technologies—800-497-4200
PS-Print from Brightwork—800-552-9876
LanSpool from Intel—916-351-2746
I-Queue! Server from Infinite Technologies—800-678-1097 or 410-363-1097

A 30-day trial version of I-Queue! Server is available on the diskette accompanying this book.

Problem

For Windows 3.0, NIC is running at IRQ 2/9 and you get occasional "Error reading network device" messages or unable to run Windows in Enhanced Mode.

Solution

This problem is relevant only to Windows 3.0. There is a file called VPICDA.386 provided by Novell that attempts to get around the interrupt problems associated with using IRQ 2/9. If you are running Windows 3.0, copy this file to your Windows system directory (usually \WINDOWS\SYSTEM) and change the "device=*vpicd" line in SYSTEM.INI (in the [386Enh] section) to "device=vpicda.386." If you're at IRQ 2, and that doesn't work, try a different IRQ.

If you are having this problem under Windows 3.1, DO NOT USE VPICDA.386. Instead, try different interrupt settings, or check with your network adapter vendor to see if a later driver is available.

Problem

NIC has shared RAM and Windows freezes; there are occasional driver errors, such as "Network Error on Server FS1: Error sending on network. Abort, Retry?" or will not run in Enhanced mode.

Solution

Windows is trying to use the memory your network card is mapping into the memory space between 640K and 1MB. You need to tell Windows not to use the memory space managed by your NIC. Add the following line to your SYSTEM.INI file (in the [386Enh] section):

```
EMMEXCLUDE=C800-CBFF
```

assuming that your NIC used 16K of RAM and the starting address is C800h. Some NICs have more than one area of shared RAM (for example, some RAM and some ROM—IBM TRN cards especially).

Additionally, some VGA cards (16 bit especially), have another problem in that they use the area between C4000 and C7FFF. Try adding the following EMMEXCLUDE line to SYSTEM.INI's [386 Enh] section:

```
EMMEXCLUDE=C400-C7FF
```

Also, if you have any memory managers like Microsoft's EMM386 or Quarterdeck's QEMM386, you will want to specifically exclude any shared RAM or ROM used by your NIC. For Microsoft's EMM386, for example, you could specify a CONFIG.SYS line something like:

```
device = c:\dos\emm386.exe noems x=c800-cfff
```

This would exclude the memory in the range of C800-CFFF. For Quarterdeck's QEMM386, the line would look like:

```
device = c:\qemm\qemm386.sys RAM EXCLUDE=C800-CFFF
```

Problem

Windows freezes when loading.

Solution

Try loading Windows with a command-line parameter of

```
/D:XSV (e.g., WIN /D:XSV).
```

Each of the letters following the /D: are equivalent to placing the following statements under the [386Enh] section header in SYSTEM.INI, one time only:

X EMMExclude=A000-EFFF
S SystemRomBreakpoint=OFF
V VirtualHDIrq=OFF

If Windows now works, use a process of elimination to determine which of the parameters was the key to your success.

WIN /D:X is most often the solution to these types of problems, which indicates that the shared RAM area used by your network adapter is not properly excluded from your memory manager or the Windows internal memory manager.

For Windows internal memory manager, you exclude this memory range with an EMMExclude=xxxx-xxxx statement under the [386Enh] section header of your SYSTEM.INI. If you are unsure of this range, use EMMExclude=A000-FFFF while troubleshooting. As an example, to exclude a 16KB range of memory at segment D000h, you would specify EMMExclude=D000-D3FF.

For the Microsoft EMM386.EXE memory manager, use a /X=xxxx-xxxx parameter to tell it what range of memory to exclude for your network card.

For the DR-DOS EMM386.SYS memory manager, use a /E=xxxx-xxxx parameter to tell it what range of memory to exclude for your network card.

Problem

Windows Setup hangs when loading.

Solution

Setup tries to determine your hardware setup and may get confused when doing so. You can use the /I switch (as in "SETUP /I") to tell Windows not to try to determine your hardware setup.

Also, Windows uses I/O address 2E0 to determine whether you have an IBM 8514 video adapter. Make sure your network adapter does not use this I/O address.

Problem

Windows freezes when loading.

Solution

Some PCs treat the COM ports as a "family." If there is a serial mouse on COM1 (using interrupt 4) and a network adapter is set to interrupt 3, it may have an interrupt conflict, depending on how the PC treats the interrupts. You may want to change the interrupt on the network adapter to see if the problem improves. If you must use an interrupt normally associated with a COM port, like interrupt 3 or 4, you may need to disable the serial ports in the BIOS setup to get Windows to work properly.

Problem

The mouse is set to COM1/IRQ4, the network board is set to IRQ3, and Windows freezes when loading.

Solution

Many network adapters ship defaulting to interrupt 3 which can create a problem with Windows when you have a serial mouse. The Microsoft Mouse driver looks at COM4, then COM3, then COM2, then COM1, to locate the serial mouse.

You may try to use the COM#IRQ= setting in the SYSTEM.INI to disable the ports as far as Windows is concerned. The setting "COM4Irq= −1" disables the port and may make the mouse driver NOT search it for a possible mouse.

Generally, though, the problem is that when you have a mouse on a serial port and a NIC on either IRQ 4 or 3, the mouse driver has blown the network connection by the time it finds the mouse, since it's generating an interrupt for COM4 at IRQ 3 and COM3 at IRQ 4 (shared with COM2 and COM1). For future reference, bus mice are generally easier to work with because of this contention. Bus mice rely on a card that plugs into an expansion slot on your computer. The card can be set to a specific IRQ—for example, 5—thus avoiding a conflict with your network card.

Problem

Windows freezes when loading.

Solution

If you are using the XMSNETx or EMSNETx shells, you may experience a memory allocation problem with Windows 3.0, which generally occurs as Windows hanging when loading. Microsoft corrected some of the memory allocation errors in versions of Windows after 3.0 (such as 3.0a and 3.1), although it is still recommended that you do not use EMSNETx with Windows (the NETWORKS.WRI file that comes with Windows 3.1 states that EMSNETx is not supported with Windows 3.1).

You could also use the conventional NETx shell file to get around the problem. If you are concerned about conventional memory, you can load NETx into high memory using QEMM or some other memory management utility.

Problem

There are errors running Windows or during Setup when NIC is set to an I/O address of 2E0h.

Solution

Windows uses this address in Setup to find certain IBM video adapters and may become confused if it finds your network adapter there. You can either change the I/O address on your network adapter or run setup with the /I parameter (as in "Setup /I"), which tells Setup not to try to identify your video type. However, it is generally considered best to change your I/O address to something different because Windows uses 2E0h as the I/O address for COM4, so it should be disabled in SYSTEM.INI.

Problem

There are SHARE errors or other strange Windows freezing errors.

Solution

If you are loading ANSI.SYS or SHARE.EXE, try removing them. Under DOS 4.0 (and above), these seem to cause some problems. Note that DOS 4.01, and some versions of DOS (notably an IBM DOS 4.01 that identifies itself as 4.00) load SHARE.EXE automatically if you have a large (greater than 32MB) driver. You should rename the SHARE.EXE file to something else so it doesn't get loaded.

Problem

DOS Applications under Windows will not work or function improperly.

Solution

Rename WIN.INI to WIN.SAV and try loading Windows, then the DOS Apps that had problems. If they work, there is some garbage in the WIN.INI file, such as ASCII codes that must be removed.

Problem

For the following DOS commands inside a Windows DOS shell the following responses are received:

```
COPY file1 file2
   Path not found  file1
TYPE filename
   Path not found  filename
EDLIN filename
   No room in directory for file
```

Solution

These commands all work fine in a normal Windows/NetWare setup. Re-run Setup and ensure that NetWare is selected as the network type. Also, try removing ANSI.SYS and SHARE.EXE from the CONFIG.SYS file.

Some bus-mastering boards, such as Thomas Conrad's token-ring boards, require an extra TSR called BUFFER.COM to be loaded to ensure that there is buffer space in low memory when a memory manager (such as Windows) is operating. You can download this file from Thomas Conrad's support BBS.

Problem

Windows appears to start running when loaded, but then clears the screen and jumps to the DOS prompt.

Solution

Sometimes if the TEMP variable is not set and no permanent swap file is defined, this can happen, especially when there is not enough space in the default directory to create the temporary swap file. Try setting TEMP to a temporary directory on your hard disk (such as "SET TEMP=C:\TEMP").

Problem

Some Ethernet cards won't work with the MAP ROOT command.

Solution

Some old Western Digital Ethercard Plus boards and drivers and Everex ethernet boards and drivers would not work correctly with the MAP ROOT command. If you have these products, you should contact the manufacturers for updated drivers.

Problem

Windows conflicts with SMC Arcnet NICS and SMC Turbo Drivers.

Solution

There are known problems with Windows running on NetWare using older SMC Turbo drivers with SMC Arcnet network adapter boards. You should contact SMC for updated Turbo II drivers if you have this hardware.

Problem

There are errors running Windows in Enhanced mode on the network.

Solution

Some general suggestions and procedures that have worked are:

1. Quarterdeck's QEMM386 seems to work well with Windows.

2. Set Token Ring cards (and possibly other boards) to occupy a range between C000-CFFF and D000-DFFF.

3. Prevent QEMM386 from using this space by using the RAM parameter in CONFIG.SYS.

4. Prevent Windows from using this space by using the EMMEXCLUDE parameter in SYSTEM.INI.

5. Provide the page frame space explicitly by using the FR parameter in QEMM386.

The following RAM addresses are generally used in the following situations:

16-bit VGA cards	C400-C7FF
IBM Token Ring Card ROM 8K	CC00-CDFF
IBM Token Ring Card Shared RAM 16K	D800-DBFF

Problem

Windows 386 Enhanced Mode is extremely slow on the network.

Solution

Apart from the suggestions in Chapter 8, you may want to set Paging=False in the SYSTEM.INI file under the [386Enh] section. This will disable temporary swap files and, by some user reports, it could decrease Windows' loading time sixfold. There are, however, some sacrifices, such as the benefits gained from swap files and the way Windows performs its memory allocation, which changes to a less-optimal configuration.

Generally, when you have 10MB or more of local RAM, you may also want to turn paging off, as this will improve local performance as well as decrease network traffic for everyone.

Problem

The message "A file necessary to run in 386 Enhanced mode could not be found: vnetware.386. Run Setup." appears when running in 386 Enhanced mode.

Solution

Run Windows Setup and reselect the network as Novell. Setup should help you copy vnetware.386 to the \WINDOWS\SYSTEM directory. This file is also located in the WINUPx.ZIP file available from Novell (currently WINUP7.ZIP). You can copy the file manually, if you prefer.

Problem

Loading Windows in Enhanced mode produces the message "VIPX.386 could not load since a proper version of IPX was not in memory."

Solution

Try reinstalling Windows. If Windows is installed with the wrong (or no) network shells, it sometimes refuses to change its notion of what's really there.

Also, verify that you really are running the latest shells. It's quite common to find another copy of IPX somewhere on your hard disk that is being used rather than the one you think. Check your DOS PATH.

Keep in mind that VIPX.386 requires IPX v3.10 or IPXODI v1.20.

Problem

Windows hangs when loading in 386 Enhanced mode on the network right after the Windows logo screen clears.

Solution

Make sure you wait at least five minutes, since Windows is trying to create a temporary swap file on the file server at this point. If you want to eliminate the delay, you can change SYSTEM.INI in the [386Enh] section to "Paging=False" to disable use of a temporary swap file, although this can create other problems, such as being unable to load several programs at once. See Chapter 5 for a full discussion of the Paging and other Enhanced mode options.

Problem

Windows runs sluggishly or freezes in Enhanced Mode running on the network with 2MB installed.

Solution

Add at least one more MB of RAM. Windows needs a fair amount of memory to function smoothly, especially on the network.

Problem

There is not enough memory to start Windows in Standard or Enhanced modes.

Solution

There's not much more you can do here: Add more RAM to the workstation or use the conventional or expanded memory shell.

Problem

You cannot run Windows on a non-dedicated NetWare 2.x file server.

Solution

Because NetWare non-dedicated file servers run in protected mode (and switch back to real mode), you generally cannot run any programs that use protected mode, as Windows does in Standard or Enhanced modes. You may be able to run Windows 3.0 in Real mode, but it's generally considered risky. Also, you will usually not be able to load programs high with non-dedicated servers because NetWare manages all of extended memory.

Problem

NWPOPUP.EXE doesn't pop up when it receives a broadcast message until you run a DOS application from Windows or specifically RUN the program from the

Program Manager. Or, NWPOPUP doesn't pop up when you're IN a DOS program, even though it's in the Load= line in WIN.INI.

Solution

The NWPOPUP.EXE that was included on older Windows distribution disks will not work properly. Make sure you have the latest version from Novell. Also, check to make sure that you don't have an older version of NWPOPUP.EXE in a different directory.

Problem

When installing Windows on a NetWare 2.1x network, Windows says the netware software version needs to be updated.

Solution

Install the latest NetWare workstation shells—Windows and the NetWare drivers check what version of the NetWare shells you have running. If they are too old, Windows will not run properly.

Problem

Windows drops to DOS when loading on an EISA machine when loading IPX into high memory (using QEMM386).

Solution

Many bus-mastering network cards have trouble when IPX is loaded in an unusual place because the relationship between the logical addresses seen by the driver linked to IPX and the physical addresses used by the hardware is no longer one-to-one. Check with the NIC manufacturer to see if they have a drive which can live with being loaded high.

Problem

When running Windows on a diskless workstation with DOS 5.0, Windows can't access the WINA20.386 file which you need with DOS 5.

Solution

To your CONFIG.SYS file try adding:

```
SWITCHES=/W
```

To the [386Enh] section of Windows SYSTEM.INI add:

```
DEVICE=[drive:][path]\WINA20.386
```

Also, you may need to run RPLFIX against the boot image file, especially if you have DOS 5. RPLFIX is in the DOSUPx.ZIP file (currently DOSUP6.ZIP). Consult Novell documentation for details.

Problem

Network adapters, such as TRX-NET, have a limited amount (4) of configuration options (you can display these by typing "IPX /d"). With only four options, you may not be able to find a non-conflicting setup.

Solution

Try using the ODI drivers, as they will let you use any configuration of RAM and I/O addresses and interrupts that the card can use. Also, a program called JUMPERS.EXE may be useful in changing IPX settings.

Problem

There is confusion over whether to use TBMI or TBMI2.

Solution

TBMI2 should be used when running Windows 3.1 in Standard mode. VIPX.386 should be used with Windows in Enhanced mode. TBMI and TASKID should be used with Windows 3.0 in Real or Standard mode.

Problem

Running NWTOOLS, either by loading it from WIN.INI or running it from the Program Manager, produces UAE errors.

Solution

Make sure that you have the updated copies of VNETWARE.386, NETWARE.DRV, VNETWARE.386, and NWPOPUP.EXE in your Windows\SYSTEM directory, and that older versions of these drivers are not also located in the Windows directory. Delete the older versions of these drivers.

Problem

The SHGEN program searches the A: and B: drives in an endless loop.

Solution

When you set up for Windows you will very likely have to regenerate your network shells. The WSGEN program is the most current for generating shells, but SHGEN (current through NetWare 2.15) can be used if you have a new IPX.OBJ. When SHGEN runs, it looks to see if it is either:

a) running on a floppy and the volume label is SHGEN-1 or

b) running on a hard drive and there is a SHGEN-1 directory below the current directory (there may also be LAN_DRV_.??? directories below the default directories. These contain additional driver files).

If the program does not find either of these cases, it can get stuck in a loop looking for them.

Either place all of your SHGEN files on a floppy labeled SHGEN-1 and run SHGEN.EXE from there, or create a directory called \NETWARE and copy the files from the SHGEN-1 floppy into the \NETWARE\SHGEN-1 directory. You should also copy SHGEN.EXE from \NETWARE\SHGEN-1 to \NETWARE and run SHGEN.EXE from the \NETWARE directory. (If you have drivers you need to link on the LAN_DRV_.??? diskettes and you are installing on a hard drive, make directories below \NETWARE for these as well. For instance, a floppy labeled LAN_DRV_.001 would have its files copied into \NETWARE\LAN_DRV_.001.)

Problem

Novell Menu System displays "Cannot find beginning of menu file" error message when exiting Windows.

Solution

Windows expects to be the only menu system in use. The Novell Menu system can be used, however, if the MENU utility and its overlay files are copied to a local drive and run from there. There are also several third-party menu utilities that will work with Windows.

Problem

EMS memory error messages are being displayed.

Solution

It's most likely not the fault of the shell. The EMS NetWare Shell (EMSNETX and EMSNET4 and EMSNET3) was written to strictly conform to the LIM EMS 4.0 specification. The EMS shell passes through any errors that are generated from the EMS manager. The problem probably resides in the EMS memory manager. Make sure it's the latest version and that it fully supports the LIM EMS 4.0 specification.

Problem

Setup displays the error "Cannot create WIN.COM."

Solution

Often this error is generated when SETUP is run with the /N option to copy network files to a workstation, but the files on the LAN have not yet been uncompressed. Use the EXPAND program (procedure is described in Chapter 5) to decompress the files and try SETUP /N again.

Problem

Error is displayed when Windows loads stating that the shell version is incorrect.

Solution

Windows takes advantage of the facilities Novell wrote into the later versions of the shell files. Many people will have to regenerate their IPX file and use a new NET file to get Windows working properly.

Problem

Windows can't find your Group (*.GRP) files.

Solution

Make sure your drive mappings are consistent. If you map F: to SYS:APPS\WIN-DOWS today but F: is mapped somewhere else tomorrow, Windows may get confused about where files should be stored, especially when different servers or volumes are mapped to the same drive letter.

Problem

Group files are corrupted.

Solution

This seems to be caused by Windows at certain times. The only known way to restore the group files is to delete the corrupted ones and either restore good ones from archive/backup or rebuild them.

Problem

There are problems receiving Broadcast Messages while in windows. They are stacked up in DOS when you exit windows. The Load=nwpopup.exe is the first line of the first section in the WIN.INI file.

Solution

First, make sure the Windows Control Panel Network dialog box shows that Broadcast Messages are Enabled.

If this still does not work, you may have a corrupted WIN.INI file. If there is a user on the network who can receive broadcast messages, make a backup of your WIN.INI, then copy that user's WIN.INI file into your directory area. If that clears up the problem, examine the two WIN.INI files to determine the difference. If they are seemingly identical, it may be control characters (such as Tabs) embedded in the WIN.INI file which can confuse Windows (or other applications) at times.

Also, check to make sure you have the latest versions of the following files: NWPOPUP.EXE, NETWARE.DRV, VNETWARE.386, VIPX.386.

Problem

There is difficulty loading NETBIOS in a DOS session.

Solution

NETBIOS should be loaded after the NetWare shell and before Windows.

Problem

Is there any way to make the shell use less memory and make this memory available for Windows?

Solution

Since Windows takes memory from all sources to meet its needs, there is no way to make the NetWare shell give Windows more memory. By selecting between regular load, load high, and EMS/XMS shells, you can control what type of memory it takes from Windows.

XMSNET does not work with DOS 5.0 loaded high, but on most machines it will work with Windows. If you have DOS 5.0, optimum setup is to have 5.0 load IPX and/or NETX high. The performance is much better than with the EMSNETX or XMSNETX option.

Problem

You are having trouble running Windows on a diskless workstation with EMM386.EXE as the memory manager. However, when you start Windows, it looks for EMM386.EXE on the boot drive. Is there any way to tell Windows to look elsewhere for the EMM386.EXE driver? Does Windows even need this file?

Solution

Yes, Windows in Enhanced mode does need to locate EMM386.EXE if it has been loaded.

You can use the /Y=path parameter when loading EMM386 to tell Windows where to later find EMM386.EXE. This is documented in the README.TXT file included with DOS 5.

Problem

There is confusion over whether to load NETBIOS TSR.

Solution

NetBIOS is rarely used on a Novell LAN except for those applications that MUST have it. Your application's documentation should state explicitly whether it needs NETBIOS loaded.

Problem

Windows once printed with NetWare correctly, but now prints pages and pages of garbage characters before or after the print job.

Solution

If things once worked but now do not, then you have to determine what has happened to cause the problem.

First, examine what you have done since the network printed correctly. Any system configuration changes or additions could have played a role. Also, consider what changes have been made to the Windows setup, such as different drivers, CAPTURE settings, and so on. Are there any new applications that won't print while others will?

Sometimes NetWare queues can become corrupted. If this queue is not working but others are, you may suspect the queue even more. You can delete the print queue (and server if you have one running), then run BINDFIX and recreate the queue (and server, if applicable) again.

Problem

There is strange Windows behavior that seemingly indicates a connection loss, such as in the following circumstances:

• You map a search drive for a non-Windows application and the map fails. If you execute a map command that specifies the server name, the command executes successfully.

- SYSCON will not execute successfully, but all of your drive mappings are intact as is the DOS path. Applications can be run from their own directories.

- WHOAMI says you are still attached to the server, but when you log out, the message "UNABLE TO GET CONNECTION INFORMATION 8801" is returned.

Let's assume you have already tried some of the basic procedures, like adding an EMMExclude line to SYSTEM.INI and using TBMI where appropriate.

Solution

Sometimes, older versions of the XMSNETX and EMSNETX have been known to cause some intermittently strange behavior. There have been some issues where Windows, your memory manager, and XMS/EMSnetx have problems. Try using NETX to see if this helps any (you can load it high in DOS 5 to save memory if you like).

Also, corrupted or old version LOGIN.EXE files can cause problems. Ensure you have a good, recent version (there is a copy in \LOGIN and \PUBLIC—you might want to compare them to see if they are identical).

Problem

When generating a new Windows-compatible shell with SHGEN, one or several of the following messages are displayed:

```
"An error occurred while linking IPX. Error = 9"
"An error occurred while linking IPX. Error = 10"
"Fatal error 10"
```

Solution

Error 9 means SHGEN could not find a file it needed. Make sure you copy the new IPX.OBJ to the SHGEN-1 diskette or into the SHGEN-1 directory if you are generating shells on a hard drive.

Also, make sure that you have enough space on the hard/diskette drive. SHGEN or WSGEN need to write out the IPX file and it may not have room, especially if you are generating the shells from a floppy.

Problem

Windows' temporary swap file WIN386.SWP gets created on the network (each time you run Windows) and you want to create it on the local drive or not at all.

Solution

One way to change this file's location under Windows 3.0 is to run Swapfile from your local Windows directory (type "Win /r swapfile"). Delete the swap file and create another permanent swap file on the local drive. Since Windows 3.0 can become "confused" about the swap file location sometimes, this procedure has been known to help. For Windows 3.1, simply use the Virtual Memory option from the 386 Enhanced section of Control Panel.

If you want to eliminate the swap file completely, you can change SYSTEM.INI in the [386Enh] section to "Paging=False" to disable use of a temporary swap file, although this can create other problems, such as being unable to load several programs at once. See Chapter 5 for a full discussion of the Paging and other Enhanced-mode options.

Problem

When you map a driver to a server's volume in DOS with the MAP command, you see the full path specified (as in F:\USER\GEORGE). In Windows, however, when you point to the F drive in File Manager, for example, your path is ignored and all you see is the root of drive F. How do you get Windows to default to the path you set rather than to the root?

Solution

Use NetWare's MAP ROOT command to set up a "fake root." For example, when you type

```
MAP ROOT F:=SYS:USER\GEORGE
```

the F drive is mapped to SYS:USER\GEORGE as a root. This fools DOS into thinking that you are currently at the root of the directory tree for that drive. For example, when you type "F:<Enter>" to change to the drive, and do a directory search (DIR), you will see the contents of the \USER\GEORGE . If you have your prompt set to PG, however, you will see that DOS thinks you are at the root of the directory tree.

The whole point is that when you run Windows, the F: drive will appear in a file manipulation dialog box (such as File Open from any application) with your full path of \USER\GEORGE. That way, you don't have to go through the tiresome process of selecting the USER subdirectory, then the GEORGE subdirectory every time you want to manipulate a file.

> **Note:** Keep in mind that this happens with search drives as well, so you may need to MAP ROOT your search drives. In addition, you must have versions of NetWare utilities that support the new MAP ROOT drives. See Chapter 5 for full details on Windows installation on NetWare.

Problem

When loading Windows with no Netware Shell, DOS environment variables that existed before Windows was loaded (such as COMSPEC, PATH, PROMPT, and so on) are inherited by a DOS session under Windows; but when the shell is loaded, these variables are lost.

Solution

Run SETUP from DOS and the Network option is set to a Novell LAN. If Windows doesn't know you are running on a Novell network, this type of error can occur.

Problem

When using Word for Windows, files that are saved to the network cannot be loaded at a later time. Also, error messages are displayed stating that the file is not accessible or the path is incorrect, yet files saved to a local hard disk load fine.

Solution

After making sure you have the correct rights to the directory area in question, add the following line in the [Microsoft Word 2.0] section of your WIN.INI:

```
NovellNet=Yes
```

Problem

You cannot use input redirection in Standard mode.

Solution

This does not work in Standard mode, although it does with Enhanced mode. Input redirection allows you to pipe text to a DOS program that requires standard DOS input. For instance, if the file Y.DAT contained a Y character and a carriage return, and you typed "del *.* < Y," when DOS asked the question "Are you sure? (Y/N)," it would use the contents of the Y file for input.

> **Note:** This is only relevant to Windows 3.0.

Problem

Windows will not run for more than a few minutes with the NetBIOS shell file loaded—the user is dumped back to DOS. However, Windows works fine without the NetBIOS shell.

Solution

NetBIOS shell versions up to 3.01 have problems running with Windows, such as the "drop to DOS" phenomenon and even erasing files on the local hard disk. You should have NetBIOS version 3.10 or later to work with Windows.

Problem

VIPX generates an error message when loading Windows. The note message says that VIPX.386 cannot be run because TBMI is loaded.

Solution

VIPX.386 (the virtual IPX driver for NetWare 386 Enhanced mode) was meant as a replacement for TBMI (the Task-Switched Buffer Manager for IPX-SPX), so you should remove TBMI (and TASKID) from your batch files if you are still using it and have VIPX installed. TBMI2 should still be used for Windows 3.1 Standard mode (TASKID is not needed), however, and TBMI should still be used for Windows 3.0 in Real or Standard mode.

Problem

MAP ROOT works at the DOS level, but File Manager freezes when displaying the directory associated with a MAP ROOT drive.

Solution

Several older IPX drivers, such as those from SMC, have been known to cause this. Make sure you have the latest IPX file.

Problem

Running Windows results in 'Network Error on Server ABC: Error sending on network' messages.

Solution

Make sure that you have valid VNETWARE.386 and VIPX.386 drivers in the \WINDOWS\SYSTEM directory, that they are the latest version, and that there is no asterisk (*) in front of their names in the SYSTEM.INI file on the "network=" line (in the [386Enh] section).

Problem

Running NetWare-compatible (DOS-based) software under Windows that uses IPX causes Unrecoverable Application Errors (UAEs) in Windows 3.0 and General Protection Faults in Windows 3.1.

Solution

Make sure you are using VIPX.386 for 386 Enhanced mode or TBMI if you are using Standard mode (TBMI2 for Windows 3.1).

Problem

Windows will not start in Enhanced mode on the network, but it will start in Standard mode with the /S switch.

Solution

Make sure you have at least 2MB of RAM to run Enhanced mode. The realistic baseline for Windows, however, is about 4MB of RAM.

Problem

Programs running in a DOS session run out of memory when they try to access extended or expanded memory.

Solution

Windows uses this memory too, so you may be out of luck if you don't have any more memory available. Try to reduce the amount of memory being used by closing non-essential applications. Also, programs like screen savers and background application launchers take up memory. Therefore, you may have to temporarily remove these.

Generally, you'll want to have at least 4MB of RAM as a minimum when running Windows. (2MB should work, but it's very slow, considering the constant swapping that inevitably takes place.)

Problem

There are problems running Windows with versions of QEMM and 386MAX.

Solution

Make sure you have versions of QEMM or 386MAX recent enough to include their Windows 3.x extensions (this should be version 5.12 or higher for both packages— QEMM was at 6.02 as of this writing and functioned very well under Windows according to user reports).

Problem

When running DOS applications under Windows, the drive mapping changes made from within one DOS application alter the drive mappings in another.

Solution

By default, the NWShareHandles parameter in the [NetWare] section of SYSTEM.INI is set to FALSE, meaning that each DOS session gets its own separate set of drive mappings. Changing this parameter to TRUE will create the situation in the Problem above, which is how some users may want their system configured.

If you do leave the NWShareHandles parameter set to FALSE, each separate DOS session will have its own set of drive mappings. Furthermore, this will consume memory from the DMP 1 memory pool on the file server, which is a limited resource on NetWare 2.x file servers. In fact, if you have too many users running multiple DOS sessions, each with a separate set of drive mappings, you can exceed the limits of the memory pool and, in some cases, bring down the file server. This memory pool in NetWare 3.x, however, is dynamic and adjusts as needed to fit the demand.

Problem

When booting from a diskless Windows workstation, Windows cannot find the WINA20.386 file (which comes with DOS 5) it needs when running under DOS 5, even though the file was placed in the boot image for the diskless machine.

Solution

Once you load the NETX portion of the NetWare shell, you lose access to the remote boot image file. To solve this problem, make sure you have added:

```
SWITCHES=/W
```

to your CONFIG.SYS file.
In addition, add the line

```
DEVICE=[drive:][path]\WINA20.386
```

to the [386Enh] section of Windows SYSTEM.INI.

You may need to run RPLFIX against the boot image file, especially if you have DOS 5. RPLFIX in the DOSUPx.ZIP file, available from Novell. Consult your Novell documentation for details.

Problem

You can't get drivers like VPICDA.386 or VNETWARE.386 to load and run.

Solution

Make sure that you have a recent VPICDA.386 driver in the \WINDOWS\SYSTEM directory, and that there is no asterisk (*) in front of its name in the SYSTEM.INI file on the "network=" line (in the [386Enh] section). Windows comes with the line "device=*vpicd" in the [386Enh] section. The asterisk tells Windows to use a driver internal to Windows. When you remove the asterisk and insert a valid filename, Windows will look for the external VPICDA.386 driver file. Note that VPICDA should only be used with Windows 3.0

Problem

With the initial release of the NetWare Windows Workstation Utilities, the USER LIST feature appears to have some problems. When you ask to display users by full name, some may not properly match the user. Furthermore, some appear to be duplicates of previous entries, although the User IDs appear to be fine. Also, the list erroneously shows PRINT SERVERS as whoever had the previous connection number.

Solution

These are problems Novell is aware of and is working to fix.

Problem

Windows is freezing—suspected shell problems.

Solution

Make sure that the IPX you are loading is v3.10 or higher (or v1.20 or higher for ODI shells), and that the VIPX.386 you are loading is the one included with the most recent VIPX.ZIP file available from Novell. You can run the NetWare NVER utility to verify that it is IPX v3.10 or greater.

Problem

While in Enhanced Mode, unpredictable behavior occurs in a DOS session, such as the environment (SET) variables becoming garbled. On the other hand, things are okay in Standard mode; the DOS session works fine when the network shell files are not loaded.

Solution

This problem usually indicates that this copy of Windows was not installed with the NetWare drivers. Run Setup from DOS and choose NetWare as the network driver. Windows will reinstall the proper driver. Also, make sure that network-specific drivers, such as VNETWARE.386 and VIPX.386, are installed in the 386Enh section of SYSTEM.INI.

Problem

A DOS application running in a Windows DOS session returns the error "EMS corrupt" on a networked machine. The problem does not occur on the same machine if not attached to the network.

Solution

Windows may be trying to use the memory your network card is mapping into the memory space between 640K and 1MB. You need to tell Windows not to use the memory space managed by your NIC. Add the following line to your SYSTEM.INI file (in the [386Enh] section)

```
EMMEXCLUDE=C800CBFF
```

assuming that your NIC uses 16K of RAM and the starting address was C800h. Some NICs have more than one area of shared RAM (some RAM and some ROM—IBM TRN cards especially).

Additionally, some VGA cards (16 bit especially) have another problem in that they use the area between C4000 and C7FFF. Try adding the following EMMEXCLUDE:

```
EMMEXCLUDE=C400-C7FF
```

Also, if you have any memory managers like Microsoft's EMM386 or Quarterdeck's QEMM386, you will want to specifically exclude any shared RAM or ROM on your NICs. If you are using Microsoft's EMM386, for example, you can include a line in CONFIG.SYS that looks like:

```
device = c:\dos\emm386.exe noems x=c800-cfff
```

This would exclude the memory in the range of C800-CFFF from use by EMM386. For Quarterdeck's QEMM386, the line would look like

```
device = c:\qemm\qemm386.sys RAM EXCLUDE=C800-CFFF
```

Problem

Your DOS sessions share drive mappings and you do not want them to. You have the statement NWShareHandles=False in the [NetWare] section of SYSTEM.INI (the default), ensuring that changes to the drive mappings in one DOS session do not affect another DOS session. Yet, if you map F: to SYS:PUBLIC in one DOS session and you look in another DOS session where drive F was once mapped to SYS:DOS, drive F: is now mapped to SYS:PUBLIC in that session as well. If this happens to you, try the solution recommended below.

> **Note:** This situation also affects drives that have been created or deleted in one DOS session but suddenly appear or disappear in another session.

Solution

If you have a TASK MODE setting in NET.CFG, it is best if you remove it.

Problem

You have difficulty running Windows with Token Ring boards.

Solution

Apparently DOS 5 or any memory management software can have conflicts with several Token Ring boards, such as Thomas Conrad's. Many have found the following addition to their NET.CFG file helpful:

```
Link Driver TCTOKSH
    NON_VDS
```

Also, placing STACKS 0,0 in the CONFIG.SYS file has helped many get Token Ring boards working correctly.

Problem

When flagging Windows application files as Execute Only, Windows doesn't run the applications properly.

Solution

You cannot flag Windows application files as Execute Only—this is a DOS/Windows limitation.

Problem

When using a NACS gateway and NASI under Windows Enhanced mode, the data flow will stop after 1000 bytes or so. If you drop DTR, you get the NASI prompt back. When you resume the port, you can get another block of data. While incoming data is lost, the data you type is still sent over the gateway. This is only a problem in Enhanced mode.

Solution

At the time of this writing, TBMI would work well with NACS/NASI, but VIPX.386 had some problems. The best solution is to look for the latest VIPX.386; if that doesn't work, use TBMI.

Problem

There seems to be a NetBIOS problem with some Token Ring configurations. You get occasional DOS lockups when first entering a DOS session.

Solution

Remove *vnetbios from Network= line in the SYSTEM.INI file. Be aware, however, that this will cause programs requiring NetBIOS not to work.

The problem is VNETBIOS is causing a deadlock from a hardware interrupt. It basically causes all LAN interrupts to stop firing. The shell can't continue until those events complete. Novell will be relaying the information to Microsoft. It will then be up to them to determine if they are going to fix it. If you don't require VNETBIOS, then a work-around is to not load it.

Problem

SmartDrive won't work on network drives.

Solution

There is no solution. SmartDrive won't work on network drives.

Problem

There are spurious errors in Windows when using the new BNETX shells.

Solution

Novell knows that there have been several problems with these shells. Keep in touch with Novell and obtain the latest version as soon as possible.

Also, keep in mind that BNETX v3.31 or higher is required for use with Windows 3.1.

Problem

When installing Microsoft (and several other vendors') products on the network, the MAP ROOT process is ignored. For example, if the Windows directory is root mapped to W:\ and an application wants to access a file in the Windows directory, then the application appends a backslash and the desired filename/directory name. The result is usually W:\\system.ini or something similar.

Many Microsoft-supplied utilities have (or once had) this problem. For example, SYSEDIT may not be able to find my WIN.INI or SYSTEM.INI because of it. This is due to the Universal Naming Convention; the \\ causes the file reference to begin at the drive's TRUE root, not the MAPPED root.

Solution

One work-around is to temporarily remove any MAP ROOT commands for the duration of an install, then put them back afterwards. This usually requires editing the PROGMAN.INI so that the group files can be properly located.

One other method is illustrated by the following scenario. Start by installing Windows on the server. Run Setup /A on drive V, for example, which has been created with the command "MAP ROOT Sx:=SYS1:WINDOWS." Next, run Setup /N to install a user version of Windows on drive W, which is defined as "MAP ROOT Sx:= SYS1:APPS\USERNAME." When you're done, the PROGMAN.INI for the user (under either 3.0 or 3.1 Windows) may have entries like these:

```
[Groups]
Group1=W:\ACCESSOR.GRP
Group2=W:\MICROSOF.GRP
Group3=W:\NOVELLNE.GRP
Group4=W:\MAIN.GRP
```

If, in the process of installing a new program that has problems with an improperly formed pathname (e.g., using W:\\SETUP.T as a directory name), remap the W: drive as MAP W:=W: (which is equivalent to keeping the same directory and search drive status, but deleting the false root); then the above fully qualified path names for group files will be incorrect.

In other words, after deleting the false root, you must change the 'Group4 = W:\MAIN.GRP' to 'Group4 = W:\BIN\USERNAME\MAIN.GRP'. If it were possible to deactivate UNC support, this process would be unnecessary.

Problem

When you type 'DIR SYS:SYSTEM' from a map rooted drive, the MAP ROOT is undone.

Solution

Don't type 'DIR SYS:SYSTEM.' Seriously, this is a known problem and is being investigated. Expect later NetWare shell revisions to accommodate this command.

Problem

Windows may hang while using WINSTART.BAT when exiting Windows. Windows will look for WINSTART.BAT each time you start the program. This allows you to load a TSR, for example, before starting Windows.

Solution

Microsoft is aware of this problem and is working on it. For now, the only solution is to remove the elements from WINSTART.BAT (and delete or rename WINSTART.BAT) and move any TSRs from your AUTOEXEC.BAT file or some other batch file that is run before Windows is loaded.

The problem stems from a memory conflict between the TSRs and Windows' use of memory. Some combinations of FILES= in CONFIG.SYS and FILE HANDLES= in NET.CFG will allow some batch files to be initiated from WINSTART.BAT. You'll simply have to experiment with these settings to see if you can get TSRs to load from WINSTART.BAT.

10 NetWare/Windows Software

This chapter provides a full discussion of each of the applications and utilities on the NetWare Power Tools for Windows diskette included with this book. Apart from a few brief comments, the documentation is provided by the software vendor. The following software is included with the disk accompanying this book and will be discussed below:

- NetScan, a network virus scanner, by McAfee Associates

- Network Application Installer (NAI), an automated, Windows-based network application installation utility, by Aleph Systems

- While You Were Out, a networked Windows phone message taking system, by Caliente International

- WSEND, a Windows SEND utility, by Steve Goulet/ GDG Systems

- WSUPER, a Windows utility that lets you switch NetWare supervisor equivalence on and off as needed, by Wolfgang Schreiber

- SHOWDOTS, a Windows utility that lets you change the NetWare shell's Show Dots parameter, by Wolfgang Schreiber

- Express-It! for Windows, a Windows-based e-mail system, by Infinite Technologies

- I-Queue!, a Windows-based NetWare print queue/print capture utility, by Infinite Technologies

The disk also includes an Install program created with Oriel for Windows, a powerful batch language processor that will help you install the utilities on the disk. For an explanation of how to run the install program, please refer to Appendix A.

NetScan by McAfee Associates

Running NetScan and Clean Under Windows

by Charles Rose

NetScan is a powerful network virus scanner program by McAfee Associates. It allows you to scan a network drive for a virus infection and, optionally, delete any infected files. NetScan is one of several products from McAfee that perform virus detection and cleanup. Among others are Viruscan—a workstation virus scanner—and Clean-up—a universal tool for disinfecting virus-ridden files without deleting them. Unfortunately, due to disk-space considerations, only the NetScan utility has been included on the disks that ship with this book.

The documentation to follow is provided by McAfee Associates and gives detailed instructions on how to use Viruscan (SCAN.EXE), Clean-up (CLEAN.EXE), and NetScan (NETSCAN.EXE). We've decided to include the entire set of documentation in order to give you a feel for how all three products can work together to help you ensure a virus-free network environment.

Note: The NetScan software (NETSCAN.EXE) is very similar to McAfee's Viruscan program (SCAN.EXE). The major difference is that NetScan can deal with Network drives—for example, NetWare volumes—where you see a reference to SCAN.EXE in the documentation to follow, you can substitute NETSCAN.EXE.

Although NetScan was not written specifically to run under Windows, it will work fine; we have provided the above icon for you to use on the Windows desktop when running NetScan.

To Install NetScan under Windows, you should first read through the McAfee documentation below, at least the Quick Start Documentation. Next, go into the Program Manager and choose File New and Program Item. Fill in the fields as follows:

Description:	NetScan
Command Line:	NETSCAN.PIF
Working Directory:	
Shortcut Key:	None
Run Minimized:	Unchecked

Then choose Change Icon followed by the Browse button. Enter the path where your SCAN.ICN icon is stored and choose OK. Your Program Item Properties window will look similar to Figure 10.1.

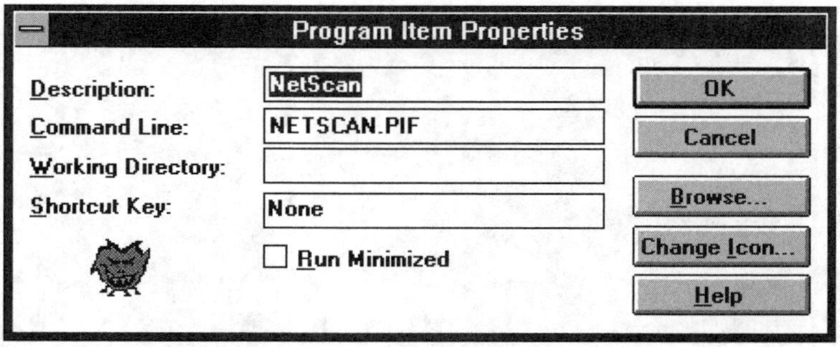

Figure 10.1 Program Item Properties window for NETSCAN.PIF.

Now run the PIF Editor and create NETSCAN.PIF. Figure 10.2 shows the first screen of a completed NETSCAN.PIF—the Advanced screen in the PIF editor should not require any changes.

Some of the important PIF settings are:

Optional Parameters	You can set this to a question mark (?) if you want to specify the command-line options each time you run NetScan, or you can set it permanently as in Figure 10.2. The options chosen are:
F:\	- Tells where to scan for viruses.
/A	- Says to check all files.
/BELL	- Ring bell if a virus is found.
/CHKHI	- Check all memory for a virus.

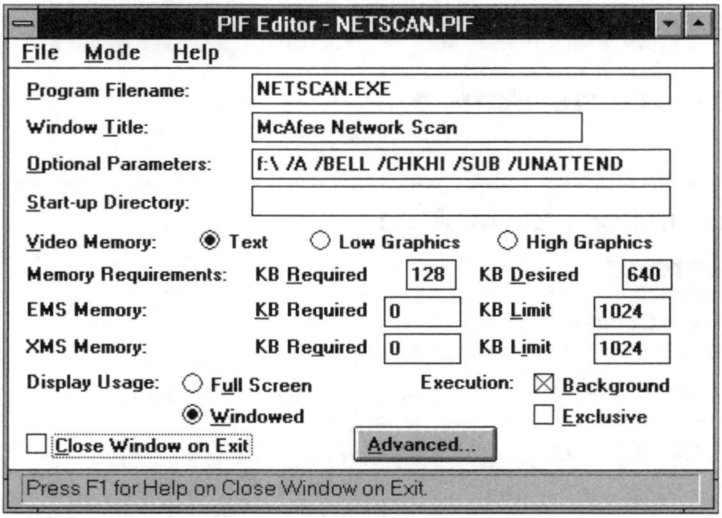

Figure 10.2 PIF Editor window with NETSCAN.PIF loaded.

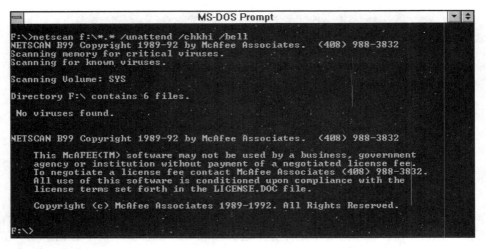

Figure 10.3 DOS window with NetScan running.

/SUB	- Look in subdirectories.
/UNATTEN	- Run in unattended mode - IMPORTANT!

Close Window on Exit	It's important that this option be turned off; otherwise, you won't see the results of the NetScan on the screen.
Execution: Background	If you want to scan for viruses in the background, this is a nice option to enable.
Display Usage	This is up to you: whether you want Windowed or Full Screen.

Figure 10.3 shows the NetScan program running in a DOS window.

Quick Start Documentation

Quick Start Instructions for McAfee Associates Programs

Written by Aryeh Goretsky.
Thanks to Mike Ramey and Alan Kearney for their comments.

McAfee Associates
4423 Cheeney Street
Santa Clara, CA 95054-0253
USA

(408) 988-3832 Telephone
(408) 970-9727 FAX
(408) 988-4004 BBS 2400 bps
(408) 988-5138 BBS HST 9600
(408) 988-5190 BBS v32 9600
CompuServe   GO VIRUSFORUM
InterNet mcafee@netcom.com

These instructions explain how to identify a virus with the VIRUSCAN program and remove the virus with the CLEAN-UP program. They are intended to provide the person with a virus infection an emergency means to identify and remove an infection. They are not meant to replace the program documentation. Please read through the documentation for detailed instructions. Files ending in a .DOC extension have been formatted for printing on a printer with a minimum of 60 lines per page. Files ending in a .TXT extension have not been formatted.

VIRUSCAN (SCAN)

1. Copy all the VIRUSCAN files to a floppy disk in drive A.
2. WRITE PROTECT THE DISK!!!
3. Insert the disk into the infected PC and type:

   A:\SCAN C: D: E:

   This will allow VIRUSCAN to run on the C:, D:, and E: drives. If you do not have D: and E: drives, leave them out.

4. If infected files are found, they may be ERASED by running VIRUSCAN with the /D (overwrite and delete) option:

   A:\SCAN C: D: E: /D

   Running VIRUSCAN with the /D option will delete files in a way that is non-recoverable. Use this option only if you do NOT want to recover any of the infected files. Otherwise use the CLEAN-UP universal virus disinfector.

5. Turn computer off to remove the virus from memory.

CLEAN-UP (CLEAN)

1. Copy all the CLEAN-UP files to a floppy disk in drive A:.
2. WRITE PROTECT THE DISK!!!
3. Power down the infected system and then boot from a clean, write protected system master diskette. This must be done to remove any viruses from memory that may interfere with the virus removal process. NOTE: If you are unable to access your hard disk after booting from a floppy, check to make sure that any special device drivers needed to use the hard disk are on the floppy and run from the CONFIG.SYS or AUTOEXEC.BAT file. AT THIS POINT IF YOU HAVE NOT DONE A BACKUP OF ANY CRITICAL FILES ON YOUR SYSTEM, DO SO IMMEDIATELY.
4. Insert the CLEAN-UP disk into the A: drive of the infected PC and type:

   A:\CLEAN C: D: E: [virus-ID-code]

   This will allow CLEAN-UP to disinfect viruses on the C:, D:, and E: drives. If you do not have D: and E: drives, leave them out.

   For the Jerusalem virus, the ID code is [JERU]. For the Stoned virus, the ID code is [STONED]. For other viruses, use the ID code generated by SCAN, or check the VIRLIST.TXT file. Remember to include the square brackets, "[" and "]."

Quick Start Instructions for McAfee Associates Programs is reprinted with permission from McAfee Associates. Last revised August 22, 1991. Copyright © 1990, 1991 by McAfee Associates. All rights reserved.

If you are disinfecting a file-infecting virus, such as the Jerusalem, it is recommended that you add the /A switch to the command line to check all files. This will ensure that the virus is removed from any overlay files that may not use the default overlay extensions recognized by CLEAN-UP. If you know that none of your programs use overlays, then the /A switch is not necessary.

If more than one virus type was detected, then CLEAN-UP will have to be run for each type of virus.

5. Turn the computer off and then re-boot from the hard disk.

AN IMPORTANT NOTE: You have now completed a virus disinfection of your computer system, however, you may have other computers and floppy disks that are infected. You now have a clean PC from which to scan and clean them. Please now take the time to read through the VIRUSCAN and CLEAN-UP documentation to show you the fastest and safest way of removing your computer virus infection.

NetScan Documentation

Documentation by Aryeh Goretsky.

McAfee Associates	(408) 988-3832 office
3350 Scott Blvd, Bldg. 14	(408) 970-9727 fax
Santa Clara, CA 95054	(408) 988-4004 BBS (25 lines)
USA	USR HST/v.32/v.42bis/MNP1-5
	CompuServe GO MCAFEE
	InterNet support@mcafee.COM

WHAT'S NEW

NETSCAN Version 99 adds detection of all new viruses detected by VIRUSCAN that are capable of spreading over a network.

For a complete list of known viruses, refer to the enclosed VIRLIST.TXT file. For a description of known viruses please refer to Patricia Hoffman's Hypertext VSUM.

Two new features was added in this release:

^G   When NETSCAN is run against a drive that does not exist, it will no longer give an error message. Instead, it will go the next drive and start scanning or quit if no other drives are listed.

^G   A new Dark Avenger Mutation Engine [DAME] virus detection routine is being used. This new algorithm will greatly speed up detection of DAME-based viruses and at the same time reduce or entirely prevent false alarms.

SYSTEM REQUIREMENTS

NETSCAN requires 320Kb of RAM and DOS 2.0 or above (some features require DOS 3.1 or above). NETSCAN works with 3COM 3/Share and 3/Open, Artisoft LANTastic, AT&T

StarLAN, Banyan VINES, DEC Pathworks, Microsoft LAN Manager, Novell NetWare, and any other IBMNET or NETBIOS compatible network operating systems. Contact McAfee Associates if you do not see your network listed.

NETSCAN is designed to check network file servers for viruses. For stand-alone and networked PC's please use VIRUSCAN instead.

NETSCAN displays messages in English, French, or Spanish.

NOTE: WRITE-PROTECT THE FLOPPY DISK CONTAINING THE NETSCAN (NETSCAN.EXE) PROGRAM BEFORE SCANNING TO PREVENT NETSCAN FROM BECOMING INFECTED BY A COMPUTER VIRUS.

NOTE: FOR NETSCAN TO CHECK ALL AREAS OF THE FILE SERVER, IT MUST BE RUN FROM AN ACCOUNT WITH GLOBAL READ AND FILESCAN RIGHTS.

OVERVIEW (Known Virus Detection)

NETSCAN Version B99 fixes a bug in release V99 (unable to scan network drive). This version (filename NETSCAN.EXE) identifies all known computer viruses and their variants identified by the current version of VIRUSCAN which can be transferred over a network.

NETSCAN can check a files, subdirectories, volume, or network drive for pre-existing computer virus infections. It will identify the virus infecting the system and the area where it was found, giving the name of the virus as well as the I.D. code used with CLEAN-UP to remove it.

Infected files can be removed with the /D switch in NETSCAN to erase the file, or with the CLEAN-UP universal virus removal (disinfection) program. CLEAN-UP is recommended because in most cases it will eliminate the virus and fully restore infected programs or system areas to normal operation.

The accompanying VIRLIST.TXT file lists describes all viruses identified by NETSCAN and their associated I.D. codes for removal by CLEAN-UP.

OVERVIEW (Unknown and New Virus Detection)

NETSCAN has three separate methods of detecting unknown and new viruses:

^G   Validation codes which can be periodically checked against to look for the changes made by a virus to files or system areas.

^G   Generic and Family virus detectors to look for new viruses which are derivatives of older viruses.

^G   External virus signatures to insert new virus signature strings on a temporary basis to NETSCAN.

SYNOPSIS (Technical Description of Known Virus Detection)

NETSCAN detects known viruses by searching the system for strings (sequences of bytes) unique to each computer virus and reporting their presence if found. For viruses which encrypt or cipher their code so that every infection of the virus is different, NETSCAN uses detection algorithms (programs) that work by statistical analysis, heurstics, or code disassembly.

SYNOPSIS (Technical Description of New/Unknown Virus Detection)

NETSCAN checks for new or unknown viruses by comparing files against previously-recorded validation (checksum) data stored in a discrete file.

NETSCAN also checks for new or unknown viruses by searching for Generic or Family virus strings. These are strings that have been found repeatedly in different viruses. Since virus writers may use the older pieces of code for new viruses, this allows NETSCAN to detect viruses which have not been written yet.

NETSCAN can be updated to search for new viruses by an External Virus Data File, which allows the user to input new search strings for viruses. (/EXT switch)

AUTHENTICITY

Before using NETSCAN for the first time, verify that it has not been tampered with or infected by a virus by using the the enclosed VALIDATE program. For instructions on using VALIDATE, please read the VALIDATE.DOC file.

The validation results for Version B99 should be:

FILE NAME: NETSCAN.EXE

SIZE: 84,181

DATE: 11-17-1992

FILE AUTHENTICATION

Check Method 1: 9701

Check Method 2: 07AB

If your copy of NETSCAN differs, it may have been damaged or have options stored in it with the /SAVE switch. Run NETSCAN with only the /SAVE option to remove any stored options and then re-run VALIDATE. Always obtain your copy of NETSCAN from a known source. The latest version of NETSCAN and validation data for NETSCAN.EXE can be obtained from McAfee Associates' bulletin board system at (408) 988-4004 or from the McAfee Virus Help Forum on CompuServe (GO MCAFEE), or the mcafee.COM anonymous ftp site on the Internet.

NETSCAN performs a self-check when run. If NETSCAN has been modified in any way, a warning will be displayed and the user prompted to either continue or quit. NETSCAN can still check for viruses, however, if NETSCAN reports that it has been damaged, it is recommended that a clean copy be obtained.

Beginning with Version 72, all of McAfee Associates' NETSCAN series are archived with PKWare's PKZIP Authentic File Verification. If you do not see an "-AV" after every file is unzipped and receive the "Authentic Files Verified! # NWN405 Zip Source: McAFEE ASSOCIATES" message when you unzip the files then do not use them. If your version of PKUNZIP does not have verification ability, then this message may not be displayed. Please contact us if you believe tampering has occurred to the .ZIP file.

COMMAND SUMMARY

IMPORTANT NOTE: WRITE-PROTECT YOUR FLOPPY DISK BEFORE SCANNING TO PREVENT INFECTION OF THE NETSCAN PROGRAM.

NETSCAN checks files and other areas of the system that can contain a computer virus. When a virus is found, NETSCAN identifies the virus and the file or system area where it was found.

NETSCAN examines files based on their extension. The default extensions supported by NETSCAN are .APP, .BIN, .COM, .EXE, .OV?, .PGM, .PIF, .PRG, .SWP, .SYS, and .XTP. Additional extensions can be added with the /EXT option, or use the /A to check all files.

Valid options for NETSCAN are:

NETSCAN {drive(s)} {options}

{drive(s)}   -Indicates a drive or drives to be scanned

Options are:

/? /H or /HELP	-Displays help screen
/A	-Scan all files, including data, for viruses
/AD	-Scan all available hard drives
/AF {filename}	-Store recovery & validation data to {filename}
/BELL	-Beep whenever a virus is found
/CERTIFY	-List files that do not have a validation code
/CF {filename}	-Check for viruses using recovery & validation data stored in {filename}
/CHKHI	-Check workstation memory from 0Kb to 1,088Kb
/D	-Overwrite and delete infected files
/E .xxx .yyy	-Scan overlay extensions .XXX and .YYY
/EXT {filename}	-Scan using external virus data from {filename}
/FAST	-Speed up NETSCAN's output (see below for specifics)
/FR	-Display all messages in French
/HISTORY {fname}	-Create infection log {fname} appending to old log
/M	-Scan workstation memory for all viruses (see below for specifics)
/NLZ	-Skip internal scan of LZEXE-compressed files
/NOBREAK	-Disable Ctrl-C and Ctrl-Brk during scanning
/NOEXPIRE	-Do not display expiration notice
/NOMEM	-Disable workstation memory check
/NOPAUSE	-Disable screen pause when scanning
/NPKL	-Skip internal scan of PKLITE-compressed files
/REPORT {fname}	-Create infection log {fname} deleting the old log
/RF {filename}	-Remove recovery & validation data from {filename}
/SAVE	-Save specified options as new default options
/SP	-Display all messages in Spanish
/SUB	-Scan all subdirectories inside a subdirectory

/UNATTEND   -Scan using DOS critical error handler (required for Novell NetWare)

@ {filename}   -using options from {filename}

OPTIONS

Following is a detailed description of NETSCAN's options. Please note the /SAVE switch modifies the NETSCAN.EXE file. This may cause other anti-viral programs to generate a warning.

/A - This option checks all files on the drive scanned. This substantially increases the time required to scan disks, so it is recommended this switch only be used when installing new software or if a file-infecting virus has been found. This option takes priority over the /E option.

/AF {filename} - This option logs recovery and validation data for .COM and .EXE files, boot sector, and partition table of a disk to a user-specified file. The log file size is about 20Kb per 1,000 files validated. Recovery from a virus using the /AF information requires the CLEAN-UP (CLEAN.EXE) program.

NOTE: Files which are immunized against viruses or contain self-modifying code should not have validation codes added to them. To prevent NETSCAN from adding validation codes to these files, a validation exception list must be created with the path and filename of each file NOT to be validated listed on each line (only one filename for each line). To put a comment in, start the line with an "*" character. This sample file contains a list of programs NOT to validate:

*LIST OF FILES NOT TO USE /AV OR /AG OPTIONS WITH *

*This is Nantucket Corp's database program, Clipper C:\CLIPPER\BIN\CLIP-
    PER.EXE

*This is Lotus Development Corp's spreadsheet program, 1-2-3 C:\123\123.COM

*This is MS-DOS 5.00's self-modifying program, SETVER C:\DOS\SETVER.EXE

*PKWare's data compression programs already perform a self-check

C:\PKWARE\PKLITE.EXE

C:\PKWARE\PKZIP.EXE

C:\PKWARE\PKUNZIP.EXE

*Stac Technologies hard disk swapping program

C:\SWAPVOL.COM

*Symantec's Norton Utilities V6.01 disk caching program

C:\NORTON\NCACHE.EXE

*WordStar Corp's word processor is self-modifying

C:\WORDSTAR\WS.EXE

The validation exception list should be an ASCII or DOS text file. If a word processor is used to create the list, be sure to save the file as ASCII or DOS Text.

/BELL - This option causes NETSCAN to beep when a virus is found.

/CF {filename} - This option checks recovery and validation data stored by the /AF option in {filename}. If a file or system area has changed, NETSCAN reports that a viral infection may have occurred. Using the /CG option adds about 25% more time to scanning.

/CHKHI - This option checks memory on the workstation NETSCAN is being run on from 640Kb to 1,088Kb. Server memory is not checked. This option cannot be used with the /NOMEM option.

/D - This option tells NETSCAN to prompt the user to overwrite and delete an infected file. Files erased by the /D option can not be recovered. If the CLEAN-UP program is available, it can be used to disinfect the file. Partition table and boot sector viruses can not be removed by the /D option and require the CLEAN-UP virus removal program.

/E .xxx .yyy - This option allows an additional extension or set extensions to be scanned. Extensions should include a period "." character and be separated by a space after the /E. Up to three extensions may be added with the /E. For more extensions, use the /A option instead.

/EXT {filename} - This option tells NETSCAN to search for viruses using virus search strings from ASCII text file {filename}, in addition to the viruses that NETSCAN looks for. For instructions creating an external virus data file, refer to Appendix A.

NOTE: The /EXT option provides users with the ability to add strings for detection of viruses on an interim or emergency basis. When used with the /D option, it will overwrite-and-delete infected files. This option is not for general use and should be used with caution.

/FAST - This option speeds NETSCAN up by displaying less on the screen, skipping checking inside of LZEXE- and PKLITE- compressed files, and examining a smaller portion of files during scanning. This may reduce the accuracy of NETSCAN.

/FR - This option tells NETSCAN to display all messages in French instead of English. This option cannot be used with the /SP (Spanish) option.

/HISTORY {filename} - This option saves the output of NETSCAN to {filename} in ASCII text file format. If {filename} exists, NETSCAN will add the results of the current scan to the end.

/M - This option tells NETSCAN to check memory on the workstation it is being run from, not the network file server's memory, for all known computer viruses that can inhabit memory. NETSCAN by default only checks memory for critical and "stealth" viruses, which are viruses which can cause catastrophic damage or spread during the scanning process. By default, NETSCAN will check memory for the following viruses:

1024	1253	1530	15xx variant
1963	1971	2153	2560
3040	337	3445-Stealth	4096
500	512	557	702
ABC	Agena	Anthrax	Antitelefonica
Aragon	arcv	B3	Blood Rage
Brain	Budo	Caz	CD
Chang	Coffee Shop	Copyr-ug	Cracky
Crusher	Dark Avenger	Davis	Dir-2
DM-330	Doom II	EEL	Empire
End-of	Evil Genius	ExeBug	Fam

Feist	Fish	Flu	FORM
Frodo Soft	Fune	Futhark	Geek
Greemlin	Green	HA	HBT
Hellween 1182	Hi	Highland	Horror
Ice9	Iernim	IOU	Jeru Variant
Joanna	Joshi	Jump4Joy	Kersplat
L1	Larry	Leech	LixoNuke
Lozinsky	Lycee	Magnum	Malaga
Malaise	Microbes	Mirror	Mocha
Monkey	Mugshot	Mummy	Murphy
NCU Li	Ninja	Nomemklatura	NOP
No-Int	Nygus	Nygus-KL	Ontario-3
Otto	P1R	PCBB11	Penza
Phantom	Piazzola	Plastique	Pogue
Pojer	Problem	Radyum	Rattle
Reaper	Reklama	Rocko	Sandwich
SBC	Scr-2	Scroll	Scythe
Sentinel	Sergant	Silence	SK
Sk1	Sma-108a	Soyun	Stealthb
Sticky	Stoned (Vari)	Sunday-2	SVC
Tabulero	Taiwan3	Ten Bytes	Tequila
Thursday 12th	Turbo	Turkey	Twin-351
V2100	V2P6	V600	Vietnamese
Walker	Whale	Windmill	Yan2050a
Youth	Zaragoza		

If any of the above viruses is found in memory, NETSCAN will stop, tell the user to power down and reboot the system from a virus-free system-bootable disk. This option can not be used with the /NOMEM option.

NOTE: Using the /M option with another anti-viral software package may result in false alarms if the other package does not remove or cipher (hide or otherwise encrypt) its virus search strings in memory.

/NLZ - This option tells NETSCAN not to look inside files compressed with LZEXE, a file compression program. NETSCAN will still check LZEXE-compressed files for viruses that may have become infected after LZEXE compression.

/NOBREAK - This option prevents Ctrl-C or Ctrl-Brk from aborting the scanning process.

/NOMEM - This option turns off all memory checks for viruses in order to speed up the scanning process. It should only be used when a system is known to be virus-free. This option can not be used with the /CHKHI or /M options.

/NOEXPIRE - This option prevents NETSCAN from displaying a warning message after 7 months warning that it may no longer be current with respect to known computer viruses.

/NOPAUSE - This option disables the "More? (H = Help)" prompt displayed when NETSCAN fills up a screen with 24 lines of text. This allows NETSCAN to run on LAN's with severe infections without requiring operator assistance.

/NPKL - This option tells NETSCAN not to look inside files compressed with PKLITE, a file compression program. NETSCAN will still check PKLITE-compressed files for viruses that may have become infected after PKLITE compression.

/REPORT {filename} - This option saves the output of NETSCAN to {filename} in ASCII text file format. If {filename} exists, NETSCAN will erase it and replace with the current scan results.

/RF {filename} - This option removes recovery and validation data from log file {filename} created by the /AF option.

/SAVE - This option stores any listed options for subsequent executions of NETSCAN. The options are stored by modifying the NETSCAN.EXE executable file itself. For example:

NETSCAN /NOMEM /REPORT C:\NETSCAN.LOG /NOPAUSE /SAVE

saves the default options to /NOMEM, /REPORT C:\NETSCAN.LOG and /NOPAUSE and will cause NETSCAN to use these options the next time it is run. If NETSCAN is run with only the /SAVE switch, all saved options are removed and the NETSCAN.EXE is returned to normal. If you do not wish to modify the NETSCAN.EXE file, use the @{filename} option instead.

NOTE: VALIDATE 0.4 must be used to validate NETSCAN V89 or above if the /SAVE option is used. /SAVE directly modifies NETSCAN.EXE in such a manner that validate codes will not match if an older version of VALIDATE is used. VALIDATE 0.4 generates correct validation results if the /SAVE option is used.

/SP - This option tells NETSCAN to display all messages in Spanish instead of English. This option cannot be used with the /FR (French) option.

/SUB - This option scans all subdirectories inside a subdirectory. Previously, NETSCAN would only recursively check subdirectories if a drive was scanned at the root level (e.g., C:). Do not use the /SUB switch if you are scanning a drive from the root level.

/UNATTEND - This option tells NETSCAN to use the DOS critical error handler when accessing files. This allows NETSCAN to skip files in use by another program instead of stopping and displaying an error message. This option requires DOS 3.10 or above.

NOTE: The /UNATTEND switch is required if you are running NETSCAN on a Novell NetWare file server.

@{FILENAME} - option allows the user to store a list of options and drives to be scanned in a configuration file. Options need to be separated by a space, while drives (disks, subdirectories, or files) need to be listed on separate lines. A sample file might look like this:

/A /BELL /NOMEM /REPORT C:\NETSCAN\NETSCAN.LOG

F:\PUBLIC

G:

The first line contains the NETSCAN options while other lines list the names of disks, subdirectories, or files to scan. The file should be an ASCII text file. If a word processor is used to create the list, be sure to save it as ASCII or DOS text.

EXAMPLES

The following examples show different option settings:

NETSCAN F: /UNATTEND   To scan drive F: on a Novell NetWare
                                        LAN for viruses

NETSCAN F: /CF C:\NETSCAN.CRC	To scan drive F: for viruses and check for unknown viruses by comparing against recovery/validation data from file NETSCAN.CRC
NETSCAN X: Y: Z: /D /A	Scans all files on drives X: Y: and Z: for viruses and prompt for erasure of any infected files, if found.
NETSCAN L: M: /E .WPM .COD	Scans drives L: and M: for viruses, including files with .WPM and .COD extensions
NETSCAN G: /EXT A:SAMPLE.ASC /BELL	To scan drive G: for known viruses and for new viruses added he external virus data file option, and beep whenever a virus is found.

EXIT CODES

After NETSCAN has finished running, it sets the DOS ERRORLEVEL. The ERRORLEVEL's returned by NETSCAN are:

ERRORLEVEL	DESCRIPTION
0	No viruses found
1	One or more viruses found
2	Abnormal termination (program error)
3	One or more uncertified files found
4	Ctrl-C or Ctrl-Break aborted scan

If a user stops the scanning process, NETSCAN will set the ERRORLEVEL to 4. If you wish to prevent users from stopping the scanning process, then run NETSCAN with the /NOBREAK option.

VIRUS REMOVAL

What do you do if a virus is found? You can contact McAfee Associates for help, their authorized agents, or use the CLEAN-UP program.

McAfee Associates can be reached by BBS, CompuServe, FAX, Internet, or Telephone and there is no charge for support calls to McAfee Associates (Authorized agents may charge normal McAfee Associates consulting rates.).

The CLEAN-UP universal virus disinfection program can disinfect virtually all reported computer viruses. It is updated with each release of the NETSCAN program to remove new viruses. CLEAN-UP can be downloaded from McAfee Associates' BBS, the McAfee Virus Help Forum on CompuServe, and the mcafee.COM and WSMR-SIMTEL20.Army.Mil sites on the Internet, or from any of the agents' BBSes listed in the enclosed AGENTS.TXT text file.

It is strongly recommended that you get experienced help in dealing with viruses if you are unfamiliar with anti-virus software and methods. This is especially true for 'critical' viruses and partition table/boot sector infecting viruses as improper removal of these viruses can result in the loss of all data and the use of the infected disk(s). [For a listing of critical viruses, see the /M switch listed under OPTIONS above.]

Before removing a boot sector or partition table-infecting virus, it is recommended that you cold boot the infected PC from a clean DOS disk and backup any critical data.

For qualified assistance in removing a virus, contact McAfee Associates directly or any of the Authorized Agents in your area. Agents may charge McAfee Associates' normal consulting rates for their services.

If you wish to remove a file-infecting virus manually, cold boot the PC from a clean (virus-free) DOS system disk and run NETSCAN with the /A and /D switches to erase all infected files. Any files removed in this manner can not be recovered.

LICENSE

NETSCAN may be copied and distributed for testing and evaluation purposes on a trial period of five (5) days. If you wish to use NETSCAN after the trial period, a license is required. Licenses are available for internal use within businesses, organizations, government agencies, and for external use by repair centers and other service organizations. License fees are based on the size of the network or number of copies required. Information on licensing can be obtained from McAfee Associates or any authorized agent listed in the AGENTS.TXT file.

TECHNICAL SUPPORT

For fast and accurate help, please have the following information ready when you contact McAfee Associates:

- Program name and version number.
- Type and brand of computer, hard disk, plus any peripherals.
- Version of DOS plus any TSRs or device drivers in use.
- Printouts of your AUTOEXEC.BAT and CONFIG.SYS files.
- A printout of what is in memory from the MEM command (DOS 4 and above users only) or a similar utility.
- The exact problem you are having. Please be as specific as possible. Having a printout of the screen and/or being at your computer be will helpful.

McAfee Associates can be contacted by BBS, CompuServe, FAX, or InterNet 24 hours a day, or by telephone at (408) 988-3832, Monday through Friday, 7:00AM to 5:30PM Pacific Time.

If you are overseas, there may be an Authorized McAfee Associates Agent in your area. Please refer to the AGENTS.TXT file for a list of McAfee Associates Agents.

OBTAINING THE LATEST VERSION OF McAFEE ASSOCIATES PROGRAMS

McAfee Associates regularly updates the VIRUSCAN series of programs every 4 to 6 weeks to add new virus detectors, new options, and fix the occasional, if infrequent, bug. To distribute these new versions, we run a multi-line BBS, CompuServe Forum, and Internet node:

BBS ACCESS

Our 25-line BBS is accessible 24 hours a day, 365 days a year, except for scheduled downtime and maintenance. All lines run US Robotics Courier HST Dual Standard ASL modems operating from 1,200bps to 14,400bps with line settings of 8 data bits, no parity, and one stop bit.

THE McAFEE VIRUS HELP FORUM ON COMPUSERVE

We are now sponsoring the McAfee Virus Help Forum on CompuServe. To reach the McAfee Virus Help Forum type GO MCAFEE at any CompuServe prompt. A free introductory membership is available. For more information, please read the enclosed COMPUSER.NOT file.

INTERNET ACCESS TO McAFEE ASSOCIATES SOFTWARE

The latest versions of McAfee Associates' anti-viral software is now available by anonymous ftp (file transfer protocol over the Internet from the site mcafee.COM). If your domain resolver does not support names, use the IP# 192.187.128.1. Enter "anonymous" for your user I.D. and your own email address for the password. Programs are located in the pub/antivirus directory. If you have any questions, please send email to support@mcafee.COM

McAfee Associates' anti-viral software may also be found at the Simtel20 archive site WSMR-SIMTEL20.Army.MIL in the PD1:<MSDOS.TROJAN-PRO> directory and its associated mirror sites WUARCHIVE.WUSTL.EDU (US), NIC.SWITCH.CH (Swiss), NIC.FUNET.FI (Finland), SRC.DOC.IC.AC (UK), and RANA.CC.DEAK.OZ.AU (Australia).

APPENDIX A: Creating a Virus String File with the /EXT Option

NOTE: The /EXT option is intended for emergency and research use only. It is a temporary method for identifying new viruses prior to the subsequent release of NETSCAN. A thorough understanding of viruses and string-search techniques is advised for using this option. A string length of 10 to 15 bytes is recommended.

The External Virus Data file should be created with an editor or a word processor and saved as an ASCII text file. Be sure each line ends with a Carriage Return/Line Feed pair.
The virus string file uses the following format:

#Comment about Virus_1

"aabbccddeeff..." Virus_1_Name

#Comment about Virus_2

"gghhiijjkkll..." Virus_2_Name

.

.

"uuvvwwxxyyzz..." Virus_n_Name

Where aa, bb, cc, etc. are the hexadecimal bytes that you wish to scan for. Each line in the file represents one virus. The Virus Name for each virus is mandatory, and may be up to 25 characters in length. The double quotes (") are required at the beginning and end of each hexadecimal string. NETSCAN will use the string file to search memory, the Partition Table, Boot Sector, System files, all .COM and .EXE files, and overlay files with the extension .APP, .BIN, .COM, .EXE, .OV?, .PGM, .PIF, .PRG, .SWP, .SYS, and .XTP. Virus strings may contain wild cards. The two wildcard options are:

Fixed Position Wildcard. The question mark "?" may be used to represent a wildcard in a fixed position within the string. For example, the string:

"E9 7C 00 10 ? 37 CB"

would match "E9 7C 00 10 27 37 CB", "E9 7C 00 10 9C 37 CB", or any other similar string, regardless of the fifth byte.

Range Wilcard. The asterisk "*", followed by range number in parentheses "(" and ")" is used to represent a variable number of adjoining random bytes. For example, the string:

"E9 7C *(4) 37 CB"

would match "E9 7C 00 37 CB," "E9 7C 00 11 37 CB," and "E9 7C 00 11 22 37 CB." The string "E9 7C 00 11 22 33 44 37 CB" would not match since the distance between 7C and 37 is greater than four bytes. You may specify a range of up to 99 bytes. Up to 10 different wildcards of either kind may be used in one virus string.

COMMENTS

A pound sign "#" at the beginning of a line will denote a comment. Use this for adding notes to the external virus data file. For example:

#New .COM virus found in file FRITZ.EXE from

#Schneiderland on 01-22-91

"53 48 45 45 50" Fritz-1 [F-1]

gives a description of the virus, name of the infected file, where and when it was found, etc.

IMPORTANT NOTICE - PLEASE READ! Due to the nature of anti-virus software, the slight chance exists that a virus may be reported in a file that is not infected by that virus.

If you receive a report of a virus which you believe may be in error, please contact McAfee Associates by telephone at (408) 988-3832, by fax at (408) 970-9727, or upload the file to our BBS at (408) 988-4004 along with your name, address, daytime telephone number, and electronic mail address, if any.

Clean Documentation

by Charles Rose

Although disk space restrictions prevented McAfee's Clean program from being included on the disk, you are nevertheless encouraged to contact McAfee Associates. Their BBS (see phone numbers on the next page) provides a quick and easy means of obtaining the most recent copy of their software, such as Clean. In case you are interested, however, the documentation for Clean is provided below.

CLEAN-UP Version 8.3B86

Documentation by Aryeh Goretsky.

McAfee Associates
1900 Wyatt Drive, Suite 8
Santa Clara, CA 95054-1529
USA

(408) 988-3832 office
(408) 970-9727 fax
(408) 988-4004 BBS 2400 bps
(408) 988-5138 BBS HST 9600
(408) 988-5190 BBS v32 9600
CompuServe   GO VIRUSFORUM
InterNet mcafee@netcom.com

SYNOPSIS

CLEAN-UP (CLEAN) is a virus disinfection program for IBM PC and compatible computers. CLEAN-UP will search through the partition table, boot sector, or files of a PC and
remove a virus specified by the user. In most instances CLEAN-UP is able to repair the
infected area of the system and restore it to normal usage. CLEAN-UP works on all viruses
identified by the current version of the VIRUSCAN (SCAN) program. CLEAN-UP can also
remove unknown viruses from .COM and .EXE files, partition tables, and boot sectors that
have had recovery information stored for them by the VIRUSCAN program.

CLEAN-UP runs on any PC with 256Kb and DOS 2.00 or above.

AUTHENTICITY

CLEAN-UP runs a self-test when executed. If CLEAN has been modified in any way, a
warning will be displayed. The program will still continue to remove viruses, though. If
CLEAN reports that it has been damaged, is recommended that a new, clean copy be
obtained.

CLEAN-UP is packaged with the VALIDATE program to ensure the integrity of the
CLEAN.EXE file. The VALIDATE.DOC instructions tell how to use the VALIDATE program.
The VALIDATE program distributed with CLEAN-UP may be used to check all further
versions of CLEAN.

The validation results for Version 8.3B86 should be:

FILE NAME: CLEAN.EXE

SIZE: 84,682

DATE: 2-3-1992

FILE AUTHENTICATION

Check Method 1: 682D

Check Method 2: 068A

If your copy of CLEAN.EXE differs, it may have been modified. Always obtain your
copy of CLEAN-UP from a known source. The latest version of CLEAN-UP and validation
data for CLEAN.EXE can be obtained off of McAfee Associates' bulletin board system at
(408) 988-4004 or from our Computer Virus Help Forum on CompuServe.

Beginning with Version 72, all McAfee Associates programs for download are archived with PKWare's PKZIP Authentic File Verification. If you do not see the "-AV" message after every file is unzipped and receive the message "Authentic Files Verified!   # NWN405 Zip Source: McAFEE ASSOCIATES" when you unzip the files then do not run them. If your version of PKUNZIP does not have verification ability, then this message may not be displayed. Please contact McAfee Associates if your .ZIP file has been tampered with.

WHAT'S NEW

Version 86-B has been released to repair a minor problem which can cause a system hang when removing the Stoned virus under certain circumstances.

Please note that we have changed our mailing address. Please direct all correspondence to the new address listed in the documentation.

CLEAN-UP Version 86 adds the option to disinfect files, boot sectors, and partition tables infected by unknown viruses, providing that recovery information had been previously saved for them with the /AG option of the VIRUSCAN program. When CLEAN is run with the /GENERIC option, it will attempt disinfection based on the recovery information stored by the VIRUSCAN program on the .COM and .EXE files and in the hidden SCANVAL.VAL file stored in the root directory of the bootable drive.

Additionally, removers for the 1992, Haifa, Lehigh, Perfume, and Slayer viruses have been added.

Please refer to the enclosed VIRLIST.TXT file for a short description of the new viruses. For a more complete description, please refer to Patricia Hoffman's VSUM listing.

OVERVIEW

CLEAN-UP searches the system looking for the virus you wish to remove. When an infected file is found, CLEAN-UP isolates and removes the virus, and in most cases, repairs the infected file and restores it to normal operation. If the file is infected with a less common virus, CLEAN-UP will then display a warning message and prompt the user, asking whether to overwrite and delete the infected file. Files erased in such a manner are non-recoverable.

Before running CLEAN-UP, verify the virus infection with the VIRUSCAN (SCAN.EXE) program. SCAN will locate and identify the virus and provide the I.D. code needed to remove it. The I.D. is displayed inside the square brackets, "[" and "]." For example, the I.D. code for the Jerusalem virus is displayed as "[Jeru]". This I.D. must be used with CLEAN-UP to remove the virus. The square brackets "[" and "]" MUST be included.

If SCAN finds an unknown virus in a file that had previously had recovery information stored for it, it will notify the user that an infection has occurred. It will not, however, display an I.D. code.

NOTE: When CLEAN is run with the /GENERIC option to disinfect files or system areas based on the recovery information stored by SCAN, no I.D. code should be used.

Please refer to the VIRUSCAN documentation for instructions in adding recovery information to your system.

The common viruses that CLEAN-UP is able to remove successfully and repair and restore the damaged programs are:

555	730	748	903
1008	1024	1253	1260
1575/1591*+	170x*	1992	2000

2100	2560	3445	4096*+
Air Cop*	Alabama+	Alameda	Antitelefonica
Ashar*	Azusa	Beeper	Black Monday+
Bloody!	Boys	Cara	Curse
Dark Avenger*+	DataLock+	December 28+	Devil's Dance
Dir-2	Disk Killer*	EDV*	Empire*
Enigma	Fellowship+	Filler	Fish+
Flash	Flip*+	Form	Generic Boot
Generic MBR	Ghost	Haifa	Invader*+
Irish	Jerusalem*+	Joshi	KeyPress*+
Korea*	Lazy	Lehigh	Liberty+
Lisbon*	Loa Duong	Michelangelo	Miky
Murphy*+	Music Bug	New Jerusalem+	Nomenclature
Pakistani Brain*	PayDay+	Perfume	Ping Pong*
Plastique*+	Plastique	Possessed	Print Screen-2*
R-11+	RPKS	Slayer	Slow+
Stoned*	Striker+	SBC	SVC*+
SunDay+	Sunday 2+	Suriv03+	Taiwan 3+
Taiwan 4+	Tequila	Tokyo	Topo
Typo Boot	V800	V-801	VACSINA*+
Vienna*	Violator*+	Whale*+	Yankee Doodle*+
ZeroBug			

* Denotes virus with more than one strain
+ Denotes virus which attaches to overlays

AN IMPORTANT NOTE ABOUT .EXE FILES: Some viruses which infect .EXE files can not be removed successfully in all cases. This usually occurs when the .EXE file loads internal overlays. Instead of attaching to the end of the .EXE file, the virus may attach to the beginning of the overlay area, and program instructions are overwritten. CLEAN-UP will truncate files infected in this manner. If a file no longer runs after being cleaned, replace it from the manufacturer's original disk.

AN IMPORTANT NOTE ABOUT THE STONED VIRUS: Removing the Stoned virus can cause loss of the partition table on systems with non-standard formatted hard disks. As a precaution, backup all critical data before running CLEAN-UP. Loss of the partition table can result in the LOSS OF ALL DATA ON THE DISK.

OPERATION

IMPORTANT NOTE: POWER DOWN YOUR SYSTEM AND BOOT FROM A CLEAN SYSTEM DISK BEFORE BEGINNING. RUN THE CLEAN-UP PROGRAM FROM A WRITE-PROTECTED DISK TO PREVENT INFECTION OF THE PROGRAM.

Power down the infected system and boot from a clean, write-protected system diskette. This step will insure that the virus is not in control of the computer and will prevent reinfection. After cleaning, power down the system again, reboot from the system disk, and run the VIRUSCAN program to make sure the system has been successfully disinfected. After cleaning the hard disk, run the VIRUSCAN program on any floppies that may have been inserted into the infected system to determine if they have been infected.

CLEAN-UP will display the name of the infected file, the virus found in it, and report a "successful" disinfection when the virus is removed. If a file has been infected multiple times by a virus (possible if the virus does not check to see if it has already attached to a file) then CLEAN-UP will report that the virus has been removed successfully for each infection.

To run CLEAN-UP type:

CLEAN d1: ... d10:   [virus ID] /A /CHKHI /E .xxx /FR /GENERIC

                                          /MAINT /MANY /M /REPORT d:filename /NOPAUSE

Options are:

/A	- Examine all files for viruses
/E .xxx .yyy .zzz	- Clean overlay extensions .xxx .yyy .zzz
/FR	- Display messages in French
/GENERIC	- Clean unknown viruses (see below for details)
/MAINT	- Clean DOS 4.0+ damaged boot sector
/MANY	- Check and disinfect multiple floppies
/NOPAUSE	- Disable screen prompting
/REPORT d:filename	- Create report of cleaned files
/SP	- Display messages in Spanish
d1: ... d10:	- indicate drives to be cleaned
[virus ID]	- Virus identification code - provided by the VIRUSCAN program when it detects a virus. For a complete list of codes, see the accompanying VIRLIST.TXT file.

NOTE: Brackets [ ] are required.

The /A option will cause CLEAN to check all files on disk. This should be used if an overlay-infecting virus is detected.

The /E option allows the user to specify an extension or set of extensions to clean. Extensions must be separated by a space after the /E and between each other. Up to three extensions may be added with the /E. For more extensions, use the /A option.

The /FR option tells CLEAN-UP to display all messages in French instead of English.

The /GENERIC option is used to clean files or areas of the system that have been infected with a new (unknown) virus. For /GENERIC to work, the PC must previously (prior to infection) have had SCAN with the /AG option run on it to store recovery information.

The /MAINT option is used to clean hard disks partitioned with DOS 4.0 or above that have been damaged by a boot sector or partition table infecting virus. Attempts to access disks damaged in such a manner result in an "invalid media" message being displayed. The /MAINT option will only clean the partition table and boot sector, not the files.

The /MANY option is used to clean multiple floppy diskettes. If the user has more than one floppy disk to check for viruses, the /MANY option will allow the user to check them without having to run CLEAN multiple times.

The /NOPAUSE option disables the "More..." prompt that appears when CLEAN fills a screen with data. This allows CLEAN-UP to run on a machine with multiple infections without requiring operator intervention when the screen fills up with messages from the CLEAN program.

The /REPORT option is used to generate a listing of disinfected files. The resulting list can be saved to disk as an ASCII text file. To use the report option, specify /REPORT on the command line, followed by the device and filename.

The /SP option tells CLEAN-UP to display all messages in Spanish instead of English.

EXAMPLES

The following examples are shown as they would be typed in on the command line.

CLEAN C: D: E: [JERU] /A	To disinfect drives C:, D:, and E: of the Jerusalem virus, searching all files for the virus in the process
CLEAN A: [STONED]	To disinfect floppy in drive A: of the Stoned virus
CLEAN C:\MORGAN [DAV] /A	To disinfect subdirectory MORGAN on drive C: of the Dark Avenger, searching all files for the virus in the process
CLEAN B: [DOODLE] /REPORT C:YNKINFCT.TXT	To disinfect floppy in drive B: of the Yankee Doodle virus, searching all files in the process, and creating a report of disinfected files named YNKINFCT.TXT on drive C:
CLEAN C: /GENERIC	To disinfect drive C: of an unknown virus using recovery information stored on the drive by SCAN's /AG option.

REGISTRATION

A registration fee of $35.00US is required for the use of CLEAN-UP by individual home users. Registration is for one year and entitles the holder to unlimited free upgrades off of McAfee Associates BBS or CompuServe Computer Virus Help Forum. When registering, a diskette containing the latest version may be requested. Add $9.00US for diskette mailings. Only one diskette mailing will be made.

Registration is for home users only and does not apply to businesses, corporations, organizations, government agencies, or schools, who must obtain a license for use. Contact McAfee Associates for more information.

Outside of the United States, registration and support may be obtained from the Agents listed in the accompanying AGENTS.TXT file.

TECH SUPPORT

In order to facilitate speedy and accurate support, please have the following information ready when you contact McAfee Associates:

- Program name and version number.

- Type and brand of computer, hard disk, plus any peripherals.

- Version of DOS you are running, plus any TSRs or device drivers in use.

- Printouts of your AUTOEXEC.BAT and CONFIG.SYS files.

- The exact problem you are having. Please be as specific as possible. Having a print-out of the screen and/or being at your computer will help also.

McAfee Associates can be contacted by CompuServe Forum, BBS or fax twenty-four hours a day, or call our business office at (408) 988-3832, Monday through Friday, 8:30AM to 6:00PM Pacific Standard Time.

McAfee Associates
1900 Wyatt Drive, Suite 8
Santa Clara, CA 95125-4617
USA

(408) 988-3832 office
(408) 970-9727 fax
(408) 988-4004 BBS 2400 bps
(408) 988-5138 BBS HST 9600
(408) 988-5190 BBS v32 9600
CompuServe GO VIRUSFORUM
InterNet mcafee@netcom.com

REGISTRATION INFORMATION

MCAFEE ASSOCIATES HOME USER LICENSE

NOTICE TO HOME USER: CAREFULLY READ THE FOLLOWING LEGAL AGREEMENT. YOU MUST PROMPTLY REGISTER YOUR USE OF THE SOFTWARE PROVIDED WITH THIS AGREEMENT (THE "SOFTWARE") BY COMPLETING AND FORWARDING TO MCAFEE ASSOCIATES ("MCAFEE") THE REGISTER.DOC FILE CONTAINED IN THE SOFTWARE.

1. LICENSE GRANT. If you are a home user, McAfee grants to you, as an individual, a non-exclusive right to use one copy of the object code version of the SOFTWARE associated with this license for personal use on your computer. This license to use the SOFTWARE is conditioned upon your compliance with the terms of this Agreement. You are entitled to evaluate the software on a royalty free basis for five days. Use after the five day evaluation period is further conditioned upon payment of the license fee specified in this REGISTER.DOC file. This license is effective for one year from the date of your first use or receipt of the REGISTER.DOC file by McAfee, whichever first occurs. You agree you will only copy the SOFTWARE as necessary to use it in accordance with this license.

2. COPYRIGHT. The SOFTWARE is protected by United States copyright law and international treaty provisions. You acknowledge that no title to the intellectual property in the SOFTWARE is transferred to you. You further acknowledge that title and full ownership rights to the SOFTWARE will remain the exclusive property of McAfee or its suppliers, and you will not acquire any rights to the SOFTWARE except as expressly set forth in this license. You agree that any copies of the SOFTWARE will contain the same proprietary notices which appear on and in the SOFTWARE.

3. REVERSE ENGINEERING. You agree that you will not attempt to reverse compile, modify, translate, or disassemble the SOFTWARE in whole or in part.

4. LIMITED WARRANTY. McAfee warrants that the SOFTWARE will perform substantially in accordance with the accompanying written materials for a period of ninety (90) days from the date of purchase. Any implied warranties relating to the SOFTWARE are limited to ninety (90) days.

5. CUSTOMER REMEDIES. If the SOFTWARE does not conform to the limited warranty in Section 4 above ("Limited Warranty"), McAfee's entire liability and your sole and exclusive remedy shall be, at McAfee's option, either to (a) correct the error or (b) help you work around or avoid the error. The Limited Warranty is void if failure of the SOFTWARE has resulted from accident, abuse, or misapplication. Any replacement SOFTWARE will be warranted for the remainder of the original Limited Warranty period.

6. NO OTHER WARRANTIES. MCAFEE DOES NOT WARRANT THAT THE SOFTWARE IS ERROR FREE. EXCEPT FOR THE EXPRESS LIMITED WARRANTY IN SECTION 4

("LIMITED WARRANTY"), MCAFEE DISCLAIMS ALL OTHER WARRANTIES WITH RESPECT TO THE SOFTWARE, EITHER EXPRESS OR IMPLIED, INCLUDING BUT NOT LIMITED TO IMPLIED WARRANTIES OF MERCHANTABILITY, FITNESS FOR A PARTICULAR PURPOSE AND NONINFRINGEMENT OF THIRD PARTY RIGHTS. SOME JURISDICTIONS DO NOT ALLOW THE EXCLUSION OF IMPLIED WARRANTIES OR LIMITATIONS ON HOW LONG AN IMPLIED WARRANTY MAY LAST, OR THE EXCLUSION OR LIMITATION OF INCIDENTAL OR CONSEQUENTIAL DAMAGES, SO THE ABOVE LIMITATIONS OR EXCLUSIONS MAY NOT APPLY TO YOU. THIS WARRANTY GIVES YOU SPECIFIC LEGAL RIGHTS AND YOU MAY ALSO HAVE OTHER RIGHTS WHICH VARY FROM JURISDICTION TO JURISDICTION.

7. SEVERABILITY. In the event of invalidity of any provision of this license, the parties agree that such invalidity shall not affect the validity of the remaining portions of this license.

8. NO LIABILITY FOR CONSEQUENTIAL DAMAGES. IN NO EVENT SHALL MCAFEE OR ITS SUPPLIERS BE LIABLE TO YOU FOR ANY CONSEQUENTIAL, SPECIAL, INCIDENTAL OR INDIRECT DAMAGES OF ANY KIND ARISING OUT OF THE DELIVERY, PERFORMANCE OR USE OF THE SOFTWARE, EVEN IF MCAFEE HAS BEEN ADVISED OF THE POSSIBILITY OF SUCH DAMAGES. IN NO EVENT WILL MCAFEE'S LIABILITY FOR ANY CLAIM, WHETHER IN CONTRACT, TORT OR ANY OTHER THEORY OF LIABILITY, EXCEED THE LICENSE FEE PAID BY YOU, IF ANY.

9. GOVERNING LAW. This license will be governed by the laws of the State of California as they are applied to agreements between California residents entered into and to be performed entirely within California. The United Nations Convention on Contracts for the International Sale of Goods is specifically disclaimed.

10. ENTIRE AGREEMENT. This is the entire agreement between you and McAfee which supersedes any prior agreement or understanding, whether written or oral, relating to the subject matter of this license.

Should you have any questions concerning this license agreement, or if you desire to contact McAfee for any reason, please call (408) 988-3832, fax (408) 970-9727, or write: McAfee Associates, 3350 Scott Boulevard, Building 14, Santa Clara, California 95054-3107.

MCAFEE SOFTWARE USE AGREEMENT

USE OF McAFEE SOFTWARE PROGRAMS

Use the form below to register to use McAfee series of software programs for personal home use on a single computer. Registration is for personal (home, non-business) use only. Any business (for profit or non-profit), corporate, institutional, or governmental use of our programs requires a Business/Institution/Government License. Business/Institution/Government License information may be requested by completing the "Request for Information" form in the LICENSE.DOC file and returning it to McAfee by fax or mail.

BBS SysOp's running no-charge, publicly-accessible systems may use the software free-of-charge on their BBS system—that's our way of saying thank you.

Send completed Registration Forms to:

McAfee Associates
3350 Scott Boulevard, Building 14
Santa Clara, California
95054-3107 USA

Or send to any of McAfee's AUTHORIZED AGENTS listed in the AGENTS.TXT file.

McAFEE REGISTRATION FORM for Individual Home Users ONLY

PROGRAM		# COPIES	AMOUNT
CLEAN-UP	($35 per copy)	_____	$ _____
VIRUSCAN	($25 per copy)	_____	$ _____
VSHIELD	($25 per copy)	_____	$ _____
SCAN for Windows (includes VIRUSCAN)	($35 per copy)	_____	$ _____
SCAN for OS/2 V2.0 (does NOT include VIRUSCAN)	($35 per copy)	_____	$ _____
SENTRY	($25 per copy)	_____	$ _____
CCP	($15 per copy)	_____	$ _____
MCONFIG	($15 per copy)	_____	$ _____
THE CONFIG MGR. (includes CCP and MCONFIG)	($25 per copy)	_____	_____
TARGET	($20 per copy)	_____	_____

DISK** $9 for Disk Handling Fee (add if a disk is
requested. A single handling fee is charged
regardless of the number of programs registered.) $ _____

Specify disk: 360K, 5-1/4" _____   Other _____

SALES TAX   California residents add 7.25%
(Santa Clara County residents add 8.25%) $ _____

                                     TOTAL $ _____

PAYMENT BY:

Check/Money Order No. _____ enclosed for $ _____

OR CHARGE TO: MasterCard __   Visa __   Expiration Date _____

Card Number   _____

Card Issued To   _____

Signature _____

MAILING ADDRESS:

Name _____

Address _____

City/State/Province_____

Country/Postal Code _____

Telephone (Voice/FAX/Modem) _____

**Disks are available at the time of registration only. Disks are shipped
U.S. Mail first class in the United States and Airmail to foreign
countries. Upgrades are available through the McAfee Associates
BBS or CompuServe only and will not be mailed to users.

BUSINESS/INSTITUTION/GOVERNMENT REQUEST FOR INFORMATION FORM

Please mail _____ or FAX _____ license information.
We have approximately _____ DOS-based systems.
Send to:
Name_____ Dept. _____
Company_____
Address _____

City/State/Province _____
Country/Postal Code _____
Telephone _____ FAX _____
Send to: McAfee Associates
             3350 Scott Boulevard, Building 14
             Santa Clara, California 95054-3107 USA

Or send to any of the AUTHORIZED AGENTS listed in the AGENTS.TXT file
For questions, orders and problems call
(M-F, 7:00am-5:30pm PT)   (408) 988-3832 Business
For FAXs (24 hours, Group III FAX)   (408) 970-9727 FAX
Bulletin Board System
(24 hours, 32 lines,1200-14.4K baud, US Robotics HST DS) (408) 988-4004 BBS

Information on VALIDATE

VALIDATE is a file-authentication program that may be used to check other programs for signs of tampering. VALIDATE uses two discrete methods to generate Cyclic Redundancy Checks (CRC's), which are then displayed for the user to compare against the known value for the program(s) validated. The known validation data can be published by the author of the program or be obtained from a trusted information database. The dual CRC checking provides a high degree of security.

To confirm that a program is in its original, untampered state, run the VALIDATE program on it, record the validation data produced, and compare it against the record in the online database. If they match, then it is highly improbable that the program has been modified.

To run VALIDATE, type:

VALIDATE d:\path\filename.ext

The VALIDATE program will then display the following information:

Size: (#/bytes)
Date: (file creation date)
File Authentication

VALIDATE Version 0.4. From McAfee Associates, (408) 988-3832. NOTE: VALIDATE version 0.4 is being released so that VALIDATE will remain compatible with the /SAVE option of SCAN. The new /SAVE option changes the SCAN.EXE file, and the new VALIDATE will be able to compensate for the changes, so that the validation results before and after the /SAVE switch will be identical. This in no way impairs the validating process.

Check Method 1: (a four digit CRC)
Check Method 2: (a four digit CRC)

The VALIDATE program may be copied and distributed at no charge as long as it is distributed whole and intact and unmodified in any way, along with this file. Please report virus infections and reports of program tampering to:

McAfee Associates
1900 Wyatt Drive, Suite 8
Santa Clara, CA 95054-0253
USA
(408) 727-4559 telephone answering machine

The validation data for VALIDATE.COM, version 0.4 is:

Size: 12,197
Date: 03-24-92
File Authentication
Check Method 1: D5BB
Check Method 2: 166F

SUPPORT ON COMPUSERVE

McAfee Associates now offers an online service through CompuServe that not only gives you access to our information and staff members, but also allows you to communicate with thousands of our other users on CompuServe as well. On CompuServe you can enjoy:

- Quick reponses to your questions about McAfee Associates software, directly from us! Find out progress on upgrades, updates, new features, and disk replacement.

- Around-the-clock technical support for all of McAfee Associates anti-viral software. Find out how to best use our software with your system. Learn solutions for common problems.

- Access to updates. Download the latest versions of McAfee Associates software.

- Access to public domain, user-written, and shareware programs available for downloading. All virus-free.

- An avenue for learning. Learn how others utilize McAfee Associates anti-viral software to fit their needs. Keep up to date on the latest third-party products available for McAfee Associates anti-viral software.

Not only can you get support for McAfee Associates' software on CompuServe, you can also access CompuServe's many other services. These include support for computer hardware and software products from over 200 companies, news, weather, sports, travel services, reference database, and business information.

If you are already a CompuServe member, you can access this service by typing GO MCAFEE at any CompuServe prompt.

FREE COMPUSERVE INTRODUCTORY MEMBERSHIP

As a McAfee Associates customer, you're entitled to a free introductory membership on CompuServe, which includes a private User ID and password, a US$15.00 introductory usage credit, and a free subscription to COMPUSERVE Magazine.

To receive your free CompuServe Introductory Membership, complete and return this form. Or call one of the telephone numbers below and ask for Representative 309.

NORTH AMERICA
United States and Canada   (800) 848-8199   *
                                    (614) 457-0802

OVERSEAS TELEPHONE NUMBERS TO ACCESS COMPUSERVE THROUGH A GATEWAY (Do not contact for CompuServe Membership)

SOUTH AMERICA
Argentina   +54 (01) 322-1864, 5934
Brazil   +55 (11) 2842433
(outside of Brazil)   +55 (11) 1081212
Chile   +56 (02) 696-8807
Venezuela   +58 (02) 793-2984, 2384, 6894

EUROPE
Germany   0130 37 32   *
                                    +49 (89) 66550 111
Belgium   +352 405637
Switzerland   155 31 79   *
United Kingdom   0800 289 378   *
                                    +44 (272) 255 111

PACIFIC RIM
Australia   008 02 5240   *
                                    +61 (02) 411 8603
Japan (via NIFTY-Serve)   0120 22 1200   *
                                    +81 (03) 3221-7363
Korea   +82 (02) 7966104
                                    080-022-7400   *
New Zealand   0800 44 6113   *
Taiwan   +886 (02) 515-0330

*Indicates a telephone number that is toll-free within the country indicated.

MAIL TO:

(UNITED STATES and CANADA)   (UNITED KINGDOM)
COMPUSERVE   COMPUSERVE
5000 Arlington Centre Blvd.   FREEPOST (BS6971)
P.O. Box 20212   P.O. Box 676
Columbus, OH 43220-9988   Bristol BS99 1NZ
USA   UNITED KINGDOM

(GERMANY)   (AUSTRALIA and NEW ZEALAND)
COMPUSERVE   COMPUSERVE PACIFIC
Jahstrasse 2   Fujitsu Australia Ltd

Postfach 1169
D-8025 Unterhaching/Muenchen
DEUTSCHLAND

475 Victoria Avenue
Chatswood, NSW 2067
AUSTRALIA

(JAPAN)
NIFTY Corporation
Kojimachi Koyo Bldg.
1-20 Kojimachi
Chiyoda-ku
Tokyo 102
JAPAN

(KOREA)
POS-Serve
PC Communication Department
POSDATA CO., Ltd.
10/F, Daejan Jedang Bldg.
7-23, Shinchun-dong, Songpa-ku
Seoul, KOREA

(TAIWAN)
Taiwan Telecom Network
Services Co Ltd
15/F, 120 Chien-kuo N. Road
Section 2, Taipei
TAIWAN R.O.C

(ARGENTINA)
CompuServe S.A. Argentina
Florida 671 E.P. 1005
Buenos Aires
ARGENTINA

(CHILE)
Chilepac
Gerencia Red de Datos
Morande 147
Santiago
CHILE

(VENEZUELA)
CompuServe C.A. Venezuela
Plaza Venezuela - Torres Capriles
Pis 4, Oficina 401
Caracas
VENEZUELA

CUT THE FORM AT THE LINE ABOVE, ANSWER ALL THE QUESTIONS BELOW, AND THEN MAIL TO COMPUSERVE AT THE ADDRESS AT THE BOTTOM OF THE FORM.

_____ YES! Please send me a free CompuServe Introductory Membership from Representative 309, the McAfee Virus Help Forum.

NAME _____
COMPANY NAME _____
ADDRESS1 _____
ADDRESS2 _____
CITY _____ STATE/PROVINCE _____
ZIP/POSTAL CODE _____
COUNTRY _____
McAFEE ASSOCIATES PROGRAM(S) _____

This offer is limted to first-time members only. Only one Introductory Membership will be given to a customer.

LICENSE INFORMATION

PLEASE FEEL FREE TO (i) UPLOAD THIS SOFTWARE TO ANY ELECTRONIC BULLETIN BOARD, (ii) DEMONSTRATE THE SOFTWARE AND ITS CAPABILITIES OR (iii) GIVE COPIES TO POTENTIAL USERS, SO THAT OTHERS MAY HAVE THE OPPORTUNITY TO OBTAIN A COPY FOR USE IN ACCORDANCE WITH THE LICENSE TERMS CONTAINED IN THIS FILE.

BUSINESS/INSTITUTION/GOVERNMENT LICENSE. If you are a business, institution, or government agency, the first of the three licenses in this file pertains to you. Forms to request information regarding this license are at the end of this file.

SERVICE LICENSE. If you are a business using the software programs for checking client and customer diskettes and systems, the second of the three licenses in this file pertains to you.

SHAREWARE DISTRIBUTION LICENSE. If you are a shareware distributor, the third of the three licenses in this file pertains to you.

HOME USER LICENSE. If you are an individual end user whose use is not on behalf of a business, organization, or government agency, the license in the REGISTER.DOC file pertains to you. Registration forms are also located in the REGISTER.DOC file.

McAFEE ASSOCIATES BUSINESS/INSTITUTION/GOVERNMENT LICENSE

NOTICE TO USERS ("COMPANY"): CAREFULLY READ THE FOLLOWING LEGAL AGREEMENT. COMPANY'S USE OF THIS SOFTWARE IS CONDITIONED UPON COMPLIANCE BY COMPANY WITH THE TERMS OF THIS AGREEMENT. THE SOFTWARE MAY BE EVALUATED FOR FIVE DAYS ON A ROYALTY FREE BASIS. CONTINUED USE AFTER EVALUATION IS CONDITIONED UPON PAYMENT BY COMPANY OF THE NEGOTIATED LICENSE FEE SPECIFIED IN A CONFIRMATION LETTER FROM MCAFEE ASSOCIATES ("MCAFEE").

The Software may not be distributed by Company to any outside corporation, organization, or government agency. This license authorizes Company to use the number of copies described in the confirmation letter from McAfee and for which Company has paid McAfee the negotiated license fee. If the confirmation letter from McAfee indicates that Company's license is "Corporate-Wide", this license will be deemed to cover copies duplicated and distributed by Company for use on any additional incremental machines purchased or leased by Company during the Term, at no additional charge. This license will remain in effect for two years from the date of the confirmation letter from McAfee authorizing such continued use or such other period as is stated in the confirmation letter (the "Term"). If Company does not obtain a confirmation letter and pay the applicable license fee, this license expires at the end of the five day evaluation period. All updates must be accessed and downloaded from McAfee's bulletin board, the McAfee Virus Forum on CompuServe or McAfee's Internet node. Access instructions for the Company's licensed user bulletin board are included in the confirmation letter. In the case where Company is licensing more than 50 copies of the Software, all updates will also be provided in diskette form at no charge as they occur or quarterly, whichever is less frequent, during the term of this license.

I. *SINGLE POINT OF CONTACT*. Support for Software bug reports and other product issues will be handled through a single point of contact within the Company. Company shall identify the contact individual when placing its order with McAfee or McAfee's Authorized Agent. There will be no charge for support of the Software when channelled through such individual. Support requests from other organizational areas will be billed at normal hourly support rates.

II. *INFECTION SUPPORT.* Telephone, BBS, CompuServe and Internet support for virus infections is available at no additional charge. On-site support may be obtained from a McAfee Authorized Agent, as available, at a negotiated hourly rate plus travel time and expenses.

III. *EMPLOYEE HOME USE OPTION.* In the case where Company is licensing more than 50 copies of the Software, McAfee will license the Software for home use by employees if requested by Company, in writing, within the first year of the license. The cost for this option is 20% of the standard site license fee for that number of employee home use machines.

IV. *GENERAL TERMS.*

COPYRIGHT. The Software is protected by United States copyright laws and international treaty provisions. Company acknowledges that no title to the intellectual property in the Software is transferred to Company. Company further acknowledges that full ownership rights to the Software will remain the exclusive property of McAfee or its suppliers, and Company will not acquire any rights to the Software except as expressly set forth in this license. Company agrees that any copies of the Software made by Company will contain the same proprietary notices which appear on and in the Software.

REVERSE ENGINEERING. Company agrees that it will not attempt, and will use its best efforts to prevent its employees from attempting to reverse compile, modify, translate, or disassemble the Software in whole or in part.

LIMITED WARRANTY. McAfee warrants that the Software will perform substantially in accordance with the accompanying documentation for a period of ninety (90) days from the date McAfee receives payment.

COMPANY REMEDIES. If the Software does not conform to the limited warranty above ("Limited Warranty"), McAfee's entire liability and Company's sole and exclusive remedy shall be, at McAfee's option, either to (a) correct the error, (b) help Company work around or avoid the error or (c) authorize a refund, so long as the Software is destroyed by Company. The Limited Warranty is void if failure of the Software has resulted from accident, abuse, or misapplication. Any replacement Software will be warranted for the remainder of the original Limited Warranty period.

NO OTHER WARRANTIES. MCAFEE DOES NOT WARRANT THAT THE SOFTWARE IS ERROR FREE, IDENTIFIES ALL KNOWN VIRUSES OR MAY NOT OCCASIONALLY REPORT A VIRUS IN A FILE NOT INFECTED BY THAT VIRUS. EXCEPT FOR THE EXPRESS LIMITED WARRANTY ABOVE, MCAFEE DISCLAIMS ALL OTHER WARRANTIES WITH RESPECT TO THE SOFTWARE, EITHER EXPRESS OR IMPLIED, INCLUDING BUT NOT LIMITED TO IMPLIED WARRANTIES OF MERCHANTABILITY, FITNESS FOR A PARTICULAR PURPOSE AND NONINFRINGEMENT OF THIRD PARTY RIGHTS.

SEVERABILITY. In the event of invalidity of any provision of this license, the parties agree that such invalidity shall not affect the validity of the remaining portions of this license.

NO LIABILITY FOR CONSEQUENTIAL DAMAGES. IN NO EVENT SHALL MCAFEE OR ITS SUPPLIERS BE LIABLE FOR CONSEQUENTIAL, INCIDENTAL OR INDIRECT DAMAGES OF ANY KIND ARISING OUT OF THE DELIVERY, PERFORMANCE OR USE OF THE SOFTWARE, EVEN IF MCAFEE HAS BEEN ADVISED OF THE POSSIBIL-ITY OF SUCH DAMAGES. IN NO EVENT WILL MCAFEE'S LIABILITY FOR ANY CLAIM, WHETHER IN CONTRACT, TORT OR ANY OTHER THEORY OF LIABILITY, EXCEED THE LICENSE FEE PAID BY COMPANY.

EXPORT. Company agrees that it will not export or re-export the Software to North Korea, Vietnam, Cuba, Iran, or Iraq without the appropriate United States or foreign government licenses.

GOVERNING LAW. This Agreement will be governed by the laws of the State of California as they are applied to agreements to be entered into and to be performed entirely within California. The United Nations Convention on Contracts for the Interna-tional Sale of Goods is specifically disclaimed.

U.S. GOVERNMENT RESTRICTED RIGHTS. If the Software is acquired (i) for use by DoD, use, duplication or disclosure by the Government is subject to the terms of this license unless superseded by 252.227-7013(c)(1)(ii) or (ii) for use by civilian agencies, use, reproduction or disclosure is subject to the terms of this license unless super-seded by 52.227-19.

ENTIRE AGREEMENT. This Agreement together with any McAfee confirmation letter constitute the entire agreement between Company and McAfee which supersedes any prior agreement, including any prior license from McAfee, or understanding, whether written or oral, relating to the subject matter of this Agreement. The terms and conditions of this Agreement shall apply to all orders submitted to McAfee and shall supersede any different or additional terms on purchase orders from Company.

Should you have any questions concerning this license agreement, or if you desire to contact McAfee for any reason, please call (408) 988-3832, fax (408) 970-9727, or write: McAfee Associates, 3350 Scott Boulevard, Building 14, Santa Clara, California 95054-3107.

McAFEE ASSOCIATES SERVICE LICENSE

NOTICE TO SERVICE PROVIDERS ("COMPANY"): CAREFULLY READ THE FOLLOWING LEGAL AGREEMENT. COMPANY'S USE OF THIS SOFTWARE IS CONDITIONED UPON COMPLIANCE BY COMPANY WITH THE TERMS OF THIS AGREEMENT AND PAYMENT BY COMPANY OF THE NEGOTIATED LICENSE FEE SPECIFIED IN A CONFIRMATION LETTER FROM MCAFEE ASSOCIATES ("MCAFEE").

The Software may not be distributed by Company to any outside corporation, organi-zation or government agency. This license authorizes Company to use the number of copies described in the confirmation letter from McAfee and for which Company has paid McAfee the negotiated license fee. The Software must remain on diskette, may not be copied to a hard drive, and must be removed from the client/customer site when the Company representative leaves the site. This license will remain in effect for two years from the date of the confirmation letter from McAfee authorizing such use or such other period as is stated in the confirmation letter (the "Term"). All updates must be accessed and downloaded from McAfee's bulletin board, the McAfee Virus Forum on CompuServe or McAfee's Internet node. Access instructions for the Company's licensed user bulletin board are included in the confirmation letter.

I. *SINGLE POINT OF CONTACT.* Support for Software bug reports and other product issues will be handled through a single point of contact within the Company. Company shall identify the contact individual when placing its order with McAfee or McAfee's Authorized Agent. There will be no charge for support of the Software when channelled through such individual. Support requests from other organizational areas will be billed at normal hourly support rates.

II. *INFECTION SUPPORT.* Telephone, BBS, CompuServe and Internet support for virus infections is available at no additional charge.

III. *GENERAL TERMS.*

COPYRIGHT. The Software is protected by United States copyright laws and international treaty provisions. Company acknowledges that no title to the intellectual property in the Software is transferred to Company. Company further acknowledges that full ownership rights to the Software will remain the exclusive property of McAfee or its suppliers, and Company will not acquire any rights to the Software except as expressly set forth in this license. Company agrees that any copies of the Software made by Company will contain the same proprietary notices which appear on and in the Software.

REVERSE ENGINEERING. Company agrees that it will not attempt, and will use its best efforts to prevent its employees from attempting to reverse compile, modify, translate, or disassemble the Software in whole or in part.

LIMITED WARRANTY. McAfee warrants that the Software will perform substantially in accordance with the accompanying documentation for a period of ninety (90) days from the date McAfee receives payment.

COMPANY REMEDIES. If the Software does not conform to the limited warranty above ("Limited Warranty"), McAfee's entire liability and Company's sole and exclusive remedy shall be, at McAfee's option, either to (a) correct the error, (b) help Company work around or avoid the error or (c) authorize a refund, so long as the Software is destroyed by Company. The Limited Warranty is void if failure of the Software has resulted from accident, abuse, or misapplication. Any replacement Software will be warranted for the remainder of the original Limited Warranty period.

NO OTHER WARRANTIES. MCAFEE DOES NOT WARRANT THAT THE SOFTWARE IS ERROR FREE, IDENTIFIES ALL KNOWN VIRUSES OR MAY NOT OCCASIONALLY REPORT A VIRUS IN A FILE NOT INFECTED BY THAT VIRUS. EXCEPT FOR THE EXPRESS LIMITED WARRANTY ABOVE, MCAFEE DISCLAIMS ALL OTHER WARRANTIES WITH RESPECT TO THE SOFTWARE, EITHER EXPRESS OR IMPLIED, INCLUDING BUT NOT LIMITED TO IMPLIED WARRANTIES OF MERCHANTABILITY, FITNESS FOR A PARTICULAR PURPOSE AND NONINFRINGEMENT OF THIRD PARTY RIGHTS.

SEVERABILITY. In the event of invalidity of any provision of this license, the parties agree that such invalidity shall not affect the validity of the remaining portions of this license.

NO LIABILITY FOR CONSEQUENTIAL DAMAGES. IN NO EVENT SHALL MCAFEE OR ITS SUPPLIERS BE LIABLE FOR CONSEQUENTIAL, INCIDENTAL OR INDIRECT DAMAGES OF ANY KIND ARISING OUT OF THE DELIVERY, PERFORMANCE OR USE OF THE SOFTWARE, EVEN IF MCAFEE HAS BEEN ADVISED OF THE POSSIBILITY OF SUCH DAMAGES. IN NO EVENT WILL MCAFEE'S LIABILITY FOR ANY CLAIM,

WHETHER IN CONTRACT, TORT OR ANY OTHER THEORY OF LIABILITY, EXCEED THE LICENSE FEE PAID BY COMPANY.

EXPORT. Company agrees that it will not export or re-export the Software to North Korea, Vietnam, Cuba, Iran, or Iraq without the appropriate United States or foreign government licenses.

GOVERNING LAW. This Agreement will be governed by the laws of the State of California as they are applied to agreements to be entered into and to be performed entirely within California. The United Nations Convention on Contracts for the International Sale of Goods is specifically disclaimed.

U.S. GOVERNMENT RESTRICTED RIGHTS. If the Software is acquired (i) for use by DoD, use, duplication or disclosure by the Government is subject to the terms of this license unless superseded by 252.227-7013(c)(1)(ii) or (ii) for use by civilian agencies, use, reproduction or disclosure is subject to the terms of this license unless superseded by 52.227-19.

ENTIRE AGREEMENT. This Agreement together with any McAfee confirmation letter constitute the entire agreement between Company and McAfee which supersedes any prior agreement, including any prior license from McAfee, or understanding, whether written or oral, relating to the subject matter of this Agreement. The terms and conditions of this Agreement shall apply to all orders submitted to McAfee and shall supersede any different or additional terms on purchase orders from Company.

Should you have any questions concerning this license agreement, or if you desire to contact McAfee for any reason, please call (408) 988-3832, fax (408) 970-9727, or write: McAfee Associates, 3350 Scott Boulevard, Building 14, Santa Clara, California 95054-3107.

McAFEE ASSOCIATES SHAREWARE DISTRIBUTION LICENSE

NOTICE TO SHAREWARE DISTRIBUTORS ("DISTRIBUTOR"): CAREFULLY READ THE FOLLOWING LEGAL AGREEMENT. DISTRIBUTOR'S RIGHT TO DISTRIBUTE THIS SOFTWARE IS CONDITIONED UPON COMPLIANCE BY DISTRIBUTOR WITH THE TERMS OF THIS AGREEMENT.

1. *LICENSE GRANT.* McAfee Associates ("McAfee") grants to Distributor a nonexclusive, worldwide right to distribute the object code version of the Software as shareware. This license to distribute the Software is conditioned upon Distributor's compliance with the terms of this Agreement. Distributor will not copy the Software except as necessary to use it in accordance with this license, and Distributor is granted no right to modify or sublicense the Software. Distributor may download the Software files from McAfee's electronic bulletin board system at 408-988-4004, settings are 8NI, ANSI or TTY emulation, and full duplex, from the McAfee Virus Forum on CompuServe or McAfee's Internet node. All files of this Software must be distributed bundled together, with the Software .COM and .EXE files bundled with the LICENSE.DOC, REGISTER.DOC and AGENTS.TXT file. All Software distribution must be via diskettes (which are either write-protected or notchless) or electronic transmission (in which case the original archive file from McAfee must be used). Distributor is prohibited from installing copies of the Software on hard drives and distributing such hard drives.
2. *NO SUBLICENSE FEE.* Distributor may not charge its customers for the Software other than a nominal fee for the diskette.

3. *COPYRIGHT.* The Software is protected by United States copyright laws and international treaty provisions. Distributor acknowledges that no title to the intellectual property in the Software is transferred to Distributor. Distributor further acknowledges that full ownership rights to the Software will remain the exclusive property of McAfee or its suppliers, and Distributor will not acquire any rights to the Software except as expressly set forth in this license. Distributor agrees that any copies of the Software made by Distributor will contain the same proprietary notices which appear on and in the Software.

4. *REVERSE ENGINEERING.* Distributor agrees that it will not attempt, and will use its best efforts to prevent its employees from attempting to reverse compile, modify, translate, or disassemble the Software in whole or in part.

5. *LIMITED END USER WARRANTY.* McAfee warrants the Software TO END USERS ONLY pursuant to the terms and conditions of the end user license and no warranty is extended to Distributor. In the event the Software does not conform to the limited warranty described in the end user license, McAfee will provide the end user with a solution in accordance with the terms of the end user license. Distributor agrees to provide McAfee with reasonable assistance in providing warranty assistance to end users.

6. *NO OTHER WARRANTIES.* MCAFEE DOES NOT WARRANT THAT THE SOFTWARE IS ERROR FREE, IDENTIFIES ALL KNOWN VIRUSES OR MAY NOT OCCASIONALLY REPORT A VIRUS IN A FILE NOT INFECTED BY THAT VIRUS. EXCEPT FOR THE EXPRESS WARRANTIES GRANTED TO THE END USER IN THE END USER LICENSE AGREEMENT, MCAFEE DISCLAIMS ALL OTHER WARRANTIES WITH RESPECT TO THE SOFTWARE, EITHER EXPRESS OR IMPLIED, INCLUDING BUT NOT LIMITED TO IMPLIED WARRANTIES OF MERCHANTABILITY, FITNESS FOR A PARTICULAR PURPOSE AND NONINFRINGEMENT OF THIRD PARTY RIGHTS.

7. *SEVERABILITY.* In the event of invalidity of any provision of this license, the parties agree that such invalidity shall not affect the validity of the remaining portions of this license.

8. *NO LIABILITY FOR CONSEQUENTIAL DAMAGES.* IN NO EVENT SHALL MCAFEE OR ITS SUPPLIERS BE LIABLE FOR CONSEQUENTIAL, INCIDENTAL OR INDIRECT DAMAGES OF ANY KIND ARISING OUT OF THE DELIVERY, PERFORMANCE OR USE OF THE SOFTWARE, EVEN IF MCAFEE HAS BEEN ADVISED OF THE POSSIBILITY OF SUCH DAMAGES.

9. *EXPORT.* Distributor agrees that it will not export or re-export the Software to North Korea, Vietnam, Cuba, Iran or Iraq without the appropriate United States or foreign government licenses.

10. *GOVERNING LAW.* This Agreement will be governed by the laws of the State of California as they are applied to agreements to be entered into and to be performed entirely within California. The United Nations Convention on Contracts for the International Sale of Goods is specifically disclaimed.

11. *U.S. GOVERNMENT RESTRICTED RIGHTS.* If Distributor provides the Software for use by DoD, Distributor agrees to insure that use, duplication or disclosure by the Government will be subject to the terms of this Agreement unless superseded by 252.227-7013(c)(1)(ii). If Distributor provides the Software for use by civilian agencies, Distributor agrees to insure that use, reproduction or disclosure is subject to the terms of this Agreement unless superseded by 52.227-19.

12. *ENTIRE AGREEMENT.* This Agreement constitutes the entire agreement between Distributor and McAfee which supersedes any prior agreement, including any prior license from McAfee, or understanding, whether written or oral, relating to the subject matter of this Agreement.

Should you have any questions concerning this license agreement, or if you desire to contact McAfee for any reason, please call (408) 988-3832, fax (408) 970-9727, or write: McAfee Associates, 3350 Scott Boulevard, Building 14, Santa Clara, California 95054-3107.

BUSINESS/INSTITUTION/GOVERNMENT REQUEST FOR INFORMATION FORM

Please mail _____ or FAX _____ license information.
We have approximately _____ DOS-based systems.
Send to:
Name _____ Dept. _____
Company _____
Address _____
_____
City/State/Province _____
Country/Postal Code _____
Telephone _____ FAX _____

Send to:

McAfee Associates
3350 Scott Boulevard, Building 14
Santa Clara, California
95054-3107 USA

Or send to any of the AUTHORIZED AGENTS listed in the AGENTS.TXT file

For questions, orders and problems call

(M-F, 7:00am - 5:30pm PT):	(408) 988-3832 Business
For FAXs (24 hour, Group III FAX):	(408) 970-9727 FAX
Bulletin Board System (24 hour, 32 lines, 1200 - 14.4K baud, US Robotics HST DS):	(408) 988-4004 BBS

Virus List for NetScan

The following list outlines the major characteristics of the known IBM PC and compatible virus strains identified by SCAN. The number of known variants of each virus is also listed. This number is listed in parenthesis beside the name of the strain. The total number of known viruses is summed at the end of the list. The Clean-Up virus I.D. code is included in brackets.

	Virus Uses STEALTH Techniques	Virus Uses Self-Encryption	Virus Installs Self in Memory	Infects COMMAND.COM	Infects COM files	Infects EXE Files	Infects Overlay Files	Infects Floppy Diskette Boot	Infects Fixed Disk Boot Sector	Infects Fixed Disk Partition Table-A	Increase in Infected Program's	
Virus	**Disinfector**	1 v	2 v	3 v	4 v	5 v	6 v	7 v	8 v	9 v	A v	**Size**	**Damage**
1 [N1]	Clean-Up	.	.	x	x	x	.	.	.	.	.	11240	O N
007 [007]	Clean-Up	.	.	x	x	x	x	.	.	.	.	1773	OPD
1008 [1008]	Clean-Up	.	x	x	x	x	.	.	.	.	.	1008	OPDL
1014 [1014]	Clean-Up	.	.	x	x	x	.	.	.	.	.	1014	OP
1024 (2) [Alf]	Clean-Up	.	.	x	x	x	.	.	.	.	.	1024	O
1024PSRC [PS10]	Clean-Up	.	.	x	x	x	.	.	.	.	.	1024	OPL
1030 [1030]	Clean-Up	.	.	x	.	.	x	x	.	.	.	1030	OPL
1067 [1067]	Clean-Up	.	.	x	x	x	.	.	.	.	.	1067	OPL
1210 [1210]	Clean-Up	.	.	x	.	x	.	.	.	.	.	1210	OPL
1241 [1241]	Clean-Up	.	.	x	x	x	.	.	.	.	.	1241	OPL
1244 [1244]	Clean-Up	.	.	x	.	x	x	x	.	.	.	1244	OPL
1253 - Boot [1253]	M-Disk	.	.	x	.	.	.	.	x	x	x	N/A	BOPDL
1253 - COM [1253]	Clean-Up	.	.	x	x	x	.	.	.	.	.	1253	OPDL
1260 (4) [V2P2]	Clean-Up	.	x	.	.	x	.	.	.	.	.	1260	P
1280 [1280]	Clean-Up	.	x	.	.	x	.	.	.	.	.	1168	PF
1339 [1339]	Clean-Up	.	.	x	x	x	x	x	.	.	.	1339	OPL
1376 [1376]	Clean-Up	.	.	x	x	x	x	x	x	.	.	1376	OPL
1381 [1381]	Clean-Up	.	.	.	.	.	x	x	.	.	.	1381	OP
1385 [1385]	Clean-Up	.	.	x	x	x	.	.	.	.	.	1385	OPL
1392 [1392]	Clean-Up	.	.	x	x	x	x	.	.	.	.	1392	OPL
1452 [1452]	Clean-Up	.	.	x	x	.	.	.	.	.	.	1452	OP
1530 [1530]	Clean-Up	.	.	.	.	x	x	.	.	.	.	1530	PO
1559/1554 (2) [1559]	Clean-Up	.	x	x	x	x	x	.	.	.	.	1554	OPL
1575/1591 (5) [15xx]	Clean-Up	.	.	x	x	x	x	.	.	.	.	Varies	O P L
1605 (2) [Jeru]	Clean-Up	.	.	x	x	x	x	.	.	.	.	1605	LOPD
1661 [1661]	Clean-Up	.	.	x	x	x	.	.	.	.	.	1661	OPL
1677 [1677]	Clean-Up	.	.	x	x	x	.	.	.	.	.	1677	OPL
1720 (4) [1720]	Clean-Up	.	.	x	.	x	x	x	.	.	.	1720	FOPL

Name	Action	Pattern	Result	Code
1835 [1835]	Clean-Up	. . . . . x	1835	OFP
1840 [Alf]	Clean-Up	. . x . . x x . . .	1840	OPLD
191 [Tiny]	Clean-Up	. . . x x	191	LOP
1963 [1963]	Clean-Up	x . x x x x x . . .	1963	OPLD
1971/8 Tunes (2) [1971]	Clean-Up	. . x . x x x . . .	1971	OP
1992 [1992]	Clean-Up	. x x x x x	1746	LFP
1992B [1992B]	Clean-Up	. x . . . x	Overwrites	
2153 [2153]	Clean-Up	. . x x x x	2168	PDL
2330 [2330]	Clean-Up	. . x x x x x . . .	2330	OPL
2559 [2559]	Clean-Up	. . . . . x	2559	LOP
2560 [2560]	Clean-Up	x . x . x x	2560	OP
205 [205]	Clean-Up	. . . x x	205	PL
203 [203]	Clean-Up	. . . x x	203	PD
262 [262]	Clean-Up	. . x x x	262	OPL
2622 [2622]	Clean-Up	. . x x x x x x x x	2622	OPLD
2930 [Spain]	Clean-Up	. . x . x x	2930	P
310 [GS]	Clean-Up	. . x x x	310	OPL
337 [337]	Clean-Up	. . x x x	337	OL
302 [302]	Clean-Up	. . x x x	302	OP
344 [344]	Clean-Up	. . . x x	344	PL
384 [OW]	Clean-Up	. . . x x x	384	DPL
3040 [3040]	Clean-Up	x . x . x x	3183	DPO
355 [355]	Clean-Up	. . . x x	355	DPL
3445 [4096]	Clean-Up	x x x . x x	3445	OPDL
365 [365]	Clean-Up	. . x x x	365	OPL
370-B [370]	Clean-Up	. . . . x	370	P
382 (2) [Pir]	Clean-Up	. . . x x x	Overwrites	LOP
439 [439]	Clean-Up	. . x x x	439	OP
405 [Burger]	Clean-Up	. . . . x	Overwrites	PF
408 [408]	Clean-Up	. . x x x	408	LOP
4096 (9) [4096]	Clean-Up	x . x x x x x . . .	4096	DOPL
482 [482]	Clean-Up	. . x x x	482	OP
487 [487]	Clean-Up	. . . . x	487	P
4915 [OW]	Clean-Up	. . . . . x	Overwrites	
500 [500]	Clean-Up	. . x x x	500	LOP
510 [VHP]	Clean-Up	. . . x x	510	OL
512 (5) [512]	Clean-Up	x . x x x	N/A	OPL
5120 (3) [5120]	Clean-Up	. . . x x x x . . .	5120	OPDL
555 [BWish]	Clean-Up	. . x x x x x . . .	555	OPL
557 [557]	Clean-Up	. . x . . x	557	DPL
560 [560]	Clean-Up	. . x x x	560	OPL
621 [621]	Clean-Up	. . . x x	621	OPD

Name	Tool	Marks	Size	Flags
644 [644]	Clean-Up	. x . . x x	644	LD
651 [Alf]	Clean-Up	. . x . x	651	OPD
654 [640]	Clean-Up	. . . . x	654	P
702 [702]	Clean-Up	. . . x x x	702	PF
709 [CSL]	Clean-Up	. x x x x	709	OP
733 [733]	Clean-Up	. . . x x x	733	OPDL
737 [GN]	Clean-Up	. . x x x x	737	OPL
748 [748]	Clean-Up	. . x x x	748	ODL
765 [765]	Clean-Up	. . x . . x x . . .	765	OPL
777 [777]	Clean-Up	. . x x x	777	OP
7808 [7808]	Clean-Up	. . x x x x x . . .	7808	OPLD
789 [Zar]	Clean-Up	. . x x x	789	OL
7th Son (4) [7S]	Clean-Up	. . . x x	350	OP
812 (2) [812]	Clean-Up	. . x x x x x . . .	812	OD
834/Arab Virus [Ar]	Clean-Up	. . x . x	834	OP
855 [GN]	Clean-Up	. . x x x x x . . .	855	OPL
8000 [OW]	Clean-Up	. . . . . x	7529	OPL
903 [903]	Clean-Up	. . x x x	903	OP
905 [905]	Clean-Up	. . . . x	905	P
923 [923]	Clean-Up	. . x x x x x . . .	923	OPLD
A-403 [A-403]	Clean-Up	. . x x x	Overwrites	L
ABC [ABC]	Clean-Up	. . x . . x	2972	LPOD
Abraxas [Abrx]	Clean-Up	. x . x x x	546	OPD
Acid [Acd]	Clean-Up	. . . x x x	Overwrites	
Ada [Ada]	Clean-Up	. . x x x	2600	OPL
Agena [Agn]	Clean-Up	. . x x x x	738	PDL
AGI-Plan [AGI]	Clean-Up	. . . x x	1536	OPL
Ah [Alf]	Clean-Up	. . x x x	1173	BLOP
AIDS [N1]	Clean-Up	. . . . x x	Overwrites	P O L
AIDS II [A2]	Clean-Up	. . . . x x	Spawning	O
AIDS Trojan (13) [Aids]	Clean-Up	. . . . x	Overwrites	P
AirCop (3) [AirCop]	Clean-Up	. . x . . . . . x . .	N/A	BO
Akuku (2) [Akuku]	Clean-Up	. . . x x x	891	LOP
Alabama (3) [Alabama]	Clean-Up	. . x . . x	1560	OPL
Albanian [Alb]	Clean-Up	. . . x x	606	DPL
Alfa (2) [Alf]	Clean-Up	. . x x x x x . . .	1150	LOP
Amstrad (7) [Amst]	Clean-Up	. . . . x	847	P
Andre [And]	Clean-Up	. x x . x x	3648	PD
Andre2 [And]	Clean-Up	x x x . x x	3568	PDL
Anna [Anna]	Clean-Up	. . . x x	742	PLO
Anthrax - Boot (2) [Atx]	M-Disk	. . x x	N/A	BOPD

Name	Action	Pattern	Size	Code
Anthrax - File (4) [Atx]	Clean-Up	. . x x x x	1206	OPD
ANT [Ant]	Clean-Up	. . . . x	770	OPL
Anti-D [GR]	Clean-Up	. . x x x	945	OPL
Anti-Pascal (3) [AP]	Clean-Up	. . . x x	605	LLOP
Anti-Pascal II (4) [G3]	Clean-Up	. . . x x	400	B
Anti-Tel [A-Vir]	Clean-Up	x x x . . . . . x . x	N/A	BFLO
Arcv-1 [ARC]	Clean-Up	. . . . x x	826	DL
Arcv-2 [ARC]	Clean-Up	. . . . . x	692	LPO
Arcv-3 [ARC]	Clean-Up	. . . x x	657	LPO
Argentina [GR]	Clean-Up	. . x x x	1249	OPD
Arka [Ark]	Clean-Up	. x x x x	1909	OD
Arma [Arma]	Clean-Up	. . x x x	1079	OP
Armagedon (3) [Arma]	Clean-Up	. . x x x	1079	OP
Ash [Ash]	Clean-Up	. . . . x	280	PLD
ASP-472 [472]	Clean-Up	. . x x x x x . . .	472	LOP
Astra [AST]	Clean-Up	. x . x x	976	LDP
AT144 [144]	Clean-Up	. . . x x	144	OP
Atas [Ata]	Clean-Up	. x . x x	384	LOD
August 16 [A16]	Clean-Up	. . . x x	631	OP
Australian [GD]	Clean-Up	. . x x x x x . . .	1433	OPLD
Azusa (2) [Azusa]	Clean-Up	. . x . . . . x . x	N/A	DOBL
B3 [B3]	Clean-Up	. . x x x	483	PL
BackTime [BT]	Clean-Up	. . x x x	528	LOP
Bad Boy (4) [BB]	Clean-Up	. . x x x	1000	OPD
BadGuy (3) [IB]	Clean-Up	. . . x x	265	OL
Banana [OW]	Clean-Up	. . . . x	Overwrites	OD
Bandit [Ban]	Clean-Up	. . x x x x x . . .	988	LOP
Barcelona [Barc]	Clean-Up	. . x . x	1792	OPL
Beast [Bea]	Clean-Up	. . . x x	429	OPD
BeBe [BeBe]	Clean-Up	. . . x x	1004	OPD
Beeper (2) [Beep]	Clean-Up	. . x . x	482	OPD
Best Wishes [BWish]	Clean-Up	. . . x x x x . . .	1024	OPD
Beta [Bet]	Clean-Up	. . . . x	1117	LOP
Beware [Bwr]	Clean-Up	. . . . x	442	P
Black Monday (3) [BMon]	Clean-Up	. . x x x x x . . .	1055	LOPD
Blaze [OW]	Clean-Up	. . x x x x	Overwrites	OP
Bljec (8) [Blj]	Clean-Up	. . . x x	369	OP
Blood (2) [Blood]	Clean-Up	. . . x x	418	LOP
Blood-2 [Blood]	Clean-Up	. . . . x	427	OD
Blood Lust [Blus]	Clean-Up	. x . x x	Overwrites	
Blood Rage	Clean-Up	. . x x x	450	DP

Name	Method	Pattern	Value	Code
Bloody! [Bloody]	Clean-Up	. x x . . . . . x . . x	N/A	B
Bob [Bob]	Clean-Up	. . x x x	718	OPL
Bow [5856]	Clean-Up	. . x x x x	5856	OD
Boys (3) [Boys]	Clean-Up	. . x x x	500	OD
Brainy [Bry]	Clean-Up	. . x x x	768	O
Brothers [Bro]	Clean-Up	x . . x . x x x . . .	2045	LOP
Budo[OW]	Clean-Up	. . . . . x x	Overwrites	
Burger (28) [Burger]	Clean-Up	. . . x x x	Overwrites	P
Burghofer [Bgh]	Clean-Up	. . x x x	525	LOP
Busted [Bst]	Clean-Up	. . . x x	Overwrites	O P L
C [CV]	Clean-Up	. . . . x x	N/A	P
CADKill [GN]	Clean-Up	. . x x x x x . . .	1163	OPD
Cancer [Pix]	Clean-Up	. . . . x	1480	OPD
Cannabis (2) [CB]	Clean-Up	. ? x . . . x . . .	N/A	BLO
Cansu [Can]	Clean-Up	. . x . . . . x . x	N/A	O
Capital [Cpt]	Clean-Up	. x . x x	927	LFO
Cara [Cara]	Clean-Up	. . x x x	1024	FLOP
Carioca (6) [Carioca]	Clean-Up	. . x . x	951	OP
Cascade/170x (14) [170x]	Clean-Up	. x x . x	1701	OP
Casc1621 [Cas]	Clean-Up	. x x x x	1704	PDL
Casino [Casino]	Clean-Up	. . x x x	2332	OPL
Casper (2) [Casper]	Clean-Up	. x . x x	1200	LOPD
Catman [Ctm]	Clean-Up	. . x . . . . x . x	N/A	O
Caz [Zar]	Clean-Up	. . x x x x x . . .	1204	LOP
CB-1530 [1530]	Clean-Up	. . . x x x x . . .	1530	LOP
CD [CD]	Clean-Up	. x x . x x x . . .	2161	OLDP
CD-10 [D2]	Clean-Up	x x x	N/A	LFO
Cerburus [Cerb]	Clean-Up	. . x x x	1353	LPD
Chad [Chad]	Clean-Up	. . . x x	751	DL
Chang [Cha]	Clean-Up	. . x x x x	1773	PDL
Chaos [GenB]	M-Disk	. . x . . . . x x .	N/A	BODF
Chaser [Chs]	Clean-Up	. . . . . x	994	DP
Cheeba [Che]	Clean-Up	. x x x x x	1698	DL
Cheeba (2) [CHB]	Clean-Up	. x x x x x x . . .	1683	LOP
Chemist [G1]	Clean-Up	. . x x x	650	OPL
Chrisj13	Clean-Up	. . . x x	709	ODP
Christmas Tree [XA1]	Clean-Up	. x . . x	1539	FOPL
Christmas Violator[Vienna]	Clean-Up	. . . x x	5302	OPD
Cinderella [GS]	Clean-Up	. . x x x	390	OPL
CkSum [Cks]	Clean-Up	. . x x x	1233	PO
Clonewar [Clw]	Clean-Up	. . . . . x	Spawning	

Virus	Disinfector	Pattern	Size	Codes
Coahuila [Coa]	Clean-Up	. . . x x	454	PL
Code Zero	Clean-Up	. . x x x	652	PLO
Coffee Shop [Cf]	Clean-Up	. x x . x x	1568	PLOD
Color [GM]	Clean-Up	. . x x x	802	OPD
Com16850 [C16]	Clean-Up	. . . . . . x . . .	Spawning	
Cop-Mpl [COP]	Clean-Up	. . . x x x	1113	LOP
Copyright [1193]	Clean-Up	. . x x x	1193	L
Copyr-ug [1193]	Clean-Up	. . x x x	1208	LPD
Cossiga [1241]	Clean-Up	. . x . . x x . . .	899	OPL
Cracker Jack [CRJ]	Clean-Up	. . . . x	Varies	LOP
Cracky [Crk]	Clean-Up	. . . x x	648	LPD
Crash [Zar]	Clean-Up	. . . .	See Note	
Crazy Eddie [Crazy]	Clean-Up	. . x ? x x . . . x	Varies	F L O P
Crazy Imp [Imp]	Clean-Up	x . . x x x	1445	OPL
Creeper [Crp]	Clean-Up	. . x x x	475	OPL
Crew-2480 [GM]	Clean-Up	. . . x x	2480	LOP
CRF [CRF]	Clean-Up	. . . x x	270	OP
Criminal [Crm]	Clean-Up	. . x x x	2615	P
Crumble [Crm]	Clean-Up	. x . x x x	778	PLD
Crusher [Crsh]	Clean-Up	x x x . . x . . . x		LOP
CSL (2) [CSL]	Clean-Up	. . x x x	457	LOP
Curse Boot [Curse]	M-Disk	. . x . . . . x x .	321	BO
CV4 [CV4]	Clean-Up	. . x x	321	PL
Cyber [Cybr]	Clean-Up	. . . x x x	1092	PL
D-Tiny (4) [DT]	Clean-Up	. . x x x x	124	L
Dada [Dd]	Clean-Up	. x . . . x x . . .	1363	OPD
Damage [Alf]	Clean-Up	. . x x x x x . . .	1063	ODP
Dark Avenger (11) [Dav]	Clean-Up	. . x x x x x . . .	1800	OPL
Darth Vader (6) [512]	Clean-Up	. . x x x	Varies	O L P
Datacrime/1168 (3) [Crime]	Clean-Up	. x . . x	1280	PF
Datacrime-2 [Crime-2]	Clean-Up	. x . . x x	1514	PF
Datacrime II-B [Crime-2B]	Clean-Up	. x . x x x	1917	P
DataLock [Data]	Clean-Up	. . x x x x x . . .	920	OP
Davis [Davis]	Clean-Up	. . x . . x	1965	OP
Day10 [D10]	Clean-Up	. . . x x	674	FLOP
DBASE [Dbase]	Clean-Up	. . x . x	1864	DOP
Death [Dth]	Clean-Up	. . . . x x	671	PDL
Dedicated [DAME]	SCAN /D	x x x x x	Varies	O P L
Define [Def]	Clean-Up	. . . x x x	Overwrites	L O P
Deicide [Dei]	Clean-Up	. . . . x	Overwrites	F L O P

Name		Marks	Size	Code
Demolition [Dmo]	Clean-Up	. . x x	1585	LOP
Demon (5) [Dem]	Clean-Up	. . . x x	Overwrites	F L O P
Den Zuk (5) [GenB]	Clean-Up	. . x . . . . x . .	N/A	OB
Dest1-2 [Dst1]	Clean-Up	. . . x x	478	OPL
Dest3 [Dst3]	Clean-Up	. . x x x	478	DLP
Destructor [Destr]	Clean-Up	. . x x x x x . . .	1150	OP
Devil's Dance (2) [Dance]	Clean-Up	. . x . x	941	DOPL
Dima [Dima]	Clean-Up	. . x x x	1024	DP
Diogenes [Dio]	Clean-Up	. . x x	846	PO
Dir Virus [Dir]	Clean-Up	x . . x x	691	OPD
Dir-2 910 [910]	Clean-Up	x . x x	910	OPD
Dir-2/CD 1x (3) [D2]	Clean-Up	x x x x x x x . . .	1024	OLDP
Disk Killer (4) [Killer]	Clean-Up	. . x . . . . x x .	N/A	BOPDF
Dismember [Dsbr]	Clean-Up	. x . x x	288	LOP
DM (3) [GS]	Clean-Up	. . x x	400	LOP
DM-B [Dmb]	Clean-Up	. . x x x	400	P
DM-330 [DM300]	Clean-Up	. . x x x	400	LOP
Do Nothing [Nothing]	Clean-Up	. . x . x	608	PDL
Dodo [Dod]	Clean-Up	. . x x	408	O
Doodle (14) [Doodle]	Clean-Up	. . . x . x x . . .	2885	OP
Doom II [Dm2]	Clean-Up	. . x . x x . . .	2504	OPDL
Dot-789 [789]	Clean-Up	. . x x x	801	OPD
Dot-801 [I-F]	Clean-Up	. . x x x	803	PL
Dot Killer [Dot]	Clean-Up	. . x x x	944	OP
Druid [OW]	Clean-Up	. . . . . x	Overwrites	
DTR [DTR]	Clean-Up	. . . x x x	2219	PD
Dust [OW]	Clean-Up	. . . x x	45	PDL
Dutch [Dt]	Clean-Up	. . x x x x . . .	555	DOP
Ed [Ed]	Clean-Up	. . x x x x	794	PDO
Edcl [Edc]	Clean-Up	. . x x x	1615	PDL
EDV (2) [EDV]	Clean-Up	x . x . . . . x x x	N/A	BO
Einstein [Ein]	Clean-Up	. . x . . x	878	LOP
Eliza [El]	Clean-Up	. . . x x	1193	LOP
EMF [EMF]	Clean-Up	. . . x x	404	OPL
Empire (3) [Emp]	Clean-Up	. x x . . . . x x .	N/A	OP
End-of [Eof]	Clean-Up	. . x x x	783	OPL
Enemy [Enm]	Clean-Up	. . x x x x x . . .	1285	OPD
Enigma [Eng]	Clean-Up	. x x . . x x . . .	1755	OP
Enola [Eno]	Clean-Up	. . x x x x	1878	PDL
Error [Er]	Clean-Up	. . . . . x x . . .	628	OP
ETC [ETC]	Clean-Up	. . x x x	572	ODLP
Europe-92 [E92]	Clean-Up	. . x x x	728	OLD

Name	Action	Pattern	Size	Codes
Evil Genius [Egn]	Clean-Up	. . x x x x	963	OPD
Explode [OW]	Clean-Up	. . x x	229	OPDF
Exterminator [M45]	Clean-Up	. . x x x x	451	ODL
F-Word [FW]	Clean-Up	. . x x x	417	O
Farcus [Farc]	Clean-Up	. . x . . . . x x x	N/A	BOPL
Father Christmas [VHP]	Clean-Up	. . . x x	1881	OP
Fear [DAME]	SCAN /D	. . x x x x	Varies	O P L
Feist [Fst]	Clean-Up	. . x x x x x . . .	670	OPL
Fellowship (4) [Fellow]	Clean-Up	. . x . . x	1022	OPDL
Fgt [GN]	Clean-Up	. . . x x	651	P
Fich [Fch]	Clean-Up	. . x x x	896	OPL
Fil [Fil]	Clean-Up	. . x x x	1658	PD
Filler [Filler]	Clean-Up	x . x . . . . x . x	N/A	BFLO
Fingers [Sub]	Clean-Up	. . x x x x x . . .	1322	OPD
Fish (2) [Fish]	Clean-Up	x x x x x x x . . .	3584	OPL
Fish Boot [GenB]	Clean-Up	. . x . . . . x . x	N/A	O
Flash [Flash]	Clean-Up	. . x x x x	688	OPDL
Flip (5) [Flip]	Clean-Up	. x x x x x x . . .	2343	OPDL
Flu-2 [Fl2]	Clean-Up	. x x x x x	2112	P
Forger2 [For]	Clean-Up	. . x . . x	1000	PD
Form (4) [Form]	Clean-Up	. . x . . . . x x .	N/A	BOD
Francois [Fra]	Clean-Up	. . x . . . . x . x	N/A	O
Free [Free]	Clean-Up	. . . . x	692	P
Frere Jacques [Mule]	Clean-Up	. . x . x x x . . .	1811	OP
Fri13-nz [Fnz]	Clean-Up	. . . . x	512	DPO
Friday 13th COM [Fri13]	Clean-Up	. . . . x	512	P
Frogs [Frg]	Clean-Up	. . x x x	1500	OP
FamC [GC]	Clean-Up			
FamD [GD]	Clean-Up			
FamE [GE]	Clean-Up			
FamH [GH]	Clean-Up			
FamJ [GJ]	Clean-Up			
FamM [GM]	Clean-Up			
FamN [GN]	Clean-Up			
FamQ [GQ]	Clean-Up			
FamR [GR]	Clean-Up			
FamS [GS]	Clean-Up			
FamV1 [G1]	Clean-Up			
FamV2 [G2]	Clean-Up			
FamV3 [G3]	Clean-Up			
FamV4 [G4]	Clean-Up			

Name	Disinfectant	Pattern	Size	Type
Filedate [FDt]	Clean-Up	. . . . . x	553	OLP
Frodo Soft [FSof]	Clean-Up	. x . x x	563	ODP
Frodo-458 [F458]	Clean-Up	. x . x x	563	ODP
Fu Manchu (4) [Fu]	Clean-Up	. . x . x x x . . .	2086	OP
Fune [Fune]	Clean-Up	. . x x x x	921	LPD
Futhark [Futh]	Clean-Up	. . x x x	640	DP
Geek [GK]	Clean-Up	. . x x x x	466	OP
Generic Boot [GenB]	Clean-Up	. . x . . . . x x .	N/A	BLO
Generic File [GenF]	Clean-Up	. . x ? x ? ? . . .	Varies	P
Generic MBR [GenP]	Clean-Up	? . x x	See Note	FLO
Gergana (9) [Gerg]	Clean-Up	. . . x x	184	PO
Get Password 1 [Jeru]	Clean-Up	. . x . x x x . . .	1914	OPL
Ghost Boot [Ghost]	Clean-Up	. . x . . . . x x .	N/A	BO
Ghost COM [Ghost]	Clean-Up	. . . . x	2351	BP
Ghost Dos-62 [Gho]	Clean-Up	. . . . x . . x x .	2351	BP
Gliss [Gls]	Clean-Up	. . . . x	1247	P
Goblin [CRJ]	Clean-Up	. . x x x	1951	OPL
Gomb [Gomb]	Clean-Up	. x x x x	4091	P
Gosia [Gs]	Clean-Up	. . x x x	466	LOP
Got-you [GY]	Clean-Up	. . . . . x	3052	LP
Gotcha (4) [G4]	Clean-Up	. . x x x x x . . .	806	O
Gotcha [Gto]	Clean-Up	. . x x x x	879	O
Grapje [Gr]	Clean-Up	. . . x x	1039	LOP
Greemlin [Alf]	Clean-Up	x . x x x x x . . .	1146	OPLD
Green [Gre]	Clean-Up	. . . x x	743	LD
Green Catapillar [Gcat]	Clan-Up	. . x x x x	1575	LDO
Growing Block [GD]	Clean-Up	. . x x x x x . . .	1446	OPLD
Grunt [Grnt]	Clean-Up	. . . x x	344	PO
Guppy [Guppy]	Clean-Up	. . x x x	152	OP
H-2 [H-2]	Clean-Up	. . x x x x x . . .	1962	O
HA [HA]	Clean-Up	. x x x x x	1472	OLD
Hacktic [Hck2]	Clean-Up	. . . . . x	Overwrite	
Hafen [Hafn]	Clean-Up	. . . . . x	809	P
Haifa [Hf]	Clean-Up	x x x x x x x . . .	2351	LOP
Halloechen [Hal]	Clean-Up	. . x x x x x . . .	2011	LOP
Halloween [HW]	Clean-Up	. . . x x x	10000	LOP
Happy N. Y. [HNY]	Clean-Up	. . x x x x x . . .	1865	OP
Happy [Hpp]	Clean-Up	. . . x x	453	OP
Hara [kiri]	Clean-Up	. . . x x x	5488	ODP
Hary [Hary]	Clean-Up	. . x x x x	997	OLP
Hastings [Hst]	Clean-Up	. . . . x	N/A	OL
HBT [HBT]	Clean-Up	. . x . x x	396	OPD

Virus	Scanner	Pattern	Size	Code
Hellween 1182 [1182]	Clean-Up	. x x . x x	1376	P
Here [Hre]	Clean-Up	. . . . x	N/A	O
Hero (2) [G3]	Clean-Up	. . x x x x x . . .	506	OLP
Hero-394 [HrB]	Clean-Up	. . . . x	394	LOP
Hi [Hi]	Clean-Up	. . . . . x	460	DP
Highland[High]	Clean-Up	. . x . x	477	DO
Hitchcock [Hitc]	Clean-Up	. . . x x	1121	OP
Holland Girl (6) [Sylvia]	Clean-Up	. . . . x	1332	P
Holo/Holocaust (3) [Hl]	Clean-Up	x . x x x	3784	OPLD
Horror [Hrr]	Clean-Up	. x x x x x	2319	PL
Horse (7) [Hrs]	Clean-Up	. . x x x x x . . .	1154	OP
Horse Boot [DRP]	Clean-Up	. . x x x . . x x .	N/A	B
HS [G4]	Clean-Up	. . x x x x x . . .	4103	OPL
Huge [Huge]	Clean-Up	. . x x	3072	PLO
Hungarian [Hng]	Clean-Up	. . x x x x	695	OL
Hybrid [Hyb]	Clean-Up	. . . x x	1306	OPL
Hydra (12) [G3]	Clean-Up	. . . x x	Varies	L O P
Hymn (3) [Hymn]	Clean-Up	. . x x x x x . . .	642	OPD
I-B (5) [IB]	Clean-Up	. . . x x	Varies	F
IB Demonic [OW]	Clean-Up	. . . x x	451	PDL
Ice 9 [I9]	Clean-Up	. . x . x	639	POD
Icelandic (3) [Ice-3]	Clean-Up	. . x . . x	642	OP
Icelandic II [Ice-3]	Clean-Up	. . x . . x	661	O
Icelandic-3 [Ice-3]	Clean-Up	. . x . . x	853	OP
Idle [Idle]	Clean-Up	. . x . x x	2332	PO
Ieronim [Ier]	Clean-Up	. . x . x	570	PDO
IKV528 [G2]	Clean-Up	. . . x x	528	OP
III [III]	Clean-Up	. x . x x	1016	P
Incom [Inc]	Clean-Up	. . . . x	648	OP
Infinity [Inf]	Clean-Up	. . . x x	732	OP
Inrud-B [Intr]	Clean-Up	. . . . . x	1333	PD
Invader (8) [Invader]	Clean-Up	. x x . x x x x x .	4096	BLOPD
Invol Virus [Inl]	Clean-Up	. . . . x x	1413	OPLD
IOU [IOU]	Clean-Up	. x x x x	2088	OLP
Iraqi Warrior [Lisbon]	Clean-Up	. . . x x	777	OPLD
Israeli Boot [Iboot]	Clean-Up	. . x . . . . x . .	N/A	BO
IT [IT]	Clean-Up	. . x x x	454	O
Italian Pest (3) [Murphy]	Clean-Up	. . x . x	1910	LOP
ItaVir (3) [Ita]	Clean-Up	. . . . . x	3880	OPLB
Japan [C-J]	Clean-Up	. . x x x x	600	O P
JD [JD]	Clean-Up	. . x x x	158	P

Name	Method		Size	Flags
Jeff (3) [Jeff]	Clean-Up	. . x x	828	O P D F
Jerk (2) [Jrk]	Clean-Up	. . x x x	1077	L O P
Jeru1663 [J1663]	Clean-Up	. . x x x x x . . .	1663	O P D
Jerusalem (48) [Jeru]	Clean-Up	. . x . x x x . .	1808	O P
Joanna [Joa]	Clean-Up	. x x x	986	P D L
JoJo (3) [JoJo]	Clean-Up	. . x . x	1701	O P
Joke [JK]	Clean-Up	. . . . x	N/A	P
Joker (3) [Joke]	Clean-Up	. . x x x	N/A	O P
Joshi (4) [Joshi]	Clean-Up	x . x . . . x x x	N/A	B O D
Joshua [Jsh]	Clean-Up	. . . . x x . . .	965	O P L
July 13th [J13]	Clean-Up	. x . . . x	1201	O P D L
July 26 [J26]	Clean-Up	. . x x	205	O P
Jump4Joy [J4J]	Clean-Up	. . x x x x . . .	2225	O D
June 16th [June16]	Clean-Up	. . x x	1726	F O P L
Justice [Jus]	Clean-Up	. x x x	1242	O P
JW2 (2) [Jab]	Clean-Up	. x x x x	1812	L O P
K [K]	Clean-Up	. . x x x x . . .	4928	O P L
Kalah [GR]	Clean-Up	. . x x x	390	O P L D
Kamikaze [Kami]	Clean-Up	. . . . . x . . .	Overwrites	P
Karin [GN]	Clean-Up	. . x x	1090	L O P
KBug [Kbu]	Clean-Up	. x . x x	1598	P O
Kemerov (3) [Kem]	Clean-Up	. . x x	257	L O P
Kemerov (5) [Keme]	Clean-Up	. x x x	Varies	O L P D
Kennedy (4) [Tiny]	Clean-Up	. x . x	308	O P
Kersplat [Ker]	Clean-Up	. x x x x x . . .	670	O P L
Keypress [Key]	Clean-Up	. x x x x	1232	O L P
Keypress (4) [Key]	Clean-Up	. x x x x	1232	O P D
Kiev [Kiev]	Clean-Up	. . x x	483	L O P
Kiev-1 [K1]	Clean-Up	. . x x x	483	P O L
Kilroy [Klr]	Clean-Up	. x . . . . x . x	N/A	O
Klaeren [GH]	Clean-Up	. x x x x x x . . .	981	O P L D
KODE4 [K4]	Clean-Up	. . x x	399	O P L
Korea (4) [Korea]	Clean-Up	. . . . . x x .	N/A	B O
Krivmous [Krv]	Clean-Up	. x . x x	993	P O
KU-448 [KU]	Clean-Up	. . x x	448	L
Kukaturbo [Kakt]	Clean-Up	. x x x	Overwrites	P
Kuzmitch [Kzm]	Clean-Up	. . . x	1064	P O
L1 [L1]	Clean-Up	. x x x	144	O D
Label [Label]	Clean-Up	. x x x	Overwrites	P
Lamer [Lam]	Clean-Up	. x . . x	1040	P D
Lanc [Lan]	Clean-Up	. . x x	5476	O D
Lanc5476 [Lan]	Clean-Up	. . x x	5476	O D
Lanc5882 [Lan]	Clean-Up	. . x x	5476	O D

Name	Type												Size	Codes
Larry [Lar]	Clean-Up	.	.	x	x	x	x	.	.	.	.	.	507	P D L
Lazy [Lazy]	Clean-Up	.	.	x	x	x	.	.	.	.	.	.	720	O P
LCV [LCV]	Clean-Up	.	.	.	.	x	.	.	.	.	.	.	N/A	P
Leapfrog Virus (3) [Leap]	Clean-Up	.	.	x	x	x	.	.	.	.	.	.	516	O P D
Leech [Leech]	Clean-Up	x	x	x	x	x	.	.	.	.	.	.	934	O P L D
Lehigh (2) [Lehigh]	Clean-Up	.	.	x	x	.	.	.	.	.	.	.	N/A	P F
Leper AOD [OW]	Clean-Up	.	.	.	.	x	.	.	.	.	.	.	Overwrites	
Leprosy (7) [Vip]	Clean-Up	.	.	x	x	x	x	x	.	.	.	.	Overwrites	P O L
Leprosy-3 (4) [Lep3]	Clean-Up	.	.	.	x	x	.	.	.	.	.	.	Overwrites	L O P
Leprosy-B [Vip]	Clean-Up	.	.	.	x	x	.	.	.	.	.	.	Overwrites	P O L
Les [Les]	Clean-Up	.	.	.	x	x	.	.	.	.	.	.	205	P D L
Lib1172 (2) [1186]	Clean-Up	.	.	x	x	.	.	.	.	.	.	.	1172	L O P
Liberty (13) [Liberty]	Clean-Up	.	.	x	x	x	x	x	.	.	.	.	2862	O P
Lisbon (2) [VHP]	Clean-Up	.	.	.	.	x	.	.	.	.	.	.	648	P
Little Brother [LB]	Clean-Up	.	.	x	.	.	x	.	.	.	.	.	307	P D L
Little Brother 349 [LB]	Clean-Up	.	.	x	.	.	x	.	.	.	.	.	349	P D L
Little Brother 361 [LB]	Clean-Up	.	.	x	.	.	x	.	.	.	.	.	361	P D L
Little Girl [LG]	Clean-Up	.	.	x	x	x	x	.	.	.	.	.	1008	P D L O
Little Pieces [LPC]	Clean-Up	.	.	x	.	x	x	.	.	.	.	.	1374	O P
LixoNuke [Lix]	Clean-Up	.	.	x	.	.	x	.	.	.	.	.	1024	D P
Loa Duong [Loa]	Clean-Up	.	.	x	.	.	.	.	.	x	x	x	N/A	B O P L
Love Child (3) [LC]	Clean-Up	.	.	x	x	x	.	.	.	.	.	.	488	O D
Lozinsky (4) [Loz]	Clean-Up	.	.	.	x	x	.	.	.	.	.	.	1023	O P D
Lucifer [Alf]	Clean-Up	x	.	x	x	x	x	x	.	.	.	.	1086	O P D L
Lycee [Lyc]	Clean-Up	x	.	x	x	x	x	x	.	.	.	.	1788	P O D
LZ [LZ]	Clean-Up	.	.	.	.	x	.	.	.	.	.	.	Spawning	O
LZ 2 [LZ2]	Clean-Up	.	x	.	.	.	x	.	.	.	.	.	8847	L P
M-128 [M128]	Clean-Up	.	.	x	x	x	.	.	.	.	.	.	128	L
Macedonia [1385]	Clean-Up	.	.	x	.	x	.	.	.	.	.	.	400	L O P
Madismo [Mds]	Clean-Up	.	.	.	.	.	x	.	.	.	.	.	Overwrites	
Magnum [Mgm]	Clean-Up	.	.	x	.	x	x	.	.	.	.	.	2560	P L D
Malage [Mlg]	Clean-Up	.	.	x	x	x	x	x	x	x	x	.	2626	O P L
Malaise [Mls]	Clean-Up	.	.	x	x	x	x	.	.	.	.	.	1371	L D P
Malsmsey[OW]	Clean-Up	.	.	.	x	x	.	.	.	.	.	.	Overwrites	
Malmsey2 [Malm]	Clean-Up	.	.	.	.	.	x	.	.	.	.	.	1717	L D P
Maltese Amoeba [Irs]	Clean-Up	.	x	x	x	x	x	x	.	.	.	.	2505	O P L
Mannequin [Mn]	Clean-Up	.	.	x	x	x	x	x	.	.	.	.	778	O P L D
Manola [Mno]	Clean-Up	.	.	x	x	x	.	.	.	.	.	.	957	L P
Manta [Mant]	Clean-Up	.	.	.	x	x	.	.	.	.	.	.	1077	L O P
Marauder [Mar]	Clean-Up	.	.	.	x	x	.	.	.	.	.	.	860	O P L
Mardi Bros. (3) [Mardi]	Clean-Up	.	.	x	.	.	.	.	.	x	x	.	N/A	B O

Name	Tool	Detection	Bytes	Codes
Mayak [Mayk]	Clean-Up	x x x x x x	2339	D P O
McWhale [MCAF]	Clean-Up	. . . . x x	1125	D P L
Medical [Med]	Clean-Up	. . x x	189	D P O
Mexican Mud [Mex]	Clean-Up	. . x x	575	P L
Mface [Mfc]	Clean-Up	. x x x	1441	O P L
MG (4) [MG]	Clean-Up	. x x x	500	L O P
MGTU Virus (4) [MGTU]	Clean-Up	. . x x	273	O P D
Michaelangelo [Mich]	Clean-Up	. x . . . . x x x	N/A	B O
Microbes [Micro]	M-Disk	. x . . . . x x .	N/A	BOD
Miky [Miky]	Clean-Up	. x x x x x . . .	2350	O P L
Mini Virus (4) [M45]	Clean-Up	. . x x	Varies	O P
Minsk-GH [Mgh]	Clean-Up	x . x x x x . . .	1478	P D L
Mir (2) [DAV]	Clean-Up	. x x x x x . . .	1745	O P L
Mirror (2) [Mirror]	Clean-Up	. x . . x . . .	928	O P
MIX1 (4) [Ice]	Clean-Up	. x . . x . . .	1618	O P
Mix2 [MX2]	Clean-Up	. x x x x x . .	2280	O P
Moctezuma [MC]	Clean-Up	. x x x x x . .	2208	L O P
Mono [G1]	Clean-Up	. x x x . . .	1063	L O P
Monxla (3) [VHP]	Clean-Up	. . x x . . .	939	O P
Monxla-B [MXB]	Clean-Up	. . x x	535	O P L
Mosquito [Mosq]	Clean-Up	. x x . . x x . .	1028	O D P
Mozkin [Hf]	Clean-Up	. x x x x x x . .	2357	L O P
MPC [MPC]	Clean-Up	. . x . . x x . .	689	O P L
MPS 1.1 [M11]	Clean-Up	. . x x	469	L O P
Mr. Vir [MV]	Clean-Up	. . x x	508	L P D
MPS 3.1 (3) [MPS]	Clean-Up	. . x x	640	L O P
MSTU [GN]	Clean-Up	. . x x x . . .	531	L O P
Mugshot [Msht]	Clean-Up	. . . . . x . .	700	L P D
Mule [Mule]	Clean-Up	. x x x x	4126	L P O
Mule (2) [Mule]	Clean-Up	. x x x x	4171	O P D
Multi [M123]	Clean-Up	. . x x	123	L O P
Multi-2 [Ml2]	Clean-Up	. x x x x x x . .	927	L O P
Mummy [Mum]	Clean-Up	. x x . . x x . .	1374	L
Munich [Mnc]	Clean-Up	. . x x	Varies	O P
Murphy (6) [Murphy]	Clean-Up	. x x x x x . . .	1277	O P
Music Bug (11) [MBug]	Clean-Up	. x . . . . x . x	N/A	B O
Mutant (8) [Mut]	Clean-Up	. . x x	123	L O P
Mutation Engine [DAME]	SCAN /D	x x x x x	Varies	O P
Nazi [Ram]	Clean-Up	. . . . x	N/A	O P
NCU Li [Li]	Clean-Up	. x . . x	1704	O P D
Necrophilia [Nec]	Clean-Up	. x x x	Varies	O PL D

Virus	Tool	Pattern	Size	Flags
New Sunday [NSun]	Clean-Up	. . x . x x x . . .	1636	O P L D
New-1701 [1701]	Clean-Up	. . x x x	1701	L P L
Newcom [Alf]	Clean-Up	. . x x x	3045	O
Nina [Nina]	Clean-Up	. . x x x	256	O P D
Nines Compliment [Nns]	Clean-Up	. . x x x	705	O P L
Ninja [Nja]	Clean-Up	. x x . x x	1634	O P D
No-Int [Stoned]	Clean-Up	. . x . . . . x . x	N/A	O
No Wednesday [NWed]	Clean-Up	. x . . x	520	O L P
Nobock [Nbk]	Clean-Up	. . . . x	440	L O P
Nomenclature (4) [Nom]	Clean-Up	. . x x x x x . . .	1024	O P D
NOP [NOP]	M-Disk	. . x . . . . x . x	N/A	N/A
NPox 2.0 [NPX]	Clean-Up	. . x x x x	2048	D P L
NPox 2.1 [NPX]	Clean-Up	. . x x x x	1774	D P L O
Null [NL]	Clean-Up	. . . x x	733	P
Nygus-KL [Nkl]	Clean-Up	. . x . x x	757	P D
Off Stealth [SVC50]	Clean-Up	x . x x x x x . . .	1689	O P D
Ohio [Ohio]	Clean-Up	. . x . . . . x . .	N/A	B O
Omt [417]	Clean-Up	. . . x x	413	P D L
Ontario [Ont]	Clean-Up	. x x x x x	Varies	O P D
Ontario 3 [Ont]	Clean-Up	. . x x x x x . . .	744	O P L
Oropax (5) [Oro]	Clean-Up	. . . x	2773	P O
P1 (7) [P1r]	Clean-Up	. x x . x	Varies	O P D L
P529 [529]	Clean-Up	. . x x x	529	O P D
PA-5792 [PA]	Clean-Up	. . . . . x	5792	O P L
Padded [Pad]	Clean-Up	. . . x x	2589	O P L
Pakistani Brain (8)[Brain]	Clean-Up	. . x . . . . x . .	N/A	B
Parasite [Par]	Clean-Up	. . . x	1132	P O
Parasite2B [Ps2]	Clean-Up	. . x x	903	P O F
Paris [Paris]	Clean-Up	. . x x x x . . .	4909	O P D L
Parity [G2]	Clean-Up	. . x x	441	O P D
Particle Man [PMN]	Clean-Up	. . x x	690	P L O
Pas-4260[OW]	Clean-Up	. . . x x	Overwrites	
Pas-5220 [P5220]	Clean-Up	. x x x x . . .	5220	P L D
PathHunt [Ph]	Clean-Up	. . . x x . . .	1231	D L O P
Patient [Pt]	Clean-Up	. . x . x x x . .	1504	L O P
Payday [Jeru]	Clean-Up	. . x . x x x . .	1808	P
PC Flu [802]	Clean-Up	. . x x x . . .	802	L O P
PCBB11 [PCB]	Clean-Up	. . x x	1677	P
PCBB3072 [PCB]	Clean-Up	. . x x	1677	P
PCBB5B [PCB]	Clean-Up	. . x x	1677	P

Name	Tool	Pattern	Size	Codes
PCV [PCV]	Clean-Up	x . x . x x	1904	L O P
Peach [Pch]	Clean-Up	. . x x x x	889	P
Pentagon [Pentagon]	M-Disk	. . . . x . .	N/A	B
Penza [Pnz]	Clean-Up	. . x x x x	700	D P
Perfume (2) [Fume]	Clean-Up	. . . . . x	765	P
Pest (8) [Murphy]	Clean-Up	. . x x x x x . . .	1910	O P L
Phantom [Pht]	Clean-Up	. . x x x	2253	O P
PI [PI]	Clean-Up	. . x . . x	1568	D P
Piazzola [Pia]	Clean-Up	. . x . x	874	O P
Pig [Pig]	Clean-Up	. . x x x	407	O P L
Ping Pong-B (7) [Ping]	Clean-Up	. . x . . . . x x .	N/A	O B
Pirate [Pir]	Clean-Up	. . . x x	Overwrites	L O P
Pitch [Ptch]	Clean-Up	. . x x x	593	O D L
Pixel (5) [Pix]	Clean-Up	. . . x x	779	O P
Plague (3) [Plg]	Clean-Up	. . . . x x	Overwrites	
Plastique (9) [Plq]	Clean-Up	. . x x x x x . . .	3012	O P D
Platinum [GE]	Clean-Up	. x . . . x x . . .	1489	O P L D
Plov [Plov]	Clean-Up	. . x x x x x . . .	1000	L O P
Plutto [Plu]	Clean-Up	. . . x x	602	L O D
Poem [Pm]	Clean-Up	. . x x x	1825	F L O P
Pogue [Pog]	SCAN /D	. x x . x	Varies	L O P
Pojer [Poj]	Clean-Up	. . x x x x	1919	P D L
Polimer [Polimer]	Clean-Up	. . . x x	512	O P D
Polish-2 [Pol2]	Clean-Up	. . x x x	512	O P D
Polish Tiny [Plt]	Clean-Up	. . . x x	150	P D
P-45 [P45]	SCAN /D	. . . . x	N/A	P
Polish 217 [P217]	Clean-Up	. . . x x	217	O
Polish-583 [P583]	Clean-Up	. . . x x	583	P P D
Possessed (6) [Poss]	Clean-Up	. . x x x x x . . .	2443	L O P
Pregnant [Prg]	Clean-Up	. . x x x	1199	L O P
Prime [Prm]	Clean-Up	. x . x x	580	P D
Prime Evil B [PEB]	Clean-Up	. . . x x	580	P D
Print Screen (2) [PrtScr]	M-Disk	. . x . . . . x x .	N/A	B O D
Prism [Flip]	Clean-Up	. . x x x x x x . x	2153	B F L O P
Problem [Prb]	Clean-Up	. . x x x x	856	L P D
Psycho [Psc]	Clean-Up	. . . . x	N/A	O
QMU [QML]	Clean-Up	. . x x x x	1513	F L O P
QP3 [1530]	Clean-Up	. . x x x x x . . .	1028	L O P
Quake-o [Qo]	Clean-Up	. . x . . x	532	L D
Queen's [GenB]	Clean-Up	. . x . . . . x . x	N/A	O B
Quiet [Qt]	Clean-Up	. . x x x	2063	O P
R-10 [R10]	Clean-Up	. . x x x	500	O

Virus	Tool	Signature	Size	Codes
R-11 [R11]	Clean-Up	x . x x x	700	O
Radyum[Rad]	Clean-Up	. . x x	448	O P L
Rage [Rag]	Clean-Up	. . . x x	575	L O P
Ram [Ram]	Clean-Up	. . x . x x x . . .	Varies	L O P
Rattle [Rttl]	Clean-Up	. . x x x	615	P D
Raubkopi [Raub]	Clean-Up	. . . x x x	Varies	L O P
Reaper	Clean-Up	. . x . x x	1072	F L D
Rebo-715 [R175]	Clean-Up	. . . x x	715	L P
RedX (2) [Redx]	Clean-Up	. . . x x	796	O P
Reklama [Rkm]	Clean-Up	. . . x x	2723	P D L
Relzfu [233]	Clean-Up	. . x x x	233	O P L
Reset [RST]	Clean-Up	. . . x x	440	O P
RMIT [RMIT]	Clean-Up	. . . x x x	Overwrites	L O P
RNA [RNA]	Clean-Up	. . . x x x x . . .	7296	O P L
Rocko [Roc]	Clean-Up	x . x x x x x . . .	666	P D
RPVS [453]	Clean-Up	. . x x x	453	O P
S-847 [Pix]	Clean-Up	. . x . x	850	O L D
Saddam [Saddam]	Clean-Up	. . x x x	919	O P D L
Sadist [Sadt]	Clean-Up	. . . . . x	1436	P O
Sandwich [Sand]	Clean-Up	. . x . x	1172	P D L
Saratoga [Doodle]	Clean-Up	. . x . . x	656	P L B
Saturday [Sat14]	Clean-Up	. . x . x x	669	P L
Saturday 14th (3) [Arma]	Clean-Up	. . x . x x x . . .	685	F O P L
SBC [SBC]	Clean-Up	x x x . x x x . . .	1024	L O P
Scott's Valley [2133]	Clean-Up	. x x . x x x . . .	2133	L O P D
Screaming Fist [Scr]	Clean-Up	. . x x x x x . . .	711	O P L
Screaming Fist-2 [696]	Clean-Up	. . x x x x x . . .	696	O P L
Scream 2 [Sc2]	Clean-Up	. x x x x x x . . .	1324	O
Scribble [OW]	Clean-Up	. . . x x x	Overwrites	
Scroll [Scl]	Clean-Up	x x x x x	1306	O L P
SCT [SCT]	Clean-Up	. . . . x	N/A	P
Scythe2D [Scy]	Clean-Up	. x x x x	1208	D O
Sergeant [Ser]	Clean-Up	. . x x x	122	L D
Secrets [OW]	Clean-Up	. . . x x x	Overwrites	
Semtex [Set]	Clean-Up	. . x x x	1000	L O P
Sentinel (3) [Sent]	Clean-Up	. . x x x x x . . .	4625	L O P D
Sentinel-X [BCV]	Clean-Up	. . x x x x x . . .	4625	L O P D
Sh [Sh]	Clean-Up	. . . x x x x . . .	Overwrites	L O P
Shadow (3) [Sha]	Clean-Up	. . x x	723	O P
Shake (2) [Shake]	Clean-Up	. . x . x	476	O P
Shield [Shd]	Clean-Up	. . x . x	127	O

Shirley[Shl]

Name	Program	Marks	Size	Flags
Silence [S1l]	Clean-Up	. . . x x	555	P L
Silly Willy [SilW]	Clean-Up	. . . x x x	2313	P D
Silver3b [OW]	Clean-Up	. . . x x x	2071	P D
Simulati [Sim]	Clean-Up	. . . . x	1257	L O P
Sis (2) [Sis]	Clean-Up	. . x x x x x . . .	2380	O P L
Skism [Jeru]	Clean-Up	. . x . x x x . . .	1815	O P
Sk [Sk]	Clean-Up	. . x . x	1147	P L
Sk1 [Sk1]	Clean-Up	. . x . x	1147	P D
Slayer [Slay]	Clean-Up	. . x . x x x . . .	5120	O P L D
Slovak [Slv]	Clean-Up	. . . . x	1771	P D
Slow (5) [Slow]	Clean-Up	. x x . x x x . . .	1721	O P L
Sma-108a [Sma]	Clean-Up	. . x x x	108	O D L
Small-38 [M45]	Clean-Up	. . . . x	38	O P L
Smily [G2]	Clean-Up	. . x x x	1987	O P L
Socha [SCH]	Clean-Up	. . . . x	N/A	P
Solano (4) [Sub]	Clean-Up	. . x . x	2000	O P L
Something [658]	Clean-Up	. . x x x	658	L O P
Sorry (3) [Sorry]	Clean-Up	. . x x x	731	O P
Sov (3) [Sov]	Clean-Up	. . . x x	545	L O P
Soyun [Soy]	Clean-Up	. . x x x x	2064	L P D
Spanish [Spain]	Clean-Up	. . x x x x x . . .	2930	O L P
Spanish April Fool [D28]	Clean-Up	. . x . . x x . . .	1400	O
Spanz [Spz]	Clean-Up	. . x x x	663	O D
Spar [Spar]	Clean-Up	. . x x x x	1255	O P
Spyer [Spyer]	Clean-Up	. . x . x x	1181	O P
Spyer (3) [GD]	Clean-Up	. . x . x x x . . .	1181	O P
Squawk [Sqk]	Clean-Up	. . x x x x x . . .	852	O P L
Squeaker [Sqe]	Clean-Up	. . x x x x x . . .	1091	L O P
Squisher [Squ]	Clean-Up	x . x x x	Overwrites	
SQR [SQR]	Clean-Up	. . x x x	9977	O P L
Staf [Staf]	Clean-Up	. . x x x	2083	O P L
Stahl Platte [Sta]	Clean-Up	. . . x x	750	O P
Star Dot [Sdot]	Clean-Up	. . . . . x	604	P D
Star Dot (4) [Sdot]	Clean-Up	. . x . x	Varies	O P L
Stardot-801 (3) [IF]	Clean-Up	. . . x x x	604	D F L O P
Sticky [ML2]	Clean-Up	. x x x x x x . . x	1407	L O D F
Stink [Sti]	Clean-Up	. . . . x	1254	L O P
Stink2 [Sti2]	Clean-Up	. . . x x	306	P D
Stone-90 [VHP]	Clean-Up	. . . x x	961	O P
Stoned [Stoned]	Clean-Up	. . x . . . . x . x	N/A	O
Striker [STR]	Clean-Up	. . x x x	461	D O P F

```
Subliminal (3) [Sub]      Clean-Up  . . x x x . . . .  1496   O P
Suicide [Sui]             Clean-Up  . . . x x x . . .  1992   P D
Sunday (6) [Sunday]       Clean-Up  . . x . x x x . .  1636   O P
Sunday-2 [Su2]            Clean-Up  . . x x x x x . .  2877   L O P
Suriv 402 [GR]            Clean-Up  . . x x x . . . .  897    L O P
Suriv A (2) [SurivA]      Clean-Up  . . x . x . . . .  897    O P
Suriv B [Surivb]          Clean-Up  . . x . x x x . .  1813   P O
Surrender [707]           Clean-Up  . . x x x x x . .  513    O P L
SVC 5.0/6.0 (2)           Clean-Up  x x x x x x x . . x 3103  B L O P
  [SVC50]
Sverdlov (2) [Sv]         Clean-Up  . . x x x x x . .  1962   O P
SVir (4) [Svir]           Clean-Up  . . . . . x . . .  512    L O P
Swap Boot [Swb]           Clean-Up  . . x . . . . x .  N/A    B
Swiss 143 [Gtc]           Clean-Up  . . . x x . . . .  143    O P D
Swiss Phoenix [SPh]       Clean-Up  . x x x x x . . .  927    O P L
SX [SX]                   Clean-Up  . . x x x . . . .  800    L O P
Sylvia [Sylvia]           Clean-Up  . . x . x . . . .  1332   L O P
Sys Virus [Sys]           Clean-Up  x x x x x x x . .  N/A    O P D
Syslock/3551              Clean-Up  . x . . x x . . .  3551   P D
  [Syslock]
Tabulero [Tab]            Clean-Up  . . x . . x . . .  2062   P D
Taiwan (11) [Taiwan]      Clean-Up  . . . . x . . . .  708    P
Taiwan3 [T3]              Clean-Up  . . x x x x x . .  2905   O P D L
Taiwan4 [JeruA]           Clean-Up  . . x x x x x . .  2576   O P D
Telecom Boot [Tele]       M-Disk    . x x . . . . . x x N/A   B P
Telecom File [Tele]       Clean-Up  . x x . x . . . .  3700   B P O D
Telekom [GTk]             Clean-Up  . . . x x . . . .  1077   P O L
Tequila [Teq]             Clean-Up  x x x . . x . . . x 2468  O P F L
Terror (3) [Ter]          Clean-Up  . . x x x x x . .  1085   O P F
Tester [TV]               Clean-Up  . . x x x . . . .  1000   O P
Thursday 12th [T12]       Clean-Up  . . x . x x . . .  2175   P D
TimeMark [Tim]            Clean-Up  . . x . . x . . .  1076   P D
Timid [Tmd]               Clean-Up  . . . x x . . . .  306    L O P
Timid305 [Timid]          Clean-Up  . . . x x . . . .  305    L O P
Timid-LM [TLM]            Clean-Up  . . . x x . . . .  305    L O P
Tiny (31) [Tiny]          Clean-Up  . . . x x . . . .  163    O P
Tiny 133 [T133]           Clean-Up  . . . x x . . . .  133    O
TMTM [TMTM]               Clean-Up  . x . x x . . . .  441    O D
Todor [Tdr]               Clean-Up  . . . x x x . . .  1993   O P
Tokyo [Tokyo]             Clean-Up  . . x . . x . . .  1258   L O P
Tony [Tn]                 Clean-Up  . . . x x . . . .  200    L O P
Topo [Topo]               Clean-Up  . . x . x . . . .  1542   L O P
Traceback (3) [3066]      Clean-Up  . . x . x x . . .  3066   P
```

Name	Action	Pattern	Size	Flags
Traveller [GN]	Clean-Up	. . x x x x . . .	1220	L O P
Triple Shot [3Sht]	Clean-Up	. . . . . . x . .	Companion	
Troi [GS]	Clean-Up	. . x x x	322	O P L
Troi Two [Tr2]	Clean-Up	. . x x x x . . .	322	P D
Tuesday (2) [Alf]	Clean-Up	. . x . x x x . .	1163	O P L P
Tula [Tula]	Clean-Up	. . x x x	419	O P D
Tumen [Tum]	Clean-Up	. . x x x	1663	P L D
Tumen V0.5 [Tum5]	Clean-Up	. . x x x	1663	O P L D
Tumen V2.0 [Tum2]	Clean-Up	. . x x x	1092	O P L D
Turbo (2) [Pol2]	Clean-Up	. . x x x	448	L O P
Turkey [Trk]	Clean-Up	. . x . x	1661	P L D
Twin-351 [Twin]	Clean-Up	x . x . x x . . .	351	L O P
Twin Peaks[OW]	Clean-Up	. . . x x	Overwrites	
Typo Boot (2) [TBoot]	Clean-Up	. . x . . . . x x .	N/A	O B
Typo/Fumble/712 (2) [712]	Clean-Up	. . x . x	867	O P
Ucender [Jeru]	Clean-Up	. . x x x x x . .	1783	O P L
Unk [Unk]	Clean-Up	. . x x x x . . .	1015	P
USSR (11) [USSR]	Clean-Up	. x . . . x . . .	575	O
USSR 1049 [Alf]	Clean-Up	. . x x x	1049	O P L
USSR 2144 (8) [U2144]	Clean-Up	. x x x x x x . .	2144	L O P D
USSR 256 (5) [U256]	Clean-Up	. x . x x	256	P D
USSR 257 [U257]	Clean-Up	. x . x x	257	P D
USSR 3103 [SVC]	Clean-Up	x x x x x x x . . x	3103	B L O P
USSR 311 [U311]	Clean-Up	. . . . x	321	O P
USSR 394 [U394]	Clean-Up	. x . x x	394	P D
USSR 492 [U492]	Clean-Up	. . . . x	492	O P
USSR 516 (4) [Leap]	Clean-Up	. . x x x	516	O P
USSR 600 [U600]	Clean-Up	. x . x x	600	P D
USSR 696 [GR]	Clean-Up	. x . x	696	P D
USSR 707 [U707]	Clean-Up	. x . x x	707	P D
USSR 711 [U711]	Clean-Up	. x . . x	711	P D
USSR 830 [U830]	Clean-Up	. . x x x	830	O P
USSR 948 [U948]	Clean-Up	. x . . x x x . .	948	O P D
V-Label [Label]	Clean-Up	. . x x x x . . .	Overwrites	L P
V1-Not [OW]	Clean-Up	. . . x x	Overwrites	
V1_1 [OW]	Clean-Up	. . . x x	Overwrites	
V2_0 [OW]	Clean-Up	. . . x x	Overwrites	
V1_0 [OW]	Clean-Up	. . . x x	Overwrites	
V1028 [QP2]	Clean-Up	. . x x x x . . .	1028	O P L
V125 [M128]	Clean-Up	. . x x x	125	P
V1463 [1452]	Clean-Up	. . . x x	1463	O P

Virus	Scanner	Pattern	Size	Codes
V2000 (3) [RKO	Clean-Up	. . x x x x x . . .	2000	O P L
V2100 (5) [RKO]	Clean-Up	. . x . x x	2100	O P D L
V270 [268P]	Clean-Up	. . . x x	270	O P L D
V299 [V299]	Clean-Up	. . . . x	299	O P D
V2P2 [V2p2]	Clean-Up	. x . . x	Varies	L O P
V2P6 [V2P6]	Clean-Up	. x . . x	Varies	L O P
V400 (5) [MCE]	Clean-Up	. . x . x	Varies	O P D
V483 [G3]	Clean-Up	. . x x x	483	O P
V5 [V-5]	Clean-Up	. . . x x x	547	O D
v600 [v600]	Clean-Up	. . x x x	600	O P L
V800 (3) [V800]	Clean-Up	x x x . x	800	O P L
V801 [V801]	Clean-Up	. . x x x x x . . .	801	O P L
V82 [V801]	Clean-Up	. x . . . x x x x x	2000	O P L
V914 [914]	Clean-Up	. . . . x	914	O P
V961 [V961]	Clean-Up	. . x x x	961	O P
VA [VA]	Clean-Up	. . x . . x	1651	O P L
Vacsina (19) [Vacs]	Clean-Up	. . x . x x x . . .	1206	O P
Vcomm (5) [Vcomm]	Clean-Up	. . . . . x	1074	O P L
VCL {Con]	Clean-Up	. . x x x	576	O P
VCL-HEEVE	Clean-Up	. . x . . x	514	O P
VDV-853 [VDV]	Clean-Up	. . . x x	853	O P L
Venge-E [OW]	Clean-Up	. . x x x	1132	L P D
VHP (7) [VHP]	Clean-Up	. . . x x	Varies	L O P
VHP-2 [VHP2]	Clean-Up	. . . . x	N/A	P O
Victor (2) [Victor]	Clean-Up	. . x x x x x . . .	2458	P D L
Vienna/648 (49) [Lisbon]	Clean-Up	. . . . x	648	P
Vietnamese [Vt]	Clean-Up	. x x x x	950	P D L
Violator (5) [Vienna]	Clean-Up	. . . x x	1055	O P D
Viper [Vip]	Clean-Up	. . . x x x	Overwrites	L O P
Virus90 [V9]	Clean-Up	. x x x	857	P D L
Virus-101 [V101]	Clean-Up	. x x x x x x x . .	2560	P
Virus-90 [90]	Clean-Up	. . x . x	857	P
VM [VM]	Clean-Up	x . x x x x	3291	P L D
Voronezh (2) [Vor]	Clean-Up	. x x x x x x . . .	1600	O P D
Vote/Vote1000[Vot]	Clean-Up	. . . x x	1000	P D L
VP [VP]	Clean-Up	. . . x x	913	L O P
Vriest [1241]	Clean-Up	. . x x x	1280	L O P
VTS [VTS]	Clean-Up	. . . . x	N/A	P
VVF-34 [vvf]	Clean-Up	. . x . x x	1628	P L
W13 (4) [G2]	Clean-Up	. . . . x	532	O P
Walker [Wlk]	Clean-Up	. . x x x x	3861	O P L

Virus	Scanner	Marks	Size Increase	Flags
Walkabout [Walk]	Clean-Up	. x x x x x	573	O D L
Warrior [War]	Clean-Up	. . x . . x	1024	O
Warrior 2 [war2]	Clean-Up	. . . . x	1024	O P
Whale (34) [Whale]	Clean-Up	x x x x x x x . . .	9216	L O P D
Why_win [Why]	Clean-Up	. . . x x	1328	L P
Windmill [Wm]	Clean-Up	x . x . . . . . x . .	N/A	B
WinVir [WinVir]	Clean-Up	. . . . . x	854	P D
Wisconsin (3) [Wisc]	Clean-Up	. x . x x	825	O P D
Wolfman (3) [Wolf]	Clean-Up	. . x x x x	2064	O P
Wonder [Wond]	Clean-Up	. . . . x x	Overwrites	L O P
Wordswap (4) [Ws]	Clean-Up	. . x x x x	Varies	D F L O P
WWT (3) [WWT]	Clean-Up	. . . x x	Varies	L O P
Xabaras [Xab]	Clean-Up	. . . . . x	Overwrites	L O P
Xuxa [GR]	Clean-Up	. . x x x	1413	O P L
Xpeh [XP]	Clean-Up	. . x . x x	4016	O P D
Yale/Alameda (3) [Alameda]	Clean-Up	. . x . . . . x . .	N/A	B
Yan2505a [Yan]	Clean-Up	. . x . x x	2899	P O
Yankee [Doodle]	Clean-Up	. . x . x x	2899	P O
Yankee - 2 [Doodle2]	Clean-Up	. . . x x	1961	P O
Yap [Yap]	Clean-Up	. x x x x	6258	L O P
Youth [Yth]	Clean-Up	. . x x x	640	L P D
Yukon [OW]	Clean-Up	. . . x x	Overwrites	
Z10 [Z10]	Clean-Up	. x . x . x	704	P L
Zaragosa [Zar]	Clean-Up	. . x x x x x . . .	1159	L O P
Zeppelin [Zpp]	Clean-Up	. x . x x	1508	P L O
Zero Bug/1536 [Zero]	Clean-Up	. . x . x	1536	O P
ZeroHunt [Hunt]	Clean-Up	x x x . x	N/A	O P D
ZK900 [Z900]	Clean-Up	. x x x x	900	L O P
ZRK (3) [ZRK]	Clean-Up	. . x x x x x . . .	2968	O L P
ZU1 [ZU1]	Clean-Up	. . x x x	473	P L O
ZY [ZY]	Clean-Up	. . . x x	924	P L

Total Number of Viruses, including variants: 1561

LEGEND:

Size Increase:

N/A   Virus does not attach to files.

None   Virus does not change file size (uses unused space in file or manipulates file linkages)

Overwrites - Virus overwrites beginning of file; no file size change

All Others - The length in bytes by which a file will increase when infect

Damage Fields:

B - Corrupts or overwrites the boot sector

D - Corrupts data files

F - Formats or overwrites all/part of disk

L - Directly or indirectly corrupts file linkage

O - Affects system run-time operation

P - Corrupts program or overlay files

Characteristics:

x - Yes

. - No

Disinfectors:

Clean-Up   - Clean-Up universal virus disinfector

SCAN /D   - VIRUSCAN with /D option

SCAN /D /A   - VIRUSCAN with /D and /A options

MDISK /P   - MDISK with "P" option (See Note)

All Others   - The name of disinfecting program

NOTES

SCAN /D OPTION
The SCAN /D options will overwrite and then delete the entire infected program. The program must then be replaced from the original diskette or a backup. Files removed in this manner can not be recovered by UNDELETE programs. If you wish to try and recover an infected program then use the above-named disinfector.

MDISK
MDISK can be used to repair virus-infected master boot record (partition table) code and boot sector code on DOS 3.00 to 4.01 partitioned diskettes. For replacing the MBR code on MS-DOS 5.00 partitioned hard disks, use the FDISK.EXE program with the undocumented /MBR switch.

OVERLAY-INFECTING VIRUSES AND THE /A OPTION
If a virus infects Overlay Files (Item 7) Clean-Up should be used with the /A option when removing the virus.

GENERIC BOOT SECTOR [GENB], MBR [GENP] AND FAMILY [FAMx] VIRUSES
In order to detect non-specific (new or unknown) viruses, VIRUSCAN contains code that will search files and system areas of a disk for virus-like mechanisms. If such code is found in the Master Boot Record (partition table), SCAN will report the presence of a Generic Partition Table [GenP] virus. If such code is found in the DOS Boot Sector, SCAN will report the presence of a Generic Boot Sector [GenB] virus. If

such a virus is reported, it can be removed by running CLEAN-UP with the appropriate I.D. code, however, please forward a copy of the virus to McAfee Associates for analysis prior to doing so.

Please note that some security and anti-viral programs which replace the MBR with custom code may be reported as the [GenP] virus. If you are running such a program, deinstall it and re-run VIRUSCAN.

The Family viruses are a number of viruses, usually very recent, using standard viral code. SCAN is able to detect them through generic detection, but CLEAN does not have the ability to remove those. As with the GENB and GENP viruses, please forward a copy of any viruses of this sort to McAfee Associates for analysis and identification.

OVERWRITING VIRUSES AND THE [OW] CLEAN-UP CODE

Viruses that overwrite sections of programs with their own code do permanent, irreparable damage to the infected file. The user will find the infected program impossible to execute. Viruses designated with the [OW] CLEAN-UP code are not able to be cleaned, and CLEAN-UP will prompt the user with a message warning that the file cannot be repaired and must be deleted.

McAfee Agent Listing

McAFEE ASSOCIATES AGENT LISTING
November 16, 1992

McAfee Associates	(408) 988-3832 office
3350 Scott Boulevard, Building 14	(408) 970-9727 fax
Santa Clara, CA 95054-3107	(408) 988-4004 BBS (25 lines)
USA	USR HST/v.32/v.42bis/MNP 1-5
	support@mcafee.COM InterNet
	GO MCAFEE CompuServe

In order to provide the global community with anti-virus coverage in a timely manner, McAfee Associates has established an Agents program to provide service, sales and support for McAfee Associates products around the world. If you do not see your country listed, please contact McAfee Associates directly. A listing of United States Agents has been added to the end of this file.

ARGENTINA
RAN Ingenieria de Sistemas
Address: Cosquin 10-5o. C
                Buenos Aires 1408
Contact: Maria Jose Alvarez Hamelin
Telephone: +54 (1) 642-3689
Fax: +54 (1) 334-7802

AUSTRALIA
Computer Virus Clinic
Address: P.O. Box 106
                Moorebank, N.S.W. 2170
Contact: Colin Keeble
Telephone: +61 (02) 822-4303 Sydney

Fax:	+61 (02) 822-4304
BBS:	+61 (02) 602-9237 [9600bps, v.32, 24hrs]
Telephone:	+61 (03) 335-4677 Melbourne
Fax:	+61 (03) 335-4656
Telephone:	+61 (08) 234-5287 Adelaide
Fax:	+61 (08) 234-5324
Telephone:	+61 (07) 261-3565 Queensland
Fax:	+61 (07) 261-2059

AUSTRALIA

Computerware for Micros

Telephone:	(008) 882-875 National Toll Free
Fax:	+61 (08) 363-1974 National
BBS:	+61 (08) 362-4293 National

ADELAIDE - HOME OFFICE

Address:	23 Magill Road
	Stepney, Adelaide, S.A. 5096
Contact:	Priestly Hillam
Telephone:	+61 (08) 362-8200

SYDNEY BRANCH

Contact:	John Hillam
Telephone:	+61 (02) 252-3546
Fax:	+61 (02) 252-3353
BBS:	+61 (08) 311-1036

MELBOURNE BRANCH

Contact:	Michael O'Sullivan
Telephone:	+61 (03) 663-4868
Fax:	+61 (03) 663-7466
BBS:	+61 (03) 888-5932

BRISBANE BRANCH

Telephone:	+61 (07) 285-2339
Fax:	+61 (07) 363-1974
BBS:	+61 (07) 804-0239

PERTH BRANCH

Contact:	Rob Edwards
Telephone:	+61 (09) 357-0818
BBS:	+61 (09) 307-8075

CANBERRA BRANCH

Contact:	David Fabris
Telephone:	+61 (06) 259-1814
BBS:	+61 (06) 259-2062

TOWNSVILLE BRANCH

| BBS: | +61 (077) 79-1546 |

AUSTRALIA

Doctor Disk (Perth Office)

Address:	77 Bulwer Street
	Perth, WA 6000
Contact:	Greg Golden
Telephone:	+61 (09) 328-2011 (Perth Office)

Fax:	+61 (09) 328-9661 (Perth Office)
BBS:	+61 (09) 244-2111 (Perth Office)
Telephone:	+61 (02) 281-2099 (Sydney Office)
Telephone:	+61 (03) 690-9100 (Melbourne Office)
Telephone:	+61 (07) 831-0151 (Brisbane Office)
Telephone:	+61 (08) 332-2354 (Adelaide Office)
Toll-Free:	(008) 999 755 (outside of Perth Metro Area)

AUSTRIA

ComIn Terramar Handelsgesmbh

Address:	Nikolsdorfergasse 8/8
	A-1050 Wien
Contact:	Ronald Schmutzer
Telephone:	+43 (1) 545-3731
Fax:	+43 (1) 545-3339
BBS:	+43 (1) 545-3338

BAHRAIN

Deena International Commercial Agency

Address:	P.O. Box 5168
	Al Zahra Bldg., 1st Floor
	SH Issa Al Kabeer Rd.
	Manama
Contact:	Ehab Al-Maskati
Telephone:	+973 261 247
Fax:	+973 230 418
Telex:	8613 DICA BN
Cable:	DICANTER

BELGIUM

Impakt nv

Address:	Ham 64
	B-9000 Gent
Contact:	Frank Lateur
Telephone:	+32 (91) 25 35 49
Fax:	+32 (91) 33 00 78
BBS:	+32 (91) 23 40 16

BELGIUM

Softserve Distributors

Address:	Dynamicalaan 16 b20
	B-2601 Wilrijk
Contact:	Arthur Schrey
Telephone:	+32 (3) 830 59 92
Fax:	+32 (3) 830 25 92

BERMUDA

Applied Computer Technologies

Address:	P.O. Box HM 2091
	Hamilton, HM HX
Contact:	Craig Clark
Telephone:	(809) 295-1616
Fax:	(809) 292-7967
BBS:	(809) 292-7376 [U.S. Robotics HST 14.4K]
	(809) 292-1774 [v.32bis]

BERMUDA

Business Systems Ltd.

Address:	P.O. Box HM 2445
	Hamilton, HM JX
Contact:	Richard Miller
Telephone:	(809) 295-8777
Fax:	(809) 295-1149

BRAZIL

COMPUSUL Consultoria e Comercio de Informatica Ltda.

Address:	Rua Emboabas, 68-1o andar
	04623-Sao Paulo, SP
Contact:	Andre Pitkowski
Telephone:	+55 (11) 533-7331
Fax:	+55 (11) 530-6822
BBS:	+55 (11) 247-8246 [1200-14,400 bps, v.32/v.32bis]
	(call for BBS numbers in other cities)

BRAZIL

Maple Informatica Ltda.

Address:	R. Maranhao, 554 cj. 26
	01240 Sao Paulo, SP
Contact:	David Rotenberg
Telephone:	+55 (11) 826-5311
Fax:	+55 (11) 826-5375

BRAZIL

NUPEC Ltda

Address:	Av. Visconda de Suassuna, 823/313
	Boa Vista - Recife - CEP 50.050
Contact:	Anatolio de Paula Crespo
Telephone:	+55 (81) 222-0698
Fax:	+55 (81) 222-0698

CANADA

Asgard Technologies

Address:	175 Hunter Street East Suite #313
	Hamilton, Ontario
	CANADA L8N 4E7
Contact:	Michael B. Cameron
Telephone:	(416) 529-9284
Fax:	(416) 529-9186

CANADA - British Columbia

Concise Systems Corp.

Address:	#25 - 1925 Bowen Road
	Nanaimo, BC
	CANADA V9S 1H1
Contact:	Walter Anderson or Carol Sanders
Telephone:	(604) 756-1604
Fax:	(604) 756-0123

CANADA

DOLFIN Developments Ltd.

Address:	2904 South Sheridan Way
	Oakville, Ontario

```
                                CANADA  L6J 7L7
         Contact:             John Reid
         Telephone:           (416) 829-4344
         Fax:                 (416) 829-4380
         DOLFIN Developments- Montreal
         Address:             2690B Pitfield, Bureau 100
                              St-Laurent, Montreal, Quebec
                              CANADA  H4S 1G9
         Contact:             Simon Borduas
         Telephone:           (514) 333-7240
         Fax:                 (514) 333-7165
         BBS:                 (514) 735-5769
         DOLFIN Developments- West
         Address:             Maison Chadwick House
                              1842 - 14th Street SW
                              Calgary, Alberta
                              CANADA  T2T 3S9
         Contact:             Terry O'Hearn
         Telephone:           (403) 229-3454
         Fax:                 (403) 229-3507
```

CANADA - Edmonton

```
         LOGICORP Data Systems Ltd
         Address:             Suite 301, 11044 - 82nd Avenue
                              Edmonton, Alberta
                              CANADA  T6G 0T2
         Contact:             Peter Altrogge
         Telephone:           (403) 433-2830
         Fax:                 (403) 439-2134
```

CANADA - Edmonton

```
         Programmers Guild Products
         Address:             4652 - 99th Street
                              Edmonton, Alberta
                              CANADA  T6E 5H5
         Contact:             George Woycenko
         Telephone:           (403) 438-5897
         Fax:                 (403) 434-3957
```

CANADA - Ottawa

```
         Schultz Computers
         Address:             1825 Woodward Drive
                              Ottawa, Ontario
                              CANADA  K2C 0R4
         Contact:             John Schultz
         Telephone:           (613) 727-0589
         Fax:                 (613) 727-1264
```

CHILE

```
         Rigg S.A.
         Address:             Avda. Salvador 1068
                              P.O. Box 10.295
                              Santiago
         Contact:             Ricardo Gutierrez
```

Telephone:	+56 (2) 225-0222
Fax:	+56 (2) 225-0240

CZECHOSLOVAKIA

AEC Ltd.

Address:	Sumavska 33
	612 64 BRNO
Contact:	Jiri Mrnustik, MSc.
Telephone:	+42 (5) 7112 line 502
Fax:	+42 (5) 013 501

CZECHOSLOVAKIA

NKOP elektronik Ltd.

Address:	Coboriho 2
	949 01 NITRA
Contact:	Peter Zoldos
Telephone:	+42 (87) 419 780
Fax:	+42 (87) 413 958

DENMARK

Danadata

Address:	Vestergade 58
	8100 Aarhus
Contact:	Steen Pedersen
Telephone:	+45 (86) 18 28 44
Fax:	+45 (86) 18 28 92
BBS:	+45 (86) 13 89 83 [1200-9600bps/v.32/24 hours]

FINLAND

ICL Data Oy/PC-Hotline (Kayttotuki)

Address:	P.O. Box 458
	SF-00101 Helsinki
Contact:	Kari Ilonen or Erkki Mustonen
Telephone:	+358 (0) 567 4248
Fax:	+358 (0) 567 4160
BBS:	+358 (0) 567 2200 [U.S. Robotics Dual Standard]

FINLAND

SAFECO OY

Address:	Kirvuntie 22
	02140 Espoo
Contact:	Hannu Ohrling
Telephone:	+358 (0) 512 1100
Fax:	+358 (0) 515 151
BBS:	+358 (9)0 512 2483
MCI Mail:	540-0324

FRANCE

VIF "La Pepiniere"

Address:	111, avenue de Lodeve
	34000 Montpellier
Contact:	Pascal Jour
Telephone:	+33 67 58 18 36
Fax:	+33 67 58 26 61

GERMANY

BBT Electronics

Address:	Hundsmuhler Str. 12
	W-2900 Oldenburg
Contact:	David Thorlton - Marketing
	Ralf Fischer - Support
Telephone:	+49 (0) 441-950930
Fax:	+49 (0) 441-504481
BBS:	+49 (0) 441-9509333

GERMANY

BFK edv-consulting GmbH

Address:	Humboldystrasse 48
	W-7500 Karlsruhe 1
Contact:	Christoph Fischer
Telephone	+49 (721) 96201-1
Fax:	+49 (721) 96201-99

GERMANY

Nane Juergensen

Address:	Alpenstrasse 52
	8038 Grobenzell
Contact:	Nane Jurgensen
Telephone:	+49 (8) 1425-3030
Fax:	+49 (8) 1425-4641
CompuServe	100021,414

GERMANY

Kirschbaum Software, GmbH

Address:	Kronau 15
	W 8091 Emmering b. Wbg.
Contact:	Josef Kirschbaum
Telephone:	+49 (0) 8067-1016
Fax:	+49 (0) 8067-1053

GERMANY

K.H. Kitroschat, Ingenieurbuero für Neue Technik

Address:	Naabstrasse 9
	W-4006 Erkrath
Contact:	Karl-Heinz Kitroschat
Telephone:	+49 (0) 2104 48626
Fax:	+49 (0) 2104 449 555

GERMANY

NoVIR Apura GmbH

Address:	Hochofenstrasse 19-21
	2400 Lubeck 14
Contact:	Peter Boehm
Telephone:	+49 (0) 4513 06066
Fax:	+49 (0) 4513 09600
BBS:	+49 (0) 4513 05267
BTX:	*NoVIR#

GERMANY

R. Bucker EDV

Address:	Nordhemmer Straße 94
	W 4955 Hille 1
Contact:	Peter Bucker

Telephone:	+49 (0) 5703-2829
	+49 (0) 5703-3610
Fax:	+49 (0) 5703-3648

GHANA

Network Computer Systems Ltd.

Address:	PO Box 2649
	Accra
Contact:	Anne Grant
Telephone:	+233 (21) 773372
	+233 (21) 772279
Fax:	+233 (21) 772279
Telex:	3047/48 BTH25 GH

GIBRALTAR

Interactive Systems Ltd.

Address:	PO Box 397
	15A Tuckey's Lane
Contact:	Jim Watt
Telephone:	+350 73285
Fax:	+350 73385

GREECE

TopNet Computers Ltd.

Address:	15 Mpakopoulou St.
	154 51 Neo Psixiko
	Athens
Contact:	Dimitrios Georgiadis
Telephone:	+30 (1) 647 6066
	+30 (1) 647 5378
Fax:	+30 (1) 672 6629

HONG KONG

Terabyte Computer Consultants Ltd.

Address:	Room 1004, 10/F, Tung Wah Mansion
	199-203 Hennessy Road
	Wan Chai
Contact:	Isabel Chan
Telephone:	+852 (0) 598-0046-51
Fax:	+852 (0) 598-0892

HUNGARY

Pik-SYS Company Ltd.

Address:	Szentmiklosi u.18
	H-1213 Budapest
Contact:	Maria Pistar
Telephone:	+36 (1) 276-0864
Fax:	+36 (1) 276-5714

ICELAND

Tolvur og Fjarskipti

Address:	Dugguvogi 2
	104 Reykjavik
Contact:	Jim Hayward or Ari Thor Johannesson
Telephone:	+354 (9) 2 46657
	+354 (9) 1 679900

Fax:	+354 (9) 1 683489
BBS:	+354 (9) 1 670990
	+354 (9) 1 677999
	+354 (9) 1 995151
BBS NUA:	274011991000

INDIA

COMTEC (India), A Division of Microassociates Consultants

Address:	11 Sneh, D. S. Babrekar Road
	Dadar, Bombay 400028
Contact:	Mr. Mandar Dange
Telephone:	+91 (22) 5562767
	+91 (22) 452812
Fax:	+91 (22) 5115904
	+91 (22) 4223968

INDIA

Foremost Systems P. Ltd.

Address:	2G, Kashmir Emporium Bldg.
	P.m. Road
	Bombay 400 034
Contact:	Siddharth Mehta
Telephone:	+91 (22) 2862602
Fax:	+91 (22) 4922841
Telex:	011-82579 (Attn: Sid Mehta)

INDONESIA

P.T. Yakin Aman

Address:	#15-16, Block FX-1
	Jalan Kelapa Gading Boulevard
	Jakarta 14240
Contact:	M.A. Sunardi
Telephone:	+62 (21) 451-0072
Fax:	+62 (21) 451-2731

IRELAND

Systemhouse Technology Group Ltd.

Address:	39-40 Upper Mount Street
	Dublin 2
Contact:	Dermot Williams or Stephen Kearon
Telephone:	+353 (1) 615 445
Fax:	+353 (1) 615 323
BBS:	+353 (1) 288-5634
	+353 (1) 283-1908 [U.S. Robotics HST]

ISRAEL

Chief Data Recovery Company

Address:	15 Ha'banim Street
	PO Box 499
	Nes-Ziona 70400
Contact:	Nemrod Kedem
Telephone:	+972 (8) 400 070
Fax:	+972 (8) 403 295
BBS:	+972 (3) 966 7562 [v.32bis/v.42bis/14400bps]
	+972 (3) 967 3919 [v.32bis/v.42bis/14400bps]

+972 (3) 967 3499 [v.32bis/v.42bis/14400bps]
+972 (3) 967 3256 [MNP5/2400bps]

ITALY
Ultimobyte Editrice, SRL
Address:	Via A. Manuzio, 15
	20124 Milano
Contact:	Adalberto Fontana
Telephone:	+39 (2) 655-5306
Fax:	+39 (2) 65.55.061

JAMAICA
W.T.G APTEC Systems Ltd.
Address:	"The Towers"
	25 Dominca Drive
	Kingston 5
Contact:	Arnold McDonald
Telephone:	(809) 929-9250
Fax:	(809) 929-8296

JAPAN
LINK Co., Ltd.
Address:	Rosebud Gotanda Bldg 10F
	8-8-15 Nishi-Gotanda
	Shingawa-ku
	Tokyo 141
Contact:	Akira Watanabe
Telephone:	+81 (3) 3493 5850
Fax:	+81 (3) 3493 5188

KOREA
Myung-Je Corporation
Address:	3Fl, HWAIL B/D, 828-23
	Yeogsam-Dong, Kangnam-Ku
	Seoul
Contact:	Park Dong Myung
Telephone:	+82 (2) 563-5381
	+82 (2) 567-0473
Fax:	+82 (2) 553-7412

KUWAIT
Sultan Systems
Address:	Salem Mubarak Street
	Bldg. 17, Block 49, 5th Floor
	Safat 13132
Contact:	Mohanned Hassanin
Telephone:	+965 572 3153
	+965 572 3155
Fax:	+965 572 3152

MALAYSIA
MCSB Systems (M) Sdn Bhd
Address:	Ground Floor, Wisma Mirama
	Jalan Wisma Putra
	50460 Kuala Lumpur
Contact:	Mr. Mok Fork Chuan

Telephone:	+60 (3) 241 7400
Fax:	+60 (3) 248 8010

MAURITIUS

J. Kalachand & Co. Ltd.

Address:	20 A&B Lord Kitcheter Street
	Port-Louis
Contact:	Ramesh Kalachand
Telephone:	+230 212-6313
Fax:	+230 208-8244

MEXICO

Ingenieria Y Technologica Avanzada, S.A. de C.V.

Address:	Barranquilla 134-B
	Col. Altavista
	Monterrey, Neuveo Leon, 64840
Contact:	Raul Quintanilla Martinez
Telephone:	+52 (83) 469865
Fax:	+52 (83) 469865
BBS:	+52 (83)58 1477 [U.S. Robotics HST]
	+52 (83)59 9848 [1200/2400 bps]
	+52 (83)59 9849 [1200/2400 bps]

MEXICO

McAfee Associates, Mexico, S.A. de C.V.

Address:	Ave. Nuevo Leon No.253, Desp. 501
	Col. Escandon, C.P. 11800, Mexico D.F.
Contact:	Arturo De la Mora Carrasco
	Felipe Lopez Gomez
	Patricia De la Mora
Telephone:	+52 (5) 273-1361
	+52 (5) 273-0954
Fax:	+52 (5) 273-1019
BBS:	+52 (5) 590-5988 [1200-9600 bps]

MEXICO

Mundo PC, S.A.

Address:	Rio San Lorenzo No. 507-A OTE
	Garza Garcia, N.L. 66220
Contact:	Bill Schaefer
Telephone:	+52 (8) 378-34-48

NETHERLANDS, THE

CPU Communications & Products United C.V.

	SALES OFFICE
Address:	Jacob van Maerlandstraat 86-90
	5216 JM 's Hertogenbosch
	PO Box 1878
	5200 BW 's Hertogenbosch
Contact:	Rick Wezenaar
Telephone:	+31 (73) 141252
Fax:	+31 (73) 140437
BBS:	+31 (73) 124674 [14,400bps]
	+31 (73) 130204 [2400 bps]

SUPPORT OFFICE
Address: Verzamlegebouw Zuid
                 Strevelsweg 700/302
                 3083 AS Rotterdam
                 PO Box 5011
                 3008 AA Rotterdam
Contact: Fred Janssen or Fred de Koning
Telephone: +31 (10) 4102233
Fax: +31 (10) 4808555
BBS: +31 (10) 4103188 [14,400bps]
                 +31 (10) 4103022 [2400bps]

NETHERLANDS ANTILLES

Micro Computer Consultants
Address: Fokkerweg 30
                 Muskus Building
                 Willemstad Curaco
Contact: Edison Maduro
Telephone: +599 (9) 61 31 61
Fax: +599 (9) 61 61 19

NEW ZEALAND

Computer Software Library of NZ, Ltd.
Address: WaiPoPo 3 R.D.
                 Timaru
Contact: Bill Strauss
Telephone: +64 (3) 615-9333
Fax: +64 (3) 615-9333
BBS: +64 (3) 615-9313
Mobile Phone: +64 (25) 32-8443

NORWAY

ND ServiceTeam A/S
Address: Olaf Helsetsv. 5
                 Postboks 6448 Etterstad
                 0605 Oslo
                 Arne Bergersen
Telephone: +47 (2) 627500
Fax: +47 (2) 627501

PAKISTAN

Computer Connection (PVT) LTD.
Address: 19-1/A, Block 6, P.E.C.H.S.
                 Sharea Faisal
                 Karachi
Contact: (Mr.) Asim I. Shaikh
Telephone: +92 (21) 438 839
Telephone: +92 (21) 449 343
Fax: +92 (21) 447 266

PHILIPPINES

Mannasoft Technology Corporation
Address: Suite 105 Mid-Land Mansion
                 839 Pasay Road, Makati

	Metro Manilla
Contact:	Hans C. Dee
Telephone:	+63 (2) 87 63 19
	+63 (2) 813-41-62
	+63 (2) 813-41-63
Pager Service:	+63 (2) 869 11 11
FAX:	+63 (2) 812 93-10

PORTUGAL

Fobis, Informatic e Gestao, Lda.

Address:	Praca de Londres 3-1.Dt
	P-1000 Lisboa
Contact:	Nuno Pinto
Telephone:	+351 (1) 848 31 84
Fax:	+351 (1) 848 17 77

SAUDI ARABIA

Gulf Stars Computer Systems

Address:	PO Box 52908
	Riyadh 11573
Contact:	Anwar Qahwash
Telephone:	+966 (1) 432-8222
Fax:	+966 (1) 465-3156
Telex:	407602 GSCS SJ

SINGAPORE

Asiasoft (S) PTE. LTD.

Address:	No. 8, Aljunied Avenue 3, Oakwell Bldg.
	Singapore 1438
Contact:	Lai Lee Tat
Telephone:	+65 742 6000
Fax:	+65 742 7000
BBS:	+65 741 8707

SINGAPORE

Computerware for Micros
(see AUSTRALIA for address)

Contact:	Edmund Lim
Telephone:	+65 339-3238
Fax:	+65 338 5117
BBS:	+65 448-3395

SINGAPORE

MCSB Systems (S) Pte Ltd.

Address:	5 Little Road
	#05-01 Cemtex Industrial Building
	Singapore 1953
Contact:	Ivan Wainewright
Telephone:	+65 382-7600
Fax:	+65 382-5700

SPAIN

DATAMON, SA Central

Address:	Corcega, 485
	08025 Barcelona
Contact:	Carmen Mestres

Telephone:	+34 (3) 207-2704
Fax:	+34 (3) 457-1370

SPAIN

DATAMON, SA - Macroservice

Address:	C/Infanta Mercedes, 83
	28020 Madrid
Contact:	Diego Saez
Telephone:	+34 (1) 571 52 00
Fax:	+34 (1) 571 19 11

SWEDEN

Virus Help Centre - MAIN Office

Address:	Box 7018
	S 811 07 Sandviken
Contact:	Mikael Larsson
Telephone:	+46 (26) 100518
Direct Phone:	+46 (26) 275740
Mobile Phone:	+46 (10) 295 5551
Fax:	+46 (26) 275720
BBS:	+46 (26) 275710 [U.S. Robotics Dual Standard]
	+46 (26) 275715 [U.S. Robotics HST]
Fidonet:	2:205/204 or 2:205/234
VirNet:	9:461/101 or 9:461/111
Internet:	vhc@abacus.hgs.se

Virus Help Centre - GAVLE Office

Address:	Box 1237
	S 801 37 Gavle
Contact:	Ola Larsson
Mobile Phone:	+46 (10) 295-5552
Fidonet:	2:205/212
VirNet:	9:461/112
Internet:	vhcola@abacus.hgs.se

SWITZERLAND

DASIKON AG

Address:	Sandbueelstrasse 6
	CH-8604 Volketswil
Contact:	Marcus Laeubli
Telephone:	+41 (1) 945-5970
Fax:	+41 (1) 946-0545
BBS:	+41 (1) 945-5077

TRINIDAD & TOBAGO

Opus Networx

Address:	P.O. Box 972
	Port of Spain, Trinidad & Tobago
	West Indies
Contact:	Peter Wimbourne
Tel:	(809) 628-3105
Fax:	(809) 622-6878
BBS:	(809) 628-5023

UNITED KINGDOM

International Data Security

Address:	9 & 10 Alfred Place
	London WC1E 7EB
Contact:	Oliver Mills
Telephone:	+44 (71) 631 0548
	+44 (71) 436 2244
Fax:	+44 (71) 580 1466
BBS:	+44 (71) 580 4800

URUGUAY

Datamatic

Address:	25 de Mayo 635 Piso 6
	Montevideo 11100
Contact:	Ivonne Chabaneau
	Juan Camps (technical)
Telephone:	+598 2 96 18 42
Fax:	+598 2 96 27 71

VENEZUELA

Lantech Ltd.

Address:	Edit. La linea, Ave. Libertador
	Torre A - Piso 15
	Caracas
Contact:	Vladimir Castillo
Telephone:	+582 781 4655
Fax:	+582 781 7454

ZAMBIA

KBM Software Plaza

Address:	P.O. Box 320139
	Woodlands
	Lusaka
Contact:	(Mrs.) Kasonde B. Shakalima
Telephone:	+260 (1) 260 151
Fax:	+260 (1) 260 151

UNITED STATES

Advanced Computer Networks

Address:	260 Old Nyack Turnpike
	Spring Valley, NY 10977
Contact:	Lazer Milstein or David Adams
Telephone:	(914) 425-5858
Telephone:	(800) 383-0257 Order inquriry
Fax:	(914) 425-4306
BBS:	(914) 425-2304

UNITED STATES

Advanced Computer Technologies

Address:	108 Main Street
	Norwalk, CT 06851
Contact:	Larry McNally
Telephone:	(203) 847-9433
Fax:	(203) 847-2475

UNITED STATES - Pacific Northwest

Al Mashburn & Associates

Address:	7406 - 27th Street West, Suite 8
	Tacoma, WA 98466
Contact:	Al Mashburn
Telephone:	(206) 565-8641
Fax:	(206) 565-3134

UNITED STATES

Barish & O'Brien Consulting

Address:	19 West 44th Street, Suite 300
	New York, NY 10036
Contact:	David Barish
Telephone:	(212) 221-1600
Fax:	(212) 221-1658

UNITED STATES - New England

Beehive Computer Company

Address:	#2 Industrial Park Drive
	Concord, NH 03301
Contact:	Jeff Parkerson
Telephone:	(603) 226-2993
Fax:	(603) 226-2070

UNITED STATES - Midwest

Blue Chip Computer Company

Address:	3085 Woodman Drive
	Dayton, OH 45420
Contact:	Jim King
Telephone:	(513) 299-4594
Fax:	(513) 298-5798

UNITED STATES - Northern California

C&P Solutions

Address:	14428 Union Avenue
	San Jose, CA 95124
Contact:	Luis Paz
Telephone:	(408) 559-4049
Fax:	(408) 559-8645

UNITED STATES

CDT, Inc.

Address:	3110 Rhapsody Court
	Colorado Springs, CO 80920
Contact:	Glen Sandusky
Telephone:	(719) 260-0567
Fax:	(719) 531-5256

UNITED STATES

CompuNet, Inc.

Address:	8080 Madison Avenue, Suite 202
	Fair Oaks, CA 95286
Contact:	Noel Morgan
Telephone:	(916) 965-3112
Fax:	(916) 965-5713

UNITED STATES

ComputerLand of Sioux Falls, SD

Address:	3809 South Western Avenue
	Sioux Falls, SD 57105
Contact:	Eric Hosen
Telephone:	(605) 338-5263
Fax:	(605) 338-7130

UNITED STATES

The Computer Station

Address:	2600 South King Street, Suite 207
	Honolulu, HI 96826
Telephone:	(808) 942-7747
Fax:	(808) 942-5119
BBS:	(808) 247-7328

UNITED STATES - South

Computer Generations, Inc.

Address:	P.O. Box 71
	Hendersonville, TN 37077-0071
Contact:	Cliff Jones
Telephone:	(615) 865-1418
Fax:	?

UNITED STATES - Midwest

Computer Maintenence, Inc.

Address:	1433 Fullerton Avenue, Suite M
	Addison, IL 60101
Contact:	Dan Eremenchuk
Telephone:	(708) 953-1555
Fax:	(708) 953-1441

UNITED STATES - South

Computer Security Plus, Inc.

Address:	3900 South Tampa Avenue
	Orlando, FL 32809
Contact:	Padgett Peterson
Telephone:	(407) 352-6027
Fax:	(407) 352-6027
BBS:	(407) 352-6027
Internet:	padgett%tccslr.dnet@mmc.com

UNITED STATES - South

Computers For Business

Address:	2843 Pembroke Road
	Hollywood, FL 33020
Contact:	David Bennett
Telephone:	(305) 920-9604
Fax:	(305) 921-6131

UNITED STATES - Southern California

Creative Business Concepts, Inc.

Address:	25231 Paseo de Alicia
	Laguna Hills, CA 92653
Contact:	Rick Shafer

Telephone: (714) 855-9445
Fax: (714) 855-0532

UNITED STATES - South

Crystal Data Systems
Address: 2104 West Ferry Way
                     Huntsville, AL 35801
Contact: Doug West
Telephone: (205) 883-4233
Fax: (205) 883-4293

UNITED STATES

DataLan Corporation
Address: 50 Main Street, Suite 1000
                    White Plains, NY 10606
Contact: John Arnold
Telephone: (914) 682-2022
Fax: (914) 682-2123

UNITED STATES

DataTek Computer Services
Address: 547 Wunder Street
                    Reading, PA 19602-2005
Contact: Kirk Wentzel
Telephone: (215) 374-2097
BBS: (215) 374-3735

UNITED STATES - South

Data Integrity
Address: 5301 North Federal Highway, Suite 130
                    Boca Raton, FL 33487
Contact: Neil Kutchera
Telephone: (407) 998-7540
Fax: (407) 998-7587

UNITED STATES - Southern California

FOCAL
Address: 15500 Erwin Street, Suite 2002
                    Van Nuys, CA 91411
Telephone: (818) 376-6598
Fax: (818) 376-6594

UNITED STATES

Genoa Group
Address: 7334 South Alton Way, Unit H
                    Englewood, CO 80112
Contact: William L. Ross
Telephone: (303) 770-5747
Fax: (303) 742-2449

UNITED STATES - Northern California

GW Associates
Address: 149 Forest Side Avenue
                    San Francisco, CA 94217
Contact: George Wertheim
Telephone: (415) 661-0968
                    (510) 577-3528
Fax: ?

UNITED STATES
Hornbeck's

Address:	406 Walnut Street
	Red Bluff, CA 96080
Contact:	Kevin Evenson
Telephone:	(916) 527-1201
Fax:	(916) 529-3621

UNITED STATES - Midwest
Inacomp-Decatur, IL

Address:	1690 Houston Drive
	Decatur, IL 62526
Contact:	Marshall Sperry
Telephone:	(217) 875-7611
Fax:	(217) 875-7611

UNITED STATES - East
Innovative Business Solutions

Address:	222 W Grand Avenue
	Montvale, NJ 07645
Contact:	Richard Verlaque
Telephone:	(201) 391-0200
Fax	(201) 291-9803

UNITED STATES - New York
International Security Technology Inc.

Address:	99 Park Avenue, 11th Floor
	Mail Stop: US Re
	New York, NY 10022
Contact:	Robert V. Jacobson
Telephone:	(212) 557-0900
Fax:	(212) 808-5206

UNITED STATES - East
Jetics Inc.

Address:	8229 Boone Blvd. Suite 860
	Vienna, VA 22182
Contact:	Wayne Carpenter
Telephone:	(703) 893-4404
Fax:	(703) 821-0710

UNITED STATES - Great Lakes States
James C. Shaeffer and Associates (formerly Jim's Consulting Services)
Detroit Office:

Address:	5025 Venture Drive
	Ann Arbor, MI 48108
Contact:	James C. Shaeffer (formerly Jim Shaeffer)
Telephone:	(313) 741-9527
Fax:	(313) 741-9528
Mobile:	(313) 670-7354 (If no answer, please leave name and number)
cc:Mail:	(313) 741-9533 Name: James C. Shaeffer, PO: JCS_PO
BBS:	(313) 741-9529 [PPI 14,400bps v.32/v.42bis 8N1 line settings]

Chicago Office:

Address:	744 Fox Hunt Trail

Deerfield, IL 60015
Contact: David Shook
Telephone: (312) 399-9364
Fax: (313) 741-9528
cc:Mail: (313) 741-9533 Name: David C. Shook, PO: JCS_PO
BBS: (313) 741-9529 PPI 9600Bps v.32/v.42bis 8N1 line settings

UNITED STATES
Joseph Head Cooper Consulting
Address: 321 West Craig Place
                 San Antonio, TX 78212
Contact: Joe Cooper
Telephone: (512) 736-2383

UNITED STATES
Kortek Industries
Address: 2000 Bering Drive, Suite 400
                 Houston, TX 77057
Contact: John Heaney
Telephone: (713) 783-0024
Fax: (713) 783-7649

UNITED STATES
M.S. Business Center
Address: 6161 El Cajon Blvd., Suite B-15
                 San Diego, CA 92115
Telephone: (619) 583-4960
Fax: (619) 583-9375

UNITED STATES
Micro Networks of America
Address: 320 Main Street
                 Farmington, CT 06034
Contact: Paul Dandrow
Telephone: (203) 678-7400
Fax: (203) 678-9437

UNITED STATES - Northern California
Microplus Systems Technologies
Address: 1020 East El Camino Real
                 Sunnyvale, CA 94087
Contact: Ralph Manildi or Bui Han
Telephone: (408) 737-2525
Fax: (408) 737-2402

UNITED STATES - South
Micro Tech Systems
Address: 1832 Banbury Road
                 Charleston, SC 29414
Contact: Curtis Clark
Telephone: (803) 763-5596
Fax: ?

UNITED STATES - Southeast
Monterey-Waldec, Inc.
Address: 4899 West Waters Avenue
                 Tampa, FL 33634

Contact: Andy Swenson
Telephone: (813) 882-9066
Fax: (813) 882-9910

UNITED STATES
NETLAN
Address: 29 West 38th Street
                    New York, NY 10018
Contact: Al Berg
Telephone: (212) 768-2273
Fax: (212) 768-2201
BBS: (212) 764-3876

UNITED STATES
Network Engineering & Comm.
Address: 14718 NE 87th Street
                    Redmond, WA 98052
Contact: Dan Kidd
Telephone: (206) 861-1778
Fax: (206) 891-1704

UNITED STATES
NHFA
Address: 577 Isham Street, Suite 2B
                    New York, NY 10034
Contact: Norman Hirsch
Telephone: (212) 304-9759 ext. 1
Fax: (212) 304-9759
BBS: (212) 304-9759 ext. 3

UNITED STATES - Pacific Northwest
OverFlow Corporation
Address: 8950 SW Burnham Street
                    Portland, OR 97223-6103
Contact: Jenice Shaw
Telephone: (503) 598-1871
Fax: (503) 598-1876

UNITED STATES - Northern California
PCS Networks
Address: 5900-T Hollis Street
                    Emeryville, CA 94608
Contact: Tim Cuny
Telephone: (510) 655-6500
                    (415) 986-1800
Fax: (510) 655-9298

UNITED STATES - Northern California
Peacham Cybernetics
Address: 10710 Baxter Avenue
                    Los Altos, CA 94024
Contact: Fritz Schneider
Telephone: (408) 739-3303
Fax: (408) 739-3204
CompuServe: 71043,1117
Internet: 71043.1117@compuserve.COM

UNITED STATES - West

Pueblo Group

Address:	6318 E. Calle Cappela
	Tucson, AZ 85710
Contact:	Bill Logan
Telephone:	(602) 321-2075
Fax:	(602) 881-8474
BBS:	(602) 747-5236
Internet:	blogan@solitud.fidonet.org

UNITED STATES

Ramcom Technology

Address:	PO Box 3491
	Flagstaff, AZ 86003-3491
Contact:	Ron Moore
Telephone:	(602) 779-3204
Fax:	(602) 779-3204
BBS:	(602) 779-3265

UNITED STATES

Rational Elegance

Address:	14636 NE 42nd Place #N202
	Bellevue, WA 98007-3311
Contact:	Robert Gryphon
Telephone:	(206) 885-5499
Cellular:	(206) 940-1124
Fax:	(206) 885-5499

UNITED STATES

Sparrow Copmuter Systems, Inc

Address:	616 S. Broad Street
	Lansdale, PA 19446
Contact:	Bill Mann
Telephone:	(215) 368-9500
Fax:	(215) 368-9522

UNITED STATES

SSDS, Inc. - HEAD OFFICE

Address:	Special Products and Government Support
	PO Box 71827
	Ft. Bragg, NC 28307
Contact:	John H. Kida
Telephone:	(703) 827-0805 ext. 204 [24 hour voice mail]
BBS:	(919) 867-0754 [1200-14,400 bps, v.32]
Internet:	jhk@washington.ssds.com

SSDS, Inc. - AUSTIN OFFICE

Address:	3102 Bee Caves Rd, Suite C
	Austin, TX 00000-0000
Contact:	Gilbert Silva
Telephone:	(512) 329-5731
Fax:	(512) 329-5726

SSDS, Inc. - HUNTSVILLE OFFICE

Address:	200 West Coute Square, Suite 988
	Huntsville, AL 35801

Contact: Matt Petty
Telephone: (205) 534-8383

SSDS, Inc. - RALEIGH OFFICE
Address: 3101 Poplarwood Court, Suite 108
                  Raleigh, NC
Contact: John Noss
Telephone: (919) 954-0400
Fax: (919) 954-0403

SSDS, Inc. - WASHINGTON, DC OFFICE
Address: 8150 Leesburg Pike, Suite 1100
                  Vienna, VA 22182
Contact: Patrick Siemon
Telephone: (703) 827-0806
Fax: (703) 827-0716

SSDS, Inc. - CHICAGO OFFICE
Address: 1755 Park Street, Suite 180
                  Naperville, IL 60504
Contact: Mark Kilgore
Telephone: (708) 778-7737
Fax: (708) 778-7740

SSDS, Inc. - SEATTLE OFFICE
Address: 1309 - 114th Ave SE, Suite 104
                  Bellevue, WA 98004
Contact: Brett Burris
Telephone: (206) 453-9141

SSDS, Inc. - DENVER OFFICE
Address: 6595 S. Dayton Suite 3000
                  Englewood, CO 80111
Contact: Del Blackketter
Telephone: (303) 790-0660
Fax: (303) 790-1663

UNITED STATES - Eastern Seaboard

Tecnimat/TDS
Address: 180 South Ban Brunt Street
                  Englewood, NJ 07631
Contact: Sheree Parke
Telephone: (201) 569-4200
Fax: (201) 569-2274

UNITED STATES

Typetronics Business Systems Inc
Address: 5717 North 7th Street
                  Phoenix, AZ 85014
Contact: Roger Smith
Telephone: (602) 274-7253
Fax: (602) 274-7636

UNITED STATES - New England

VacciVirus
Address: 84 Hammond Street
                  Waltham, MA 02154

Contact:	Roger Aucoin
Telephone:	(617) 893-8282
Fax:	(617) 893-3770

UNITED STATES

ValCom More than Computers Inc.

Address:	2249 Pinehurst Drive
	Middleton, WI 53562
Contact:	Gary Hoffman
Telephone:	(608) 836-8180
Fax:	(608) 836-7401

UNITED STATES

Wang Laboratories

Address:	7500 Old Georgetown Rd
	Bethesda, MD 20814
Contact:	Bill Repine
Telephone:	(301) 657-5028
Fax:	(301) 657-5971

Network Application Installer (NAI) 2.0 (by Aleph Systems)

by Charles Rose

Network Application Installer (NAI) by Aleph Systems is a flexible utility that lets you install Windows software in a networked environment. NAI helps the network administrator automate many of the network application installation tasks that are normally repetitious and tedious, and that often lead to human error.

WINSTALL 2.0

PREFACE

New Features

For those users who have purchased or evaluated earlier versions of WINSTALL (formerly known as N.A.I.), here is a list summarizing the major enhancements in release 2.0:

Environment and Application-Specific Variables

In addition to the support provided for user-specific variables, WINSTALL now fully supports environment variables (up to 5) and also supports application-specific variables (up to 3) as well. WINSTALL can substitute any or all of these variables within the file modifications, in source and destination paths for files to copy, and in the command line, icon path, and working directories. Environment and user-specific variables can also be written to the WINSTALL network log file as well.

Additional File Modifications

WINSTALL now provides a means of automatically modifying information within the AUTOEXEC.BAT and CONFIG.SYS files, plus one other ASCII file per application .DAT file. These modifications are in addition to the earlier support for modifications to the WIN.INI and SYSTEM.INI files.

File Copy Improvements

The copying of files during installation has been improved in several ways. First of all, the speed of the copy operation has been vastly increased. Second, the destination files now have the same date and time as the source files. Finally, WINSTALL offers an array of options for handling copy operations when the destination file already exists.

WINSTALL Network Log

WINSTALL now offers the option of logging all its operations to a file on the server. WINSTALL will log all activities by users and administrators, including error messages and WINSTALL configuration changes. User-specific variables and environment variables can be logged along with each entry to help identify the user.

Special Handling of the WIN.INI [Fonts] Section

Because multiple programs modify the WIN.INI [Fonts] section, WINSTALL now accords the [Fonts] section the same special treatment it has always provided to the [Extensions], [OLE], and [Embedding] sections. This special treatment enables the REMOVE APPLICATION operation to remove only the entries in these sections that were added during the installation of the application, preserving any entries belonging to other applications.

Message Display Options

WINSTALL now provides the option of displaying a short message to the end user before or after an installation or removal operation.

Program Call Option

Release 2.0 extends the reach of the WINSTALL program by providing an option to automatically call any other program at the conclusion of an installation or removal. Called programs can include other Windows applications, DOS applications, upgrade or installation routines for specific software packages, even .BAT files. WINSTALL will even pass command line parameters to called programs.

Miscellaneous Enhancements and Improvements

A number of small improvements and enhancements have also been added to release 2.0, including the ability to create a working directory if it does not exist when an application is installed, and the ability to remove an empty working directory when an application is removed, the removal of empty directories when an application is removed, improved error checking throughout the program, and checking for valid DOS filenames where appropriate.

Compatibility with Prior Releases

WINSTALL 2.0 is backwards compatible with all prior releases of N.A.I. The executable programs in earlier versions of the program had different names and used somewhat different file formats. Earlier versions of the end user program were called NAI.EXE. The current version of the end user program is WINSTALL.EXE. Earlier versions of the administrative program were called NAIMAINT.EXE; the current version is WINSTADM.EXE.

The WINSTALL.EXE program can read and execute application .DAT files created with all versions of the NAIMAINT.EXE program, so there is no need to immediately update application .DAT files as soon as you install the new version.

The WINSTADM.EXE administrative program can read application .DAT files created with all versions of the NAIMAINT.EXE program, **but application .DAT files created by WINSTADM.EXE are not compatible with any versions of NAI.EXE or NAIMAINT.EXE.**

The WINSTADM.EXE will, on startup, look for its own configuration file, WINSTADM.CFG. If it does not find that file, it will then look for the NAIMAINT.EXE configuration file, NAIMAINT.CFG. It can read NAIMAINT.CFG. If the working directory changes, however, WINSTADM.EXE will create a new configuration file, and NAIMAINT.EXE will be unable to use that file.

What WINSTALL (Network Application Installer) Is

One of the great advantages of a PC LAN file server is that administrators can provide their entire user community with access to a software program simply by installing a single copy of the program on the server. Unfortunately, many Microsoft Windows applications are not amenable to this approach, because Windows programs often require specific changes to the environment of each PC where the application is to run. For example, a Windows application install routine is likely to make changes to the user's WIN.INI file, to create special, application-specific .INI files, to create special .DLL files, etc. The application may not run, or may not run properly, without these changes. Until now, the only means of meeting the need for these local configuration changes was to make them manually to each PC on the LAN or else to run the application install routine on each PC on the LAN.

WINSTALL, the Network Application Installer, eliminates these problems, allowing a LAN administrator to install a Windows application only once, and providing end users on the LAN with the means of installing in their local workspace (or removing from their workspace) any Windows application with a click of the mouse. The convenient operation of WINSTALL makes quick work of adding new applications or upgrading installed applications to the latest release.

WINSTALL was initially designed to enable users to install applications which would run from the file server, but it can work equally well as a method of distributing full applications to each PC's local hard disk, especially now that the speed of the file copy operation has been increased.

In addition, whether you run your Windows applications locally or from the file server, WINSTALL's removal option provides end users with the most effective tool available to help keep their local Windows configurations up to date and free of extraneous, leftover files and information. This option alone may be reason enough to install WINSTALL on your file server.

An important feature of WINSTALL is that it provides the ability to install any Windows program, and an unlimited number of Windows programs, without purchasing any additional modules or waiting for their development. You simply install an application once, note the modifications it makes, and then create the necessary WINSTALL module yourself in minutes, using the WINSTALL Administration Program from within Windows! Your users are instantly provided with the means of installing the new application at the click of a mouse.

WINSTALL is flexible enough to allow you to work the way you want to. You can adapt WINSTALL to your environment, no matter what your requirements are, thanks to features such as the ability to modify any ASCII file during the installation process, the ability to display custom messages to your end users at the beginning and/or end of an installation (or removal) process, and the ability to call any other program, even a .BAT file, at the end of the installation or removal.

Although some new applications now include a node install program which makes the necessary configuration changes on the local workstation, WINSTALL provides you with better control over the configuration and the process, provides the end user with superior ease of use, and offers the unique ability to remove the entire application from the local configuration at any time, with a simple click of the mouse.

When WINSTALL installs an application, it performs these critical actions automatically:

1. Modifies any or all of these files as required:

    WIN.INI

    SYSTEM.INI

    AUTOEXEC.BAT

    CONFIG.SYS

    One additional ASCII file of your choice

2. Copies any needed files to the local disk.
3. Installs the appropriate icons in the local workspace.
4. Calls an external program, if configured to do so.
5. Displays a custom message to the user at the start and /or end, if so configured.
6. Updates the WINSTALL network log, if enabled.
7. Updates the user's private list of installed applications (file NAI.INI).

Some applications may require as little in the way of local configuration changes as the single act of placing an icon in the local workspace, but WINSTALL is helpful even with these simple installations because it relieves the end user of having to know or enter anything concerning directories or executable file names; the icon can be installed in the workspace by a simple click of the mouse with no chance of typographical errors or other miscues, and the WINSTALL network log, if enabled, will track the installation for the administrator's records.

How WINSTALL Works

WINSTALL consists of two programs: WINSTALL.EXE, which the end user runs to install or remove programs, and WINSTADM.EXE, which the LAN administrator runs to configure WINSTALL.EXE to make applications available for automatic installation and removal.

WINSTALL.EXE

When a user clicks on the WINSTALL icon, the program WINSTALL.EXE reads (from the file WINAPPS.LST) the list of applications available to be installed or removed.

WINAPPS.LST also contains information on a number of WINSTALL configuration options. For example, it tells WINSTALL whether or not the *REMOVE APPLICATION* function is enabled, allowing users to remove applications as well as to install them. In addition, WINAPPS.LST contains the configured options for several other features, including environment variables, prompts for User-specific variables, configuration options concerning the WINSTALL network log, and instructions on what to do during a file copy operation when the destination file already exists.

When the user selects an application to install or remove, WINSTALL reads the data file (filename.DAT) for that application. The .DAT file tells WINSTALL what changes to make to the user's local configuration for the installation or removal of that application, as well as what other actions to take in conjunction with the installation or removal. For example, the application .DAT file may instruct WINSTALL to display a custom message before beginning the installation.

WINSTALL then automatically makes the changes, including placing the icon on the user's workspace, and lets the user know that the installation was successful. A typical application can be completely installed in this manner in under 10 seconds!

WINSTADM.EXE

Five types of data files are associated with the WINSTALL programs:

WINAPPS.LST	(The list of applications available for installation or removal)
Application .DAT files	(Instructions to WINSTALL.EXE for installation and removal of particular applications)
WINSTADM.CFG	(the administrative program configuration file)
NAI.INI	(the user's private WINSTALL log file)
any filename	(the WINSTALL network log file)

All are ASCII text files, but each has its own specific format. To avoid requiring the LAN administrator to understand and remember the details of those formats (although they are fully described later in this document), and to avoid inadvertent errors in file formats, all these files are created and maintained by means of an additional program: WINSTADM.EXE (except for NAI.INI, which is created and maintained automatically by the end user program, WINSTALL.EXE, and the WINSTALL network log, which is updated by both programs as needed).

WINSTADM.EXE allows the LAN administrator to create new application .DAT files and modify or delete existing application .DAT files, at the same time updating WINAPPS.LST, the list of available applications that users see when they run WINSTALL.EXE. WINSTADM.EXE also permits the LAN administrator to enable or disable the *REMOVE APPLICATION* function in WINSTALL.EXE, to control the use of user-specific variables and environment variables, to configure the WINSTALL network log function, and to specify what to do during a copy file operation if the destination file already exists.

INSTALLATION

User Files

The user files (WINSTALL.EXE, WINAPPS.LST, and all the application .DAT files) should all reside in the same directory on the file server. Users need not have write access to this directory.

Each user must have the files VBRUN100.DLL and DISKSTAT.DLL in the Windows directory, and the WINSTALL icon in the workspace.

LAN Administrator Files

WINSTADM.EXE and WINSTADM.CFG can reside in same directory as the user files, or, for better security, they can reside in another directory. (The *CURRENT WORKING DIRECTORY* field on the main screen of WINSTADM.EXE allows the LAN administrator to specify the location of the user files). The LAN administrator must have read, write, and delete privileges for the directory where the user files reside and for the directory where the maintenance files reside.

The LAN administrator must have VBRUN100.DLL in his local Windows directory and the WINSTADM icon in his workspace.

RUNNING WINSTALL

Choosing an Application to Install

When the user clicks on the Network Application Installer icon, the WINSTALL.EXE program reads the file WINAPPS.LST, which lists all the applications available for

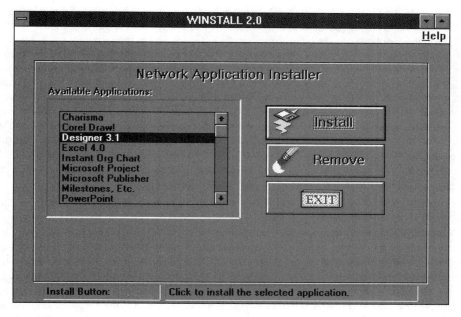

Figure 10.4 WINSTALL.EXE Main Screen.

installation. WINSTALL then presents the main screen, containing the full listing of all applications available for installation.

To install an application, the user simply clicks once on the desired application in the list and then clicks on the *INSTALL APPLICATION* Button.

If WINSTALL discovers that the user has already installed this application, it will offer a choice of canceling the installation or performing a re-installation.

If the application is configured to present a custom message before the installation, WINSTALL displays it and waits for the user to click on the *OK* Button to proceed or the *CANCEL* Button to back out of the installation.

WINSTALL will display a completion bar to indicate its progress as it makes the necessary configuration changes and copies the required files to the user's local disk.

The final step in the installation is the placing of the application icon(s) in the user's Windows workspace. If the application .DAT file specifies the creation of a separate icon group, WINSTALL will create that group and place the icon(s) in it; if the application specifies that the icons be added to an existing group, WINSTALL will do that, creating the group if it does not already exist; otherwise, it will place the icons in whatever is the active group on the end user's workspace at the time of the installation.

If the application is configured to call another program at the end of the installation process, WINSTALL displays a message to the user that a called program is loading, and WINSTALL runs the called program.

If the application is configured to present a custom message after the installation, WINSTALL displays it and waits for the user to click on the *OK* Button.

Choosing an Application to Remove

To remove an application, the user clicks on the application in the application list and then clicks the REMOVE APPLICATION Button. At this point, WINSTALL reads the application .DAT file and then, after displaying a custom message (if specified in the application .DAT file), removes the appropriate WIN.INI lines, files, etc., from the user's local configuration, again displaying a completion bar to keep the user apprised of the progress.

If the application .DAT file specifies that the icons for the application belong in a separate icon group, WINSTALL will remove the group and any icons it contains from the end user's local workspace. On the other hand, if the application .DAT file specifies that the icons belong in an existing group or in whatever the active group is at the time of installation, WINSTALL will not remove any icons from the user's workspace; instead, at the end of the removal process, WINSTALL will advise the user that the icon may not have been removed and will provide simple instructions on how to do so manually. At the end of the process, if a program is specified to be called, WINSTALL displays a message to the user that a called program is loading, and WINSTALL runs the called program. If a custom message is configured to be displayed at the end of the process, WINSTALL displays it and waits for the user to click the *OK* Button.

WINSTALL ADMINISTRATION

Administrative Program Startup

When the LAN administrator clicks on the WINSTADM.EXE icon, the program looks for the file WINSTADM.CFG in the WINSTADM.EXE program directory. If this file is found, WINSTADM.EXE reads it to discover where the correct version of the file WINAPPS.LST is located. If WINSTADM.CFG is not present, then WINSTADM.EXE looks for WINAPPS.LST in the WINSTADM.EXE program directory. If WINAPPS.LST is not found, WINSTADM.EXE informs the LAN administrator, but proceeds anyway, providing the opportunity to create a new WINAPPS.LST or to change the working directory to one which does contain a WINAPPS.LST file.

WINSTADM.EXE reads the file WINAPPS.LST to build its list of installable applications before displaying the initial screen.

This screen offers the options of setting the working directory, configuring the user-specific variables, configuring the runtime options, plus several choices regarding the list of available applications. Create a new application entry in the list, modify an existing application entry, insert an application into the list, or remove an existing application from the list.

Setting the Working Directory

To enable the security of keeping WINSTADM.EXE in a directory separate from the WINSTALL.EXE program, the file WINSTADM.CFG, which WINSTADM.EXE reads on startup, is kept in the same directory as WINSTADM.EXE. This file stores the location of the last working directory, the directory where WINSTALL.EXE, WINAPPS.LST, and the application .DAT files are kept. If this configuration file is missing, WINSTADM.EXE sets the working directory to the directory where WINSTADM.EXE itself is located.

The current working directory is displayed in a modifiable field on the WINSTADM.EXE main screen. When that directory is changed, WINSTADM.EXE immediately switches to the specified directory and loads the WINAPPS.LST file from that directory, if there is one. If it does not find a WINAPPS.LST file in the specified directory, it informs you and begins by presenting a blank list of applications. Any changes will result in the creation of a new WINAPPS.LST in whatever the working directory is at that time; the actual file will be created either when the WINSTADM.EXE program is exited, or when the working directory is changed.

Setting the User-Specific and Environment Variables

WINSTALL supports the use of up to three separate, global (non-application-specific), user-specific variables plus up to five separate environment variables during the installation and removal of applications. (WINSTALL also supports application-specific variables, which are stored in each application .DAT file and which are then used only in the installation or removal of that specific application. Application-specific variables are covered in their own section, below.) User-specific and environment variables allow installations to vary according to information that may be unique to each user. For example, if you want to install certain files for an application in a directory that is named differently for each user, WINSTALL's user-specific variable feature enables you to do so.

If you choose to implement the global user-specific variables, WINSTALL will prompt each user at runtime for the unique information you need. After receiving this information from the user, WINSTALL will use it during the installation or removal of applications by substituting the unique, user-specific information for special codes ($VAR codes) it encounters in the application .DAT files. Environment variables work in much the same way, except that the user is prompted only if the specified variable is not present in his environment.

User-specific variables are implemented in two steps: First, you must instruct WINSTALL what information to request from the user or to gather from the environment. Second, you tell WINSTALL, in each application .DAT file, what to do with that information.

To tell WINSTALL what information you need from the user or the environment, click on the *SET USER-SPECIFIC VARIABLES* Button on the WINSTADM.EXE Main Screen. The User-Specific Variables screen will appear, with three blank data entry fields labeled *PROMPT 1, PROMPT 2*, and *PROMPT 3*, and 5 more blank data entry fields labeled *Environment Variable 1, Environment Variable 2*, etc.

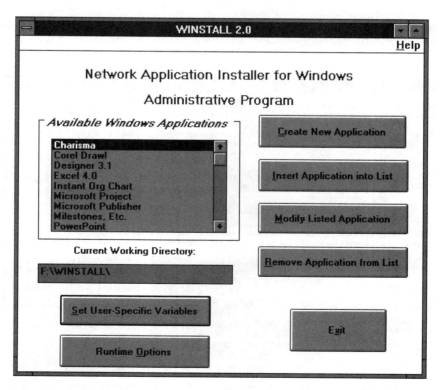

Figure 10.5 WINSTADM.EXE Main Screen.

You may enter information in any or all of these fields. For example, if you wanted to place certain application files in a directory named according to the user's network username, you could enter for *PROMPT 1*, the following text:

Username

If information has been entered for *PROMPT 1*, *PROMPT2*, or *PROMPT3*, then when an end user runs WINSTALL and selects the *INSTALL APPLICATION* or *REMOVE APPLICATION* option for the first time, WINSTALL will present a screen asking for the unique, user-specific information you specify, prompting him with whatever text you enter in the *PROMPT 1, PROMPT 2*, and/or *PROMPT 3* fields.

NOTE: Use of the user-specific variables feature is entirely optional: WINSTALL will only prompt for those fields where you have actually entered information, and if you do not enter information for any of the fields, WINSTALL will not request any information from the users and will not attempt to implement any user-specific installation parameters.

To continue the example above, if you entered the text shown above, then WINSTALL would present a screen instructing the user as shown in Figure 10.7.

When the user enters the requested information, WINSTALL will proceed with the installation or removal, substituting the text supplied by the user for the corresponding $VAR codes encountered within the application .DAT file.

Thus, the second step in implementing user-specific variables is to place the $VAR codes into the application .DAT files as required. WINSTALL will interpret $VAR codes wherever it finds them within text to be added to the WIN.INI and SYSTEM.INI files, to be added to the AUTOEXEC.BAT, CONFIG.SYS and other ASCII files, within directories and

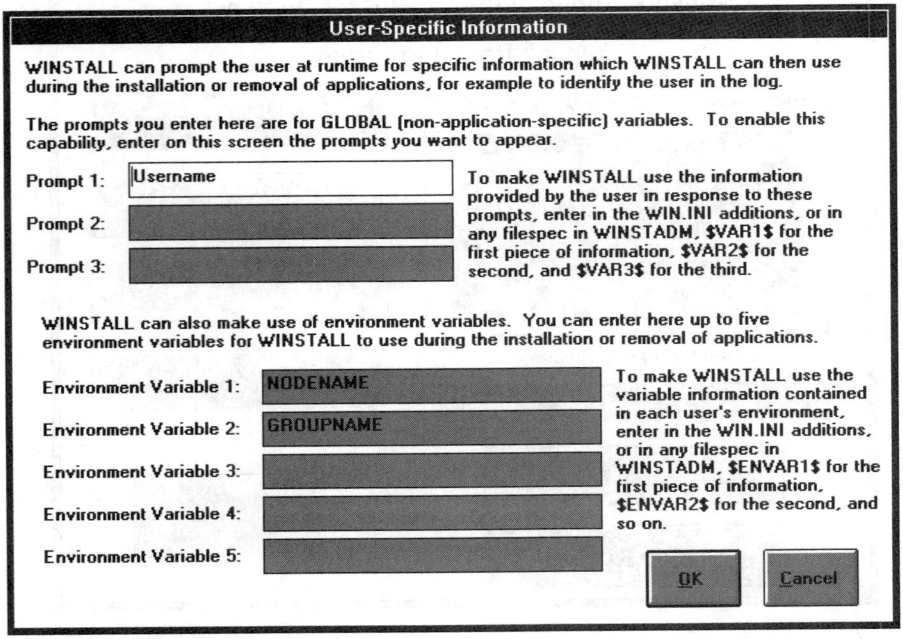

Figure 10.6 WINSTADM.EXE User-Specific Variables Screen.

filenames specified in the FILES TO COPY fields of the Add/Modify Application screen, and in the directories and filenames in the ICONS TO INSTALL fields. Each of these areas is explained in detail in its own section, below.

Each of the three available user-specific variables has a different $VAR code. For the variable corresponding to *PROMPT 1*, you would enter *$VAR1$* (note both the leading and trailing *$* characters) in the application .DAT file. For the variables corresponding to *PROMPT 2* and *PROMPT 3*, you would enter *$VAR2$* and *$VAR3$*, respectively.

To continue the example, if you had instructed WINSTALL to prompt the end user for his network username, and he had entered BWILSON in response, then WINSTALL would substitute BWILSON for the $VAR code $VAR1$ whenever that code appears during the installation. So, if you had indicated that a file should be copied to the destination directory F:\$VAR1$\, WINSTALL would copy the files to the F:\BWILSON\ directory, creating it in the process, if necessary.

Likewise, if you had the line *DOC-PATH=F:\$VAR1$\DOCS* in the WIN.INI Additions section of an application, what WINSTALL would actually add to the user's WIN.INI file would, in the case of our example user, be this:

DOC-PATH=F:\BWILSON\DOCS\

WINSTALL will only prompt the user for this information once during each execution of WINSTALL.EXE. If the user installs several programs without exiting WINSTALL.EXE, the program will remember the responses he provided for the first installation and use them whenever a subsequent application .DAT file contains a $VAR code. If the user exits WINSTALL.EXE, however, the information he provided is not retained and must be re-entered when the first application is installed or removed during subsequent executions of WINSTALL.EXE.

If you enter information in any of the Environment Variable fields, then WINSTALL will look in the user's environment for an environment variable that matches what you have entered, and it will substitute for the appropriate $VAR code the value that it finds in the user's environment. The environment $VAR codes are *$ENVAR1$*, *$ENVAR2$*, etc.

So to modify the above example slightly, if you entered *USERNAME* in the Environment Variable 1 field, then WINSTALL would look for a *USERNAME=* string in the user's

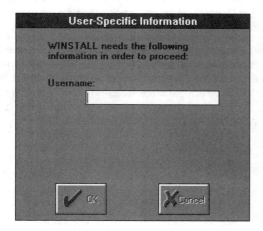

Figure 10.7 WINSTALL.EXE User-Specific Variable Screen.

environment. If it was found, then WINSTALL would substitute for *$ENVAR1$* the value following *USERNAME=* in the user's environment. If it was not found, then if WINSTALL encountered the *$ENVAR1$* string within an application .DAT file, it would prompt the user to enter his USERNAME and WINSTALL would then substitute for that string the information provided by the user.

NOTE: If you enter *SET* from the DOS prompt and press *RETURN*, DOS will list all the current environment variables and their values. So, in this example, if the user had *USERNAME=BWILSON* in his environment, WINSTALL would find it and substitute *BWILSON* for the *$ENVAR1$* string anywhere it is found in an application .DAT file.

If any of the fields on the User-Specific Variables Screen are changed, then a new WINAPPS.LST file will be created when WINSTADM.EXE is exited or the working directory is changed, whether or not the list of installed applications has changed.

Setting the Runtime Options

On the WINSTADM.EXE main screen is a *SET RUNTIME OPTIONS* Button. Clicking this button will bring up the Runtime Options Screen, where you are able to configure the WINSTALL network log, the Files to Copy options, and the WINSTALL Remove option.

If any of the Runtime Options settings are changed, then a new WINAPPS.LST file will be created on exit from WINSTADM.EXE, or when the working directory is changed, whether or not any changes were made to the application list itself.

SETTING THE WINSTALL NETWORK LOG OPTIONS

Log Filename Field. At the top of the screen is the WINSTALL Network Log Filename field. If you wish to enable the network logging feature, then enter in this field the full pathname of the file to which you want WINSTALL to log its activities. Note that all WINSTALL users must have read and write access to this file.

Log Enabled Checkbox. Beneath the Log Filename field is the Network Log Enabled Checkbox. If this box is checked and a valid DOS filename is entered in the Log Filename field, then the WINSTALL Network Log function is enabled.

Enabling/Disabling the Log. When the network log function is enabled, WINSTALL will place an entry in the log each time a user attempts to install or remove an application with WINSTALL, and WINSTADM.EXE will also add an entry each time an administrator makes a change to the WINSTALL configuration.

Items to Log. The WINSTALL Runtime Options Screen contains a listing of all user-specific and environment variables. If you have not entered information for any of these variables in the Set User-specific Variables Screen, then they are all grayed out and disabled. Any variables for which you have entered information appear in the list as the information you have entered, and they are not disabled. Clicking beside one of these to place an X in the corresponding checkbox will instruct WINSTALL to log that variable with each log entry.

Logfile Format. Log entries in general follow this format:

    date,time=application installed/removed [error]

    variable=value

    variable=value

If user-specific variables or environment variables are being logged, then these items will appear on successive lines immediately following the main log entry. Main log entries are separated by blank lines.

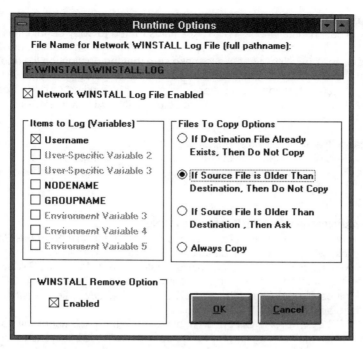

Figure 10.8 WINSTADM.EXE Runtime Options Screen.

The following is a short sample from a WINSTALL network log:

03-31-1992,12:20:10=Network Log Enabled

USERNAME=Benson

03-31-1992,12:22:16=F:\LANAPPS\WINAPPS.LST MODIFIED

Logfile changed from F:\WINLOG\WINSTALL.LOG to F:\WINLOG\WINSTAL2.LOG

USERNAME=Benson

03-31-1992,13:23:50=CHARISMA.DAT REMOVED

USERNAME=Benson

03-31-1992,14:46:15=Designer Install ABORTED: File Copy or Delete Failed

USERNAME=Williams

03-31-1992,14:48:25=DESIGNER.DAT UPDATED

USERNAME=Benson

03-31-1992,14:52:42=Designer INSTALLED

USERNAME=Williams

04-02-1992,07:38:38=Working Directory changed from F:\LANAPPS\ to G:\TESTAPPS

USERNAME=Benson

SETTING THE FILES TO COPY OPTIONS

During most application installations, WINSTALL is instructed to copy certain files from the file server to the local hard disk or to the user's private area on the file server. As WINSTALL begins to copy a file, it checks to make sure that the destination file does not already exist. If WINSTALL finds that the destination file does already exist, it will take one of several courses of action, configurable here, on the Runtime Options Screen. Depending on which radio button you have selected, WINSTALL will take one of the following four actions:

1. If the destination file already exists, do not copy the file.
2. If the source file is older than the destination file, then do not copy the file.
3. If the source file is older than the destination file, then ask the user whether or not to copy the file.
4. Always copy the file.

ENABLING/DISABLING THE WINSTALL REMOVE OPTION

The final option available on the Runtime Options Screen is the *WINSTALL REMOVE OPTION* Checkbox, which enables or disables the *REMOVE APPLICATION* option in WINSTALL.EXE. When a new WINAPPS.LST file is created (on exit from WINSTADM.EXE or when the working directory is changed), the current setting of the *REMOVE OPTION* Checkbox determines whether or not the *REMOVE APPLICATION* option in WINSTALL is enabled or disabled.

When the *REMOVE APPLICATION* option is disabled, WINSTALL users will not see the *REMOVE* Button on their screen and will not be able to use WINSTALL.EXE to remove from their local configurations any of the listed applications.

Creating a New Application Entry or Modifying a Listed Application Entry

To create a new application entry in the list of available applications, simply click on the CREATE NEW APPLICATION Button. At this point, WINSTADM.EXE brings up the Add Form, which contains 4 blank data entry fields and eight data entry buttons.

To modify the entry for a listed application, click on the desired application in the list and then click on the *MODIFY LISTED APPLICATION* Button. WINSTADM.EXE will bring up the Modify Form, which is identical to the Add Form, except that the data entry fields will display whatever information was found in the application .DAT file for the application you have chosen to modify.

DATA ENTRY FIELDS

WINSTALL List Name. In the first field on the Add/Modify Form, *WINSTALL LIST NAME,* enter the name of the application exactly as you would have it appear in the WINSTALL application list.

.DAT File Name. The next field, *.DAT FILE NAME,* holds the DOS filename of the file which WINSTALL will use to store the changes needed to install this application. The extension *.DAT* will automatically be appended to the name entered here.

Files to Copy. If a Windows application requires that any files be present on the user's local hard disk, these should be specified in the *FILES TO COPY* fields. Enter in the *SOURCE* field the filename, including drive and full path, of the file to be copied to the local disk. DOS wild cards (* and ?) are supported, but please read the discussion of **Wild Card Deletions** in the **Reference Notes** section of this document for important implications of using wild cards.

If drive and/or path is omitted from the *SOURCE* field, WINSTALL will look only in the WINSTALL directory itself.

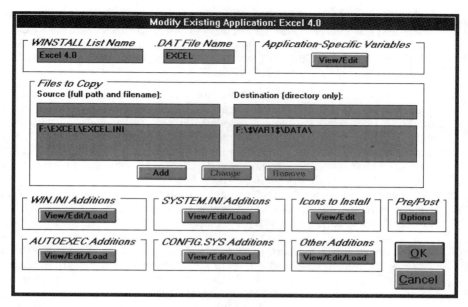

Figure 10.9 WINSTADM.EXE Add/Modify Screen.

If a source file is not found during installation, WINSTALL will inform the user of that fact and abort the installation.

When you add a file to be copied to the list, NAIMAINT will check to see if the source file you have specified is, in fact, found where you have indicated it should be. If the file is not found, NAIMAINT will inform you of that fact, though it will not prevent you from adding it to the list.

Enter in the *DESTINATION* field the drive and path of the local copy of the file that WINSTALL will create at installation time (NOTE: omit the filename—WINSTALL will automatically create the destination file with the same name as the source file).

If drive and/or path is omitted from the *DESTINATION* field, WINSTALL will default to the drive where Windows is located and to the Windows directory.

If a specified destination directory is not present on the user's local hard disk, WINSTALL will create it automatically during the installation. During a REMOVE operation, WINSTALL will remove destination directories if they are empty after the files specified in the application .DAT file have been removed.

If you need to place files in a directory or path that is unique to each user, you can do so by making use of WINSTALL's variable feature. If WINSTALL encounters the codes *$VAR1$, $VAR2$,* or *$VAR3$* anywhere in a destination path, then during the installation or removal process, it will substitute for that code whatever information it has obtained from the user. Similarly, if *$ENVAR1$, $ENVAR1$, $ENVAR3$, $ENVAR4$,* or *$ENVAR5$* appear, the appropriate environment variable information will be substituted. If you have a need for information specific to a particular application, WINSTALL provides application-specific variables for that purpose. The codes which instruct WINSTALL to substitute application-specific variable information are *$APPVAR1$, $APPVAR2$,* and *$APPVAR3$*. For a complete explanation of this feature, please see the **User-Specific and Environment Variables** section, above, and the **Application-Specific Variables** section, below.

NOTE: If the *DESTINATION* field is left blank (or if you enter *@WINDOWS* as the destination directory), WINSTALL will copy the file(s) to the user's Windows directory (for example, C:\WINDOWS), whatever it may be. If you enter *@SYSTEM* in the *DESTINATION* field, WINSTALL will copy the file(s) to the user's Windows System directory (for example, C:\WINDOWS\SYSTEM), whatever that may be.

The *SOURCE* and *DESTINATION* fields are arranged as two data entry fields, each above a list. The two lists are linked. Once a source and destination have been entered, they will drop together down into their respective lists. To add another pair, click on either data entry field and type in the desired information, or click the *ADD* Button. Once both fields have been completed, they are added to the lists automatically when a TAB or mouse click passes the focus to another object or field on the screen, when the *ADD* Button is clicked, or when the *OK* Button is clicked.

To delete a file from the list, click on either the source or destination list to select the desired pair, then click on the *REMOVE* Button.

To modify an existing source and destination pair, either select the pair by clicking on either one in the list, and then click on the *CHANGE* Button, or double-click on either entry in its list. Either method will remove the pair from their lists and place them in the data entry fields above, where they can be modified and added once again to the lists. As with adding new information, the modified information is added to the lists when a TAB or mouse click passes the focus to another object or field, when the *ADD* Button is clicked, or when the *OK* Button is clicked.

APPLICATION-SPECIFIC VARIABLES BUTTON

The *APPLICATION-SPECIFIC VARIABLES VIEW/EDIT/LOAD* Button brings up a screen with three data entry fields. The three application-specific variables are analogous to the three user-specific variables, but they also have certain differences.

As with the user-specific variables, what you enter in the data entry fields on this screen will be used as prompts for the user at runtime. And, as with the user-specific variables, WINSTALL will substitute the information provided by the user for certain $VAR codes (in this case, *$APPVAR1$*, *$APPVAR2$*, and *$APPVAR3$*).

On the other hand, WINSTALL will ask the user for this information only if it is found in the .DAT file being used for the current installation or removal. And WINSTALL will not

Figure 10.10 WINSTADM.EXE Application-Specific Variables Screen.

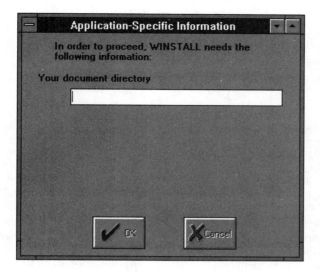

Figure 10.11 WINSTALL.EXE Application-Specific Variable Screen.

retain the information provided in response beyond the end of the single installation or removal process. Unlike the "global" user-specific and environment variable information, this information is "local" to the single application .DAT file in which it appears.

So, if you need a user's word processing document directory, for example, you could enter in the field for Prompt 1:

Your private word processing document directory

When a user runs WINSTALL to install the application, WINSTALL will present a screen such as the above, asking the user to please enter his private word processing directory. WINSTALL will then substitute the information the user provides in response for any occurrence of the string $APPVAR1$ in the .DAT file.

WIN.INI ADDITIONS BUTTON

When the *WIN.INI ADDITIONS VIEW/EDIT/LOAD* Button is clicked, WINSTADM.EXE displays the WIN.INI Additions Editor. In the editor, you can type in or load any changes to the WIN.INI file which must be applied to a user's configuration to install the application, up to 350 lines total.

NOTE: Different WIN.INI headings, and (sometimes even different lines within the same heading) are manipulated in different ways, according to their function within Windows. For details on how WINSTALL handles these additions, see the **Shared WIN.INI Headings** section, and **Special WIN.INI Headings** section, below.

If the *VIEW/EDIT/LOAD* Button is clicked during a *MODIFY* operation, or if WIN.INI additions have been entered earlier during an *ADD* operation, the WIN.INI Editor will display the changes and allow their further modification.

This editor is a full ASCII editor with buttons to perform the following functions:

- Load text from a file

- Append text from a file

- Save text to a file

- Cut selected text to the Windows Clipboard

- Paste text from the Clipboard

- Delete all text in the editor

- Delete all text in the editor, except selected text

- Quit without saving changes

- Exit and save the changes in the application .DAT file.

The text you enter in the WIN.INI Additions Editor can have embedded in it the codes for any or all of the three types of variables: *$VAR1$, $VAR2$, $VAR3$, $ENVAR1$, $ENVAR2$, $ENVAR3$, $ENVAR4$, $ENVAR5$, $APPVAR1$, $APPVAR2$*, and/or *$APPVAR3$*. These codes instruct WINSTALL to substitute in their place whatever user-specific information it has obtained from the environment or from the end user at runtime. More information on these options is provided in the **User-Specific and Environment Variables** section, and in the **Application-Specific Variables** section, above.

WINSTALL treats certain headings within the WIN.INI file in a special way. For complete information on which headings these are and what the special treatment is, please see the *SPECIAL WIN.INI Headings* section, below.

SYSTEM.INI ADDITIONS BUTTON

When the *SYSTEM.INI ADDITIONS VIEW/EDIT/LOAD* Button is clicked, WINSTADM.EXE displays the SYSTEM.INI Additions Editor. This editor functions exactly like the WIN.INI Additions Editor, except that any changes you type in or load here will be applied to the

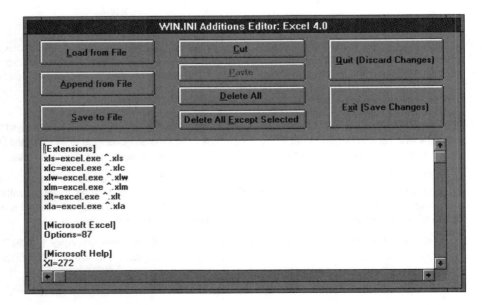

Figure 10.12 WINSTADM.EXE Win.Ini Additions Editor.

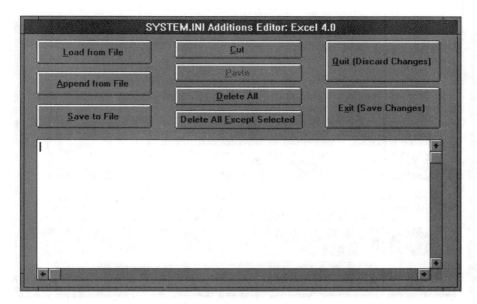

Figure 10.13 WINSTADM.EXE SYSTEM.INI Additions Editor.

user's SYSTEM.INI file when WINSTALL installs the application. The SYSTEM.INI Additions Editor will allow the entry of up to 100 lines of text to be added to the SYSTEM.INI file. The SYSTEM.INI Additions Editor will also substitute user-specific information for the three types of variable codes at runtime.

ICONS TO INSTALL BUTTON

WINSTALL needs three to five pieces of information in order to install an icon on the user's workspace. Pressing the *ICON VIEW/EDIT* Button brings up the Icons Screen, where this information can be entered.

Icon Group Radio Buttons. At the top of the screen is a group of three radio buttons permitting you to select where you want the icons for this application to be installed. By default, the *ADD TO CURRENT (ACTIVE) ICON GROUP* Button is selected. This choice will instruct WINSTALL to place the icons in whatever Program Manager group is active at runtime. The user can then move that icon to another group or leave it where it has been placed.

Selecting the *ADD TO EXISTING ICON GROUP* Button will cause a data entry field to appear beside the radio buttons. In this field, enter the name of the existing icon group where you want the icons placed. If WINSTALL does not find a group by this name in the user's configuration, it will create it.

NOTE: The icon group name is the text which appears in the icon group title bar on the Windows workspace.

To install all the icons for an application in their own separate icon group, click on the *CREATE SEPARATE ICON GROUP* Button and enter the desired group name in the data field which appears beside the radio buttons. WINSTALL will create this icon group in the user's configuration at install time, unless the group already exists, in which case WINSTALL will simply add the icons to this existing group.

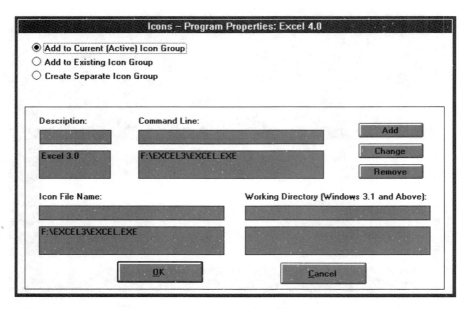

Figure 10.14 WINSTADM.EXE Icons to Install Screen.

NOTE: When WINSTALL is REMOVEing an application, its treatment of the icons varies, depending on which icon group radio button is selected for that application. If the application .DAT file instructs WINSTALL to create a separate icon group, then WINSTALL will delete that entire icon group when it removes the application. Otherwise, WINSTALL will NOT remove any icons; instead, it will conclude the removal process with a message to the user indicating that the icons may still be present in his workspace and providing simple instructions on how the user can remove those icons manually.

Because some Windows applications install more than one icon, the information required for installation of icons is presented in three fields which, like the SOURCE and DESTINATION Fields for FILES TO COPY, are presented as data entry fields above linked lists:

Description. In the *DESCRIPTION* Field, enter the text that you would like to appear below the icon in the user's workspace.

Command Line. In the *COMMAND LINE* Field, enter the drive and full path and filename of the executable file for the application. You may use the $*VAR* codes within this field to instruct WINSTALL to substitute user-specific information at runtime. For further details, see the **User-Specific and Environment Variables** section, and the **Application-Specific Variables** section, above.

Icon File Name. If the icon to be used for the application comes from other than the application's executable file, enter in the *ICON FILE NAME* Field the drive and full path and filename of the file from which to extract the icon. If this field is left blank, WINSTADM.EXE will automatically fill it in with the path and filename of the application's executable file. You may use the $*VAR* codes within this field, too, to instruct WINSTALL to substitute user-specific information at runtime. For further details, see the **User-Specific and Environment Variables** section, and the **Application-Specific Variables** section, above.

Working Directory. Beginning with release 3.1, Windows offers the option of specifying a working directory for each application. This directory is where the application will by default look for and save its documents or data files. When a user runs WINSTALL, the program checks to see what version of Windows the user is running. If the version is 3.1 or above, WINSTALL will install the directory entered in this field as the application's working directory. If the version is 3.0, WINSTALL will ignore any information in this field. As with the *Command Line* and *Icon File Name* fields, you may use the *$VAR* codes within this field to instruct WINSTALL to substitute user-specific information.

As it installs the icon, WINSTALL will check for the existence of the working directory, if one is specified in the application .DAT file. If that directory does not exist, WINSTALL will create it.

During a REMOVE operation, WINSTALL will remove the working directory if it is empty.

The same techniques for adding, removing, and modifying pairs of source filenames and destination directories apply to the sets of icon descriptions, command lines, icon file names, and working directories (see the **Files to Copy** section, above). The only differences are that the icon file name, if left blank, will automatically default to the path for the executable filename, and the working directory may be left blank if desired.

When these fields are complete, clicking the *OK* Button saves the changes and returns the Add/Modify Screen.

When the fields on the Add/Modify Screen have been filled in and the WIN.INI Changes and Icon Information have been entered, click the *OK* Button to create the new application .DAT file and update the list of applications.

PRE/POST OPTIONS BUTTON

When you click on the PRE/POST OPTIONS Button, WINSTADM.EXE presents the Pre/Post Options Screen, with 6 data entry fields for you to specify messages and actions for WINSTALL to perform before and/or after installing or removing applications.

Text Files to Display Fields. The Pre/Post Options screen contains 4 fields for the filenames of ASCII text files to display before installation, after installation, before removal, and/or after removal of the application. Enter in any or all of these fields the full path and filename

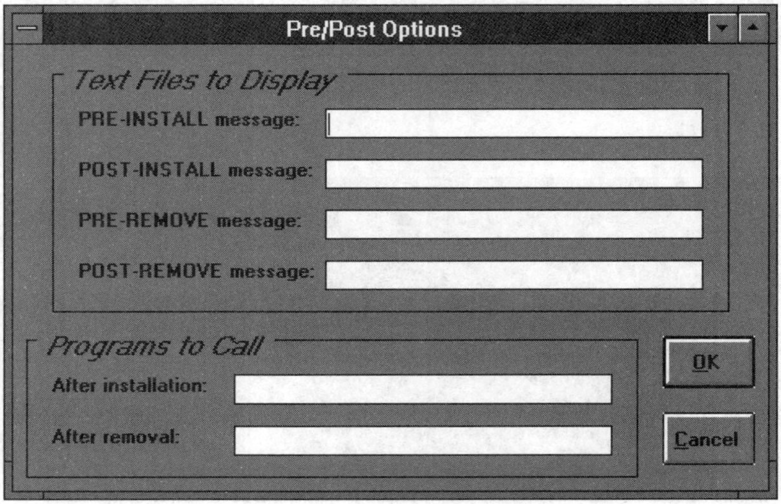

Figure 10.15 WINSTADM.EXE Pre/Post Options Screen.

of ASCII text files to display to the user at the specified point in the installation or removal process. You may choose to display as many or as few of these messages as you like. The only limitations are that every WINSTALL user must have read access to the files you specify, and the files should be no wider than about 60 characters (width limitations may vary due to Windows' proportional fonts) and no longer than 12 lines.

If a text file is to be displayed prior to installation or removal, the user will have a choice of clicking the OK Button to proceed with the operation or a CANCEL Button to back out of the operation.

If a text file is to be displayed at the conclusion of the installation or removal process, the user will have only an OK Button to remove the message from the screen. The conclusion text files take the place of the usual WINSTALL conclusion messages, so you should include in them the information that the installation or removal is complete, plus any directions you want the users to have concerning icon removal or placement, etc.

Programs to Call Fields. WINSTALL offers you the opportunity to extend its functionality by providing the means of calling another program or batch file at the conclusion of any installation or removal process. Simply enter in the appropriate Program to Call data entry field the full path and filename (plus any desired command line parameters), and WINSTALL will call this program at the conclusion of the installation or removal process. This step will take place immediately after the display of the concluding message, if you have configured the .DAT file to display a concluding message.

AUTOEXEC.BAT ADDITIONS BUTTON

The *AUTOEXEC.BAT ADDITIONS VIEW/EDIT/LOAD* Button, like the corresponding button for WIN.INI Additions and SYSTEM.INI Additions, brings up a full function ASCII editor, but this screen has a number of other data fields as well.

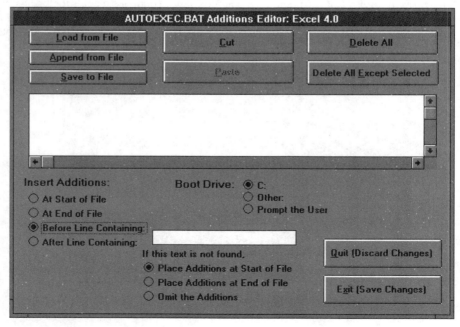

Figure 10.16 WINSTADM.EXE AUTOEXEC.BAT Additions Screen.

AUTOEXEC.BAT Additions Editor. The editor allows the input of up to 25 lines of text for addition to the AUTOEXEC.BAT file. As with the text in the WIN.INI and SYSTEM.INI editors, this text can be typed in at the keyboard, pasted from the clipboard, or loaded from a file.

The Insert Additions Radio Buttons. The placement of the added text within the AUTOEXEC.BAT file is governed by the selection among the Insert Additions Radio Buttons. The added text can be placed at the beginning of the file or at the end of the file or before or after the first line containing a key text string.

To instruct WINSTALL to place the added text at the start or end of the file, click on the appropriate radio button.

To key the placement of the added text to existing text within the AUTOEXEC.BAT file, select either the *BEFORE LINE CONTAINING* or the *AFTER LINE CONTAINING* radio button. When you click to select either of these buttons, more fields will appear on the screen.

The Key Text Field and Alternate Placement Radio Buttons. When either the *BEFORE LINE CONTAINING* or the *AFTER LINE CONTAINING* Button is selected, a Key Text Field will appear to the right of the selected button. Enter in this field the text you want WINSTALL to find in order to properly locate the added lines within the AUTOEXEC.BAT file.

Below the Key Text field are the Alternate Placement Radio Buttons. Select the appropriate one of these three buttons to instruct WINSTALL what to do with the additions if the key text is not found in AUTOEXEC.BAT. You may tell WINSTALL to place the additions at the start of the file or at the end of the file or to omit the additions entirely.

The Boot Drive Radio Buttons. In order to locate the right AUTOEXEC.BAT file, WINSTALL needs to know what drive the end user booted from. The default choice is the C: drive, but you may specify any other drive or instruct WINSTALL to ask the user at install time by clicking on the corresponding button. If you click on *OTHER*, a small data entry field will appear to the right of the word *Other*. Enter in that field the letter for the end user's boot drive.

CONFIG.SYS ADDITIONS BUTTON

If you click on the *CONFIG.SYS ADDITIONS VIEW/EDIT/LOAD* Button, you will bring up yet another ASCII editor, this one identical in appearance and function to the AUTOEXEC.BAT Additions Editor, except that changes entered here will be applied to the CONFIG.SYS file.

OTHER ADDITIONS BUTTON

Clicking on the OTHER ADDITIONS VIEW/EDIT/LOAD Button brings up an editor very similar to the AUTOEXEC.BAT and CONFIG.SYS Additions Editor, but with one difference. This editor allows you to enter up to 25 lines of text to be added to any ASCII file of your choice, so instead of a selection of Boot Drive Radio Buttons, you are presented with a Text Filename data entry field, where you can enter the full path and filename of the file to apply the additions to, and a checkbox to indicate whether or not you would like WINSTALL to create the file if it is not found.

NOTE: WINSTALL executes the instructions in the Other Additions section of the .DAT file *AFTER* it copies the files specified in the Files to Copy fields. Therefore, you can use this section to modify "generic" text files, including .INI files, that have been copied to the local disk as part of the same application installation process.

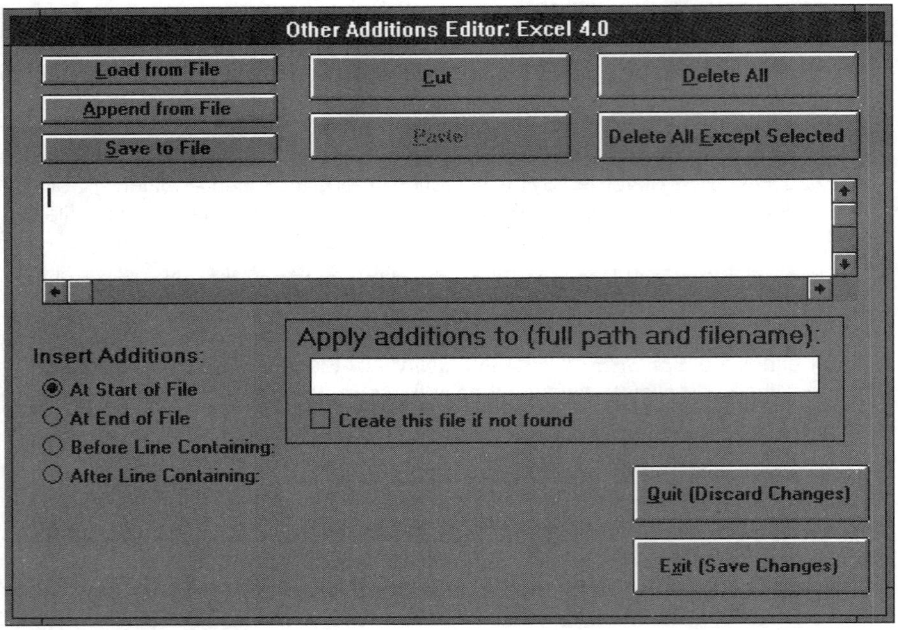

Figure 10.17 WINSTADM.EXE Other Additions Screen.

Inserting an Application into the List

When you click on the *INSERT APPLICATION INTO LIST* Button, WINSTALL presents a blank data field and a list box of application .DAT files in the Current Working Directory.

This feature enables you to add an existing .DAT file to the list. For example, if an application .DAT file had been created in another directory, it could be copied to the current working directory and it and its application added to WINAPPS.LST by using the *INSERT APPLICATION INTO LIST* Button. The text entered into the first field will appear in the *AVAILABLE APPLICATIONS* listing in WINSTALL (and also in the WINSTADM.EXE program), while the .DAT file selected from the list will provide WINSTALL with the information it needs to install or remove that application from the user's configuration.

SUGGESTIONS

WINSTALL Configuration

You might consider running several copies of WINSTALL on the same file server. (This is a no-extra-cost configuration option, because WINSTALL is licensed by file server, not by the number of copies in use or by the number of nodes or users). For example, you might want to make certain applications available to everyone but other applications available only to certain users. To accomplish this, you could create two directories containing WINSTALL, each with a different WINAPPS.LST appropriate to the groups of users having access to it.

Using two directories, two copies of WINSTALL.EXE, and two separate WINAPPS.LST files would also allow you to control which applications users can remove and which they cannot remove; you would simply enable the *REMOVE APPLICATION* option in one WINAPPS.LST file but not in the other.

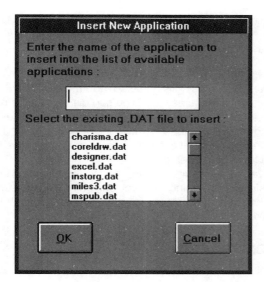

Figure 10.18 WINSTADM.EXE Insert Application Screen.

.DAT File Creation

Lately, some new Windows programs have included a file which describes all changes made by the installation process. These files make creating a .DAT file very easy.

In absence of such a file, it may be easiest to create a brand new Windows configuration on a drive which does not have one (or on a PC which does not have one, if you have the luxury of being able to reserve a PC for this type of work), and install the application onto the file server from that configuration. If you make a backup of the WIN.INI, SYSTEM.INI, AUTOEXEC.BAT, and CONFIG.SYS files and a printout of the WINDOWS, SYSTEM, and ROOT directories before installing the application, you can quickly and easily identify any changes by comparing them with what you find after the installation. Make a point of checking the file dates, especially in the SYSTEM directory; more and more applications are now updating during their installation processes some of the .DLL files which are shared by multiple applications.

For changes to the WIN.INI, SYSTEM.INI, AUTOEXEC.BAT, CONFIG.SYS, and other ASCII files, use the corresponding Additions Editors built into WINSTADM.EXE. An easy way to pull these changes into a .DAT file without retyping is to follow this procedure:

1. Run WINSTADM.EXE and select *CREATE NEW APPLICATION.*
2. At the Add Form, click on the *WIN.INI ADDITIONS VIEW/EDIT/LOAD* Button to enter the WIN.INI Additions Editor.
3. Click on the *LOAD FROM FILE* Button, and specify the WIN.INI file from the configuration used to load the application to the file server.
4. Once the WIN.INI file is loaded, select only the text which was added during the installation of the application.
5. Click on the *DELETE ALL EXCEPT SELECTED* Button, and you will have in the editor only those changes applicable to the application you are adding. (The original WIN.INI file is not modified.)

This same procedure will work equally well for any changes to the SYSTEM.INI, AUTOEXEC.BAT, CONFIG.SYS, and OTHER files, using the corresponding *ADDITIONS VIEW/EDIT/LOAD* Button from the Add Form.

Application Updates

When a new version of an application you are using is released, add the new version to WINAPPS.LST, but leave the old version in place as well. (You can distinguish the new version by adding a version number to the end of the List Name, and by using a different .DAT filename.) Instruct your users to use WINSTALL to remove the old version and then to install the new version. After you are satisfied that everyone has upgraded, remove the old version from WINAPPS.LST and from the file server.

If the upgrade would best be served by preserving some of the files or other data from the old version rather than wiping it all out and starting over, you can edit the old version's .DAT file and remove from it the information you want to remain after the REMOVE operation. If it is not listed in the .DAT file, then WINSTALL will not remove it.

INITIAL END USER WINDOWS CONFIGURATIONS

You can configure the Windows setup program to automatically install the WINSTALL icon in the Main program group (or any other program group) of every Windows installation. That way, you can let end users finish the job themselves by installing whatever Windows applications they need through WINSTALL.

It is also very quick and easy to install local copies of Windows from a file server. Consult the Windows documentation for instructions on how to set Windows up to best allow this type of installation.

Three easy steps enable the Windows setup program to automatically install WINSTALL to each new Windows installation:

1. Copy the files VBRUN100.DLL and DISKSTAT.DLL into the directory on the file server, or onto one of the diskettes, from which you will install Windows. If you are going to be installing Windows from diskettes, note the number of the diskette to which you have copied these two .DLL files. If they do not fit onto any of the Windows diskettes, it will be simplest if you copy them manually into each Windows directory immediately after the Windows setup program completes.
2. In the same directory on the file server, (or on the first diskette, if you are installing Windows from diskettes) open the file SETUP.INF with the Windows Notepad or any other ordinary text editor.

   If you have copied the files VBRUN100.DLL and DISKSTAT.DLL to the Windows directory on the file server or to the first diskette, add the following line to the [win.apps] section:

   1:VBRUN100.DLL, "Visual Basic Runtime Module"

   1:DISKSTAT.DLL, "Art Krumsee's VB Extension"

   The first character in this line (the number 1 in the example above) specifies on which Windows diskette the setup program can expect to find the .DLL file. If you are installing Windows from a file server, diskettes will not be involved, so you can just use the number 1. If you will be installing Windows on each network node from diskettes, this number should correspond to the number of the diskette to which you have copied the .DLL file. In either case, these lines will assure that the required .DLL files are automatically copied into the Windows directory of each new Windows installation. If you have been unable to copy the .DLL files to one of the Windows diskettes, do not add this line.

3. Finally, add to the [Main] section, the line which will create the WINSTALL icon in the Program Manager *Main* Group (or in whatever group you want the WINSTALL icon to appear):

"WINSTALL",F:\NETAPPS\WINSTALL.EXE

For the path *F:\NETAPPS*, substitute the drive and directory where you have installed WINSTALL and the application .DAT files.

Installing Windows Applications to Run Locally

Heavy network use and a need for better performance may encourage you to load Windows applications on each PC's local hard disk. WINSTALL can make quick work of this type of installation, too, saving many hours of tedious support effort. The same procedures suggested for installing Windows applications on a network drive and running them from networked PCs will work for installing a separate copy of each application on each PC. The .DAT file will differ, of course, in what files are specified to be copied to the local disk, and in the path to the executable file and icon, but the principles remain the same. Obviously, you will be copying many more files, so each installation will take a bit longer than if the applications are to be run from the file server. In either situation, though, WINSTALL can enable all your end users to do the job themselves—quickly and easily, without the possibility of confusion.

REFERENCE NOTES

Backup Files

WIN.INI

When a user runs WINSTALL, the program makes a backup copy of the WIN.INI file, named WININI.TMP. When the program concludes, if it has changed the WIN.INI file, it renames WININI.TMP to WININI.BAK (first deleting any existing file named WININI.BAK). If it has not changed the WIN.INI file, it deletes WININI.TMP.

AUTOEXEC.BAT, CONFIG.SYS, and Other ASCII Files

In each case, if WINSTALL modifies one of these files, it preserves the original with a .BAK extension, deleting in the process any earlier .BAK files if they exist.

Application .DAT Files

If a new application .DAT file is created as a result of modifications to an existing .DAT file, the original .DAT file is preserved with a .BAK extension. (Again, if an earlier .BAK file exists, it is deleted to allow the current version to use that file name).

WINAPPS.LST

When the file WINAPPS.LST is updated, the previous version is retained with a .BAK extension. As with WIN.INI and the Application .DAT files, only the last version of WINAPPS.LST is preserved as WINAPPS.BAK.

File Formats

Formats for all data files associated with WINSTALL.EXE and WINSTADM.EXE are fully described here. All of these files are flat ASCII files, so they can be edited manually with the Windows Notepad, or any other ordinary text editor. However, the information provided here is intended for reference only; these files are created and maintained by the WINSTADM.EXE program (except for NAI.INI, which is created and maintained automatically by the WINSTALL.EXE program) and under normal circumstances should require no manual editing whatsoever. Because of the many parameters they contain and the intricate nature of the modifications which WINSTALL makes to a user's configuration, it is strongly recommended that these files be manually edited only in an emergency and even then only by someone who well understands how WINSTALL works.

WINAPPS.LST

```
;=========================================================
;FILE WINAPPS.LST
;WINDOWS APPLICATIONS LIST FOR WINSTALL rel. 2.0
;=========================================================
;WINSTALL Runtime Options:
REMOVE=ENABLED
NETLOG=ENABLED
LOGFILE=F:\WINSTLOG\WINSTALL.LOG
LOGITEMS=VAR1 VAR2 ENV1 ENV3
COPYFILES=ALWAYS
;User-specific information:
$VAR1=First Name
$VAR2=Last Name
$VAR3=
$ENVAR1=USERNAME
$ENVAR2=GROUPNAME
$ENVAR3=NODENAME
$ENVAR4=
$ENVAR5=
;Format for application list is:
;Application List Name ¦ Application .DAT file name
Charisma ¦ CHARISMA
CorelDraw ¦ CORELDRW
Designer 3.1 ¦ DESIGNER
Excel 4.0 ¦ EXCEL
Instant Org Chart ¦ INSTORG
Milestones, Etc. ¦ MILES3
Packrat ¦ PACKRAT
Powerpnt ¦ POWERPNT
Project for Windows ¦ PROJECT
Word for Windows 2.0 ¦ WFW
;=========================================================
; WINSTALL 2.0 (Network Application Installer for Windows)
; (c) Copyright 1991, 1992 by Aleph Systems
; All rights reserved.

; 7319 Willow Avenue, Takoma Park, MD 20912
; (301)270-4458
;=========================================================
;End of file WINAPPS.LST
;=========================================================
```

Notes

Blank lines and lines beginning with ; are ignored.

Before the list of applications, the runtime options lines must appear. The first two options are *REMOVE=* and *NETLOG=*. The only recognized values for these two options are *ENABLED* and *DISABLED.* The *REMOVE=* setting determines whether or not the *REMOVE* Button appears in the WINSTALL program, enabling users to remove listed applications from their local configurations. The *NETLOG=* setting determines whether or not the WINSTALL network log is enabled.

The *LOGITEMS=* option lists all the global user-specific variables and environment variables which are to be logged to the WINSTALL network log. User-specific variables are here specified as *VARn*, where n is the number of the variable (between 1 and 3). Environment variables are specified as *ENVn*, where n is the number of the variable (between 1 and 5). The items are separated by spaces.

The *COPYFILES=* option determines how WINSTALL is to handle copy operations where the destination file already exists. The value must be one of the following:

NODESTINATION   (copy only if the destination file does NOT already exist)

OLDDESTINATION   (if the destination file is newer than the source file, then do not copy)

PROMPT   (if the destination file is newer than the source file, then ask the user)

ALWAYS   (always do the copy)

User-specific variables are indicated in the WINAPPS.LST file by the *$VAR1=*, *$VAR2=*, and *$VAR3=* lines. If the line is empty following the "=", then the variable is not in use. If a variable is in use, then the text which follows the "=" will be used by the WINSTALL.EXE program to prompt the user for the specific information needed at installation time.

Environment variables are indicated in the WINAPPS.LST file by the *$ENVAR1=*, *$ENVAR2=*, *$ENVAR3=*, *$ENVAR4=*, and *$ENVAR5=* lines. If the line is empty following the "=", then the variable is not in use. If a variable is in use, then the text which follows the "=" will be used by the WINSTALL.EXE program to search the user's environment for the specific information needed at installation time. If the text is not found in the environment, then WINSTALL will prompt the user for it.

In the application list section of WINAPPS.LST, each line represents one application, with the display name of the application (what the user sees in the list of available applications) first, followed by a vertical bar and then the filename (no path, no extension) of the data file containing the information needed to install the program.

Application .DAT Files

```
;==========================================================
;File DESIGNER.DAT (WINSTALL rel. 2.0 .DAT file for DESIGNER 3.1)
;==========================================================
;Application-Specific Variables:
$APPVAR1=
$APPVAR2=
$APPVAR3=
PREINSTALL=
POSTINSTALL=
PREREMOVE=F:\WINSTALL\PREREM.TXT
POSTREMOVE=
INSTALLSHELL=
REMOVESHELL=
[Extensions]
drw=designer.exe ^.drw
```

```
shw=mgxslide.exe ^.shw
[Micrografx]
Designer 3.1=F:\DESIGNER
Libraries 4.0=F:\MGXLIBS
CLIPART=F:\MGXCLIP
Libraries=F:\MGXLIBS
[Clipboard Formats]
MGX_DRAW=0,"Micrografx Picture"
MGX_PICT=0,"In*a*Vision or Windows Draw Picture"
[Micrografx Outline Fonts]
BSBEZIER=F:\MGXLIBS\BITFONTS,MGXBITBZ,BSBEZ.FTM,0,15
BSSPEEDO=F:\MGXLIBS\SPDFONTS,MGXBITSP,BSSPD.FTM,0,20
URWBEZIER=F:\MGXLIBS\URWFONTS,MGXURWBZ,URWBEZ.FTM,0,6
[MGXTIFF]
Format=64
Device=1
Compression=2
[MGX_DRW_OUTPUT]
CPI=480
[CGMIN]
CPI=4052
TypeOfCGM=Harvard Graphics
ShowProfile=0
[Designer 3.1]
Warning=1
AutoPaste=0
Format=64
AutoPaste=0
BOOT=C
PLACEMARKER=
KEY=SMARTDRV
ALTPLACEMARKER=
[START AUTOEXEC.BAT]
BOOT=C
PLACEMARKER=
KEY=
ALTPLACEMARKER=
[START CONFIG.SYS]
F:\DESIGNER\DESIGNER.INI @WINDOWS
FILE=
CREATE=ENABLED
PLACEMARKER=
KEY=
ALTPLACEMARKER=
[START OTHER]
XGROUP=Main
F:\DESIGNER\DESIGNER.EXE,Designer,F:\DESIGNER\DESIGNER.EXE,,,,F:\$VAR1
$\DATA
;========================================================
;WINSTALL 2.0: Network Application Installer for Windows
; © Copyright 1991, 1992 by Aleph Systems
```

; All rights reserved.

; 7319 Willow Avenue, Takoma Park, MD 20912
; (301)270-4458
;==
;End of File DESIGNER.DAT

Notes
Blank lines and lines beginning with ; are ignored.
Eight headings appear in the .DAT file , and they should appear in this order:

@APPVARS
@WIN.INI
@SYSTEM.INI
@AUTOEXEC.BAT
@CONFIG.SYS
@FILES
@OTHER
@ICONS

Beneath the @APPVARS heading are listed the following items:

$APPVAR1=

$APPVAR2=

$APPVAR3=

PREINSTALL=

POSTINSTALL=

PREREMOVE=

POSTREMOVE=

INSTALLSHELL=

REMOVESHELL=

Each item will be listed, but if no text follows the equal sign, then the feature or variable will go unused.

The $APPVARn keys specify the application-specific variables to be used with the installation and removal of this application. Any text following the equal sign will be used to prompt the user for the information needed. If nothing follows the equal sign, then the variable is not in use, and the appearance of its $VAR code later in the .DAT file will cause an installation or removal failure.

Text following the equal sign on the PREINSTALL line specifies the full path and filename of an ASCII text file to display at the start of the installation process. The text following the equal sign on the POSTINSTALL line specifies a text file to display following the installation process. The PREREMOVE and POSTREMOVE lines fulfill the same function for the removal process.

Text following the equal sign on the INSTALLSHELL and REMOVESHELL lines specifies the full path and filename of an executable file (.BAT, .COM, or .EXE) to be called by WINSTALL.EXE at the conclusion of the installation or removal process.

Any changes to the user's WIN.INI file must appear below the *@WIN.INI* heading, exactly as they are to appear in the user's WIN.INI file. If there are no changes to WIN.INI, the heading must still appear, but it would be followed on the next uncommented line by the *@SYSTEM.INI* heading.

Any changes to the user's SYSTEM.INI file must appear below the *@SYSTEM.INI* heading, exactly as they are to appear in the user's SYSTEM.INI file. If there are no changes to SYSTEM.INI, the heading should still appear, but it would be followed on the next uncommented line by the *@AUTOEXEC.BAT* heading.

The next heading, *@AUTOEXEC.BAT*, has four key values and a subheading indicating the beginning of the actual changes to be installed.

The *BOOT=* line specifies the user's boot drive. This value can be any letter of the alphabet or *PROMPT*, the latter meaning that WINSTALL.EXE should ask the user for his boot drive.

The *PLACEMARKER=* line specifies the location within the AUTOEXEC.BAT file where the changes should be placed. This value can be *START*, *END*, *BEFORE*, or *AFTER*. *START* will place the additional text at the very beginning of the file; *END* will place it at the very end. *BEFORE* and *AFTER* instruct WINSTALL.EXE to key the placement either before or after the first line containing the key text, specified after the equal sign on the *KEY=* line.

The *ALTPLACEMARKER=* line instructs WINSTALL.EXE as to where the changes should go if the *PLACEMARKER=* line is set to either *BEFORE* or *AFTER* and the key text is not found in the AUTOEXEC.BAT file. Valid entries for the *ALTPLACEMARKER=* line are *START*, *END*, and *OMIT*.

Following the *ALTPLACEMARKER=* line is the subheading, *[START AUTOEXEC.BAT]*. Any additions to the AUTOEXEC.BAT file will follow this subheading, exactly as they are to appear in the user's AUTOEXEC.BAT file after installation. $VAR codes are valid within this text.

If the installation will make no changes to AUTOEXEC.BAT, these lines should all still appear, but no text would follow the equal signs, and no text would follow the *[START AUTOEXEC.BAT]* subheading. The subheading would be followed on the next uncommented line by the *@CONFIG.SYS* heading.

The format of the *@CONFIG.SYS* section is identical to that of the *@AUTOEXEC.BAT* section. This section describes changes to be made to the user's CONFIG.SYS file. The four key values which appear here are the same as those for the *@AUTOEXEC.BAT* section, and they permit the same valid entries for each. All of the actual changes to be made to the user's CONFIG.SYS file appear following the *[START CONFIG.SYS]* subheading. $VAR codes are valid within this text.

Any files which must be copied to the user's local hard disk must appear below the *@FILES* heading, in the following format:

sourcefile destinationdirectory

DOS wildcards (* and ?) are OK, but please see the discussion of **Wildcard Deletions** later in the **Reference Notes** section. The *sourcefile* must include drive and path. The *destinationdirectory* assumes the drive where Windows was started, unless another drive is specified in the path. Any directory in the *destinationdirectory* will automatically be created on the user's local drive, if necessary.

If the *destinationdirectory* is omitted, or if *@WINDOWS* appears in its position, the file(s) will be copied to the user's Windows directory (where his WIN.INI file is found— usually C:\WINDOWS). If *@SYSTEM* appears in the *destinationdirectory* position, then the file(s) will be copied to his Windows\System directory, wherever that may be (usually C:\WINDOWS\SYSTEM).

If you need to place a user-specific directory into the *destinationdirectory*, WINSTALL provides full support for user-specific, environment, and application-specific variables. Within the *destinationdirectory*, you would insert the appropriate $VAR code, and WINSTALL will substitute at runtime the corresponding variable information. See the **User-Specific and Environment Variables** section, and the **Application-Specific Variables** section, above, for complete details.

If no files need to be copied, the heading must still appear, but it would be followed on the next uncommented line by the *@OTHER* heading. The *@OTHER* section describes changes to be made to any ASCII file in the end user's configuration, including files just copied there by the instructions in the *@FILES* section. This section has five key values and a subheading. The first key line, *FILE=*, contains the full path and filename of the ASCII file to modify. The second key, *CREATE=*, instructs WINSTALL as to whether or not to create this file if it is not found. Valid entries are *ENABLED* (meaning to create the file if not found) and *DISABLED* (meaning to ignore the *@OTHER* section entirely if the file is not found).

The other three keys, *PLACEMARKER=*, *KEY=*, and *ALTPLACEMARKER=*, are identical to the corresponding keys in the *@AUTOEXEC.BAT* and *@CONFIG.SYS* sections in both their function and their acceptable values.

The *[START OTHER]* subheading precedes the actual additions to be made to the specified ASCII file, which appear here exactly as they are to be entered in the user's file. $VAR codes are valid within this text.

The *@ICONS* section follows the *@OTHER* section. Information for each icon to be created in the user's workspace must follow the *@ICONS* heading. If the icons are to go in a separate icon group, then the name of that group should appear in the first uncommented line beneath the *@ICONS* heading, in the following format:

GROUP=groupname

If the icons are to go into an existing icon group, then the name of that group should appear in the first uncommented line beneath the *@ICONS* heading, in the following format:

XGROUP=groupname

The *GROUP=* or XGROUP= line is optional. If it is omitted, WINSTALL will install the icon(s) in the icon group which is current (active) at runtime.

Each icon to be placed must have a line in this final section of the .DAT file. The format for the icon information is as follows:

executablefilename,displayname,iconpath,,,,workingdirectory

The *executablefilename* should include a full, specific path to the program file to be executed when the icon is double-clicked. $VAR codes are valid within the *executablefilename*.

The *displayname* is whatever should appear beneath the icon in the user's workspace.

The *iconpath* indicates the file from which to draw the icon; it may be different from the executable file. $VAR codes are valid within the *iconpath*. Only the comma should separate the items (no spaces or tabs).

The *workingdirectory* specifies the default data directory for the application (in version 3.1 and above of Windows—if the end user is running an earlier version of Windows, the *workingdirectory* information is ignored). $VAR codes are valid within the workingdirectory. (NOTE: the *workingdirectory* must be preceded by exactly 4 commas.)

NOTE: If any of these items are omitted, it is important that the commas appear anyway. Only the commas should separate the items (no spaces or tabs).

At installation time, WINSTALL will create the *workingdirectory* on the user's disk if it does not already exist. If WINSTALL is used to remove the application, it will remove the *workingdirectory* from the user's disk if that directory is empty.

The group specified in the *GROUP=* line will be automatically created by WINSTALL, and all icons specified will be created in this group. If a group is specified in the *XGROUP=* line instead of a *GROUP=* line, that group will be automatically created by WINSTALL if it does not already exist, and all icons specified will be created in this group. If no *GROUP=* or *XGROUP=* line appears, the icons will be created in the group which is current (active) in the user's Windows workspace at the time when the installation is performed. While it is technically not necessary to include any icon information (the *@ICONS* heading must still appear in the .DAT file, though), the user would have no way to run the program after installation if no icon was installed.

WINSTADM.CFG

```
;===========================================================
;File WINSTADM.CFG (WINSTADM.EXE Config file)
;Comments begin with;
;Blank lines are ignored
;===========================================================
;File WINSTADM.CFG (WINSTADM.EXE rel 2.0 Config file)
;Comments begin with;
;Blank lines are ignored
;===========================================================
DATDIR=F:\WINSTALL\
;===========================================================
;WINSTALL 2.0: Network Application Installer for Windows
; © Copyright 1991, 1992 by Aleph Systems
; All rights reserved.

; 7319 Willow Avenue, Takoma Park, MD 20912
; (301)270-4458
;===========================================================
;End of File WINSTADM.CFG
;===========================================================
```

Notes

Blank lines and lines beginning with ; are ignored.

The only valid configuration option is the location of the working directory, specified in the *DATDIR=* line. All other lines must either be blank or begin with a semicolon.

NAI.INI

[Programs]

Designer 2.0=10:03:23,01/07/92

Excel 3.0=14:02:45,02/14/92

PowerPoint=14:03:15,02/14/93

Word for Windows 2.0=14:04:00,02/14/92

Notes

Blank lines and lines beginning with ; are ignored.

This file is a standard format Windows application initialization file. In the current release, the only valid heading is *[Programs]*. Each line beneath that heading has to the left of the equal sign the Application List Name of the application installed by WINSTALL To the right of the equal sign is the time of installation, followed by a comma and the date of installation.

In the current release, this file is used only during the WINSTALL Install Application function, to determine whether or not an application has been installed previously. Later releases will employ this file for the purpose of automatically determining when an application upgrade is needed.

Icon Groups

If an application .DAT file specifies that a separate icon group be created, then the *REMOVE* operation of WINSTALL will automatically remove that group and all its icons from the user's workspace. If the .DAT file specifies installing the icons into an existing icon group or into the icon group which is current (active) at runtime, then the *REMOVE* operation will make no attempt to remove any icons. Instead, when the rest of the removal process is complete, WINSTALL will inform the user that the icon(s) may remain in the workspace and may have to be removed manually. Simple instructions for removing an icon are included in this message.

Note that during the installation of an application, the CREATE SEPARATE ICON GROUP and ADD TO EXISTING ICON GROUP work the same way. That is, if the icon group does not exist, WINSTALL will create it and install the icons in it. On the other hand, if the specified icon group *does* exist, then WINSTALL will simply add the icons to those already in the specified group.

The difference between these two choices arises only when WINSTALL removes the application. The *REMOVE* operation for any application specifying CREATE SEPARATE ICON GROUP will remove the entire icon group and all the icons it contains, whether they are part of the application being removed or not. In contrast, the *REMOVE* operation for an application specifying ADD TO EXISTING ICON GROUP will remove no icons or icon groups. Instead, it will behave exactly the same as the ADD TO CURRENT (ACTIVE) ICON GROUP option: it will inform the user that the icons may have to be removed manually, and it will at the same time provide some brief instructions on how to do so.

Reinstallation Check

When a user clicks the *INSTALL APPLICATION* Button in WINSTALL, the program checks the user's local configuration to determine whether or not the selected application is already installed. WINSTALL keeps in the user's Windows directory the file NAI.INI, a log of all applications it has installed and the date and time it installed them. If WINSTALL does not find an application listed as having been installed in the NAI.INI file—and does not encounter a match between the [Extensions] heading in the WIN.INI additions section of the application .DAT file and the user's WIN.INI file, it assumes that the application has not been installed. If WINSTALL believes that the application is currently installed, it will give the user the option of aborting the installation or reinstalling the application.

Because of idiosyncrasies in various Windows applications and the way that they share files and WIN.INI headings, WINSTALL assumes that an application is NOT currently installed unless it finds the application listed as having been installed in the NAI.INI file or it finds in the WIN.INI [Extensions] section the extensions specified in the application .DAT file. If neither of these conditions exists, WINSTALL will assume that the application is not installed.

If WINSTALL reinstalls an application (whether or not it is aware that it is reinstalling), the affected WIN.INI sections will be entirely rewritten according to the information in the .DAT file, and the files specified in the .DAT file will replace any by the same name which are already located on the user's local disk, and new icons will be added to the user's workspace.

Shared WIN.INI Headings

Certain applications share WIN.INI headings with other applications. For example, a number of Microsoft applications use the [Microsoft Help] heading in WIN.INI, while a number of applications from Micrografx, Inc. share the [Micrografx] heading. If a user has installed in his configuration two applications which share a heading, this heading may cause temporary problems if WINSTALL is used to remove one of the two applications.

In such a case, the remaining application will find that the heading it needs is missing from WIN.INI. If you suspect that WINSTALL has removed a shared WIN.INI heading, try reinstalling the remaining application. The reinstallation will replace the missing heading and the remaining application should then work as before.

Special WIN.INI Headings

For most WIN.INI headings, WINSTALL treats the entire heading and all the lines beneath it as a single unit, installing it or removing it whole cloth. However, WINSTALL treats five WIN.INI headings in a special fashion. The *[Windows], [Extensions], [Embedding], [OLE],* and *[Fonts]* headings are all known to be shared. Therefore, WINSTALL inserts or deletes from these headings only the information which the application .DAT file specifies belongs under them. The result is that for these five headings, each application .DAT file will affect the only the lines it specifies; all other lines beneath these headings will remain untouched.

In addition, two lines within the *[Windows]* heading are handled in a unique fashion. The *RUN=* and *LOAD=* lines are never removed or replaced. Instead, if an application .DAT file specifies text to be inserted in one of these two lines, the WINSTALL install application process will simply add it to what is already there (if anything); likewise, the remove application process will remove from these lines only the text specified in the application .DAT file. All other text on these lines will be left intact.

SYSTEM.INI Headings

For SYSTEM.INI headings, WINSTALL inserts or deletes only the information which the application .DAT file specifies belongs under them. The result is that for the SYSTEM.INI file, each application .DAT file will affect the only the individual lines it specifies; all other lines will remain untouched.

Wild Card Deletions

WINSTALL supports the use of DOS wildcards (* and ?) in the specification of files to be copied. However, this support has important safety implications for WINSTALL's application removal feature. WINSTALL includes special safeguards to prevent the application removal feature from inadvertently causing damage to a user's Windows configuration or other areas of his local PC. Nevertheless, the application removal feature is very powerful, and it is important for a LAN administrator to understand how it operates in order to be certain that it works as intended. Remember that the application removal feature can be disabled from within the WINSTADM.EXE program.

If a user clicks on the *REMOVE APPLICATION* Button in WINSTALL, the program will attempt to remove from the local configuration whatever files the application .DAT file specifies as required to be copied to the local configuration during installation of the application. If the source files are specified by complete filenames, they are simply deleted one by one, by complete filename. This method is completely safe.

However, if these files are specified by means of wildcards, WINSTALL follows a cautious procedure for their removal, to avoid removing any files other than those intended:

1. WINSTALL first looks for the individual filenames in the specified source directory on the file server. If files matching the file specification are found in the source directory, then WINSTALL uses these names in the removal process: it deletes each of these filenames one by one from the user's local configuration. In other words, if the .DAT file specifies F:\FONTS*.FNT as the source file and C:\FONTS\ as the destination directory, WINSTALL will look in the F:\FONTS\ directory for files with the .FNT extension. If it finds, say, FONT1.FNT, FONT2.FNT, and FONT3.FNT, then it will perform three separate deletions on the local drive, equivalent to the following series of DOS commands: DEL C:\FONTS\FONT1.FNT, DEL C:\FONTS\FONT2.FNT, and DEL C:\FONTS\FONT3.FNT.

2. With certain exceptions for reasons of safety (see #3, below), if the file server does not contain any files matching the source file specification in the .DAT file, then WINSTALL performs a wild card deletion of files matching the specification on the local configuration. For example, if the source file specification reads F:\FONTS*.FNT but the F: drive holds no files with the .FNT extension in the \FONTS\ directory (perhaps because the application has been removed from the file server), then WINSTALL will perform on the local drive the equivalent of the following DOS command: DEL \FONTS*.FNT.

3. *If the destination directory is the WINDOWS or SYSTEM directory or the ROOT directory of any drive, then WINSTALL will not delete files specified in the .DAT file by the use of wildcards unless it can discover the individual filenames from the file server,* as discussed in #1, above. In other words, **if** the .DAT file specifies files by the wildcard method **and** the source files are not found in the source directory **and** the destination for those files is the WINDOWS directory, or the SYSTEM directory, or a ROOT directory, **then** WINSTALL will **not** delete the files.

WINSTALL Capacities and Limitations

The WINSTALL program includes the following limitations:

Maximum applications per WINAPPS.LST file	100
Maximum WIN.INI additions per application .DAT file	350 lines
Maximum separate WIN.INI headings per application .DAT file	20
Maximum WIN.INI [Windows] additions per application .DAT file	5 lines
Maximum WIN.INI [Extensions] additions per application .DAT file	50 lines
Maximum WIN.INI [Embedding] additions per application .DAT file	50 lines
Maximum WIN.INI [OLE] additions per application .DAT file	50 lines
Maximum WIN.INI [Fonts] additions per application .DAT file	75 lines
Maximum SYSTEM.INI additions per application .DAT file	100 lines
Maximum AUTOEXEC.BAT additions per application .DAT file	25 lines
Maximum CONFIG.SYS additions per application .DAT file	25 lines

Maximum OTHER ASCII file additions per application .DAT file	25 lines
Maximum number of icons per application .DAT file	20

LICENSE AGREEMENT

Disclaimer

This program is provided without any express or implied warranties whatsoever. Because of the diversity of conditions and hardware under which this program may be used, no warranty of fitness for a particular purpose is offered. The user is advised to test the program thoroughly before relying on it. The user must assume the entire risk of using the program. The manufacturer assumes no liability of any kind.

Licensing Information

This copyrighted program is NOT free. This is an evaluation copy: you are permitted to **test** it in your network to see if it will prove useful to you. **If you do actually put it into use,** you are legally obligated to license your copy from the manufacturer, Aleph Systems. You are encouraged to pass copies of this evaluation program along to others for their evaluation, but please include all of the files, and please encourage others to license their copies as well. This program can save you enormous amounts of time, effort, and money: if you use WINSTALL to install even one application on most of the nodes in an average sized network, you will have saved enough time to easily cover the expense of a license.

An invoice/order form is provided for your convenience.

To keep licensing as simple and equitable as possible, this program is licensed on a per-file server basis. For the purposes of this license, a server is defined as any computer from which the program is made available to be run. In other words, even if you are not running WINSTALL from a dedicated file server (for example, in a peer-to-peer network which has no dedicated file servers), any computer from which the WINSTALL program is made available is considered a file server and requires its own WINSTALL license. You may elect to run multiple copies of this program on a single server; in this case, you still need only a single license. However, if you install a copy of this program on a second file server, you are obligated to purchase an additional license to run WINSTALL on that second file server.

For pricing information on licenses for 10 servers or more or on upgrades from previous releases, please contact Aleph Systems directly, by mail at 7319 Willow Avenue, Takoma Park, MD 20912, by CompuServe mail at 71371,635, or by telephone at (301)270-4458.

Anyone distributing this program for any kind of remuneration must first contact Aleph Systems for authorization.

While You Were Out (by Caliente International)

by Charles Rose

While You Were Out is a capable Windows-based phone message management system. It can be used effectively in a networked environment to help you take office messages from different locations and distribute them to the proper employees. You can do away with those pink notepads with WYWO.

While You Were Out ReadMe File

Caliente International   April 14, 1992
[IMPORTANT!!! READ ALL OF THIS DOCUMENT]

To Our Customers,

Thank you for your interest in While Your Were Out and Caliente International. Our name says it all: We're HOT! To prove it, you've just installed While You Were Out 3.0(WYWO), the Windows 3.0/3.1 office messaging system.

Inspired by the universal telephone message note, you already know how to use WYWO. Installed on a MS DOS 3.1 or higher compatible network, users can send and receive messages which look just like their familiar phone messages. They're password protected and encrypted for privacy. WYWO notifies you of new messages. Messages are organized into New and Old message lists. Once read, new messages are automatically saved to the old message list. The contents of a message can be saved either to a printer, file, or the clipboard for pasting into another Windows 3.0 application. WYWO has extensive online help.

===> INSTALL AND PRODUCT OVERVIEW FOLLOWS THIS GREETING <===

While You Were Out 3.0 Highlights:
WYWO 3.0 is a major upgrade to our popular product:

Semiautomated installation.

Assign users to one or more logical work groups (comes in handy with large licenses!).

Modify message contents after they have been read.

Forward a read message to another user or group.

Object sensitive pop-up menus accessed by the right mouse button.

Users can now search their message lists by any WYWO message field. (From, Company, Date, Time, etc.)

Enhanced message printing. Print up to 4 messages per page with access to any installed printer and fonts.

Please view the evaluation file WYWO.HST for more details about these features and those of previous versions of While You Were Out.

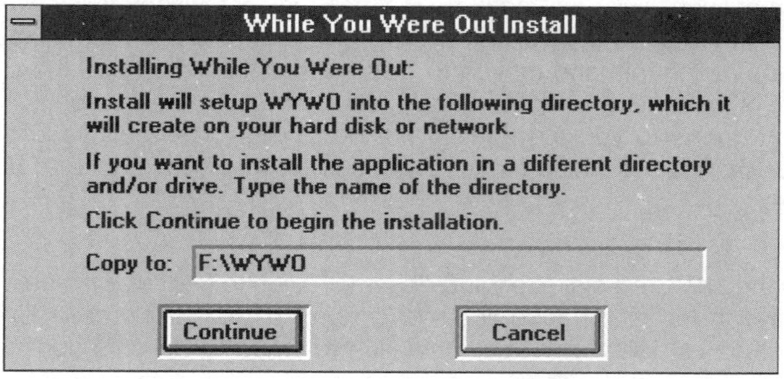

Figure 10.19 While You Were Out Install window.

Figure 10.20 Install completed window.

COMPANY NEWS

We've installed a 24 hour bulletin board service for our customers. The Caliente International Hot Line will provide online access to revisions of WYWO and technical support. In the future you will be able to order Caliente International software electronically.

>>>The BBS Hot Line is 203 667-2768.

Available for download April 30, 1992: Electronic Documentation. We've done away with paper manuals. Our new on-line documentation will become part of our existing help system. Our tech writer and illustrator are doing an excellent job! Please contact us at (203) 667-2159 if you want a diskette mailed to you.

ORDERING WHILE YOU WERE OUT 3.0

For your convenience, we've included an order form which is located in the ORDER.FRM file. Simply print the file. Fill in the information and mail or fax it to us. Our fax numbers are (203) 667-2159 or (203) 665-7382.

We hope you enjoy using WYWO 3.0. Please let us know how WYWO and Caliente International can better service your office in the future. Those of you with CompuServe accounts can send e-mail to our account: 70324,2055. Of course you can always reach us by telephone or fax.

INSTALL AND PRODUCT OVERVIEW

License Statement

This software and accompanying manual is copyrighted and is therefore protected by the Copyright Laws of the United States and copyright provisions of various international treaties. The effect of such laws and treaties is that you may not, without a license from Caliente, copy or distribute the booklet or software. The software and manual may be used by any number of people and moved to different locations provided there is no possibility of either of them being used simultaneously on two or more networks.

Caliente hereby grants to you the right to make archival copies of the enclosed software solely for the purpose of protecting yourself from loss or damage of such enclosed software.

Warranty

Caliente warrants the enclosed diskettes and documentation to be free from defects in materials and workmanship for a period of 60 days from the date of purchase. Caliente will replace any defective diskette or documentation returned to Caliente during such warranty period. Replacement is the exclusive remedy for any such defects, and Caliente shall have no liability for any other damages.

Likewise, click the WYWO sheet itself, and a menu with functions associated with an entire message is displayed.

By clicking the Help button, you can get help on using any of WYWO's functions. This is the on-line manual.

Version 3.0 now has on Options screen which is available by clicking the Options button from the message create sheet of WYWO. From this screen you can set the following:

Default user:	The person normally using a particular workstation.
Default user group:	Group the default user will normally send and receive messages.
New message notification time:	How often WYWO will search for new message or not at all.
Notification window handling:	When notified of new messages, should the user be required to respond to the notification dialog window or let the window stay in the background.
Message save options:	When saving a message to the printer, file, or clipboard, save the message field identifiers such as To, From, Date, etc. with the message or not.

If you would like WYWO to be loaded each time you run windows so it always checks for incoming messages, add WYWO.EXE to the Load= line of the WIN.INI file.

To specify a specific default user name when running WYWO, pass the name on the command line for the WYWO icon or from the Program Manager. This name will override the default user name specified in the Options screen.

RUNNING THE WMONITOR.EXE PROGRAM

WMONITOR.EXE acts as a system message rack/message board similar to the message racks used on many secretaries' desks. It is great for those users with or without a network that want to monitor all new WYWO messages that come in at a central location. WMONITOR will check for all new messages in the system at 30-second intervals and display the names of users with new messages. The users can then read their messages from WMONITOR by double-clicking on their name or selecting their name and clicking the Read Messages button. WMONITOR can be used in two modes: One for displaying new message names as a message board which will show the number of new messages as small WYWO sheets following the user's name, or by displaying a message rack with a picture of the number of WYWO sheets sitting in their message "slot."

WMONITOR will only display users who belong to the group specified in the Options screen of WYWO installed on the same workstation. To monitor other groups, simply access WYWO and click the Options button to select another default group.

VERSION HISTORY OF WHILE YOU WERE OUT

Version 3.02	Enhanced Print capabilities by graphically printing messages to look like actual While You Were Out message sheets including selectable fonts (including Script) and printers. Also added ability to print one message, all new messages, all old messages, or all messages as a result of a search operation. Prints up to four messages per page.

Version 3.01	Allowed date and time formats for WYWO to reflect international settings from Windows.
	Added ability to have WYWO added to the WIN.INI Load= line when WYWO is first run.
	Internal speed enhancements for saving new messages.
Version 3.0	Moved the Options function to an Options button available in edit mode.
	Added the ability to edit messages that have been read, new or old.
	Added the ability to search through old messages and through messages satisfying a previous search criteria.
	Added the ability to forward a message.
	Added User Groups to all programs reducing the number of users that will be viewed in WYWO and WMONITOR.
	Added ability to send or forward messages to a User Group which will send a message to every user belonging to that group.
	Added popup menu support for most main functions through the use of the right mouse button.
	Added a WVERSION.DLL file for controlling the number of users and combined features of WYWO, WSETUP, and WMONITOR.
	Fixed bug of WSETUP not deleting files and directories of deleted users.
Version 2.22	Added ability to be notified of new messages while reading new and old messages.
	When WYWO is run from WMONITOR, any new messages read will remain as new messages until the message is read without being run from WMONITOR. Also, Read Mode is entered automatically once WYWO is launched from WMONITOR.
Version 2.21	Fixed bug with delete key not working in edit mode and causing an error opening a file.
	Fixed bug with message field not getting cleared on entering read mode.
	Fixed bug with time and date fields in edit mode not displaying the current time.
	Fixed bug with modifying existing message types in WSETUP.
	Fixed bug with '&' characters disappearing and causing the following character to have an underscore when reading messages.
	Fixed bug with user being notified of a new message while entering a read password.
	Fixed bug in WMONITOR with the Message Rack scrollbar being displayed if more than four users have messages and the mode is switched to the Message Board.

If entering read mode and no new messages exist, the first old messages will automatically be displayed if they exist.

If the current user has a read password, it must be entered each time read mode is entered.

Added ability to use the up and down arrow keys to move between edit fields in edit mode.

Allowed the RETURN key to be used as a carriage return in the message field instead of requiring the ALT key to be pressed.

When the Default User is changed, new messages for that user will immediately be checked.

Forced the WYWO.HLP file to be in the same directory as the WYWO.EXE.

Improved performance when flagging old messages to be deleted.

Version 2.2

Removed restriction of not informing user of new messages if that user sends a message to himself. This can be accomplished by setting the New Message Delay Time to 0 (off).

The Default User in the Options menu now sets the default user of the current execution of WYWO. The User function will allow messages from other users to be read, but once read mode is exited the default user becomes the current user.

Added option for New Message Notification Message Box to require a response so the message would have to be answered before continuing with other programs.

Added a focus identification to all of the WYWO programs for the Listboxes and Combo Boxes to identify when they have the input focus.

Fixed a bug that would not delete old messages if the user had over 80 messages on file.

Version 2.12

Fixed New Message Delay Time = 0(Off) bug which did not disable the new message alarm when WYWO was loaded with a delay time of 0, only when it was changed from the options screen.

Fixed WSETUP bug of not being able to use the tab key to move to the user-name listbox.

Added keyboard shortcut keys for all buttons in both WSETUP and WMONITOR that can be accessed with the ALT key.

If WYWO is launched from WMONITOR and the Exit button is pressed, WYWO will exit completely and not be minimized.

If WSETUP is closed from the system menu and users have been added or deleted, the user will be asked if he/she would like to save the changes.

All WYWO Message Types are now created and modified by the WSETUP program and stored in a WMSGTYPE.DAT file in the WYWO directory so they are now defined on a global scale instead of for each individual user. The User Message types have been taken out of WYWO Options and the WYWO.INI file.

Added an Exit button for WSETUP. The Save button will now save either the user names or message types depending on the screen being displayed and will not exit the program.

If WYWO and/or WMONITOR are running when WSETUP is saving data, they will be updated to reflect the changes made in WSETUP.

All functions in WYWO, WSETUP, and WMONITOR are now completely usable without a mouse.

Version 2.11

WYWO will no longer cause Windows to display a device error message box when the drive WYWO is on is unavailable when checking for new messages.

Fixed moving message filed bug when changing users while reading messages in WYWO.EXE.

Fixed bug in WMONITOR that wouldn't allow the minimized icon to be restored to normal size.

Version 2.1

Took all options out of WIN.INI and placed them in WYWO.INI.

WYWO now comes in 20-, 50-, and 100-user versions.

General internal changes to both WYWO and WSETUP to improve performance and functionality.

Allows multiple copies of WYWO to be running, but only with different users.

Enhanced WSETUP to have the general look of the WYWO program.

Added a Cancel option to the WSETUP program. You must use the Save button to actually save any new users and to delete old users and files.

Eliminated the Path option for the INI file. WYWO will load the WYWO.DAT file from the directory in which it finds WYWO.EXE and WSETUP.EXE.

Increase the size of the message data to 300 characters and made the message field scrollable to accommodate the new size. This requires the execution of the WCONVERT program to convert all old and new messages on the system. Run WCONVERT from the WYWO directory.

If only one user exists, that user becomes the default To: user for sending messages.

If WYWO is minimized and the user has new messages waiting to be read, the caption on the icon will display the number of new messages waiting.

Allowed movement among input fields by use of the Enter or Return key for quicker data entry.

Added a new Operator field. If no operator is entered, the current user's name is placed in this field.

Added a WYWO Options screen. Accessed from the Help menu after clicking on the Help button.

Options	A Default User can be selected.
	User-defined message actions can now be added to the existing message types (ie. Telephoned, Urgent, Will Call Back, Etc.).
	New Message Alarm Time determines how often (0 to 60 seconds) WYWO will look for new messages sent to the default user.
	Added an option for the Save function that determines how message info is saved to the clipboard, printer, or to file: Specify whether headings (ie. To, From, Date, Time, etc) are included with the message.
	Added WMONITOR.EXE, a WYWO Message monitor which will display all users who have new messages waiting and the number of messages. WMONITOR will check for new messages every 30 seconds to give up-to-the-minute results.
	If WMONITOR is running and a new message is sent from WYWO, WYWO will immediately notify WMONITOR to update its new message display.
	WYWO, WSETUP, and WMONITOR have been fixed to eliminate the problem of a disappearing icon when more than one is running or when other programs start using WYWO's icon or vice-versa.
Version 2.01	The Exit button will now minimize WYWO and return to the Edit mode instead of completely exiting the program. Exiting the program can be accomplished by double-clicking the closer box of WYWO or selecting Close from the System Menu.
	If sending a message to yourself, WYWO will not bring up the "New Messages" information.
	Fixed uppercase only message type for "Called To See You" while in read mode.
Version 2.0	Initial While You Were Out release.

INSTALLATION INFORMATION FILE

This is the Installation Information file for installing the WINSTALL Example application and sources onto your system.

You can compare the format and data in this file to the example file that you can find in DEMODSKS\DEMO.INF

The only changes that have been made from that file to this, is that the appropriate information has been inserted to cause it to install the sample code, and the comments that describe the data have been removed.

[dialog]	caption = "While You Were Out Install"
[data]	defdir = C:\WYWO
[disks]	1 =., "While You Were Out Install"
[needed.space]	minspace = 180000

```
[wywo.copy.wywostuff]          #wywo.main,   0:

[wywo.main]                    1:WYWO.EXE,        "WYWO.EXE"
                               1:WSETUP.EXE,      "WSETUP.EXE"
                               1:WMONITOR.EXE,    "WMONITOR.EXE"
                               1:WVERSION.DLL,    "WVERSION.DLL"
                               1:WYWO.HLP,        "WYWO.HLP"
                               1:WYWO.HST,        "WYWO.HST"
                               1:README.TXT,      "README.TXT
                               1:ORDER.FRM,       "ORDER.FRM"

[progman.groups]               "While You Were Out",WYWO.GRP

[While You Were Out]           "WYWO",            WYWO.EX
                               "WYWO Setup",      WSETUP.EX
                               "WYWO Monitor",    WMONITOR.EX
```

ORDER FORM

While You Were Out Commercial Version 3.0 Order Form

You can use this order form to order the commercial version 3.0 of WYWO For Windows. Order by mail, phone, fax, or CompuServe Email to one of the following:
CompuServe: 70324, 2055
VOICE: (203) 667-2159   FAX: (203) 667-2159 or (203) 665-7382
CUSTOMER BBS: (203) 667-2768   Call for the current release of WYWO!
Mail to: Caliente International
         Suite 201, 2596 Berlin Tpke.
         Newington, CT 06111

Caliente, send me:

While You Were Out For Windows – Version 3.0

_____ 5 User License(s)	@ $ 99.95 ea	$ _____
_____ 10 User License(s)	@ $ 199.95 ea	$ _____
_____ 20 User License(s)	@ $ 349.95 ea	$ _____
_____ 50 User License(s)	@ $ 750.00 ea	$ _____
_____ 100 User License(s)	@ $1,250.00 ea	$ _____

Larger-user licenses and unlimited-user licenses are available, please call.

→ 40% discount when ordered directly form Caliente International!

                                              – Discount $ _____
Floppy Disk Size: ( ) 5-1/4"   ( ) 3-1/2"   TOTAL $ _____

Payment by: ( ) CHECK (MAIL ONLY)   ( ) MC   ( ) VISA
Name_____
Company (ONLY if company address) _____
Address _____
_____
_____

Voice Phone _____   FAX _____
Card # _____   Exp. Date _____
Signature of cardholder _____

WSEND *(by Steve Goulet, GDG Systems)*

by Charles Rose

Windows SEND (WSEND) is a Windows version of the popular NetWare command-line utility, SEND. Normally, you would have to open a DOS window and type SEND "message," but with WSEND, you can send messages to any user on the network while in Windows.

WSEND.TXT

WINDOWS SEND Version 1.4b
by GDG Systems.
Release Date: February 25, 1991
Author: Steve Goulet

INTRODUCTION

Windows Send is a utility program designed to send broadcast messages to users or groups across a Netware LAN. It basically provides the same functionality as the DOS based SEND command provided by Novell Netware, except that it is designed to work under Microsoft Windows 3.0.

REQUIREMENTS

All that is required to run WINDOWS SEND is that you must be running Windows 3.0 or above and that you have a Novell Netware based LAN running Netware 2.1 or above.

INSTALLATION

Installation of WINDOWS SEND is very straightforward. The executable program WSEND.EXE (and its associated library WSENDDLL.DLL) must be copied somewhere in the DOS Path or in the current directory. To run the program, go to the 'File Run' option in the Program Manager menu and type WSEND.EXE in the dialog box.

You may decide to have WSEND.EXE executed automatically every time you start windows. To do this, edit your WIN.INI file and append the text 'WSEND.EXE' to the end of the line. If you wish, you can also add the WSEND.EXE icon to one of your program groups. Consult your DOS and WINDOWS manual for further details.

NOTE: If you are running WINDOWS on your Netware LAN, to receive broadcast messages, you must have the Netware drivers for WINDOWS properly installed and you must have NWPOPUP.EXE specified on the load line in your WIN.INI file.

INSIDE WINDOWS SEND

When WINDOWS SEND is loaded, it scans the network for all logged in users and all groups. These names go into a list box from which you can select the target of your message. The text of the message that you wish to send is to be typed into the first edit field on the screen.

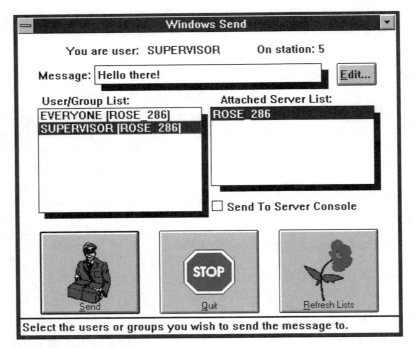

Figure 10.23 Window Send main screen.

Once you have entered your message and you wish to send it, press the SEND button. If you wish to close the WINDOWS SEND application, select the CLOSE button. It is assumed however, that most users will open WINDOWS SEND and leave it as an icon throughout their windows session. Because of this and the fact that other users may log into or log out of the network, the user/group combo list box may become out of date. If you wish to update your list, press the REFRESH LISTS button. We could have made rereading the list automatic but on some slower networks the delay in reading the user list can be as much as 15 seconds.

The other list box on the window shows you the servers that you are currently attached to. If you wish to send a message to a user who is logged into another network that your network is bridged to, you must attach to that network (consult you network administrator for details). When Windows Send is loaded or the REFRESH LISTS button is hit these attached networks are scanned and added to the list box. When you select a new attached network to send messages to, the userlist list box is automatically read and updated with users from that network.

ENHANCEMENTS

Version 1.4b incorporates coding changes which take advantage of the DOS Protected Mode Interface (DPMI) which allows WSEND to function properly in all three Windows modes, REAL STANDARD AND ENHANCED. This version also optimizes the functionality of the main "push buttons" and reduces flicker.

Version 1.3 of Windows SEND incorporates two major new features over previous versions. The first is that one can now select as many users or groups from the User/group list box or as many servers from the Servers list box as one wishes. This enables you to send one message to several people simultaneously. The other main feature is that messages can also be sent directly to, the server console. There are also a number of cosmetic changes.

REGISTRATION

WINDOWS SEND Version 1.4b is currently being marketed as shareware. Subsequent versions may NOT be available as shareware and the prices outlined below may not be valid for new releases. To obtain a registered single user copy and a valid registration number of WINDOWS SEND please send $20.00 per copy US funds ($15 plus $5.00 for shipping and handling) to:

GDG Systems
4451 PH Mathieu.
Lachenaie Qc
Canada
J6W 5L6

A single site license of WSEND is available for $200 US per server. This site license gives the owner the right to install WSEND on as many PC's as are attached to a SINGLE server. Multiple servers require multiple site licenses. (i.e., if your corporation has 3 Novell servers connected through bridges and you wished all users on all servers to get a copy of WSEND, this would cost $600 regardless of how many people are connected to each server).

Please make checks or money orders payable to GDG Systems. GDG Systems phone number is (514) 597-9755.

Steve Goulet can also be contacted via Compuserve at 72421,2733.

WSUPER *(by Wolfgang Schreiber)*

by Charles Rose
WSUPER is a handy tool that lets you switch supervisor equivalence on or off when needed. You might want to turn supervisor equivalence off for security reasons when you don't need to take advantage of your supervisory rights. This utility lets you manage that capability in Windows.

WSUPER.DOC

WSUPER.ZIP

Title: WSUPER.EXE: switch SUPERVISOR equivalence on/off
Keywords: SUPERVISOR EQUIVALENCE RIGHTS SECURITY UTILITY WINDOWS
Enhanced Windows version of the NetWare/DOS tool SUPER.ZIP (NetWire NovLib 16). WSUPER.EXE allows you to switch SV equivalence on/off when needed. Do your daily work as normal user, and be SV only when needed. No security gap, since you have to have SV equivalence before being able to switch it on/off. (Public domain by Wolfgang Schreiber)

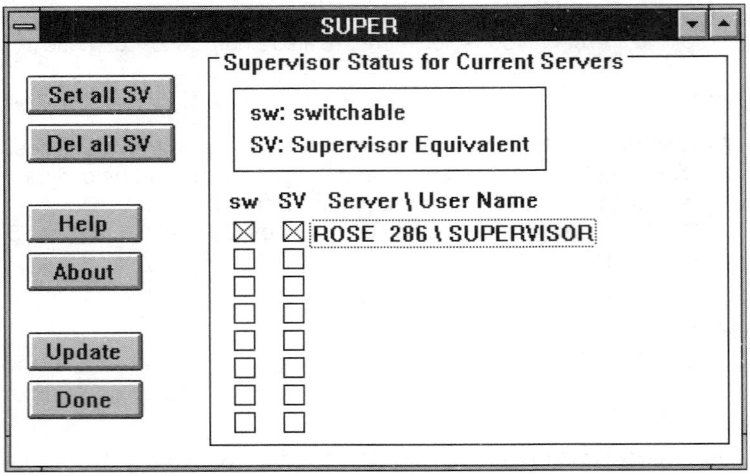

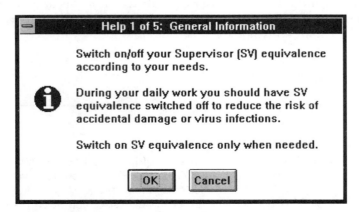

Figure 10.24 WSUPER Main window.

Background

"SUPER" can modify the security byte of your bindery property SECURITY_EQUALS to 0x22 (read/write object). This allows the user to change his/her own security equivalences. Then the Supervisor equivalence can be removed/added as needed.

SUPER allows a user who is Supervisor equivalent to do the daily work as normal user, while Supervisor equivalence is available when needed. This reduces the risk of accidental damage to files caused by viruses, carelessness, or unattended workstations.

The NetWare tool SECURITY.EXE will notice that the bindery access level is not set to default. This is intended.

This program was written by Wolfgang Schreiber in Borland's Turbo Pascal for Windows.

A DOS version is available on NetWire (NovLib 16) as SUPER.ZIP.

Figure 10.25 WSUPER Help screen #1.

ShowDots *(by Wolfgang Schrieber, SHOWDOTS.ZIP)*

by Charles Rose

ShowDots lets you toggle the NetWare shell's Show Dots parameter. The Show Dots parameter is necessary in Windows if you want to see the "." and ".." directory entries in Windows applications, such as in the Open File dialog box.

SHOWDOTS.DOC

The program SHOWDOTS.EXE

- can change the setting for the shell variable "SHOW DOTS" any time. Under Windows the setting should be 'ON'
- requires a shell version NET?.COM v3.01 or higher
- is available as a Windows or DOS program

ExpressIt! for Windows *(by Infinite Technologies)*

by Charles Rose

ExpressIt! for Windows is a powerful, MHS-compatible e-mail system for NetWare. Often compared to Word Perfect and Da Vinci's e-mail packages, ExpressIt! for Windows holds its own as a full-function e-mail system. Infinite also provides support and answers questions in their own section in the NOVVEN forum on CompuServe.

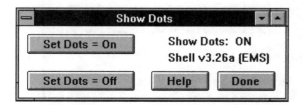

Figure 10.26 ShowDots Main Window.

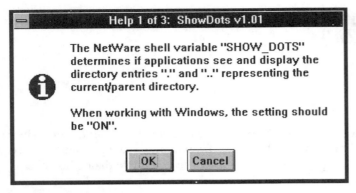

Figure 10.27 ShowDots Help screen #1.

ExpressIt! Files

This document describes and identifies the files shipped with ExpressIt!
ExpressIt! Windows Version (EXPWIN.ZIP):

EXPWINM.EXE   Executable Program for ExpressIt! Windows Version.

EXPWINM.HLP   Help file for ExpressIt! Windows Version.

Standard ExpressIt! Utility Programs (EXPDOS.ZIP, EXPWIN.ZIP & EXPUTL.ZIP):

FAKEMHS.EXE   Utility to create the standard MHS directory structure, allowing ExpressIt! to run without MHS installed.

EXINSTAL.EXE   Program to initialize the 30-day "counter" for the ExpressIt! 30-day trial version.

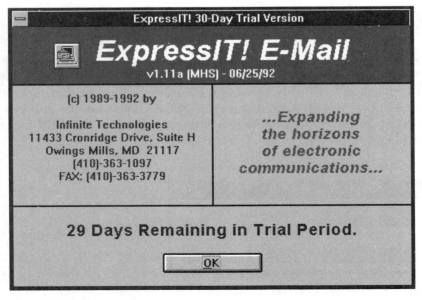

Figure 10.28 ExpressIT! opening window.

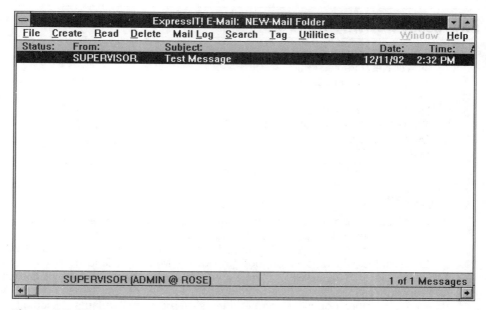

Figure 10.29 ExpressIt! main window.

REGEX.EXE — Utility to define ExpressIt!'s MHS Application code, POSTMAST, to MHS. (Only necessary if you will be manually defining your users to MHS via the MHS Directory Manager.)

EXSETUP.EXE — Utility to automatically define all NetWare users to the MHS Directory Manager. EXSETUP should be run after adding/deleting any users to/from the NetWare bindery.

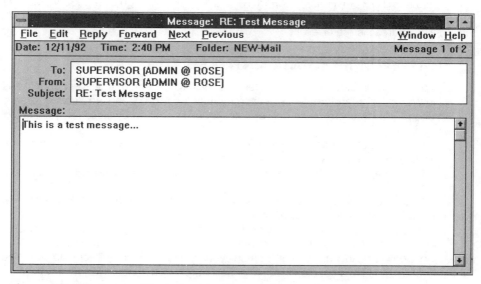

Figure 10.30 ExpressIT! window showing received mail.

ExpressIt! Documentation

ExpressIt! Electronic Mail
(Novell NetWare Version)
30 Day Evaluation Copy
User's Guide
Infinite Technologies
11433 Cronridge Drive, Suite H
Owings Mills, MD 21117
(410)-363-1097
FAX: (410)-363-3779

OVERVIEW

ExpressIt! Electronic Mail is a comprehensive electronic mail system for your Novell NetWare network that runs in less than 2KB of resident workstation memory. (As low as 0 bytes overhead on properly configured 386-based PCs!) A Windows version is also available.

ExpressIt! provides native support for Novell's Message Handling Service (MHS). While MHS is *NOT REQUIRED* to run ExpressIt!, MHS enhances ExpressIt! by offering delivery services facilitating dial-in/dial-out communications, as well as connectivity via gateways to other popular electronic mail systems and standards, including CompuServe, X.400, SMTP, MCIMail and popular mainframe and minicomputer based electronic mail systems.

In addition to the network version of ExpressIt! e-mail, Infinite Technologies offers ExpressIt!ExpressIt! Remote to provide dial-in access to MHS-based e-mail from your notebook, laptop, or home PC.

This 30-day trial version of ExpressIt! is designed to allow you to get a feel for ExpressIt! before you buy it. The trial version includes all features of the commercial version of ExpressIt!, with the exception of limited documentation.

If you have *any* questions while evaluating ExpressIt!, please do not hesitate to contact Infinite Technologies for support. Call us at 410-363-1097, or send e-mail through MHS (CSERVE or NHUB) to SUPPORT @ INFINITE. Through CompuServe Mail, send a message to >MHS:SUPPORT @ INFINITE or 73270,405. (The >MHS:SUPPORT @ INFINITE address is preferred.)

OVERVIEW OF THE INSTALLATION PROCESS

ExpressIt! is an Electronic Mail system that bases its method of delivery upon the Novell NetWare MHS Standard. MHS, an acronym for Message Handling Service, is an e-mail transport mechanism which delivers messages submitted by files in a specific location and format.

For local delivery of e-mail, ExpressIt! does not rely on MHS, but performs its local delivery by using the MHS directory structure and file formats.

It is because of this capability that ExpressIt! can be used with or without MHS installed.

If you are *only* communicating with users on a Local Area Network, you can use this version of ExpressIt! as it is, without MHS.

If you need to communicate with other hosts or gateway processes, you will probably need to install MHS as a transport mechanism. If you do not currently own a copy of MHS and would like to purchase it, contact your dealer or Infinite Technologies. You can purchase MHS at a special discount price if purchased bundled together with ExpressIt!

RELATED ZIP FILES (if downloaded from CompuServe):

XPRESS.ZIP	Complete 30-day trial version of ExpressIt! for DOS and Windows plus related utilities. (includes all files in EXPDOS.ZIP, EXPWIN.ZIP and EXPUTL.ZIP)
EXPDOS.ZIP	30-day trial version of ExpressIt! DOS Version
EXPWIN.ZIP	30-day trial version of ExpressIt! Windows Version
EXPUTL.ZIP	Utility programs for ExpressIt!

INSTALLING EXPRESSIT! IN THE NOVELL NETWARE ENVIRONMENT *WITHOUT* MHS

INSTRUCTIONS IF YOU ARE INSTALLING THE EXPRESSIT! 30-DAY TRIAL VERSION *WITHOUT MHS* (or if you will be installing MHS at a later time)

IMPORTANT: PLEASE print out this document and read these instructions through once very carefully before attempting the actual installation procedure. As you perform the installation, check each box after each step has been successfully completed.

☐ 1. These procedures assume that you will not be running Novell's MHS at this time. If you are installing or have already installed MHS, proceed to the next section.

☐ 2. Sign on to your file server as SUPERVISOR or a SUPERVISOR equivalent.

☐ 3. Creating the MHS Directory Structure (FAKEMHS)
We need to create the directory structure that MHS would normally do for us. Execute the FAKEMHS.EXE program that is in the \EXPRESS.IT!\UTILS directory of your distribution disk.

FAKEMHS will:

☐ a. Ask you for the name of the NetWare Volume on which to install the "fake" MHS directory Structure. On most systems, this will be SYS: but if you have more than one NetWare Volume you may want to consult with your Network Supervisor for the appropriate Volume ID.

☐ b. Ask you for the "fake" MHS host name. You will be shown the name of your NetWare file server, and in most instances this will be acceptable. If you would like to use a different name, enter it now.
MHS Host Names are limited to 8 characters or less.

☐ c. After creating all files and directories, FAKEMHS will display the MV setting that you will need to include in your system login script. Copy this statement accurately.

EXAMPLE: DOS SET MV="FS/SYS:\\"

Where FS is the name of your file server, and SYS: is the name of the NetWare Volume you entered in step 2) above.

☐ d. The environmental variable MV (Master Volume) is used by ExpressIt! to locate the "fake" MHS directories and related files. This variable must be set to use ExpressIt!
Verify that the two settings above are set correctly by logging in to your network after these changes have been made.

☐ 4. Execute EXINSTAL.EXE from the \EXPRESS.IT!\UTILS directory of your installation diskette. This program initializes ExpressIt! to your file server.

☐ 5. Copy the following ExpressIt! user programs from the \EXPRESS.IT!\DOS directory on the ExpressIt! distribution diskette to SYS:PUBLIC (or other appropriate directory) on your file server:

EXPRESSM.COM, EXPRESSM.OVR, EXPRESSM.HLP, EXPSWAP.OVR and CHKMHS.COM.

☐ 6. If you wish to use ExpressIt! Windows, copy the following user programs from the \EXPRESS.IT!\WINDOWS directory on the ExpressIt! distribution diskette to SYS:PUBLIC (or other appropriate directory) on your file server:

EXPWINM.EXE and EXPWINM.HLP

☐ 7. Copy the following ExpressIt! supervisor programs from the \EXPRESS.IT!\UTILS directory on the distribution diskette to the MHS\EXE (or other appropriate) directory:

EXSETUP.EXE and REGEX.EXE

EXNICNAM.EXE, EXMHSNAM.EXE, EXNOMHS.EXE, MAILRITE.EXE and EX

CLEAN.EXE (included in XPRESS.ZIP & EXPUTL.ZIP)

☐ 8. To define *ALL* of your NetWare users to ExpressIt!, we will be using an ExpressIt! utility called EXSETUP.EXE.

☐ a. EXSETUP will be copying the USER NAME and the FULL NAME from your NetWare configuration into your e-mail setup, so review your NetWare Users and check each user's full name with SYSCON before running EXSETUP.

☐ b. If you need to limit which users will be defined to ExpressIt!, use the NetWare SYSCON utility and edit the FULL NAME field for each user that will NOT be defined to ExpressIt! so that the first character of the name is a period.

EXAMPLE: user: BACKUP

fullname: .Tape Backup Operator

☐ c. Execute EXSETUP, which will:

1. Define ExpressIt!'s application code of POSTMAST to MHS or the "fake" MHS.
2. Copy all user information from your NetWare bindery into the e-mail user directory. If you are using MHS, EXSETUP will eliminate the need to manually add users with the MHS Directory Manager.
3. Convert NetWare users into e-mail user names. If you have user names that are longer than 8 characters or names that contain invalid characters, you will be prompted for alternate names.
4. Convert NetWare groups into public ExpressIt! mailing lists. If group names are over 8 characters in length, or contain invalid characters, you will be prompted for an alternate mailing list name.

NOTE: As you add, modify, and delete users from your network, you will need to run EXSETUP to keep the e-mail directory and the NetWare bindery synchronized.

5. Prompt for the installation of ExpressIt!'s Directory Assistant, which allows on-line access to user lists from other hosts running ExpressIt! and Directory Assistant.
SINCE YOU ARE NOT USING MHS, ANSWER NO TO THIS QUESTION.

INSTALLING EXPRESSIT! IN THE NOVELL NETWARE ENVIRONMENT *WITH* MHS

INSTRUCTIONS IF YOU ARE NOT INSTALLING THE EXPRESSIT! 30-DAY TRIAL VERSION *WITH MHS*

IMPORTANT: PLEASE print out this document and read these instructions through once very carefully before attempting the actual installation procedure. As you perform the installation, check each box after each step has been successfully completed.

☐ 1. Sign on to your file server as SUPERVISOR or a SUPERVISOR equivalent.

☐ 2. IF YOU NEED TO INSTALL MHS:
If you have not already installed NetWare MHS, do so now following the instructions provided in Novell's MHS Installation and Operations Guide.

☐ a. Installing MHS will create an \MHS directory structure and modify the NetWare System Login Script to include the following statements:

MAP INS S1:=FS/SYS:MHS\EXE
DOS SET MV="FS/SYS:\\"

Where FS is the name of your file server.
The \MHS\EXE directory is included in the search path as this is where the executable portions of MHS are stored.
The environmental variable MV (Master Volume) is used by both ExpressIt! and NetWare MHS to locate the MHS directories and related files. This variable must be set to use ExpressIt!

☐ b. Verify that the two settings above are set correctly by logging in to your network after these changes have been made.

☐ c. Execute MHS and establish a name for your hub, as outlined in the MHS Installation and Operations Guide.

NOTE: DO NOT define your users to MHS at this time. (ExpressIt! includes the EXSETUP utility which will automate this process.)

☐ 3. Execute EXINSTAL.EXE from the \EXPRESS.IT!\UTILS directory of your installation diskette. This program initializes ExpressIt! to your file server.

☐ 4. MHSNotify for notification of incoming remote e-mail: (included in XPRESS.ZIP, EXPUTL.ZIP & MHSNFY.ZIP)
The Infinite Technologies MHS Demo Diskette includes a copy of our MHS Notify! utility, which is a TSR that should be loaded before MHS on the MHS mail server only to notify users of incoming MHS mail. When e-Mail comes in remotely, or across an internetwork connection, MHS does not notify the user. MHS Notify! sends a broadcast message to notify users of incoming e-mail.

☐ a. Copy MHSNOTFY.COM from the \MHSNOTFY directory on the MHS Demo diskette to the MHS\EXE directory.

☐ b. Execute MNINSTAL.EXE from the \MHSNOTFY directory on the MHS Demo diskette.

☐ c. Create a STARTMHS.BAT file that gets run each time you load MHS that includes these commands:

MHSNOTFY
MHS
MHSNOTFY /U

NOTE: The /U parameter uninstalls MHSNOTFY. For additional information regarding MHS Notify! please refer to the MHSNOTFY.DOC file on the MHS Demo Diskette.

☐ 5. Copy the following ExpressIt! user programs from the \EXPRESS.IT!\DOS directory on the ExpressIt! distribution diskette to SYS:PUBLIC (or other appropriate directory) on your file server:

EXPRESSM.COM, EXPRESSM.OVR, EXPRESSM.HLP, EXPSWAP.OVR and CHKMHS.COM.

☐ 6. If you wish to use ExpressIt! Windows, copy the following user programs from the \EXPRESS.IT!\WINDOWS directory on the ExpressIt! distribution diskette to SYS:PUBLIC (or other appropriate directory) on your file server:

EXPWINM.EXE and EXPWINM.HLP

☐ 7. Copy the following ExpressIt! supervisor programs from the \EXPRESS.IT!\UTILS directory on the distribution diskette to the MHS\EXE (or other appropriate) directory:

EXSETUP.EXE, REGEX.EXE, EXNICNAM.EXE, EXMHSNAM.EXE, EX-NOMHS.EXE, MAILRITE.EXE, and EXCLEAN.EXE

☐ 8. EXDA for exchanging user directories between sites (optional): (included in XPRESS.ZIP and EXPUTL.ZIP)
Copy the following ExpressIt! Directory Assistant utilities from the \EX-PRESS.IT!\UTILS directory on the distribution diskette to the MHS\EXE (or other appropriate) directory:

EXDA.EXE, EXDALV1.EXE, EXDALV2.EXE, NOEXDA.EXE, SHOWEXDA.EXE.

☐ 9. IF MHS HAD PREVIOUSLY BEEN INSTALLED AND YOU WANT TO DEFINE ONLY A FEW USERS TO EXPRESSIT!:

☐ a. Run the REGEX.EXE utility from the \MHS\EXE directory. REGEX defines "POSTM-AST" as a valid application.

☐ b. Use the MHS Directory Manager to define ExpressIt! users with the application code POSTMAST.

☐ 10. IF YOU ARE NOT USING MHS, OR THIS IS A NEW INSTALLATION WITH MHS:
To define *ALL* of your NetWare users to ExpressIt!, we will be using an ExpressIt! utility called EXSETUP.EXE.

☐ a. EXSETUP will be copying the USER NAME and the FULL NAME from your NetWare configuration into your e-mail setup, so review your NetWare Users and check each user's full name with SYSCON before running EXSETUP.

☐ b. If you need to limit which users will be defined to ExpressIt!, use the NetWare SYSCON utility and edit the FULL NAME field for each user that will NOT be defined to ExpressIt! so that the first character of the name is a period. EXAMPLE: user: BACKUP
                    fullname: .Tape Backup Operator

☐ c. Execute EXSETUP, which will:
   1. Define ExpressIt!'s application code of POSTMAST to MHS or the "fake" MHS.
   2. Copy all user information from your NetWare bindery into the e-mail user directory. If you are using MHS, EXSETUP will eliminate the need to manually add users with the MHS Directory Manager.

3. Convert NetWare users into e-mail user names. If you have user names that are longer than 8 characters or names that contain invalid characters, you will be prompted for alternate names.

4. Convert NetWare groups into public ExpressIt! mailing lists. If group names are over 8 characters in length, or contain invalid characters, you will be prompted for an alternate mailing list name.

NOTE: As you add, modify, and delete users from your network, you will need to run EXSETUP to keep the e-mail directory and the NetWare bindery synchronized.

5. Prompt for the installation of ExpressIt!'s Directory Assistant, which allows on-line access to user lists from other hosts running ExpressIt! and Directory Assistant. Call Infinite Technologies for additional information if you are considering using this facility during your trial period.
EXDA.EXE, the Directory Assistant gateway is included in the XPRESS.ZIP and EXPUTL.ZIP files.

LOADING EXPRESSIT! (DOS Version)

To load ExpressIt! into memory, simply type EXPRESSM [ENTER]. When ExpressIt! is executed, ExpressIt! checks to see if you have any unread mail waiting for you. If so, the ExpressIt! main menu is displayed. New messages are marked with NEW at the right hand side of the screen. If no new mail is waiting, or when you press [ESC] from the main menu, ExpressIt! is loaded into resident memory.

ExpressIt! will display the version number, memory management technique used, conventional memory usage, and the hot-key.

AN IMPORTANT NOTE: ExpressIt!, like other memory-resident programs, should not be loaded via the NetWare System Login Script. It is recommended that a batch file be created to execute ExpressIt! as well as any other TSR after the System Login Script is completed (for example using the Login Script EXIT "BATCHFIL" command). ExpressIt! should then be un-installed from memory (EXPRESSM /U) when the user logs out. This, too, can be done via a batch file.

If setting up batch files is inconvenient, ExpressIt! can be loaded in a workstation's AUTOEXEC.BAT file. A small utility, CHKMHS.COM, which is included with ExpressIt!, can be executed from the System Login Script to check for new mail. When CHKMHS is executed, if new mail is waiting, CHKMHS will pop-up the resident portion of ExpressIt!. Since CHKMHS itself is not a memory resident program, it may be safely executed from the System Login Script.

For notification of new mail, ExpressIt! uses the NetWare message broadcast facility (e.g., SEND command). The commercial version of ExpressIt! ships with a companion utility, CastAway!, which provides for a non-intrusive new mail notification. CAST-AWAY.COM, if used, should be loaded into memory before EXPRESSM.COM. (CAST-AWAY.COM is included in XPRESS.ZIP, EXPUTL.ZIP & CASTAW.ZIP.)

LOADING EXPRESSIT! (Windows Version)

For best results, we recommend that you configure Windows to automatically load ExpressIt! when Windows is started. This can be done by including EXPWINM.EXE in the "load=" statement of your WIN.INI file (e.g., load=EXPWINM.EXE).

When configured in this manner, ExpressIt! will check to see if you have any new unread mail waiting for you when Windows loads, and will "pop-up" over the program manager if any new mail is waiting.

It is also recommended that the NetWare Windows Message Broadcast Utility (NWPOPUP.EXE), also be included in the WIN.INI "load=" statement, as NetWare broadcasts are used to notify recipients of new mail.

COMMAND-LINE PARAMETERS (DOS)

To control certain aspects of ExpressIt!'s operation, you can specify command-line parameters when loading ExpressIt! A list of command-line parameters include:

/U	Un-installs (or unloads) ExpressIt! from resident memory.
/NR	Runs ExpressIt! in non-resident mode. This is the preferred way to run ExpressIt! under multi-tasking environments such as Quarterdeck's DesqView, Microsoft Windows, or Software Carousel. A Windows version of ExpressIt! is available from your dealer.
/NE	Tells ExpressIt! not to use expanded memory.
/NX	Tells ExpressIt! not to use extended memory.
/ND	Tells ExpressIt! not to use disk overlays.
/D	Tells ExpressIt! to ignore expanded and extended memory and use a disk overlay.
/NU	Tells ExpressIt! not to use "upper" memory blocks (memory between 640KB and 1MB) provided by 80386 based memory managers like QEMM and 386-to-the-MAX.
/Q	Loads ExpressIt! "quietly" and does not check for new mail. By default, if new mail is waiting, ExpressIt! will pop-up when loading. This parameter skips the check for new mail.

ENVIRONMENT VARIABLES (DOS)

ExpressIt! also recognizes several DOS environment variables to configure different modes of operation. Environment variables are set using the DOS SET command from the DOS command prompt or a batch file (e.g., SET VARIABLE=VALUE).

COLOR=MONO. Tells ExpressIt! to format its screen displays in black and white (monochrome). While ExpressIt! can usually detect the display mode and act accordingly, this setting may be necessary for some composite monitors and laptop PCs.

VGASAVE=OFF. When ExpressIt! is popped up over a graphics display, it will make every effort to restore the screen cleanly upon exit. However, one technique that is used to save and restore the state of the VGA adapter is not properly supported by all third party VGA adapters. Should you encounter a situation where the video display is "corrupted" when popping up ExpressIt! or exiting ExpressIt!, try placing SET VGASAVE=OFF in your AUTOEXEC.BAT file.

EXLPT=LPTx. Allows you to redirect message printouts from ExpressIt! to a device other than LPT1. Simply replace LPTx with a valid DOS device or filename.

EXDEFDIR=DRIVE:\DIRECTORY. Specifies a default directory path to be used for attached files and ASCII file import and export.

EXADDRBOOK=Address Book. Specifies the default address book to display when entering the mailing list screen.

EXSORT=USER or FULL. Default sort order for user lists, sort by user name or by full name.

MHS11=TRUE. ExpressIt! will send mail in MHS 1.1 format, even if a later version of MHS is detected as present.

EXENHKB=OFF. Disables ExpressIt!'s use of enhanced keyboard function calls, even if an enhanced keyboard is detected. Use this option if your keyboard is dead when you pop-up ExpressIt!

EXMBOX=ALT [or EXMBOX=d:\path]. Normally, ExpressIt! stores messages in the Novell MAIL directories.

EXMBOX=ALT tells ExpressIt! to store messages in an EXMBOX directory underneath of the MHS\MAIL\USERS\USERNAME directory structure.

EXMBOX=d:\path tells ExpressIt! to store messages in a user subdirectory underneath of d:\path.

EXVIDEO=BIOS. This option tells ExpressIt! to display screen output through PC BIOS function calls rather than writing directly to video output. If your monitor displays snow while running ExpressIt!, try setting this option.

EXHOSTPROMPT=NO. Disables the "route via preferred hub" option when a user sends a message to a host that has not been defined to MHS.

EXFULLNAMESORT=NONE. Disables the last,first name parsing in the address book screens.

EXPRESSIT! NOVELL NETWORK ONLY SETTINGS

EXSEND=NO. ExpressIT! will not use the NetWare message broadcast facility (e.g., SEND) for new mail notification.

EXPRESSIT! REMOTE AND NON-NOVELL NETWORK ONLY SETTINGS

USR=username. ExpressIt! will attempt to read the current user name from the network. Setting the USR variable will override this setting.

PWD=password. Specifies the MHS password to go with the USR setting above.

EXMHSHUB=ON. This option tells the non-Novell Network version of ExpressIt! to include a main menu option of F10 to run MHS.

CHANGING THE EXPRESSIT! HOTKEY (DOS)

Command line parameters can be used to change the ExpressIt! default hot-key if [ALT+M] conflicts with a hot-key used by another application. However, ExpressIt! can use a combination of [ALT] or [CTRL] and any alphabetic key, [A] through [Z] or function key, [F1] through [F12] as its hot-key.

The hot-key can be specified when ExpressIt! is loaded, and changed at any time by re-executing ExpressIt!, followed by any of the following:

#	Tells ExpressIt! to use [CTRL] instead of [ALT] in the hot-key.
%	Tells ExpressIt! to use [CTRL][ALT] instead of just [ALT] in the hot-key.
&	Tells ExpressIt! to use [CTRL][LEFT SHIFT] instead of [ALT] in the hot-key.
!	Tells ExpressIt! to use [ALT][LEFT SHIFT] instead of [ALT] in the hot-key.
A–Z	Any alphabetic character from [A] to [Z] can be specified to work in conjunction with [ALT] or [CTRL] in the hot-key.
Fxx	Any function key [F1]-[F12] can be specified to work in conjunction with [ALT] or [CTRL] in the hot-key.

Examples:

EXPRESSM	defaults to the [ALT]-[M] hot-key, or if ExpressIt! has already been loaded, the hot-key is not changed.
EXPRESSM X	tells ExpressIt! to use [ALT]-[X] as its hot-key.
EXPRESSM #Z	tells ExpressIt! to use [CTRL]-[Z] as its hot-key.
EXPRESSM F12	tells ExpressIt! to use [ALT]-[F12] as its hot-key.
EXPRESSM %F5	tells ExpressIt! to use [CTRL]-[ALT][F5] as its hot-key.
EXPRESSM &Z	tells ExpressIt! to use [CTRL]-[LEFT SHIFT]-[Z] as its hot-key.

NOTE: Because the "%" symbol is interpreted specially in DOS batch files, use %% instead, for example: EXPRESSM %%F5.

EXPRESSIT! QUICK REFERENCE

Main Menu Function Keys

[UP ARROW]	Previous Message
[DN ARROW]	Next Message
[PG UP]	Previous Screen of Messages
[PG DN]	Next Screen of Messages
[HOME]	First Message
[END]	Last Message
[ENTER]	Read Message
[DEL]	Delete this message
[F1]	Help
[F2]	Create Message
[F8]	View Mail Log
[F9]	Utilities

Reading Messages

[DEL]	Delete Message
[F1]	Help
[F3]	Reply to Message
[F4]	Forward Message
[F6]	Receive Attached File
[F9]	Message Utilities
[ESC]	Return to Main Menu
[UP ARROW]	Go to previous line
[DN ARROW]	Go to Next Line
[PG UP]	Previous Page of Message
[PG DN]	Next Page of Message
[PRTSC]	Print Message

[–]	Display Previous Message
[+]	Display Next Message

Message Editing Keys

[LEFT]	Move One Character Left
[RIGHT]	Move One Character Right
[CTRL]-[LEFT]	Move One Word Left
[CTRL]-[RIGHT]	Move One Word Right
[UP ARROW]	Move Up One Line
[DN ARROW]	Move Down One Line
[PG UP]	Move to Previous Page
[PG DN]	Move to Next Page
[CTRL]-[PG UP]	Move to First Line
[CTRL]-[PG DN]	Move to Last Line
[HOME]	Move to Beginning of Line
[END]	Move to End of Line
[TAB]	Move To Next Line
[INS]	Turn Insert On or Off
[DEL]	Delete this Character
[BACKSPACE]	Delete Character Backwards
[CTRL]-[END]	Delete to end of this line
[F6]	Attach a File
[F9]	File Utilities
[F10]	Send this Message
[ALT]-[F10]	Send Message Registered
[ESC]	Abort this Message

Cut & Paste

ExpressIt! allows you to move, delete and copy text by providing special keys to cut and paste.

To Cut or Copy text, you must first mark the text, then either cut or copy the text. Once you have cut or copied the area of the message, ExpressIt! will place the text in it's clipboard, from which you can paste the text into another area of the message ... or even another message.

[SHIFT]-[DN ARROW]	Mark the current line of text
[SHIFT]-[UP ARROW]	Mark the previous line of text
[SHIFT]-[CTRL]-[LEFT]	Mark the word to the left
[SHIFT]-[CTRL]-[RIGHT]	Mark the word to the right
[SHIFT]-[HOME]	Mark to beginning of line
[SHIFT]-[END]	Mark to end of line
[SHIFT]-[LEFT/RIGHT]	Mark character

[SHIFT]-[CTRL]-[PG UP]	Mark to beginning of message
[SHIFT]-[CTRL]-[PG DN]	Mark to end of message
[CTRL]-[INS]	Copy marked text
[SHIFT]-[DEL]	Delete text, and copy to clipboard
[SHIFT]-[INS]	Paste clipboard text into message
[DEL]	Delete marked text only

EXPRESSIT! UTILITIES

ExpressIt! includes several utility programs for different purposes.

CastAway!

CastAway! is a memory resident utility that when loaded prior to ExpressIt!, provides for unobtrusive notification of new mail. Try it, you'll like it...refer to CASTAWAY.DOC for more information.

MAILRITE

MAILRITE is a utility for the NetWare environment to ensure that all users have the appropriate rights to send and receive ExpressIt! e-Mail.

It ensures that the group EVERYONE has WOC (or WC under NetWare 386) rights to the SYS:MAIL directory, so that they can send mail, and additionally ensures that all users have NetWare mailboxes, and rights to read and delete files from their own mailbox.

EXCLEAN

EXCLEAN is a utility for the NetWare environment that is intended to clean up stray temporary files, and reclaim disk space used up by mailboxes which are not in use. In most environments, EXCLEAN should be run once a month, or possibly more often as part of a backup procedure.

EXCLEAN performs one other important diagnostic function. Users upgrading from NetWare 286 to NetWare 386 may experience random mailbox errors several weeks after their upgrade. EXCLEAN corrects the situation that causes this problem.

COMPATIBILITY NOTES

ExpressIt! automatically detects most monitor configurations to determine whether to format displays as color or monochrome. However the following details potential problems and resolutions when using ExpressIt! with certain video combinations:

IBM 8514/A Display Adapter (PS/2)

The PS/2 BIOS incorrectly identifies this adapter/monitor combination as a VGA monochrome monitor. Reading this information, ExpressIt! will format the display as monochrome. As this is a BIOS problem, other applications, most notably Microsoft Word 5.0, will also experience this problem. On workstations equipped with this combination, the program 8514FIX.COM on the ExpressIt! distribution diskettes should be added to the workstation AUTOEXEC.BAT file. 8514FIX.COM is not a memory-resident program.

Composite Monitors

Composite Monitors are monochrome monitors connected to color graphic adapters. ExpressIt! will in many instances identify these monitors as color monitors. To override this automatic video detection, add the command SET COLOR=MONO to the workstation

AUTOEXEC.BAT file. When loaded, ExpressIt! scans the DOS environment for this setting. When set, ExpressIt! will always format the display as monochrome.

Popping up over EGA & VGA Graphics

ExpressIt! will pop-up over EGA & VGA graphics modes. However, on EGA equipped systems, upon returning to your application, the screen colors may be completely changed. In the case of Lotus 1-2-3 Release 3, the color may change from white on a black background to black on an orange or brown background. To prevent this problem, the program EGAFIX.COM on the ExpressIt! distribution diskettes should be added to the workstation AUTOEXEC.BAT file. EGAFIX.COM is a memory-resident program and will take approximately 500 bytes of workstation memory.

EGAFIX can also be used with other memory-resident programs to prevent similar screen discoloration with either EGA or VGA monitors.

VGA Screen Blanks or Is Corrupted

When ExpressIt! is popped up over a graphics display, it will make every effort to restore the screen cleanly upon exit. However, one technique that is used to save and restore the state of the VGA adapter is not properly supported by all third party VGA adapters. Should you encounter a situation where the video display is "corrupted" when popping up ExpressIt! or exiting ExpressIt!, try placing SET VGASAVE=OFF in your AUTOEXEC.BAT file.

PRODUCTS FROM INFINITE TECHNOLOGIES

Infinite Technologies offers innovative and easy-to-use software solutions, designed primarily for the networked environment.

We back our products with dependable service and special attention to individual requirements. All of our programs are easy to learn and use, and are designed to increase your efficiency.

We also want to help keep you up-to-date with product information and updates. You can do this by subscribing to our MHS Librarian! mailing list.

To join, send a message via MHS (CSERVE or NHUB) to LIBRARY @ INFINITE with SUBSCRIBE on your subject line. (CompuServe users can send a message to MHS:Library@Infinite via CompuServe Mail.)

We also anticipate opening a section in the PCVEN forum area of CompuServe in the near future.

NETWORK UTILITIES

- I-Queue! - Simplifies network printing and print queue management in the Novell NetWare environment. From within a small memory resident popup (0 to 2-1/2KB), I-Queue! allows users to easily change NetWare print queues and modify "capture" parameters. I-Queue! is compatible with Novell's PRINTCON/PRINTDEF and adds global PRINTCON support for Novell's own utilities. Queue management capabilities include: delete/reorder print jobs, move/copy jobs between queues, and hold/delayed printing. Now includes a Windows version!

- CastAway! - A better NetWare broadcast message trap. Get NetWare message notification (e.g., SEND) without your PC locking up until you press CTRL-ENTER! Get notified of new messages while in graphics based applications! All in 0 to 1-1/2KB of conventional memory!

- PopIT! - Gain pop-up access to almost ANY program with less than 2-1/2 KB overhead. Network administrators — access SYSCON, RCONSOLE, FCONSOLE and all of your favorite network utilities without leaving your current application.

- OnCall! - A memory resident "Chat" utility for Novell NetWare, that runs in between 0 and 2-1/2 KB of workstation memory. Simple, straightforward, and easy to use.

EXPRESSIT! ELECTRONIC MAIL

ExpressIt! Electronic Mail -The ExpressIt! Electronic Mail product family includes the following products:

- ExpressIt! - The network version of ExpressIt!, including the MHS-compatible DOS version, which runs in less than 2KB of resident memory.

- ExpressIt! Remote - A remote version of ExpressIt! (DOS) customized for use on stand-alone/remote PCs. Includes Personal MHS and allows users to send and receive mail with any MHS-based electronic mail system. Includes the ability to run the MHS Connectivity Manager from within the 2KB TSR without exiting your current application.

- ExpressIt! Windows Client - An upgrade for the network version of ExpressIt! offering native support for the Microsoft Windows environment, and a wealth of additional features.

- ExpressIt! Remote Windows - A remote version of the Windows version of ExpressIt! customized for use on stand-alone/remote PCs. Includes Personal MHS and allows users to send and receive mail with any MHS-based electronic mail system.

A special Windows-based MHS configuration utility eliminates the need to use the MHS Directory Manager.

All versions of ExpressIt! include ExpressIt! Directory Assistance, facilitating automatic exchange of user directories between ExpressIt! hosts.

MHS GATEWAYS AND UTILITIES

- MHS Scheduler - An MHS mail agent that provides greater flexibility in configuring when MHS will connect to a host. On a host-by-host basis, the MHS administrator can configure different frequencies of forced connections based on different times of the day, with separate weekday, weekend, and holiday scheduling possible. MHS gateways and internetwork connections can also be scheduled. The companion RunIT! utility simplifies the creation of batch file gateways...now you can run your tape backup system on your MHS server.

- MHS Librarian! - An MHS Gateway that allows users to request information to be forwarded to them via MHS. Requests are made by placing a keyword in the "SUBJECT" field of the message that you address to the library. A list of files may be requested by sending a message with the keyword of INDEX. The system Admin can also configure MHS Librarian so that selected users can request files or directories other than those that appear in the index. Security is provided by a password program that generates unique daily passwords, a fixed password, or you can create your own password utility.

MHS Librarian! also supports "discussion lists," similar to the "list server" concept on the internet.

- PageIT! - An MHS gateway connecting MHS-based electronic mail systems to full text alphanumeric pagers. Once configured, sending messages to an alphanumeric pager is as simple as sending a message from your favorite MHS application.

- ForwardIT! - An MHS mail agent for automatically forwarding MHS-based electronic mail messages. ForwardIT! can forward (or copy) messages addressed to an MHS address to an alternate address.

ForwardIT! is most useful in the MHS remote e-mail environment. By remote, we refer to field workers or business travelers who operate ExpressIt! Remote, or other MHS compatible remote software, on a PC or laptop to access their electronic mail from a distant location. Examples could include a salesperson between sales calls, a business traveler in a hotel room, or work-at-home scenarios.

Without ForwardIT!, when mail is sent to a recipient's office address, MHS does not allow for a remote user to dial into the network and retrieve mail waiting at their office address. Mail addressed to this office address can only be picked up at the office.

In order to send a message to the user's MHS remote, the sender must assume responsibility for sending a copy of the message to the remote MHS address.

With ForwardIT!, the user leaves a forwarding address at the office, and while they're out, all messages will be forwarded, or copied, to their forwarding address, giving users transparent access to their electronic mail while away from the office.

This forwarding address can be any valid MHS address, including addresses via MHS gateways.

- MhsQ! - An MHS gateway interface to NetWare print queues. Messages can be sent via MHS to a NetWare print queue. This capability can be useful for MHS remote sites and/or MHS enabled applications for generating printed output and/or reports.

MhsQ! can also redirect print queues on one file server to a remote print queue on another file server via MHS.

- MHSNotify! - A TSR which runs on the MHS mail server only, and automatically notifies recipients of new electronic mail received from remote MHS sites, or across internetwork connections. An excellent alternative to MHSALERT for DaVinci e-mail users! (MHSNotify! is bundled with ExpressIt!)

REQUESTING TRIAL VERSIONS VIA MHS

30-Day Trial Versions of many Infinite Technologies Products can be requested via MHS. For more information, send an MHS message to LIBRARY @ INFINITE via CSERVE or NHUB, with a subject line of INDEX.

DOWNLOADING TRIAL VERSIONS FROM COMPUSERVE

30-Day Trial Versions of many Infinite Technologies Products are available on Compu-Serve! Look for the following files in the NOVLIB Forum, Library 15 or 17:

XPRESS.ZIP	ExpressIt! Electronic Mail (NetWare) (DOS and Windows versions combined)
EXPDOS.ZIP	ExpressIt! Electronic Mail (NetWare) (DOS Version)
EXPWIN.ZIP	ExpressIt! Electronic Mail (NetWare) (Windows Version)
XPRES2.ZIP	ExpressIt! Electronic Mail (Remote & non-NetWare) (DOS and Windows versions combined)
POPIT.ZIP	PopIT!
ONCALL.ZIP	OnCall!
CASTAW.ZIP	CastAway!
IQUEUE.ZIP	I-Queue!
MHSCED.ZIP	MHS Scheduler
PAGEIT.ZIP	PageIT!
4WARD.ZIP	ForwardIT!
MHSNFY.ZIP	MHSNotify!
MHSLIB.ZIP	MHS Librarian!
MHSQ.ZIP	MhsQ!

And don't miss our *FREE* utilities (in NOVLIB Library 16 or 17):

NETERR.ZIP	Network error handlers (CRITTER, SHATTACH) to reboot unattended workstations and clear network errors.
MHSACT.ZIP	Automatically re-activate deactivated MHS internetwork hosts without operator intervention.
MHSSWP.ZIP	Redirect MHS swap files to a local drive or VDISK.
CREATQ.ZIP	Create NetWare print queues on a volume other than SYS:
MHSBPL.ZIP	Configure MHS 1.5C host to host communications to use the B+ protocol.
SENDIT.ZIP	Send MHS messages from the DOS command line or batch files.

Browse NOVLIB on the keyword INFINITE for a complete listing of all Infinite Technologies uploads!

BRO /KEY:INFINITE /LIB:ALL
FOR MORE INFORMATION, CONTACT:

Infinite Technologies
11433 Cronridge Drive, Suite H
Owings Mills, MD 21117
+1-410-363-1097
FAX: +1-410-363-3779
MHS: Support @ Infinite
CompuServe: MHS:Support @ Infinite (or 73270,405)
Internet: Support@Infinite.MHS.CompuServe.com

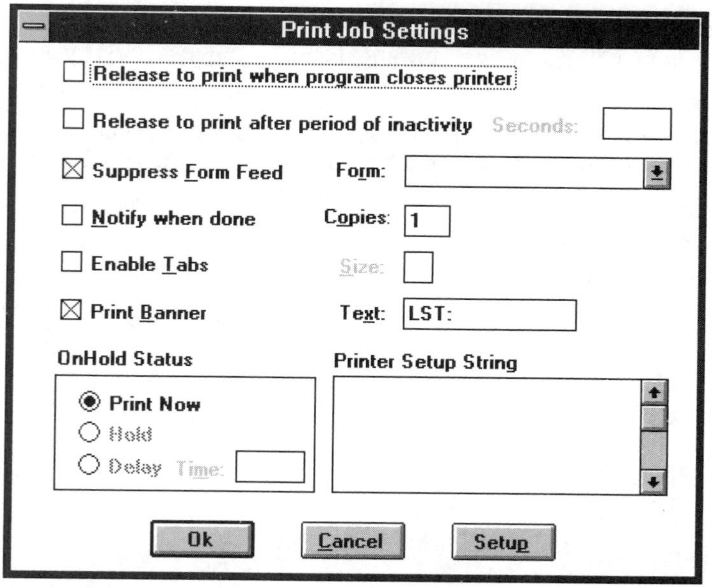

Figure 10.33 I-Queue! print job settings window.

I-Queue! also includes the following additional utilities:

OnHold is a TSR which allows users to submit print jobs that can automatically be placed "on hold," or delayed for printing at a later time.

DefCap allows you to modify CAPTURE parameters from the command-line, but only modifies the specified parameters, leaving all others intact.

Com2Lpt allows you to redirect serial (COM) port output to a parallel (LPT) port, provided that your application prints through the BIOS or DOS, and not directly to the serial port hardware.

CreateQ allows you to create NetWare print queues where the temporary files are stored on a volume other than SYS:.

Also available from Infinite Technologies is I-Queue! Server, a TSR print server for Novell NetWare networks. I-Queue! Server boasts Windows compatibility and 2 to 4 times the printing speed of Novell's RPRINTER, among other capabilities. I-Queue! Server can be downloaded separately as IQS.ZIP, and is available in a special bundle offer with I-Queue! (See the ordering information later in this document.)

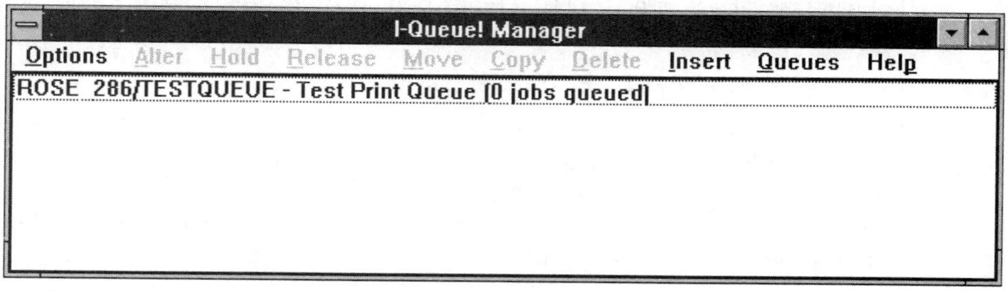

Figure 10.34 I-Queue! Manager window.

INSTALLING I-QUEUE!

1. LOGIN TO YOUR FILE SERVER AS SUPERVISOR OR A SUPERVISOR EQUIVALENT.
2. COPY I-QUEUE! TO YOUR SERVER.

Copy I-Queue!'s program files into SYS:PUBLIC or another appropriate directory on your file server. The following files are required to be accessible to all I-Queue! users.

DOS Version:

IQ.COM

IQ.OVR

IQ.HLP

VIDEO.OVR

IQPOPUP.COM

ONHOLD.EXE

DEFCAP.EXE

CREATEQ.EXE

COM2LPT.COM

NOTE: If you are running other Infinite Technologies' utilities, they share a common VIDEO.OVR file. Use the VIDEO.OVR with the most recent date stamp.

Windows Version:

IQW.EXE

IQW.HLP

IQMW.EXE

IQMW.HLP

3. RUN IQINSTAL OR IQSERIAL TO INITIALIZE I-QUEUE!

Run IQINSTAL.EXE to initialize the I-Queue! 30-day trial period.

If this is a purchased copy, run IQSERIAL to initialize I-Queue! for your network.

4. RUN PRINTDEF TO DEFINE YOUR NETWORK PRINTERS (DOS Version ONLY).

This option is not required if you are only running I-Queue! Windows version.

I-Queue! runs best when PRINTDEF has been used to create setup strings that can be made available for users.

Execute the Novell PRINTDEF utility and select "Print Devices."

NetWare comes with drivers for a variety of different printer types (the .PDF files located in SYS:PUBLIC). It is best to use these as a starting point. Select "Import Print Device" and enter SYS:PUBLIC as the path under "Source Directory." This will give you a list of available printer definition files (PDFs). Import that definitions for any printer types that you use on your network with PRINTDEF.

Refer to your NetWare documentation for additional information on PRINTDEF.

5. RUN IQSETUP TO CONFIGURE I-QUEUE! (DOS Version ONLY).

This option is not required if you are only running I-Queue! Windows version.

The IQSETUP.EXE utility allows you to define some additional information for use by I-Queue!

Most importantly, the "Queue Defaults" option allows you to define a descriptive name and default printer type definition for each NetWare print queue. This way, when selecting setup strings for jobs directed to a particular queue, you can press <Insert> in I-Queue! to see a list of pre-defined setup strings for the type of printer to which the queue is directed.

Printer types must first be defined using the NetWare PRINTDEF utility, as described in #4 above.

Additional options in IQSETUP include:

"Enable Q_OPERATORS to Move/Copy print jobs" - In order for I-Queue! to be able to move and/or copy jobs between print queues, special rights must be given to the user. This option will grant all necessary rights to the defined Queue Operators of a queue. Queue operators are defined in the NetWare PCONSOLE utility.

"Copy SUPERVISOR's Printcon.Dat to each user" - NetWare's PRINTCON job config-uration information is maintained on a user-by-user basis, i.e., each individual has their own Printcon.Dat configuration file. Most LAN administrators would prefer to create one Printcon.Dat file that is shared by all users. This option copies the SUPERVISOR's Printcon.Dat file to all users.

"Make SUPERVISOR's Printcon.Dat GLOBAL" - This option copies the SUPERVISOR's Printcon.Dat file to SYS:PUBLIC for use as a global Printcon.Dat file. If you select this option, you will need to also select the option that follows.

"Modify NetWare utilities to support Global Printcon" will configure the NetWare utilities PRINTCON, NPRINT and CAPTURE to work with this global Printcon.Dat file.

"Modify NetWare utilities to support Local Printcon" reverses the modifications made by the previous option.

6. DEFINE DEFAULT WINDOWS PRINT DRIVERS FOR I-QUEUE! WINDOWS:

One of the most important features of I-Queue! Windows is its ability to have default Windows print drivers defined for each NetWare print queue.

When I-Queue! Windows is initially installed, the system administrator should establish a default Windows print driver for each print queue.

This can be done via the I-Queue! Manager program (IQMW.EXE or the "Manage Queue" button in I-Queue!).

Within I-Queue! Manager, select "Queues" from the main menu bar, highlight a queue, and select the "Options" button. The "Default Printer" defines the Windows print device that should be associated with this queue as a default.

It is recommended that you specify a descriptive name for each print queue, and define an associated Windows print driver.

7. PREREQUISITE NETWARE DLLS (WINDOWS VERSION)

I-Queue! Windows uses several of the NetWare Windows DLLs. Specifically, NWBIND.DLL, NWCONN.DLL, NWPRTQUE.DLL, NWSERVER.DLL and NWWRKSTN.DLL are required.

A copy of these DLLs can be obtained from the NOVLIB forum on CompuServe. The current filename is WINUP6.ZIP in NOVLIB Library 5, but it is subject to change.

8. INSTALLATION / CONFIGURATION COMPLETE - PROCEED TO LOADING I-QUEUE!

LOADING I-QUEUE! (DOS)

To load I-Queue!, simply type IQ.

If you wish to take advantage of the additional capabilities of the OnHold utility to enable submitting print jobs that are automatically put on hold or delayed for later printing, then you should also load the ONHOLD.EXE program into memory.

Optional commandline parameters for IQ.COM include:

/NR	tells I-Queue! to run non-resident. This is recommended when running under a task switching environment or Microsoft Windows.
/NE	tells I-Queue! not to use Expanded memory for swapping.
/NX	tells I-Queue! not to use Extended memory for swapping.
/NU	tells I-Queue! not to use 386-to-the-MAX or QEMM upper memory blocks to reduce conventional memory overhead.
/D	tells I-Queue! not to use Expanded or Extended memory for swapping, and to swap to disk. (I-Queue! will swap to disk by default if insufficient expanded or extended memory is available.) Note: I-Queue! creates a swap file in C:\ or the directory specified via the DOS TMP environmental variable. I-Queue! is NetWare aware, so multiple workstations can safely use the same TMP directory.
/U	unloads or de-installs I-Queue!.

You can also change I-Queue!'s default hotkey of <ALT>-<Q> via the command line with the following command line parameters:

#	Tells I-Queue! to use <CTRL>instead of ALT in the hot-key.
%	Tells I-Queue! to use <CTRL>-<ALT> instead of just <ALT> in the hot-key.
&	Tells I-Queue! to use <CTRL>-<LEFT SHIFT> instead of <ALT> in the hot-key.
!	Tells I-Queue! to use <ALT>-<LEFT SHIFT> instead of <ALT> in the hot-key.
A-Z	Any alphabetic character from A to Z can be specified to work in conjunction with <ALT> or <CTRL> in the hot-key.
Fxx	Any function key (F1–F12) can be specified to work in conjunction with <ALT> or <CNTRL> in the hot-key.

Examples:

IQ alone defaults to the <ALT>-<Q> hot-key, or if I-Queue! has already been loaded, the hot-key is not changed.

IQ X tells I-Queue! to use <ALT>-<X> as its hot-key.

IQ #Z tells I-Queue! to use <CTRL>-<Z> as its hot-key.

IQ F12 tells I-Queue! to use <ALT>-<F12> as its hot-key.

IQ %F5 tells I-Queue! to use <CTRL>-<ALT>-<F5> as its hot-key.

IQ &Z tells I-Queue! to use <CNTRL>-<LEFT SHIFT>-<Z> as its hot-key.

IQ !F1 tells I-Queue! to use <ALT>-<LEFT SHIFT>- <F1>as its hot-key.

POPPING UP I-QUEUE! (DOS)

Press the I-Queue! hot-key defined when loading I-Queue!, and the I-Queue! menu will be displayed.

For more information about the I-Queue! menu options, press <F1> for help.

If you wish to pop-up I-Queue! from within a batch file without pressing the hot-key, execute the command IQPOPUP.COM after I-Queue! has been loaded.

A couple of additional configuration options should be mentioned.

If you want users to default to the Printcon Job Configuration selection window when popping up I-Queue!, set the following DOS environmental variable: SET IQQUICK=Y

If you experience problems where your video display is corrupted when popping up or exiting I-Queue!, this is due to a bug in your VGA card's BIOS. Load the small memory-resident utility VGASAVE.COM provided in the IQUEUE.ZIP file before loading IQ.COM on any workstations that exhibit this behavior.

SPECIAL I-QUEUE! SETTINGS (DOS)

The IQQUICK environmental variable can be used to configure certain operations of I-Queue! DOS.

Issue a SET IQQUICK= command in your AUTOEXEC.BAT file or system login script to configure the desired mode of execution.

IQQUICK=q

When I-Queue! is popped up, the user is immediately prompted for a print queue selection. After a queue is selected, if the user presses Enter, they exit I-Queue! If Escape is pressed they remain in I-Queue!

IQQUICK=Q

Similar to IQQUICK=q, except that the user always remains in I-Queue! until they exit.

IQQUICK=j

When I-Queue! is popped up, the user is immediately prompted for a printcon job selection. After a job is selected, if the user presses Enter, they exit I-Queue! If Escape is pressed they remain in I-Queue!

IQQUICK=J

Similar to IQQUICK=j, except that the user always remains in I-Queue! until they exit.

LOADING I-QUEUE! (WINDOWS)

I-Queue! Windows is separated into two executable programs:

IQW.EXE is the program that allows you to modify your current "CAPTURE" parameters.

IQMW.EXE is the program that allows you to manage print queues and jobs already in the print queue. (IQMW.EXE is automatically executed when you select the "Manage Queues" option in IQW.EXE.)

You can use the File New option in Program Manager to define one or both programs to a program group (or the startup group).

For help within I-Queue! Windows, press F1 at any time.

USING ONHOLD!

OnHold is a small (<3k) TSR that changes the default action of CAPTURE/NPRINT. Normally print jobs are created without a hold on them allowing them to be printed immediately. OnHold causes print jobs to be created with a USER_HOLD, preventing them from being printed. This allows the user or an operator to schedule them to print at a later time, to move them to another queue, or change any parameters that may need to be changed.

Command usage:

OnHold	Installs OnHold (if already installed it enables OnHold)
OnHold /D	Disables OnHold (leaving it resident)
OnHold /U	Un-installs OnHold

For average usage with I-Queue!, it is recommended that you load OnHold with the /D parameter (initially disabled), and then use I-Queue! to put a hold or delay on jobs.

USING DEFCAP!

The DefCap utility allows you to modify CAPTURE parameters from the command-line, but only modifies the specified parameters, leaving all others intact.

For example, if you have a particular application that requires a higher timeout and no added form feed, you can issue the command DEFCAP TI=80 NFF. This maintains all other current CAPTURE parameters, and only changes TI=80 and NFF.

DEFCAP supports the following parameters:

DefCap V1.0
© Copyright 1991 by Infinite Technologies
Usage: defcap [options]

Options:

/A	Autoendcap
/B	enables Banner
/B= <name>	enables Banner and set banner text to <name>
/C= <number>	number of copies
/FF	FormFeed
/L<printer>	Local printer #
/LPTx	Local printer #
/NA	NoAutoendcap
/NB	No Banner

/NFF	No FormFeed
/NOT	Notify when printed
/NN	No Notify
/NT	No Tab expansion
/SH	SHow options
/Tabs=<#>	Tab size
/Ti=<#>	TImeout count (seconds)

USING CREATEQ!

The CreateQ utility allows you to create NetWare print queues that store their temporary queue files on volumes other than SYS:

USAGE:

CreateQ <queuename> <pathname>

1. Login as supervisor and map a drive to the volume where you want queue files stored.

   Ex. (assuming you have a volume named VOL1)

   MAP Q:=VOL1:

   Q:

2. Create a "containing" directory to hold the actual queue directories.

   Ex.

   MD\QUEUES

3. Create a queue using CREATEQ

   Ex. (creating a new queue name NEWQUEUE)

   CREATEQ NEWQUEUE VOL1:QUEUES

4. Use PCONSOLE to add users, operators, and servers.

USING COM2LPT!

The Com2LPT utility allows you to redirect output being sent to COM ports to an LPT port, so that it can be redirected to a network print queue.

   However, this utility will only work with programs that perform their serial output using BIOS or DOS functions. Programs that print directly to the serial port are out of luck.

   USAGE:

/U	unloads Com2Lpt from memory, only if Com2Lpt was the last program loaded into memory.
/C#	where # is the COM port to be redirected to an LPT port.
/L#	where # is the destination LPT port (0 to cancel redirection).

PRODUCTS FROM INFINITE TECHNOLOGIES

Infinite Technologies offers innovative and easy-to-use software solutions, designed primarily for the networked environment.

We back our products with dependable service and special attention to individual requirements. All of our programs are easy to learn and use, and are designed to increase your efficiency.

We also want to help keep you up-to-date with product information, updates, and technical support.

These services are provided via the following mechanisms:

On the CompuServe Information Service, Infinite Technologies offers support and product updates in Section/ Library 4 of the Novell Vendor Forum (NOVVEN).

Via MHS (through CSERVE or NHUB), you can address technical support and/or product information inquiries to SUPPORT @ INFINITE.

You can also subscribe to our MHS Librarian! mailing list, which will include notices of product updates. To join this mailing list, send a message via MHS (CSERVE or NHUB) to LIBRARY @ INFINITE with SUBSCRIBE on your subject line. (CompuServe users can send a message to MHS:Library@Infinite via CompuServe Mail.)

For an index of files available via LIBRARY @ INFINITE, send a message with INDEX on your subject line.

NETWORK UTILITIES

- I-Queue! - Simplifies network printing and print queue management in the Novell NetWare environment. From within a small memory resident popup (0 to 2-1/2KB), I-Queue! allows users to easily change NetWare print queues and modify "capture" parameters. I-Queue! is compatible with Novell's PRINTCON/PRINTDEF and adds global PRINTCON support for Novell's own utilities. Queue management capabilities include: delete/reorder print jobs, move/copy jobs between queues, and hold/delayed printing. NOW INCLUDES A WINDOWS VERSION!

- I-Queue! Server - Turn printers attached to any network workstation into shared network printers. Two to four times faster than RPRINTER, compatible with work-stations running Windows, and compatible with printer ports that do not provide "hardware interrupt support."

- LockIT! - Intelligent Security for DOS & Windows workstations on Novell NetWare networks. LockIT! addresses the problem of users leaving workstations unattended, and the security issues that this presents. Unlike other solutions that will reboot or logout a workstation after a period of "inactivity," potentially leading to data loss, LockIT! locks out keyboard input until you enter your NetWare password...even allowing unattended processes to continue executing.

- CastAway! - A better NetWare broadcast message trap. Get NetWare message notification (e.g., SEND) without your PC locking up until you press CTRL-ENTER! Get notified of new messages while in graphics based applications! All in 0 to 1-1/2KB of conventional memory!

- PopIT! - Gain pop-up access to almost ANY program with less than 2-1/2 KB overhead. Network administrators—access SYSCON, RCONSOLE, FCONSOLE and all of your favorite network utilities without leaving your current application.

ORDERING I-QUEUE!

I-Queue!, the NetWare Printing Toolbox, is currently available for $199, for unlimited use on a single file server.

I-Queue! Server is currently available for $149, for unlimited use on a single file server. Or, both can be purchased together as the I-Queue! Bundle for $249, for unlimited use on a single file server.

Dealer inquiries are invited!

Please rush me ____ copies of the I-Queue! Bundle for $249 each $ _____
Please rush me ____ copies of I-Queue! Toolbox for $199 each $ _____
Please rush me ____ copies of I-Queue! Server for $149 each $ _____
     Disk Size: ____ 3-1/2"   ____ 5-1/4"
Maryland residents add 5% sales tax $ _____
Shipping and Handling (UPS Ground Service)* $ __ 8.00 __
TOTAL $ _____

Name _____
Company _____
Address _____
City _____ State _____ Zip _____
Country _____
Telephone Number _____
FAX Number _____
CompuServe ID _____
MHS Address _____ (via _____)
Method of Payment: ____ Visa   ____ Master Card   ____ Check Enclosed
     Card # _____
     Name of Cardholder _____
     Signature _____
     Expiration Date _____

*Overseas payments by Visa or Master Card only. There will be an additional charge applied for shipping costs to reflect the actual cost of shipment.

INFINITE TECHNOLOGIES
11433 Cronridge Drive, Suite H
Owings Mills, MD 21117
(410) 363-1097

FAX your credit card orders – (410) 363-3779

- OnCall! - A memory resident "Chat" utility for Novell NetWare, that runs in between 0 and 2-1/2 KB of workstation memory. Simple, straightforward, and easy to use. NOW INCLUDES A WINDOWS VERSION!

EXPRESSIT! ELECTRONIC MAIL

ExpressIt! Electronic Mail - The ExpressIt! Electronic Mail product family includes the following products:

- ExpressIt! - The network version of ExpressIt!, including the MHS-compatible DOS version, which runs in less than 2KB of resident memory.

- ExpressIt! Remote - A remote version of ExpressIt! (DOS) customized for use on stand-alone/remote PCs. Includes Personal MHS and allows users to send and receive mail with any MHS based electronic mail system. Includes the ability to run the MHS Connectivity Manager from within the 2KB TSR without exiting your current application.

- ExpressIt! Windows Client - An upgrade for the network version of ExpressIt! offering native support for the Microsoft Windows environment, and a wealth of additional features.

- ExpressIt! Remote Windows A remote version of the Windows version of ExpressIt! customized for use on stand-alone/remote PCs. Includes Personal MHS and allows users to send and receive mail with any MHS-based electronic mail system.

A special Windows based MHS configuration utility eliminates the need to use the MHS Directory Manager.

All versions of ExpressIt! include ExpressIt! Directory Assistance, facilitating automatic exchange of user directories between ExpressIt! hosts.

MHS GATEWAYS AND UTILITIES

- MHS Scheduler - An MHS mail agent that provides greater flexibility in configuring when MHS will connect to a host. On a host-by-host basis, the MHS administrator can configure different frequencies of forced connections based on different times of the day, with separate weekday, weekend, and holiday scheduling possible. MHS gateways and internetwork connections can also be scheduled. The companion RunIT! utility simplifies the creation of batch file gateways...now you can run your tape backup system on your MHS server.

- MHS Librarian! - An MHS Gateway that allows users to request information to be forwarded to them via MHS. Requests are made by placing a keyword in the "SUBJECT" field of the message that you address to the library. A list of files may be requested by sending a message with the keyword of INDEX. The system Admin can also configure MHS Librarian so that selected users can request files or directories other than those that appear in the index. Security is provided by a password program that generates unique daily passwords, a fixed password, or you can create your own password utility.

  MHS Librarian! also supports "discussion lists," similar to the "list server" concept on the internet.

- PageIT! - An MHS gateway connecting MHS-based electronic mail systems to full text alphanumeric pagers. Once configured, sending messages to an alphanumeric pager is as simple as sending a message from your favorite MHS application.

- ForwardIT! - An MHS mail agent for automatically forwarding MHS based electronic mail messages. ForwardIT! can forward (or copy) messages addressed to an MHS address to an alternate address.

  ForwardIT! is most useful in the MHS remote e-mail environment. By remote, we refer to field workers or business travelers who operate ExpressIt! Remote, or other MHS compatible remote software, on a PC or laptop to access their electronic mail from a distant location. Examples could include a salesperson between sales calls, a business traveler in a hotel room, or work-at-home scenarios.

Without ForwardIT!, when mail is sent to a recipient's office address, MHS does not allow for a remote user to dial into the network and retrieve mail waiting at their office address. Mail addressed to this office address can only be picked up at the office.

In order to send a message to the user's MHS remote, the sender must assume responsibility for sending a copy of the message to the remote MHS address.

With ForwardIT!, the user leaves a forwarding address at the office, and while they're out, all messages will be forwarded, or copied, to their forwarding address, giving users transparent access to their electronic mail while away from the office.

This forwarding address can be any valid MHS address, including addresses via MHS gateways.

- MhsQ! - An MHS gateway interface to NetWare print queues. Messages can be sent via MHS to a NetWare print queue. This capability can be useful for MHS remote sites and/or MHS enabled applications for generating printed output and/or reports.

    MhsQ! can also redirect print queues on one file server to a remote print queue on another file server via MHS.

- ExpressIt! MHS Directory Assistant - A directory services gateway that automatically creates and updates user routes in a multi-host workgroup environment. Add a user at one host within the workgroup, and the user route will automatically be created at all other hosts within the workgroup. Add a new host to your workgroup, and the host and user lists will automatically be added to other hosts within the workgroup. (Directory Assistant is bundled with ExpressIt! but is also available separately.)

- MHSNotify! - A TSR which runs on the MHS mail server only, and automatically notifies recipients of new electronic mail received from remote MHS sites, or across internetwork connections. An excellent alternative to MHSALERT for DaVinci e-mail users! (MHSNotify! is bundled with ExpressIt!)

REQUESTING TRIAL VERSIONS VIA MHS

30-Day Trial Versions of many Infinite Technologies Products can be requested via MHS. For more information, send an MHS message to LIBRARY @ INFINITE via CSERVE or NHUB, with a subject line of INDEX.

DOWNLOADING TRIAL VERSIONS FROM COMPUSERVE

30-Day Trial Versions of many Infinite Technologies Products are available on CompuServe! Look for the following files in NOVVEN Library 4:

XPRESS.ZIP	ExpressIt! Electronic Mail (NetWare) (DOS and Windows versions combined)
EXPDOS.ZIP	ExpressIt! e-Mail (NetWare) (DOS Version)
EXPWIN.ZIP	ExpressIt! e-Mail (NetWare) (Windows Version)
XPRES2.ZIP	ExpressIt! e-Mail (Remote & non-NetWare) (DOS and Windows versions combined)
REMDOS.ZIP	ExpressIt! e-Mail (Remote & non-NetWare) (DOS Version)
REMWIN.ZIP	ExpressIt! e-Mail (Remote & non-NetWare) (Windows Version)

POPIT.ZIP	PopIT!
ONCALL.ZIP	OnCall!
CASTAW.ZIP	CastAway!
IQUEUE.ZIP	I-Queue!
IQS.ZIP	I-Queue! Server
LOCKIT.ZIP	LockIT!
MHSCED.ZIP	MHS Scheduler
PAGEIT.ZIP	PageIT!
4WARD.ZIP	ForwardIT!
MHSNFY.ZIP	MHSNotify!
MHSLIB.ZIP	MHS Librarian!
EXDA.ZIP	ExpressIt! MHS Directory Assistant
MHSQ.ZIP	MhsQ!

And don't miss our *FREE* utilities (also in PCVENF Library 13):

NETERR.ZIP	Network error handlers (CRITTER, SHATTACH) to reboot unattended workstations and clear network errors.
CREATQ.ZIP	Create NetWare print queues on a volume other than SYS:
LOGIN.ZIP	Load TSRs from the NetWare Login Script without losing available memory!
MHSACT.ZIP	Automatically re-activate deactivated MHS internetwork hosts without operator intervention.
MHSSWP.ZIP	Redirect MHS swap files to a local drive or VDISK.
MHSBPL.ZIP	Configure MHS 1.5C host to host communications to use the B+ protocol.
SENDIT.ZIP	Send MHS messages from the DOS command line or batch files.

Plus, other helpful text files and reports:

MHSGAT.TXT	NetWare MHS and Gateways overview
DOSMEM.TXT	PC Memory management/architecture overview
WINTIP.TXT	Windows vs. NetWare Troubleshooting Tips

...and stay tuned for MORE!!!

FOR MORE INFORMATION, CONTACT:
Infinite Technologies
11433 Cronridge Drive, Suite H
Owings Mills, MD 21117
+1-410-363-1097
FAX: +1-410-363-3779
MHS: Support @ Infinite
CompuServe: MHS:Support @ Infinite (or 73270,405)
Internet: Support@Infinite.MHS.CompuServe.com
Technical Support provided on the CompuServe Information Service in NOVVEN Section 4.

11 Net Tools by Automated Design Systems

Introduction to Net Tools

Automated Design Systems was one of the first providers of Windows-based software for NetWare. Net Tools (formerly Windows Workstation) has been improved and revised for several years and is now at version 4.1. The current version provides a robust Applications Manager, a network security module, a flexible network script language, a network print manager, and a network applications metering utility. All but the print manager and metering software are included with this book.

With the Net Tools Applications Manager you can do the following:

- Launch applications with a multi-user icon-based interface.

- Centrally create and tailor network menus according to user's rights.

- Hide program groups, subgroups, and items from users depending on network membership or username.

- Globally enable/disable pull-down menu options, such as remove File/Run or File/Exit.

- Display program group items horizontally, vertically, or as text only.

- Execute applications/scripts via network and personal startup groups.

- Create customized context-sensitive on-line Help.

- View technical support data on Windows, DOS, and the network.

- Document network menu structure and rights.

  With the Net Tools network security module, you can do the following:

- Automatically secure and require password access for unattended workstations without exiting Windows.
- Secure the screen on demand or after a pre-set period of inactivity.
- Encrypt and decrypt files for added security.
- Schedule the execution of commands, such as backups or file transfers.
- Set personal reminder messages with "snooze" capabilities.
- Send intercom messages to users or LAN groups across multiple servers.

  With the Net Tools network scripting language, you can do the following:

- Write "network-aware" scripts to update .INI files and distribute software.
- Dynamically update .INI files on the LAN or local hard drives without exiting Windows.
- Centrally manage software distribution and updates.
- Set path and drive mappings "on the fly."
- Write scripts using conditional logic, interactive dialog boxes, and environment variables.

Release Notes

Net TOOLS™ (formerly Windows Workstation) Version 4.1c for Novell NetWare
Rev. February 1993
Net TOOLS is available for Novell NetWare 2.1 or higher, Microsoft LAN Manager 2.0 or higher, and Banyan Vines 4.10(5). It requires Microsoft DOS 3.3 or higher and Microsoft Windows 3.X or higher.

This document contains important information on Net TOOLS that is not included in the Net TOOLS manuals (*Net TOOLS Menu Administrator's Guide*, *Net TOOLS Print Administrator's Guide*, and *Net TOOLS Meter Administrator's Guide*) or in the on-line Help files. **Please read it completely before attempting installation.**

If you find it necessary to contact our Technical Support Department for assistance, please refer first to the "Getting Support" section of Chapter 1 of your Net TOOLS Menu or Print manual for the procedure. Note that the serial number of your software now appears in the About box of Applications Manager, Print Manager, and Print Editor as well as on the installation diskettes.

Contents

New Installation Information

For your convenience, the Net TOOLS Setup program automatically installs Net TOOLS Menu, Print, and Meter.

❑   **Installing Net TOOLS comprises three important and distinct steps:**

1.   Running the Net TOOLS Setup program (WWSETUP.EXE) from within Windows.

To install Net TOOLS, follow the procedure in Chapter 2, "Installation and Configuration," of the *Net TOOLS Menu Administrator's Guide*. For this special release of Net TOOLS, the Setup program installs all three Net TOOLS products automatically. Contrary to the instructions in the manual, you do not have to explicitly tell Setup to install Print and Meter after Menu.

2.   Setting up and configuring both network and personal printers using the Net TOOLS Print Editor (WWPEDIT.EXE). For further information, see the *Net TOOLS Print Administrator's Guide*.

3.   Using Net TOOLS Menu's Administration mode to set up new network groups and assign corresponding user access rights. For further information, see the *Net TOOLS Menu Administrator's Guide*.

Upgrading a Previous Release of Net TOOLS

If you are upgrading to Release 4.1 from a previous version of Net TOOLS, please read this section *first*, then turn to "General Information."

❑   **Upgrading to Net TOOLS 4.1 comprises three important and distinct steps:**

1.   Launching the Net TOOLS Setup program (WWSETUP.EXE) from within Windows.

To install Net TOOLS, follow the procedure in Chapter 2, "Installation and Configuration," of the *Net TOOLS Menu Administrator's Guide*. For this special release of Net TOOLS, the Setup program installs all three Net TOOLS products automatically. Contrary to the instructions in the manual, you do not have to explicitly tell Setup to install Print and Meter after Menu.

2.   Using the Net TOOLS Print Editor program
(WWPEDIT.EXE) to upgrade your existing network printer
database.
3.   Running the Net TOOLS Print Manager program
(WWPRINT.EXE) at each workstation to update the personal
printer information.

Upgrade Information

❑   **Upgrading to Windows 3.1.** If you are also
upgrading to Windows 3.1, install Net TOOLS 4.1 *first*
since it is compatible with both Windows 3.0 and 3.1. If
you are placing printer drivers in a shared network
directory, be sure that you have separate shared
directories and correct search paths for Windows 3.1
and Windows 3.0 so that you do not mix driver
versions.

❑   **Upgrading 3.0 & 3.1 Menus.** Applications
Manager replaces older versions of Workstation Menu.
Menus created in versions 3.0 and 3.1 of Workstation
Menu can be converted for use with Applications
Manager. If a menu item used a script in Workstation
Menu, Applications Manager converts the menu item
with the script. Menu items created with Quick Menu
are converted to a program item unless it contains a list
files mask, i.e., *.DOC, *.TXT. When Quick Menu
includes a list files mask, Quick Menu is converted to a
script by Applications Manager in order to provide the
list files option.

•   As Applications Manager converts menus, it
will prompt for passwords that were set in Workstation
Menu for individual menu item access. If you do not
provide the correct password, that particular menu item
will not be converted.

•   Passwords set in the Menu Configuration
Editor for exiting to DOS and access to menu
configuration are not directly transferable. These
features can be incorporated separately through the
Administration mode. For specific information see
Chapter 4, "Net TOOLS Administration," of the *Net
TOOLS Menu Administrator's Guide*.

- Passwords set in the Menu Configuration Editor for exiting to DOS and access to menu configuration are not directly transferable. These features can be incorporated separately through the Administration mode. For specific information see Chapter 4, "Net TOOLS Administration," of the *Net TOOLS Menu Administrator's Guide*.

❏ **Printer Database Upgrade.** Windows 3.1 printer drivers have a different format than Windows 3.0. To prevent incompatibilities, Net TOOLS Release 4.1 automatically marks each printer database according to the Windows version that created it (e.g., WWPRINT.31). Print Manager will not load a printer database unless its version correctly matches the version of Windows being run.

- If you have an existing printer database created under Windows 3.0 and you wish to run Windows 3.1, the upgrade process will attempt to automatically update printer information it knows has changed between the two versions. All data is automatically backed up as part of the upgrade process. Printer drivers from third-party manufacturers (those not included with the standard Windows 3.1 drivers) will *not* be automatically updated and will require manual installation.

- This upgrade process applies to driver records, network printers and connected personal printers. Locations, printer descriptions, icons and network options are not affected.

- Administrators still have the option of building a completely new database with Windows 3.1 information.

- If you plan for some users to run Windows 3.0 while others use Windows 3.1, you *must* maintain a separate printer database for each. In addition, you must maintain the database for Windows 3.0 users using WWPEDIT running under Windows 3.0. This is done by setting the WWPATH parameter in the WWPRINT section of each WIN.INI to point to the desired database. A script for automating this procedure is provided in the "Updating Network Printers" section of this document.

Updating Your Menu Database

Use the following procedure to upgrade your Net TOOLS programs and menu database:

❑ **Installation directory.** We require that you install the Net TOOLS 4.1 upgrade into a new directory.

1. Run WWSETUP.EXE from within Windows and specify a new installation directory.

   To install Net TOOLS, follow the procedure in Chapter 2, "Installation and Configuration," of the *Net TOOLS Menu Administrator's Guide*. For this special release of Net TOOLS, the Setup program installs all three Net TOOLS products automatically. Contrary to the instructions in the manual, you do not have to explicitly tell Setup to install Print and Meter after Menu.

2. Copy your pre-4.1 .APP, .WWR and/or .DB files to the new directory you specified.

3. Copy your printer database to this new directory including the WWPRINT directory, its subdirectories (DRIVERS, DB, HELP and WININI) and their contents.

4. Import the groups you want as menus using Administration mode and the procedure outlined under "Merging Existing Groups into Applications Manager" in Chapter 3, "Applications Manager," of the *Net TOOLS Menu Administrator's Guide*.

❑ **Upgrading to a new WWEXT.WWR file.** Previous versions of Net TOOLS Menu did not include the ability to restrict the Command option in the Alarm Options dialog box. When a new .WWR file is written, the default setting is for the Command option to be enabled. If you do *not* want users to run commands from Alarm, disable the Command option by checking it off in the Net TOOLS Security - Restrictions box in Net TOOLS Administration and saving the file.

Updating Your Printer Database

❑ **If you plan to upgrade to Windows 3.1**, you *must* also upgrade your database to be compatible with the 3.1 drivers. Use this procedure to document your database information *before* you upgrade:

1. Install Net TOOLS 4.1 Print first using Windows 3.0.

2. Run the WWPEDIT.EXE program under Windows 3.0 and choose the Configure/Print Database option.

3. Select "Include .WI Files" and "All Printers."

4. Press Print. This creates a WWPRINT.TXT file that contains all of your existing printer database information, which can be printed out or viewed by a text editor for reference as you upgrade.

❑ **Personal Printer Index.** When updating from version 3.0 to 4.1 of Net TOOLS, you may need to re-enter the personal printers for each workstation due to version 3.0 incorrectly storing the NetWare Internet Address. Releases of Net TOOLS after version 3.0 do not have this problem.

Updating Network Printers

With Windows 3.1 installed, follow these instructions to update your network printers:

1. Run Windows 3.1.

2. Edit the WWPATH parameter in the WWPRINT section of your WIN.INI file to point to your printer database.

   • This entry may be entered by drive letter or server\volume. For example, if you want to move the directories to the NETTOOLS directory, use:

   WWPATH=<drive:>\NETTOOLS

   or

   WWPATH=SERVER\VOLUME:NETTOOLS

3. Run WWPEDIT.EXE.

   - You will get a message box indicating that Print Editor has detected a 3.0 database while running under Windows 3.1. Selecting "Yes" will back up your existing printer database and automatically upgrade it for Windows 3.1 compatibility. Selecting "No" will abort the process.

4. Click "Yes" to upgrade the database.

   - Print Editor will back up your printer database by copying the DB and WININI subdirectories to a WWPRINT.30 subdirectory at the same level as your WWPATH directory. For example, if your WWPATH is X:\NETTOOLS\WWPRINT, WWPEDIT will create a directory X:\NETTOOLS\WWPRINT.30 with corresponding DB and WININI subdirectories and automatically copy over the appropriate files.

   - If WWPEDIT finds an existing WWPRINT.30 directory it will display a warning message box. You may either click "Cancel" to abort the upgrade or click "Continue" to overwrite any files that may exist in the directory and proceed with the upgrade.

   - Print Editor will completely update your Driver and Network Printer information including adding appropriate driver records as required for Windows 3.1 compatibility.

5. When the upgrade process concludes, you will receive a message indicating that your database has been successfully upgraded or that a problem was encountered. *If the upgrade was unsuccessful, your database has not been changed.* Check the UPGRADE.LOG ASCII file located in the WWPATH directory for the specific reason the upgrade was unsuccessful, correct the problem and try the upgrade again.

6. You can optionally convert the backup database directory into a database for any Windows 3.0 users by creating Help and Drivers subdirectories in WWPRINT.30 and copying over the appropriate files. If you rename your WWPRINT directory to WWPRINT.31, you can use the following MultiSet script to have Print Manager automatically use the correct database for your corresponding Windows 3.0 and 3.1 users.

   SETINI *win.ini wwprint wwpath=x:\nettools\wwprint.+$winver*
   RUN *wwprint.exe*

Updating Personal Printers

Follow these instructions to update your personal printers:

1. Ensure that each personal printer is connected and correctly configured *before* you begin. Personal printers that are not connected will *not* be upgraded properly and will require the printer to be completely reinstalled.

2. Run the Windows 3.1 Setup program to update each user's initialization files to Windows 3.1.

3. Run WWPRINT.EXE at each user's workstation that has a personal printer connected.

   • When Print Manager is run under Windows 3.1, personal printer information for the workstation is automatically upgraded and the results are recorded in an ASCII file called LOCAL.LOG located in the DB subdirectory of WWPATH.

4. Check the LOCAL.LOG file for any additional steps you may need to perform.

   • If the user has a personal printer whose model is not already in the printer database, the administrator must add the model record manually. For example, if you have a HP LaserJet IID as a network printer and a HP LaserJet Series II as a personal printer, the driver record would be changed to specify the IID because there is not a valid Series II driver record in Windows 3.1. Since the user would not have the appropriate permissions to update the driver database, Print Manager adds a line to the LOCAL.LOG file for you that indicates that a Series II driver record should be added.

General Information

New Features in Release 4.1c

❏ **Windows for Workgroups Compatibility:** Net TOOLS 4.1c supports Microsoft's Windows for Workgroups product.

Applications Manager

❏ **Applications Manager and DDE.** Applications Manager provides a DDE interface that is equivalent in format and functionality to that of Windows Program Manager. In order for Applications Manager to receive DDE commands, Program Manager cannot be running. Designate Applications Manager as your shell by editing the Shell= line in the SYSTEM.INI to read Shell=APPMAN.EXE. (If Program Manager is running concurrently with Applications Manager, DDE calls will be received only by Program Manager.)

❏ **Files used by Applications Manager from the Net TOOLS directory.**

APPMAN.WWR	Net TOOLS Menu restriction file for Applications Manager. Contains menu defaults, menu bar restrictions and logo information. Applications Manager reads this file upon startup.
WWEXT.WWR	Net TOOLS Menu restrictions file for Net TOOLS Security. Contains restrictions and logo information. Security reads this file upon startup and checks it periodically when running.
NETMENU.INI	Initialization file for Applications Manager. Contains a list of network group files.
WWNET.INI	Specifies which network DLL to use.

*.APP	Network group files which include Rights information.

❏ **User-specific files found in the same directory as WIN.COM, WIN.INI and SYSTEM.INI:**

PERMENU.INI	Initialization file for Applications Manager that contains a user's personal options and personal group files. This file must be located in the same directory as the user's WIN.COM, WIN.INI and SYSTEM.INI.
*.APP	Personal group files.
*.RCT	Rectangle file. Windows appearance information for network groups that the user has altered.
APPMAN.ORD	Group ordering file. The order in which the groups are displayed in the user's workspace.

❏ **Sending a Trouble Ticket**, described on page 3-49 of the *Net TOOLS Menu Administrator's Guide*, will be supported in the next release of Net TOOLS.

Net TOOLS Administration

❏ **Setting up the Trouble Ticket**, described on pages 4-15 and 4-16 of the *Net TOOLS Menu Administrator's Guide*, will be supported in the next release of Net TOOLS.

Print Manager/Print Editor

❏ **Auto EndCap Option.** Printer databases created with versions of Net TOOLS earlier than 4.1b will have both the Enable and the Permit Change options disabled. If you are using the 4.1b PDRIVERS.DB, the default states are for the Auto EndCap option to be disabled and Permit Change by users to be enabled.

❑ **Micrografx Driver Support.** To ensure compatibility with Micrografx and other special drivers, the file WWPRINT.INI must be in the same directory as the WWPRINT and WWPEDIT files. This file, which stores information on handling drivers and alternate driver names, is used by Print Manager and Print Editor. Editing WWPRINT.INI is not recommended.

Due to the nature of the Micrografx drivers, the printer description and location will not appear in third-party application printer setup boxes. Instead, the model name displays for these printers.

❑ **386 Enhanced Mode Printing Problems.** If you are experiencing problems printing while in 386 Enhanced mode, you may want to direct your print jobs to LPT1.OS2 and LPT2.OS2 instead of LPT1, LPT2 and LPT3. To do so, edit the WIN.INI to include the following line under the [WWPRINT] section: USEOS2=1

MultiSet Script Language/MultiSet Editor

❑ **Sample Scripts.** The following Sample Scripts are located in the Examples subdirectory of the Net TOOLS 4.1 directory. You may view them in Notepad or edit them from the MultiSet Editor (MSEDIT.EXE). Be sure to read the comments in each script which indicate when you need to substitute information for your specific network configuration.

The Examples subdirectory also contains various text files that offer technical tips and techniques for optimizing Net TOOLS Menu.

BULLETIN.SET	This script displays different files in a bulletin board depending on parameters in an .INI. Can also be set to run once per day.
EXCELEXE.SET	This script demonstrates some of the conditional actions that can precede launching an application.
MAPPINGS.SET	This script uses a PIF to call a batch file. It displays the current mappings.

WINWORD2.SET SETWORD2.SET	The WINWORD2.SET file checks if the user is set up for Word for Windows 2.0. If he is not, it runs the SETWORD2.SET script to set it up. This is faster than keeping everything in one script since the set up is not scanned each time the user runs Word for Windows.
WPWIN.SET	This script runs a PIF for WordPerfect. When WordPerfect is launched the WIN.INI is checked for a three-letter ID value that is required for the network version of WordPerfect. If no ID is found, the user is prompted to enter the ID. The ID is then stored in the WIN.INI.
WWINSTALL.SET	This script sets a user's .INI file up for running Applications Manager and Print Manager. It also collects information about the user's setup into a common .INI file.

Net TOOLS Meter

❏ **Meter Installation.** The Setup program installs Net TOOLS Meter as a part of the installation process. It is no longer necessary to copy the Meter program files into the Net TOOLS directory as described in Chapter 1 of the *Net TOOLS Meter Administrator's Guide*.

❏ **Module Name Exceptions.** Certain Windows applications can escape usage activity being reporting in Meter's graphs due to the filenames that are registered. Two examples are Micrografx Designer and Charisma. In both cases, register the DESIGNER.BIN and CHARISMA.BIN files instead of the .EXE files in order to meter activity. These .EXE files are files that load the programs; the program code is located in the .BIN files for each application.

❏ **NetWare 386 Rights.** The user rights to the WWMETER directory recommended in the *Net TOOLS Meter Administrator's Guide* are for NetWare 286. Note that the rights required for NetWare 386 are Read, Write and File Scan [RWF]. Refer to the following chart for a comparison list:

NetWare 286	NetWare 386
Read	Read
Write	Write
Open	Read Write
Create	Create
Delete	Erase
Parental	Supervisor, Access Control
Search	File Scan
Modify	Modify

❏ **Unlocatable Domain Files.** If you cannot locate your Meter domain file, you may wish to create a new domain file. To recreate the domain file, you must first delete the username WindowsWorkstation using Novell's SYSCON or other equivalent utility. This username, created with the Register Server option, was set up by the program in order to log in and out of file servers. You must also delete the WWMETER directory and its contents from volume SYS of the registered server. If you attempt to register a server without performing the above steps, Meter will not display the server in the list of available servers since it considers the server(s) already registered.

❏ **Meter and Dynamic Data Exchange (DDE).** Meter DDE gives you the ability to export Net TOOLS Meter data into any application that supports the BIFF record format, such as Microsoft Excel. Once transferred, you can manipulate and present the data in any way the application allows. You can view the data in tabular format, enter it into a database, create different graphs, etc.

METERDDE.EXE is the DDE server that exchanges data between the requesting application or Meter and the .MTR files residing on the various servers where the usage data is written by WWMARKER.EXE.

❏ **DDE Format.** When a DDE request is made, the DDE server returns a BIFF block of the appropriate size. The number of rows in the BIFF block is specified in the request; each row contains data from one interval. There is one column in the block for each application in the request. The first column is the date/time for the data in that row. The format of the DDE request is as follows:

METERDDE | *domain file, group name[,userid[,password]]!end*
time,rows,resolution:application1[,application2 ...]

The following are definitions of the terms included in the DDE request
command line:

domain file   A full path specification to the Domain file that contains
information on the Domain you wish to use.   Domain
filenames have the .MTD file extension.

Example: F:\WINAPPS\WW\ADS.MTD

group name   The internal name of a Domain and/or Reporting
Group. This name indicates the subset of the Domain
for which you are requesting data.

To retrieve data for the entire Domain, repeat the
Domain's filename, without the extension. Example:
ADS

To retrieve data for a particular Reporting Group, use
the Domain name followed by a period and the name of
the Reporting Group. Example: ADS.Marketing

userid   The userid Meter DDE uses when logging in to servers.
This entry is not required; you will be prompted for the
userid if it is omitted. (It is not used in either example
below.)

password   The password associated with the userid specified. As
with the userid, you will be prompted if necessary. (It
is not used in either example below.)

end time   The time of the last row of data requested, specified in
seconds since January 1, 1970. If omitted, this field
defaults to the current time.

rows   The number of rows of data requested.

resolution   The size of an interval in seconds. This value should be
an exact multiple of the interval specified in the System
Options box in the Meter Administration program.
Example: 900 (15 minutes)

applicationN   The module name of an application for which you are
requesting data. Module names are displayed in the
Meter Administration list box. Example: MSWORD,
WWPRINT, EXCEL.

Samples. ADS provides two sample Excel spreadsheets with the Net
TOOLS Meter program to illustrate how to formulate DDE requests and
uses for them.

❏ *Example 1:* METER.XLS is an example of a hard-coded spreadsheet.
You can create similar spreadsheets by following these steps:

1. Drag-select a range of cells two columns wide and several rows tall.

2. In the formula bar, type:

=METERDDE | *domain file, group name!0,rows,1800:application1*

replacing the italics with appropriate values. *rows* must match the
number of rows you drag-selected. In METER.XLS, the formula bar
is:

=METERDDE | 'F:\WINAPPS\WW\DOMAIN.MTD,DOMAIN'!'0,49,
1800:EXCEL,WWPRINT'

3. Press Ctrl+Shift+Enter.

This creates an array and fills in the entire shaded area with data from
Meter. If you wish to get data for multiple applications, you may do
so by shading an additional column and adding the applications to
the end of the application list.

Note: METER.XLS is merely an example of how to hard-code a
spreadsheet. To make it more functional, use Formula Replace to
change the Domain file and group name to valid ones for your
environment and then enter the correct number of rows and
application names. See Example 2 for an alternate method.

❏ *Example 2:* MTRDDE.XLS (along with MTRDDE.XLM) is an example of
an Excel Macro that can be used to hide the complexity of the data
request format.

1. Run Microsoft Excel and open the METERDDE.XLS file.

2. From the DATA menu, select Import Meter Data (or use the shortcut key, ^A).

3. Fill in each field in the dialog box with an appropriate value.

    • For Group Name, follow the rules given earlier in this section.

    • Enter application names separated by commas. Example: MSWORD, WWPRINT

    • Select a Domain.

    • For Number of Rows, enter the number of intervals for which you want data.

    • You can normally accept the defaults for the other fields. If you change them, follow the rules on the previous page.

4. Select OK.

    Excel formats the data request for you according to the values provided. The macro does little checking of the input data, so be careful to enter the information correctly.

❑ **Additional Graph Option.** There is an additional command on the Options menu of the graph menu bar that is not described in the *Net TOOLS Meter Administrator's Guide*. Options/Legend turns the Legend display on and off in the graph window. The command is checked in the drop-down menu if the legend displays. If the window contains more than one graph, the command applies to the active child window. Turning off the Legend allows a graph to occupy the full child window.

❑ **Exiting Windows on Metered Workstations.** Administrators should be aware that metered data may not be accurate if users do not properly exit from Windows. When a user powers off his workstation while WWMarker is in the process of updating a .MTR file, there is a small chance that the count will be affected. This is due to the .MTR file being locked as the user shuts down the workstation. While the file is in a locked state, other metered workstations cannot write their data to the .MTR file. If a user logs back in immediately, the file will automatically return to the unlocked state, avoiding a 15-minute timeout that would otherwise occur.

Running Net TOOLS Menu in Stand-Alone Mode

❏ **Stand-Alone Mode.** Users who have Applications Manager designated as the shell and attempt to run Windows when not logged into the network will receive an error. In order for a user to successfully run Windows both on and off the network, the program files must also be copied to the local hard disk and the program added to the path.

❏ When running Net TOOLS Menu in stand-alone mode, certain features are not available:

- In stand-alone mode, Net TOOLS Administration cannot be accessed with <CTRL><ALT><A>. To run Administration, choose File/Run from the Applications Manager menu bar, then specify WWADMIN.EXE; or double-click on the program's icon if it is an item in one of your groups.

- Network Groups and the Network Info menu items are not available.

- MultiSet Script Language is available in the stand-alone version, however, network commands such as attach, login_name, map, memberof, p_station, rights, username, etc. are not available.

- The Intercom module of Net TOOLS Security is not available.

- **Support for Other Script Languages.** On occasion, a user may want a third-party script language to enter a password for a stand-alone version. In order to accomplish this task, a WIN.INI parameter **must** be specified to allow the script program to insert a "stand-alone" password for the user for Secure Station. Use a text editor to add the following line to the [SECURE] section of the WIN.INI file:

        [SECURE]
        NOTMODAL=1

Net TOOLS 4.1c Files

ADMAMAN.DLL	ADS Support Library
ADMEXT.DLL	ADS Support Library

ADMIN.APP	Personal Group file for LAN Administrator
ADMIN.INI	Regulates entry into Administration mode
ADS_EGA.FON	Screen fonts for EGA monitors; used by Net TOOLS Meter
ADS_VGA.FON	Screen fonts for VGA monitors; used by Net TOOLS Meter
ADSUTILS.DLL	ADS Support Library
APPMAN.EXE	Applications Manager program
APPMAN.WWR	Default Applications Manager restrictions file
COMMDLG.DLL	Microsoft redistributable DLL
DEFAULT.HLP	Help displayed if no printer-specific HyperHelp exists
DRIVERS.TXT	File copied into DRIVERS directory
HELP.WWH	Help about Print Manager HyperHelp itself
KEYLIB.DLL	ADS support library, used by Secure Station
LZEXPAND.DLL	Microsoft redistributable DLL
MAIN.APP	Network Group file
METER.XLS	Sample spreadsheet in Excel
METERDDE.EXE	Reads metered data files created by WWMARKER.
MSEDIT.EXE	MultiSet Editor program
MTRDDE.XLM	Excel 2.1 macro to bring Meter data into Microsoft Excel through DDE
MTRDDE.XLS	Sample spreadsheet in Excel
MULTISET.EXE	MultiSet program
NETWARE.DLL	A stub that allows applications requiring network access to run stand-alone

NW*.DLL	Novell Support Libraries (3 files)
PDRIVERS.DB	Printer drivers database
PRTUPD.INF	Printer Upgrade data file
README.WRI	Readme file providing information on Net TOOLS 4.1c
SHELL.DLL	Microsoft redistributable DLL
STARTUP.APP	Network Startup Group file
TOOLHELP.DLL	Microsoft redistributable DLL
WININI.TXT	Text file copied into WININI directory
WWADMIN.EXE	Net TOOLS Administration program
WWADMIN.HLP	Net TOOLS Menu Help file used in Administration mode
WWBOARD.EXE	Bulletin Board program
WWEDIT.HLP	MultiSet Help file
WWENCODE.EXE	File Encryption/Decryption program
WWENV.EXE	Program used by MultiSet to control the environment
WWEXT.EXE	Net TOOLS Security program
WWEXT.WWR	Default Security restrictions file
WWHELP.EXE	Print Manager HyperHelp program
WWHELP.HLP	Net TOOLS Menu Help file for users
WWMARKER.EXE	Program that records application usage activity on each workstation; used with Net TOOLS Meter
WWMETER.EXE	Net TOOLS Meter Administration and graphing program
WWMETER.HLP	Net TOOLS Meter Help file

WWNET.INI	Specifies network DLL to load; used by ADSUTILS.DLL
WWNETWAR.DLL	ADS Support Library
WWPEDIT.EXE	Net TOOLS Print Editor program
WWPEDIT.HLP	Print Editor Help file
WWPINDEX.SYS	Used by Print Manager HyperHelp
WWPRINT.EXE	Net TOOLS Print Manager program
WWPRINT.INI	Contains information on handling special drivers
WWPRINT.TXT	Text file copied into the WWPRINT directory
WWPRTUPD.INF	Printer upgrade data file
WWSETUP.EXE	Net TOOLS Setup program
WWSETUP.INF	Information file used by Setup program
WWTSR.EXE	DOS TSR allowing Secure Station to monitor keyboard activity while running a DOS application in 386 Enhanced Mode.
WWVER.EXE	Displays information about ADS DLLs

Administrator's Guide

Menu

Software for Network Administration

Net TOOLS and Microsoft Windows

Net TOOLS runs in an environment called Microsoft Windows, created by Microsoft Corporation. An extension of the MS-DOS operating system, Microsoft Windows gives a standard look and feel to Net TOOLS and all other Windows applications.

With Microsoft Windows, you can take advantage of these additional features of the Windows environment:

- Running multiple applications: You can run several applications under Windows at one time and easily switch between them, creating an integrated work environment.

- Windows control of the DOS environment: From the Windows environment, you can easily access all Windows and non-Windows applications, files, directories, and disks, and control all DOS-related tasks such as directory management and disk formatting.

To run Net TOOLS under Microsoft Windows, you need to license and install Microsoft Windows version 3.0 or higher. Please contact your dealer, distributor or Automated Design Systems, Inc., for more information.

Automated Design Systems, Inc.
375 Northridge Road
Suite 270
Atlanta, Georgia 30350 USA

(404) 394-2552
(404) 394-2191 FAX

Printed and reproduced in the United States of America

End-User License Agreement
Limited Warranty and Damage Disclaimer

PLEASE READ THIS NOTICE BEFORE OPENING THE PACKAGE CONTAINING THE SOFTWARE PROGRAM AND RELATED MATERIALS, IF ANY (COLLECTIVELY THE "PRODUCT").. OPENING THE PACKAGE OR USING ITS CONTENTS CONSTITUTES YOUR COMPLETE AND UNCONDITIONAL ACCEPTANCE OF THE TERMS AND CONDITIONS OF THIS END-USER LICENSE AGREEMENT ("AGREEMENT"). IF YOU DO NOT AGREE WITH THESE TERMS AND CONDITIONS, PROMPTLY RETURN THE UNOPENED PACKAGE TO THE POINT OF PURCHASE FOR FULL REFUND. SHOULD YOU HAVE ANY QUESTIONS CONCERNING THIS AGREEMENT, YOU MAY CONTACT AUTOMATED DESIGN SYSTEMS, INC., BY WRITING AUTOMATED DESIGN SYSTEMS, INC., 375 NORTHRIDGE ROAD, SUITE 270, ATLANTA, GA 30350.

License: Automated Design Systems, Inc. ("Licensor") hereby grants to you a non-exclusive, non-transferable and non-assignable license to use the computer software programs in object code form ("Software") on a single processing unit ("file server"). You agree that you will not sublicense, rent, lease, sell, assign, or transfer the Product or share your rights under this license with a third party. You may make one (1) copy of the Software for backup purposes and agree to affix Licensor's copyright and other proprietary rights notices to such copy.

Ownership: You acknowledge and agree that all right, title, and interest in and to the Product are and shall remain with Licensor. This Agreement conveys to you only a limited right of use revocable in accordance with the terms of this Agreement.

Limited Warranty: Licensor warrants to you that for a period of ninety (90) days from the date you receive this Product the magnetic media contains an accurate reproduction of the Software. This limited warranty covers only the original user of the Product. Licensor does not warrant that the Product will be free from error or will meet your specific requirements. Except for the warranties set forth above, the Product is licensed "as is", and LICENSOR DISCLAIMS ANY AND ALL OTHER WARRANTIES, WHETHER EXPRESS OR IMPLIED, INCLUDING WITHOUT LIMITATION, ANY IMPLIED WARRANTIES OF MERCHANTABILITY AND FITNESS FOR A PARTICULAR PURPOSE. Some states do not allow limitations on how long implied warranty lasts, so the above limitations may not apply to you. This warranty gives you specific legal rights, and you may also have other rights which may vary from state to state.

Limitation of Liability: You acknowledge and agree that in no event will Licensor, its affiliates, or any officers, directors, employees or agents thereof be liable to you or any third party for injury or damage caused directly or indirectly by the Product, including but not limited to, incidental, special, consequential, indirect or exemplary damages, and legal expenses or loss of good will, whether based on contract, tort or otherwise arising out of or resulting from or in connection with the use of or inability to use or performance of the Product, even if Licensor has been advised of the possibility of such damages or costs. Some states do not allow the exclusion or limitation of incidental or consequential damages so the above limitation or exclusion may not apply to you.

U.S. Government Restricted Rights: The Product is provided with RESTRICTED AND LIMITED RIGHTS. Use, duplication or disclosure by the U.S. Government is subject to restriction as set forth in FAR S52.227-14 (June 1987) Alternate III (8) (3) (June 1987), FAR S52.227-19 (June 1987), or DFARS S52.227-7013 (c) (1) (iii) (June 1987) as applicable. Contractor/manufacturer is Automated Design Systems, Inc., 375 Northridge Road, Suite 270, Atlanta, GA 30350.

Term & Termination: The limited license granted to you is effective from the date you open this package and shall continue until terminated. You may terminate it at any time by returning the Product to Licensor. The license will also terminate automatically if you fail to comply with any term or condition of this Agreement. You agree upon termination for any reason to return the Product together with any copies to Licensor.

Severability: Should any term of this Agreement be declared void or unenforceable by any court of competent jurisdiction, such declaration shall have no effect on the remaining terms hereof.

Governing Law: This Agreement is governed by and construed in accordance with the laws of the State of Georgia.

Chapter 1

Introduction

Welcome to **Net TOOLS Menu,** a collection of software utilities that greatly enhances the networking capabilities of Windows by providing convenient centralized menu management, workstation security, message delivery across the network, and scripting capability.

This chapter provides an overview of **Net TOOLS Menu,** instructions on how to use this manual and on-line Help, information about different networks, and details on registering your copy to receive technical support.

Net TOOLS Menu was formerly called **Windows Workstation.**

Topics in this chapter

An Overview of Net TOOLS Menu
Checking the Contents of Your Package
Registering Net TOOLS Menu
How to Use the Documentation
System Requirements for Running Net TOOLS Menu
Network Considerations
If You Are New to Microsoft Windows
Learning about Net TOOLS Menu
Getting On-Line Help
Getting Started Quickly with Net TOOLS Menu
Getting Support for Net TOOLS Menu

An Overview of Net TOOLS Menu

Net TOOLS Menu is an extension to the Windows environment that provides the essential management tools needed to integrate Windows applications on your local area network.

Applications Management Tools

Applications management tools are defined as the components of a local area network that offer users an easy-to-use interface to the resources of the network. **Net TOOLS Menu** is comprised of three applications management tools: an **Applications Manager**, **Script Language**, and **Net TOOLS Security**.

The central hub for managing applications over a LAN is a menu system. **Applications Manager** provides a true, multi-user graphical menu system designed specifically for the network user. It is through **Applications Manager** that application and file resources of the network may be presented to users in a logical, intuitive fashion.

The **Script Language, "MultiSet,"** is a powerful batch language that works along with **Applications Manager** to carry out application management commands. In addition, **MultiSet** can also be used with other Windows menu systems, such as Program Manager, to provide them network awareness.

Net TOOLS Security, "Secure Station," provides security at the workstation level above and beyond standard network security provisions. **Secure Station** offers network password protection to unattended workstations. Its screen saver patterns provide privacy for important or sensitive documents during periods of user inactivity. Other components of **Net TOOLS Security** include **Net TOOLS Intercom,** which allows important messages from the LAN Administrator or other users to be delivered across the network, and **Net TOOLS Clock,** which allows the user to set alarm messages and schedule programs to execute at predefined times.

In these ways, **Net TOOLS Menu** breaks new ground by providing a common network user interface to network operating systems. This means that the same commands and actions are used to interact with different network operating system platforms.

Moreover, **Net TOOLS Menu** seamlessly delivers the best features of your network to all Windows applications. It is designed to serve both the end-user and the LAN Administrator alike. For the end-user, the complexities of the network and its resources are completely masked from view. For the LAN Administrator, tight control over network features through a flexible network front-end eliminates potential administrative headaches.

Checking the Contents of Your Package

Before you install **Net TOOLS Menu**, please check the contents of the package. If something is missing from the package or is damaged in any way, please contact the dealer/distributor where you purchased the software or call Automated Design's Customer Service Department at (404) 394-2552.

Documentation - Your package should contain documentation with these titles:

- *Net TOOLS Menu Administrator's Guide* (this book)

- *Release Notes*

Additional copies of this documentation are available from your local dealer or directly from Automated Design Systems, Inc.

Diskettes - **Net TOOLS Menu** contains two sets of diskettes: one set for 5-1/4" disk drives and one set for 3-1/2" disk drives.

Miscellaneous - In addition to the Registration Card, your package may include other useful material about **Net TOOLS Menu** or other topics that may be of interest to you.

Registering Net TOOLS Menu

To register your purchase of **Net TOOLS Menu**, simply complete and return the Registration Card provided in your package. Be sure to return a card for each copy of **Net TOOLS Menu** you have purchased to ensure that you will receive technical support and product update information without delay.

How to Use the Documentation

Net TOOLS Menu's documentation provides many ways to find information quickly. Whether you read documentation only as a last resort, read all of it before you start, or just refer to it as you work, we hope that you will find it helpful in quickly finding the information you need.

The following table lists and briefly describes each part of **Net TOOLS Menu**'s documentation.

Using Net TOOLS Menu's Documentation

Refer to...	When...
Administrator's Guide (*this book*)	Working with **Net TOOLS Menu** to use, configure or manage the various modules. You'll find complete information about using and configuring the various components of **Net TOOLS Menu** organized by module.
Release Notes File	Looking for late-breaking information about using **Net TOOLS Menu**. Release Notes can be found on the Setup diskette as README.TXT and can be viewed with any text editor or viewer such as **Net TOOLS Bulletin Board**.

System Requirements for Running Net TOOLS Menu

The minimum system requirements to run this version of **Net TOOLS Menu** are:

- An 80286-based computer or equivalent.

- 2 megabytes of memory.

- One 1.2MB (5-1/4") or 720K (3-1/2") disk drive.

- MS-DOS 3.3 or later, or equivalent.

- Microsoft Windows version 3.0 or later.

- A local area network running Novell's NetWare 286 version 2.1 or higher, Novell's NetWare 386 version 3.0 or higher, LAN Manager 2.0 or higher, or Banyan VINES 4.10(5).

- A monitor and adapter card for Hercules, EGA, or VGA graphics, or other high-resolution graphics card compatible with Windows version 3.0 or later.

For optimal performance, we recommend at least a 386/SX-16 processor and 4 megabytes of memory. Because Windows is processor- and memory-intensive, greater resources in these areas will provide more satisfying performance.

Network Considerations

This manual contains instructions for installing, configuring, and using **Net TOOLS Menu** in a NetWare, LAN Manager, or Banyan VINES environment. Where differences exist among the networks, NetWare terminology is used "generically." Network-specific information is presented where necessary.

Terminology

The following table summarizes the differences among NetWare, LAN Manager, and Banyan terminology:

NetWare	LAN Manager	Banyan VINES
supervisor	administrator	member of Admin List
search path	the user's path	the user's path
search drive	a directory on the user's path	a directory on the user's path
login	log on	login
Syscon	NET ADMIN	Manage
server/volume:	\\server\sharename:	N/A

NetWare Rights

The user rights referenced throughout this document are for NetWare 386. If you are using NetWare 286, refer to the following list for the equivalent NetWare 386 rights:

NetWare 386	NetWare 286
Read	Read
Write	Write
Read Write	Open
Create	Create
Erase	Delete
Supervisor, Access Control	Parental
File Scan	Search
Modify	Modify

LAN Manager Rights

The rights a user can have to a particular network path under LAN Manager are:

R - Read from files

C - Create new files

D - Delete files

A - Attributes

P - Permissions

W - Write to files

NetWare Considerations

The EMS NetWare shells (EMSNETX) are not supported when running Windows in Enhanced mode and could cause problems. The correct shell to use is the NETX.COM shell.

LAN Manager Security

The Enhanced Workstation version of LAN Manager 2.0 supports two levels of security, share level security and user level security. Share level security allows each shared resource on the server to be protected by a password. Any user knowing the password can use the shared resource. Share level security is completely compatible with MS-NET and LAN Manager 1.0 security. The Basic Workstation version of LAN Manager 2.0 supports only share level security.

Net TOOLS Menu was designed for user level security. When operating under share level security, certain features such as **Secure Station** will work in standalone mode, prompting users for a password for use during the current session.

NETLOGON must be running on the server in order to use user level security.

Banyan VINES Considerations

Due to the nature of an enterprise network (large number of users and the large geographic area that it may cover) remote access calls are inherently slow. In addition, if a server does not respond to a remote call, the process is even slower. To eliminate lengthy delays, Windows restricts the portions of the network it looks at when enumerating lists and users to the local group@organization. The default is for the local group@organization, e.g., *@my group@my org. Therefore, even though you may be accessing resources in various groups and organizations, only local group information is provided by default. The Access Rights dialog box in Administration mode and the "Member of Lists" in the Network Information dialog box are two examples of where **Net TOOLS Menu** must provide this information.

Administrators may edit the default setting to view additional items, groups and organizations by creating masks. See "Changing the Default VINES Network Group" in Chapter 2, "Installation and Configuration." This option is set centrally so that any changes will affect all users.

Applications Manager requires the StreetTalk Directory Assistance utility in order to assign rights to users for access to network program groups, items and scripts. If StreetTalk is not available, the list box in the Access Rights dialog box will be empty.

If You Are New to Microsoft Windows

Net TOOLS Menu operates in the graphical operating environment called Microsoft Windows. With Windows, you can use drop-down menus and icons to choose commands and start programs -- you don't have to memorize or type complex commands. Windows can be thought of as a "manager" that allows you to use graphics on the screen to manipulate your computer, its memory, programs and files.

Unlike character-based programs, Windows programs excel at displaying both graphics and text on the screen. Windows provides a truly WYSIWYG (what you see is what you get) environment where the printed page looks nearly identical to the screen display. With Windows, several different applications and/or files can be opened at once, and it is easy to switch back and forth between them. More importantly, all the programs share similar features, providing the user a familiar environment to work in.

With Windows, the mouse is used to point to commands and icons on the screen. The mouse is easy to use--just slide it on a flat surface to move the pointer or cursor on the screen. By moving the pointer and pressing the mouse button, you can use **Net TOOLS Menu** commands and features.

This manual assumes that you have installed Windows and are familiar with its operation. For more information about working with a mouse and Windows, see the Microsoft Windows documentation.

Learning about Net TOOLS Menu

Net TOOLS Menu combines Microsoft Windows and your network into one easy-to-use graphical environment. It provides "integration tools" such as a customized menuing system and program scripts. In addition, **Net TOOLS Menu** adds ready-to-run utilities for security, data encryption, work group messaging and alarm clock features.

You will want to make certain that you spend some time thinking about how you can use the tools **Net TOOLS Menu** offers to best serve your networking needs. This chapter will present some opportunities to discover how Windows and networks come together and are enhanced by using **Net TOOLS Menu**.

How Do I Learn Net TOOLS Menu?

You can learn to use **Net TOOLS Menu** in a variety of ways to suit your needs and experience. The following table suggests some approaches to learning **Net TOOLS Menu**.

Chapter 1

Approaches to Learning Net TOOLS Menu

If you...	Do this...
Are new to Windows	Learn about working with the mouse and with general Windows concepts by reading the Microsoft Windows documentation.
Want to learn how to install and configure **Net TOOLS Menu**	Read Chapter 2 in this guide.
Want to learn about using **Net TOOLS Menu** modules	Read Chapters 3 through 6 in this guide.
Want to learn how to set up and use **Applications Manager's** menuing system	Read Chapter 3 in this guide.
Want to learn how to set restrictions for features in **Applications Manager** and **Net TOOLS Security**	Read Chapter 4 in this guide.
Want to learn about **MultiSet, Net TOOLS Menu**'s network scripting language	Read Chapter 5 in this guide.
Want to learn about **Net TOOLS Security** features	Read Chapter 6 in this guide.

Getting On-Line Help

Net TOOLS Menu's on-line Help feature provides information about using the product, how to use Help and how to use the keyboard shortcuts for menu commands. **Net TOOLS Menu** also presents information on Windows basics for users who may be unfamiliar with Microsoft Windows.

For ease of learning, **Net TOOLS Menu** uses the standard Windows Help interface provided by Microsoft. The user can display on-line Help by choosing any command from the Help menu in **Applications Manager** or other **Net TOOLS** modules. The following table describes each command on the Help menu.

Commands on the Help menu

Command	Function
Index	Opens the Windows Help program with an index of Help topics.
Keyboard	Presents keyboard shortcuts for **Net TOOLS Menu**.
Basic Skills	Presents concepts and techniques for using Microsoft Windows and Windows applications such as **Net TOOLS Menu**.
Commands	Defines the drop-down menu option found in **Net TOOLS Menu**.
Procedures	Presents a "how-to" for **Net TOOLS Menu**.
Glossary	Presents a recap of special terms used in the **Net TOOLS Menu** on-line Help and documentation.
Using Help	Opens the Help file supplied by Microsoft for using Windows Help.

System Help

System Help is general help about the program and how to operate its features. **Net TOOLS Menu** makes use of the standard Help facilities for Windows (WINHELP.EXE). System Help is available in each module of **Net TOOLS Menu** by choosing the Help option on the menu bar. Most dialog boxes also have a Help button that displays information pertaining to that particular dialog box.

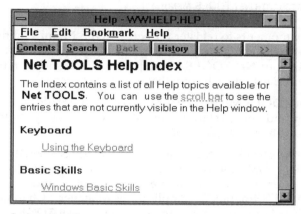

System Help Screen.

Application Help

Application Help is customized help that the LAN Administrator makes available to the user on particular application procedures. Customized help can be created for groups, subgroups and program items in **Applications Manager**. In **Applications Manager**, customized help is available to users by pressing SHIFT+F1 and then choosing a selected group, subgroup or item for which help text exists. For more information about Application Help, see the section on creating help text in Chapter 3.

Getting Started Quickly with Net TOOLS Menu

Net TOOLS Menu includes tools for organizing, administering and using network applications under Microsoft Windows. Getting started with **Net TOOLS Menu** is fast and easy--just follow the instructions below outlining what to do first.

- **TO GET STARTED WITH NET TOOLS MENU:**

1. Take a few moments to register for **Net TOOLS Menu** Technical Support by completing and returning the Registration Card included in your **Net TOOLS Menu** package. You should return a Registration Card for each copy that you have purchased.

2. Install **Net TOOLS Menu** on your network. For details on installation and how to start and exit the program, see Chapter 2, "Installation and Configuration."

3. Configure **Applications Manager** and **Net TOOLS Security** for your network applications. For details about configuration and setting user restrictions, see Chapter 2, "Installation and Configuration," Chapter 3, "Applications Manager," Chapter 4, "Net TOOLS Administration," and Chapter 6, "Net TOOLS Security."

Getting Support for Net TOOLS Menu

If you should need assistance using **Net TOOLS Menu**, our Technical Support Department is available to help you from 8:30 am - 5:30 pm EST Monday through Friday at (404) 394-2552.

In order to receive technical support, you must have a registered copy of **Net TOOLS Menu**. If you need assistance before we have received your Registration Card, we will accept your registration information over the phone.

Before you call for support, please consult the relevant section of this manual for help. If you are unable to find your answer in the manual, please have the following information available for the technical support representative:

Important information for technical support:

Topic	Explanation
Net TOOLS Menu Serial Number (required)	The serial number of your **Net TOOLS Menu** is found in the **Applications Manager** About box. To display this box, choose Help and then About. The serial number is also on the installation diskette.
Network Operating System	**Net TOOLS Menu** supports Novell NetWare 2.1 or higher, Microsoft LAN Manager 2.0 or higher and Banyan VINES 4.10(5).
Workstation Configuration	This includes model of CPU, network interface card, memory configuration, disk configuration.
Version of **Net TOOLS Menu**	The version of **Net TOOLS Menu** may be found in the **Applications Manager** About box; it is also printed on your installation diskette.
Version of Microsoft Windows	The version of Windows is available by running WINVER.EXE and may also be found in the Program Manager About box.

You may prefer to send your questions to our Technical Support Department via Fax or the Bulletin Board Service.

BBS: (404) 394-7448

FAX (404) 394-2191

To reach the **Net TOOLS** forum in CompuServ, type **GO ADSINFO**.

Chapter 2

Installation and Configuration

Net TOOLS Menu is easy to install -- just run the Setup program located on the Setup diskette and specify the drive and directory where **Net TOOLS Menu** is to be installed. Setup installs **Net TOOLS Menu** automatically, copying the appropriate files from the product diskettes to your network. After installing **Net TOOLS Menu**, you will have the option to install any other **Net TOOLS** products you may have purchased, such as **Print** or **Meter**. When you finish running the Setup program, you will need to configure **Net TOOLS Menu** for the users and administrators in your organization.

Important: You must run the Setup program to install **Net TOOLS Menu**. The **Net TOOLS Menu** files are compressed on diskette. If you copy these files yourself, important setup procedures may be bypassed, causing unpredictable results.

Topics in this chapter

Installing Net TOOLS Menu
Net TOOLS Menu Components
Configuring Net TOOLS Menu
Starting Net TOOLS Menu
Exiting Net TOOLS Menu Applications

Installing Net TOOLS Menu

Installing **Net TOOLS Menu** is a very simple process and should take only a few minutes.

- **TO INSTALL NET TOOLS MENU:**

1. Log on to the network.

   Log on to the file server on which **Net TOOLS Menu** is to be installed.

   Since you will need certain rights for creating subdirectories and files on the server, we recommend that you log in with Supervisor equivalent rights.

2. Start Microsoft Windows.

   The installation program is a Windows application and, therefore, requires that you install the product while running Windows. If you do not have Microsoft Windows installed on your workstation or available to you on the network, please refer to the Windows manual for assistance in installing your Windows software.

3. Insert the **Net TOOLS Menu** Setup diskette into the disk drive.

4. Run WWSETUP.EXE. You can start WWSETUP in either of the following ways:

   - Issue the File/Run from Windows Program Manager, and type <drive>:WWSETUP, where <drive>: is the drive letter that contains the **Net TOOLS Menu** Setup diskette. The Setup program will load, displaying its logo.

   - Use the Windows File Manager. Change the current directory to the drive that contains the Setup diskette, (A: or B:), then double-click on WWSETUP.EXE.

5. The Setup program's initial screen displays. It indicates the default drive and directory in which **Net TOOLS Menu** will be installed. You can type in another drive and directory, if desired. A server name\volume: may be substituted for the drive.

```
┌─────────────────────────────────────────────────────┐
│ ▭              Net TOOLS Setup                       │
│                 Applications Manager                 │
│  will be installed in the following directory, which will be created on your hard disk. │
│                                                      │
│  If you want to install the application in a different directory and/or drive, type the │
│                     name of the directory.           │
│                                                      │
│  Select Continue to begin the installation.          │
│                                                      │
│  Copy to:  ┌──────────────────────────────────────┐  │
│            │ F:\NETTOOLS                          │  │
│            └──────────────────────────────────────┘  │
│   ┌────────────┐      ┌────────────┐    ┌────────────┐│
│   │  Continue  │      │   Cancel   │    │    Help    ││
│   └────────────┘      └────────────┘    └────────────┘│
└─────────────────────────────────────────────────────┘
```

Setup Program's initial screen.

The Setup program installs **Net TOOLS Menu** program files, which consist of the executable and help files, dynamic link libraries, and other files that are necessary for the **Net TOOLS Menu** program to run.

On a network, the **Net TOOLS Menu** program files must be placed in an area that is accessible to all users of **Net TOOLS Menu.** The program files MUST be placed on the user's search path.

Enter the drive letter, or the server name and the volume name, followed by the directory name where the **Net TOOLS Menu** program files will be stored.

Example: F:\NETTOOLS

            or

            MYSERVER\SYS:\NETTOOLS

6. As Setup is copying the required files to their destinations, a dialog box displays and details the copy process. You may stop the installation process at any time while this dialog box is displayed.

Chapter 2

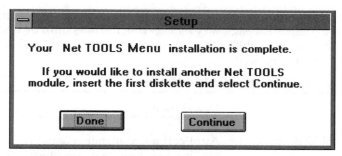

The Net TOOLS Menu Setup dialog box.

You may be prompted to insert additional diskettes.

Note: Please do not remove the diskette from the source drive until prompted to do so by the Setup program.

When **Net TOOLS Menu** is installed, the following dialog box displays:

The Installation Complete dialog box.

7. If you are installing only **Net TOOLS Menu**, choose Done.

If you have purchased another **Net TOOLS** product, such as **Print** or **Meter**, and want to install it now, insert the first installation diskette for that product and choose Continue.

Installation Considerations

- During installation if the program files directory is pointing to a previous version of **Net TOOLS Menu** (formerly **Windows Workstation**), no configuration or group files are installed. This prevents the deletion of customized files.

- If you are updating an existing **Windows Workstation** installation and **Workstation Menu** is executing as your shell, do not attempt to install the new version of **Net TOOLS Menu** in the same directory. You will receive a Sharing Violation Error message because the **Workstation** program is already in use and cannot be written over. Instead install the new version in a different directory. After installation, change your path to the directory in which the new version is installed.

Net TOOLS Menu Components

Net TOOLS Menu has been developed using a modular approach. This makes network design easy by allowing the integrator or LAN Administrator the flexibility to choose which components work best for the particular installation.

Modules included with Net TOOLS Menu

Module	Description
APPMAN.EXE	**Applications Manager,** a network applications and file management tool.
WWEXT.EXE	**Net TOOLS Security,** which includes **Secure Station, Net TOOLS Intercom** and **Net TOOLS Clock**.
WWENCODE.EXE	File Encryption/Decryption command line feature. For the format of this command see Chapter 6, "Net TOOLS Security."

MULTISET.EXE	**MultiSet Script Language.**
WWBOARD.EXE	**Bulletin Board.**

Using administration tools, you can customize **Net TOOLS Menu** in a variety of ways for use on the network.

Administration tools included with Net TOOLS Menu

Tool	Description
APPMAN.EXE	**Applications Manager,** which you can run in Administration mode to control user access to groups and applications.
WWADMIN.EXE	**Administration,** a utility for setting user restrictions in **Applications Manager** and **Net TOOLS Security.**
MSEDIT.EXE	**MultiSet Script Language Editor.**

Because **Net TOOLS Menu** acts as a network extension to Microsoft Windows, it is suggested that **Net TOOLS Menu** be included in your Windows startup procedure to ensure that complete, easy-to-use network functionality is available to the user at all times.

Applications Manager's .INI files

Applications Manager does not use the WIN.INI to store settings; rather, it uses .INI files of its own.

.INI Files Used by Applications Manager

Filename	Description
NETMENU.INI	This file contains a list of all the Network Group files defined while in Administration mode. When you Save Workspace in Administration mode, NETMENU.INI is created in the directory from which **Applications Manager** was started. You may move NETMENU.INI to another directory on the user's path, since **Applications Manager** searches for that file along the user's path. Use a file management utility such as File Manager to move the file.
PERMENU.INI	This file contains references to Personal Group files and the user-defined settings. It is automatically placed in the user's Windows directory when the user issues a Save Workspace command in User mode. **Applications Manager** does not search the path for PERMENU.INI. If the user deletes or moves this file, **Applications Manager** is unable to find it and will create another in the Windows directory. However, any information on personalized settings or groups previously written to the file will not be included in the new one.
WWNET.INI	This file specifies the network-specific DLL that must be used for **Applications Manager** to interface with the network. This file must be in the NETTOOLS directory.

ADMIN.INI   This is a 0-byte file in the **Net TOOLS Menu** program directory that acts as the gate keeper to Administration mode. When you toggle into Administration mode by pressing <CTRL> + <ALT> + <A>, ADMIN.INI is opened. If you attempt to toggle into Administration mode while another user is already in that mode, the following message displays: "Access denied. Another user is currently in Administration mode." This message may also display if you do not have [RWFCDM] rights to the **Net TOOLS Menu** directory or if the file is flagged Read Only.

Configuring Net TOOLS Menu

Once you have installed **Net TOOLS Menu**, you need to configure the software for users and administrators in your network environment. This section describes the configuration tasks.

Note: Before proceeding with the configuration process, we suggest that you become familiar with **Net TOOLS Menu** by running the program and reading through the rest of this manual.

Granting rights to the Net TOOLS Menu directory

You must grant users and administrators rights to the **Net TOOLS
Menu** directory.

Rights to be granted

Network	Default Directory	User	Administrator
NetWare	SERVER\\VOL: NETTOOLS	[RF]	[RWFCDM]
LAN Manager	\\SERVER\SHARENAME \NETTOOLS	[R]	[RWC]
Banyan	Z:\NETTOOLS	Read Permis.	Control Permis.

Note: Do not flag files in the **Net TOOLS Menu** directory.

Setting Up Administrators

You must set up any additional users who will use Administration
mode. **Net TOOLS Menu** allows the administrator to create and
change *network* groups and items only while in Administration mode.
Add the following section to the WIN.INI file for each user who will
be using Administration mode:

```
[WWAdmin]
NetworkSecurity=ADMEXT.DLL
ApplicationsManager=ADMAMAN.DLL
```

Loading Applications Manager as the Windows Shell

Applications Manager can be defined as the shell for Microsoft Windows by:

- Editing each user's SYSTEM.INI file as described below.

  and

- Updating each user's search path to include the directory containing the **Net TOOLS Menu** program files (.EXE, .DLL). This directory **must** be on each user's search path.

This will cause **Applications Manager** to be loaded automatically for access to applications, files and network utilities.

- **TO UPDATE A USER'S SYSTEM.INI FILE:**

1. Using the text editor of your choice, edit the individual user's SYSTEM.INI file.

2. In the [BOOT] section, change the SHELL= line to read SHELL=APPMAN.EXE.

3. Save the modified SYSTEM.INI with the new settings.

You can automate the above procedure by running the following **MultiSet** script:

SETINI SYSTEM.INI BOOT SHELL=APPMAN.EXE

(For further information about **MultiSet** scripts, see Chapter 5.)

Using Startup Groups

If you have created a startup group for your users, the programs or scripts contained in that group will execute automatically each time you start up **Applications Manager** (if **Applications Manager** is running as your Windows shell). The default startup group that is shipped with **Net TOOLS Menu** loads as icons the **Net TOOLS Security** applications. The startup group is equivalent to the load= and run= lines in the WIN.INI file.

Each user may have one network and one personal startup group.

Net TOOLS Menu Startup Groups

Type	Description
Network	The administrator creates a network startup group by naming a network group STARTUP.APP. The programs and scripts in STARTUP.APP execute after **Applications Manager** loads. After execution, STARTUP.APP closes, hiding the network startup group from all users. When the administrator toggles **Applications Manager** into Administration mode, however, the startup group loads and displays for editing. Network startup groups support subgroups and the "rights" features of **Net TOOLS Administration**.
Personal	Users can create and maintain personal startup groups by naming a personal group PERSTART.APP. After executing the network startup group, PERSTART.APP executes its programs and scripts. Unlike the network startup group, PERSTART.APP remains active, displaying all program group items for editing.

Network and personal startup groups and their paths are specified in the NETMENU.INI and the PERMENU.INI files, respectively. The NETMENU.INI, which all users share, is updated as the administrator creates or deletes network program groups. The PERMENU.INI is updated as each user creates or deletes personal program groups.

> **Note:** The load= and run= lines in the WIN.INI file are still executed when there is a startup group. If an application is referenced in these lines and also in the startup group, **Applications Manager** will attempt to launch it twice.

Setting the TEMP Variable

If the TEMP environment variable is not already set, you must set it. This variable specifies a directory that is used by **Net TOOLS Menu** to temporarily store data.

The directory specified by the TEMP variable must physically exist. For example, if you have SET TEMP=C:\WINDOWS\TEMP in your AUTOEXEC.BAT file, you must create the directory TEMP in C:\WINDOWS if it does not already exist.

Securing DOS Applications

A terminate-and-stay resident program (TSR) called WWTSR.EXE is included with the **Net TOOLS Security** program files. In 386 Enhanced mode, this program enables **Secure Station** to support DOS applications just as it supports Windows applications. WWTSR **must** execute before Windows is launched. You may want to consider centrally launching this TSR from a batch file specified in the login script. (In Standard mode, **Secure Station** does not monitor DOS applications since they are effectively "asleep" when Windows is in use.)

In addition, the TEMP variable **must** be set and pointing to an existing directory in order for WWTSR.EXE to communicate properly with **Secure Station**.

Adding the LAN Manager WWServer Service

WWSetup adds a service, WWServer, to the primary and backup servers in the domain to which the user logged in. This service allows **Secure Station** to verify user passwords and **Net TOOLS Intercom** to enumerate groups. When using **Net TOOLS Menu** on networks with multiple domains, WWSetup should be run on each domain server so that WWServer is active whenever users log in to the domain.

If a server was not active when WWSetup was run or if automatic setup fails, you can manually add WWServer as a service by following these steps:

1. Copy WWSERVER.EXE to the SERVICES subdirectory on every affected server.

2. Modify the LANMAN.INI for every affected server as follows:

- In the [workstation] section, increment the value of numservices.

- In the [server] section, add WWSERVER to the srvservices list.

- In the [services] section, add the line
  wwserver=services\wwserver.exe.

- Create a [wwserver] section and add the line
  install=services\wwserver.exe.

Changing the Default VINES Network Group

In a VINES environment, the default setting for **Applications Manager** is to look only at the local group because of the slow process of checking all items, groups and organizations across the network.

You can customize the items, groups and organizations that will display by editing the WWNET.INI file. Initially, the absence of masks indicates the default setting.

- The wildcards * and ? are allowed. *@*@* indicates all items at all groups at all organizations. If you choose this option there is no need to list other masks. When typing in masks you must enter a mask for the local group for it to continue to display.

- Multiple mask statements create an OR condition. That is, information is returned that meets any of the conditions on any line.

- Masks begin with Mask1 and must appear in consecutive order. A break in the mask sequence stops the reading of masks. For example., if you jump from Mask2 to Mask4, the program will discontinue reading the section when no Mask3 is found.

Here is a sample modified WWNET.INI file:

[VINES]
Mask1=*@Sales@Atlanta (Set the default group)
Mask2=*@Marketing@* (View all users and lists having Marketing as group)
Mask3=R????@*@Remote (Return any item that begins with R and has a maximum of 5 characters **and** is a Remote organization.)

Starting Net TOOLS Menu

You can load **Applications Manager** as the Windows shell or start the program manually. If configured to load as the Windows shell, **Applications Manager** starts automatically when you start Windows.

You may start **Applications Manager** manually by running the program APPMAN.EXE from the File/Run option of your Windows shell (e.g., Program Manager) or by choosing the program from File Manager.

Applications Manager's Initial Display

When **Applications Manager** is executed, the workspace does not display any program groups. Several sample group files with .APP extensions are included in the **Net TOOLS Menu** directory for your use. You can also merge existing Program Manager (.GRP) group or earlier versions of Windows Workstation (.DB) groups.

Follow this procedure to merge groups:

1. Hold <ALT> <CTRL> while you type <A> to enter Administration mode.

2. Choose File/New/Network Group.

3. Click in the Filename edit box.

4. Select the Browse button.

5. Select a group (.APP file for the sample groups or .GRP for your Program Manager groups) you want to appear in **Applications Manager** and choose OK.

   Do not select ADMIN.APP (the personal menu) unless you want it converted into a network group.

6. Complete the New Network Group dialog box and choose OK.

Repeat this procedure for each group you want to add. See Chapter 3, "Applications Manager," for more information.

Starting Windows with Command Line Parameters

You can use a command line parameter to load an application as Windows starts. For example, if you wish to have Word for Windows run after Windows starts, type the following command line parameter from the DOS prompt:

   WIN WINWORD.EXE

Setting Personal Passwords for Secure Station in a Banyan Environment

Since **Net TOOLS Menu** is unable to access a user's VINES network password, each user must set a personal password at the start of each session. For information about Secure Station passwords, see Chapter 6, "Net TOOLS Security."

Exiting Net TOOLS Menu Applications

When you are through working with the various components of **Net TOOLS Menu,** you can exit quickly.

If **Applications Manager** is your Windows shell, exiting it will also close Windows.

- **TO EXIT NET TOOLS MENU APPLICATIONS:**

1. Choose Exit from the **Applications Manager** File menu or press ALT+F4 at the same time.

   If necessary, **Applications Manager** prompts you to save changes when you attempt to exit.

   The Exit Applications Manager message box displays with a Save Workspace check box. If the Save Workspace on Exit menu item is checked on, the default action in this box will be to save. You may check the box in the exit message off at this time. Unchecking this box does not alter the status of the Save Workspace on Exit menu item, however.

2. Choose OK.

Chapter 3

Applications Manager

Applications Manager includes easy-to-use tools for creating, administering and accessing network resources in the Windows environment. It is intended for use by the LAN Administrator to organize and manage standardized menus for network groups and by end-users to add their own customized groups to the workspace.

This chapter presents procedures on creating, maintaining and working with Network (Administrator-defined) and Personal (user-defined) Groups and their contents. It also covers the range of display and operating mode options that are available to the Administrator or to the end-user.

Topics in this chapter

What Is Applications Manager?
Running Applications Manager in Administration Mode
Running Applications Manager as the Shell
Working with Group Windows
Building Applications Manager Groups
Saving Groups and Your Workspace
Editing Groups, Subgroups and Items
Running Programs from Applications Manager
Selecting Display Options
Checking System Resources
Exiting Applications Manager

What Is Applications Manager?

Applications Manager contains a graphical menuing system for organizing programs into single or multi-user groups for easy network access. Some highlights of **Applications Manager's** features include:

- Complete centralized control of Network Group and Subgroup design

- User rights and password assignments for multi-level network security

- Easy access to administrative options from any workstation

- Creation of application-specific help screens

- Customized groups for users' personal files

- Integration with **MultiSet** scripting language

- Multiple choices for viewing and arranging the workspace

- Hierarchical or flat group access

Applications Manager serves as a hub for logically managing both Windows and non-Windows network resources. It is an organization of Network and Personal Groups and their respective Subgroups, all of which may contain items that run programs or scripts.

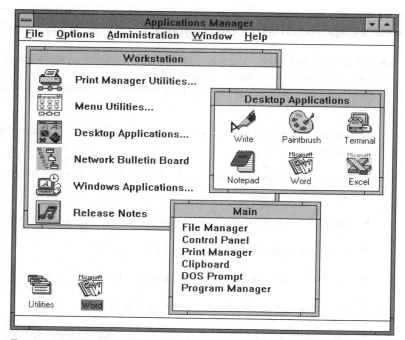

The Applications Manager window showing group windows and icons.

Using its administrative options, you may create as many Network Groups and related Subgroups as you have system resources for, add application items to them and assign rights to restrict their use to specific LAN groups or users. **Applications Manager** users may also add their own Personal Groups and customize their workspace settings, if these options are available to them.

If you choose to run **Applications Manager** as the Windows shell, it will load automatically each time Windows is run. While you are running applications, **Applications Manager** is always available, either in the background or minimized as an icon at the bottom of the screen.

Applications Manager and its administrative features are closely integrated and as easily accessible as executing a key sequence. The program's flexibility allows you to define the selection of menu bar options and features that you make available to groups of users by placing the file with these settings on their path. Updating groups and programs is virtually transparent to users, allowing them to continue working during the process.

Running Applications Manager in Administration Mode

In addition to building a system of groups and applications in **Applications Manager**, you will want to set default options restricting its functions. Many of these options, which are set in the **Net TOOLS Administration** program, determine how **Applications Manager** appears to users and which menu bar items, Network Groups and applications are available. Other options, such as the ability to add Network Groups or set user rights, are only activated when a LAN Administrator uses a key sequence to change modes.

Applications Manager can be run in two modes: User mode and Administration mode. In User mode only the menu bar items and default options defined by an Administrator for a LAN group's use are available. In Administration mode, *all* of **Applications Manager's** menu items and options are available, *plus* additional commands related to Network Groups and Administration Setup.

The integrated design of these two programs makes it convenient to perform related tasks in **Net TOOLS Administration,** while using **Applications Manager** to create or edit groups. Use the following procedures to enter Administration mode and to run the **Administration** program:

- From the **Applications Manager** window, use the key sequence Ctrl+Alt+A to toggle into Administration mode. A message box may prompt you for the password assigned to the current .WWR file. Executing this key sequence automatically gives you access to the Administration menu now visible in the menu bar.

  Choose Setup from the Administration menu to launch the program. The currently opened APPMAN.WWR file automatically displays for editing. At this point, you may open other **Applications Manager** files, **Net TOOLS Security** files or create new .WWR files of either type.

  OR

- Choose File/Run from the menu bar in your Windows shell and enter WWADMIN.EXE in the command line box.

If **Applications Manager** is not currently running and you want to start it in Administration mode directly, type APPMAN.EXE /A in the File/Run command line box.

You will be prompted to enter a password when you attempt to open .WWR files if a password has been set in **Administration**. Your product is shipped without a password so there is no initial password prompt. You may set a password after setup by choosing Options/Change Password in the **Net TOOLS Administration** menu bar and entering your own password. You will not be required to enter a password for a password-protected file if you have logged into the network with supervisor-equivalent privileges.

In addition to providing a menu item to access the Administration program, toggling **Applications Manager** into Administration mode offers you access to other options not available to users:

- All **Applications Manager** menu bar options, even those that you may have restricted to network users, are available to you.

- The File/New/Network Group menu item is available and the group-, subgroup- and item-related dialog boxes allow you to set rights.

- The File/New/New Workspace item, which lets you create a new NETMENU.INI file or modify a NETMENU.INI file on any attached server.

- The File/Save Workspace As item lets you clone the present workspace to a different server.

- The Commit Changes item is available on the Administration menu. Use this command to propagate changes to LAN groups and users made in the Syscon utility to **Applications Manager's** Network Groups. Users are notified of any changes committed by this command the next time they attempt to start **Applications Manager** or open an affected group or item.

- No passwords are required to use groups or items.

When you want to end your session, repeat the key sequence to toggle back to user mode. The Administration item no longer displays in the menu bar.

See Chapter 4, "Net TOOLS Administration," for an in-depth discussion of **Applications Manager's** administrative functions and procedures.

Running Applications Manager as the Shell

The Windows shell is the application that automatically runs whenever you start Windows. Unless you specify otherwise, Program Manager is the Windows shell. To take full advantage of **Net TOOLS Menu's** broad range of network features, you should specify **Applications Manager** as the shell. The directory containing the **Applications Manager** program files must be on each user's path.

To change the shell, modify the shell= line in the SYSTEM.INI file on each user's workstation to read:

```
shell=APPMAN.EXE
```

You can edit this file using any text editor such as Windows Notepad. Save the above change and exit Windows.

Or you can run the following **MultiSet** script:

SETINI SYSTEM.INI BOOT SHELL=APPMAN.EXE

The next time the user runs Windows, **Applications Manager** displays as the shell. The user now has all the standard features and accessories of Windows plus the enhanced networking capabilities of **Applications Manager**.

> **Note:** As a safeguard against errors, be sure to create a copy of the SYSTEM.INI file before editing it.

The **Net TOOLS Menu** EXE and DLL files must be installed on each user's search path. If **Applications Manager** is the shell and the DLLs and EXEs cannot be located, Windows will not load and an error will result. (The error message indicates that Program Manager "cannot be found," when actually it is the **Applications Manager** EXE and DLL files that cannot be located.) In order for a user to successfully run Windows both on and off the network, the program files must also be copied to the local hard disk and the directory containing them added to the path. This procedure is permissible under your software license agreement.

Working with Group Windows

A typical **Applications Manager** display at startup includes an arrangement of open group windows and a collection of group icons at the bottom of the workspace. Depending on the combination of group windows, the number of programs that execute at startup and the settings selected, the look of the workspace will vary.

Because **Applications Manager** is a Windows program, its workspace appearance and features look and respond in similar ways to most other Windows applications. To access and run an item contained in a group or a subgroup, you open the group window and choose the program's icon. Once you have started a program, you can minimize the group window to an icon to reduce clutter on your workspace.

The following sections describe several common procedures involved in working with **Applications Manager's** windows.

- **To OPEN A GROUP WINDOW OR PROGRAM ITEM:**

1. Select the icon of the group, subgroup or item you want to open.
2. Choose Open from the File menu

   OR

   Double-click on the group's icon.

   You will be prompted for a password if one has been set when you attempt to open a group or item.

   The selected group window is restored to the size and arrangement in effect when you last closed it.

- **To MINIMIZE A GROUP WINDOW TO AN ICON:**

1. Select the window you want to minimize.
2. Choose its Minimize box (down arrow)

   OR

   Choose Minimize from its Control menu.

The group window displays as an icon at the bottom of the workspace.

- **To REARRANGE GROUP WINDOWS:**

During the course of working with several open group windows, they start overlapping or hiding one another. The Window menu offers two display choices to rearrange group windows neatly within the workspace: **Cascade** and **Tile**.

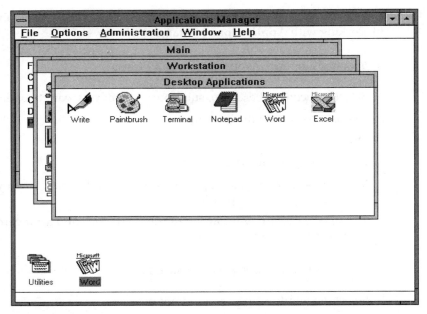

Applications Manager arranged with cascading windows.

The **Cascade** command displays all windows in a uniform size and an overlapping view so that the title bar of each window is visible.

Chapter 3

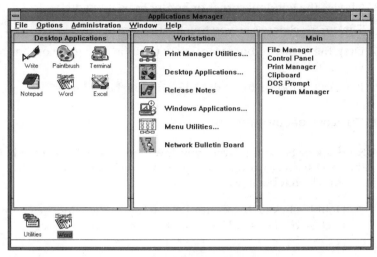

Applications Manager arranged with tiled windows.

The **Tile** command arranges all the open windows so that each fills a portion of the workspace without overlapping. The size of a tiled window will vary depending on the number of windows open on your workspace.

Each additional window that is opened displays on top of the rearranged workspace. Choose the Tile or Cascade again to include the new window in the arrangement.

● **TO RESIZE GROUP WINDOWS:**

Changing the size the **Applications Manager**'s group windows follows standard Windows procedures. Since group windows often contain several item icons, some of them might be out of view after resizing. Checking Auto Arrange Icons on in the Options menu assures that the icons will be automatically rearranged in the resized window. You may also redistribute icons manually after resizing by choosing the Arrange Icons command from the Window menu.

1. Select the window to be resized.

2. Choose the window corner or border to be moved.

   The cursor changes as you touch either area.

3. Drag the corner or border to a new position, using the outline as your guide.

4. Release the mouse to set the new window boundaries.

● **TO CLOSE GROUP WINDOWS:**

A Network or Personal Group window closes as an icon at the bottom of the workspace. A program item window closes back into the group to which it belongs.

   ● Double-click on the Control menu box of the window you want to close or choose Close from its drop-down menu

     OR

   ● Choose the Close all command from the Window menu to close all open windows.

● **TO CLOSE SUBGROUP WINDOWS:**

Depending on which procedure you use to close subgroups, they respond differently.

   ● Double-click on the Control menu box of the subgroup window or choose Close from that menu to close the window back into the parent group to which it belongs.

     OR

   ● Choose the down-arrow from the window to minimize the group at the bottom of the workspace. (If the hierarchical option is active, this action will close the subgroup as above.)

Building Applications Manager Groups

Applications Manager consists of an arrangement of Network Groups, Personal Groups, Subgroups and Items representing programs or scripts. You build a menu system by creating the number of groups or subgroups you need and adding items representing executable filenames or scripts to each unit. This customized set of groups and subgroups is graphically represented by multiple windows and icons on your **Applications Manager** workspace.

Group files may contain as many subgroups and/or program items as you choose. There are three ways to build the contents of a group:

- Merging existing Windows Program Manager groups.

- Merging group menus from earlier versions of **Workstation Menu**.

- Adding individual applications or scripts with the New/Item command or by copying or moving elements from another group or subgroup.

To meet security needs in the LAN environment, **Applications Manager** also provides multi-level security features. You may assign access rights to Network Groups and their subgroups as well as to the program items they contain. In addition, all groups, subgroups, and items can be password protected to further control user access.

All group files are automatically assigned the default .APP extension, but they will accept other extensions. Network Groups are saved to the directory where your **Applications Manager** program files reside unless you specify otherwise. Personal Group files are saved to the user's Windows directory by default.

> **Note**: You must explicitly save a newly created or a modified group in **Applications Manager**.

The following sections describe the procedures involved in building and maintaining groups, subgroups and program items.

Merging Existing Groups into Applications Manager

Applications Manager is capable of merging both Program Manager's group files and menu database files created in earlier versions of **Workstation Menu**. If you are already using standard Windows groups or have **Net TOOLS Menu** group menus customized to your network needs, it's simple to transfer their contents to **Applications Manager** groups. To merge another type of group file to a Network Group in **Applications Manager**, you must be in Administration mode. Personal Group files can be converted to Network Group files, but not vice versa.

● **TO MERGE AN EXISTING GROUP FILE:**

1. Follow the general procedures for adding new Network or Personal Groups as detailed in the sections below.

2. Type the filename of the existing group in the text box, including the path if necessary.

   OR

   Use the Browse button to search for the files with either .GRP (Program Manager) or .DB (**Workstation Menu**) file extensions. Choose OK in the Browse dialog box.

Shortcut: If you want to merge multiple .GRP or .DB files, you can use DOS wildcards to locate all the files of that type in the current directory. For example, typing *.GRP in the filename text box will merge all the Program Manager groups in the directory to **Applications Manager** groups. If you experience a problem, enter the full path to the directory in the text box.

---

3. Choose OK again.

Workstation Menu files are interpreted hierarchically, with submenus translated into subgroups. Both types of merged files display in the currently selected icon view.

> **Note**: When you merge a .DB file to an **Applications Manager** .APP file, the new .APP cannot be read by the earlier version of **Workstation Menu**.

Adding Network Groups

The LAN Administrator creates Network Groups in Administration mode for use by particular LAN users and groups who require common program access. By assigning rights to Network Groups and their contents, you can determine which groups or users on the network will have access to them. Network Groups are protected from modification by users, who do not have access to the New/Network Group item or to Network Group Properties.

You may wish to customize the startup group shipped with the program or create your own to distribute to network users. Any group that you create with the filename "startup.app" will automatically load the program items or scripts included in it each time you start **Applications Manager.**

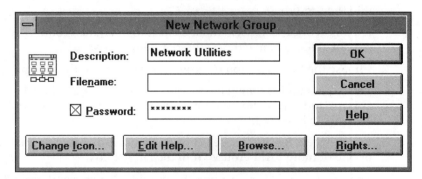

The New Network Group dialog box.

> **Note:** To add a Network Group, you must be in Administration mode.

- **TO ADD A NEW NETWORK GROUP:**

1. Select New/Network Group from the File menu.

The New Network Group dialog box displays.

2. Type the description and/or filename of the new group in the text boxes. Network Group files are saved to the program directory. If you want to save them to another location, use the Save Group As command followed by Save Workspace. (See the section "Saving Groups and Your Workspace" for procedures.)

The description appears in the title bar or below the group's icon. It's best to keep the description entry brief (less than 25 characters) to prevent overlapping of titles on your workspace.

> **Shortcut**: If you only enter the description and press OK, the .APP extension is automatically appended to the first 8 characters of your entry to create a filename. If you only enter the filename and press OK, the description is automatically created from the filename.

- The following optional procedures will customize the Network Group you are creating:

1. If you wish to assign a password, check the Password box and type it in the text box.

If a password is set, users must enter it to open the group. They are not able to change the Network Group password.

2. Choose the Rights button to assign access rights to the group.

The Access Rights dialog box displays with a list box of LAN Groups and Users. If you do not specify, the program default is for all users to have rights.

3. In the Access Rights box, select one or more individual user names or one or more LAN groups from the left list box.

The Groups and Users list box shows all LAN users and groups on your default server. As you select a LAN group in the list, the names of the users assigned to it display in the lower list box. You may choose any combination of individual users and LAN groups available. The entry <all users> is the default in the Granted Rights box.

4. Choose the Add button after each selection or double-click on an entry to move it to the Granted Rights box.

The Remove button is available to remove entries from the Granted Rights list.

5. Choose OK to assign rights and return to the New Network Group dialog box.

6. To create group-specific help, choose the Edit Help button and refer to the section on Editing Help.

7. Choose OK again to add the new Network Group.

Adding Personal Groups

In addition to the Network Groups created by the LAN Administrator, **Applications Manager** allows end-users to create and maintain groups for their personal applications and preferences. In the **Applications Manager** workspace, it's easy for users to switch between assigned Network Groups and their own Personal Groups.

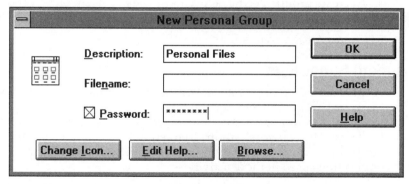

The New Personal Group dialog box.

- **TO ADD A NEW PERSONAL GROUP:**

1. Select New/Personal Group from the File menu.

   The New Personal Group dialog box displays.

2. Type the description and/or filename of the new group in the text boxes. Personal Group files are saved to the user's Windows directory. If you want to save them to another location, use the Save Group As command followed by Save Workspace. (See the section "Saving Groups and Your Workspace" for procedures.)

   The description appears in the title bar and below the group's icon. It's best to keep the description entry brief (less than 25 characters) to prevent overlapping of titles on your desktop.

   > **Shortcut**: If you only enter the description and press OK, the .APP extension is automatically appended to the first 8 characters of your entry to create a filename. If you only enter the filename and press OK, the description is automatically created from the filename.

3. If you wish to assign a password, check the Password box and type it in the text box.

4. To create group-specific help, choose the Edit Help button and refer to the section on Editing Help.

5. Choose OK again to add the new Personal Group.

Adding Subgroups

A subgroup is a group of items that can be contained in a Network or Personal Group or in another subgroup. Subgroups further help you to organize your applications into logical units for convenient access by users. The Network Group "Marketing," for example, might have subgroups named Presentations or Reports containing the applications used in those activities.

When you add a new subgroup, it is assigned to the currently selected group or subgroup, whether it is an open window or an icon. If you wish, you may create a series of subgroups, each "nested" in the higher level group or subgroup. A subgroup's contents and settings are saved in the parent group's .APP file when you select the Save Workspace or Save Group As commands. Likewise, when you delete a group or subgroup, the subgroups within these units are deleted.

The procedure for creating subgroups is the same for both Network and Personal Groups. For subgroups linked to Network Groups, however, it is possible to set rights for user access.

Chapter 3

The New Subgroup dialog box.

● **TO ADD A NEW SUBGROUP TO A GROUP:**

1. Select New/Subgroup from the File menu.

   The New Subgroup dialog box displays with the name of the group it is assigned to in the title bar. The new subgroup will be assigned to the currently selected group.

2. Type the description of the new group in the text box.

   The description appears in the title bar and below the subgroup's icon. It's best to keep the entry brief to prevent overlapping of titles on your workspace.

3. If you wish to assign a password, check the Password box and type it in the text box.

4. If you wish to change the default icon for the subgroup, choose the Change Icon button and follow the procedures in the "Changing Icons" section.

5. To create subgroup-specific help, choose the Edit Help button and refer to the section on Editing Help.

6. To assign access rights to a subgroup in a Network Group, follow steps 2 through 5 above in "Adding Network Groups."

7. Choose OK to assign rights and return to the New Subgroup dialog box.

8. Choose OK again to add the new subgroup.

Adding Program Items to Groups and Subgroups

An item is an element within a Network or Personal Group or a subgroup that represents a program or a script created with MultiSet scripting language. It is represented by either an icon with a text label or by text alone, depending on the display chosen. Double-clicking an item's icon or text title starts the program or script associated with it.

You may add items to a group by using the File menu option or by moving or copying items from other groups open on your desktop. The Script button displays the **MultiSet Script Editor** window for creating application management commands using its MultiSet scripting language.

If an item is being added to a Network Group or subgroup, the dialog box displays a Rights option for assigning access rights to that program. The Rights button is not available for Personal Group items. The Edit Help button allows you to create application-specific help for the item.

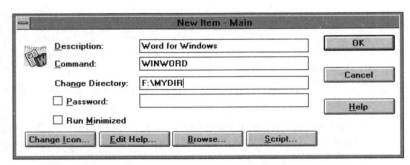

The New Item dialog box as it displays for a Network Group.

● TO ADD A PROGRAM ITEM TO A GROUP OR SUBGROUP:

1. With the group or subgroup to which you want to add an item selected, choose New/Item from the File menu.

The New Item dialog box displays with the name of the selected group in the title bar.

2. Enter the description for the program item.

The description is any alphanumeric combination from 1 to 50 characters that appears below the group's icon. It's best to keep the description brief (less than 25 characters) to prevent overlapping on your desktop.

You may designate a speed key for an item by typing an ampersand (&) in front of the letter you want as a speed key. For example, &Excel will place an underline under the "E." To include the ampersand character in the displayed name, type two ampersands (A&&L creates A&<u>L</u>). The & is included in the total number of description characters.

3. Enter the name of the program file to be executed by this item in the Command text box.

For example: To add an item for Microsoft Word for Windows, type WINWORD in the text box (the extension is automatically appended to the command)

   OR

Use the Browse button to locate the filename from the lists of available network drives and directories.

4. Choose OK.

● The following optional procedures will customize the program item:

1. Enter a path and directory name in the Change Directory text box.

By using the Change Directory text box, you can specify a different current directory -- for example, the location of the files you use with that application.

2. If you wish to assign a password, check the Password box and type it in the text box.

A password consists of any alphanumeric combination from 1 to 10 characters in length. Users will be prompted for a password when they open the item.

3. To create item-specific help, choose the Edit Help button and refer to the section on Editing Help.

4. Check the Run Minimized box if you want the application to load as an icon instead as an open window.

5. Choose OK again to add the item.

Using the Script Option

MultiSet is a network scripting language, similar in use to DOS batch files, that provides you with centralized control of applications management. **Applications Manager** and the **MultiSet Script Language Editor** are closely integrated to enhance the network tools available to you. The Script button in the New Item and Item Properties boxes displays the **MultiSet Editor**.

● **TO ADD A SCRIPT TO A GROUP OR SUBGROUP:**

1. Type a description in the New Item dialog box to activate the Script button.

2. Choose the Script button.

   The **MultiSet Editor** displays with an empty window showing the description in its title bar.

3. Enter the script you want to add using the **MultiSet** commands and procedures described in the chapter on **MultiSet Script Language** in this manual.

The following is an example of a **MultiSet** script:

```
; Check to see if the user is attached to the server where the ;
application resides.
IF NOT (USERNAME <server>) THEN ATTACH
<server>\LOGIN_NAME
; Check to see if the user has rights, if so, run the application and ;
display a list of his files.
```

```
; If not, issue a message for him to see his Administrator.
IF (RIGHTS <server>\sys:winapps\excel "ROS") THEN
   BEGIN
            MAP L:=<server>\sys:winapps\excel
            PATH ADD L:\winapps\excel
            CD "F:\USERS\"+LOGIN_NAME+"\DOCS"
            $file = LISTFILES *.xls  "Please select the
document to load: "
            RUN NORMAL excel.exe $file
   END
   ELSE
   MESSAGE OK "Sorry, you have insufficient rights to this
   application.  Please see your Administrator."
```

4. Save the script using File/Save Item and exit **MultiSet Editor.**

   The New Item dialog box now shows the grayed entry *Script* in the Command text box and the Change Directory box is disabled.

5. Choose OK.

See Chapter 5, "MultiSet Script Language," for a complete description of creating and using scripts.

> **Note**: A script cannot be detached from an item. To "disassociate" an item and a script, you must delete the item and then add it again without specifying a script.

Changing Icons

The icons representing a group, subgroup or item may be changed in the associated New and Properties dialog boxes. If you do not select an icon, the default icon will be assigned. The default filename for the icon source file in the Change Icon box is APPMAN.EXE for groups and subgroups or the command line for a program item. You can specify an icon associated with a .EXE file or the .ICO file containing the icon itself.

Since all DOS applications are automatically assigned the Windows DOS icon, you may want to change these icons.

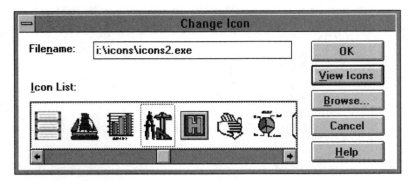

The Change Icon dialog box.

● TO CHANGE THE ICON:

1. Choose the Change Icon button in either a New or Properties box.

   The Change (Group or Item) Icon dialog box displays.

2. Select a new icon from the icon list that displays

   OR

   Choose the Browse button to select another .EXE file with icons associated with it or the .ICO file containing the desired icon.

   The Icon List box displays the available icon(s) for the selected file.

3. Choose an icon from the list and then OK.

4. Choose OK again in the New or Properties box.

   OR

   You may type the icon source filename and extension directly in the Filename text box. Then choose the View Icons button or touch ENTER to display the icon(s). Choose one and then OK.

Browsing Files

The Browse feature allows you to look through lists of network or local drives, directories and associated files for selection. It is helpful when you are unsure of a program or group filename and want to search through available network directories. The procedure for using the Browse button is the same in the various dialog boxes in which it occurs.

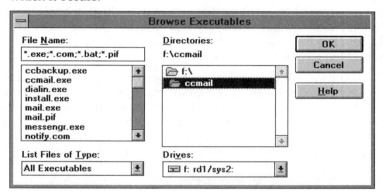

The Browse dialog box.

- **TO BROWSE LISTS OF AVAILABLE DIRECTORIES AND FILES:**

1. Choose the Browse button.

   The Browse dialog box displays a list of available drives and directories and a list of associated files. You may change the file specification shown if you want to browse for particular extensions such as .APP or .GRP by typing over the default entry in the Filename text box.

2. Choose a drive from the Drives box and/or a directory from the Directories list box.

3. Choose a filename from the choices in the Files list box or type one in the text box.

   You can use the List Files of Type box to limit the filename display to files with a specific extension.

4. Choose OK to insert that filename in the Command text box in the previous dialog box.

Editing Help

In addition to the on-line help available through the Help menu and Help buttons on all dialog boxes, **Applications Manager** features a Help editor for creating context-sensitive Help for groups and applications. The Edit Help button is found in the New Group, Subgroup and Item dialog boxes as well as in the Properties boxes. Using a standard Edit menu, the Edit Help box allows you to create customized help text for Network Groups and Items and users to write help for their Personal Groups.

Once you've written help text for a group or item, it is available to users in two ways. Selecting a group or program icon produces a quick help message in the status bar at the bottom of the window (if the status bar is enabled). When you touch SHIFT+F1 with an icon selected, **Applications Manager** displays the help text you've written on programs or procedures related to the currently selected icon.

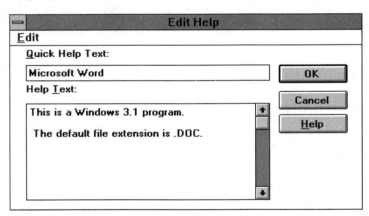

The Edit Help dialog box with sample quick and full help text entries.

• TO CREATE AND EDIT CONTEXT-SENSITIVE HELP:

1. Choose the Edit Help button from a New or Properties box.

   The Edit Help dialog box displays with blank boxes for a new group or item or with current text for existing groups or items.

2. Type a brief entry in the Quick Help Text box.

3. TAB and type new text or edit existing text in the Help Text box.

   Both help entries are optional; you may include just one if you want.

4. Choose OK.

5. Choose OK again in the New or Properties box.

6. To test the feature, choose the icon of the group or item for which you have just written help. The quick help line displays in the status bar if it is enabled. Touch SHIFT + F1 to display the longer help text for the group or item that icon represents.

The following commands can be used in the Edit Help dialog box to create help text:

Right Arrow	Moves the text cursor one character to the right.
Left Arrow	Moves the text cursor one character to the left.
Up Arrow	Moves the text cursor up one line.
Down Arrow	Moves the text cursor down one line.
Home	Moves the text cursor to the first character in the line.

End	Moves the text cursor to the space after the last character in the line.
Page+Up	Moves the thumb one screen toward the top of the box.
Page+Down	Moves the thumb one screen toward the bottom of the box.
Ctrl+Tab	Moves the cursor a Tab space within the box.
Ctrl+Enter	Moves the cursor to the next line with the text box.
Ctrl+Home	Moves the text cursor to the first line in the box.
Ctrl+End	Moves the text cursor to the end of the box.
Ctrl+Right	Moves the cursor to the end of the word.
Ctrl+Left	Moves the cursor to the beginning of the word.
Ctrl+Backspace	Undo
SHIFT+Del	Cut
Ctrl+Ins	Copy
SHIFT+Ins	Paste
Del	Clear
SHIFT+Left Arrow	Highlights the character to the left of the text cursor.
SHIFT+Right Arrow	Highlights the character to the right of the text cursor.

SHIFT+Up Arrow	Highlights one line of text to the left of the text cursor.
SHIFT+Down Arrow	Highlights one line of text to the right of the text cursor.
SHIFT+Home	Highlights from the text cursor to the first character in the line.
SHIFT+End	Highlights from the text cursor to the last character in the line.

Saving Groups and Your Workspace

The three save options on the File menu are used to store the elements of the groups and subgroups you create and the personal settings you have selected for your **Applications Manager** workspace. Saving your workspace before exiting assures that it will look the same as when you last used it.

When you save new groups, subgroups or items to **Applications Manager** the information is saved in the .APP file created for each group. These are binary files that store data about groups and the elements they contain. For each Network Group created, the program creates a .RCT file in the user's Windows directory. These files contain the user's preferences about size and the screen location of Network Groups. The customized settings regulating how **Applications Manager** looks and the specific groups a user has access to are stored in the user's PERMENU.INI file.

To save additions or changes, you must either choose the File/Save Workspace menu item or have Save Workspace on Exit checked on the Options menu. Save Workspace on Exit saves the current selections, options, window states, sizes and locations as well as the group information. If this option is checked, your changes will be saved automatically each time you exit **Applications Manager**.

The Save Group As command saves the currently selected group to the filename and path you specify. Use this File menu option when you want to save an .APP file to another location or to change its name. Save Group As saves the .APP files and any subgroup and item changes made to them. The Save Workspace command saves both the workspace settings and the groups.

Since the Save Group As command saves only the elements of a group, it is convenient to use it as you are making changes to a group and do not yet want to distribute those changes to network users. When you are ready to make the group available to users, use Save Workspace to save both group files as well as any changes to workspace settings.

If you are in Administration mode, you can use the File/Save Workspace As command to clone the current workspace to another server.

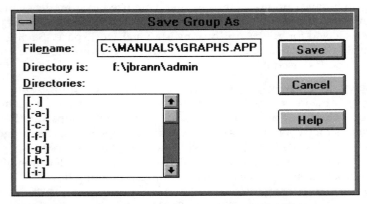

The Save Group As dialog box with a typical path and filename.

● **TO SAVE A GROUP TO A NEW PATH AND FILENAME:**

1. Choose Save Group As from the File menu.

   The Save Group As dialog box displays the current filename and path.

2. Enter the new filename. Include the drive letter and directory, using the list box if necessary.

3. Choose Save.

4. Choose Save Workspace from the File menu or have Save Workspace on Exit active in order to update the reference to the group file in the NETMENU.INI file.

Naming Group Files

You may specify the path in either a Server/Volume format or use a drive format (for example, F:\directory\filename.APP). **Applications Manager** converts the format to Server/Volume when it is written into the NETMENU.INI file. This ensures that the file will be found no matter how the drives are mapped.

Applications Manager uses standard DOS naming conventions for .APP filenames. If a filename is entered that already exists, the group associated with that file is loaded. If a description is entered but no filename, **Applications Manager** automatically assigns the first 8 DOS-legal characters of the description and an .APP extension to it. You may assign a file extension other than .APP. However, the filename (first 8 characters) must be unique. For example, you may **not** use both GROUP.APP and GROUP.XYZ.

> **IMPORTANT**: NetWare DLL versions 1.30 and earlier do not convert MAP ROOTed drives correctly. To avoid a possible problem, use a Server/Volume designation instead of a map-rooted drive letter in specifying the location of a network group file.

> **Note:** If you attempt to exit Administration mode after making unsaved changes, you are prompted to save group changes. Selecting "Yes" saves not only the groups but any changes to workspace settings as well.

Printing the Workspace

Users can use the File/Print Workspace command to print their
personal group information and PERMENU.INI file to an ASCII text
file. In Administration mode, you can use this command to print
network groups, default menu settings, restrictions, and the
NETMENU.INI file.

● **To PRINT THE WORKSPACE TO AN ASCII FILE:**

1. Choose Print Workspace from the File menu.

   The Print Options dialog box displays.

The Print Options dialog box.

2. Check the INI Files box to include INI file information in the report.
   If you are running **Applications Manager** in Administration mode,
   you can check the Restrictions box to include menu defaults and
   restrictions.

3. Use the Group Selections box to select the Personal or Network
   Groups to include in the report.

4. In the Output File text box, enter the name of the ASCII file to which the report is to be "printed." The default file extension is .RPT.

OR

Choose the Save As button and select the file from a list box.

5. Choose Print.

Editing Groups, Subgroups and Items

You can easily change the contents of Groups and Subgroups and the details for items using the editing commands on the File menu. In addition to using the menu bar commands, a "drag and drop" mouse action allows you to copy and move subgroup and item icons from one open group window to another. The copied or moved icon assumes the display style of the destination window.

The Properties options allows you to view and edit any of the details that define a group, subgroup or item. To display the Properties dialog box, select the item or minimize the group window and select its icon.

> **Note**: You must be running **Applications Manager** in Administration mode to make any changes to a Network Group other than repositioning the icons within the window or moving the window.

- **TO COPY ITEMS OR GROUPS:**

1. Select the icon of the program item or subgroup you wish to copy.

2. Choose Copy from the File menu.

   The Copy dialog box displays with the name of the group and the item.

3. Choose a destination from the list of available groups in the combo box.

4. Choose the Copy button.

The icon for the copied item displays in the open destination group window.

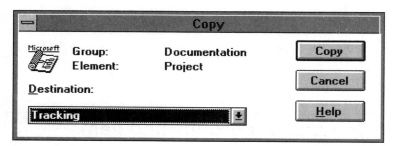

The Copy dialog box.

Mouse Shortcut:

Hold the CTRL key down while you drag the icon you wish to copy from the open source group window to the open destination window. Using this same technique within a single window creates a duplicate of that item within the group or subgroup.

● **TO MOVE ITEMS OR GROUPS:**

1. Select the icon of the program item or subgroup you wish to move.

2. Choose Move from the File menu.

   The Move dialog box displays with the name of the group and the item.

3. Choose a destination from the list of available groups in the combo box.

4. Choose the Move button.

   The icon for the moved item displays in the open destination group window.

The Move dialog box.

Mouse Shortcut:

Drag the icon you wish to move from the open source group window to the open destination window. Using this same technique within a single window repositions the icon according to the current display choice.

● **To delete groups, subgroups or items:**

1. Select the icon of the group, subgroup or item you wish to delete.

2. Choose Delete from the File menu.

3. Depending on the check boxes you have checked in the Options/Confirmation dialog box, you are prompted for confirmation to delete groups, subgroups or items.

4. Choose Yes in the message box to delete your selection.

> **Note:** Deleting a group results in removing all of the group's subgroups.

Keyboard Shortcut:

Choose the Delete key to delete the selected icon or open window and select Yes in the message box if one displays.

● TO VIEW AND CHANGE PROPERTIES:

1. Select the icon of the group, subgroup or item for which you wish to change details related to filename, password, icon, help text, script, etc.

2. Choose Properties from the File menu.

   The Properties dialog box displays with the existing data.

3. Enter your changes in the text boxes.

   The Change Icon, Edit Help and Browse buttons are available to change properties related to those commands.

4. Choose OK.

The Network Group Properties dialog box.

> **Note**: You must be running **Applications Manager** in Administration mode to display the Group Properties dialog box for a Network Group, subgroup, or item.

Mouse Shortcut:

Pressing the right mouse button when the cursor is on a group, subgroup, or item opens the Properties dialog box.

Running Programs from Applications Manager

With programs and scripts logically organized into Network and Personal Groups and associated subgroups, it's quick to locate and run an application using **Applications Manager**. To start an application, the group or subgroup window in which it is located must be open with the item's icon selected.

● TO RUN A PROGRAM IN A GROUP:

Choose Open from the File menu with the item you want to run selected (If you've set a speed key for the item, you can select it quickly by pressing that key.)

OR

Double-click on the icon you want to run.

The program window opens. If the Run Minimized box is checked in the New or Properties box, the program loads as an icon at the bottom of the workspace.

● TO RUN A PROGRAM THAT IS NOT IN A GROUP:

1. Choose Run from the File menu.

   The Run dialog box displays.

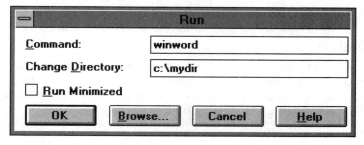

The Run dialog box.

2. In the Command box, type the program's name and optionally path and command line parameters (for example c:\windows\notepad myfile.txt).

OR

Choose the Browse button to display the Browse dialog box, which lets you select the path and filename from list boxes.

3. You can use the Change Directory to type the path you want to change to (make current) when the program is executed.

4. Check the Run Minimized box if you want the application to run minimized, with the icon appearing at the bottom of the screen.

5. Choose OK.

Shortcut: The Run dialog box maintains a history of the last 25 items entered during this session. To display prior commands or directories, position the cursor in the Command or Change Directory box and press the up or down arrow key.

Selecting Display Options

The Options menu allows you to set preferences that regulate elements of **Applications Manager**'s operation and display. You can turn most of these choices on or off by checking the menu item. A check mark indicates the option is active. The Confirmation and Wallpaper options display dialog boxes for selecting preferences. The settings selected in the Options menu are stored in each user's PERMENU.INI file when the workspace is saved.

Hierarchical

The way you access group windows to open their subgroups and programs is determined by the status of the Hierarchical option. This setting is group-specific, so access to one group may be Hierarchical and to another group "flat" or non-hierarchical.

- Checking Hierarchical on means that access is only allowed to a group and the direct line of parent groups up to the top-level group. Selecting a group closes all subgroups (children) and groups that are on the same level (siblings). Users cannot change this option for a Network Group.

- When Hierarchical is not checked, all open group and subgroup windows are accessible at the same time. For example, if a subgroup is open, you can access it and its parent group at the same time. Working this way is particularly helpful if you are copying or moving items from one level group to another. (Although convenient for maintenance purposes, this could lead to a large number of open windows, which could affect performance.)

Status Bar

The status bar at the bottom of the **Applications Manager** window displays definitions of menu items as you scroll down a menu's items. It also displays Quick Help information when you select a group or program icon. When a program or script is executing or **Applications Manager** is saving or exiting, the status bar indicates the operation in progress.

Auto Arrange Icons

When the Auto Arrange Icons option is checked on the icons in a group will be automatically rearranged to accommodate the new window area that results from resizing.

Minimize on Use

Checking Minimize on Use on will minimize the **Applications Manager** window to an icon at the bottom of the screen each time you run an application from one of its groups.

Confirmation

The Confirmation dialog box allows you to choose whether confirmation messages will display when you select the Delete command for groups, subgroups and items or the Save Workspace command from the File menu. If a box is checked you will see a confirmation box each time you choose one of these commands. If a box is not checked, **Applications Manager** will execute the command without showing a warning message.

To prevent inadvertently deleting a group, subgroup or item, it is advisable to activate the confirmation option for these elements. If you prefer to work with this option off, remember that you may exit **Applications Manager** without saving a group or the workspace if you wish to undo a delete made in error.

To turn confirmation messages on for one or more of the four commands, check the corresponding box and choose OK.

The Confirmation dialog box with all boxes activated.

Save Workspace on Exit

Save Workspace on Exit sets the default setting for exiting. Checking this setting on ensures that the changes made to both groups and to the appearance of the workspace will be saved when you exit **Applications Manager**.

If this option is checked in the menu bar, your changes will be saved automatically each time you exit **Applications Manager**. If it is not checked on, you can still save changes on exiting by checking the Save Workspace box in the Exit prompt. Checking this box off in the Exit message only applies to the *current* session. It does not alter any default settings in effect.

Wallpaper

The Wallpaper option allows users to change background patterns or graphic images from within **Applications Manager**. You can display any available bitmap file (.BMP file extension) by selecting its filename in the Wallpaper dialog box.

The Wallpaper dialog box.

● **TO SELECT A WALLPAPER FILE:**

1. Choose Wallpaper from the Options menu.

   The Wallpaper dialog box displays with the Windows directory as the current directory.

2. Choose a bitmap file from the drop-down list box
   OR

   Choose Browse to display another directory containing bitmap files and make your selection.

3. Select Center or Tile to center the bitmap on the screen or arrange it in a tiled pattern.

4. Choose the OK button.

Checking System Resources

The **Applications Manager** Help menu contains three information items that offer extensive statistics on a user's current system configuration: Network Info, Windows Info and DOS Info. Each of these Help items displays read-only information on the current workstation. It is intended to help with troubleshooting if you encounter a problem while running **Applications Manager** or other **Net TOOLS Menu** products.

In addition, each of the main and secondary Info Help windows features a Print button so you can print out and review any of the available information. Choosing the Print button in any of the three main Information windows, prints the data in that window plus the data in all lower-level windows.

The Help menu also contains a Trouble Ticket item, which allows users to send Network, Windows, DOS, and Personal Workspace information to designated users and groups for diagnostic purposes.

Following is an alphabetical listing of the terms included in the system information boxes accessed through the Help menu. Each entry describes the term and indicates in which box you can find that information.

AUTOEXEC.BAT   TSRs, the Windows Temp Variable and the path to local directories are set in the AUTOEXEC.BAT. Many systems also use the AUTOEXEC.BAT to load the network shells and log in to the network and/or launch Windows.

To view AUTOEXEC.BAT, select DOS Info from the Help menu, then press the System Files button. If **Applications Manager** cannot identify your boot device, it will offer you the option of browsing for it.

Capture information Correct network printing depends on redirecting printer ports to network queues. If users are unable to print to a network printer or if output is not showing a local printer, check the redirection information to ensure that print files are being sent to the correct destination. Spooling options are also shown here.

To view Capture information, select Network Info from the Help menu, press the Connection Info button. Scroll down until the Capture information is visible.

CONFIG.SYS DOS device drivers are loaded in the CONFIG. SYS file. The number of file handles, disk buffers and the command interpreter are also set here.

To view CONFIG.SYS, select DOS Info from the Help menu, then press the System Files button. If **Applications Manager** cannot identify your boot, device it will offer you the option of browsing for it.

Disk Space Available If you are running Windows in enhanced mode with a temporary swapfile, performance can be severely degraded if the paging drive becomes nearly full. Windows gives erratic behavior when it is low on memory. If users are reporting a significant slowdown of Windows, check to make sure there is sufficient room on the paging drive and delete any unneeded files. Temporary files can accumulate in the temp directory and are likely candidates for erasure.

To view the disk space available on local drives, select DOS Info from the Help menu.

Drive Mapping Table Drive redirection is the heart of network file sharing. Maintaining the correct drive mapping is much more complicated in the Windows multitasking environment. "File not found" messages can indicate that the drive mappings may not be what the program expects.

To view drive mapping information, select Network Info from the Help menu, press the Connections button. Scroll down until the Drive Mapping Table is visible.

DOS Version Although Windows is compatible with DOS 3.0 or higher, compatibility with different versions of DOS is not 100 percent, and some problems will only show up with particular versions of DOS.

To view the DOS Version, select DOS Info from the Help menu.

DLL Versions Applications Manager uses the Novell Windows DLL to support network functions. Check to ensure that users have the latest version of the DLLs.

To view the DLL version, select Network Info from the Help menu.

Full Name Users identify themselves to the network using their login name. Using Syscon, you can also assign the full name to the account.

To view the full name, select Network Info from the Help menu. The full name appears on the User ID line after the dash.

Group Memberships Groups simplify network security administration. By granting rights to groups or making scripts dependent on group membership, you can allow many users access at once. This list allows you to check the users in a group.

To view Group Membership information, select Network Info from the Help menu, press the Connection Info button. Scroll down until the Group Membership heading is visible.

INI files Users preferences are stored in *.INI files. The two most important INI files are the SYSTEM.INI, which holds the hardware-related parameters, and the WIN.INI, which contains global status information.

To view the SYSTEM.INI and WIN.INI, select Windows Info from the Help menu, press the INI Files button.

Local Hard Disks Windows will run faster when loaded on a local hard disk. However, if Windows runs out of space on the hard disk, its performance will suffer. Make sure there is sufficient space on the hard disk for a temporary swapfile.

To view local hard disk information, select DOS Info from the Help menu.

Login Name The login name identifies the user to the network for security purposes. It can also be used to identify personal directories and personal configuration files.

To view the login name, select Network Info from the Help menu. The login name displays to the right of the User ID heading.

Login Script The login script is where a user's network configuration, especially the drive mappings, is set.

To view the login script, select Network Info from the Help menu and press the Login Script button.

Memory Map Any device drivers and TSRs loaded before Windows is started will remain active during a Windows session. The memory map allows you to check which devices and TSRs are loaded and the order of their location in memory.

To view the Memory Map, select DOS Info from the Help menu.

NetBIOS Many network programs use NetBIOS as their interface to the network. Novell provides a NetBIOS Emulator that can be loaded on top of IPX.

To view NetBIOS information, select Network Info from the Help menu.

Network Number Novell assigns each cable system a number to enable routing between systems. The number shown here is the cable system that the user is attached to.

To view Network number, select Network Info from the Help menu.

Path DOS will search for programs not found in the current directory in the directories listed in the path environment variable. Windows, NetWare utilities and **Net TOOLS Menu** should be on the path. Other commonly used program directories can also be included.

To view the Path, select DOS Info from the Help menu, then press the Environment button.

Station ID Station ID uniquely identifies each workstation on the network. This is also known as the physical station ID.

To view Station ID, select Network Info from the Help Menu.

Search Drives Since network paths can be very long, Novell saves environment space by adding a reference to the current directory of a network drive in the path DOS environment variable and then maps a drive to the desired directory. This can cause problems if the current directory of a search drive is changed. If the user receives a "program not found" message, check that the search drives are still properly mapped.

To view Search Drives, select Network Info from the Help menu, press the Connections button. Scroll down until the Search Drives heading is visible.

Security Equivalences Security equivalences grant one user all the rights of other users. The user is equivalent to any group he or she is a member of. Administrative users are sometimes made equivalent to supervisor to save time logging in and out.

To view security equivalences, select Network Info from the Help menu, press the Connections button. Scroll down until the Security Equivalences list is visible.

Servers Attached Users must establish a connection and account ID with a server before accessing any resources on that server. Since users are limited in the number of servers they can attach to, large networks may require users to attach and detach from servers as they need resources.

To view servers the user is attached to, select Network Info. from the Help menu and press the Connection Info button.

Shell Programs make all network requests via the NETx.COM network shell. It is important to have the latest version of the network shell to support software properly.

To view the version of NETx.com, select Network Info from the Help menu.

SHELL.CFG/NETCFG The behavior of the Novell shell can be modified by parameters within a text file named either SHELL.CFG or NET.CFG. The Novell shell looks in the current directory for this file when it is loaded. For Windows, it should include turning on show dots (for directory walking) and allocating 60 network file handles.

To view the SHELL.CFG file, select Network Info from Help and press the Configuration button. If the program cannot find the file, it will allow the user to browse for it, which may cause the user to change the path. The administrator, however, can circumvent this problem by setting an environment variable named NETCFG that points to the location of the SHELL.CFG.

Set the variable in either the system login script or the AUTOEXEC.BAT file on the user's system by adding the line: SET NETCFG = drive:\path or SET NETCFG=C:\NETWORK. If you have not set this variable, the user will receive an error message when attempting to print this information from the Network Info dialog box.

SYSTEM.INI The SYSTEM.INI contains the hardware-specific information needed to start up windows. All Windows system drivers, enhanced mode drivers and virtual machine information is available here. The SYSTEM.INI is only read at startup; changes have no effect until Windows is restarted.

To view the SYSTEM.INI, select Windows Info from the Help menu, then press the INI Files button.

Swap File Size The swap file is where Windows stores virtual memory pages when they are bumped for other pages. The size of the swap file plus the amount of real (conventional plus extended) memory is the amount of memory that Windows is currently using. Windows will always leave a certain amount of disk space on paging.

To view the swap file size, select Windows Info from the Help menu.

Swap File Types Swap files can be temporary, which Windows will create and expand on the fly, or permanent, which are created by the swap file program and fixed in size. Permanent swap files are faster than temporary swap files but can only be utilized on local hard drives.

To view the swap file type, select Windows Info. from the Help menu.

User ID Novell handles network security on the basis of user IDs. Internally, it uses a number Users see the IDs as login names and full names.

To view the user ID, select Network Info from the Help menu.

WIN.INI The WIN.INI holds the user setup information about printers, applications, and the Windows appearance. Many applications, including **Net TOOLS Menu**, also write user preference information in the WIN.INI.

To view the WIN.INI, select Windows Info from the Help menu, then press the INI Files button.

WINDIR When WIN.COM loads, it defines the WINDIR variable as the directory where it was found. Windows will look for the SYSTEM.INI and WIN.INI, as well as other INI files, in the WINDIR directory. Other Windows parameters have defaults based on the WINDIR variable.

To view the WINDIR variable, select DOS Info from the Help menu, press the Environment button.

Windows Drivers Windows communicates with the operating system through a set of drivers. Sometimes when drivers are not installed, Windows will not run. However, with the network drivers left off Windows will still run, but some network functions will not work correctly.

To view the Windows Drivers, select Windows Info from the Help menu, then press the Drivers button.

Windows Environment Windows makes a copy of the DOS environment at startup and provides it to Windows applications. DOS applications use the original DOS environment.

To view the Windows environment, select DOS Info from the Help menu, then press the Environment button.

Windows Mode Windows has three modes of operation: real, standard and enhanced. Windows' performance differs among the three modes, especially with regard to DOS applications.

To view the Windows mode information, select Windows Info from the Help menu.

Windows Setup The Windows setup program checks the hardware and the network and installs the correct drivers in the SYSTEM.INI. It does not recognize all hardware, and it will not recognize the network if the network shells are not loaded (if the network is not loaded when Windows is installed).

To view the Windows Setup, select Windows Info from the Help menu, then press the Drivers button.

Windows Version To view the Windows version, select Windows Info from the Help menu.

LAN Manager-Specific Information

The following information is provided in the Network Information dialog box, available through the Help menu:

- Full Name
- LANMAN.INI file
- Log on Domain
- Network drives
- Groups
- Printer connections
- Redirector version
- Station ID
- Servers
- User ID

Trouble Ticket

Applications Manager's Trouble Ticket feature lets a user send Network, Windows, DOS, and Personal Workspace information through electronic mail to designated users and groups for diagnostic purposes. Using the **Net TOOLS Administration** program, the administrator determines which categories of information users can send (Network, Windows, DOS, and/or Personal Workspace) and the users and groups who will receive the information.

The Trouble Ticket option is available only if you are running a mail program that supports the Messaging Application Programming Interface (MAPI).

● **TO SEND A TROUBLE TICKET:**

1. Choose Trouble Ticket from the Help menu.

   An electronic mail dialog box appears with the Trouble Ticket message addressed to the user and groups predefined by the administrator and the Network, Windows, DOS, and/or Personal Workspace information attached to the message.

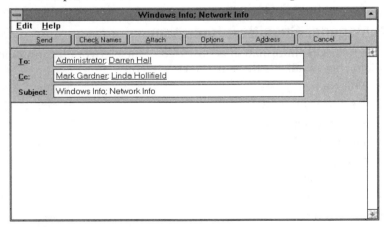

Electronic mail dialog box.

2. Enter a message, if desired, and choose Send.

Exiting Applications Manager

While you are working in applications, **Applications Manager** is running in the background or iconized at the bottom of the screen. If **Applications Manager** is your Windows shell, exiting it will also close Windows.

Applications Manager prompts you to save changes if you attempt to exit without saving unless Save Workspace on Exit is checked on the Options menu or no changes have occurred during the session.

- **TO EXIT APPLICATIONS MANAGER:**

1. Choose Exit from the File menu.

   The Exit Applications Manager message box displays with a Save Workspace check box. If the Save Workspace on Exit menu item is checked on, the default action in this box will be to save. You may check the box in the exit message off at this time. Unchecking this box does not alter the status of the Save on Exit menu item, however. (If the check box is grayed, you cannot change the setting even if the box is checked.)

2. Choose OK to exit **Applications Manager** and Windows.

Chapter 4

Net TOOLS Administration

Net TOOLS Administration is the utility program that assigns restrictions to global aspects of **Applications Manager** and **Net TOOLS Security**. Using **Administration's** features, you can build configuration files that define the menu bar items, program options and default settings available to all users on the network. **Net TOOLS Administration** provides both convenient and secure access to centralized management of these two network programs.

Topics in this chapter

How Does Net TOOLS Administration Work?
Starting Net TOOLS Administration
Creating and Editing .WWR Files
Saving .WWR Files
Setting Applications Manager Restrictions
Setting Net TOOLS Security Restrictions
Exiting Net TOOLS Administration

How Does Net TOOLS Administration Work?

Net TOOLS Administration builds the configuration files that contain the information restricting access to the program features of **Applications Manager** and **Net TOOLS Security**. With **Administration's** commands, you can select preferences for menu bar items and defaults, program options and logo displays. These customized settings are saved with a default filename and extension (.WWR) and must be placed in a location on the user's current path. When either **Applications Manager** or **Net TOOLS Security** starts, it first reads the associated .WWR file and displays the program's menu bar and options according to these settings.

To regulate use of certain **Applications Manager** and **Net TOOLS Security** features, you may use a combination of **Administration's** restrictions. For example, to enforce workstation security you would require that the Secure Station feature be active on each workstation and also set the secure timeout range. To ensure that users run **Applications Manager** with the predefined options, you would set menu defaults and then remove the corresponding items from the menu bar.

The diverse requirements of different network groups or users can be addressed by creating multiple .WWR files, each including a different selection of restrictions. By placing a particular .WWR on a user's path, you determine which set of **Net TOOLS Security** or **Applications Manager** options he or she can access.

Using **Net TOOLS Administration** is quick and easy while maintaining a high degree of security. Whether you are at your own workstation or at a user's, if **Applications Manager** is available you can use it to access Administration mode and then run the **Net TOOLS Administration** program.

Starting Net TOOLS Administration

Use either of the following procedures to run the **Net TOOLS Administration** program:

- From the **Applications Manager** window, use the key sequence Ctrl+Alt+A to toggle into Administration mode. This action may prompt you for the password assigned to the current .WWR file. (If a password has not been set or if you log in as supervisor, you are not prompted.)

  This action automatically gives you access to the Administration menu now visible in the title bar. Choose Setup from the Administration menu to launch the program. The currently opened APPMAN.WWR file automatically displays for editing. At this point, you may open other **Applications Manager** files, **Net TOOLS Security** files or create new .WWR files of either type.

  OR

- Choose File/Run from the menu bar in your Windows shell and enter WWADMIN.EXE in the command line box.

> **Note:** To access Administration mode, your WIN.INI file must contain a [WWAdmin] section. For further information, see "Setting Up Administrators" in Chapter 2, "Installation and Configuration."

If **Applications Manager** is not currently running and you want to start it in Administration mode directly, type APPMAN.EXE /A in the File/Run command line box.

> **Banyan Note:** To access Administration mode, a Banyan administrator must have control permissions to the directory where the NETMENU.INI file is located

> **Note:** We recommend that you assign a password to the .WWR files in **Net TOOLS Administration** to keep unauthorized users from editing the rights files. As an added security measure, the administrator can move the WWADMIN.EXE file to a location that is on his or her path but not available to users.

Changing the Password

If you have set password for a .WWR file, **Net TOOLS Administration** requires that you enter it each time you attempt to open that file. Since the product is shipped without a password, you will want to set an initial password and change it periodically. The Change Password command is available on the Options menu when you are editing both **Applications Manager** and **Net TOOLS Security** .WWR files.

The Change Password dialog box.

- To reset the password, choose Options/Change Password on the **Administration** menu bar and enter your own password.

  The Password Confirmation box requires that you enter the password a second time. Passwords, which are not case sensitive, appear "blind" for security reasons when entered in the text box.

Creating and Editing .WWR Files

The File menu's New command displays a submenu with the items **Applications Manager** and **Net TOOLS Security.** (Depending on the edition of **Net TOOLS Menu** you have purchased, only one item may be available.) When you select one of these items, the commands on the Options menu correspond to your choice. The title bar and message line indicate which type of .WWR file you are currently creating or editing.

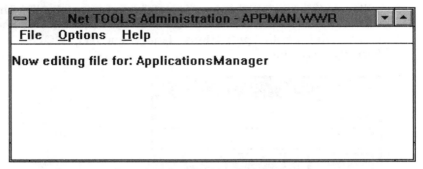

The Net TOOLS Administration window with an APPMAN.WWR file open.

Although the Options menu varies for **Applications Manager** and **Net TOOLS Security**, the procedures for defining and saving .WWR files are identical. If you work with both types of files in the same session, be sure to save your changes to one file before opening the next.

- **TO CREATE A NEW .WWR FILE:**

1. Choose New and either the **Applications Manager** or **Net TOOLS Security** item from the File menu.

   The **Administration** window indicates that you are editing either an **Applications Manager** (APPMAN.WWR) or **Net TOOLS Security** (WWEXT.WWR) file.

2. Set a password.

3. Use the items on the Options drop-down menu to set restrictions for the .WWR file you are creating. (See the sections on setting **Applications Manager** and **Net TOOLS Security** restrictions later in this chapter.)

4. Choose Save As from the File menu to save the file.

   By default, .WWR files are saved to the current directory. The **Applications Manager** program reads the first APPMAN.WWR file on the user's path and creates a menu bar and settings that reflect the restrictions you have defined. Likewise, the **Net TOOLS Security** program reads the first WWEXT.WWR file on the user's path and starts the program according to the .WWR settings.

> **Note**: The password in effect when you save a .WWR file is the one you will be prompted for when you attempt to reopen it.

● **To OPEN AN EXISTING .WWR FILE:**

1. Choose Open from the File Menu.

   The Open File dialog box displays.

2. Select either the APPMAN.WWR or WWEXT.WWR file from the Files list box, changing network drives and directories if necessary.

3. Choose OK.

   The **Administration** window indicates the type of file you are editing and the Options menu commands correspond to that type.

4. Enter a password if prompted for one. (If a password has not been set, you are not prompted.)

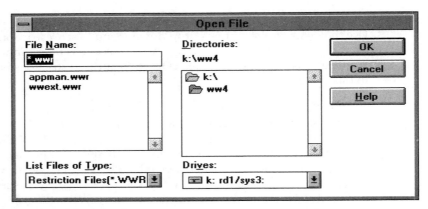

The Open File dialog box.

Saving .WWR Files

The procedure for saving .WWR files applies to both **Applications Manager** (APPMAN.WWR) and **Net TOOLS Security** (WWEXT.WWR) restriction files. It is important to retain the names automatically assigned to each of these files in order for each program to read its respective .WWR file for restrictions. You may want to change a .WWR filename as a temporary administrative convenience or for backup purposes. However, be sure to reassign the file's default name when you want to use it again.

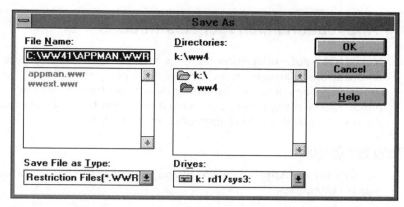

The Save As dialog box.

● **TO SAVE A NEW .WWR FILE:**

1. Choose Save As from the File menu.

   The Save As dialog box displays with the default filename and extension for the type of file **(Applications Manager** or **Net TOOLS Security)** you are saving. The default directory is the location of the **Net TOOLS Menu** program files. Use the Drives and/or Directories boxes to change the drive and directory for the .WWR file's location.

2. Choose Save.

In addition to new files, use the Save As command to change the name or directory location of a .WWR file. Use the File/Save command to save changes to existing .WWR files.

You are prompted to save changes to a .WWR file when you attempt to open another **Net TOOLS Administration** file and when you select Exit without first saving your changes.

Setting Applications Manager Restrictions

Net TOOLS Administration offers you the flexibility to configure the **Applications Manager** menu bar items and program defaults for different groups of users. By setting the status of menu bar items and removing the corresponding item from the menu bar, you can control the way **Applications Manager** looks and functions.

Menu Bar Defaults

Defaults for the **Applications Manager** menu bar can be set in three general categories:

View: Horizontal, Vertical and Text.

Options: Save Workspace on Exit, Hierarchical, Status Bar, and Minimize on Use.

Confirmation: Delete Group, Subgroup, Item and Save Workspace.

Default settings that pertain to individual windows (Horizontal, Vertical and Text views and the Hierarchical option) apply to newly created group windows. For example, if you set the default view to Text, existing windows with Horizontal or Vertical displays are not affected. New group windows will automatically be assigned the current default setting -- Text, in this case.

See Chapter 3, "**Applications Manager**" for a detailed explanation of how these menu items affect usage.

The Applications Manager - Menu Bar Defaults dialog box.

● **TO SET MENU BAR DEFAULTS:**

1. Choose Menu Bar Defaults from the Options menu.

   The Menu Bar Defaults dialog displays.

2. Choose items that you want as defaults by selecting a single radio button from the View group box and checking one or more of the check boxes.

   Checking an item means the default setting for that item is on (active) and it will show a check next to it on the **Applications Manager** menu.

3. Choose OK.

   When you save your restrictions to the current .WWR file and place the file on a user's path, **Applications Manager** reflects these settings the next time it is run or when you attempt to open a group or item affected by the changes.

> **Note:** The Menu Bar Defaults dialog box lets you set default settings for selected **Applications Manager** menu items. These are simply initial settings. A user may override these defaults by changing these settings for his or her workstation. To prevent a user from changing these settings, you must restrict the menu items controlling these settings from appearing on the user's menu.

Menu Bar Restrictions

The Menu Bar Restrictions dialog box contains an identical model of the **Applications Manager** menu bar for choosing the menu items that the program will display. Checking items that you want to restrict access to toggles them on (active) or off (inactive) in the drop-down menus. By checking items off, you actually remove them from the menu bar that is made available to users.

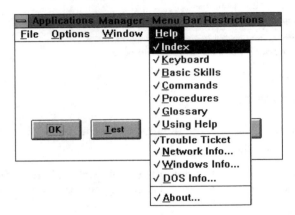

The Applications Manager - Menu Bar Restrictions dialog box in Edit mode.

By selecting only the menu choices you want certain groups of users to have, you are able to regulate their use of network resources. For example, you may want to set a menu bar default for Save Workspace on Exit and then remove that item from the menu in order to prevent users from resetting it.

The Menu Bar Restrictions dialog box initially displays in Edit mode with the Test button active. Once you have checked a menu item off, you can view the actual look of the restricted menus by choosing the Test button. You are now in Test mode where you can see exactly which **Applications Manager** menu items will be available to users. You can toggle in and out of Test and Edit mode by selecting the corresponding button.

As administrator, you have complete control over the configuration of the **Applications Manager** menu bar. You can restrict any item on the menu bar and pull-down menus. If all of the items on a pull-down menu are restricted, the item is removed from the menu bar. You edit the APPMAN.WWR file to restrict menu bar items.

- **TO SET MENU BAR RESTRICTIONS:**

1. Choose Menu Bar Restrictions from the Options menu.

   The Menu Bar Restrictions dialog box displays in Edit mode with **Applications Manager's** full menu bar and four buttons.

2. Choose one of the items from the menu bar.

   For a new APPMAN.WWR file, the drop-down menus show all items checked on, or in an active state. If you are editing an existing file, the menu's state represents currently set restrictions which you may change.

3. Check off the item that you want to remove from the menu bar.

   Each time you check an item the drop-down menu closes, so you must repeat this process for each item you want to remove on all four menus. Removing all items from submenus results in removal of the menu item.

4. Choose the Test button and then each of the menu bar items to view a Test-mode version of the drop-down menus you just customized. Only the items that were checked on appear in the menu now.

5. Choose the Edit button to return to Edit mode.

6. Choose OK if all menu bar restrictions have been set.

To edit previously set restrictions, follow the above procedure, toggling on or off the existing settings you need to change.

Considerations

- When File/Run is restricted, users cannot run a program that is not on the menu. However, it is possible to run programs using the Command feature in the Net TOOLS Clock/Alarm Options dialog box. Net TOOLS Alarm's Command feature may be restricted in Net TOOLS Administration in the WWEXT.WWR file. See "Setting Net TOOLS Security Restrictions" later in this chapter.

- Using the System Control box for exiting Windows is also disabled when File/Exit is restricted.

- If the Save Workspace on Exit option is restricted to users, the Save Workspace check box in the exit dialog box will be gray. If the menu bar default is on, this box will show a check even though it is grayed. If the option is not restricted, the user is able to check it on or off.

Logo Display

The **Net TOOLS Menu** logo that displays automatically each time **Applications Manager** or **Net TOOLS Security** starts can be customized. You can replace this logo with another Windows Metafile (.WMF) or a bitmap file (.BMP) or select "None" from the drop-down list box if you don't want to display a logo.

The Administration program does not check for the existence of the file you enter here so you may create it at a later time. If you don't specify a file extension, the program appends .WMF. In addition to selecting a logo, you may edit the logo's background colors.

Checking the Allow User Customization check box on gives **Applications Manager** and **Security** users the ability to change the logo file and color for their own workstation. (See the next section, "Customizing a User's Logo," to learn how a user can change the logo display.)

The Logo Display dialog box.

- **TO CHANGE THE LOGO DISPLAY:**

1. Choose Logo Display from the Options menu.

   The Logo Display dialog box shows the default logo name in the text box.

2. Choose the down-arrow to select another .WMF from the list box or the entry "none."

   OR

   Choose the Browse button to view other available .WMF files. Select one in the Browse Logo dialog box and choose OK.

3. Edit the logo background color by replacing the default settings with new values between 0 and 255 for each color.

4. Choose OK.

Customizing a User's Logo

If you have allowed users to customize the **Net TOOLS Menu** logo, they may substitute another graphics file or modify the color of the logo that displays on their workstations. To do this, the settings in each user's WIN.INI file will need to be edited.

The **Net TOOLS** logo displays for each of two modules: **Applications Manager** and **Net TOOLS Security**. If the user has more than one module on his or her system, the logo will only display for the first module run.

In the [WindowsWorkstation] section of the user's WIN.INI file, add the following parameter:

Logo File=<filename>

Replace <filename> with the name of the Windows Metafile (.WMF) or bitmap file (.BMP) that contains the user's customized logo. This file must be on the user's path.

If you want to disable the logo display, enter "Logo File="; do not specify a filename.

To modify the background color of the logo display, add the following parameter to the [WindowsWorkstation] section of the user's WIN.INI file:

Logo Background=<Red_n> <Green_n> <Blue_n>

Replace <Red_n>, ,Green_n>, and <Blue_n> with RGB values between 0 and 255. An example is:

Logo Background= 30 40 50

> **Note**: It is not possible to modify the logo in Evaluation copies of **Net TOOLS Menu.**

Trouble Ticket

The Trouble Ticket item on the **Applications Manager** Help menu lets users send their Network, Windows, DOS, and/or Personal Workspace (PERMENU.INI) information to designated users and groups through electronic mail. This tool is intended for diagnostic purposes.

As administrator, you define what categories of information users can send and the users and groups who will receive this information.

● **TO SET UP THE TROUBLE TICKET:**

1. Choose Trouble Ticket from the Options menu.

The Trouble Ticket dialog box displays.

Trouble Ticket dialog box.

2. From the User/Group Destinations box, select the users and groups who can receive Trouble Ticket information.

3. Under Attachments check the categories of information that will be sent with the Trouble Ticket—Network, Windows, DOS, and/or Personal Workspace.

4. Choose OK.

Setting Net TOOLS Security Restrictions

Using the options available in the Net TOOLS Security - Restrictions dialog box, you are able to customize **Net TOOLS Security's** features for your network needs. If **Applications Manager** is the workstation shell, placing the customized **Security** modules in the network startup group would ensure that they load automatically at each workstation.

When you build a **Net TOOLS Security** .WWR file, you can choose which of the three **Security** modules your network users will run: Clock, Intercom and/or Secure Station. You may set restrictions enabling or disabling any of the modules or requiring users to run Secure Station. In addition, you can specify a filename and color for the logo that displays at startup and allow users to customize it.

The Options menu includes Change Password and Logo Display items, which are described earlier in this chapter:

- For procedures on modifying the logo display, see the section "Logo Display" in this chapter.

- For procedures on changing the password, refer to the section "Changing the Password" in this chapter.

The Options/Restrictions menu item offers the following options:

Net TOOLS Security modules and available options

Module	Options	Results
Clock	Enable	Clock displays whenever program runs
	Command	Lets users run programs from the Alarm Options dialog box
Intercom	Enable Send	Users can send network messages
	Enable Receive	Users can receive network messages
Secure Station	Enable	Secure Station feature is available, but use is optional
	Require	Secure Station feature is enforced (and users cannot close Secure Station from the Task List)
	Enable Messages	Leave Message feature is active

Timeout range limit	Users can only set timeout value within the set range
Action upon double-click on Secure Station icon	Action will display the menu *or* invoke security immediately
Directory for screen saver display	This entry will display as default location of screen saver files

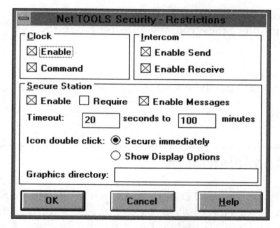

The Net TOOLS Security - Restrictions dialog box.

● **TO SET RESTRICTIONS ON SECURITY MODULES:**

1. Choose Restrictions from the Options menu.

   The Net TOOLS Security - Restrictions dialog box displays.

2. To enable the Clock, Command, Intercom (Send and Receive) and Secure features, check the corresponding box.

A check in the box indicates the feature is active. You may select one, two, three, or all four features to be active.

3. Additionally, in the Secure Station group box you may:

Check the Require box to enforce use of Secure Station. (If you require the use of Secure Station, users cannot close Secure Station from the Task List.)

Enter the Timeout limits within which users can set the timeout range for Secure Station.

Choose the radio button indicating the action performed when users double click on the icon (secure now or display options).

Enter the directory location of screen saver graphics. Secure Station will list graphics files from this directory in the Secure Station Options box.

4. Choose OK.

For details on using the **Security** modules, see the Chapter 6, "**Net TOOLS Security**."

Exiting Net TOOLS Administration

When you are ready to exit **Net TOOLS Administration**, choose Exit from the File menu. If you have not saved your changes during the session, a message box requests that you save them. Choosing Yes in this box saves the changes in the current .WWR file and closes the program. Choosing No disregards any changes you may have made and exits.

If you have run the **Administration** program from **Applications Manager**, selecting Exit only closes the **Administration** program.

Note: Although you have exited the program, you remain in Administration mode until you re-enter the key sequence Ctrl+Alt+A to return to user mode.

Chapter 5

MultiSet Script Language

MultiSet is a scripting language designed for LAN integrators and administrators. It provides the mechanisms necessary to make applications and files transparently available to users on the network.

This chapter presents procedures to create **MultiSet** scripts with the **MultiSet Editor** using scripts with menuing front-ends such as **Applications Manager** and Windows Program Manager. It also describes in detail the **MultiSet** commands.

Topics in this chapter

Scripts: Building an Integrated Net TOOLS Menu
How Do I Create a Script?
Automatically Executing Scripts
Managing MultiSet Scripts
How Do I Use MultiSet with Other Menu Systems?
MultiSet System Variables
How to Use the MultiSet Commands
The MultiSet Commands

Scripts: Building an Integrated Net TOOLS Menu

MultiSet scripts provide you with the features and flexibility needed to integrate Windows applications on a local area network. **MultiSet** is also the tightly integrated with **Applications Manager**. By creating **MultiSet** scripts, you can transparently manage the use of files and applications across the network within the Windows and DOS environments.

Following is a list of some of the actions **MultiSet** can perform through scripts:

- Attach to other file servers on your network.

- Assign a drive letter to network drives for use by your applications.

- Display important information on the Bulletin Board.

- Run or load multiple programs with a single command.

- Change or add information to your .INI files such as the WIN.INI or the SYSTEM.INI.

- Dynamically update your environment's search path for each Windows application.

MultiSet is both similar to and different than other scripting languages for Windows. It is similar in the way it allows users to perform multiple operations using a single command. Its differences, however, are more important. It was written specifically to integrate Windows applications on a network.

Many of the **MultiSet** commands are designed for use by LAN Administrators and experienced end-users. However, even if you are a novice user, you may easily use some of **MultiSet**'s more basic commands to change directories and run or load multiple programs.

How Do I Create a Script?

MultiSet scripts are created using the **MultiSet Editor**. The **MultiSet Editor** is similar to Windows Notepad, but it allows you to work on more than one script at a time through its Multiple Document Interface (MDI). You can view, write, edit, copy and print scripts in the script windows of **MultiSet Editor**. The editor also checks syntax, (that is, the "grammar" of your script statements) and allows you to test the script while you are editing it (Run Script).

- **TO OPEN THE MULTISET SCRIPT EDITOR:**

1. Choose **MultiSet Script Editor** from the startup group provided with **Applications Manager** if that program is your shell.

    OR

2. Choose MSEDIT.EXE in the File Manager or Program Manager.

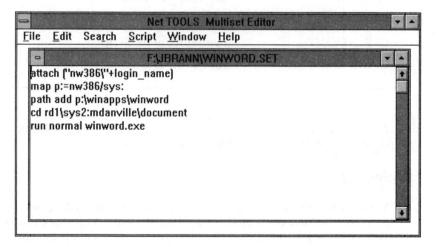

The MultiSet Editor window.

Editing a script is handled the same way in **MultiSet Editor** as in any other Windows editors. However, in addition to providing the same editing features used throughout Windows, **MultiSet Editor** offers various additional editing techniques. The following sections explain each of these techniques.

Special Cursor Movement Keys

Since composing and editing scripts relies heavily upon using the keyboard, **MultiSet Editor** includes a number of special keys for quickly moving around in a script.

Special Cursor Movement Keys

Press this	To move to the
CTRL+RIGHT	Next word
CTRL+LEFT	Previous word
HOME	Beginning of a line
END	End of a line
CTRL+HOME	Beginning of the script
CTRL+END	End of the script

Note: You can move the insertion point continuously by holding down any of these key combinations.

Finding Text

You can easily search for and edit commands in your **MultiSet** scripts by using the Find command on the Search menu. With this command, you can look for a character, word or group of characters or words in a script.

When you choose the Find command, **MultiSet Editor** starts a search at the cursor insertion point or at the end of any text that is currently selected. When it reaches the end of the script, it will discontinue the search and display any appropriate messages.

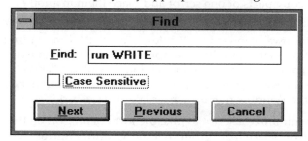

The Find dialog box.

- **TO FIND TEXT:**

1. Position the insertion point where you want to start your search.

2. Choose Find from the Search menu.

   The Find dialog box displays.

3. In the Find dialog box, enter the text you want to find.

4. Select the Case Sensitive check box if you want to match capitalization exactly.

   Otherwise, **MultiSet Editor** will find, for example, instances of both *Main* and *main*.

5. Choose Next (or press ENTER) to start the search. Pressing Previous will search in a backwards direction.

   MultiSet Editor searches for the text and selects the first occurrence. If there are no occurrences of the text in the script, **MultiSet Editor** displays a message that the text searched for was not found.

To continue searching for the next occurrence of the text, press F3. To find previous occurrences, press F4.

Editing multiple scripts

With **MultiSet Editor's** Multiple Document Interface (MDI), it is possible to have more than one script open at a time. This feature allows you to copy parts of one script and place them in another script.

Following Windows' standard MDI rules, **MultiSet Editor's** Window menu allows you to view multiple scripts on the screen at one time. Each script is contained and edited in a window called a "child" window. You can easily manage their display with the commands found under the Window menu such as Tile and Cascade.

You may also minimize a script to take the form of an icon on the application's workspace (background of the **MultiSet Editor** window). Other commands found under the Window menu allow you to arrange the icons on the application workspace or to close all windows simultaneously.

You may select which script, or child window, to take the focus by selecting it from the list of opened scripts in the Window menu. The scripts are numbered in the order in which they were opened. The script that is currently in focus is denoted by a check mark beside its number, path and filename.

Checking the syntax of a script

MultiSet Editor will automatically try to help you write scripts that will work properly. The Check Syntax command on the Script menu does what its name implies--checks the syntax of your script. This assures you that the command's parameters and expressions have been used properly. In addition, your syntax will be checked every time you run a script from the editor.

As errors are discovered, a syntax error message box displays, and the cursor moves to the line and location of the invalid command.

- To check the syntax of a script:

1. Select the window that contains the script in which you would like to check syntax.

2. Choose Check Syntax from the Script menu or press CTRL+C.

Running a script from MultiSet Editor

As a convenience for testing, the **MultiSet Editor's** Script menu also includes a Run Script command. This will invoke **MultiSet** to run the script that is in the window currently in focus. If any errors are detected during the script's execution, a syntax error message will display and the cursor will move to the line and location of the offending command.

- **TO RUN A SCRIPT FROM THE MULTISET EDITOR:**

1. Select the window that contains the script you wish to run.

2. Choose Run Script from the Script menu or press CTRL+R.

Automatically Executing Scripts

You can automatically execute **MultiSet** scripts. If you use **Applications Manager** as your Windows shell, use one of the following methods to execute the file:

- If you are going to run **Net TOOLS Security**, create a startup group which contains the **Net TOOLS Security** program. As **Net TOOLS Security** launches, the CONFIG.SET script executes, if it has been created. This script provides the administrator with a centralized method to update users' Windows environments as they launch Windows, whether their Windows personal files (WIN.INI, SYSTEM.INI, etc.) are on the network or the local hard drive.

- If you do not run **Net TOOLS Security**, place a script file in the startup group. As Applications Manager loads, the script file will execute. This file must have a .SET extension.

If you do not designate **Applications Manager** as your shell, **Applications Manager** startup groups will not function. In this case, execute a script at startup by placing either WWEXT.EXE (which will launch CONFIG.SET) or the name of the .SET file on the Load= or Run= line of the WIN.INI file.

> **Note:** MULTISET.EXE should not be included on the Run= or Load= lines of the WIN.INI file. Specifying the MultiSet executable will cause a system lock-up, as the parameter for the .SET filename will never be found. You can prevent this by designating only the name of the .SET file, for example EXCEL.SET.

The .SET File Extension

For MultiSet to execute along with the designated .SET file, make sure that the .SET extension has been associated with the MultiSet program in the [Extensions] section of the WIN.INI file, for example:

SET=MULTISET.EXE ^.SET

Managing MultiSet Scripts

You may Open and Save **MultiSet** script files much the same way you would any other text or data file -- by using the commands located on the File Menu. These commands include New, Open, Save and Save As. In addition, you may also Print your scripts to the default printer. Shared **MultiSet** scripts should be placed on the user's search path or other directory where they will be accessible.

How Do I Use MultiSet with Other Menu Systems?

Net **TOOLS Menu's** modular nature allows you to choose which components work best for your particular installation. While **MultiSet** has been designed to work seamlessly with **Applications Manager**, it works very well with any other menu system, such as Windows Program Manager, protecting your investment in those products.

Although Windows Program Manager was designed to be used in a stand-alone configuration, you may extend both its capabilities and its reach to the network through **MultiSet**. Because **MultiSet** handles the execution of other programs, Program Manager can run **MultiSet**, which will, in turn, run the application of your choice.

The first task in this process is to create a small **MultiSet** script using the command language discussed in this chapter.

- **TO CREATE AND SAVE YOUR MULTISET SCRIPT:**

1. Select the **MultiSet Script Editor** from the startup group provided with **Applications Manager** if it is your shell or run MSEDIT.EXE from the Program Manager or File Manager.

2. Create your script using the instructions found in the "How Do I Create a Script?" section of this chapter.

3. Save your script to the location of your choice with a .SET file extension. The location should be on your search path so Program Manager can find it when Windows is loaded.

Using a script in Program Manager

Now that the script has been created, you can place the .SET file into Program Manager and assign an icon to it.

- **TO PLACE THE SCRIPT INTO PROGRAM MANAGER:**

1. Switch to Program Manager. If Program Manager is not loaded, then run PROGMAN.EXE from the File/Run menu of File Manager.

2. Select the Group Menu of your choice into which you want to place the script.

3. Choose New from the File menu.

   The New Program Object dialog box displays.

4. Select Program Item and choose OK.

   The Program Item Properties dialog box displays.

5. Enter the description for your script.

6. In the Command Line text box, type the name of the script, for example *WINWRITE.SET*.

7. Select Change Icon. Use the Change Icon dialog box to associate an icon with the script.

8. In the Program Item Properties dialog box, Click on OK.

This will add the script to your Program Manager group menu. For more information on Windows Program Manager, refer to the *Windows User's Guide*.

Now, whenever you select the script from your Program Manager menu, **MultiSet** will actually be in control, just as if you were running it from **Applications Manager**. In addition, by placing your scripts in a search path over the network, **MultiSet** allows you to centrally manage the way Program Manager operates, a capability which is impossible without **MultiSet**.

Using a script in File Manager

As another alternative, you may also run your scripts from the File Manager. By double-clicking on a .SET file, **MultiSet** will automatically execute the selected script.

MultiSet System Variables

MultiSet allows you to change your environment and to read it. There are three commands that set your environment. These are PATH ADD, SET, and SETPATH. There are two ways to read your environment: with the GETPATH command and by using the environment variable enclosed in percentage signs (%) in an expression.

$ENVMODE

When you are running Windows in standard or enhanced mode, there are two environments. One environment is used for Windows applications and one for DOS applications. To control which environment you will affect or read in a **MultiSet** script, you set the **MultiSet** system variable $ENVMODE.

When changing the environment, there are three recognized states for this variable:

To set the environment for DOS applications, you should set this variable to "DOS".

For Windows applications, you should set it to "Windows". This is also the default setting, which applies if the script does not set $ENVMODE.

For both DOS and Windows applications, you should set it to "BOTH".

When reading the environment, there are only two recognized states for $ENVMODE (there is no setting for both, since the two environments could be different):

To read the DOS environment, set $ENVMODE to "DOS".

To read the Windows environment, set $ENVMODE to anything else. If the script does not set $ENVMODE, it will read the Windows environment, since "Windows" is the default setting.

MultiSet expands the Windows environment as needed. After the first change is made to the Windows environment by **MultiSet**, there are two separate environments. Windows applications launched prior to the first environment change use the environment that was set when Windows was launched. Windows applications launched after the first environment change use the new environment which is maintained by **MultiSet**.

Environment Space

When making changes to the DOS environment space you may receive an "out of environment space" error message. Due to a Windows limitation, the DOS environment cannot be expanded once Windows is launched. Existing environment space, however, can be reused. You can work around this limitation by setting dummy variables in DOS to reserve the environment space before loading Windows.

You can set DUMMY to xxxxxxxxxxxxxxxxxxxxxxxxxxxxxxx, for example, before launching Windows to reserve the environment space. Then reassign the environment space in the script, as in the following example which adds a directory to the path:

```
$ENVMODE=DOS
SET DUMMY=""
PATH_ADD F:\WP
RUN WP.EXE
```

Restoring the Environment Setting

When you set the environment for DOS applications, **MultiSet** changes the environment, launches the DOS application and restores the environment to its original state. Due to the slow speed of some systems, COMMAND.COM is unable to finish launching before **MultiSet** restores the environment. To correct this occurrence, you may want to increase the value for the MSENVRESTORE= parameter in the [WindowsWorkstation] section of your WIN.INI file from the 1000 millisecond default setting.

$WINVER

The variable, $WINVER reflects the Windows version you are running. The variable will contain "30" for Windows 3.0 and "31" for Windows 3.1.

How to Use the MultiSet Commands

MultiSet is similar to a programming language, although much easier to understand. Like most languages, it has a set of rules for putting the parts of a script together in a meaningful way. These rules are called syntax.

Usually, a **MultiSet** statement is made up of a command followed by its parameters. Each command expects a parameter or group of parameters. For example, the ATTACH command expects the parameter of what to attach to. Its parameters are *server* or *server/username*.

Understanding statement syntax

Scripts also need to follow certain rules for formatting commands and programming statements, although they are not case sensitive (words may be typed in upper or lower case). The following table lists the syntax conventions used in **MultiSet**:

Syntax conventions for MultiSet

Convention	*Description*
Commands	Words that appear in capital letters are commands. Commands must be spelled exactly as shown.
Variables	Words printed in italics are variables. Variable information is provided by input from the user or from the results of other commands, such as MEMBEROF or LOGIN_NAME. User-defined variables are shown by $var. User-defined variables may be used anywhere text is required.

[|]	Square brackets enclose parameters that are *optional* to the command. Items enclosed within square brackets are not required in the statement, but they can be used to make a statement clearer or to add options. When you type an optional word in a command format, do not include the brackets. When two or more items may be used interchangeably, they are separated by a vertical bar.
(. . .)	Ellipses indicate that the command or variables immediately preceding can be repeated as many times as necessary. The commands or variables must be separated by a space or other punctuation that is listed in the command's syntax.
%VARIABLE%	You may pass environment variables freely within your **MultiSet** scripts by using the format %VARIABLE%. For example, to pass the COMSPEC variable, use %COMSPEC%.
Other characters	Any other characters or punctuation included in a command format should be typed exactly as shown.
Special symbols	When using special symbols (! = +, etc.) in strings, the string must be enclosed in double quotes. A space is also considered a special symbol. When a section name contains a space, e.g., [Microsoft Word], enclose it in double quotes - "Microsoft Word".

Some of the commands in this reference include more than one acceptable form of syntax. In such cases, you may use any of the forms.

Command expression format

You should use the following format to compose an expression for use with **MultiSet** command scripts:

variable = expression
command
BEGIN
    command
     ...
END

IF expression THEN

    statement

ELSE

    statement

Words Reserved as MultiSet Commands

Words designated as **MultiSet** commands must be enclosed in double quotes if you want to use them as literals. For example:

    SETINI WIN.INI WINDOWS "RUN"="WWEXT.EXE"

Since RUN is a **MultiSet** command, enclose it in double quotes to keep **MultiSet** from trying to execute the Run command.

WIN.INI Entries that Display in Double Quotes

Some entries in the WIN.INI are enclosed in double quotes. When indicating these strings in a **MultiSet** script, enclose the string in an additional set of double quotation marks to keep **MultiSet** from treating the text as a literal. For example, the conversion section for Microsoft Word encloses some keynames in double quotes.

CONV1="WordPerfect 5.1" G:\WINAPPS\WINWORD\CONV-WP5.DLL
    ^.DOC

When writing a script to set this line in the WIN.INI, WordPerfect must be enclosed with a double set of double quotation marks and the entire string must be enclosed in double quotation marks. Note that Microsoft Word is enclosed in double quotation marks since it contains a space.

SETINI WIN.INI "Microsoft Word" CONV1="""WordPerfect 5.1""
    G:\WINAPPS\WINWORD\CONV-WP5.DLL ^.DOC"

Combining Strings

Use the + sign to combine strings. For example:

CD "F:\"+LOGIN_NAME+"\sheets"

The MultiSet Commands

The following sections are provided as a reference to the **MultiSet** commands. Each command is organized into four sections. The following table describes these sections:

Subheading definitions for this chapter

Subheading	Definition
Purpose	Provides a short description of the command and explains why you might use it.
Command Syntax	Lists the complete command format.
Returns	Shows the value that is returned for each command.
Examples	Provides examples of how the command can be used. May also provide suggestions of how to use a command in conjunction with another command.

The **MultiSet** commands and parameters are case insensitive. While we have used uppercase to denote the commands and lowercase to denote the parameters, this is only done for ease of reading.

ATTACH

Purpose

Checks current file server attachments. If you are already attached (as USERNAME), the command returns "TRUE", otherwise, prompts user for *username/password*. The *username* can be supplied as an optional parameter. This will prompt the user only for a password. (This command does not apply in a LAN Manager environment. If encountered in a script, it is skipped over.)

The Attach dialog box.

Command Syntax

ATTACH *server[/username]*
$var = ATTACH *server[/username]*

Returns

If the user is already attached to the server, the command returns "TRUE". If the user is not attached, the command returns "" and brings up the Attach dialog box.

Example

To attach to file server MYSERVER as user SUPERVISOR, you would type the following in the **MultiSet** script:

ATTACH myserver/supervisor

If the user is already attached on the server specified, the user is not prompted and "TRUE" is returned. You can also check to see if a user is currently attached to a file server by using the USERNAME command, described below. If a user is already attached and they attach again, all drive mappings to that server are lost.

If any programs or data files were running from those drives, Windows may be in an unstable state. The following script is a simple example of how to check if an attachment exists and then conditionally attach to a server:

IF NOT (USERNAME myserver) THEN
　　　ATTACH myserver\jim

CD

Purpose

Changes the current working directory for **MultiSet** to a new directory on the same drive letter or to a new drive letter and directory. As new commands are issued or applications are launched with **MultiSet**, they will assume the new working directory. (This command offers enhanced functionality over the CD DOS command in that it allows you to change the current drive as well as the current directory.)

Command Syntax

CD [drive:]directory

$var = CD [drive:]directory

Returns

If the command is successful, it returns the value of the new current directory. If the command fails, it returns "".

Example

To change to directory D:*myfiles**docs* you would type:

CD d:\myfiles\docs

The CD command can be used before a LISTFILES command. This will move you to a desired directory before listing the files of your choice.

The CD command cannot contain a *server/volume* designation. It must use a drive letter if you want to move to a drive other than that of your current working directory. You may use the MAP command to define a new drive:\directory.

> **Note:** If the CD command is followed by a RUN command and the application you are running uses a PIF (Program Information File) with a change directory command, the PIF change directory command overrides the **MultiSet** CD command.

COPY

Purpose

To copy a file or files from one directory, drive or server to another.

Command Syntax

COPY [server\volume:][directory\]filename |

   wildcard [[server\volume:][directory\]

   [filename | wildcard]]
                 or
   COPY [drive:][directory\]filename | wildcard

   [[drive:][directory\][filename | wildcard]]

$var = COPY[server\volume:][directory\]

filename | wildcard [[server\volume:]

[directory\] [filename | wildcard]]
> or

$var = COPY[drive:][directory\]filename | wildcard

[[drive:][directory\][filename | wildcard]]

Returns

If the command is successful, it returns "TRUE". If the command
fails, it returns "".

Example

COPY updated files to a workstation from a server.

COPY admin\sys2:appl*.* c:\appl

COPY admin\sys2:batch\autoexec.bat c:\autoexec.bat

DELETE

Purpose

To delete a file or files from a directory, drive or server.

Command Syntax

DELETE [server\volume:][directory\] filename |

wildcard
> or

DELETE [drive:][directory\]filename | wildcard

$var = DELETE[server\volume:][directory\]

filename | wildcard
> or

$var = DELETE[drive:][directory\]filename | wildcard

Returns

If the command is successful, it returns "TRUE". If the command fails, it returns "".

Example

DELETE can be used to remove old files that are no longer necessary.

> DELETE c:\pater*.bak

Banyan Consideration

When using the DELETE command in a script, first use a CD (change directory) command to move to the directory containing the files to delete. Then use the DELETE command to delete the files. **Do not** designate a path to the file(s) that you want to delete.

DELINI

Purpose

Delete a section or individual parameter from a specified Windows .INI file. The .INI files must reside in the subdirectory that contains your Windows startup files in order for Windows to find it. If you do not specify an individual parameter, the entire section is deleted.

Command Syntax

> DELINI *filename.ini section [parameter]*

Returns

If the command is successful, it returns "TRUE". If the command fails, it returns "".

Example

> DELINI win.ini Extensions txt

This will remove the "txt=" parameter from the Extensions section of the WIN.INI file.

DISPLAY

Purpose

Displays one or more text files in a multiple document display. The first DISPLAY command in a script launches the **Workstation Bulletin Board**. Additional Display commands open new windows in the **Bulletin Board**.

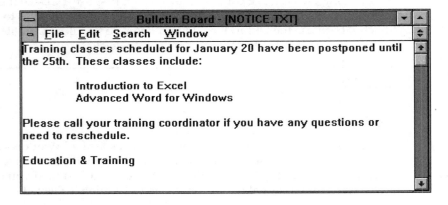

The Bulletin Board window.

Command Syntax

DISPLAY *[server/volume:filename]* | *[drive:][dir\ ]filename*

$var = DISPLAY *[server/volume:filename]* | *[drive:][dir\ ]filename*

Returns

If the command is successful, it returns "TRUE". If the command fails, it returns "".

Example

Messages or notices can be displayed for users as they login each day or as information needs to be disseminated over the LAN. One practical use might be to list the week's training classes or important events. By using the DISPLAY command with the MEMBEROF command you can dynamically present customized messages to various groups of people:

```
IF (MEMBEROF accounting) THEN

BEGIN
        MAP Q:=MYSERVER\SYS2:NEWS
        DISPLAY Q:\NEWS\ACCTNEWS.TXT
END
```

The Bulletin Board will remain on screen until closed by the user. The user can optionally copy text to the Clipboard and print the messages.

EXISTS

Purpose

Determines if a particular file exists on the specified path.

Command Syntax

EXISTS [server\volume:]directory\filename

Returns

If the command is successful, it returns "TRUE". If the command fails, it returns "".

Example

```
IF EXISTS EXCEL.EXE THEN

        EXIT
```

In this example, the script will check the user's current directory for the file EXCEL.EXE. If it exists, the script terminates.

EXIT

Purpose

The EXIT command terminates execution of a **MultiSet** script. EXIT may be used more than once in a script.

Command Syntax

EXIT

Returns

There is no return value.

Example

IF (USERNAME myserver) THEN

EXIT

This will exit the **MultiSet** script if the user is attached to file server "MYSERVER."

FDISPLAY

Purpose

Displays a designated text file in a window with a vertical scroll bar and an OK button. Used to pop up a text file for informational purposes.

Command Syntax

FDISPLAY [server\volume:]directory\file

Returns

"TRUE" if file is displayed. Otherwise, returns "".

Example

IF (MEMBEROF "admin") THEN

FDISPLAY "backup.log"

The above example will display the file "backup.log" for a member of the group ADMIN.

GETINI

Purpose

Retrieves values from sections in the WIN.INI or other .INI files.

Command Syntax

$var = GETINI *filename.ini section entry*

Returns

The text in the INI file if found. Otherwise, "".

Example

$var = GETINI *win.ini windows spooler*

This will get the value of *spooler=* from the [Windows] section of the file WIN.INI and put it in user variable $var.

$shell = GETINI *system.ini boot shell*

This example allows you to determine which shell is being loaded as the user launches Windows.

GETPATH

Purpose

Gets current path information from the DOS environment. Helps in allowing a user to view or edit his path manually.

Command Syntax

$variable = GETPATH

Returns

The current path setting.

Example

$currentpath = GETPATH

$newpath = PROMPT "Enter New Path" $currentpath

IF $newpath THEN

SETPATH $newpath

Displays the current PATH environment variable setting from variable $currentpath and then prompts the user to make changes to the path. When the changes have been made, the script will update the environment with the new path. The path can also be added to the environment with the SET command.

See the section "MultiSet System Variables" earlier in this chapter for details on environment variables and the GETPATH command.

GOTO

Purpose

Jumps to *label* and continues the execution of a **MultiSet** script. Labels are defined by the :label statement.

Command Syntax

GOTO   *label*

Returns

There is no return value.

Example

```
IF (USERNAME myserver) THEN
        GOTO showmsg
ELSE
BEGIN
        ATTACH myserver\userid
        MAP p:=myserver\sys:userid
END
:showmsg
DISPLAY myserver\sys:msgs\bbs.txt
```

IF...THEN...ELSE

Purpose

You can use the IF...THEN command to make the **MultiSet** script perform commands conditionally. The expression used in evaluating the IF statement will be TRUE if the expression is anything except "". If the expression is anything more than a single operator, enclose it in parenthesis. The keywords IF and THEN must appear on the same line. You may nest IF statements within the IF-THEN-ELSE logic. BEGIN-END statements can be used to group commands to be executed inside the IF statement.

Comparison operators are used to compare user variables or identifiers. A string or variable is evaluated as True if it contains any characters. Otherwise, it is False. The following operators are available:

Operators used to compare variables

Operators	Description
a = b	Compares a with b and returns "TRUE" if they are equal, otherwise returns "".
a <> b	Compares a with b and returns "TRUE" if they are not equal.
NOT(a)	If a is True, returns "". If a is False, returns "TRUE".
a AND b	If a is True and b is True returns "TRUE", else returns "".
a OR b	If a is True or b is True returns "TRUE", else returns "".

Command Syntax

IF *expression*THEN

    command

[ELSE
    command]

Returns

There is no return value.

Example

```
$myname = LOGIN_NAME
IF NOT ($myname) THEN
BEGIN
        IF (MESSAGE OKCANCEL "Log in now?") THEN
        BEGIN
                IF NOT (ATTACH myserver) THEN
                BEGIN
                        MESSAGE OK "Login cancelled."
                        GOTO fail
```

```
                    END
                    ELSE
                                GOTO success
            END
            ELSE
            BEGIN
                    MESSAGE OK "Fine."
                    GOTO fail
            END
    END
    ELSE
            GOTO fail
    :success
    MESSAGE OK "Login successful."
    :fail
```

The example above can determine whether a user is currently logged into the network and provide him with a mechanism for logging in.
IF (MEMBEROF acctsrv\accounting) THEN

    RUN NORMAL excel.exe

ELSE

    MESSAGE OK "You are not authorized to run this program."

EXIT

If the user is a member of the group "accounting" on the current server and is a user on server "accsrv", then a drive is mapped and a file is displayed.

ISNETWORK

Purpose

Checks to see if the network software is loaded on the current PC. May be used to conditionally run **MultiSet** scripts that pertain to local rather than network operation if the network is not available.

Command Syntax

$var = ISNETWORK

Returns

Returns "TRUE" if the network software has been loaded and attachments can be made, otherwise returns "".

Example

IF (ISNETWORK) THEN

GOTO connect

If the network is available, Goto the script section labeled :connect.

LISTFILES

Purpose

Presents the user with a file selection list box using multiple file and wildcard specifications with a title of *text*. *Filespec* is composed of multiple filespecs separated by semicolons (;) in order to display files in a particular directory for a user selection. Returns the path/filename selected or "" if the Continue button is selected. Selecting Cancel will stop the execution of the script.

```
┌────────────────────────────────────────────────────────┐
│ ─                      List Files                        │
│ Please select a document to load:                       │
│                                              ┌────────┐  │
│ File Name:  [                            ]   │   OK   │  │
│                                              └────────┘  │
│ Files In:     f:\jbrann\ww42                ┌─────────┐  │
│ ┌───────────┐                               │Continue │  │
│ │42mchp1.doc│▲  Directories                 └─────────┘  │
│ │42mchp2.doc│                               ┌─────────┐  │
│ │42mchp3.doc│   ┌────────┐▲                 │ Cancel  │  │
│ │42mchp4.doc│   │[..]    │                  └─────────┘  │
│ │42mchp5.doc│   │[-a-]   │                               │
│ │42mchp6.doc│   │[-b-]   │                               │
│ │42mdde.doc │   │[-c-]   │                               │
│ │42mgloss.doc│▼ │[-f-]   │                               │
│ └───────────┘   │[-g-]   │▼                              │
│                 └────────┘                               │
└────────────────────────────────────────────────────────┘
```

The List Files dialog box.

Command Syntax

$var = LISTFILES *filespec1[;filespec2...] title*

Returns

The path\filename of the file selected, or "" if Continue is selected. If the Cancel button is selected, script execution stops.

Example

$file = LISTFILES *.doc;*.txt "Please select a document to load:"

This will display a list box of all files with *.doc* and *.txt* extension, and place the title "Please select a document to load:" at the top of the list box. Returns path/filename of file selected to the user variable $file.

To display the files of a particular drive and/or subdirectory use the LISTFILES command in conjunction with a CD command like this:

CD "F:\"+LOGIN_NAME+"\sheets"

$file = LISTFILES *.XL*;*.wk1 "Please select a spreadsheet:"

RUN NORMAL excel.exe + " " + $file

The CD will change the current working directory to the *sheets* subdirectory of the logged-in user and the LISTFILES will display the Excel and Lotus files in the directory.

As the user selects a file, he may choose to move to a different drive or subdirectory to find the file that he requires. As he moves through the subdirectories and drives, **MultiSet** keeps track of his location and will pass this information to the application that is launched with the file that he selects. With this feature, the user is always assured of being able to find and save his files to a familiar location from which the file came.

For example, if the user executed the script above, but decided to load a file from the N:\SHARE subdirectory, he could select the N:\SHARE drive and subdirectory from within the LISTFILES dialog box. Then when Excel is launched, it would take on that subdirectory as the current working directory. As he opened or saved files, he would see the files in the N:\SHARE subdirectory. To prevent the current working directory from changing due to a user selection in LISTFILES, you can issue a second CD command after the LISTFILES command to return the user to the proper directory before launching Excel.

LOGIN_NAME

Purpose

Returns the current username on the primary server.

Command Syntax

$var = LOGIN_NAME

Returns

Username on the primary server. This is usually the server that the user first logged in to. If "" is returned, the user is either not logged in or the network is not present. See the ISNETWORK command for information on determining whether the user has networking software loaded.

Example

$myname = LOGIN_NAME

The user's login name on the primary server will be placed in the variable $myname. See the example in LISTFILES for another example of LOGIN_NAME.

MAP

Purpose

The MAP command can be used to map a specified drive to a given file server, volume and directory.

Command Syntax

MAP [root] *drive:=[server/]volume:[/directory]*

Returns

If the command is successful, it returns "TRUE". If the command fails, it returns "".

Example

MAP P:=myserver/sys:\eng\jim

Maps the specified drive to the given directory. Directory refers to the directory path, beginning with the volume name.

MAP ROOT F:=server/sys:\public\mail

If the optional keyword root is specified, the directory specified in the command will become the root directory for the drive being mapped. In the example command above, F:/ will give access to the files in the MAIL subdirectory. You will not be able to do a change directory (CD) command on drive F: to access the files in the PUBLIC directory.

> **Note**: Some software does not function properly when using drives with a directory mapped as the root.

LAN Manager Note

This command can be used to map a specified drive to a given file server, sharename and directory. For LAN Manager, the syntax is:

MAP drive:=[\\server\]sharename[\directory] [optional password]

Banyan Note

This command can be used to map a drive to a given file service and optional directory. For Banyan VINES, the syntax is:

MAP drive:"fileservice@group@organization[@\optional directory]"

Here is an example of the command:

MAP F:="Winapps@Marketing@Atlanta

The Map command supports false roots when a directory path is added to the end of the command:

MAP F:="Data@Marketing@Atlanta@\DocFiles

MEMBEROF

Purpose

Determines if the user is a member of the network group called *group name*. Groups are defined with the utilities supplied with your network operating system. For example, in Novell NetWare, you create groups through the SYSCON utility.

The server specified in this command is checked. If a server is not specified, the primary server is checked.

Command Syntax

MEMBEROF [server/] *group name*

Returns

If the user is a member of the group, it returns "TRUE". If the command fails, or user is not a member, returns "".

Example

IF (MEMBEROF sales) THEN

CD f:\sales\records

If the user is a member of the group sales, changes current directory and drive to f:\sales\records.

MESSAGE

Purpose

Produces a message box with buttons showing *text*. The *type* can be OK for an OK button, OKCANCEL for an OK and a CANCEL button, YESNO for a Yes and a No button, and YESNOCANCEL for a Yes, a No and a Cancel button.

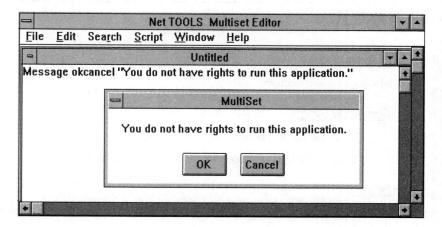

A typical Message dialog box

Command Syntax

MESSAGE *type text*

Returns

If the command is successful or the user selects OK, it returns "TRUE". If the command fails or the user selects CANCEL, it returns "". If the user selects Yes, the command return "YES". If the user selects No, the command returns "NO"

Example

$continue = MESSAGE YESNO "Delete selected file?"

This will display the text in a message box with both YES and NO buttons and set user variable $continue with either "YES" or "NO" depending on which button is pressed.

MESSAGE OK "Not logged in."

This will display the text "Not logged in" in a message box with just an OK button.

MKDIR

Purpose

Makes a new directory.

Command Syntax

MKDIR *[server/volume:dir]* | *[drive:][dir\]*

$var = MKDIR *[server/volume:dir]* | *[drive:][dir\]*

Returns

If the command is successful, it returns "TRUE". If the command fails, it returns "".

Example

To create d:*myfiles**docs* you would type:

MKDIR d:\myfiles\docs

PATH ADD

Purpose

Adds a drive and directory path to the global path. This new path is appended to the end of the current global path and is available to all applications that are launched through **MultiSet** including standard DOS applications.

PATH ADD is an important tool for the administrator as it eliminates the need for multiple drive mappings and search drive mappings to the same volume of a server. When applications are launched with underlying scripts, each script can map drives "on the fly" to ensure the proper execution of a program.

It is important to use correct pathing techniques to ensure that your **MultiSet** scripts work smoothly. The command syntax requires a complete path to the executable to ensure that an executable file can still be found if a drive mapping changes.

Command Syntax

PATH ADD *[drive:][dir\]*

Returns

If the command is successful, it returns "TRUE". If the command fails, it returns "".

Example

PATH ADD c:\winapps\winword

This will add the new path *c:\winapps\winword* to the current global path, making the programs in that directory available to the user on the search path. This is the equivalent of MAP INSERTing a Search Drive in Novell's NetWare or changing your path in DOS with the PATH command.

Each subsequent time that this command is run, it will check to see if you already have the requested path on your search path. If it is, it will not add it again.

> **Note**: PATH ADD does not affect DOS boxes.

See the section "MultiSet System Variables" earlier in this chapter for details on environment variables and the PATH ADD command.

P_STATION

Purpose

Returns the physical station ID number of the workstation in 12 hexadecimal digit format. This number is usually stored in the network interface card either as a factory burned-in address (as it is with Ethernet) or in a definable setting (as it is with ARCNet or Token Ring). The P_STATION command is very useful for conditionally running a program like a print server based on the workstation's hardware ID.

Command Syntax

    P_STATION

Returns

The physical station ID number as text if the user is logged into the network.

Example

IF (P_STATION = "104225987657") THEN

BEGIN

RUN NORMAL pserver.exe

EXIT

END

Will check the value of P_STATION first and use it in the IF statement.

LAN Manager Note

This command returns the physical station (local machine) ID number as defined in LANMAN.INI. This ID number is returned as text whether or not the user is logged into the network.

PROMPT

Purpose

Prompts user for *text* by showing text and putting *default* in the edit box. If no text is in the edit box, or CANCEL is pressed, "" is returned; otherwise, the text in the edit box is returned. This command can be used to request a variable from the user during the execution of the script. The results of the command can be used by other **MultiSet** commands as variables.

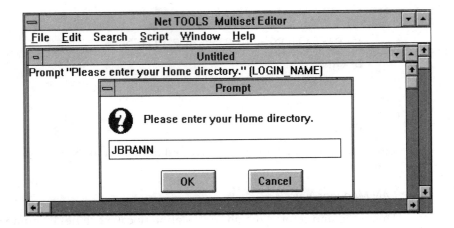

A typical Prompt dialog box.

Command Syntax

PROMPT "text" " default"

Returns

The text that the user entered in the edit box if OK is pressed, else "".

Example

$oldpath = GETPATH

$newpath = PROMPT "Please edit your path settings." $oldpath

SETPATH $newpath

RENAME

Purpose

To rename a file or files.

Command Syntax

RENAME filename | wildcard filename | wildcard

$var = RENAME filename | wildcard filename | wildcard

Returns

If the command is successful, it returns "TRUE". If the command fails, it returns "".

Example

RENAME can be used to change the name of a file. For example, if you keep multiple AUTOEXEC.BAT files, you might use this command.

RENAME autoexec.bat autoexec.net

RENAME autoexec.rnm autoexec.bat

RIGHTS

Purpose

Determines a user's access rights to a particular network path. If a filename is included in the path, the user's access rights to that file are also checked.

Command Syntax

RIGHTS [server\volume:path\[filename]] flags | [drive:] [dir] [\file]

Returns

If the user has *at least* the rights specified in "flags," it returns "TRUE". If the user has fewer rights, it returns "". Flags include:

R = Read from Files

O = Open Files

S = Search Directory

C = Create New Files

D = Delete Files

M = Modify File Names/Flags

P = Parental Rights

W = Write to Files

Example

IF ($access = RIGHTS myserver\sys:excel "ROS") THEN

RUN MAXIMIZE EXCEL.EXE

ELSE

MESSAGE OK "Sorry, you have insufficient rights."

This will verify that the user has at least ROS rights in the directory myserver\sys:excel before attempting to run the program.

LAN Manager Note

The command syntax in a LAN Manager environment is:

RIGHTS [\\server\sharename\path\[filename]] flags |
    [drive:][dir][\file] flags

The flags include:

R = Read from files

C = Create new files

A = Attributes

P = Permissions

D = Delete files

W = Write to files

RMDIR

Purpose

Removes a directory.

Command Syntax

RMDIR *[server/volume:dir]* | *[drive:][dir\]*

$var = RMDIR *[server/volume:dir]* | *[drive:][dir\]*

Returns

If the command is successful, it returns "TRUE". If the command fails, it returns "".

Example

To remove d:*myfiles**docs* you would type:

RMDIR d:\myfiles\docs

RUN

Purpose

Runs a program using *showtype* as the initial display mode. *Showtype* can be either "icon," "normal," or "maximize." Icon will cause the application to load as an icon. Normal will cause the program to run in its window that would be displayed upon a normal startup. Maximize will cause the application being run to take over full screen after it has been launched.

If a variable holds the command line for a program, be sure to include a space between the EXE filename and the variable ("CLOCK.EXE" + " " + $file).

Command Syntax

RUN *[showtype] [path\]program [commandline]*

> RUN [*showtype*] "[*path*]*program* [*commandline*]"

Returns

If the command is successful, it returns "TRUE". If the command fails, it returns "".

Example

> $file = LISTFILES *.doc "Enter the file to be spellchecked."
>
> RUN NORMAL c:\winspell\spell.exe + " " + $file

OR

> RUN ICON "notepad.exe readme.txt"

The first example will run *spell.exe* from the *c:\winspell* directory in the *normal* mode using the results of the LISTFILES command as the command line argument. The second example will run Notepad, loading the file readme.txt.

SET

Purpose

Sets the DOS environment variable to a specified value.

Command Syntax

> SET *envvar* = "*value*"

Returns

If the command is successful, it returns "TRUE". If the command fails, it returns "".

Example

> SET HOME = "F:\"+LOGIN_NAME

For the user FRED, this will set the DOS environment variable HOME to equal F:\FRED.

See the section "MultiSet System Variables" earlier in this chapter for details on environment variables and the SET command.

SETINI

Purpose

Sets or changes or creates a value in a section of a specified Windows .INI file. New sections can be created in existing .INI files; the .INI file must have already been created. The .INI files must reside in the subdirectory that contains your Windows startup files in order for Windows to find it.

Command Syntax

SETINI *filename.ini section parameter = value*

Returns

If the command is successful, it returns "TRUE". If the command fails, it returns "".

Example

SETINI *system.ini boot shell=appman.exe*

This will set the value of shell= in the [boot] section of system.ini to APPMAN.EXE.

SETPATH

Purpose

Sets the global path to *newpath*. *Newpath* can be the result of a function or a variable. This command can be used with the GETPATH command to allow the user to manually change his current path.

Command Syntax

SETPATH *newpath*

Returns

If the command is successful, it returns "TRUE". If the command fails, it returns "".

Example

$result = SETPATH   "c:\;c:\dos;c:\winword"

Sets the search path to "c:\;c:\dos;c:\winword" and returns the result to the user variable $result. See "GETPATH" for another example of how to use SETPATH.

See the section "MultiSet System Variables" earlier in this chapter for details on environment variables and the SETPATH command.

USERNAME

Purpose

This function is useful for determining if a user is attached to a server. If attached, returns the user's name for the requested server.

Command Syntax

USERNAME *server*

Returns

User's name if attached, otherwise it returns "".

Example

```
IF NOT(USERNAME server1) THEN
    IF NOT(ATTACH (server1 + "\"+LOGIN_NAME)) THEN
            EXIT
```

The IF statement checks to see if the user is attached to *server1*. If the user is not attached, the script will prompt the user for a password using his current LOGIN_NAME (from his primary server) and attempt to attach to server1 using it. If this is not successful, the script is exited.

Net TOOLS Security

Net TOOLS Security offers these useful applications to make your use of the Windows environment more convenient and productive:

- **Secure Station,** which secures your workstation after a user-defined period of mouse and keyboard inactivity and covers the screen with a Screen Saver pattern. This application also lets you encrypt and decrypt files.

- **Net TOOLS Intercom,** which lets you send messages to and receive messages from other users on the network.

- **Net TOOLS Clock,** which provides an alarm feature that lets you set up messages to be displayed on your workstation or commands to be executed at specified times.

The LAN Administrator can restrict the extent to which users can use **Secure Station,** send and receive messages, and use **Net TOOLS Clock.** The LAN Administrator can also enforce security. For further information, see Chapter 4, "Net TOOLS Administration."

Topics in this chapter

Starting Net TOOLS Security
Secure Station
Secure Station Options
Secure Now
Exiting Screen Saver Mode
Leaving a Message
File Encryption/Decryption
Net TOOLS Intercom

Starting Net TOOLS Security

To manually start **Net TOOLS Security**, choose the File/Run option from **Applications Manager** or one of the other Windows shell programs (such as Program Manager or File Manager) and run WWEXT.EXE.

To load **Net TOOLS Security** when Windows is launched, add WWEXT.EXE to the network startup group.

Secure Station

A graphical user interface such as Microsoft Windows presents a new challenge for workstation security. Having multiple applications on the screen at one time on an unattended workstation magnifies the problem of securing sensitive information and application access. **Secure Station** is designed with the multitasking, graphical environment in mind.

In order to regain access to your computer, you must provide your LAN password or an optional temporary password that you assign. Creating a temporary password allows you to provide others with temporary access to your computer without compromising your network security.

If an incorrect password is entered, **Secure Station** remains in Screen Saver mode. Once a correct password is entered, however, you are returned to the point in your application(s) at which you left off.

> **Note**: **Secure Station** will also inform you of the number of failed passwords attempted in your absence. If more than 5 failed attempts were made, the LAN Administrator is also notified by the network notification service.

Secure Station also lets you do the following:

- Manually secure your workstation immediately.

- Permit other people to leave messages on your secured terminal.

- Protect data through file encryption.

> **Note**: A menu item or dialog box item is grayed if the LAN Administrator has not given you access to **Secure Station** or one of its features.

Secure Station Password in a Banyan Environment

When **Net TOOLS Menu** starts, the user is prompted for the password to be required by **Secure Station**. This password is retained for the duration of the **Net TOOLS Menu** session, but it must be entered each time **Net TOOLS Menu** is started.

Display Option

You can select the graphics pattern to be displayed by Screen Saver from several predefined choices in the Pattern combo list box.

A special feature allows you to select a "Jumping Prompt," which generates a personalized message as the Screen Saver display. If you select the Jumping Prompt display option, you can also enter your own Screen Saver message in the Prompt text box.

For a preview of the graphic image you have selected, choose the Test button.

The Pattern combo list box also lists Windows Metafiles (.WMF) and bitmaps (.BMP), which are explained below, from your Windows directory or the graphics directory specified by the LAN Administrator.

Graphics File Formats

A graphic image such as a corporate logo can be displayed as a Screen Saver graphics pattern. Screen Saver interprets Windows Metafiles and bitmap files, standard graphics formats supported by many leading graphics applications. To use a corporate logo or graphic in Screen Saver, create it in a compatible application and export the file in a Windows Metafile format, giving it a .WMF extension, or in a bitmap format, giving it a .BMP extension. Place the file on your search path or current directory. (Refer to the export section of your graphics application program for more information.) The largest possible Metafile size is 64K.

Enter the Metafile or bitmap filename (and optionally pathname) in the Pattern combo list box or use the Browse option to specify the path and file.

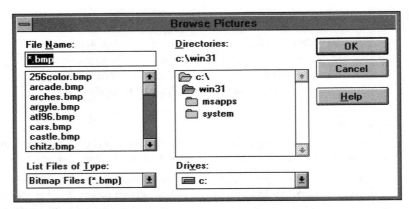

The Browse Pictures dialog box.

- **TO CHANGE SECURE STATION OPTIONS:**

1. Click the **Secure Station** icon. The Secure menu displays.

2. Choose Options from the Secure menu.

   The Secure Station Options dialog box displays.

3. Modify the options as necessary.

4. Choose OK.

> **Note:** Double-clicking the **Secure Station** icon displays the Secure Options dialog box if the LAN Administrator has set the option for this action.

Secure Now

As a security or privacy feature you can run **Secure Station** immediately without waiting for the time-out period to elapse.

- **TO LOCK YOUR WORKSTATION MANUALLY:**

1. Click the **Secure Station** icon. The Secure menu displays.

2. Choose Secure Now from the Secure menu.

   Your workstation is secure and the Screen Saver pattern covers the other applications on your screen.

> **Note:** Double-clicking the **Secure Station** icon secures the workstation immediately if the LAN Administrator has set the option for this action.

Exiting Screen Saver Mode

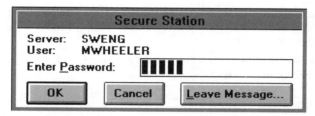

The Secure Station dialog box.

- **TO EXIT SCREEN SAVER MODE:**

1. Press any key or move the mouse.

2. If the workstation is password-secured, the Secure Station dialog box displays. Enter your LAN password or temporary password, whichever is applicable.

3. Choose OK.

Leaving a Message

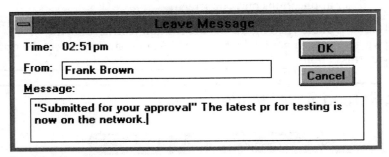

The Leave Message dialog box.

When a workstation is in Screen Saver mode, you can leave an electronic message for the user.

- **TO LEAVE A MESSAGE:**

1. Press any key.

2. When the Secure Station box displays, choose Leave Message.

3. The Leave Message dialog box displays. Enter your name in the From text box and your message in the Message text box.

4. Choose OK.

Chapter 6

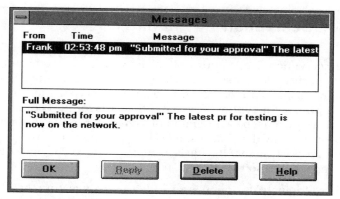

The Messages dialog box.

If someone has left a message, you will see the Messages dialog box after exiting Screen Saver mode.

- **TO REVIEW MESSAGES:**

1. Exit Screen Saver mode as described earlier in this chapter.

2. When the Messages dialog box displays, select the desired message. The text of message displays in the Message text box.

3. Choose Delete to delete the message.

   You can exit the Messages dialog box before deleting all messages. In this case, a minimized Messages icon displays on your screen and your messages are retained.

> **Note:** The LAN Administrator can disable the Leave Message feature in **Net TOOLS Administration**.

File Encryption/Decryption

The File Encryption/Decryption option allows you to encode and decode your disk files for security. Data encryption is a form of "scrambling" used to protect sensitive data. To encrypt a file, you provide a private Encryption Key that is the basis for the coding scheme. The key must be a minimum of 4 characters and can contain any displayable ASCII characters. File Decryption reverses the encryption process so that the file is again readable to you and usable to your applications software.

The Delete Original File option is an added security feature that deletes or erases the original file after it has been encrypted or decrypted.

You may also encrypt or decrypt a file by setting command line parameters in the File/Run menu option in **Applications Manager** or one of the other Windows shell programs (such as Program Manager or File Manager) or using the **MultiSet Script Language** (if installed).

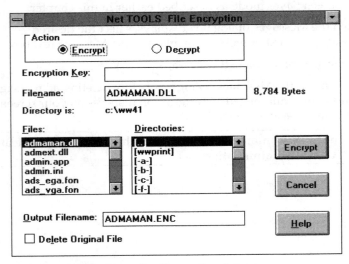

The Net TOOLS File Encryption/Decryption dialog box.

- **TO ENCRYPT OR DECRYPT A FILE:**

1. Click the **Secure Station** icon. The Secure menu displays.

2. Choose Encrypt/Decrypt a File from the Secure menu.

   The File Encryption/ Decryption dialog box displays.

3. Select the Encrypt or the Decrypt radio button to access either of the two available modes.

4. Enter your Encryption/Decryption Key (minimum of any 4 ASCII characters) in the corresponding text box.

5. In the Encrypt File/Decrypt File text box (whichever is displayed), enter the filename and optionally pathname of the file to be encrypted/decrypted. You can also select the path and filename from the list boxes.

6. The selected filename is automatically displayed in the Output File text box with a default extension. Change the output filename as desired.

> **Caution:** Be sure to remember your Encryption Key. You must provide the same key when you decrypt your files. There is no way to decrypt a file without the correct Encryption Key. In addition, use caution when selecting Delete Original File. You may want to save a copy of the file on another disk before selecting this option.

7. For extra security, you can check the Delete Original File box. This deletes the original file once it is encrypted.

8. Choose the Encrypt/Decrypt button, depending on which mode you are using.

TO ENCRYPT OR DECRYPT A FILE USING THE COMMAND LINE:

1. Choose the File/Run menu option from **Applications Manager** or one of the other Windows shell programs (such as Program Manager or File Manager).

2. In the text box, enter WWENCODE, the path and filename of the file to be encrypted or decrypted and the appropriate options from the following examples:

/E Encrypts and stores the result in the designated directory and filename (WWENCODE F:\PATH\FILENAME /E F:\PATH\FILENAME.ENC).

/D Decrypts and stores the result in the designated directory and filename (WWENCODE F:\PATH\FILENAME /D F:\PATH\FILENAME.DEC).

/K Optionally provides the Encryption/Decryption Key in the command line (WWENCODE F:\PATH\FILENAME /E F:\PATH\FILENAME.ENC /K 1234).

If the /K option is not provided, the Key dialog box prompts you for the missing key. In this case, enter your key and choose OK. See the box above on using caution when assigning a key.

> **Note**: To invoke the Encryption/Decryption option from the command line, **Net TOOLS Security** must currently be running.

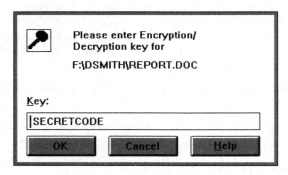

The Key dialog box.

In addition, you may set environment variables for paths and filenames using the **MultiSet** format (%VARIABLE%). (See the chapter on the MultiSet Script Language for more information.)

Net TOOLS Intercom

Net TOOLS Intercom allows you to send and receive network messages. It is designed to intercept messages from the supervisor's console as well as send and receive messages between workstations logged into the network. Users can optionally send messages to multiple users, groups of users or users logged into different servers.

The following sections present procedures for sending messages, receiving messages and replying to received messages. They also detail procedures for customizing your preferences for receiving incoming messages.

How Do I Send a Message?

You send a message by double-clicking the Intercom - Send icon or by using the Send Message command on the Intercom menu. The Intercom - Send dialog box allows you to select a server, a predefined group of users, and one or more individual users to receive your message.

The Server combo box offers the option of selecting a file server other than your default server. When you select a server, a new list of groups and logged-in users displays for that server.

When you choose a group of users from the Groups list box, **Net TOOLS Intercom** automatically selects the members of the selected group or groups. These group members are defined by the LAN Administrator through the network group definition utilities supplied with the network operating system.

> **Note:** The message can be up to 40 characters long. When entering a message, bear in mind that your user ID is included in this total.

> **LAN Manager Note:** Under LAN Manager, the length of the message can be up to 128 characters. A message of up to 128 characters can be sent from a DOS workstation to another DOS workstation. Messages longer than 128 characters will be truncated. (A variable length message can be sent from an OS/2 workstation, OS/2 server, or DOS workstation.)

Sending a message to a single user

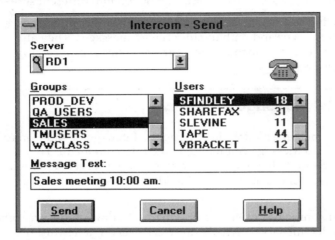

Intercom - Send dialog box.

- **TO SEND A MESSAGE TO A SINGLE USER:**

1. Double-click the Intercom - Send icon. Or choose Send Message from the Intercom menu.

   The Intercom - Send dialog box displays.

2. Select the receiver's name from the Users list box.

   Under LAN Manager, if you choose Other from the Users list box you will be prompted to supply the recipient's login name, computer name or message alias.

3. Enter a message of up to 40 characters.

4. Choose Send.

Net TOOLS Intercom confirms delivery of your message by displaying the words "Message Sent" above the message text box.

> **Note**: When sending a message to a single user after sending one to either a group or multiple users, be aware that the previous selections do not automatically clear unless you change servers. To avoid inadvertently sending a message to previously selected users, choose any highlighted entries again to deselect them or reselect the server.

Sending a message to multiple users

Sending a single message to multiple users requires that you highlight each user to which the message should be sent. The User list box conforms to the normal multiple-select list box conventions. To select more than one item from the list, continue choosing users until all relevant ones are highlighted.

- **TO SEND A MESSAGE TO MULTIPLE USERS:**

1. Double-click the Intercom - Send icon.

   Or

2. Choose Send Message from the Intercom menu.

   The Intercom - Send dialog box displays.

3. Select each receiver's name from the Users list box. To deselect, click on the entry again.

4. Enter a message of up to 40 characters.

5. Choose Send.

   Net TOOLS Intercom confirms delivery of your message to the users and displays a message box indicating the users that did *not* receive the message.

Using the Keyboard

- TAB to the Users list box and move to a name in the User list box using the arrow keys. Touch the SPACEBAR to select or deselect that name.

Sending a message to a predefined group of users

Net TOOLS Intercom allows you to send a single message to a predefined group of users. It uses the groups that have been defined by your LAN Administrator through the network's own group definition tools. For example, in NetWare groups can be defined through the SYSCON utility.

- **TO SEND A MESSAGE TO A GROUP OF USERS:**

1. Double-click the Intercom - Send icon.

   Or

2. Choose Send Message from the Intercom menu.

   The Intercom - Send dialog box displays.

3. Select the group from the Groups list box.

   The users currently logged in will be highlighted in the Users list box.

4. Enter a message of up to 40 characters.

5. Choose Send.

   Net TOOLS Intercom confirms delivery of the message by displaying the words "Message Sent" above the message text box.

It is possible to send a message to multiple groups. As you select each group from the Groups list box, the users in that group that are currently logged on will automatically be selected in the Users list box. You may select or deselect individual users by following the instructions for sending a message to multiple users.

> **Note**: You may send a message to users on only one file server at a time. When the Send dialog box displays, the default server is listed in the combo box and the groups and users on that server are listed in their respective locations. To send a message to users on a different server, you must select that server from the server combo box.

Viewing file server attachments

As you log in to the network each day, you connect to at least one file server that is your "home" or "primary" server. It is most likely the server that stores your files. During this process, you may also attach to other servers on the network to use their resources. **Net TOOLS Intercom** allows you to view your file server attachments. (This feature does not apply to LAN Manager networks, where the concept of attaching to a server does not exist.)

- **TO VIEW YOUR FILE SERVER ATTACHMENTS:**

1. Double-click the Intercom - Send icon.

   Or

2. Choose Send Message from the Intercom menu.

   The Intercom - Send dialog box displays.

3. Choose the left Server pop-box (magnifier) in the Intercom - Send dialog box.

   The Attach/Detach File Server dialog box displays.

4. Use the scroll bars to view the file servers on your network.

5. Choose OK to close the dialog box.

The Attach/Detach File Server dialog box.

The dialog box contains a list of all recognized servers on your network. For those servers to which you are connected, a user name and status displays with the server name.

Attaching to a different file server

As you view your server attachments, you may wish to attach to another server to share its resources. To attach to a server you must have a valid login name and password for that server. If you try to attach to a server on which your password has expired, you are prompted for a new password. If you do not want to enter a password at this time, select Cancel. (This feature does not apply to LAN Manager networks.)

- **TO ATTACH TO A DIFFERENT FILE SERVER:**

1. Select a file server to which you are currently not attached from the File Servers list box.

2. Enter your user name and password in the corresponding boxes.

3. Choose Attach.

   The list box will be updated to display the user name and status of the selected server.

4. Choose OK.

Detaching from a server

Detaching from a server can be a risky decision. Because of the nature of Windows applications, an application must always be able to locate its program files. If you detach from a server in **Net TOOLS Intercom**, you may remove an important resource that another application you are running may need. **Net TOOLS Intercom** will warn you of such potential problems. (This feature does not apply to LAN Manager networks.)

- **TO DETACH FROM A FILE SERVER:**

1. Select a file server to which you are currently attached from the File Servers list box.

2. Choose Detach.

.A warning message may be displayed if you are currently using
the resources of the selected file server. Make your decision to
detach with caution. The list box will be updated to display the
user name and status of the selected server.

3. Choose OK.

How Do I Receive a Message?

Net TOOLS Intercom periodically polls all file servers to which you
are attached for incoming messages that have been sent from other
users, the supervisor's console, or other applications that make use of
the network's native messaging feature.

Incoming message options

Move	
Close	Alt+F4
About...	
Send Message...	
√ Accept Messages	
√ Display Message on Screen	

Intercom options with default settings.

Net TOOLS Intercom provides two options for receiving incoming
messages:

Display Messages on Screen

When the Display Messages on Screen option is enabled, incoming
messages will pop up over the Windows application you are currently
running.

When Display Messages on Screen is disabled, the Messages icon
flashes and beeps at the bottom of the screen.

Accept Messages

When Accept Messages is enabled, incoming messages will be received according to the status of the Display Messages on Screen option.

No notification is received when the Accept Messages option is disabled. Additionally, users attempting to send messages to you will be notified that the message was not delivered.

The default setting is for both Accept Messages and Display Messages on Screen to be enabled. In this mode, when **Net TOOLS Intercom** receives a message from another user, it immediately displays the message on your screen.

If your Administrator has restricted the Send command, the default options for receiving messages are as follows: Accept Messages is enabled; Display Messages on Screen is disabled.

> **Note**: All messages sent from the file server console will automatically override the user's option settings and immediately display the message on the user's screen.

The options you choose for incoming messages will be stored for future **Net TOOLS Menu** sessions.

- **TO CHANGE YOUR INCOMING MESSAGE OPTIONS:**

1. Click the Intercom - Send icon to access the **Net TOOLS Intercom** menu.

2. The Accept Messages option may be checked as the default setting, allowing your workstation to receive messages. Although it is recommended that you keep this feature enabled, you can disable it by choosing the menu option. The check mark will disappear.

3. The Display Messages on Screen option may be checked as the default setting, allowing you to receive Message Slips on the screen. To have messages displayed as icons, choose the menu option to remove the check mark.

4. If you choose to accept the defaults after viewing the menu, click in a blank area outside the drop-down menu.

Receiving a message

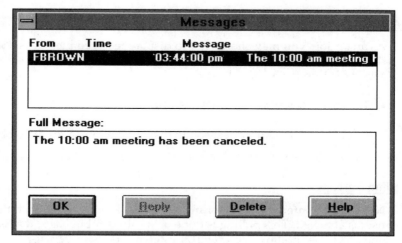

A message displayed on the screen.

- **TO REVIEW MESSAGES:**

1. In the Messages dialog box, select the desired message. The text of message displays in the Full Message text box.

2. Choose Delete to delete the message or Reply to send a response.

   Net TOOLS Intercom makes it easy to send a reply message to an incoming message. Choosing the Reply button displays the Intercom - Send dialog box with the originator's name highlighted and the original message in the message box. You may forward the original message to another person or group or delete the message text and type your reply. If the message was sent from a file server console, from a user not currently logged into the network, through the Leave Message feature, or if Intercom-Send is disabled, the Reply button will be grayed, indicating that it is not possible to reply to that message.

You can exit the Messages dialog box before replying to or deleting all messages. In this case, a minimized Messages icon displays on your screen.

Receiving a message as an icon

As an option, you may choose not to display received messages. (See "Incoming Message Options.") When you receive a message, the Messages icon flashes and beeps.

- **TO VIEW AN INCOMING MESSAGE FROM THE ICON:**

1. Double-click the Messages icon to display the Messages dialog box.

2. Follow the instructions above in "Receiving a message."

Polling Servers

Net TOOLS Intercom polls for messages on all servers to which the user is attached. This polling is done on a round-robin basis, that is, one server per polling. **Net TOOLS Intercom** polls servers for messages at 2-second intervals by default. This interval may be changed by setting the value of MessagePollTime= in [message] section of the WIN.INI file to the desired number of seconds. On heavily loaded networks and/or file servers, it may be desirable to increase the poll interval time, reducing network traffic.

> **LAN Manager Note:** Under LAN Manager, **Net TOOLS Intercom** also polls for messages, and the polling time can be changed as described in the previous paragraph.

LAN Manager's WinPopup and Intercom

WinPopup is a Windows program provided with LAN Manager DOS Workstation that allows users to receive but not send network messages. The LAN Manager NetPopup service will launch WinPopup if it is active while Windows is loading. To prevent messages from displaying twice, **Net TOOLS Intercom** will not receive messages while WinPopup is active.

To make use of the additional features that **Net TOOLS Intercom** provides, such as replying to a message, WinPopup must be disabled. To accomplish this, copy ADSPOPUP.EXE to the existing WINPOPUP.EXE located in each user's Windows subdirectory. The new file should be named WINPOPUP.EXE but contain ADSPOPUP.EXE. This will bring up a version of WINPOPUP that **Net TOOLS Intercom** can disable when it is launched. If a user is running Windows from his or her local hard disk, we have provided a **MultiSet** script called WWLANM.SET that can be added to the user's Startup group. This script copies ADSPOPUP.EXE to the existing WINPOPUP.EXE when the user starts **Net TOOLS Menu**.

Net TOOLS Clock

In addition to providing a useful timepiece icon on your Windows desktop, **Net TOOLS Clock** allows you to keep a tickler file of reminders to send to yourself during the day or to schedule the automatic execution of programs, such as daily backup procedures and file transfers.

The following sections discuss procedures for setting the Alarm Clock, responding to Alarm Clock messages, using the Snooze Timer features, cleaning up old alarm settings and changing the look of the desktop clock.

Clock Options: Analog, Digital & Second Hand

Net TOOLS Clock can display the time of day in several different ways. The analog version of the clock icon displays the hour and minute hands with an optional second hand. The digital version incorporates a segmented "LED" display with an optional am/pm indication.

Digital and Analog Clock modes.

- **TO CHANGE YOUR CLOCK DISPLAY OPTIONS:**

1. Click the Clock icon. The Clock menu displays.

2. Select Analog if you want to display the analog version of the clock or Digital to display the digital version. A check mark displays next to your choice.

3. When displaying the Analog clock, you can choose whether to display the second hand. A check mark displays next to Show Second Hand if the second-hand display feature is turned on. Click the Show Second Hand menu option to toggle this feature on or off.

Net TOOLS Clock works closely with Windows to display the time based on your Control Panel preferences. For example, the clock can optionally display the time in 24-hour format with the digital clock option selected. The date displayed under the icon is also tied to the date format defined through Control Panel. See your *Microsoft Windows User's Guide* for more information about setting time and date preferences through Control Panel.

Chapter 6

How to Schedule an Alarm Message or Command?

Net TOOLS Clock's alarm feature is a flexible way of reminding yourself of important events and executing commands (programs or groups of programs) at predefined times.

This flexibility extends to the frequency of the reminder or command. With **Net TOOLS Clock**, you may program an alarm message or command using one of four frequency options.

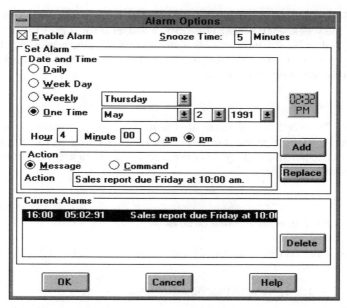

The Alarms Options dialog box.

Daily

The Daily option generates the message or command each day of the week, including Saturday and Sunday, at the same time. Daily alarm messages and commands continue to occur each day until removed from the tickler file.

Weekday

The Weekday option generates the message or command on the days Monday through Friday only. This option is useful for tape backups or file transfers that must be performed each day of the work week, but would be redundant on weekends. Weekday alarm messages and commands continue to occur Monday through Friday until removed from the tickler file.

Weekly

The Weekly option generates the message or command on a particular day of the week, each week. This option is useful for reminding yourself of weekly appointments such as staff meetings. Weekly alarm messages and commands continue to occur on the preset day and time until removed from the file.

One Time

The One Time option will generate the message or command on a particular date at a particular time. **Net TOOLS Clock** automatically removes the alarm message or command from the tickler file after successful completion.

- **TO SCHEDULE AN ALARM MESSAGE OR COMMAND:**

1. Choose Set Alarm from the Clock menu. (Or double-click the Clock Icon.)

   The Alarms Options dialog box displays.

2. Select the Frequency: Daily, Weekday, Weekly, or One Time.

   If you select Weekly, select the day of the week from the adjacent drop-down list box. If you select One Time, select the month, day and year from the adjacent boxes.

3. Enter the hour and minute and choose "am" or "pm."

4. Select either the Message or Command radio button.

> **Note:** The Administrator can disable the user's ability to run commands in Net TOOLS Alarm by disabling the Clock/Command option in the WWEXT.WWR rights file.

5. If setting an alarm message, enter up to 40 characters in the text box. The message will appear on the screen at the designated time.

   If scheduling a command, enter the name of the executable program or **MultiSet** command to run at the designated time. Be sure that the event generated by this command is finished and all files are closed when the network's backup procedure is scheduled to take place.

> **Note:** You can use **MultiSet** to execute a series of commands or events. (See Chapter 5, "MultiSet Script Language.")

6. Choose Add to add the new entry to the list box.

   Repeat steps 1 through 6 as necessary to schedule additional messages or commands.

7. Choose OK to save your tickler file entries in the WIN.INI file.

Revising an Alarm Message or Command

You can revise a scheduled alarm message or command as needed.

- **TO REVISE AN ALARM MESSAGE OR COMMAND:**

1. Choose Set Alarm from the Clock menu.

   The Alarms dialog box displays. The scheduled messages and commands appear in the Current Alarms list box.

2. Select the message or command you want to change.

3. Change the information in the Set Alarm and Action sections of the dialog box as needed.

4. Choose Replace to update the entry in the list box.

5. Choose OK to save your changes in the tickler file.

Removing an Alarm Message or Command

Scheduled daily, weekday, or weekly messages and commands continue to be displayed or performed at the preset time until removed from the tickler file. (One-time messages and commands are deleted upon successful completion.)

You can remove alarm messages and commands that are no longer needed from the tickler file.

- **TO REMOVE AN ALARM MESSAGE OR COMMAND:**

1. Choose Set Alarm from the Clock menu.

   The Alarms dialog box displays. The scheduled messages and commands appear in the Current Alarms list box.

2. Using the scroll bar to view all the available messages and commands in the list box, select the one to be removed.

3. Choose Delete.

   The selected messages or command is removed from the list box.

4. Choose OK.

- **TO REMOVE AN ALARM MESSAGE UPON RECEIPT:**

   If you want to remove an alarm message from the tickler file when the message displays on the screen, choose the Delete button.

   The message disappears and is permanently removed from the tickler file.

Snooze Timer

When an alarm message is displayed at the preset time and date, you may choose to "snooze" the message. By doing this, you start a timer that causes the message to reappear after a definable period of time. You may choose to snooze the message as many times as you like.

- **TO SET THE SNOOZE TIMER DEFAULT:**

1. Choose Set Alarm from the Clock menu.

   The Alarms dialog box displays.

2. Enter default snooze time in minutes in the Snooze Time box.

3. Choose OK.

You may choose to change the Snooze Timer for individual reminder messages. This can be done when the message is displayed.

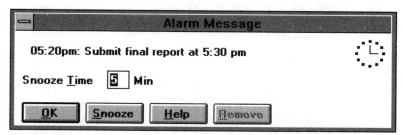

Alarm Message dialog box.

- **TO SNOOZE AN ALARM MESSAGE:**

1. When an alarm message displays on screen, choose the Snooze button to snooze the message for the default time.

2. If you want to change the snooze time for this message, enter the snooze time in minutes in the Snooze Time text box.

> **Note**: Changing the Snooze Time when receiving an alarm message will not change the default setting for the Snooze time. It will only affect that particular message.

Disabling the Alarm

The Alarm Clock can be disabled by toggling off the Enable Alarm check box in the Alarms dialog box.

• **TO DISABLE ALARM FUNCTIONS:**

1. Choose Set Alarm from the Clock menu.

   The Alarms dialog box displays.

2. If the Enable Alarm check box contains an X, click the check box to toggle the alarm function off.

3. Choose OK.

Glossary

.WWR files APPMAN.WWR and WWEXT.WWR files contain the preferences set by the LAN Administrator.

Active A window or icon that is currently selected and to which the next keystroke or command will apply.

Application filename The name of an application's executable file.

Application Help Context-sensitive, customized help files that can be created and modified by a LAN Administrator for **Applications Manager** users.

Cascade Arrangement of open windows so that they overlap one another with the title bar of each visible.

Check box A small box within a dialog box that turns an option on or off when it is checked.

Choose To perform an action that carries out a command in a menu or dialog box.

Click Press, then release, the left mouse button. The left mouse button is assumed unless the directions specifically state the right mouse button.

Clipboard A temporary Windows storage area for holding text or data that you are copying or moving.

Combo box A combo box is made up of a one-line text box and a list box that is displayed on demand. To display the list box, click the down-arrow pop-box and make the selection from the list box. The list box automatically closes. To close the list box without making a selection, click the down-arrow pop-box again. In **Applications Manager**, some combo boxes have a left pop-box displaying a magnifier, which leads to additional options relevant to the dialog box.

Command button A rectangular button in a dialog box that carries out or cancels an action when chosen. The OK button, which carries out a command, is usually the default button. The cancel button cancels the command without applying any settings.

Context-Sensitive Help Help that is available for a specific command or option. To display the context-sensitive Help cursor (pointer plus question mark), press SHIFT+F1 and select the group, subgroup, or item for which you need help.

Control menu box Displays the standard Windows control menu containing these commands: Restore, Move, Size, Minimize, Maximize, and Close in addition to special commands of a particular application. Click on it to display the Control menu; double-click on it to exit Windows.

Decryption Reverses the encryption process so that the files are again readable and usable to your applications software.

Default button The default button is the one automatically chosen when you press ENTER in a dialog box. The default button is indicated by its heavier border.

Device driver A program that controls how your computer and a particular device, such as a printer or plotter, interact.

Dialog box A box of options and information that appears when you choose a command that requires more information, which you provide by filling in the dialog box. Commands that display dialog boxes are followed by ellipses (...) on menus.

Double-click To rapidly click the left mouse button twice in quick succession. Selects and executes in one step. Double-clicking is often used as a shortcut for a longer procedure.

Drag To press and hold down the mouse button while moving the mouse to reposition a window.

Drag and drop To move an item or subgroup to another group or subgroup by dragging the item or subgroup icon and dropping it in the destination group or subgroup window.

Encryption A form of coding or "scrambling" files to protect sensitive data.

Focus The focus shows where the next action will take place. In dialog boxes, the focus is indicated by a dotted underline or outline for most options or by a blinking insertion point in text boxes.

Grayed A term applied to a command or option that appears in the menu or box but that is inactive.

Hierarchical Activating this **Applications Manager** option means that access is only allowed to the selected group or subgroup.

Highlighted Indicates an item is selected and will be affected by your next action. A highlighted item appears in reverse video. A highlighted icon displays its name in reverse video box.

Icon A small symbol that represents an application that is running in memory. Clicking once on an icon displays its system menu; double-clicking restores the window to its previous size.

Inactive A window or icon that is not currently selected.

Insertion point The place where text that you type is inserted. In a text box, it appears as a flashing vertical bar.

Item An element of a group or subgroup representing an application or script.

LAN group A group as defined by the LAN operating system.

LAN user A user as defined by the LAN operating system.

List box Displays a list of choices for a given subject. To select an item in a list box, click on the desired item. The highlight shows which item is selected. Use the scroll bar to display more items in a list box. To select more than one item, continue clicking on other items in the box.

Maximize box A button in the top right corner of the window that enlarges the window to fill the entire screen.

MDI window A multiple document interface such as that displayed in **Applications Manager** and **MultiSet Editor.**

Menu bar The horizontal line near the top of an application window, just below the title bar, that contains names of available menus or commands. Also called the "main menu" or "action bar."

Message bar Displays program messages and quick definitions of the selected menu choice.

Minimize box A button in the top right corner of the window that reduces the window to an icon.

Module name A hardcoded name that is read from the executable filename.

MultiSet A batch file language designed specifically for the Windows environment that carries out application management commands.

NETMENU.INI file The **Applications Manager** file that contains references to the Network Group (.APP) files and the initial location of the window.

Network Group An **Applications Manager** group created by a LAN Administrator when in Administration mode for use by LAN groups and users.

PERMENU.INI file The **Applications Manager** file that contains references to the Personal Group (.APP) files and the user-defined settings.

Personal Group An **Applications Manager** group created for use by an end-user.

Radio button An option that is part of a group. Selecting one option will deselect all of the others. The group is usually surrounded by a border with a title. To choose a radio button, click on it or its label. If the radio button is in focus, the spacebar will also select the option.

Rights Privileges that control how users may work with files in a given directory (for example, controlling whether or not a user may read a file, change a file, or delete a file).

Run Run allows you to execute a program that may not be included in a group. The Run command is located on the **Applications Manager** File menu.

Scroll To move the contents of a window or list box up or down within the window or list box so you can view additional contents.

Scroll bar A bar on the right side or the bottom of a window.

Shell The application that automatically displays when you start Windows.

Shortcut key A special key sequence that bypasses the menu bar and takes you directly to a dialog box or performs a command.

Speed Key A speed key refers to the underlined letters that appears in the menu options and dialog boxes. Speed keys may be defined when creating a menu. To execute an option using a speed key, type the underlined letter.

Startup group A special Personal or Network Group that causes programs and **MultiSet** scripts contained in it to be executed when **Applications Manager** starts (if **Applications Manager** is the Windows shell).

Subgroup A group created in **Applications Manager** that is a unit within another group or subgroup.

System Help Help files that document program features such as menu commands and options, operating procedures and basic Windows skills.

Text box To enter text in a text box, choose the box and type. The insertion point, a blinking vertical line, shows where the text will appear. If the text is highlighted, your typing replaces the highlighted text.

Tile Arrangement of all open windows so that each fills a portion of the workspace without overlapping.

Title bar The bar at the top of a window that contains the name of the window (usually centered). You can move a window by dragging its title bar to a new location.

Window border A heavy border around an application window. With the mouse, it is possible to change the size of the window by dragging the window border.

WIN.INI A Windows file that records most of the settings and preferences you specify in your Windows shell and in many Windows applications. Windows reads the WIN.INI each times it starts and sets up your system according to these settings.

Dynamic Data Exchange Interface

Applications Manager provides a Dynamic Data Exchange (DDE) interface that allows third-party utilities to set up their own personal groups programmatically. These DDE commands have the same format as and equivalent functionality to Microsoft Windows Program Manager DDE support.

In order for **Applications Manager** to receive DDE commands, Program Manager cannot be running. Designate **Applications Manager** as your shell by editing the Shell= line in the SYSTEM.INI to read Shell=APPMAN.EXE. (If Program Manager is running concurrently with **Applications Manager**, DDE calls will be received only by Program Manager.)

Five DDE commands are provided: CreateGroup, AddItem, DeleteGroup, ShowGroup, and ExitProgman:

[CreateGroup(GroupName[,GroupPath])]

This function creates a personal group or activates it if the group already exists, with the description passed in GroupName. The group is created with the default view mode.

The GroupPath parameter contains the pathname to use when creating the group. The GroupPath is optional and the GroupName will be propagated to the GroupPath if a GroupPath is not given. The directory specified by the <windir> environment variable is used as the default directory for this personal group file.

[AddItem(CmdLine[,Name[,IconPath[,IconIndex[,xPos,yPos]]]])]

The CmdLine contains the command line executed when the item is opened. This is at least the application executable name. If a full path is specified in CmdLine, the path is stripped from the executable filename and used in the change directory field of **Applications Manager.**

The Name field specifies text that is shown with the icon. If this field is not given, the description is the filename in the command.

The IconPath parameter passes the name of a file from which the icon is extracted. If this parameter is not specified, the filename specified in the CmdLine parameter is used as default.

The IconIndex is the offset of the icon in the IconPath file to be used for this Item. If the parameter is not specified, the first icon in the IconPath file is used.

The xPos, yPos specifies the location in the window for the Icon. This is only used if the default view mode is Horizontal.

[DeleteGroup(GroupName)]

This function deletes the personal group with the description passed in GroupName. If two personal groups exist with the same description, the first one found by **Applications Manager** is deleted.

[ShowGroup(GroupName,ShowCommand)]

This function changes the view state of the personal group specified in GroupName.

The group is minimized, maximized, or restored depending on the value in ShowCommand. It may also change the focus to the group depending on the value in Show Command.

The values of ShowCommand are:

1. Shows the window in its restored state and sets the focus to window.

2. Minimizes and sets the focus to the window.

3. Maximizes and sets the focus to the window.

4. Displays the window in its restored state. The focus is not set to the window.

5. Displays the window in its current state.

6. Minimizes the window.

7. Minimizes the window. The focus is not set to the window.

8. Displays the window in its current state. The focus is not set to the window.

[ExitProgman(bSaveState)]

This statement closes **Applications Manager**.

If bSaveState is FALSE, **Applications Manager** closes without saving; otherwise, if it is TRUE, Save Workspace is performed by **Applications Manager**.

12 Object Linking and Embedding

One of the newest features of Windows 3.1 is called Object Linking and Embedding (OLE). OLE lets you place one type of document into another to create compound documents. For instance, you could have a word processing document that contained a spreadsheet created in Excel and a picture created in Paintbrush. You could even include sound (such as a recorded phone message).

OLE is important to Windows because it promotes the specialization of software. Rather than each vendor trying to provide a word processor-spreadsheet-graphics-Email-phone-dialer-disk-defragmenter-in-one-package, software vendors can concentrate on their specialties and allow the products of their applications to be linked (or embedded) through OLE to another application.

OLE becomes even more powerful in a networked context. Let's say you have an important company spreadsheet that is linked to several different documents, such as an annual report and a financial report. When the individual responsible for maintaining the spreadsheet makes a change, that change is immediately updated in the two linked reports. If those two reports are on the screen, they will be updated in real time, right before the eyes of the viewer!

This chapter will define OLE, then provide some exercises so you can become comfortable with the concepts of linking and embedding. Although OLE can be easy to visualize, it can be difficult to conceptualize exactly how to do it until you've tried it a few times—that is, actually linked and embedded a few times yourself. Once you've tried it and can see how it works, then you can decide how you want to use it. The last section of the chapter will explain how you can use OLE on a LAN to link or embed documents from other users.

The Windows Clipboard: Predecessor to OLE

Users have always needed a way to exchange information between applications. The first method software developers used, even before Windows, was to offer import/export conversion routines between different types of applications.

The Windows Clipboard was an important element of early Windows versions because it allowed applications to share binary and text information between applications. A graphic could be (and still can be) cut from Paintbrush and pasted into Word for Windows, or several paragraphs could be copied to the Clipboard from Notepad and pasted into Write.

This flexibility was an important start but, if the graphic from Paintbrush needed changing, the user would have to load Paintbrush, load the file, copy the graphic to the Clipboard again, switch to Word for Windows, delete the old graphic, and paste in the new one.

The OLE Approach

OLE makes this process of updating information much quicker and cleaner. Building on the example in the previous section, if the Paintbrush picture was connected to Word for Windows through OLE, you could simply double-click on the picture in Word; then Paintbrush would be started and the picture would be loaded automatically. You could then modify the picture as necessary and choose "Update" followed by "Close" from the File menu in Paintbrush. The Word document would then be displayed on the screen with the updated version of the Paintbrush picture. In this way, OLE lets you modify a document that has been pasted into another without having to delete it and go through all of the steps associated with re-pasting it again. For the purposes of our discussion, assume that the document is the product of an application, whether it's a text file, spreadsheet, graphic, or whatever.

Definitions

Before we go much further, let's define some of the OLE terms you'll encounter while reading this chapter.

Object	An object is any piece of information created by a Windows application that supports OLE. We used the example of a document above, but an object can be a spreadsheet, a word processing file, a graphic drawing, or even a sound recording, as you will see in our example.
Source Document	The Source Document is any document from which an object originates. Your object could be the source document, such as an entire spreadsheet, or just part of a source document, such as a single cell. Objects are linked and embedded from a source document to a destination document.

Destination Document	This is the document into which you place your linked or embedded object.
Embedded Object	An Embedded Object is one that is copied from a source document and pasted to a destination document. When the object that has been pasted in the destination document is changed, the original object in the source document is not altered.
Linked Object	This is an object that is copied from a source document and pasted to a destination document. When the object that has been pasted in the destination document is changed, the original object in the source document is altered at the same time.
Client Application	This is an application that can accept embedded or linked objects. Write and Cardfile are client applications only; that means they can only accept embedded or linked objects—you cannot take a Write document or a Cardfile card and embed it in another document.
Server Application	This is an application whose objects can be linked or embedded in other applications' documents. Paintbrush and Sound Recorder can only provide objects to be linked or embedded; they cannot accept objects from other applications.
Client/Server Applications	Some applications can act as both clients and servers.

It is important to consider that Windows applications must be written specifically to support OLE. You should check your application's documentation to see whether it supports OLE and, if it does, whether it is as a client, a server, or both.

Packaging Objects

You may have wondered what the new Object Packager application in Windows 3.1 does. This application supports OLE as both client and server, and it allows you to place an iconic representation of an object into a document. For example, with Object Packager, you can place an iconic representation of a DOS command in a document. Next to the icon you might place text similar to "try this program . . . just press this button down here." That way, when someone reading the document presses the button, a DOS session will be loaded and the command line associated with that icon will be run. We will demonstrate how this is accomplished later in the chapter.

OLE 101: Embedding a Paintbrush Picture in a Write Document

For now, let's start by helping you become comfortable with what OLE is and what it can do. We can use several applications that come with Windows 3.1, Write, and Paintbrush, to demonstrate OLE.

Although the 'Linking' part of OLE is placed before the 'Embedding' part in the acronym, Embedding is actually simpler and we will cover it first.

Embedding allows you to make a copy of an object (remember an object can be a document, a picture, a spreadsheet, even a piece of music) and place it or "embed" it into another object. Once you have made that copy, any modifications made to the embedded object do not affect the original object. In addition, the embedded object actually becomes a part of the client application's data file. As such, a separate, independent copy of the object now exists within that data file; the original object is no longer part of the picture. Still, the embedded object remains tied to its server application, which can be called upon to edit the object at any time by simply double-clicking on the object within the client application's data file. See the next section for details on how to edit an embedded object.

To demonstrate how to embed an object, let's embed a Paintbrush picture into a Write document. In Paintbrush, we will take a bitmap (.BMP) file normally used for wallpaper and embed it into a test Write document. There are really two ways you can embed this drawing—by starting from Write or by starting from Paintbrush.

Here are the steps if you start from Write:

1. Start the Write application and type some sample text. Position the cursor where you want to place the drawing.

2. Choose the Edit menu from Write. Notice that "Links. . ." and "Insert Object. . ." are selectable (See Figure 12.1).

3. Because we wish to embed an object, Choose "Insert Object. . . ." The "Links. . ." option is used to manage linked objects.

   The Insert Object dialog box in Figure 12.2 appears. This box lists the applications registered in your WIN.INI (in the [embedding] section) that support OLE. These applications act as servers because they will export objects for linking or embedding in your application—in this case, Write.

4. Choose "Paintbrush Picture." Windows will automatically load Paintbrush (Figure 12.3) because it knows that's the application where "Paintbrush Picture"–type objects are created.

   At this point, Paintbrush is actually editing the object that will be embedded into Write. This means that any action you take from now on will affect the object (drawing) that is embedded into Write. (Note the "Paintbrush Picture in (Untitled)," which is serving as the title of our drawing. If we had saved the Write document as CARLETTR, the title would be "Paintbrush Picture in CARLETTR.") Windows "knows" where Paintbrush Picture objects come from by means of the registration database.

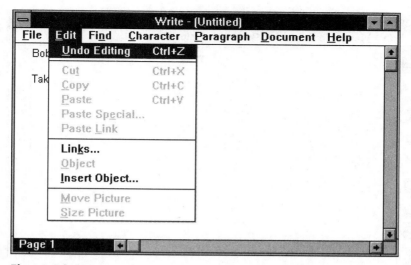

Figure 12.1 Write Edit menu showing Links and Insert Object choices.

5. Create a drawing by doodling on the screen or by reading in a drawing from the disk. Windows' wallpaper drawings are a good place to start. To open a drawing, Choose Edit Paste From and CARS.BMP as the file to load. Once this file is loaded, it will appear on your screen as shown in Figure 12.3.

6. Now you're ready to embed the drawing into your Write document. To do this, choose the Update option from the File menu. The entire screen from Paintbrush will be transferred to Write, similar to Figure 12.4.

   Note you can type below the car (the embedded object), but you have to move way down the document to do it. This is because the entire screen was copied from Paintbrush, bringing a lot of white space with the car.

You've just embedded your first object—an entire Paintbrush screen!

Now, let's suppose you just wanted to copy the car and not all of the white space around the car. To do this, you must start in Paintbrush. That way you have a bit more flexibility in the size of the drawing transferred. When you're ready, start Paintbrush and perform the following steps.

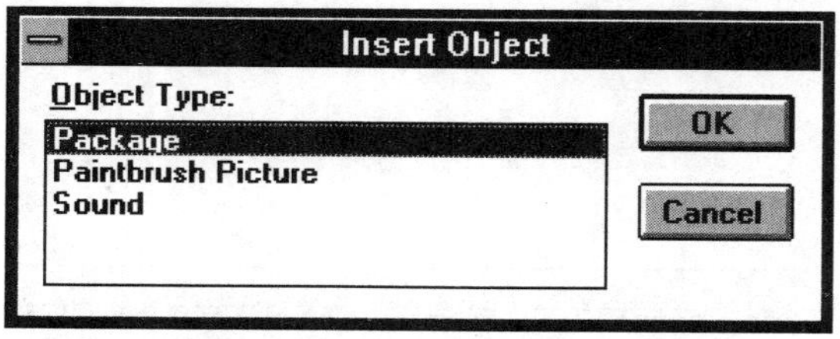

Figure 12.2 Insert Object dialog box.

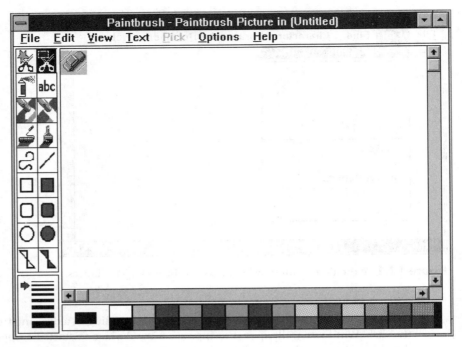

Figure 12.3 Paintbrush with embedded picture shown.

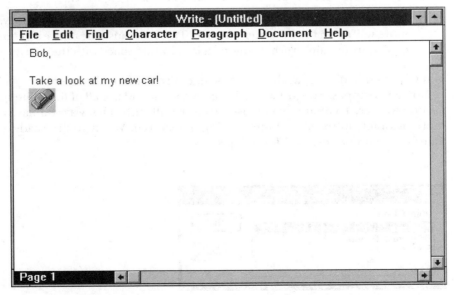

Figure 12.4 Write showing embedded object from Paintbrush.

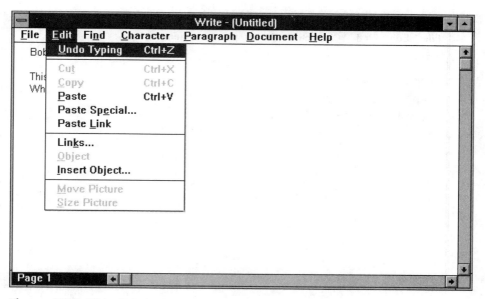

Figure 12.5 Write Edit menu showing Paste options.

1. Choose File Open and load CARS.BMP.

2. Use the scissors tool (the one on the upper right corner of the toolbar) to cut out the car. To do this, first select the scissors tool, then place the crosshairs on the upper left corner of the car drawing. Holding down the left mouse button, drag the box around the car.

3. Now that you have selected the car drawing, copy it to the clipboard by choosing Edit Copy.

4. Now we want to embed the car drawing in Write. To do this, load Write and type some text as you did in the example above. Type at least two lines and position the cursor between the lines (so we can demonstrate that we're only copying a small graphic).

5. Select the Edit menu and you will see the selections in Figure 12.5. You can use "Paste" or "Paste Special. . ." to embed an object into Write. Since Paste is the most straightforward, for now, choose Paste. Write will automatically paste the most "complete" version of an object when you choose the Paste option. That is, if it is possible to embed the object on the Clipboard, Write will automatically do so.

6. You should see your text on the lines before and after the drawing of the car, as shown in Figure 12.6.

Editing an Embedded Object

One of the best things about OLE is the direct connection between an embedded object and the server application that was used to create it. At any time, you can

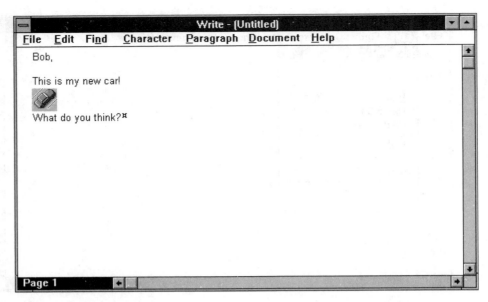

Figure 12.6 Write document with embedded graphic taking up only two lines.

simply double-click on an embedded object within a client application to have Windows open the server application used to create the object and display the object for editing. You can then edit the object as you desire. When you're done, you can have the client application updated with the changes. To demonstrate, try the following steps:

1. Close Paintbrush (if you haven't already) to satisfy yourself that it is not currently on the desktop.

2. Go back to your Write document with the car embedded in it and double-click on the car. Paintbrush will load and a copy of the car will be displayed in the upper left corner of the work area.

3. Now make a change to the car drawing. Use your imagination.

4. Update the embedded drawing in the Write document by choosing the File Update menu selection.

5. Go back to Paintbrush and load up CARS.BMP using the File Open menu selection. Move the windows so you can see both cars as shown in Figure 12.7. The original CARS.BMP should be as it originally was, without your changes.

With Embedding, you place a copy of the object into your target document. When you change that copy, the original is unaffected. With linking, any changes made to the original are immediately reflected in the copy (in real time!)—this is the primary difference between linking and embedding.

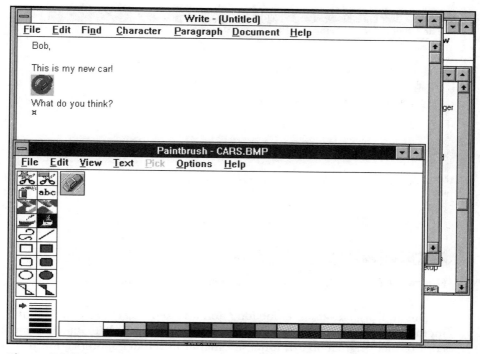

Figure 12.7 Write with modified object and Paintbrush with original (unchanged) object.

You can even embed sound recordings in a document. Load Sound Recorder, then load a sound file. Choose Copy from the Edit menu and start Write. Choose Paste from the Edit menu. You should see a microphone icon in your Write document as shown in Figure 12.8. Provided you have a PC speaker driver or a sound board installed, you can double-click on the icon to play the music.

Linking

Now that you've had a taste of embedding, let's do some linking—the two are very similar. Start in Paintbrush and perform the following steps to link a drawing to a Write document:

1. Load CARS.BMP by using the File Open menu command.

2. Select the car drawing as we did using the scissors tool above.

3. Select Copy from the Edit menu to copy the selection to the Clipboard.

4. Switch to or load the Write application and type in some text (to illustrate the text/graphic combination). Choose Paste Link from the Edit menu. You should see something similar to Figure 12.9.

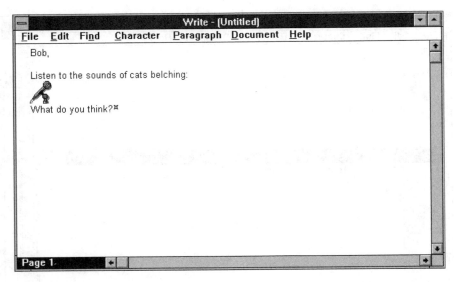

Figure 12.8 Write document with embedded Sound Recorder object.

The appearances of an embedded and a linked object are identical; it is the method of modification that is different. When you embed an object, you make a copy of that original object. It doesn't matter how much modification you make to the copy, the original will be unaffected.

Linked objects, on the other hand, are tied to specific files. For example, we made a link to the CARS.BMP in our example above. To demonstrate this, double-click on the car drawing in Write. Paintbrush will pop up in the foreground

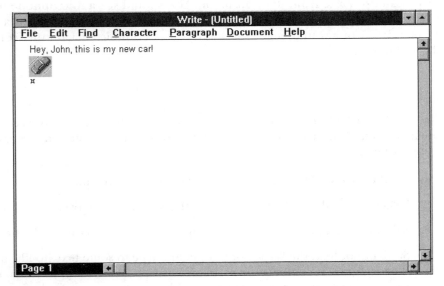

Figure 12.9 Write document with linked Paintbrush object.

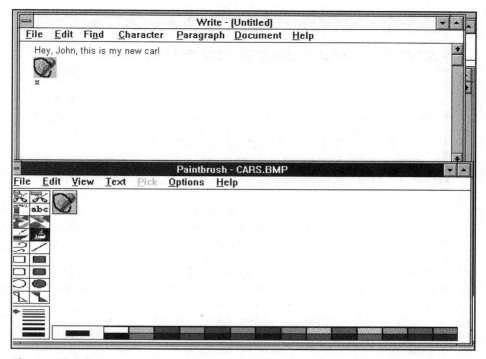

Figure 12.10 Write and Paintbrush showing changes to drawing immediately reflected in Write document.

and the CARS.BMP file will be displayed. Size and move the Write and Paintbrush windows so you can see them both on the screen, similar to Figure 12.10.

Now make a change to the car in Paintbrush; paint over it or draw a line through it. Notice that each change you make is immediately registered in the Write window. This demonstrates the power of linking (See Figure 12.10). Be aware that you must save any changes you make to a linked object to disk from within the object's server application. Otherwise, the changes will be lost.

MANAGING LINKS

Many applications provide a means of managing the links you have in a particular document. Write provides this through the "Links. . ." option in the Edit menu. When you select this option, the dialog box in Figure 12.11 is displayed.

The Links box shows the individual links you have placed in your document. There is a line for each link you have created, showing its current settings. (The "0 0 32 32" numbers show the dimensions of the drawing and where to place it.)

With this dialog box you can select how the linked objects are updated: automatically or manually. Automatic updating is the default selection. With this setting, all changes to the object are immediately reflected in the document (or documents) to which it is linked. Note that if you press the Manual button (Figure 12.11), the Manual status is reflected in the Links line.

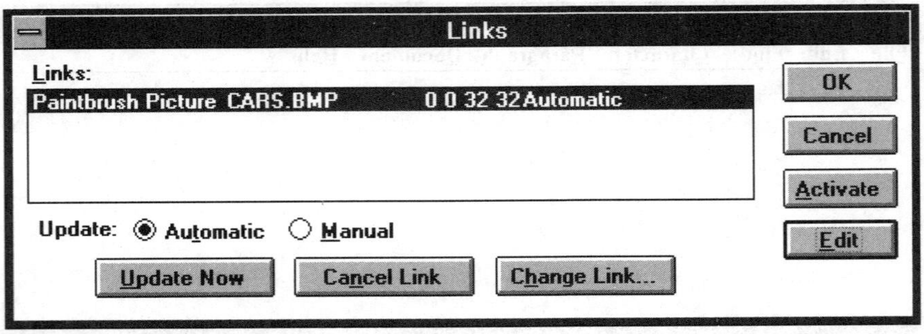

Figure 12.11 Links dialog box.

"Update Now" is used to perform manual updates. You might elect to update links manually for reasons of performance if you have a large number of links or if you have a document you do not want updated until permission or approval is granted by someone.

"Cancel Link" destroys the linkage, but leaves the object displayed in your document. To remove it completely, you will need to select the object (by clicking on it) and cut it to the clipboard or delete it completely.

"Change Link" lets you change the linked object. Remember that links are made to files, so this dialog box simply lets you choose another file—in this case, another graphic file.

The Edit button starts the application that created the object and loads the object into it for editing.

The Activate button has a different effect based on the type of object with which you are working. For a graphic file (such as the one we are working on here) Windows simply loads the drawing into Paintbrush. However, some objects such as a sound file can be "played." In this case, activate would play the sound. Activate is the action taken when you double-click on the object in the document.

LINKING MULTIPLE OBJECTS

To demonstrate how to link multiple objects (files) to one document, let's link a sound file to our example Write document. First, add a little more text to the document for embellishment, then perform the following steps:

1. Start Sound Recorder from the Program Manager.

2. Load TADA.WAV from the File menu (Open selection). You should see something similar to Figure 12.12. Press the Play button to test that your sound equipment works and the sound is being routed to it.

3. Choose Copy from the Edit menu to copy the sound object to the Clipboard. Switch back to our Write document (using ALT+TAB) and choose "Paste Link" from the Edit menu. You should now see the two drawings on your document as shown in Figure 12.13. The microphone is an iconic represen-

Figure 12.12 Sound Recorder with the TADA.WAV file loaded.

tation of the sound file, since a sound file would not look very pretty on the display. Double-click on the sound file and listen to it play.

ONE OBJECT/MULTIPLE DESTINATIONS

You may develop a need to link one source object to multiple destinations. For instance, our CARS.BMP might be a prototype drawing for a new car that you want to include in a brochure as well as in a letter to someone. The link feature is convenient here because when you change the CARS.BMP file, the picture of the car in both the brochure and the letter will be updated for the changes. That way, both documents are always current.

Let's run through the steps involved in linking one object, in this case, CARS.BMP, to multiple destinations.

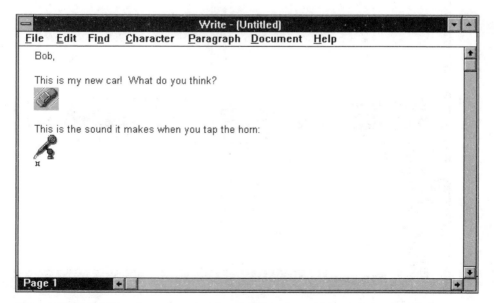

Figure 12.13 Write document showing Paintbrush and Sound Recorder objects.

1. Run Paintbrush and open the CARS.BMP file.

2. Select the car picture with the square scissors tool, as we have been doing in the examples above. Choose Copy from the Edit menu.

3. Run Write and type in some text. Choose Paste Link from the Edit menu.

4. Start another instance of Write. Type in some text and choose Paste Link from the Edit menu.

5. Position the three windows (two Write windows and one Paintbrush) so you can see the car picture in all three, as shown in Figure 12.14. Make a change to the car in Paintbrush and watch the change immediately reflected in **both** Write windows simultaneously!

Object Packager

The Object Packager's main function is to "package" embedded objects so that you can place an iconic representation of them in your documents. You'll find Object Packager's icon in your Accessories group window.

Why is this useful? The little car in CARS.BMP that we've been linking and embedding is not imposing in size, but what if we had embedded a whole screen

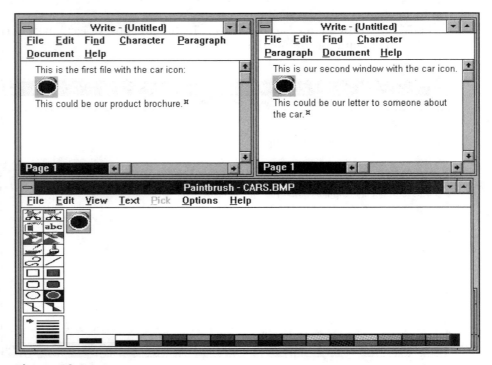

Figure 12.14 Two Write documents updated simultaneously by changing a linked Paintbrush object.

of material in our document? At some point, the size of this object might become unruly and difficult to manage.

Object Packager allows you to take an object, say a large drawing, and place an iconic representation of that object in your document (similar to the way Sound Recorder placed an iconic representation of the sound file in our document by substituting a microphone icon). When you want to view the "packaged" object, just double-click on the object to activate it—that is, start the server application that was used to create it and have the object displayed within that application.

Object Packager lets you do the following:

- Insert a complete document as a package in a destination document. (This complete document could be an actual text file, a graph, an animation, a sound file, or any conceivable object from an OLE-server application.)

  This feature can become very valuable with larger objects. For example, you wouldn't want to have *War and Peace* inserted in your business letter, but it might be nice to have an icon you could hit that would load a CD ROM browsing application to let you browse through *War and Peace.*

- Insert part of a document as a package in a destination document. (This means you can take a subset of an object—you aren't bound to take the whole thing.)

- Insert an icon representing an MS-DOS command line to be executed in a destination document. For example, you might include a note that says, "Check out this new utility I just put on the network" and place an iconic representation of the new utility in the Email file (assuming this Email application supports OLE).

  When you double-click on the icon, the utility will run in a DOS window, provided the utility is on the network in a directory that is included in your search path.

- Customize the icon that represents a packaged object. This feature lets you pick any icon you want to represent the package.

- Change the label of an icon. You change the caption for any icon.

Now let's do some packaging of our own. First, let's package a Write document and place it into another using Object Packager to illustrate how to package large text files.

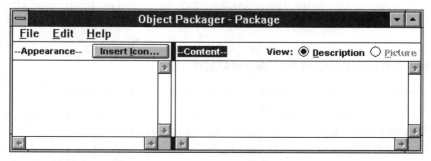

Figure 12.15 Object Packager.

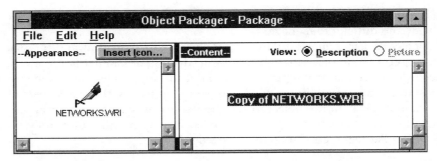

Figure 12.16 Object Packager with NETWORKS.WRI being packaged into an object.

1. Load Write and type in some text. We want to simulate a letter that includes a much longer file, but you don't want to clutter up your relatively short note by cutting and pasting in the whole file.

2. Load Object Packager. Its window is displayed as shown in Figure 12.15. There are two main windows in Object Packager; the first is labeled "- -Appearance- -" and the second is "- -Content- -." The Appearance window contains the icon and label as they will appear when pasted into your document and the Content window gives you a description or picture of the material you will be pasting.

3. We need to tell Object Packager what object we want to package. Therefore, choose Import from the File menu and select "NETWORKS.WRI" as the file we want to import. When the file is loaded, your screen should look like Figure 12.16.

   Note the Write icon with the label "NETWORKS.WRI" in the Appearance Window—this is what the icon will look like when pasted into our letter. Also look at the Content window—this is the object that is getting packaged.

4. Choose Copy Package from the Edit menu. This copies the entire packaged object to the Clipboard for embedding into our document.

5. Switch to Write and choose Paste from the Edit menu. You should now have your note in Write and the packaged object embedded into your document as shown in Figure 12.17. Double-click on the Write icon and Windows should load Write with a copy of the NETWORKS.WRI file on the screen.

CREATING OBJECTS WITH FILE MANAGER

File Manager can be used to link or embed objects in one of three different ways:

- Copy the document from File Manager to the Clipboard, then to Object Packager, and then paste into your destination document.

- Copy the document from File Manager to the Clipboard, then paste directly to the destination document.

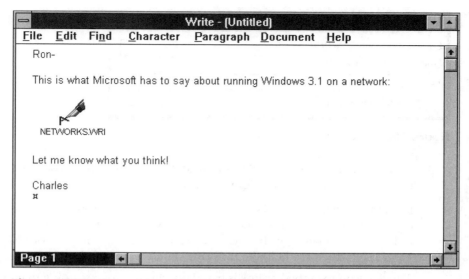

Figure 12.17 Write with packaged NETWORKS.WRI embedded in the document.

- Use the mouse to drag the document from File Manager into Object Packager, then paste the package into the destination document.

Let's run through the steps necessary to do each of these. To embed or link an object from File Manager using Object Packager:

1. Load Write and type in some text.

2. Load File Manager and select a file; click on it. It should appear highlighted on the screen as shown in Figure 12.18.

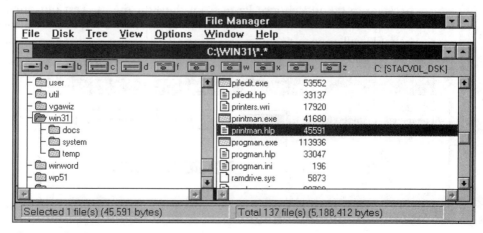

Figure 12.18 File Manager.

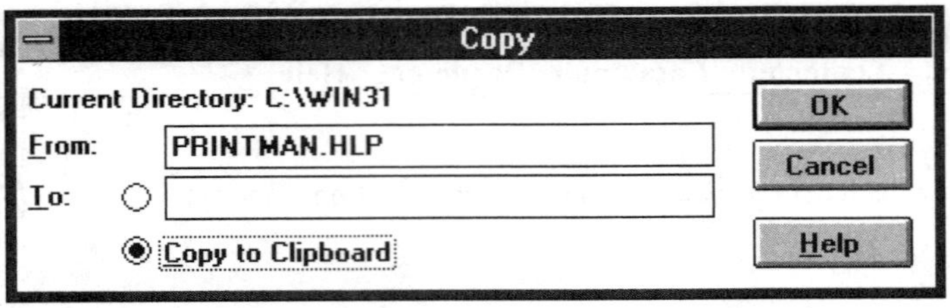

Figure 12.19 Copy dialog box.

3. Choose "Copy. . ." from the File Menu. Make sure you also choose the "Copy to Clipboard" option (See Figure 12.19).

4. Load Object Packager and select the Content window. From the Edit menu, choose Paste or Paste Link, depending on whether you want to embed or link the object later on. In this case, we are deciding the fate of PRINT-MAN.HLP which is a help file for Print Manager.

    The decision to embed or link is based on whether you are going to modify the object yourself or keep up with someone else's modifications. If you will be making the changes, you will want to embed a copy of the object. If it were linked, it would change as other folks made changes; you might not like that. However, if you want to rely on the changes made by others, then you should link the file.

    Depending on your choice, choose Paste or Paste Link. In the case of Figure 12.20, the author chose to embed (make a copy) so he chose Paste. Note the Contents window says we now have a "Copy of PRINT-MAN.HLP."

5. Time to embed this package. Choose "Copy Package" from the Edit menu to copy the package to the Clipboard.

6. Switch to your Write document. Position the cursor where you want the package to go and choose Paste from the Edit menu. Test out our new package by double-clicking on the icon. A short time later, Print Manager's help file will appear, as shown in Figure 12.21.

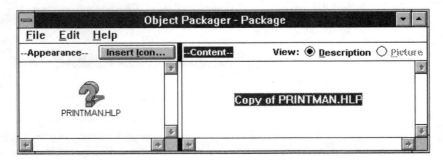

Figure 12.20 Object Packager showing PRINTMAN.HLP being packaged.

embedding the object. Finally, you must have sufficient directory rights to the object and the application that created it to perform any modifications.

Updating Linked Objects

Updating linked objects should be no problem immediately after you have created the object (the network drives are mapped the same; if you had sufficient directory rights to create the object, you will be able to edit the object also). However, when you attempt to load a different document that contains a linked object, Windows will undoubtedly check for the most recent version of the object. If you are not connected to the directory containing the source file for the object (or if you have insufficient directory rights), this update may fail and an error message may result.

Some applications are smart enough that when they detect a drive mapping change, they will search the path to see where the linked object resides "now" and update the link reference accordingly.

However, if you do not have the directory rights to a linked object, or if you do not have a network drive mapped as the linked object expects, you may get a message from the application telling you that it cannot locate the linked object (or the application that created it).

13 Windows for Workgroups

Overview

In late October 1992, Microsoft released Windows for Workgroups, a bold step toward integrating Windows and networking. Microsoft enhanced this release of Windows by adding several significant networking features. This chapter will explain those new features and walk you through the installation and configuration of Windows for Workgroups.

Additionally, there will be a detailed discussion of the networking enhancements that have been made to existing utilities, including the Windows Control Panel, Print Manager, File Manager, and Clipboard viewer which has been renamed the ClipBook Viewer. Also, Windows for Workgroups' new applications, like Microsoft Mail and Schedule+, will be discussed as well as the three new accessories: Chat, Net Watcher, and Win Meter. The icons for these new applications and accessories can be found in Program Manager's Main and Accessories group windows as shown in Figures 13.1 and 13.2.

There are two aspects of functionality provided by Windows for Workgroups. The first is its peer-to-peer networking capability, allowing workstations running Windows for Workgroups (W4W) users to access resources (like printers and disk drives) connected to other workstations running W4W. With this capability, W4W is essentially a peer-to-peer network of its own, similar to NetWare Lite or LANtastic, and is suitable for smaller offices.

The second aspect of functionality is Windows for Workgroups' ability to take better advantage of existing network environments, like Novell NetWare. At the time of this writing, however, integrating W4W into a Novell NetWare LAN environment can be somewhat difficult because of the tension existing between Novell and Microsoft Corporation.

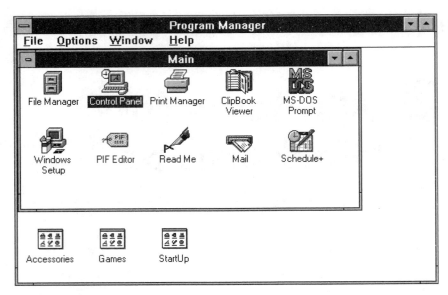

Figure 13.1 Program Manager Main group.

Novell was not invited to beta test Windows for Workgroups; therefore it is ill-equipped to support networking issues related to W4W. Additionally, W4W requires that NetWare users utilize a different protocol stack of LAN drivers based on NDIS (Network Driver Interface Specification), instead of Novell's ODI (Open Data-Link Interface). NDIS and ODI are fundamentally similar in that they are designed to allow multiple networking protocols to co-exist on the same workstation; however, they are not compatible with each other.

Figure 13.2 Program Manager Accessories group.

Before W4W, Novell users either ran the native IPX drivers, which are specific to the IPX protocol, or they ran the ODI flavor drivers, where IPX is loaded on top of the ODI layer. Through Novell's LAN Workplace products, users can also run TCP/IP on top of ODI.

Unfortunately, Windows for Workgroups insists on installing NDIS drivers and a Microsoft-supplied IPX driver that provides NetWare connectivity on top of NDIS, while W4W natively uses the NETBEUI protocol on top of NDIS. By not inviting Novell to participate in the testing of Windows for Workgroups, this Microsoft IPX driver was never certified by Novell, and its degree of compatibility with NetWare is still questionable at this time.

One thing is certain: ODI-based products, like Novell's TCP/IP stack, are not compatible with the Microsoft W4W approach. Also, not all third-party network adapters supported by NetWare have NDIS drivers.

It should also be pointed out that NETBEUI is not a protocol that is routed by NetWare file servers and routers, so W4W peer-to-peer services will not be available across different cabling segments that are connected by NetWare file servers or routers.

By introducing a new set of driver issues with W4W, Microsoft has limited the degree to which this product will be accepted in large NetWare installations. It is clear that this is part of a larger strategy where Microsoft will be challenging Novell to provide network functionality.

By the time you read this book, it is likely that one or both parties will have reached a compromise solution to make W4W more NetWare compatible. Novell already provides ODINSUP, an NDIS "shim" that emulates the NDIS protocol, running on top of Novell's ODI protocol. This alone would be sufficient for allowing W4W functionality using standard NetWare drivers; however, the ODINSUP shim currently provides support for NDIS v1.0 only, and W4W is the first networking application to require NDIS v2.0. It is likely that Novell will update ODINSUP in the near future to provide this support.

It is also likely that Novell will introduce a router NLM that will allow NetWare 3.x file servers and multi-protocol routers to pass W4W's NETBEUI packets between cabling segments.

While some of the functionality of W4W may be appealing, you'll most likely want to set up a test environment first to determine if these networking trade-offs are worth the functionality gain of W4W, until these issues are addressed.

With the above disclaimer made, let's explore the features of Windows for Workgroups to help you determine whether it would be a useful addition to your network environment.

Resource Sharing

One of the most significant benefits of Windows for Workgroups is its ability to share disk and printer resources across the network. This capability is similar to Novell's NetWare Lite or Artisoft's LANtastic which allow users to access each other's files and share each other's printers without the aid of a dedicated file server.

On a NetWare network, however, Windows for Workgroups brings you the combined functionality of NetWare and Microsoft's resource-sharing capabilities. For instance, you can attach to another user's hard drive or printer, copy files to and from that drive, and print to that printer (assuming that user wants to share the drive and printer). In the meantime, you still have access to the usual NetWare network resources.

Enhanced Windows Utilities

In addition to providing enhanced connectivity, Microsoft has upgraded several native Windows utilities with networking features. The Windows Control Panel, Print Manager, and File Manager are among these.

For example, the functionality of the Network icon in Control Panel has changed significantly, offering a whole new front-end to the Windows networking features. The original Windows 3.1 NetWare system configuration screen is still accessible through this icon, however. See "Control Panel" under "Enhanced Utilities" later in this chapter for more details on this topic.

Print Manager has been upgraded to manage the new printer sharing features of Windows for Workgroups. Microsoft also integrated Print Manager with NetWare print queues, offering a never-before-seen level of integration with NetWare printing. Print Manager can now show individual jobs in NetWare queues.

File Manager has also been improved and is now tightly coupled with the Windows for Workgroups disk drive-sharing ability. From within File Manager, you can connect to drives on other users' PCs, provided those drives have been "shared." In addition, several other enhancements make File Manager a more useful utility.

The old Windows 3.1 Clipboard Viewer has been replaced by ClipBook Viewer, a new utility that lets you manage multiple Windows clipboards and share them with other users.

Each of these new enhancements to Windows for Workgroups will be covered in detail after the Installation section in this chapter.

Three New Accessories

Windows for Workgroups includes three new "mini-applications" in the Accessories group: Chat, Net Watcher, and WinMeter. Chat lets you carry on a running dialog (i.e., "chat") with other users on the network. Net Watcher lets you monitor what resources on your computer other users are attached to and using. Win Meter gives you an analysis of your system performance.

New Applications: Mail and Schedule+

In addition to the enhanced utilities and new "mini-apps," Microsoft has included two complete productivity applications in Windows for Workgroups: Mail and Schedule+.

Mail is a complete Email application that is well-integrated into the Windows for Workgroups networking system. Schedule+ is a complete workgroup scheduling system. While neither application may be as robust as some of the mature, third-party Email and scheduling products, each makes a very useful addition to the Windows for Workgroups package.

Network DDE

Finally, Windows for Workgroups offers what some third-party vendors have been providing for Windows for a while: networked Dynamic Data Exchange (DDE). Network DDE lets applications on one user's PC send messages and communicate with an application on another user's PC.

Network DDE has tremendous potential for opening up communication across the network. It may become an important tool in the growing wave of groupware applications.

Installation

Now that you have a general idea of some features of Windows for Workgroups, let's look at installation procedures.

If you installed Windows 3.1 on NetWare, you may have suffered several bumps and bruises. If you have "gained character" through this exercise, installing Windows for Workgroups will not be as significant a task. If Windows for Workgroups is your first shot at installing a version of Windows, you will have to learn the pure Windows aspect of the installation as well as the networking aspect.

Since installing Windows on NetWare is covered in some detail in the chapters preceding this one and the procedure is the same, it will not be repeated. Instead, we will focus on the network installation aspects of the Windows for Workgroups install.

The installation procedure on a network is similar to Windows 3.1. You also have several options as you did with Windows 3.1:

1. Install full copies to each user's local hard drive.

2. Install full copies to each user's network directory.

3. Install a shared copy of Windows on the LAN and place each user's private files in their own network directory.

4. Install a shared copy of Windows on the LAN and place each user's private files on that individual's local hard drive.

Since options 1 and 2 seem rather extreme, it is recommended that you choose either option 3 or 4. Your choice will depend on such items as whether you have local drives, whether you want to burden the LAN with the additional traffic, and whether you want to do the management from the network or visit each user's PC for configuration. See Chapter 5 for a detailed discussion of these issues.

One aspect of the installation that will be different, however, is that Setup will ask for your Workgroup name, computer name, username, and password. It is recommended that everyone use the same Workgroup name, or at least decide up front which users will be in which group.

The Windows for Workgroups SETUP parameters are similar to those in Windows 3.1. The easiest method to use for the installation is to use "SETUP /A" to copy all of the Windows disks to the network server (you'll need 21 megabytes for this). Then you can run "SETUP /N" from each user's private area (either on that individual's local drive or personal directory on the network).

New Device Drivers

One aspect of Windows for Workgroups that system managers may find frustrating, at least at first, is the plethora of device drivers that must be loaded on each user's workstation. In all, there are four device drivers that must be loaded. When SETUP is run, it will ask you whether you want the workstation's CONFIG.SYS and AUTOEXEC.BAT files modified to reference these drivers along with other settings.

End-users may also find these device drivers frustrating, as they are not selectively loadable/unloadable from the DOS prompt as the standard NetWare drivers are. So, users who work sometimes on the network and sometimes in a local mode, perhaps to free up additional memory, may find this CONFIG.SYS driver approach to be extremely inconvenient.

Here is a sample of the lines added to the CONFIG.SYS file for Windows for Workgroups:

```
STACKS=9,256
LASTDRIVE=P
device=c:\protman.dos /i:C:\
device=c:\workgrp.sys
device=c:\ne1000.dos
device=c:\msipx.sys
```

The STACKS directive tells DOS how much memory to allocate for the DOS data stacks, which are used for the processing of hardware interrupts.

The LASTDRIVE statement is set, by default, to P. This means that drives A through P will appear to DOS and NetWare as local drives. Therefore, when you load the NetWare shell, the SYS:LOGIN directory will be mapped to Q:. Windows for Workgroups can only share local drive letters (A through P), hence the need for the LASTDRIVE. NetWare can map directories to any drives (including the A: and B: drives!), so if your login script maps drives below P:, don't worry about it. Also, P is not a magic drive letter—you can set this to anything you like.

Note that if you run MAP.EXE to map a drive below the last drive value, you will receive a warning: "Drive X is in use by a local drive. Do you want to assign it as a network drive? (Y/N)." You will have to enter 'Y' to continue and map the drive. The NetWare LOGIN.EXE program does not run MAP.EXE, and will not present this warning; it's only an issue if you MAP from a batch file.

The first two device drivers are generic to Windows for Workgroups. The PROTMAN.DOS line loads the Windows for Workgroups Protocol Manager. The /i switch tells PROTMAN.DOS where to look for PROTOCOL.INI (implying that you can move it around) which contains information and settings for your current hardware and software.

The WORKGROUP.SYS line loads WORKGROUP.SYS which helps with file and printer sharing.

The NE1000.DOS is an NDIS driver for the Novell NE-1000/Anthem network adapter that was in the author's system. You will need an NDIS driver for your specific network adapter on this line (NDIS is Microsoft's network adapter driver format, as ODI is Novell's).

The last driver, MSIPX.SYS, assists Windows for Workgroups in using the Novell IPX protocol.

The author's system, when booted with DOS 5.0, has 609,232 bytes of memory free. After adding these four device drivers, free memory was reduced to 522,384 bytes; therefore, the four drivers combined use 86,848 bytes of memory.

In addition, the AUTOEXEC.BAT file, as modified by SETUP, contains several lines for Windows for Workgroups:

```
NET START
MSIPX
NETX
```

The "NET START" line starts the Windows for Workgroups "Workgroup Connection." This is the NetWare Lite/LANtastic-like peer-to-peer network. Running this "NET START" line also increased the free memory on the author's machine to 592,416 bytes, bringing the total memory used by the device drivers down to 16,816 bytes (although a small TSR, PROTMAN was loaded by NET START which occupied 2544 bytes).

MSIPX is a special version of IPX that combines IPX with Microsoft's NetBEUI protocol which is used for the peer-to-peer networking in Windows for Workgroups. It consumes the same memory as the current IPX version as of this writing (16,272 bytes).

NETX is the normal DOS shell used today. EMSNETX or XMSNETX may be substituted for memory savings and the author was able to load MSIPX into high memory (using QEMM) for additional RAM savings.

MANAGING TWO NETWORKS AT ONCE

It's important to understand that when you run Windows for Workgroups and NetWare, you are essentially running two networks at once. The advantage of this is having the features of NetWare (running on the IPX protocol) plus the peer-to-peer features in Windows for Workgroups (running on the NetBEUI protocol).

As a network administrator, you may have to decide how much the peer-to-peer features will "cost": Certainly these will cost around 17K of additional RAM, plus some administrative overhead involved in setup and configuration, troubleshooting, fine-tuning, and support.

Plus, there are the security aspects—network administrators will have to consider how they will implement network security in a peer-to-peer environment. Novell provides centralized network security in NetWare (at least it's centralized at each server, and more globally with NetWare Naming Service, and even more so with NetWare 4.0). The peer-to-peer aspects of Windows for Workgroups do not provide for centralized security. Users can decide to "share" the contents of portions of their local hard drives with anyone else on the network.

Enhanced Utilities

Several of the major Windows utilities have been enhanced under Windows for Workgroups. In most cases, networking features have been added or improved, and additional features have been added to make the utility more useful. This section will explore each of these enhanced utilities in detail.

Control Panel

Although the Control Panel under Windows for Workgroups looks similar to the original Control Panel under Windows (Figure 13.3), the Network icon in Control Panel now leads to a different dialog box, as shown in Figure 13.4.

As you may recall, the Windows 3.1 version of the Network icon led to a Network settings dialog box specific to NetWare. In Windows for Workgroups, however, this button leads to a series of dialog boxes that let you do such things as configure your network card, login to the Windows for Workgroups network, install network software, and change your Windows for Workgroups password.

Computer Name is the username for the Windows for Workgroups network. It does not necessarily correspond to the NetWare user's name, but it could for convenience. The Computer name is used by others when connecting to your drives and printers. (It appears in the "Showed Shared" listings.) Also, the Workgroup name is used in a backhanded kind of way. That is, when you attempt

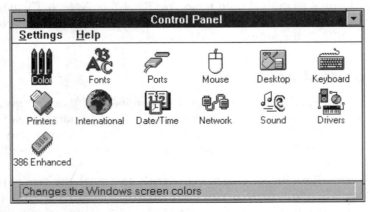

Figure 13.3 Control Panel window.

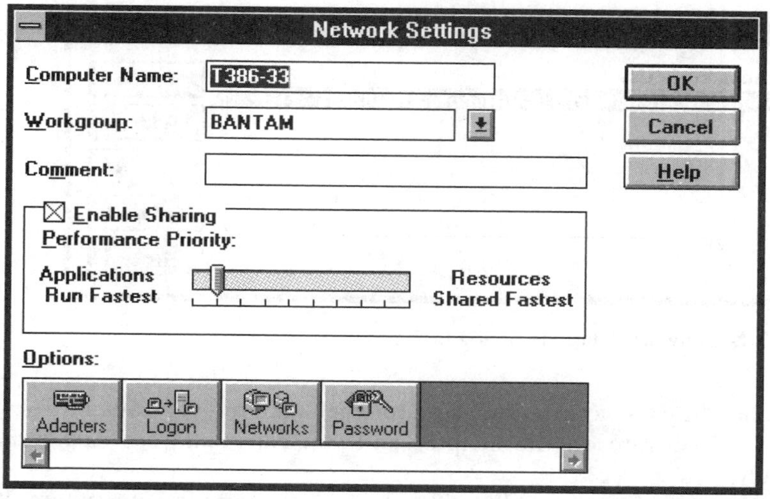

Figure 13.4 Network Settings dialog box.

to connect to a printer, the Workgroup name appears first, and the computer names in that workgroup appear (indented) below it.

The Workgroup name identifies to which workgroup the user belongs. This is done for organizational purposes mostly and helps define which users work with whom on certain projects.

In addition to their functionality in Windows for Workgroups, the Computer Name and Workgroup Name options are provided to support LAN Manager, Windows NT, and LAN Manager for Windows NT. These other "environments" also make use of the "Workgroup" concept. The sharing mechanism in Windows for Workgroups is supposed to be compatible with these products.

The Enable Sharing checkbox lets individual users choose whether they wish to share their local hard drives and printers with other users. From the sliding bar under the checkbox you can select the amount of processor time that Windows for Workgroups will devote to sharing your drive and printers at the expense of your applications.

When the bar is to the far left, few time slices are taken from your processing to share your resources with other users. This will improve your local performance, but make printing to your printers or sharing your local drives slow for other users. When the bar is to the far right, many time slices will be taken from your Windows processing, slowing down your applications, but providing quicker access for other users.

The option buttons at the bottom of the Network Settings window let you choose different configuration options. At present, these options are: Adapters, Logon, Networks, and Password.

ADAPTERS

Pressing the Adapters button produces the "Network Adapters" window shown in Figure 13.5. In this window, you can manage the network adapter or adapters you

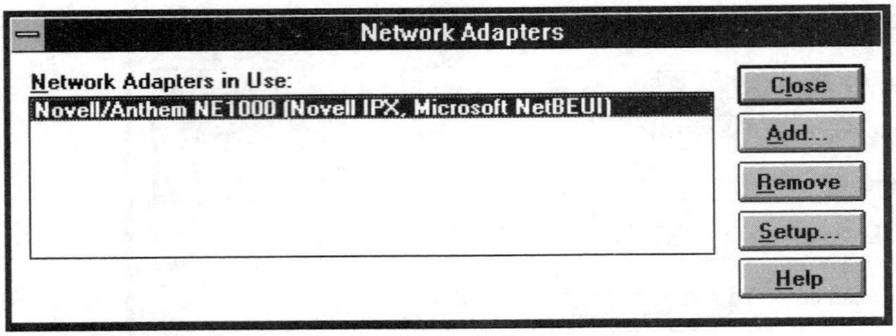

Figure 13.5 Network Adapters dialog box.

have installed in your workstation. Also, for each adapter, you can control which protocols will operate on the adapter and you can configure each protocol individually.

The Add button lets you add a network adapter driver to your system. When you press Add, Windows will prompt you to select the driver to install or to specify the directory in which the driver files are stored. Remove will delete a network adapter driver from the list.

Pressing the Setup button will bring up the adapter setup window (Figure 13.6) which lets you change the Interrupt, I/O port address, and other configuration settings that are specific to your network adapter. If you press the Protocols button in this dialog box, the dialog box in Figure 13.7 is displayed; this lets you configure the protocols associated with that adapter.

In Figure 13.7, there are two protocols defined to run on the Novell/Anthem NE1000 adapter: Microsoft NetBEUI and Novell IPX. NetBEUI is the native protocol for Windows for Workgroups and is required for the disk and printer resource sharing. IPX is the native protocol for NetWare and is required for access to NetWare.

If you have another protocol you wish to add to this list, you may select the "Unlisted or Updated Protocol" item and choose "Add ->." You will then be prompted to insert a disk containing the new protocol files.

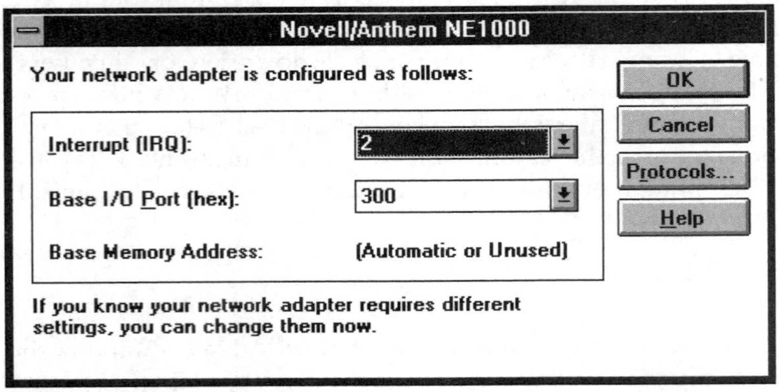

Figure 13.6 Network Adapter setup window.

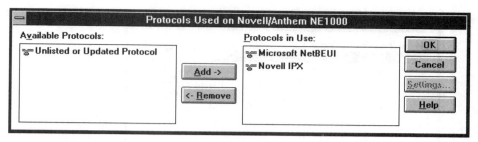

Figure 13.7 Network Adapter Protocol Configuration window.

To configure the NetBEUI or IPX protocols, click on NetBEUI or IPX, and press the Settings button. If you selected NetBEUI, you will see a window similar to Figure 13.8. The "Advanced Protocol Settings" list shows you which settings you can change. To change either the "Maximum Sessions" or "NCBS," highlight one, then manipulate the controls at the bottom of the window.

For instance, in Figure 13.8 "Maximum Sessions" is highlighted; at the bottom of the window, you can change the Value of the Maximum Sessions from the default of 10. To change the value, click on the up or down arrows beside the 10 to increase or decrease the value, then press the Set button. You can hit Revert to return to the previous value.

If you selected IPX in Figure 13.7, you will see the Novell IPX configuration window in Figure 13.9. There is only one setting you can change for IPX, the "Adapter Media Type." Pick the media type in the lower section of the window.

LOGON

Before you can connect to a resource on another Windows for Workgroups computer or to a NetWare resource, you must log on to Windows for Workgroups. This involves supplying a user name and a password associated with that user name. (You are prompted to supply the initial values for both of these during the install

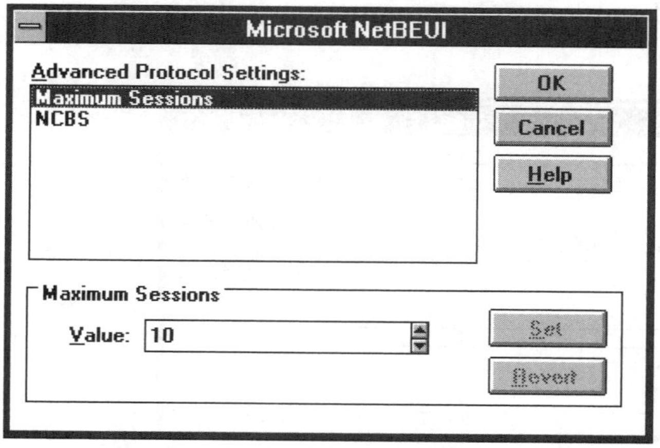

Figure 13.8 Advanced Protocol Settings for NetBEUI dialog box.

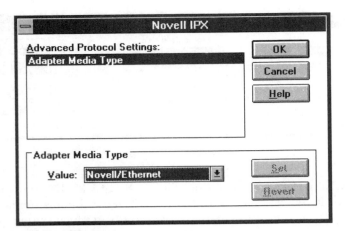

Figure 13.9 Advanced Protocol Settings for IPX dialog box.

process.) The password you supply may not necessarily match your NetWare password. See the next section for details on defining a Windows for Workgroups password.

You only need to log on to Windows for Workgroups once. That logon will remain in effect until you leave Windows for Workgroups. However, you have a choice as to when you can log on. By default, Windows for Workgroups will prompt you to log on when you attempt to connect to a drive or printer on another machine. Alternatively, you can have Windows for Workgroups prompt you to log on each time you start the program, thereby getting the logon process out of the way up front. This section will show you how to implement this setting.

Also, you can create multiple users (with different passwords) for a particular computer. To do this, type in a new user name at logon. Windows for Workgroups will prompt you for a password and create a new account for the user.

If you press the Logon button from the "Network Settings" window, you should see a display similar to Figure 13.10. (This window lets you interact with the Windows for Workgroups network and does not log you in or out of NetWare servers.)

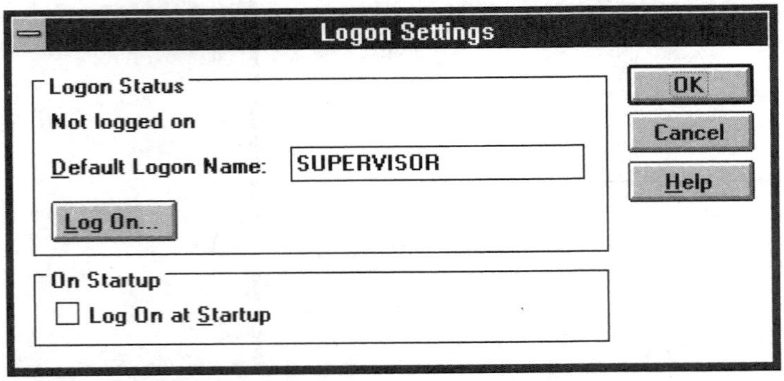

Figure 13.10 Network Settings window.

The Logon Status box shows your login status and lists your default login name. In this case, the user, SUPERVISOR is not logged in. If you are not logged in, there will be a "Log On" button in this section—press it to log onto the Windows for Workgroups network. If you are already logged in, the button will say "Log Off" instead.

At the bottom of Figure 13.10 is the "On Startup" section. You can click on the "Log On at Startup" box to have Windows for Workgroups request that you log on under your user name every time Windows starts up, rather than making you do it whenever you attempt to access a network drive or printer.

NETWORKS

If you press the Networks button from the "Network Settings" window, you should see a window similar to Figure 13.11, the "Compatible Networks" window. Here you can define which networks (other than the standard Windows for Workgroups network running on the NetBEUI protocol) will be supported. In our case, we are interested in NetWare.

If you don't see Novell NetWare listed under the "Other Networks in Use" button, highlight Novell NetWare under "Available Network Types" and press the "Add ->" button.

To modify the NetWare configuration settings, select the Novell NetWare line under "Other Networks in Use" and press the "Settings" button. You will now be presented with the Network window (Figure 13.12). As you may recall, this is what is displayed when you press the Network button from Control Panel while in Windows 3.1. See Chapter 3 for a full discussion on this window.

PASSWORD

If you press the Password button from the "Network Settings" window, you will see the "Change Logon Password" window, shown in Figure 13.13. Here you can change your Windows for Workgroups password. To do this, first select the user's name whose password you want to change. Type in the old password, enter the new password once, then enter it again for verification.

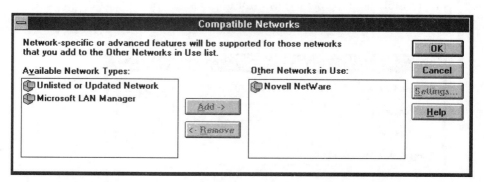

Figure 13.11 Compatible Networks window.

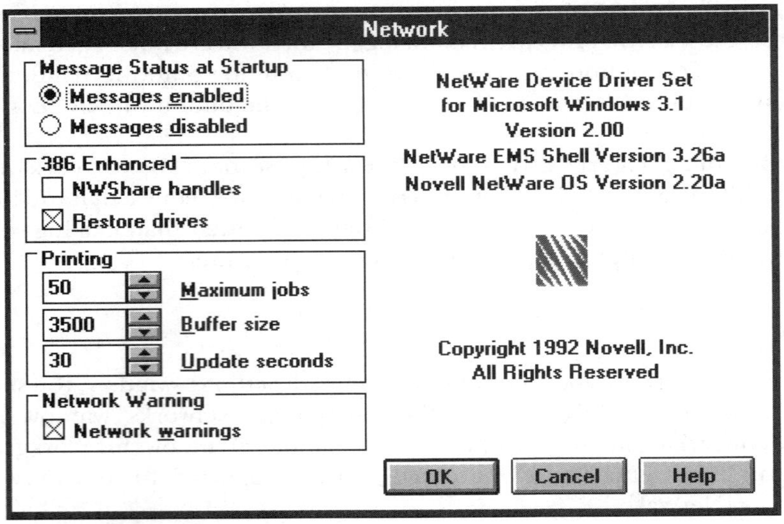

Figure 13.12 Network settings window.

Print Manager

The Print Manager has been enhanced to support the new Windows for Work-groups networking features. When you start up Print Manager, you will notice it has a different look right away, as shown in Figure 13.14.

DOCUMENT AREA

Like Windows 3.1, the main area of the Print Manager window lists the current print jobs for each printer. The status of the printer, the size of each job, and the time it was placed into the queue are displayed.

However, in Windows for Workgroups, new icons representing local non-shared printers, local shared printers, and network print queues have been added. You can see the local non-shared print queue icon next to the "HP LaserJet Series II" line in Figure 13.14. The local shared icon looks like the third icon from the left in the toolbar (it shows a hand holding a small printer, as if in offering). The network print queue icon looks like the first icon from the left in the toolbar.

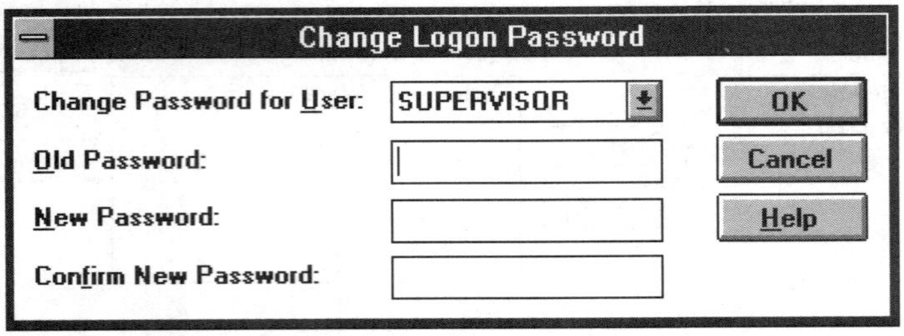

Figure 13.13 Change Logon Password.

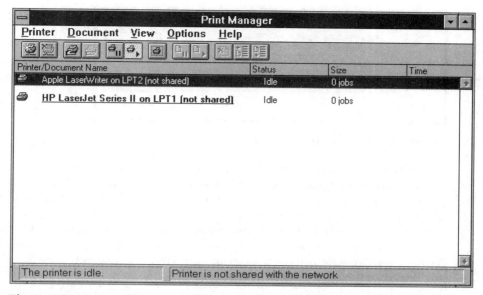

Figure 13.14 Print Manager window.

TOOLBAR

The toolbar is another valuable addition to Print Manager (and to File Manager also, as you will soon see). The toolbar lets you quickly choose common commands without taking the time to go through the pull-down menus.

It is important to realize that whenever there is a discussion of buttons on the toolbar, those same functions can also be accessed by a corresponding menu selection (and sometimes a hotkey as well, such as a Control-Key combination).

SHARING YOUR PRINTER

The two resources that can be shared in the Windows for Workgroups environment are your local drives and local printers. The share button in the toolbar lets you share a local printer with other users. When you click on the share button, you will see a window similar to Figure 13.15, "Share Printer."

In this window, you can select the printer you want to share by clicking on the down arrow and choosing the one you want. The "Share As" prompt determines the name of the printer for other users. The default name for the Apple LaserWriter is "Apple," but you could call it "Bob's Apple LaserWriter" just the same. With the Comment field you can associate another line of information about the printer for other users to read.

The password field adds an aspect of security to the sharing exercise. If you give the shared printer a password, then others will need to enter the password before they can print on your local printer.

The "Re-Share at Startup" checkbox defaults to on, which means that once you share it, it will automatically be shared every time you enter Windows. If you want this to be a one-time deal, simply click on the "Re-Share at Startup" to uncheck the box.

Share Printer

Printer:	Apple LaserWriter on LPT2 ▼
Share as:	Apple
Comment:	
Password:	☒ Re-share at Startup

OK Cancel Help

Figure 13.15 Share Printer dialog box.

Assuming you clicked on the OK button, the local Apple LaserWriter on LPT2: will be shared as "Apple." Figure 13.16 shows the new display after sharing the printer. The new icon next to the Apple LaserWriter indicates that it's a local shared printer and the "(shared as Apple)" indicates what it's called.

In addition, we have paused this queue by pressing the pause button (fifth button from the left; it cleverly looks like the pause button on tape recorders and VCRs). Also, we have printed a job from the Windows Notepad accessory—note the line after the name of the printer, which contains a document icon followed by "Local user: Notepad - BOOTLOG.TXT." This indicates that you, the local user (and not some other user on the network), sent a job from Notepad called BOOTLOG.TXT to your local Apple LaserWriter printer. You also can see that it's a 14K file and was sent at 2:37 pm (the date is cut-off to the right).

STOP SHARING

If you are tired of everyone using your printer, you can stop sharing it. This is accomplished by clicking on the Stop Sharing button (just to the right of the share

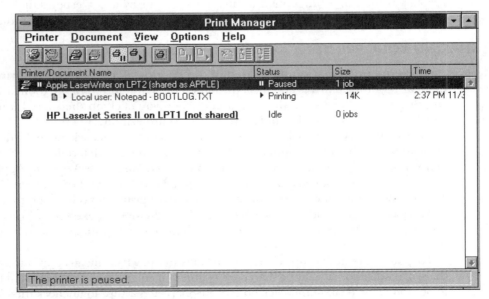

Figure 13.16 Print Manager window showing LaserJet shared as "Apple."

button in Print Manager's Toolbar—it shows a disappearing printer cradled in a hand). If you click on this button (or choose the Printer Stop Sharing Printer menu selection), you will see the "Stop Sharing Printer" window, as shown in Figure 13.17.

This window lists the printers you are currently sharing. To stop sharing the printer, simply click on the printer and click OK.

CONNECTING TO A NETWORK PRINT QUEUE

The first icon on the toolbar is the Connect Network Printer button. This connects your Windows printer driver to either a Windows for Workgroups printer that is being shared by another user or to a NetWare print queue.

Before you can print to a printer that is attached to another computer, you must install a print driver that matches the printer, and direct the output for that driver to an appropriate port on your machine. You can install a printer driver by using the Printers icon in the Control Panel.

Pressing this button (or selecting the Printer Connect Network Printer menu choice) reveals the "Connect Network Printer" window, as shown in Figure 13.18. As it stands, this window assumes that you want to connect the printer driver you had highlighted in the Print Manager main window to someone else's local printer. In reality, you are connecting a local LPT device to someone else's local printer (very similar to the NetWare CAPTURE process except the output goes to someone's local printer, not to a network print queue).

In the "Connect Network Printer" window in Figure 13.18, the "Device Name" box contains the port that will be redirected. Next is the Path to the printer you want to share. This path box contains the sharename for the printer, which includes the name of the computer the printer is on and the printer's sharename; this text string takes the form \\Computer Name\Sharename. For example, if your computer name (not your username) is SUPERVISOR and your printer's sharename is Apple, you would type \\supervisor\apple. As an alternative to using this textbox, you can build a sharename by using the Show Shared Printers On and Shared Printers listboxes as described below.

The Reconnect at Startup checkbox defaults to on; this means that Windows will automatically reconnect to this remote printer every time you start Windows for Workgroups.

Figure 13.17 Stop Sharing Printer dialog box.

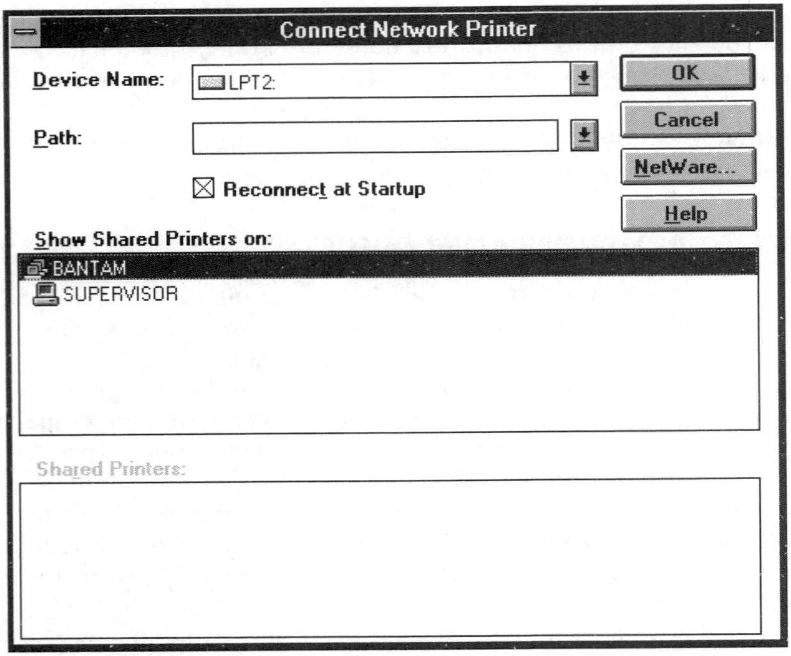

Figure 13.18 Connect Network Printer window.

The "Show Shared Printers on:" box lists workgroups and users associated with those workgroups. You can choose the workgroup/user to whom you want to connect. At the bottom of the display, you can see the shared printers to which you can connect. In this case, there are none shown.

CONNECTING TO A NETWARE PRINT QUEUE

If you don't want to connect to a local user's printer but want to connect to a NetWare print queue instead, you can click on the NetWare button from the "Connect Network Printer" window (Figure 13.18). This will result in the "Network–Printer Connections" window, shown in Figure 13.19. This same dialog box, accessible from the Control Panel/Printers selection, is discussed in detail in Chapter 3. Nevertheless, you can use this dialog box to connect an LPT port to a network server/print queue combination.

In our example, we connected the Apple LaserWriter on LPT2 to the ROSE_286/Q_TEXT print queue, and the HP Laserjet Series II on LPT1 to the ROSE_286/TESTQUEUE print queue. Figure 13.20 shows you how Print manager displays the queues.

Print Manager now shows you each job in the network's print queue. Note also the new icon of the printer with the network cable running under it denoting a network printer.

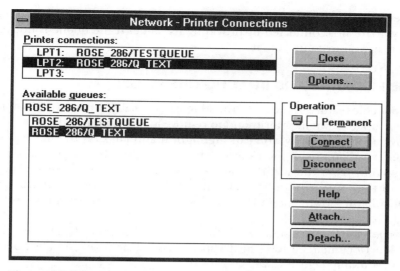

Figure 13.19 Network–Printer Connections dialog box.

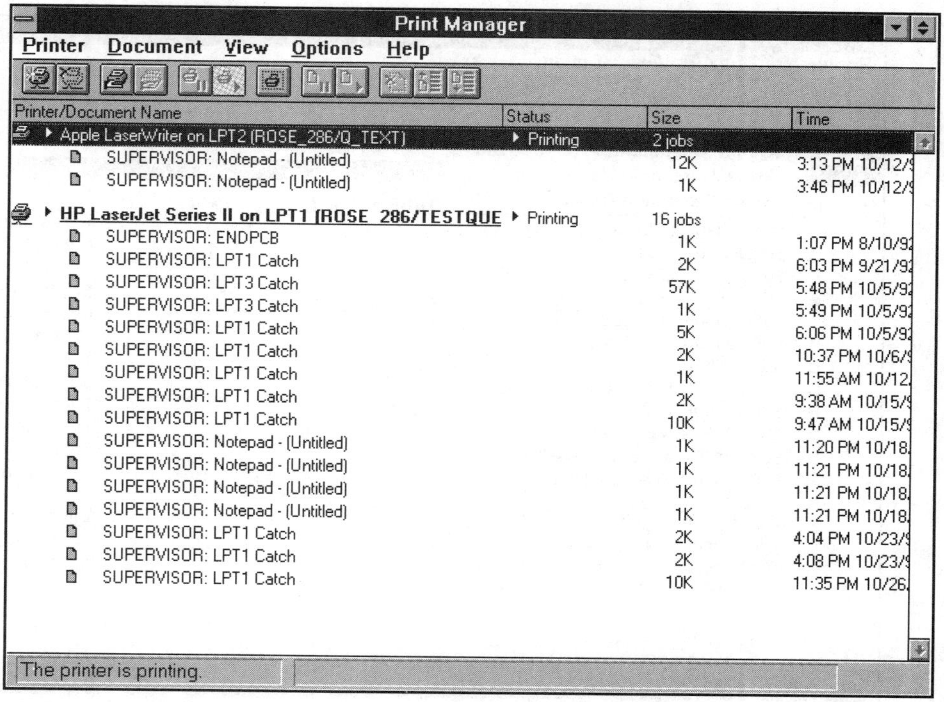

Figure 13.20 Print Manager displaying NetWare print queues.

The View Other Network printer command lets you view the contents of a queue to which you are not connected by providing its name. If the queue is not very busy, you may wish to connect to it.

MOVING JOB PRIORITIES AND DELETING QUEUE JOBS

Another valuable feature to the new Print Manager is its ability to move jobs in the print queue up or down in priority and to remove jobs from the queue.

To move a job in priority, you can highlight it and click on the move down button (farthest icon from the right on the toolbar) or click on the move up button (second from the right). You can also drag the job up or down. In addition to the toolbar buttons, you can use the "Move Document Up" and "Move Document Down" menu choices from the Document menu, shown in Figure 13.21.

To remove a job from a queue, select the job and either press the Del key, click on the Delete Document button (third from right on the toolbar), or select Delete Document, shown in Figure 13.21.

For the Windows for Workgroups shared printers, the author was able to move jobs up and down in priority and delete jobs, but was only able to delete jobs from the NetWare print queues.

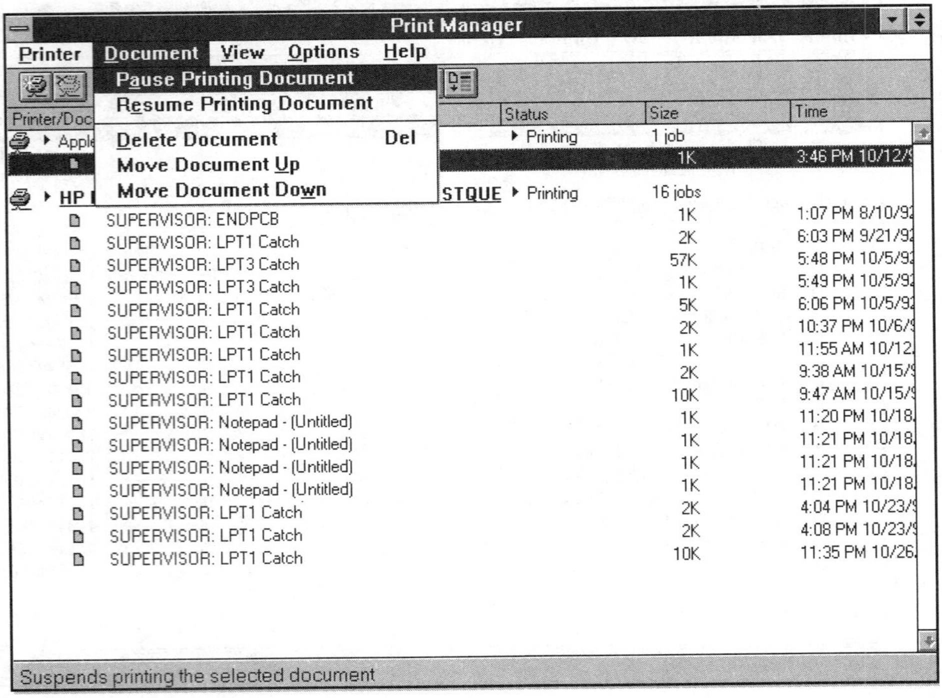

Figure 13.21 Print Manager Document menu.

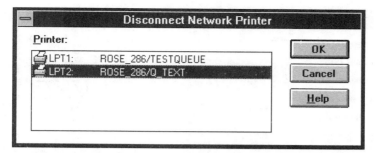

Figure 13.22 Disconnect Network Printer dialog box.

DISCONNECTING FROM NETWORK PRINT QUEUES

You may want to disconnect your local LPT ports from network print queues. To do this, press the Disconnect Network Printer button (second from the left on the toolbar) or choose the Disconnect Network Printer selection. The Disconnect Network Printer dialog box will be displayed, as shown in Figure 13.22. To disconnect a printer, select the LPT port containing the printer you want to disconnect and click on OK.

SEPARATOR PAGES

In NetWare, you can have a Banner page printed that shows who sent a specific print job and the name of the file printed. This can be useful in multi-user environments where many users share the same printer. The same functionality has been built into Windows for Workgroups; however, Banner pages are referred to as separator pages. You can have no separator page print (which is the default) or you can have a simple or standard separator page printed. In addition, you can specify a file to print as a separator page.

To specify a separator page, select the Separator Page item from the Options menu to display the dialog box in Figure 13.23. Then, select the separator page option of your choice. If you choose Custom Separator File, specify the appropriate filename in the adjacent textbox. Unfortunately, only the .CLP (Clipboard) and .WMF (Windows Metafile) file formats are supported. Windows for Workgroups does provide an application that produces these formats. The Windows 3.1 version of Clipboard Viewer produces .CLP file and many popular Windows applications support the .WMF format.

BACKGROUND PRINTING

When you print from Windows for Workgroups, your output is sent to a print queue (spooled to disk). Your print jobs, and those of other users, are then released from the queue to the printer in the order in which they arrived. That

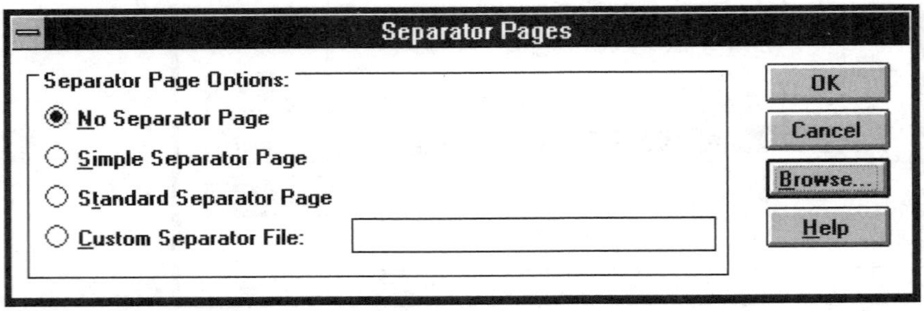

Figure 13.23 Separator Pages dialog box.

way, you can continue to work with your applications while printing takes place in the background.

Unfortunately, even though printing is a background process for Windows for Workgroups, it still must be managed; that requires allocating processor time. In fact, if there are a lot of print jobs waiting, you may notice your applications become sluggish. Fortunately, Windows for Workgroups allows you to configure the priority given to background printing.

To control background printing, select the Background item from the Print Manager's Options menu. The Background dialog box in Figure 13.24 will be displayed. This dialog box lets you control the amount of processor time devoted to background printing regardless of whether you are alerted when a printer goes inactive, or whether documents are sent directly to network queues or spooled locally first.

The last option has the most bearing on NetWare users. One of the disadvantages of Windows 3.1's Print Manager was that it could end up spooling a job twice—once on your local hard disk and again on the server—making the job take longer to print. This option lets you redirect the job to the network print queue right away rather than having to spool the job more than once.

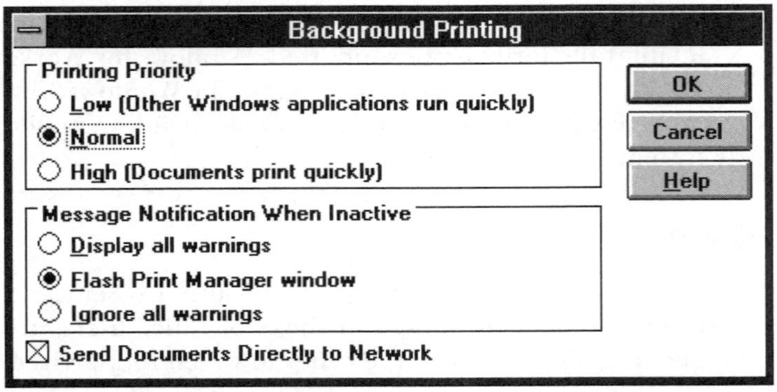

Figure 13.24 Background Printing dialog box.

File Manager

In addition to Control Panel and Print Manager, the Windows File Manager has been enhanced to support the new networking features in Windows for Workgroups. As you can see in Figure 13.25, the new File Manager looks substantially like the one in Windows 3.1 except for the addition of the toolbar (which was added to Print Manager, and is, incidentally, being added to many Microsoft products). You should also note that the icons in the File Manager window are similar in appearance and design to those in Print Manager.

CONNECTING NETWORK DRIVES

The first icon is the "Connect Network Drive" button—pressing it results in a window similar to Figure 13.26. This button can be used to connect one of your local drives to either:

- another user's local drive
- a file server/volume:directory combination

This is very similar to the NetWare MAP process, except it lets you map drives to other user's hard disks.

Using the Connect Network Drive window in Figure 13.26 is very much like using the "Connect Network Printer" window in Print Manager. In fact, the connection process is nearly identical. Press the leftmost toolbar button or choose the Disk Connect Network Drive menu option. Then, specify the local drive

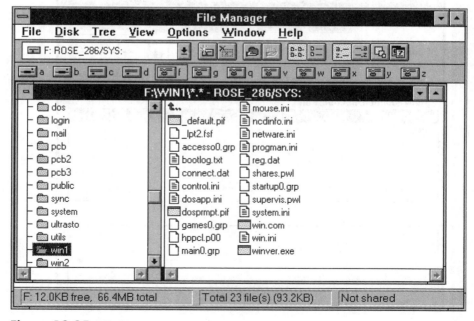

Figure 13.25 File Manager main window.

(rather than the LPT port) you want to connect to the remote machine and specify a location (directory) on that machine.

To connect to a directory on a remote Windows for Workgroups computer, first choose a local drive from the Drive drop-down listbox. Next, define a sharename for the remote directory in the Path textbox. A sharename is composed of two parts: the name of the computer the remote directory is on, followed by the directory's sharename (see "Sharing your Disk with Others" later for details on assigning sharenames to directories). This text string takes the form \\ComputerName\Sharename. For example, if the remote computer's name is ACCTG3 and the directory's sharename is BUDGET, you would type \\acct3\budget. A much easier alternative to using this textbox, however, is to build a sharename by using the Show Shared Directories on and Shared Directories listboxes below.

The Show Shared Directories on listbox shows the workgroups and names of computers that are currently on the network. The Shared Directories listbox shows the names of the shared directories on those machines. To build a sharename, first select a computer name from the Show Shared Directories on listbox. When you make a selection, the shared directories on that computer will appear in the Shared Directories box. Choose the desired directory. When you do, the Path textbox will be updated for your selection. To complete the connection, choose OK.

When you return to File Manager, the new connection will appear as a drive icon in File Manager's window. You can view the contents of the directory by clicking on the icon. In addition, you can use this drive letter to access files or run applications stored in the remote directory.

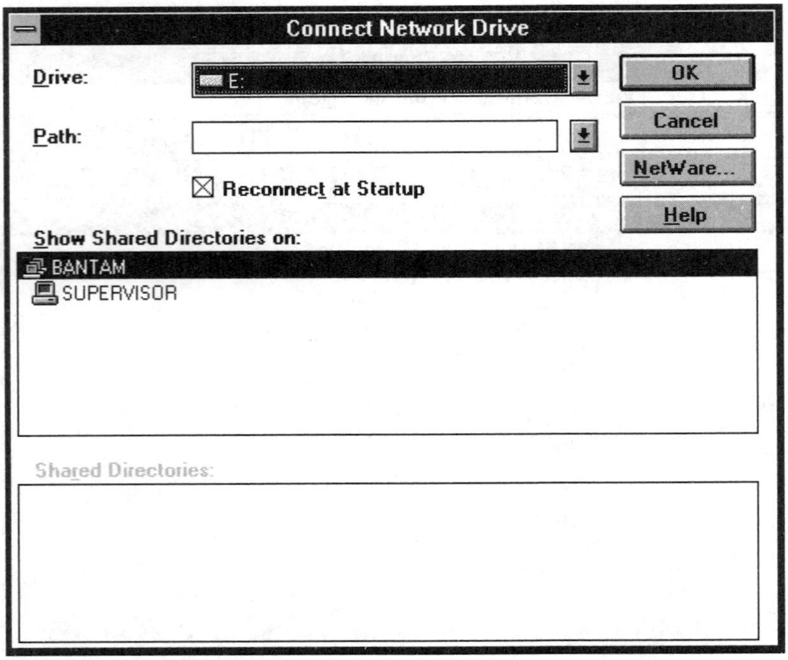

Figure 13.26 Connect Network Drive dialog box.

If you want to map your drive to a NetWare file server rather than to another user's disk drive, press the NetWare button on the "Connect Network Drive" window. When you press this button you'll see the "Network–Drive Connections" window in Figure 13.27. This is the same window you will see from the NetWare Popup utility, discussed in detail in Chapter 3. You can use this window to map local drives to NetWare directories.

> **Note:** In Figure 13.27, all of the drives through P are shown as local drives because of the "LASTDRIVE=P" in the CONFIG.SYS that Windows for Workgroups adds during the setup procedure. Windows for Workgroups cannot map drives beyond the LASTDRIVE setting to other user's disks. For example, in this case, you can only map drives using drive letters A through P to other user's disks.

DISCONNECTING NETWORK DRIVES

If you want to disconnect a network drive connection, you can press the second button from the left on the toolbar, the Disconnect Network Drive button, or choose the Disk Disconnect Network Drive menu selection. Either of these actions will reveal the "Disconnect Network Drive" window in Figure 13.28. To disconnect a drive, simply highlight a drive and press the OK button.

SHARING YOUR DISK WITH OTHERS

In order to map to another user's drive, Windows for Workgroups must be told that the user is willing to share the directory with the world. The same holds true for your machine. In fact, this lets you decide which directories you want to share and which you don't.

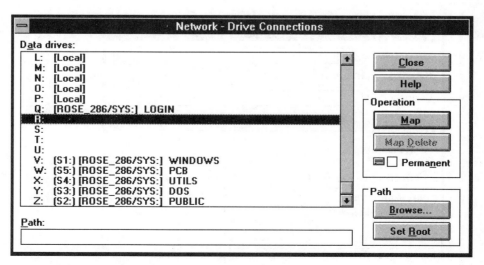

Figure 13.27 Network–Drive Connections dialog box.

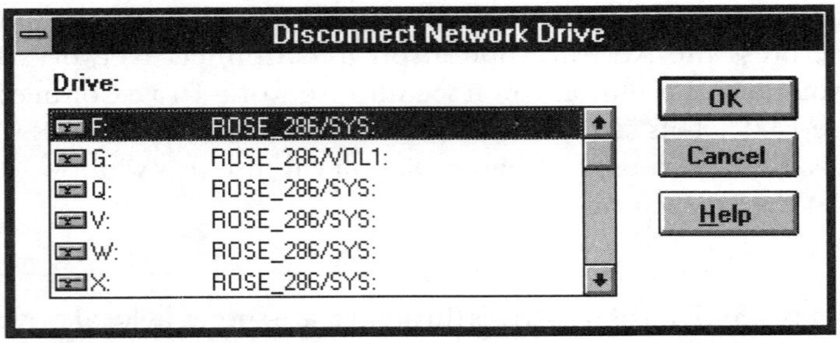

Figure 13.28 Disconnect Network Drive window.

Sharing is accomplished through the Share button (third button from the left on the toolbar) or through the Disk Share As menu selection. Press the share button (or make the menu choice) and you will see the "Share Directory" window, shown in Figure 13.29. The first item in the window is "Share Name." This is the name of the directory that other users will see. You could rename this "LOTUS SPREADSHEETS" if you want to clarify what's in the directory. The path is the DOS path to the directory you want to share (from your local drive, such as C:\LOTUS). The Comment field is available to further define the directory. Other users will also see this comment.

The "Re-Share at Startup" box defaults to on; this means that each time Windows starts it will offer this directory to others as a shared directory rather than forcing you to share it manually each time.

The Access Type box lets you define how the directory will be available to other users. The default is read-only, so users cannot delete, rename, create, or write to files in the directory. If you select Full, users will have complete access to the directory. You can also check "Depends on Password" to assign two levels of security to the directory, depending on which password the user enters.

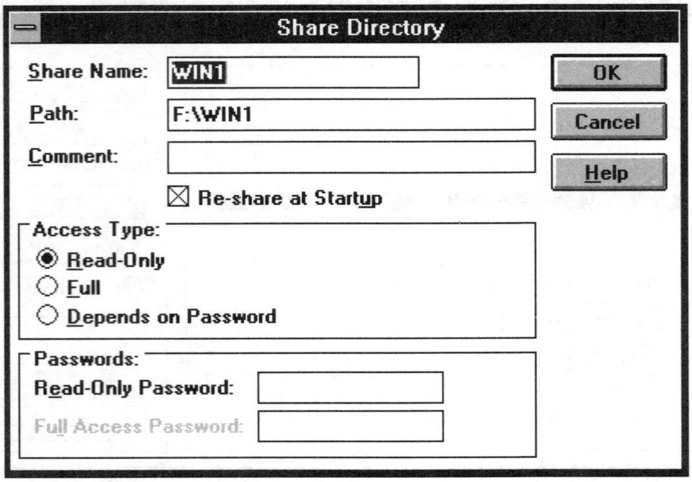

Figure 13.29 Share Directory window.

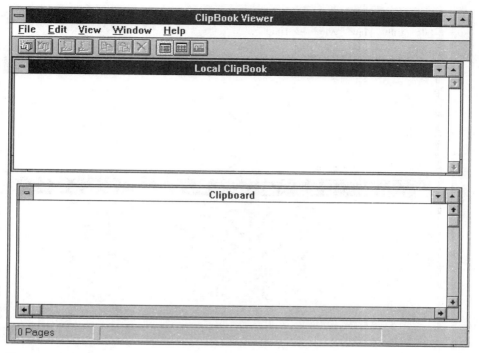

Figure 13.32 ClipBook Viewer main window.

name list format. Figure 13.35 shows the thumbnail view. The three buttons to the far left of the toolbar determine the listing format.

CONNECTING TO ANOTHER USER'S CLIPBOOK

If you want to access another user's ClipBook, press the button on the far left of the toolbar. You will then be presented with the "Select Computer" window in Figure 13.36. Here you can choose the computer to whose ClipBook you want to connect.

When you choose a computer name, a list of ClipBook items on that computer is displayed in a child window. To use one of these items, select it, then select the

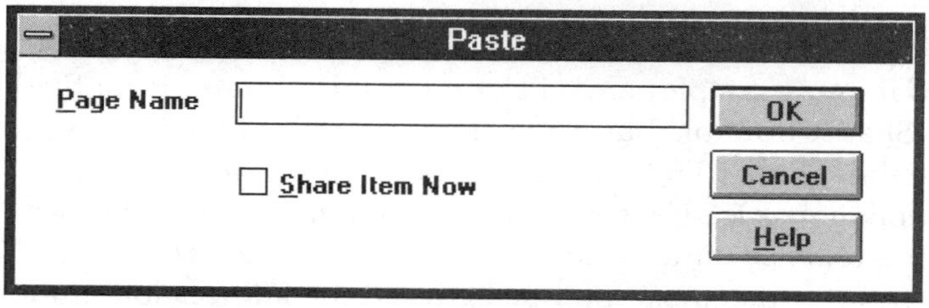

Figure 13.33 Paste dialog box.

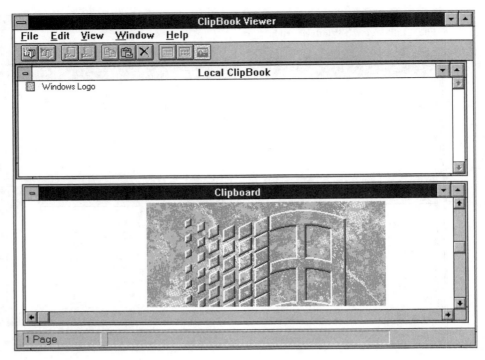

Figure 13.34 ClipBook Viewer in Name List format.

copy option from the Edit menu to copy the item to your local Clipboard. Finally, switch to the application in which you want to use the information and select its Edit Paste command.

> **Note:** Before you can access a ClipBook item from another user, that user must have made the item shareable to you. The same is true if you wish to make your ClipBook items available to other users. See the next section for details on sharing a ClipBook item.

SHARING YOUR CLIPBOOK WITH OTHER USERS

To make your ClipBook available to other users, select a ClipBook entry (we chose "Windows Logo" in our example) and click on the third button from the left in the toolbar, the "Share ClipBook" button, or choose the File Share menu selection. You will then see the "Share ClipBook Page" window in Figure 13.37.

The Sharing Options box lets you control whether the application that created the item in the Clipboard will be started when the other user connects to it. If the "host" computer is not running the application that created the information in the Clipboard, the "client" may have trouble performing a Windows link to the information.

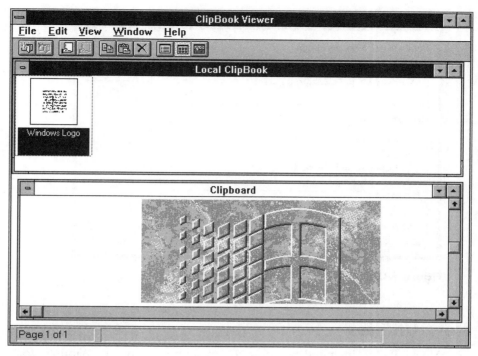

Figure 13.35 ClipBook Viewer in Thumbnail View.

The Access Type box determines whether remote users will have Read-Only, Full, or Password-Dependent access to the ClipBook page. The Passwords box lets you assign passwords to the appropriate access levels.

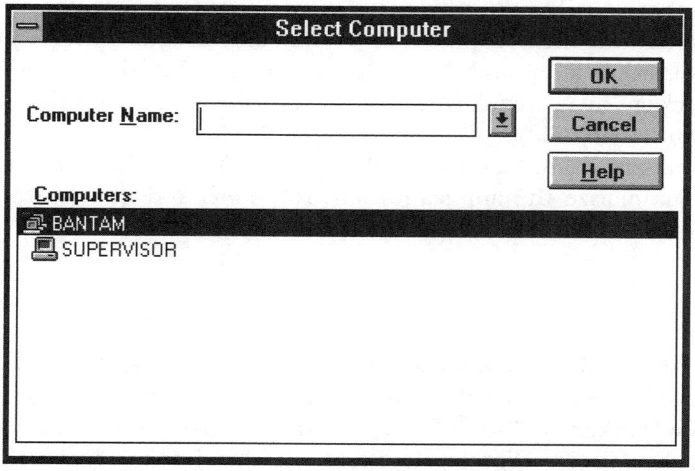

Figure 13.36 Select Computer dialog box.

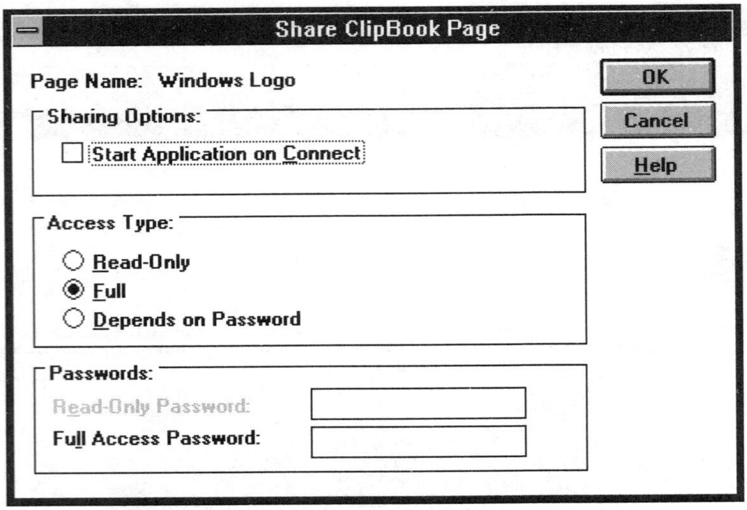

Figure 13.37 Share ClipBook Page dialog box.

New Utilities

Microsoft has included two new complete applications in Windows for Workgroups: Mail and Schedule+. Both applications are particularly appropriate to the networked environment and should prove useful. The reader should note, however, that these applications may not be as robust as some of the mature, third-party Email and scheduling products.

For instance, while this mail facility is good for local communications within your Windows Workgroup, it should be stressed that an upgrade to the full-blown Microsoft Mail and a post office is required in order to expand your Email reach outside of this workgroup. For this reason, it is still a good idea to select third-party Email applications with more robust and less expensive connectivity options. Nevertheless, this application and Schedule+ are included in the Windows for Workgroups package at no extra cost and are valuable as an introduction to electronic mail and scheduling.

Space does not permit a full discussion of each of the two applications. Instead we will briefly summarize the application environments and give you a short "walking tour" of each.

Mail

When you first start mail, you will see a window similar to Figure 13.38. If this is the first time Mail is being run on the network, the supervisor will have to choose the "Create a new Workgroup Profile" and set up a Workgroup Post Office. When you select OK, the "Create Workgroup Postoffice" window in Figure 13.39 is displayed. This dialog box lets you choose in which directory to put the Postoffice

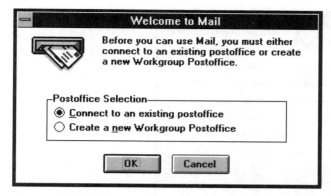

Figure 13.38 Mail Welcome window.

files. The Network button lets you connect to another user's disk if you want to place the Postoffice files there.

Once you've chosen a directory, you can fill in the Administrator Account details in Figure 13.40. You need to at least fill in the Mailbox field to specify the name of your mailbox on the system. The other fields—Phone, Office, Department, and Notes—are optional.

Once you have created the account details, you are reminded in Figure 13.41 that you just created the postoffice file on your local machine and you will need to share this drive before other users can access the post office (this is assuming that you have not done so already).

Although placing the Post Office on your machine is altruistic, it can place an undue burden on your processor, especially if a lot of users take full advantage of the Mail system. Therefore, you are better off placing the post office on either the least-used machine in your office or on the machine that belongs to someone you particularly dislike.

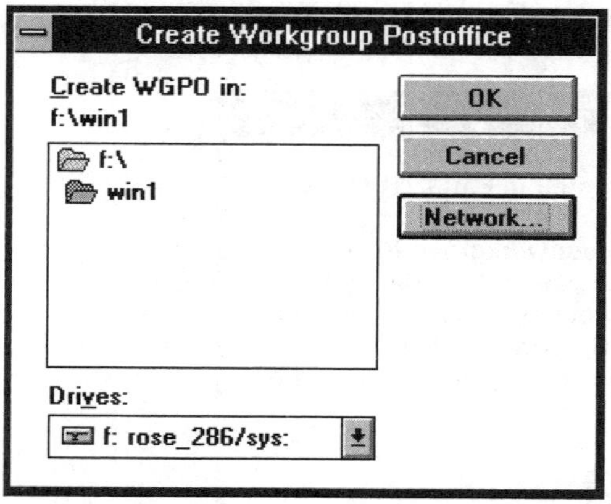

Figure 13.39 Create Workgroup Postoffice
dialog box.

Enter Your Administrator Account Details

Name:	SUPERVISOR
Mailbox:	
Password:	PASSWORD
Phone #1:	
Phone #2:	
Office:	
Department:	
Notes:	

OK   Cancel

Figure 13.40 Administrator Account Details
dialog box.

After you get the preliminaries out of the way, the main window for the Mail application appears, as shown in Figure 13.42. Icons representing mail folders appear on the left and the listing area to the right contains individual mail items within folders. A button bar at the top lets you perform specific actions on pieces of mail.

Suppose you want to send mail to someone else on the system. To do this, click on the Compose button. You will see an addressing window appear, as shown in Figure 13.43. Fill in the To: and Subject: fields, then enter your message below. Click on the Send button to send the message on its way.

When you receive mail, the mail icon in the lower right corner of the window indicates that new mail has arrived, as shown in Figure 13.44. Notice an additional line has been added, showing the source of the new mail.

If you double-click on this line, you will then see the contents of the mail item as shown in Figure 13.45. Notice that the Reply, ReplyAll, Forward, Move, and Delete buttons have turned on so you can now use them to respond to the mail item.

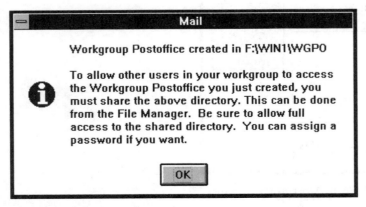

Mail

Workgroup Postoffice created in F:\WIN1\WGPO

To allow other users in your workgroup to access the Workgroup Postoffice you just created, you must share the above directory. This can be done from the File Manager. Be sure to allow full access to the shared directory. You can assign a password if you want.

OK

Figure 13.41 Post office creation reminder message window.

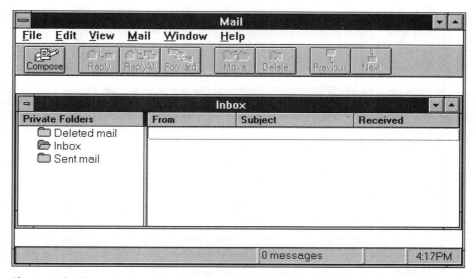

Figure 13.42 Mail main window.

Schedule+

Schedule+ works with the Mail application to provide a compact group scheduling system for a workgroup of users. When you first double-click on the Schedule+ icon located in the Main group, you will see the "Mail Sign In" window shown in Figure 13.46. This is necessary because the Schedule+ application may need to send mail to other users.

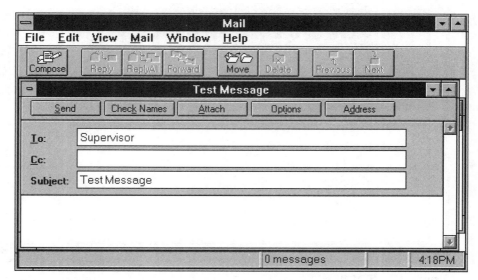

Figure 13.43 Message addressing window.

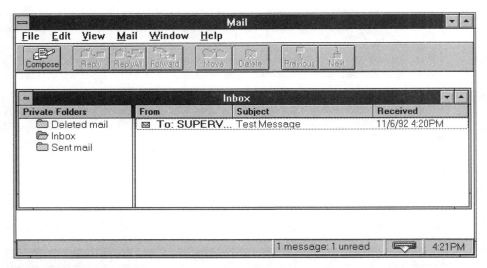

Figure 13.44 Mail main window, showing new mail.

Once you log on, the main window of Schedule+ appears, as shown in Figure 13.47. The window with your name in the title bar shows your private folder containing your Appointments, Planner, and Tasks list. Appointments are arranged by time, along with notes you may have for the day, and a calendar is displayed in the upper-right-hand corner.

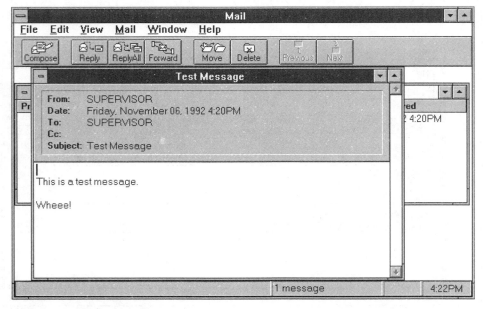

Figure 13.45 Mail item opened.

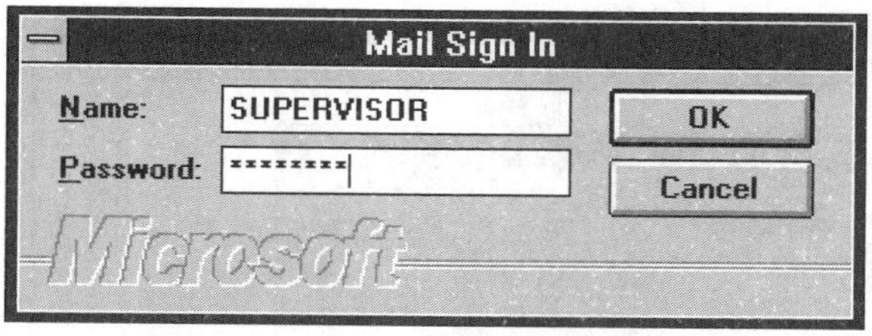

Figure 13.46 Schedule+ Mail Sign In window.

Clicking on the Planner "tab" brings up the Planner window shown in Figure 13.48. Here you can see your schedule at-a-glance and can request meetings with other users. You can also perform rudimentary conflict resolution to try to get everyone to agree on a certain time to meet.

If you click on the Tasks tab on the left of the window, you will see the Task list shown in Figure 13.49. You can see two sample tasks listed already. For each task you can assign due dates, priorities, and other characteristics.

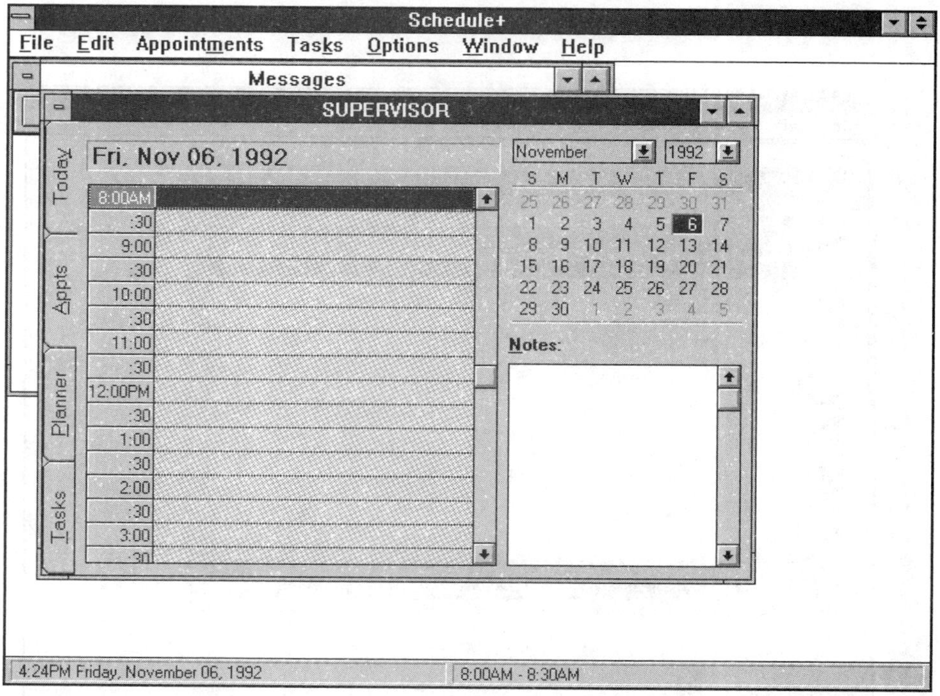

Figure 13.47 Schedule+ main window.

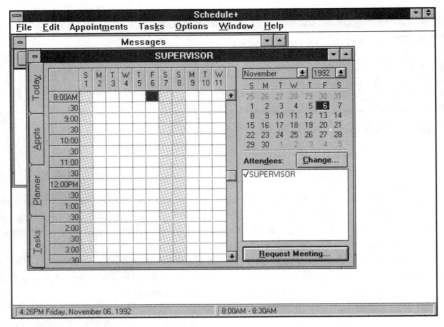

Figure 13.48 Planner window.

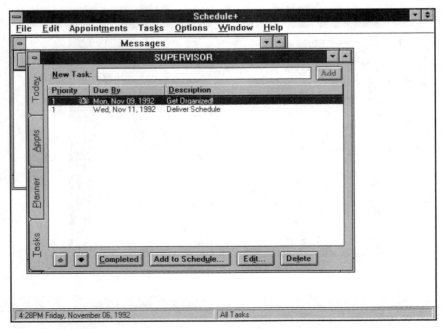

Figure 13.49 Tasks window.

New Accessories

Next, we will review the three new "mini-applications" in the Accessories group: Chat, Net Watcher, and Win Meter. Chat lets you dialog with other users on the network. Net Watcher lets you monitor to what resources on your computer other users are attached. Win Meter gives you a graphical illustration of the amount of CPU time used by your applications versus the amount of CPU time taken up by other users accessing the resources of your machine.

Chat

The main Chat window is very basic and appears in Figure 13.50. It consists of three toolbar buttons and two text windows—the window on top contains your dialog, and the window on the bottom contains the dialog you receive from your partner.

To place a call, or "Dial" as it is referred to in the Chat accessory, press the leftmost button in the toolbar (or choose Conversation Dial from the menu). You will then see the "Select Computer" dialog box shown in Figure 13.51. Simply choose the user with whom you want to chat. Since nobody else was on at the time, the author chose to chat with himself, user SUPERVISOR. When you are being called to chat, the chat icon of a ringing telephone appears in your window.

Figure 13.52 shows a chat session in progress on one computer with the author talking to himself. Normally, you would only have one Chat window up at a time and you would, of course, be talking with a remote computer (otherwise other users may suspect something).

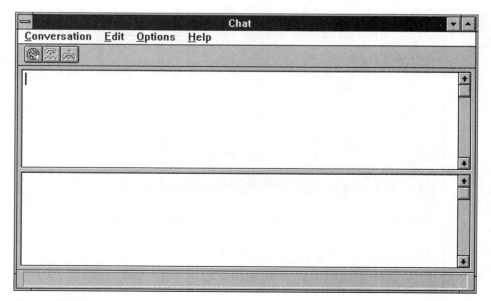

Figure 13.50 Chat window.

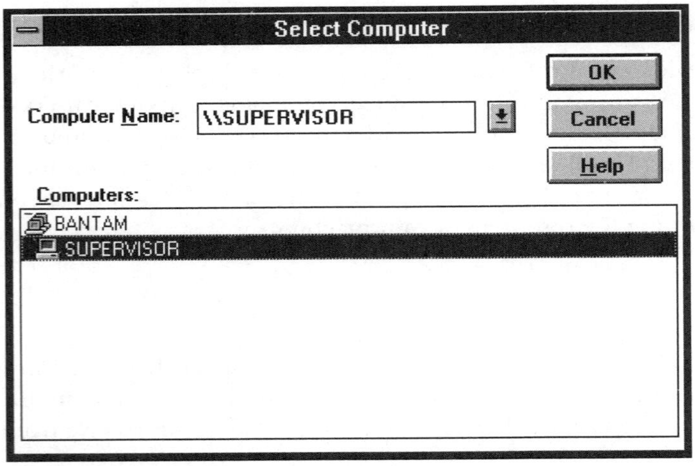

Figure 13.51 Select Computer dialog box.

WinMeter

WinMeter is an accessory that lets you determine your local system performance by gauging how much processor time is being devoted to your local applications versus sharing your resources with other users. It can be a handy tool to use to fine-tune your system.

Figure 13.53 shows the appearance of the basic WinMeter window and gives the options for the only menu item, "Settings." You can select the update interval between 5 seconds and 10 minutes. The other options are generally cosmetic.

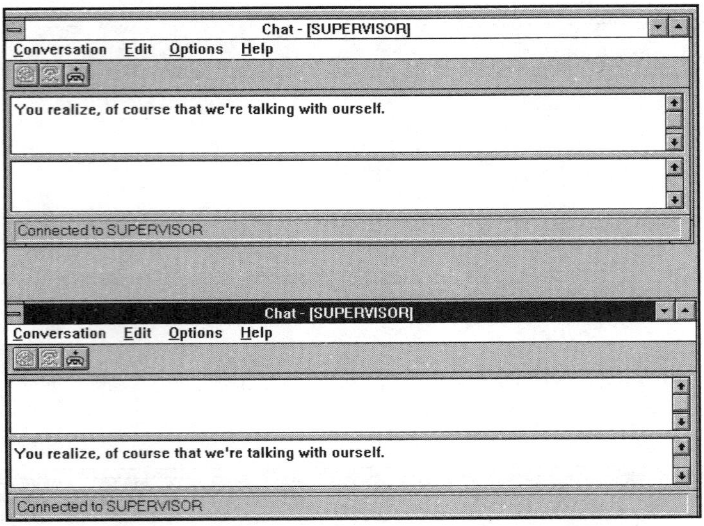

Figure 13.52 Chat session in progress.

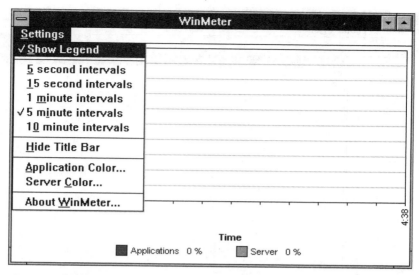

Figure 13.53 WinMeter Settings menu and main window.

If you let WinMeter run in the background while working on various projects, you can go back and check what the performance meter looks like. Figure 13.54 shows varying amounts of processor time being devoted to local applications and (so far) none to sharing resources with other users.

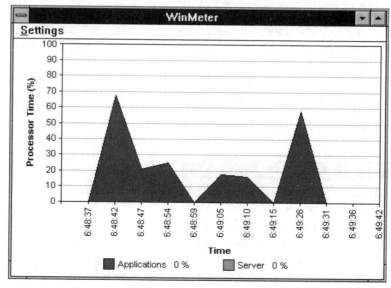

Figure 13.54 WinMeter in action.

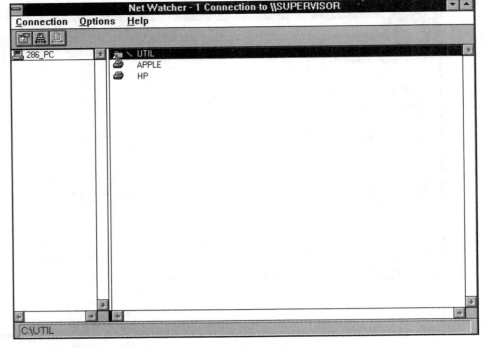

Figure 13.55 Net Watcher main window.

Net Watcher

If you are curious about who is attached to your system and what resources they are using, Net Watcher can show you this information. Figure 13.55 shows the Net Watcher window. In the example shown, a user called "286_PC" is attached to the author's local system using a directory called UTIL, and is attached to both the APPLE and HP printers.

If you select a user (286_PC in our example) and press the far left toolbar button, "Properties" (or choose Connection Properties from the menu), you will see detailed information about the remote computer that is using your resources. Figure 13.56, for example, shows the information about 286_PC.

Properties	
Computer Name:	286_PC
User Logged on:	286 PC
Network:	Microsoft Workgroup Client
Connected Since:	11/6/92 4:43:00PM (0:03:43)
Idle Time:	0:00:13

Figure 13.56 Net Watcher's Property window.

The middle button in the toolbar (or the Connection Disconnect menu choice) lets you disconnect a selected user from your machine. If you press it while the other user is sharing resources, you will receive a message like the one in Figure 13.57.

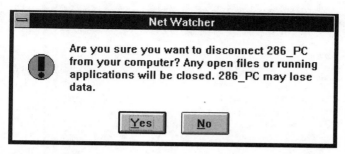

Figure 13.57 Net Watcher message.

14 Programming NetWare on Windows

Although the NetWare operating system is extremely useful as is, there are an almost unlimited number of applications and utilities that can be written to further enhance its functionality under Windows. Novell provides tools—documentation and C-function call libraries—that allow the programmer to take advantage of network resources from within a custom Windows application. As a result, the programmer can unite the elegance of the Windows GUI with the underlying power of NetWare.

This chapter explores the concepts involved in programming NetWare applications under Windows, and discusses how you can accomplish this with or without the use of Novell's function call libraries.

As you might imagine, developing for NetWare under Windows is very different (and more difficult) than developing for NetWare under DOS. Therefore, we'll start by briefly showing you the basics of programming for NetWare under DOS, then progress to programming under Windows. Along the way, we'll point out how NetWare programming concepts differ under the two environments.

After showing you the ropes, we'll roll up our sleeves and get down to some actual coding examples. First, you will be shown how to write NetWare-aware applications using Visual Basic as a programming platform. The resulting application will reveal your privileges for the current directory. Next, you will see how to create a Windows IPX chat utility (in C) that permits several users on the LAN to chat together at the same time. Finally, we'll develop a client-server database application using the Sequenced Packet Exchange (SPX) protocol. This will be accomplished using the Borland C++ environment to show how a Windows front-end application interfaces to a back-end DOS-based server on the LAN.

> **Note:** The source and executable code for all three of the example programs discussed in this chapter are included on the NetWare Power Tools for Windows diskettes that comes with this book. See Chapter 10 for details on installing the software.

What You'll Need

This chapter discusses the development of NetWare-aware Windows applications using several different types of development tools. For example, the following development tools were used to create the programs discussed in the balance of this chapter:

- Microsoft Visual Basic—An integrated Windows programming environment from Microsoft. This product allows you to create sophisticated Windows applications by using a powerful fourth-generation programming language.

- Borland C++ Development System—A powerful C/C++ programming environment from Borland International.

- The NetWare C Interface for Windows—A library of Windows dynamic-link libraries (DLLs) that provide C functions for NetWare function calls. You can get this product by contacting Novell Developer Relations at 1-800-NET-WARE. Please note that by the time you read this, Novell may have bundled this library into a product called the "NetWare Client SDK," which lets you write client applications for DOS, Windows, OS/2, and other platforms.

Since the executables are included on the disks accompanying this book, you can run any of the programs in this chapter whether you have any of the above tools. However, you will need the tools if you intend to modify the code.

Concepts

To discuss NetWare programming under Windows, you must first be comfortable with what's involved in programming each environment (NetWare and Windows) separately.

We will begin by discussing the elements of NetWare development, then focus on the Windows programming environment. While this chapter can't hope to teach you how to program in Windows or in NetWare—each topic could take volumes—it can get you started and give you some "live" working examples from wihich to learn, if you have a basic understanding of programming in C and are familiar with either environment.

NetWare Programming

When you want to connect your workstation (at the software level) to a Novell file server, you load several Terminate-and-Stay-Resident programs, the Novell shell files. These files, generally called IPX.COM and xNETX.COM (where x is blank, B, EMS, or XMS), provide the translation between DOS and the network. For example, when you type "DIR" at the command line, the workstation shell intercepts the request, sends it to the file server, receives the response, and passes the result back to DOS.

When we talk about "programming NetWare applications," we are actually talking about making calls directly to the shell files in memory. If we say "go to the server and get user BOB's object ID number," the shell will perform the communications functions for us.

When programming NetWare under DOS (without Windows) this task is accomplished by calling Interrupt 21h (or 2Fh for some other functions, like peer-to-peer communications). This interrupt is also used by DOS programmer's to access DOS services, such as Open File and Close File. (Under Windows, there are several other considerations, so it's not as easy as simply calling Interrupt 21h. We'll discuss the differences soon.)

You can use any programming language to develop NetWare applications, so long as you have access to the registers of the CPU and can make interrupt calls. Therefore, you can use C, Pascal, BASIC, Assembly, FORTH, Fortran, or another language that lets you access the lower-level functions of the PC (or link in Assembly language routines that do this).

There are two basic strategies you can use when programming NetWare applications: Code them yourself or use a code library. The decision is similar to writing a program with graphics—do you write the routines to do the graphics yourself, or do you buy a graphics library?

For those taking the first approach, you must set up and make the NetWare calls yourself. Therefore, your program must allocate space for a request buffer, the contents of which will be sent to the server and a reply buffer, to capture the packet coming back. You would have to place the appropriate values in the request buffer, initialize the reply buffer, and set up the registers.

After this is done, you're ready to call Interrupt 21h which activates the shell to make the request to the file server and place the reply into your reply buffer. When the call returns, you check the value of the AL register to see if the call was successful (0 for success).

By way of an example, suppose you wanted to find out the connection number you were using on the default server. This is the number you see next to your name when you type "USERLIST" at the DOS prompt. To do this, you can use the following C program:

```
#include <stdio.h>
#include <dos.h>

#typedef BYTE unsigned char;

BYTE GetConnectionNumber( void );

main()
{
    BYTE station;

    // Go get our connection number
    station = GetConnectionNumber();
```

```
    // And print out the results
    print( "Our connection number is %d.\n" );
}

BYTE GetConnectionNumber( void )
{
    _AH = 0xDC;

    geninterrupt( 0x21 );

    return _AL;
}
```

The program above does not contain request or reply packets, but it quickly illustrates what's involved in the simplest of NetWare API calls. In this case, you set the AH register to DCh, call Interrupt 21h, and the AL register is filled with your connection number.

On the other hand, if you were to use a function call library, like the NetWare C Interface, all you would need to do is set up your variables, call the function you need, like "GetConnectionNumber()," and then check the return value for success. To see what the program above would be like with a library, simply imagine the same code without the GetConnectionNumber() routine; this routine would be linked in.

An important point to remember, though, is that you still need to understand what's going on at the NetWare level regardless of whether you use the NetWare C Interface library or whether you code the calls yourself. In other words, you still need to know how the function calls work (what you pass to the call, what you get back, what the result of the function call will be, and so on).

Windows Programming

The Windows environment provides one of the most sophisticated and popular user interfaces for the PC today. The benefits gained by the user, however, are paid for by the developer. Developing a Windows application is considerably more involved than writing a DOS program. While this section cannot prepare you for writing Windows applications, it will give you an overview of the differences in programming NetWare applications under Windows versus under DOS.

The Windows environment has several major features that differentiate it from DOS. Foremost among them is the multi-tasking environment, where you must be courteous to other applications that may be running at the same time; you don't want to consume too many resources (memory, time, and so on) at once. Also, Windows is event-driven which means that your program reacts to what a user does ("Ok he hit the OK button, now what do we do?") rather than proactively going step-by-step through a program ("We ask him to hit the OK button, then we go do this . . . ").

Furthermore, there are several hundred function calls you can use to communicate with Windows. This, plus all of the possible messages your windows may receive, can add up to a mind-boggling array of possibilities. Also, you must be aware of how to use all of the resources available in Windows, such as windows, menus, controls, and dialog boxes.

As you learn to program in Windows, you'll become aware of the Dynamic-Link Library (DLL), which is a collection of routines that are kept in a separate file from the main executable and may be shared by different Windows programs. For instance, the Windows Common Dialog DLL (COM-MDLG.DLL) is used by many Windows programs and may be used by your programs as well. It provides resources like an "Open File" dialog box, a "Save As" dialog box, and others.

Another major difference between DOS and Windows development is that, with the introduction of Windows 3.1, all Windows programs run in the protected mode of the Intel 286/386/486 chip. This means, among other things, that your segment registers no longer point to segments—they point to selectors. A selector is an element of Intel's protected mode—you might think of it as a logical segment. A selector points to a physical segment.

This brings up an interesting point. While Windows runs in protected mode, DOS was written for and runs in real mode. To resolve this potential conflict, Microsoft came up with the DOS-Protected Mode Interface (DPMI) which lets programs running in protected mode communicate with other programs that must run in real mode (like DOS) and vice-versa.

While we won't get into DPMI programming specifics, you will see that Novell uses DPMI calls in their NetWare driver accompanying Windows in order to make NetWare function calls work correctly with Windows. This is necessary because Novell's workstation shell works only in real mode.

NetWare Programming Under Windows

Programming NetWare under Windows involves knowing how the Novell calls work and how to set them up in your program. You have the choice of making NetWare calls by setting up the registers and request/reply packets, and jumping to an entry point in NETWARE.DRV, or by using a development library like Novell's NetWare C Interface for Windows.

In Windows 3.0 and, to a greater extent in Windows 3.1, there are network functions built right into Windows, such as the Network icon in the Control Panel or the printer functions from the Control Panel that let you connect to network printers. These functions are specific to the type of network you have installed. For Novell networks, the NETWARE.DRV driver is used to provide these services. As you'll soon see, you can make calls to this driver yourself.

Here's how you can make a call to NetWare using only your low-level code (you don't need a library for this):

```
HANDLE hNetWareDrv;
long (FAR PASCAL *NetWareRequest) (void);

NetWareRequest = NULL;
hNetWareDrv = GetModuleHandle ("NETWARE");
if (hNetWareDrv != NULL) {
   (FARPROC) NetWareRequest = GetProcAddress (hNetWareDrv,
    "NetWareRequest");
}
```

If NetWareRequest != NULL, then NETWARE.DRV is loaded and available. If you're using other NetWare APIs, you could use LoadLibrary and GetProcAddress to get the API entry points.

Then, NetWareCall() passes the request and reply buffers:

```
BYTE NetWareCall (BYTE function_no, LPSTR request_buffer, LPSTR
 reply_buffer) {

    long (FAR PASCAL *NetWareRequest2) (void);
    BYTE rc;

    NetWareRequest2 = NetWareRequest;
    _asm push ds
    _asm push es
    _asm mov  ah,function_no
    _asm lds  si,request_buffer
    _asm les  di,reply_buffer
    NetWareRequest2();
    _asm pop  es
    _asm pop  ds
    _asm mov  rc,al

    return rc;

}
```

Note: The NetWareRequest2() function procedure had to be used; otherwise, Borland C++ tries to access the variable containing the procedure address relative to DS, which may be pointing to a different data segment. Using NetWareRequest2() here accessed it relative to SS instead.

Although the Windows environment is more involved than DOS, you can make NetWare calls yourself, rather than resorting to a function call library. However, be prepared to do more debugging. You should have a low-level NetWare API reference such as Novell's System Calls for DOS or the author's "Programmer's Guide to NetWare." See the appendices for a list of resources. Although making NetWare API calls under Windows is relatively straightforward, any peer-to-peer communications (like the Internetwork Packet Exchange [IPX]) will require that you use DPMI (the DOS-Protected Mode Interface) calls. When you reach that level of detail, it makes sense to purchase a library of NetWare calls for Windows like Novell's NetWare C Interface for Windows.

THE NETWARE C INTERFACE FOR WINDOWS

As of this writing, the NetWare C Interface for Windows is organized into three major DLL's:

• NWNETAPI.DLL   This DLL covers all major NetWare API function call groups, including Accounting, Bindery, File, Directory, Connection, Workstation, Print, Queue, and so on. This DLL will be used for most of your development needs.

- **NWIPXSPX.DLL** This DLL covers all of the IPX and Sequenced Packet Exchange (SPX) calls you may make from your application. Any peer-to-peer programming will involve this DLL. Also, API groups, such as the Service Advertising Protocol and the Diagnostic Services, which use IPX and SPX, will require that you use this DLL.

- **NWPSERV.DLL** This DLL includes the functions necessary to manipulate NetWare print servers. It includes the Print Server Services API.

To use the NetWare C Interface for Windows, you simply include the appropriate header files in your program and link in the library (.LIB) files (this would be NWNETAPI.LIB, NWIPXSPX.LIB, and NWPSERV.LIB). Then, when your program runs and a NetWare call is made, a NetWare DLL will be used to return the correct information.

The Windows examples in this book make calls to the NetWare C Interface for Windows. It is recommended that you obtain this toolkit from Novell if you plan to do any serious NetWare/Windows programming.

Developing NetWare Applications Using Visual Basic

Writing Windows programs in Visual Basic (VB) appeals to many because the environment simplifies so many aspects of Windows development. One of the nicer aspects of VB is that it runs entirely in Windows, so your code-run-debug-modify cycle is quick and you, the programmer, get to take advantage of the power of the user interface to quickly produce working Windows applications. Furthermore, development is done using "building blocks" provided by Microsoft—your code acts as a type of "cement" to bring everything together.

To add to this simple environment, wouldn't it be nice to make NetWare calls directly from VB? As this book goes to press, there are several companies working on DLL's that will allow you to make NetWare calls directly from VB.

For now, we will build our own "mini-library" DLL with a few calls (two or three) that we use in our example program. This is intended as food for thought if you develop applications in Visual Basic.

We have used the NetWare C Interface for Windows in our DLL to simplify matters. In other words, we make calls in Visual Basic to a DLL that we write in C. That DLL uses the NetWare C Interface for Windows to make NetWare API function calls.

We must use this intermediate step (our DLL written in C) rather than making calls directly to the Novell DLL's from VB because of limitations in Visual Basic's mechanism to call external routines. Although Novell has produced an Application Note showing how to make calls from Visual Basic to Novell DLL's directly, the writers chose to use only those calls that used data types that could be exchanged with Visual Basic. For instance, Visual Basic (as of this writing) lacks an unsigned character type passed by value, so no function calls involving this data type can be used.

Example Program

Often, the best way to learn is through an example. The first example program in this chapter displays your privileges for a given directory. This is done by displaying a window on screen (or, more accurately, a dialog box) that the user can manipulate. Figure 14.1 shows how that window appears on the screen. The main window is very simple—the elements are:

- Directory window

  Displays information about which directory is the current one

- Listbox

  Lists the rights associated with the current directory

- Combo Box

  Shows the current drive and lets the user select a different drive

- Quit button

  Lets the user quit the program

- Directory label

  Shows the current directory path

Generally the first thing done when making a Visual Basic program is to build the "Form." The Form is a white frame where you literally paste the controls you want in the window.

First, we paste the directory window, quit button, drive combo box, rights listbox, and static labels (such as "Directories:" and "Drives:"), as shown in Figure 14.2. Then we can attack the code for the Visual Basic side of our application.

Figure 14.1 RRights program main window.

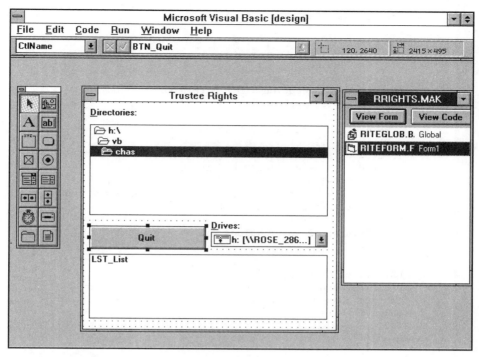

Figure 14.2 Visual Basic screen showing RRights under development.

To make calls to an external DLL (other than Windows internal DLLs), you need to declare the functions you are going to call in a global file. Our global file, RITEGLOB.BAS looks like:

```
Declare Function GetRites Lib "rightdll.dll" (ByVal hWnd%,
rights%, version%) As Integer
```

This declares a function (that we wrote in C) called GetRites. It's located in the RIGHTDLL.DLL file (covered shortly). We also tell Visual Basic that we want to pass three integers, hWnd, rights, and version. We pass hWnd by value; the others are passed by reference (a far pointer) and the function returns an integer. Now we can call GetRites in our Visual Basic code.

Next, we'll need to write some Visual Basic code to make things work together. Note that the controls described above are free-standing and work already; the directory box does indeed search the directory tree for the current drive and the drive combo box does let you search through a list of valid drives for your workstation.

However, we need to connect those controls together so they work as one cohesive application. To do this, we'll write a short Visual Basic application called RRights. Listing one shows that program.

```
Sub Form_Load ()
    Call DIR_Dirs_Change
End Sub
```

```
Sub Form_Unload (Cancel As Integer)
    End
End Sub

Sub DIR_Dirs_Change ()
    ' Show directory changed in label
    LAB_CurrentDir.Caption = DIR_Dirs.path
    ChDir DIR_Dirs.path

    ' Make call to NetWare DLL to get rights for current
    ' directory...
    item% = 0: ReturnValue% = 0: Version% = 0
    ReturnValue% = GetRites(Hwnd, item%, Version%)
    If (ReturnValue%) Then
        retVal = MsgBox("Invalid Network Drive, Error code = "+
            Str$(ReturnValue%), 16)
    End If
    Call PrintRites(ReturnValue%, item%, Version%)

End Sub

Sub DRV_Drives_Change ()
    DIR_Dirs.path = DRV_Drives.Drive
    ChDrive (DRV_Drives.Drive)
    Call DIR_Dirs_Change
End Sub

Sub PrintRites (ReturnValue%, item%, Version%)

    Dim r, w, o, c, e, a, f, m, s As Integer

    If (Version% <> 3 And Version% <> 2) Then
        retVal = MsgBox("Unsupported NetWare Version: " +
            Str$(Version%), 16)
        End
    End If

    For i = 1 To LST_List.ListCount
        LST_List.RemoveItem 0
    Next i

    r = (item% And 1)
    w = (item% And 2)
    c = (item% And 8)
    e = (item% And 16)
    a = (item% And 32)
    f = (item% And 64)
    m = (item% And 128)

    If (Version% = 3) Then
        s = (item% And 256)
    ElseIf (Version% = 2) Then
        o = (item% And 4)
    End If

    If (s) Then
        LST_List.AddItem "Supervisor (All Rights)"
    ElseIf (r And w And c And e And a And f And m And n And s And t) Then
        LST_List.AddItem "All Rights"
    End If
```

```
    If (r) Then LST_List.AddItem "Read"
    If (w) Then LST_List.AddItem "Write"
    If (c) Then LST_List.AddItem "Create"
    If (e) Then LST_List.AddItem "Erase"
    If (a) Then LST_List.AddItem "Access Control"
    If (f) Then LST_List.AddItem "File Scan"
    If (m) Then LST_List.AddItem "Modify"
End Sub

Sub BTN_Quit_Click ()
    End

End Sub
```

The following text explains each block of code in the RRights program (only six in all):

When the program starts, the Form_Load routine is run. You have the opportunity to put startup and initialization-type code here. In our example, we call the DIR_Dirs_Change routine which lists the current directory and the rights we have in that directory.

```
Sub Form_Load ()
    Call DIR_Dirs_Change
End Sub
```

The End command terminates the program and returns you to Windows. Form_Unload is run when someone wants to quit the program. You can put termination and cleanup code here if you like. In this case, no cleanup is necessary, so the program simply quits.

```
Sub Form_Unload (Cancel As Integer)
    End
End Sub
```

In the DIR_Dirs_Change routine, first the Current Directory label is set to the current path. In Visual Basic, setting the text of a control is as easy as an assignment (in Windows, it's more complicated and requires you to send a message to the control).

The ChDir routine is called, passing DIR_Dirs.path (the path specified in the directory listbox) as a parameter. This sets the path in the directory listbox as the current directory.

Next, we set up for the call to our custom-written DLL (you'll see the code for it a bit later). First, we set item, ReturnValue, and Version (all integers) to 0. Then we call GetRites and check ReturnValue to see if it's non-zero. If so, there was an error, so we print the error. Otherwise we call PrintRites (a Visual Basic subroutine) and exit the routine.

```
Sub DIR_Dirs_Change ()
    ' Show directory changed in label
    LAB_CurrentDir.Caption = DIR_Dirs.path
    ChDir DIR_Dirs.path

    ' Make call to NetWare DLL to get rights for current
    ' directory...
    item% = 0: ReturnValue% = 0: Version% = 0
```

```
        ReturnValue% = GetRites(hWnd, item%, Version%)
        If (ReturnValue%) Then
            retVal = MsgBox("Invalid Network Drive, Error code = " +
              Str$(ReturnValue%), 16)
        End If
        Call PrintRites(ReturnValue%, item%, Version%)

    End Sub
```

When you change the drive in the drive combo box, this routine sets the current drive to the one you specified. It then calls DIR_Dirs_Change to set the current directory and display the rights for it.

```
    Sub DRV_Drives_Change ()
        DIR_Dirs.path = DRV_Drives.Drive
        ChDrive (DRV_Drives.Drive)
        Call DIR_Dirs_Change
    End Sub
```

In this block of code, PrintRites simply displays the rights on the screen, as shown in Figure 14.3. The Version variable is used (it accepts two or three) to determine how to display the rights, since NetWare 286 (versions 2.15 and below) uses a different scheme for naming rights than NetWare 386 does. The model is simplistic, since you could have NetWare 286 version 2.2 and above. In this case, the program would have to test for a Minor NetWare version and pass this through but, in the interest of brevity, it has been left out.

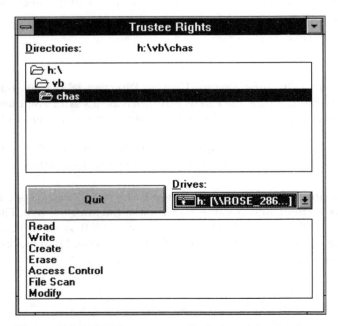

Figure 14.3 RRights program displaying rights for the current directory.

Next, the routine checks to see if a valid NetWare version was passed through. If so, the LST_List listbox is cleared out, then several flags are set or cleared. The r, w, c, e, a, f, m, s, and o variables correspond to certain rights. The code in PrintRites tests for each right, using the And operator to test bit-by-bit.

The Version variable is used to test for supervisory rights on NetWare 386 or the open right for NetWare 286. Also, a test is performed to see if all rights are available to the user.

Finally, each right flag is tested; if true, the corresponding English word is printed to the listbox to tell the user they have that right in the current directory.

```
Sub PrintRites (ReturnValue%, item%, Version%)

    Dim r, w, o, c, e, a, f, m, s As Integer

    If (Version% <> 3 And Version% <> 2) Then
        retVal = MsgBox("Unsupported NetWare Version: " +
          Str$(Version%), 16)
        End
    End If

    For i = 1 To LST_List.ListCount
        LST_List.RemoveItem 0
    Next i

    r = (item% And 1)
    w = (item% And 2)
    c = (item% And 8)
    e = (item% And 16)
    a = (item% And 32)
    f = (item% And 64)
    m = (item% And 128)

    If (Version% = 3) Then
        s = (item% And 256)
    ElseIf (Version% = 2) Then
        o = (item% And 4)
    End If

    If (s) Then
        LST_List.AddItem "Supervisor (All Rights)"
    ElseIf (r And w And c And e And a And f And m And n And s And t) Then
        LST_List.AddItem "All Rights"
    End If

    If (r) Then LST_List.AddItem "Read"
    If (w) Then LST_List.AddItem "Write"
    If (c) Then LST_List.AddItem "Create"
    If (e) Then LST_List.AddItem "Erase"
    If (a) Then LST_List.AddItem "Access Control"
    If (f) Then LST_List.AddItem "File Scan"
    If (m) Then LST_List.AddItem "Modify"

End Sub
```

The BTN_Quit_Click routine is run when the user presses the Quit button. It simply calls End to exit the program.

```
Sub BTN_Quit_Click ()
    End
End Sub
```

Although it's a fully-functional Windows program, RRights requires only a minimum of code to operate. Let's examine the C code we used to build the GetRites routine that we called in the DIR_Dirs_Change routine.

Here's the code to RIGHTDLL.C (which compiles into RIGHTDLL.DLL):

```
#include <windows.h>
#include <ctype.h>
#include <dir.h>

#include <nit.h>

// Prototypes
int FAR PASCAL GetRites( HANDLE hWnd, WORD far *rights, WORD far *ver );
WORD FAR PASCAL GetEffectiveRights( WORD serverConnID, BYTE dirHandle,
      char FAR *path, WORD FAR *rights );
BYTE FAR PASCAL GetDriveInformation( BYTE, WORD FAR *, BYTE FAR * );

#pragma argsused
int FAR PASCAL LibMain( HANDLE hInstance, WORD wDataSeg, WORD wHeapSize,
                LPSTR lpszCmdLine)
{
   if (wHeapSize > 0)
      UnlockData(0);
   return TRUE;
}

int FAR PASCAL GetRites( HANDLE hWnd, WORD far *rights, WORD far *ver )
{
    WORD connID, retVal;
    BYTE dirHandle, bRetVal, majVer, minVer, revLev;
    char message[80], path[80];

    strcpy( path, "." );

    retVal = GetNetWareShellVersion( &majVer, &minVer, &revLev );
    if ( !retVal )
        return 1;
    else
        *ver = majVer;

    bRetVal = GetDriveInformation( getdisk(), &connID, &dirHandle );
    // The following lines can be used for debugging:
    // wsprintf( message, "GetDriveInfo: connID is %X, dirHandle is %X,  returns %X",
    //      connID, dirHandle, bRetVal );
    // MessageBox( hWnd, message, NULL, MB_OK );

    retVal = GetEffectiveRights( connID, dirHandle, path, rights );
    // The following lines can be used for debugging:
    // wsprintf( message, "GetEffectiveRights returned %X, rights is %X",
    //      retVal, *rights );
    // MessageBox( hWnd, message, NULL, MB_OK );

    return retVal;
}
```

When you examine the C code to RIGHTDLL, you'll notice it's a very short DLL. It includes the required header (.h) files and declares local prototypes; there's a LibMain routine (which DLLs require) and our function, GetRites, which we call from Visual Basic.

Notice the declaration of GetRites. In Visual Basic, the first parameter was passed by value, and the other two were passed by reference. Our hWnd variable must be passed by value, while the other two, rights and ver, are passed by reference (far pointers). Also, the function returns an integer to Visual Basic.

The first step in GetRites is to set up the path variable (it contains a dot ".", the current directory). Then we make a call to Novell's NetWare C Interface for Windows DLL. We call GetDriveInformation, passing the current drive and returning the connection ID and directory handle for the current drive.

Then we call GetEffectiveRights below to see what rights the user has to the current directory. We pass the connection ID and dirHandle returned from GetDriveInformation (as well as the path variable we set up earlier), and we get back a WORD containing the rights mask in the rights variable. Finally, control returns to Visual Basic, passing the value returned from GetEffectiveRights.

Several debug lines are commented out in the source, but feel free to un-comment these lines and play with the return values. Also, error-handling and other enhancements should be added to these routines. In fact, you may want to build from this example program and work outward in a number of different directions.

When a Windows program uses external resources, as RIGHTDLL.DLL does, you'll need to create a module-definition (.DEF) file to tell the linker about the program's attributes and the resources needed. The .DEF file for RIGHTDLL.DLL looks like the following:

```
NAME            RIGHTDLL
EXETYPE         WINDOWS
DESCRIPTION     'VB-callable DLL for RRights version 1.0, Copyright
1992, Charles Rose'
STUB            'WINSTUB.EXE'
CODE            FIXED
DATA            FIXED SINGLE
HEAPSIZE        8192
STACKSIZE       8192
IMPORTS
        NWNETAPI.GetDefaultConnectionID
        NWNETAPI.GetEffectiveRights
        NWNETAPI.GetDirectoryHandle
        NWNETAPI.GetDriveInformation
        NWNETAPI.GetNetWareShellVersion
EXPORTS

        LibMain
        GetRites
```

In this DEF file, we do the standard things you would normally do in a Windows DEF file; that is, we state the name of the program, define it as a Windows EXE file, give it a description, add a stub program in case the user isn't running it under

Windows, define code and data segment flags, stack, and heap sizes. Next, we list the routines we will be importing from other DLLs, namely Novell's NWNETAPI DLL (part of the NetWare C Interface for Windows). Finally, we list the routines that are being exported to Windows and are available to be called (in this case Windows calls LibMain and our Visual Basic program will be calling GetRites).

> **Note:** The RRIGHTS.EXE program, or more accurately RIGHTDLL.EXE, must be able to find the NWNETAPI.DLL file. If it cannot find this file, an error message will be displayed.

The best way to become familiar with this (or for that matter, any) type of development platform is to play and experiment. We suggest you start with this example as a base and add features to it. The program is only a simple starting point from which you could go in several different directions.

Building Windows Applications in C

Perhaps the most flexible and popular language for Windows development is C. This section will explore a Windows chat utility, WCHAT, that was written in C, and show you how to build your own C-based Windows applications.

This section can serve neither as a tutorial in Windows programming nor as instruction for all you need to know about programming NetWare. Each of those subjects has filled entire books, such as the author's *Programmer's Guide to NetWare* (see the Appendices for further information). What we can do, however, is see the results of combining the two disciplines in applications in which the user benefits from the power of the Windows user interface coupled with the flexibility and resources available from the NetWare API.

Our example program, WCHAT, lets the user communicate with others on the LAN who are running WCHAT at the same time. It's a real-time, character-by-character, chat utility. There's essentially no limit to the number of users that may communicate at the same time.

Listing two shows the C source code for WCHAT in WCHAT.C. Figure 14.4 shows how the application appears on the screen. See Chapter 10 for details on installing the software.

```
//
// WChat — Windows "party-line" chat program for NetWare
//
// Charles Rose
//

#include <windows.h>
#include <bwcc.h>
#include <nwconn.h>
#include <nwsync.h>
#include <nwmisc.h>
#include <nxt.h>
#include "wchat.h"
```

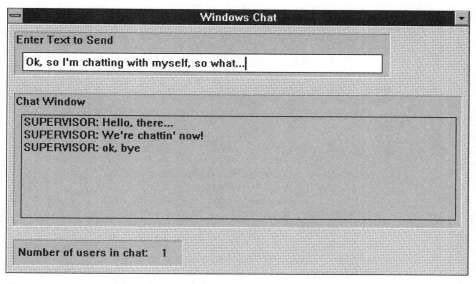

Figure 14.4 WCHAT main window.

```
#define ECBMAX 3
#define LINEMAX 120
#define CHAT_SOCKET 0x2000
#define SHORT_LIVED 0

typedef char TextLine[LINEMAX+1];

/* Local Prototypes */
long FAR PASCAL WndProc( HWND, WORD, WORD, LONG );
long FAR PASCAL EditProc( HWND, WORD, WORD, LONG );

// Windows globals
HWND hMain;
HANDLE hInst;
FARPROC lpfnOldEditProc, lpfnEditProc;
char szAppName[] = "WChat";

// NetWare globals
WORD          semaphoreValue = 127;
DWORD         semaphoreHandle;
WORD          openCount;

ECB           ECBRcv[ECBMAX];
IPXHeader     IPXRcv[ECBMAX];
TextLine      RcvPacket[ECBMAX];
ECB           ECBSnd;
IPXHeader     IPXSnd;
DWORD         IPXTaskID = 0;
WORD          socket;
IPXAddress    ourAddress;
IPXAddress    destAddress = { { 0, 0, 0, 0 },
                { 0xFF, 0xFF, 0xFF, 0xFF, 0xFF, 0xFF },
                { 0x00, 0x20 } };
int           curPkt = 0;
```

```
BOOL            processing = FALSE;
#pragma argsused
int PASCAL WinMain( HANDLE hInstance, HANDLE hPrevInstance,
        LPSTR lpszCmdLine, int nCmdShow )
{
    MSG             msg;
    HWND            hWnd, hWndTemp;
    WNDCLASS        wndclass;
    char            buffer[80];
    char            szAppName[] = "BorDlg_WChat";

    if (hPrevInstance)
    {
        hWndTemp = FindWindow (szAppName, NULL);
        if (IsIconic (hWndTemp))
                SendMessage (hWndTemp, WM_SYSCOMMAND, SC_RESTORE, 0L);
        SetFocus (hWndTemp);
        return FALSE;
    }

    /* Register window class and create window */
    wndclass.style          = CS_HREDRAW | CS_VREDRAW;
    wndclass.lpfnWndProc    = (WNDPROC) WndProc;
    wndclass.cbClsExtra     = 0;
    wndclass.cbWndExtra     = DLGWINDOWEXTRA;
    wndclass.hInstance      = hInstance;
    wndclass.hIcon          = NULL;
    wndclass.hCursor        = LoadCursor( NULL, IDC_ARROW );
    wndclass.hbrBackground  = NULL;
    wndclass.lpszMenuName   = NULL;
    wndclass.lpszClassName  = "BorDlg_WChat";

    if ( !RegisterClass( &wndclass ) )
        return FALSE;

    hMain = hWnd = CreateDialog( hInstance, szAppName , 0, NULL  );
      hInst = hInstance;

    // Display the main window
    ShowWindow( hWnd, nCmdShow );
    UpdateWindow( hWnd );

    // Subclass the edit control
    lpfnEditProc = MakeProcInstance( (FARPROC) EditProc, hInst );
    lpfnOldEditProc = (FARPROC) GetWindowLong( GetDlgItem( hWnd,
      WC_TEXT ), GWL_WNDPROC );
    SetWindowLong( GetDlgItem( hWnd, WC_TEXT ), GWL_WNDPROC, (LONG)
      lpfnEditProc );

    // Restrict send message length
    SendDlgItemMessage( hWnd, WC_TEXT, EM_LIMITTEXT, (WPARAM)LINEMAX40, 0L );

       // Enter the message loop
    while ( GetMessage( &msg, NULL, 0, 0 ) )
    {
        TranslateMessage( &msg );
        DispatchMessage( &msg );
    }

    return msg.wParam;
```

```
}

long FAR PASCAL WndProc( HWND hWnd, WORD iMessage, WORD wParam, LONG lParam )
{
    char buffer[80], *editWin;
    int buffSize, start;
    LPSTR lpGlobalBuffer;
    HANDLE hGlobalBuffer;
    POINT Point;
    WORD result;
    int i;

    switch ( iMessage )
    {
        case WM_CREATE:
            // Fire up the semaphore
            if ( OpenSemaphore( "Semaphore Test", semaphoreValue,
               &semaphoreHandle,
                            &openCount ) )
            {
                MessageBox( hWnd, "Error opening semaphore",
                   szAppName,
                            MB_OK | MB_ICONEXCLAMATION );
                DestroyWindow( hWnd );
            }

            // Initialize IPX & Open a socket & Post a listening ECB
            if ( result = IPXInitialize( &IPXTaskID, NULL, NULL ) )
            {
                sprintf( buffer, "Error initializing IPX, error = %X",
                   result );
                MessageBox( hWnd, buffer, szAppName,
                   MB_OK | MB_ICONEXCLAMATION );
                DestroyWindow( hWnd );
            }

            IPXGetInternetworkAddress( IPXTaskID, (BYTE FAR *) &ourAddress );
            socket = CHAT_SOCKET;
            if ( result = IPXOpenSocket( IPXTaskID, &socket, SHORT_LIVED ) )
            {
                sprintf( buffer, "Error opening socket, error = %X",
                   result );
                MessageBox( hWnd, buffer, szAppName, MB_OK |
                   MB_ICONEXCLAMATION );
                DestroyWindow( hWnd );
            }
            for ( i = 0; i < ECBMAX; i++ )
            {
                ECBRcv[i].ESRAddress = 0;
                ECBRcv[i].socketNumber = socket;
                ECBRcv[i].fragmentCount = 2;
                ECBRcv[i].fragmentDescriptor[0].address = ( void far *
                   )&IPXRcv[i];
                ECBRcv[i].fragmentDescriptor[0].size = sizeof( IPXRcv[i] );
                ECBRcv[i].fragmentDescriptor[1].address = ( void far *
                   )&RcvPacket[i];
                ECBRcv[i].fragmentDescriptor[1].size = sizeof(
                   RcvPacket[i] );
```

```
                    IPXListenForPacket( IPXTaskID, &ECBRcv[i] );
        }

        // Start the user check timer, every 5 seconds
        if ( !SetTimer( hWnd, 1, 5000, NULL ) )
        {
            MessageBox( hWnd, "Too many clocks or timers", szAppName,
                    MB_OK | MB_ICONEXCLAMATION );
            DestroyWindow( hWnd );
        }

        // Start the packet check timer, every 3 seconds
        if ( !SetTimer( hWnd, 2, 3000, NULL ) )
        {
            MessageBox( hWnd, "Too many clocks or timers", szAppName,
                    MB_OK | MB_ICONEXCLAMATION );
            DestroyWindow( hWnd );
        }

        break;

case WM_DESTROY:
        // Get rid of timer
        KillTimer( hWnd, 1 );
        // Close Semaphore
        if ( CloseSemaphore( semaphoreHandle ) )
          MessageBox( hWnd, "Error closing semaphore", szAppName,
                    MB_OK | MB_ICONEXCLAMATION );

        // Close socket
        IPXCloseSocket( IPXTaskID, socket );

        // Outta here
        PostQuitMessage( 0 );
        break;

case WM_SETFOCUS:
        SetFocus( GetDlgItem( hWnd, WC_TEXT ) );
        break;

case WM_TIMER:
        // Check to see what kind of timer it is

        switch( wParam )
        {
            // Timer 1:
            // Check semaphore value
            case 1:
                if ( ExamineSemaphore( semaphoreHandle,
                  &semaphoreValue, &openCount ) )
                {
                    MessageBox( hWnd, "Error examining semaphore",
                      szAppName, MB_OK | MB_ICONEXCLAMATION );

                    DestroyWindow( hWnd );
                    break;
                }
                sprintf( buffer, "Number of users in chat:  %2d",
                  openCount );
                SetWindowText( GetDlgItem( hWnd, WC_USERS ), buffer );
```

```
                break;

                // Timer 2:
                // Check listening ECB for incoming
                // If it's there use SetWindowText, etc.
        case 2:
                if ( processing == TRUE )
                    break;
                processing = TRUE;
                start = curPkt;
                while ( 1 )
                {
                    if ( !ECBRcv[curPkt].inUseFlag )
                    {
                        if ( ECBRcv[curPkt].completionCode )
                        {
                            sprintf( buffer, "Error
                              receiving packet, completion
                              code = %X\n",
                            ECBRcv[curPkt].completionCode );
                            MessageBox( hWnd, buffer,
                              szAppName, MB_OK |
                              MB_ICONEXCLAMATION );
                            DestroyWindow( hWnd );
                            return 0;
                        }
                        else
                        {
                        // Add the incoming text to our listbox
                            SendDlgItemMessage( hWnd,
WC_DISPLAY, LB_ADDSTRING, 0, (LPARAM) (LPCSTR)RcvPacket[curPkt] );
                            if ( SendDlgItemMessage( hWnd,
WC_DISPLAY, LB_GETCOUNT, 0, 0L ) > 8 )
                                SendDlgItemMessage( hWnd,
WC_DISPLAY, LB_DELETESTRING, 0, 0L );

                            // Listen for the next packet
                            IPXListenForPacket( IPXTaskID,
                              &ECBRcv[curPkt] );
                        }
                    }

                    // Advance current packet
                    if ( curPkt == ECBMAX1 )
                        curPkt = 0;
                    else
                        curPkt++;

                    if ( curPkt == start )
                        break;

                }
                processing = FALSE;
                break;

        }

        break;
```

```
                    default:
                            return BWCCDefWindowProc( hWnd, iMessage, wParam, lParam );
            }

            return 0;
}

long FAR PASCAL EditProc( HWND hWnd, WORD iMessage, WORD wParam, LONG lParam )
{
        TextLine typedText, buffer;
        WORD result, objType;
        DWORD objID;
        BYTE loginTime[7];

           // If we received a character that's a Carriage Return, send the line
           // if ( ( iMessage == WM_CHAR ) && ( wParam == 13 ) )
           {
                   // Clear the structures
                memset( &IPXSnd, NULL, sizeof( IPXSnd ) );
                memset( &ECBSnd, NULL, sizeof( ECBSnd ) );

                        // Set to broadcast (all FF's)
                memset( IPXSnd.destination.node, 0xFF, 6 );
                memset( ECBSnd.immediateAddress, 0xFF, 6 );

                        // Then setup the rest of the ECB
                ( *((WORD *)IPXSnd.destination.socket) ) = socket;

                ECBSnd.ESRAddress = 0;
                ECBSnd.socketNumber = socket;
                ECBSnd.fragmentCount = 2;

                ECBSnd.fragmentDescriptor[0].address = ( void far * )&IPXSnd;
                ECBSnd.fragmentDescriptor[0].size = sizeof( IPXSnd );

                        // Get the text we typed into the edit control
                GetWindowText( hWnd, typedText, LINEMAX+1 );
                SetWindowText( hWnd, "" );

                        // Then get our user name and construct the line to send
                GetConnectionInformation( GetConnectionNumber(), buffer,
                &objType, &objID, &loginTime );
                strcat( buffer, ": " );
                strncat( buffer, typedText, LINEMAXstrlen( buffer )-1 );

                        // Address the line as the 2nd ECB fragment (the first
                        // is the IPX header)
                ECBSnd.fragmentDescriptor[1].address = ( void far * )buffer;
                ECBSnd.fragmentDescriptor[1].size = sizeof( TextLine );

                        // Send the packet, then wait for it to complete,
                        // then check if it went out ok
                IPXSendPacket( IPXTaskID, &ECBSnd );

                while ( ECBSnd.inUseFlag )
                    IPXYield();

                if ( ECBSnd.completionCode )
                {
```

```
                        sprintf( buffer, "Error sending packet, completion
                           code = %X", ECBSnd.completionCode );
                        MessageBox( hWnd, buffer, szAppName, MB_OK | MB_ICONEXCLAMATION );
                        DestroyWindow( hMain );
                     }

                  return TRUE;
               }
            else
               return CallWindowProc( lpfnOldEditProc, hWnd, iMessage,
                  wParam, lParam );
   }

BOOL AddrCmp( char *c1, char *c2 )
{
     int i;

     for ( i = 0; i < 6; i++ )
          if ( c1[i] != c2[i] )
               return FALSE;
     return TRUE;
}
```

Perhaps the best way to understand how WCHAT works is to first try it out. (You'll find a copy on the disks that come with this book.) Load WCHAT on two workstations on your network that are running Windows and type back and forth between them. Then come back here and we will go over the program. (See Chapter 10 for details on installing the software.)

As with the Visual Basic example, discussed above, we will explain the WCHAT program several lines at a time. As with any C program, the first thing we must do is to include the relevant header files. Here we include the standard Windows header file WINDOWS.H. We use BWCC.H, Borland's Custom Controls Library header file. NWCONN.H, NWSYNC.H, NWMISC.H, and NXT.H are Novell NetWare C Interface for Windows header files. They contain the C prototypes for the NetWare functions we will use in the program. Finally, we include WCHAT.H, which contains the #defines for the constants we will be using.

```
//
// WChat -- Windows "party-line" chat program for NetWare
//
// Charles Rose
//

#include <windows.h>
#include <bwcc.h>
#include <nwconn.h>
#include <nwsync.h>
#include <nwmisc.h>
#include <nxt.h>
#include "wchat.h"
#define ECBMAX 3
#define LINEMAX 120
#define CHAT_SOCKET 0x2000
#define SHORT_LIVED 0

typedef char TextLine[LINEMAX+1];
```

```
/* Local Prototypes */
long FAR PASCAL WndProc( HWND, WORD, WORD, LONG );
long FAR PASCAL EditProc( HWND, WORD, WORD, LONG );

// Windows globals
HWND hMain;
HANDLE hInst;
FARPROC lpfnOldEditProc, lpfnEditProc;
char szAppName[] = "WChat";

// NetWare globals
WORD        semaphoreValue = 127;
DWORD       semaphoreHandle;
WORD        openCount;

ECB         ECBRcv[ECBMAX];
IPXHeader   IPXRcv[ECBMAX];
TextLine    RcvPacket[ECBMAX];
ECB         ECBSnd;
IPXHeader   IPXSnd;
DWORD       IPXTaskID = 0;
WORD        socket;
IPXAddress  ourAddress;
IPXAddress  destAddress = { { 0, 0, 0, 0 },
                { 0xFF, 0xFF, 0xFF, 0xFF, 0xFF, 0xFF },
                { 0x00, 0x20 } };
int         curPkt = 0;
BOOL        processing = FALSE;
```

WCHAT.H is also used in the resource file (WCHAT.RC). WCHAT.H consists of the following:

```
#define DIALOG_1     1
#define IDS_NAME     2
#define WC_TEXT      101
#define WC_USERS     102
#define WC_DISPLAY   103
```

Next we define some local constants that you might want to change when developing the program. Local function prototypes are defined, as well as global variables. The globals are separated into those related to Windows functions and those related to NetWare functions for better organization.

Now we're ready to define the WinMain function where Windows programs usually begin. The first thing we do in this block of code is check to see if there is another copy of WCHAT running on this workstation. If so, we check to see if it's been reduced to an icon. If it is reduced, we restore it to its former windowed state and switch control to it because we're not set up to handle multiple instances of our program. Then we register a class for our window. Next, we call CreateDialog to tell Windows to construct the window. In this case, our main window is a dialog box, rather than a standard window. We do this because we don't really need a "background" window for our application; we want to create a modeless dialog box instead. We also set a global variable, hInst, to the hInstance value.

```
#pragma argsused
```

```
int PASCAL WinMain( HANDLE hInstance, HANDLE hPrevInstance,
        LPSTR lpszCmdLine, int nCmdShow )
{
    MSG                 msg;
    HWND                hWnd, hWndTemp;
    WNDCLASS            wndclass;
    char                buffer[80];
    char                szAppName[] = "BorDlg_WChat";

    if (hPrevInstance)
    {
        hWndTemp = FindWindow (szAppName, NULL);
        if (IsIconic (hWndTemp))
            SendMessage (hWndTemp, WM_SYSCOMMAND, SC_RESTORE, 0L);

        SetFocus (hWndTemp);
        return FALSE;
    }

    /* Register window class and create window */
    wndclass.style          = CS_HREDRAW | CS_VREDRAW;
    wndclass.lpfnWndProc    = (WNDPROC) WndProc;
    wndclass.cbClsExtra     = 0;
    wndclass.cbWndExtra     = DLGWINDOWEXTRA;
    wndclass.hInstance      = hInstance;
    wndclass.hIcon          = NULL;
    wndclass.hCursor        = LoadCursor( NULL, IDC_ARROW );
    wndclass.hbrBackground  = NULL;
    wndclass.lpszMenuName   = NULL;
    wndclass.lpszClassName  = "BorDlg_WChat";

    if ( !RegisterClass( &wndclass ) )
        return FALSE;

    hMain = hWnd = CreateDialog( hInstance, szAppName , 0, NULL  );
    hInst = hInstance;
```

Here, we call ShowWindow() to display the main window on the screen and UpdateWindow to paint it. Next, we subclass the edit control in the dialog box, so that we can "get at" the text a user types. When we see that the user has pressed the Enter key, we will then send the line of text out to other workstations over the network. The last line sends a Windows message to the text box, limiting the length of the line a user can type.

```
// Display the main window
ShowWindow( hWnd, nCmdShow );
UpdateWindow( hWnd );

// Subclass the edit control
lpfnEditProc = MakeProcInstance( (FARPROC) EditProc, hInst );
lpfnOldEditProc = (FARPROC) GetWindowLong( GetDlgItem( hWnd,
  WC_TEXT ), GWL_WNDPROC );
SetWindowLong( GetDlgItem( hWnd, WC_TEXT ), GWL_WNDPROC, (LONG)
  lpfnEditProc );

// Restrict send message length
SendDlgItemMessage( hWnd, WC_TEXT, EM_LIMITTEXT, (WPARAM)LINEMAX-40, 0L );
```

The remainder of WinMain is the standard Windows message loop.

```
while ( GetMessage( &msg, NULL, 0, 0 ) )
{
    TranslateMessage( &msg );
    DispatchMessage( &msg );
}

return msg.wParam;
}
```

This next function is WndProc, which handles the messages for our main window. As is common, there is a large case statement to handle the different types of messages that it receives.

Here, WM_CREATE is sent to the window when it is born into the world. In this function, we can place all kinds of initialization code; that's just what you see here. First, we start the semaphore (a NetWare facility for controlling access to a resource) called "Semaphore Test" (named Test because we're testing things out). We will use the semaphore to count the number of people concurrently using the chat program, rather than limiting the number of users in it at once (which is what a semaphore is often used for). Without some kind of counting routine, you wouldn't know how many people were out there chatting and listening.

We use the NetWare C Interface for Windows OpenSemaphore() call to handle opening the semaphore. Then we check the return value. If it was non-zero, then there was an error; so, we put up a message box to the user stating the problem, and we call DestroyWindow to quit the application (because we consider this a fatal error).

```
long FAR PASCAL WndProc( HWND hWnd, WORD iMessage, WORD wParam, LONG lParam )
{
    char buffer[80], *editWin;
    int buffSize, start;
    LPSTR lpGlobalBuffer;
    HANDLE hGlobalBuffer;
    POINT Point;
    WORD result;
    int i;

    switch ( iMessage )
    {
        case WM_CREATE:
            // Fire up the semaphore
            if ( OpenSemaphore( "Semaphore Test", semaphoreValue,
              &semaphoreHandle, &openCount ) )
            {
                MessageBox( hWnd, "Error opening semaphore", szAppName,
                        MB_OK | MB_ICONEXCLAMATION );
                DestroyWindow( hWnd );
            }
```

Next, we call IPXInitialize(), which you must do before using any IPX or SPX functions with the NetWare C Interface for Windows. This call returns a value in IPXTaskID, which you will use in all subsequent IPX calls. This task ID helps the

NetWare shell figure out which task in the machine is talking or listening (you could have several applications in Windows concurrently trying to communicate across the LAN using IPX).

Next we call IPXGetInternetworkAddress to determine what our address is. This will be handy later if we ever need to compare our address to the addresses on the packets we receive (to see if we sent it or not).

```
// Initialize IPX & Open a socket & Post a listening ECB
if ( result = IPXInitialize( &IPXTaskID, NULL, NULL ) )
{
    sprintf( buffer, "Error initializing IPX, error = %X",
        result );
    MessageBox( hWnd, buffer, szAppName, MB_OK |
        MB_ICONEXCLAMATION );
    DestroyWindow( hWnd );
}

IPXGetInternetworkAddress( IPXTaskID, (BYTE FAR *) &ourAddress );
```

After initializing IPX we want to open the socket (like a CB radio "channel" within a particular node you want to talk on) we will be using to communicate. We call IPXOpenSocket to do this.

```
socket = CHAT_SOCKET;
if ( result = IPXOpenSocket( IPXTaskID, &socket, SHORT_LIVED ) )
{
    sprintf( buffer, "Error opening socket, error = %X", result );
    MessageBox( hWnd, buffer, szAppName, MB_OK |
        MB_ICONEXCLAMATION );
    DestroyWindow( hWnd );
}
```

Once the socket is open, we set up an array of Event Control Blocks (ECBs) that will be listening for incoming packets. These ECBs will be our ears to other workstations. For each ECB, we set the ESRAddress to 0 (no Event Service Routine). We set up the socket number and set the fragmentCount to 2. Fragments are places where the incoming (or outgoing) data comprising the packet is stored. In this case, we have two fragments: one for the packet header, and one for the actual data.

Fragment 0 is IPXRcv, an array of IPX header structures, and Fragment 1 is wRcvPacket, an array of WORDs. So, each packet consists of a 30-byte header followed by 2 bytes of data (we send so little data because communication is sent character-by-character).

Finally, we call IPXListenForPacket which posts the ECB to a queue of ECBs that are now listening for incoming packets on a particular socket.

```
for ( i = 0; i < ECBMAX; i++ )
{
    ECBRcv[i].ESRAddress = 0;
    ECBRcv[i].socketNumber = socket;
    ECBRcv[i].fragmentCount = 2;

    ECBRcv[i].fragmentDescriptor[0].address = ( void far *
        )&IPXRcv[i];
    ECBRcv[i].fragmentDescriptor[0].size = sizeof( IPXRcv[i] );
```

```
            ECBRcv[i].fragmentDescriptor[1].address =
              ( void far * )&wRcvPacket[i];
            ECBRcv[i].fragmentDescriptor[1].size = sizeof(
              wRcvPacket[i] );

            IPXListenForPacket( IPXTaskID, &ECBRcv[i] );
    }
```

One helpful resource in Windows is the timer. Windows provides timers so that you can do something every so often. In this case, we use one timer to check the semaphore to see if any users have joined us in the WCHAT program or to see if any have left. We check this every five seconds. The other timer is used to check our array of listening ECBs to see if any keystrokes have come in.

That's the end of our initialization for WCHAT. Now we will look at other messages that come into WinProc and show you how they are handled.

```
        // Start the user check timer, every 5 seconds
        if ( !SetTimer( hWnd, 1, 5000, NULL ) )
        {
            MessageBox( hWnd, "Too many clocks or timers", szAppName,
                    MB_OK | MB_ICONEXCLAMATION );
            DestroyWindow( hWnd );
        }

        // Start the packet check timer, every 3 seconds
        if ( !SetTimer( hWnd, 2, 3000, NULL ) )
        {
            MessageBox( hWnd, "Too many clocks or timers", szAppName,
                    MB_OK | MB_ICONEXCLAMATION );
            DestroyWindow( hWnd );
        }

        break;
```

WM_DESTROY messages are sent when the window is about to be closed. In this case, we kill the timers we once started, close the semaphore, close the socket, and inform Windows we're ready to leave.

```
    case WM_DESTROY:
        // Get rid of timers
        KillTimer( hWnd, 1 );
        KillTimer( hWnd, 2 );

        // Close Semaphore
        if ( CloseSemaphore( semaphoreHandle ) )
            MessageBox( hWnd, "Error closing semaphore", szAppName,
                    MB_OK | MB_ICONEXCLAMATION );

        // Close socket
        IPXCloseSocket( IPXTaskID, socket );

        // Outta here
        PostQuitMessage( 0 );
        break;
```

WM_SETFOCUS informs our Window that it received the input focus; now we make the edit control the current window so that the user can type there.

```
case WM_SETFOCUS:
    SetFocus( GetDlgItem( hWnd, WC_TEXT ) );
    break;
```

WM_TIMER messages are generated by the Windows timers. Remember that we started two different timers, so the messages they each generate will come through this section of code.

```
case WM_TIMER:
    // Check to see what kind of timer it is
```

The first timer is the one we use to check the semaphore to see if any new people have joined us or to see if any have left. We call ExamineSemaphore to check the status of the semaphore and see the new openCount. This value gets printed to a string and the static text hUsers gets updated with the new value.

```
switch( wParam )
{
    // Timer 1:
    // Check semaphore value
    case 1:
        if ( ExamineSemaphore( semaphoreHandle,
            &semaphoreValue, &openCount ) )
        {
            MessageBox( hWnd, "Error examining
                semaphore", szAppName,
                    MB_OK | MB_ICONEXCLAMATION );
            DestroyWindow( hWnd );
            break;
        }

        sprintf( buffer, "Number of users in chat:  %2d",
            openCount );
        SetWindowText( hUsers, buffer );
        break;
```

This next section of code is one of the more involved sections in the program. It deals with receiving the incoming packets, then printing other users' text to the window. The first thing we do in this block of code is check to see if we are already working in this section. If so, the processing flag will be set (this is possible because another timer period could have elapsed before we got to finish processing our incoming packets).

We also set the start variable to the current packet being viewed.

```
                // Timer 2:
                // Check listening ECB for incoming
                // If it's there use SetWindowText, etc.
    case 2:
        if ( processing == TRUE )
            break;
        processing = TRUE;
        start = curPkt;
```

First we check to see if the packet is in use. If the inUseFlag is 0, then we have received a packet.

```
            while ( 1 )
            {
                  if ( !ECBRcv[curPkt].inUseFlag )
                  {
```

Then we check to see if we received the packet intact. If not, the completionCode will be non-zero.

```
            if ( ECBRcv[curPkt].completionCode )
            {
                  sprintf( buffer, "Error receiving
                     packet, completion code = %X\n",
                        ECBRcv[curPkt].completionCode );
                  MessageBox( hWnd, buffer, szAppName,
                     MB_OK | MB_ICONEXCLAMATION );
                  DestroyWindow( hWnd );
                  return 0;
            }
            else
```

Now that we know our incoming string is OK, we will send it to the dialog box, WC_DISPLAY. Because we want to scroll the dialog box for the user, we see if more than eight messages have appeared in the dialog box. If so, we delete the one at the top (the oldest), and the dialog box scrolls to show the most recent messages.

```
            {
                  // Add the incoming text to our listbox
                  // SendDlgItemMessage( hWnd,
WC_DISPLAY, LB_ADDSTRING, 0, (LPARAM) (LPCSTR) RcvPacket[curPkt] );
                        if ( SendDlgItemMessage(
hWnd, WC_DISPLAY, LB_GETCOUNT, 0, 0L ) > 8 )
                              SendDlgItemMessage(
hWnd, WC_DISPLAY, LB_DELETESTRING, 0, 0L );
```

After we're through displaying the message, we can post the ECB back to a listening state.

```
                     // Listen for the next packet
                     IPXListenForPacket(
                     IPXTaskID, &ECBRcv[curPkt] );
            }
      }
```

This code advances to the next packet in the array. When curPkt gets to the end of the array, it is reset to 0. When it gets back around to where we started searching, the loop terminates and sets processing to FALSE.

```
                  // Advance current packet
                  if ( curPkt == ECBMAX-1 )
                        curPkt = 0;
                  else
                        curPkt++;

                  if ( curPkt == start )
                        break;

      }
```

```
                    processing = FALSE;
                    break;
                }

            break;
```

If we didn't process the message, we call BWCCDefWindowProc. The BWCC part is necessary because we're using the Borland Custom Controls library. Normally, you would just call DefWindowProc.

```
        default:
            return BWCCDefWindowProc( hWnd, iMessage, wParam, lParam );
    }

    return 0;
}
```

This routine is the subclassing code for the edit control where the user types in new messages. This function is called every time a new message is sent to that control. If the incoming message was a WM_CHAR, meaning the user typed something, and if that WM_CHAR message was for a Carriage Return (13), then send the line of text to other users.

```
long FAR PASCAL EditProc( HWND hWnd, WORD iMessage, WORD wParam, LONG
lParam )
{
    TextLine typedText, buffer;
    WORD result, objType;
    DWORD objID;
    BYTE loginTime[7];

    // If we received a character that's a Carriage Return, send the line
    if ( ( iMessage == WM_CHAR ) && ( wParam == 13 ) )
    {
```

Note the comments on the code above. We initialize the ECB in this code.

```
        // Clear the structures
    memset( &IPXSnd, NULL, sizeof( IPXSnd ) );
    memset( &ECBSnd, NULL, sizeof( ECBSnd ) );

        // Set to broadcast (all FF's)
    memset( IPXSnd.destination.node, 0xFF, 6 );
    memset( ECBSnd.immediateAddress, 0xFF, 6 );

        // Then setup the rest of the ECB
    ( *((WORD *)IPXSnd.destination.socket) ) = socket;

    ECBSnd.ESRAddress = 0;
    ECBSnd.socketNumber = socket;
    ECBSnd.fragmentCount = 2;

    ECBSnd.fragmentDescriptor[0].address = ( void far * )&IPXSnd;
    ECBSnd.fragmentDescriptor[0].size = sizeof( IPXSnd );
```

Next, we get the text the user typed, find out the name of the logged-in user, and send the packet.

```
        // Get the text we typed into the edit control
    GetWindowText( hWnd, typedText, LINEMAX+1 );
```

```
SetWindowText( hWnd, "" );
        // Then get our user name and construct the line
        // to send
GetConnectionInformation( GetConnectionNumber(), buffer,
  &objType, &objID, &loginTime );
strcat( buffer, ": " );
strncat( buffer, typedText, LINEMAXstrlen( buffer )-1 );

        // Address the line as the 2nd ECB fragment (the
        // first is the IPX header)
ECBSnd.fragmentDescriptor[1].address = ( void far * )buffer;
ECBSnd.fragmentDescriptor[1].size = sizeof( TextLine );

        // Send the packet, then wait for it to complete,
        // then check if it went out ok
IPXSendPacket( IPXTaskID, &ECBSnd );
```

These two code blocks are used to wait for the IPX Send event to complete, then check to see if the IPX packet was sent successfully. This doesn't guarantee that it was RECEIVED successfully, only that it made it out the door in good shape.

```
while ( ECBSnd.inUseFlag )
    IPXYield();

if ( ECBSnd.completionCode )
{
    sprintf( buffer, "Error sending packet, completion
      code = %X", ECBSnd.completionCode );
    MessageBox( hWnd, buffer, szAppName, MB_OK |
      MB_ICONEXCLAMATION );
    DestroyWindow( hMain );
}
```

If we didn't get a carriage return, we call the old (default) procedure for this control.

```
        return TRUE;
    }
    else
        return CallWindowProc( lpfnOldEditProc, hWnd, iMessage,
          wParam, lParam );
}
```

Finally, the AddrCmp routine is shown here for you. It is not used in the code, but could be if you wanted to compare two addresses.

```
BOOL AddrCmp( char *c1, char *c2 )
{
    int i;

    for ( i = 0; i < 6; i++ )
        if ( c1[i] != c2[i] )
            return FALSE;
    return TRUE;
}
```

Now that you've seen the code in-depth, you should take the time to modify the code, if you want to learn more about NetWare/Windows programming. Add routines to detect if you have received packets from yourself (you do in a broadcast). Also, you could add features, such as sounds, "live" character-by-character text windows, and so on. The best way to become familiar with this type of development is simply to work with it and experiment.

Client-Server Programming

One of the most popular trends in the software industry is the growth of "client-server" software architecture. This section will attempt to briefly explain the elements of client-server and provide a programming example using a Windows-based client program that communicates with a DOS-based "server"—together, the two pieces simulate a transaction-based database application.

What Is Client-Server?

The name client-server is composed of two pieces: the client and the server. When all work was done on mainframes, these two pieces were part of the same machine (although there are terminals on mainframes, they are usually "dumb" and do no actual work themselves). This is often referred to as "central processing." With the advent of the PC and the LAN, all of the work (except for file and print services) is generally done at the workstation, often referred to as "distributed processing."

Client-Server architecture represents a balance between the two extremes of central processing (mainframes) and distributed processing (PCs AND LANs). Client-Server makes optimal use of each side of the equation: The client is optimized for presentation to the user, as well as to many application-specific tasks; the server is optimized to do a certain job quickly. It takes a certain amount of input from the front-end (the client), processes that information, then returns the processed result to the client.

For example, using NetWare and Windows as elements in a client-server application, you could use Windows as the presentation element of the client. Windows provides a robust front-end that would work well for almost any client-side application.

NetWare's peer-to-peer speed and functionality allow a client to make a direct connection to the potential server. This "server" could exist as an NLM inside a file server; it could be running under OS/2 on a workstation on the LAN, it could be part of a Unix platform running TCP/IP, or it could even be part of a DOS workstation (as you will see in our C example that follows).

Generally, however, you will see servers running on a multitasking operating system like NetWare or OS/2 (or Windows, for that matter) because the server will need to service multiple clients at once. While this is possible under DOS (with a little help), other operating systems have multitasking resources built-in.

Let's examine some of the advantages of a client-server application:

• Speed

Part of the reason for going with a client-server architecture for applications is for speed. You essentially let the machine that does the task better do the job.

Also, rather than forcing each LAN workstation to do a tremendous amount of processing, you let a centralized server perform the task, thus reducing network traffic and speeding overall performance.

For example, to produce a sorted report in a non-client-server environment, each workstation that wanted the report would have to read each record in the database from the file server (each record would then travel across the network) to the workstation. The workstation would then do the sorting and present the report to the user. However, in a client-server environment, a workstation could request the sorted report. The application server would then sort the data and return only the finished report to the client, resulting in a much faster completion time (because of reduced network traffic and because the data is presumably "on" the application server).

• Security

In most cases, the data in a client-server application resides physically on the application server, so security can be more tightly controlled. This control is both in the physical sense, because the machine can be locked up, and in an electronic sense, because the application can be set up so that nobody can simply copy the data file to their local workstation—the information must be searched for and returned in more of a final, "processed" state.

• Multiple front-ends/flexibility

The flexible nature of a client-server application attracts many. The appeal is that you could have DOS, OS/2, Windows, Macintosh, or Unix front-end clients that all communicated with the same back-end server, thus creating more of an enterprise-wide application.

Now that we've summarized the theory of client-server architecture, let's see it in practice. Our code example for this section is comprised naturally of two parts: the client and the server. The client is a Visual Basic application that calls a C-coded DLL. The server is coded in C and runs under DOS. The application uses Novell's Sequenced Packet Exchange (SPX) protocol to exchange information directly between the two workstations (the information goes from one workstation to the other without having to rely on the file server).

This example is somewhat artificial in that the server is single-tasking and DOS-based; thus, it can only handle one client at a time. It is, however, meant to simulate a client-server application and give you some insight into how such an application might be constructed.

As with the two previous examples, it is recommended that you refer to the executable files on the disks included with this book and experiment with the program before exploring the code here. That way, you will have a much better idea of what the program does. See Chapter 10 for a discussion of how to install the software. To run the client-server example, start the client application from Windows on one network PC; then run the server on another PC by typing "SPXPROTO /r." Figure 14.5 shows the client application's window.

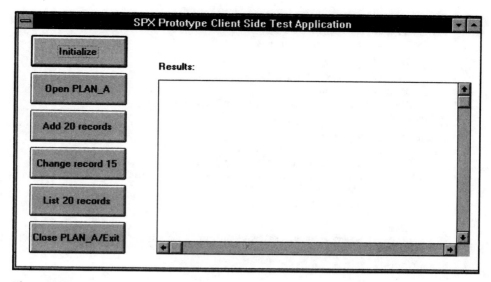

Figure 14.5 Client's window.

The Client

The code for the client side of the application follows:

```
GLOBAL.BAS

Global Const TRUE = -1
Global Const FALSE = 0

Type Pend
    SSN      As Long
    Name     As String * 40
    Dollar   As Integer
End Type

Global SSN As String * 12
Global PendRec As Pend

Declare Function CliPlanOpen Lib "clidll.dll" (ByVal hWnd%, ByVal FileName$) As
Integer
Declare Function CliPlanClose Lib "clidll.dll" (ByVal hWnd%) As Integer
Declare Function CliPlanAdd Lib "clidll.dll" (ByVal hWnd%, Plan As
Pend) As Integer
Declare Function CliPlanInfo Lib "clidll.dll" (ByVal hWnd%, ByVal SSN&, Plan As
Pend) As Integer
Declare Function CliPlanMod Lib "clidll.dll" (ByVal hWnd%, ByVal SSN&, ByVal
N$) As Integer

Declare Sub InitializeSPX Lib "clidll.dll" (ByVal hWnd%)
Declare Sub FindServer Lib "clidll.dll" (ByVal hWnd%)
Declare Sub AbortConnection Lib "clidll.dll" (ByVal hWnd%)
Declare Sub DownSide Lib "clidll.dll" (ByVal hWnd%)

.FRM CODE
```

```
Dim Plan As Pend
Dim i, SSN As Long
Dim ChangeName As String * 40

Sub Command1_Click ()
    InitializeSPX (hWnd)
    FindServer (hWnd)
    Text1.Text = "Server found and successfully attached"
End Sub

Sub Command2_Click ()
    CRLF$ = Chr$(13) + Chr$(10)
    If CliPlanOpen(hWnd, "PLAN_A") Then
        ReturnVal% = MsgBox("Error opening PLAN_A in CliPlanOpen. Exiting...", 16)
        AbortConnection (hWnd)
        DownSide (hWnd)
        End
    Else
        Text1.Text = Text1.Text + CRLF$ + "PLAN_A opened successfully"
    End If
End Sub

Sub Command3_Click ()
    Plan.Name = String$(40, 0)
    Plan.Name = "VB Test Name"
    CRLF$ = Chr$(13) + Chr$(10)

    For i = 1 To 20
        Plan.SSN = i
        Plan.Dollar = i * 5
        If CliPlanAdd(hWnd, Plan) Then
            ReturnVal% = MsgBox("Error adding record in CliPlanAdd. Exiting...", 16)
            AbortConnection (hWnd)
            DownSide (hWnd)
            End
        Else
            Text1.Text = Text1.Text + CRLF$ + "Record " + Str$(i) + "
                added successfully"
        End If
    Next i
End Sub

Sub Command4_Click ()
    CRLF$ = Chr$(13) + Chr$(10)

    SSN = 15
    ChangeName$ = String$(40, 0)
    ChangeName$ = "VBNewGuy"
    If CliPlanMod(hWnd, SSN, ChangeName$) Then
        ReturnVal% = MsgBox("Error modifying record 15 in CliPlanMod.
            Exiting...", 16)
        AbortConnection (hWnd)
        DownSide (hWnd)
        End
    Else
        Text1.Text = Text1.Text + CRLF$ + "Record 15 successfully
            modified to 'VBNewGuy'"
    End If
```

```
        End Sub

Sub Command5_Click ()
    CRLF$ = Chr$(13) + Chr$(10)

    For i = 1 To 20
        If CliPlanInfo(hWnd, i, Plan) Then
            ReturnVal% = MsgBox("Error reading record in CliPlanInfo.
                Exiting...", 16)
            AbortConnection (hWnd)
            DownSide (hWnd)
            End
        Else
            Text1.Text = Text1.Text + CRLF$ + "[" + Str$(i) + "]   " +
Str$(Plan.SSN) + " " + Str$(Plan.Dollar) + " " + Plan.Name
        End If
    Next i

End Sub

Sub Command6_Click ()
    CRLF$ = Chr$(13) + Chr$(10)
    If CliPlanClose(hWnd) Then
        ReturnVal% = MsgBox("Error closing PLAN_A in CliPlanOpen.
            Exiting...", 16)
    Else
        Text1.Text = Text1.Text + CRLF$ + "PLAN_A closed successfully"
    End If
    AbortConnection (hWnd)
    DownSide (hWnd)
    End
End Sub
```

We'll begin by looking at the client side. The client side of the application is divided into two major pieces: the Visual Basic front-end and the C DLL. The Visual Basic front-end presents information to the user and makes calls to the DLL to communicate with the application server.

The rationale of this sample application is a financial application. Individual customer files, or "plans," contain lists of transactions. Each transaction record lists a person's social security number, name, and the dollar amount of the transaction. The application is extremely simple and serves no real-world purpose other than to illustrate the concepts behind this type of program architecture.

VB CODE FOR CLIENT.EXE

This is the global declarations file (GLOBAL.BAS); it simply declares a structure called Pend, which we will use to describe a pending financial transaction (composed of a social security number, a person's name, and a dollar amount). Following that is a 12-character string called SSN and a variable called PendRec which is of type Pend.

Then we declare all of the remote functions and subroutines that we will call in the VB code. These are remote calls to the DLL that we will program in C (CLIDLL.DLL). Before we can call InitializeSPX, for example, we must first tell

Visual Basic where to find this call and what the syntax is (in this case, it expects you to pass an hWnd [a window handle] by value).

```
Global Const TRUE = -1
Global Const FALSE = 0

Type Pend
    SSN      As Long
    Name     As String * 40
    Dollar   As Integer
End Type

Global SSN As String * 12
Global PendRec As Pend

Declare Function CliPlanOpen Lib "clidll.dll" (ByVal hWnd%, ByVal
FileName$) As Integer
Declare Function CliPlanClose Lib "clidll.dll" (ByVal hWnd%) As
Integer
Declare Function CliPlanAdd Lib "clidll.dll" (ByVal hWnd%, Plan As
Pend) As Integer
Declare Function CliPlanInfo Lib "clidll.dll" (ByVal hWnd%, ByVal
SSN&, Plan As Pend) As Integer
Declare Function CliPlanMod Lib "clidll.dll" (ByVal hWnd%, ByVal
SSN&, ByVal N$) As Integer

Declare Sub InitializeSPX Lib "clidll.dll" (ByVal hWnd%)
Declare Sub FindServer Lib "clidll.dll" (ByVal hWnd%)
Declare Sub AbortConnection Lib "clidll.dll" (ByVal hWnd%)
Declare Sub DownSide Lib "clidll.dll" (ByVal hWnd%)
```

Next, we'll discuss the code associated with each button in the client window. When the user clicks on the Initialize button (Command1) in Figure 14.5, the Command1_Click subroutine is called. This routine first calls InitializeSPX (one of our C routines in CLIDLL.DLL which we will discuss in detail below), passing hWnd, the current Window handle. This variable, defined by Visual Basic, is used frequently.

Next, we call FindServer which looks for our DOS-based application server. If it was successful, FindServer returns, so we set the Text1 window to a success message. If FindServer had an error, it displays it to the user (in CLIDLL.DLL) and aborts the program since not finding a server is considered a fatal error.

```
Dim Plan As Pend
Dim i, SSN As Long
Dim ChangeName As String * 40

Sub Command1_Click ()
    InitializeSPX (hWnd)
    FindServer (hWnd)
    Text1.Text = "Server found and successfully attached"
End Sub
```

This is the code for the next button, Open PLAN_A, which calls CliPlanOpen (Client Plan Open). If CliPlanOpen was successful, it returns a 0, so we append a success message to the Text1 window. Otherwise, we terminate the application.

```
Sub Command2_Click ()
```

```
        CRLF$ = Chr$(13) + Chr$(10)
        If CliPlanOpen(hWnd, "PLAN_A") Then
            ReturnVal% = MsgBox("Error opening PLAN_A in CliPlanOpen.
              Exiting...", 16)
            AbortConnection (hWnd)
            DownSide (hWnd)
            End
        Else
            Text1.Text = Text1.Text + CRLF$ + "PLAN_A opened successfully"
        End If
    End Sub
```

This routine writes 20 records by calling CliPlanAdd 20 times. It is called by the Add 20 Records button in the client window (Figure 14.5). It passes a Plan structure to CLIDLL.DLL.

```
    Sub Command3_Click ()
        Plan.Name = String$(40, 0)
        Plan.Name = "VB Test Name"
        CRLF$ = Chr$(13) + Chr$(10)

        For i = 1 To 20
            Plan.SSN = i
            Plan.Dollar = i * 5
            If CliPlanAdd(hWnd, Plan) Then
                ReturnVal% = MsgBox("Error adding record in CliPlanAdd.
                  Exiting...", 16)
                AbortConnection (hWnd)
                DownSide (hWnd)
                End
            Else
                Text1.Text = Text1.Text + CRLF$ + "Record " + Str$(i) + "
                  added successfully"
            End If
        Next i
    End Sub
```

This routine modifies record 15 to prove that we can change the contents of a specific record. It does so by calling the CliPlanMod function from CLIENT.DLL. This block of code is initiated by clicking on the Change Record 15 button in the Client window.

```
    Sub Command4_Click ()
        CRLF$ = Chr$(13) + Chr$(10)

        SSN = 15
        ChangeName$ = String$(40, 0)
        ChangeName$ = "VBNewGuy"
        If CliPlanMod(hWnd, SSN, ChangeName$) Then
            ReturnVal% = MsgBox("Error modifying record 15 in CliPlanMod.
              Exiting...", 16)
            AbortConnection (hWnd)
            DownSide (hWnd)
            End
        Else
            Text1.Text = Text1.Text + CRLF$ + "Record 15 successfully
              modified to 'VBNewGuy'"
```

```
        End If

    End Sub
```

This routine lists the first 20 records in the plan file. It calls CliPlanInfo to get information about a specified record number. If there was an error, the client side is shut down; otherwise, the returned information is added to the text box (Text1).

```
Sub Command5_Click ()
    CRLF$ = Chr$(13) + Chr$(10)

    For i = 1 To 20
        If CliPlanInfo(hWnd, i, Plan) Then
            ReturnVal% = MsgBox("Error reading record in CliPlanInfo.
                Exiting...", 16)
            AbortConnection (hWnd)
            DownSide (hWnd)
            End
        Else
            Text1.Text = Text1.Text + CRLF$ + "[" + Str$(i) + "]   " +
                Str$(Plan.SSN) + " " + Str$(Plan.Dollar) + " " + Plan.Name
        End If
    Next i

End Sub
```

Finally, this next routine closes the file on the server and terminates the session.

```
Sub Command6_Click ()
    CRLF$ = Chr$(13) + Chr$(10)
    If CliPlanClose(hWnd) Then
        ReturnVal% = MsgBox("Error closing PLAN_A in CliPlanOpen.
            Exiting...", 16)
    Else
        Text1.Text = Text1.Text + CRLF$ + "PLAN_A closed successfully"
    End If
    AbortConnection (hWnd)
    DownSide (hWnd)
    End
End Sub
```

THE C CODE FOR CLIDLL.DLL

The following code is for CLIENT.DLL. It is to this DLL that the CLIENT.EXE Visual Basic application discussed above has been making calls. If you have reviewed the code above, you will recognize many of the routines in our custom DLL.

```
#include <windows.h>
#include <ctype.h>
#include <time.h>

#include <nxt.h>
#include <nit.h>
```

```
// Defines
#define WAITMAX             20
#define MAX_PACKETS         10
#define MAX_RECEIVE_ECBS    10
#define RETRY_COUNT         100
#define TEMPORARY_SOCKET    (BYTE)0
#define PERMANENT_SOCKET    (BYTE)0xFF
#define INVITE_SOCKET       0x0350
#define RPC_SOCKET          0X0450
#define OK              0
#define ENABLE_WATCHDOG     0xFF
#define DISABLE_WATCHDOG 0
#define MK_SOCKET(a) ( ( a[1] < 8 ) + a[0] )

// Types
typedef long int SSN;

typedef struct
{
    SSN     ssn;
    char    name[40];
    int     dollar;
} PARTINF1;

typedef struct
{
    SSN     ssn;
    char    name[40];
    int     dollar;
} PEND;

// Prototypes
void FAR PASCAL InitializeSPX( HWND hWnd );

int FAR PASCAL CliPlanOpen( HANDLE hWnd, char *planname );
int FAR PASCAL CliPlanClose( HANDLE hWnd );
int FAR PASCAL CliPlanAdd( HANDLE hWnd, PARTINF1 *plan );
int FAR PASCAL CliPlanInfo( HANDLE hWnd, SSN ssn, PARTINF1 *plan );
int FAR PASCAL CliPlanMod( HANDLE hWnd, SSN ssn, char *newName );

void FAR PASCAL SendClientPacket( HANDLE hWnd );
void FAR PASCAL FindServer( HANDLE hWnd );
void FAR PASCAL ConnectServer( HANDLE hWnd );
void FAR PASCAL AbortConnection( HANDLE hWnd );
void FAR PASCAL DownSide( HANDLE hWnd );

void FAR PASCAL IPXSetupRcvPacket( ECB *ECBptr, IPXHeader *IPXptr,
BYTE Socket[2], char *Buffer,
    WORD Buffsize, void *(ESR)() );

void FAR PASCAL IPXSetupSendPacket( ECB *ECBptr, IPXHeader *IPXptr,
BYTE Network[4], BYTE Node[6],
    BYTE destSocket[2], BYTE sourceSocket[2], char *Buffer, WORD
Buffsize, void *(ESR)() );

void FAR PASCAL SPXSetupRcvPacket( ECB *ECBptr, SPXHeader *SPXptr,
BYTE Socket[2], char *Buffer,
    WORD Buffsize, void *(ESR)() );
```

```
void FAR PASCAL SPXSetupSendPacket( ECB *ECBptr, SPXHeader *SPXptr,
BYTE Network[4], BYTE Node[6],
    BYTE destSocket[2], BYTE sourceSocket[2], char *Buffer, WORD
Buffsize, void *(ESR)() );

void FAR PASCAL SPXSetupEstConnPacket( ECB *ECBptr, SPXHeader
*SPXptr, BYTE Network[4], BYTE Node[6],
    BYTE destSocket[2], BYTE sourceSocket[2], void *(ESR)() );

void FAR PASCAL SPXSetupListenConnPacket( ECB *ECBptr, SPXHeader
*SPXptr, BYTE Socket[2], void *(ESR)() );

//Global Data
WORD            connectionID;
ECB             svrECB[MAX_PACKETS];
IPXHeader       svrIPX;
SPXHeader       svrSPX[MAX_PACKETS];
char            buff[100];
char            buff2[MAX_PACKETS][100];
BYTE            targetNetwork[4] = { 0, 0, 0, 0 };
BYTE            targetNode[6] = { 0xFF, 0xFF, 0xFF, 0xFF, 0xFF, 0xFF };
BYTE            targetSocket[2] = { 0, 0 };
BYTE            askSocket[2] = { 0, 0 };
BYTE            talkSocket[2] = { 0, 0 };
time_t          wait_secs, start_secs, start_time;
int             currPacket;

char        message[78];        /*-- Buffer to hold messages.    --*/
int         socketNumber;       /*-- Socket number to talk on.   -- */
WORD        fSocket;            /*-- File server socket number. This
                        is a place holder and not used.  --*/
DWORD       IPXTaskID = 0; // Needs to be 0 so that we allocate resources
separately

#pragma argsused
int FAR PASCAL LibMain( HANDLE hInstance, WORD wDataSeg, WORD
wHeapSize,
            LPSTR lpszCmdLine)
{
   if (wHeapSize > 0)
      UnlockData(0);
   return TRUE;
}

void FAR PASCAL InitializeSPX( HWND hWnd )
{
   HANDLE   hMem;
   int      installed;
   BYTE     major, minor;
   WORD     maxConnections, availConnections;
   WORD     maxNumECBs, maxSizeECB;
   int      ccode;
   char     message[75];

   /*-- The way SPXInitialize is now, you need to pass in the maximum
       number of ECBs that will be used along with the maximum size
       of the largest ECB to be used. The other parameters are the
       same as the C Interface. --*/
```

```
    maxNumECBs = MAX_RECEIVE_ECBS + 3;
    maxSizeECB = 576;

    installed = SPXInitialize( &IPXTaskID, maxNumECBs, maxSizeECB,
                    &major, &minor,
                    &maxConnections, &availConnections );

    if( !installed )
       {
       MessageBox( hWnd, "Error -- SPX is NOT installed!", NULL, MB_OK );
       PostQuitMessage( 0 );
       }

    /*-- There are no short lived sockets under Windows, so a NULL
       is passed in for the socket type. --*/
    ccode = IPXOpenSocket( IPXTaskID, (WORD FAR *)talkSocket, NULL );
    if ( ( ccode ) && ( ccode != 0xFF ) ) {
       wsprintf( message, "ccode from IPXOpenSocket... %02X", ccode );
       MessageBox( hWnd, message, "Status", MB_OK );
       PostQuitMessage( 0 );
       }

    ccode = IPXOpenSocket( IPXTaskID, (WORD FAR *)askSocket, NULL );
    if ( ( ccode ) && ( ccode != 0xFF ) ) {
       wsprintf( message, "ccode from IPXOpenSocket... %02X", ccode );
       MessageBox( hWnd, message, "Status", MB_OK );
       PostQuitMessage( 0 );
       }

  wsprintf( message, "Sockets open ok. talkSocket is %X askSocket is %X",
     IntSwap( *((WORD *)talkSocket) ),
     IntSwap( *((WORD *)askSocket) ) );
  MessageBox( hWnd, message, "Status", MB_OK );
}

void FAR PASCAL SendClientPacket( HANDLE hWnd )
{
    int checkPacket;

    currPacket = 1;
    // Currently, svrECB[1] is listening, so cancel the event & use it to send
       IPXCancelEvent( IPXTaskID, &svrECB[currPacket] );

    SPXSetupSendPacket( &svrECB[currPacket], &svrSPX[currPacket],
       targetNetwork, targetNode,
              targetSocket, talkSocket, buff, sizeof( buff ), NULL );
    SPXSendSequencedPacket( IPXTaskID, connectionID,
       &svrECB[currPacket] );

    start_time = time( NULL );
    while ( svrECB[currPacket].inUseFlag != OK )
    {
         IPXRelinquishControl();
         Yield();
         if ( difftime( time( NULL ), start_time ) > 1 )
         {
              start_time = time( NULL );
         }
```

```
      }

      if ( svrECB[currPacket].completionCode != OK )
      {
           wsprintf( message, "SendClientPacket:Send error in svr ECB,
             status = %x ",
                 svrECB[currPacket].completionCode );
           MessageBox( hWnd, message, NULL, MB_OK );
           MessageBox( hWnd, "Shutting client down...", NULL, MB_OK );
           AbortConnection( hWnd );
           DownSide( hWnd );
      }

      // Post svrECB[1] back to listen and check svrECB[1..MAX] for reply

      SPXSetupRcvPacket( &svrECB[currPacket], &svrSPX[currPacket],
        talkSocket, buff2[currPacket], sizeof( buff ), NULL );

      SPXListenForSequencedPacket( IPXTaskID, &svrECB[currPacket] );

      start_time = wait_secs = time( &start_secs );
      checkPacket = 1;
      while ( ( wait_secsstart_secs ) < WAITMAX )
      {
           IPXRelinquishControl();
           Yield();
           time( &wait_secs );
           if ( difftime( wait_secs, start_time ) > 1 )
           {
                start_time = time( NULL );
           }

           if ( svrECB[checkPacket].inUseFlag == OK )
           {
                if ( svrECB[checkPacket].completionCode != OK )
                {
                     if ( ( svrECB[checkPacket].completionCode == 0xED ) ||
                          ( svrSPX[checkPacket].dataStreamType == 0xFE ) )
                         MessageBox( hWnd, "Other side terminated connection",
                              NULL,MB_OK);
                     else
                     {
                       wsprintf( message, "SendClientPacket: Bad reception,
                         status = %X\nShutting down...",
                              svrECB[checkPacket].completionCode );
                         MessageBox( hWnd, message, "Status", MB_OK );
                     }
                     AbortConnection( hWnd );
                     DownSide( hWnd );
                }
                else
                {
                     movmem( buff2[checkPacket], buff, sizeof( buff ) );
                     SPXSetupRcvPacket( &svrECB[checkPacket],
                       &svrSPX[checkPacket], talkSocket,
                            buff2[checkPacket], sizeof( buff ), NULL );
                     SPXListenForSequencedPacket( IPXTaskID,
                       &svrECB[checkPacket] );
```

```
                              break;
                    }
            }
            checkPacket++;
            if ( checkPacket == MAX_PACKETS )
                checkPacket = 1;
    }

    if (  ( wait_secs  start_secs ) >= WAITMAX )
    {
        MessageBox( hWnd, "Server did not respond...shutting down",
            NULL, MB_OK );
        AbortConnection( hWnd );
        DownSide( hWnd );
    }
}

// Structure for buff now is:
//   buff[0]   = Function number
//   buff[1]   = Return code
//   buff[2n] = Passed Structure
int FAR PASCAL CliPlanOpen( HANDLE hWnd, char *planname )
{
    memset( buff, NULL, sizeof( buff ) );
    buff[0] = 0;
    strcpy( &buff[2], planname );
    SendClientPacket( hWnd );
    return buff[1];
}

int FAR PASCAL CliPlanClose( HANDLE hWnd )
{
    memset( buff, NULL, sizeof( buff ) );
    buff[0] = 1;
    SendClientPacket( hWnd );
    return buff[1];
}

int FAR PASCAL CliPlanAdd( HANDLE hWnd, PARTINF1 *plan )
{
    memset( buff, NULL, sizeof( buff ) );
    buff[0] = 2;
    movmem( plan, &buff[2], sizeof( PARTINF1 ) );
    SendClientPacket( hWnd );
    return buff[1];
}


int FAR PASCAL CliPlanInfo( HANDLE hWnd, SSN ssn, PARTINF1 *plan )
{
    memset( buff, NULL, sizeof( buff ) );
    buff[0] = 3;
    movmem( &ssn, &buff[2], sizeof( SSN ) );
    SendClientPacket( hWnd );
    movmem( &buff[2], plan, sizeof( PARTINF1 ) );
    return buff[1];
}
```

```
int FAR PASCAL CliPlanMod( HANDLE hWnd, SSN ssn, char *newName )
{
    memset( buff, NULL, sizeof( buff ) );
    buff[0] = 4;
    movmem( &ssn, &buff[2], sizeof( SSN ) );
    strcpy( &buff[2+sizeof(SSN)], newName );
    SendClientPacket( hWnd );
    return buff[1];
}

void FAR PASCAL FindServer( HANDLE hWnd )
{
    int status, segmentNumber = 1;
    char objectName[48], propertyName[16];
    char propertySecurity, propertyHasValue, moreProperties;
    BYTE objectHasProperties, objectFlag, objectSecurity;
    long sequenceNumber;
    BYTE moreSegments, propertyFlags;
    WORD objectType;
    IPXAddress serverAddress;
    char value[128];
    DWORD objectID = 0xFFFFFFFF;

    // Scan the bindery for the server we want...
    MessageBox( hWnd, "About to call ScanBinderyObject", NULL, MB_OK );
    status = ScanBinderyObject( "*", (WORD) OT_JOB_SERVER,
      &objectID, objectName,
            &objectType, &objectHasProperties, &objectFlag,
              &objectSecurity );
    if ( status )
    {
        wsprintf( message, "Error in ScanBinderyObject, error code
          = %X\n", status );
        MessageBox( hWnd, "Shutting client down...", NULL, MB_OK );
        DownSide( hWnd );
        return;
    }
    else
    {
        MessageBox( hWnd, "ScanBinderyObject successful, calling
          ReadPropertyValue", NULL, MB_OK );
        status = ReadPropertyValue( objectName, objectType,
          "NET_ADDRESS", segmentNumber, value, &moreSegments,
                                  &propertyFlags );
        if ( status )
        {
            wsprintf( message, "Error in ReadPropertyValue, error
              code = %X\n", status );
            MessageBox( hWnd, "Shutting client down...", NULL,
              MB_OK );
            DownSide( hWnd );
            return;
        }
        else
        {
            movmem( value, &serverAddress, sizeof( serverAddress ) );
```

```
                  MessageBox( hWnd, "ReadPropertyValue ok, doing our
                     movmem's and message print", NULL, MB_OK );
                  movmem( serverAddress.network, targetNetwork, 4 );
                  movmem( serverAddress.node, targetNode, 6 );
                  movmem( serverAddress.socket, targetSocket, 2 );
                  //*( (int *)targetSocket ) = IntSwap( *( int *)targetSocket ) );
                  wsprintf( message, "Job server is listening on socket %X.\n",
                         IntSwap( *( (WORD *)serverAddress.socket ) ) );
                  MessageBox( hWnd, message, "Status", MB_OK );
            }
      }

MessageBox( hWnd, "Calling application server...", "Info", MB_OK );

strcpy( buff, "Test Server #1" );
IPXSetupSendPacket( &svrECB[currPacket], &svrIPX, targetNetwork,
   targetNode, targetSocket,
      askSocket, buff, sizeof( buff ), NULL );

IPXSendPacket( IPXTaskID, &svrECB[currPacket] );

start_time = time( NULL );
while ( svrECB[currPacket].inUseFlag != OK )
{
      IPXRelinquishControl();
      Yield();
      if ( difftime( time( NULL ), start_time ) > 1 )
            start_time = time( NULL );
}

if ( svrECB[currPacket].completionCode != OK )
{
      wsprintf( message, "FindServer:Send error in svr ECB,
         status = %x Aborting.",
            svrECB[currPacket].completionCode );
      MessageBox( hWnd, message, NULL, MB_OK );
      DownSide( hWnd );
}

// Setup again and listen for response

IPXSetupRcvPacket( &svrECB[currPacket], &svrIPX, askSocket,
   buff, sizeof( buff ), NULL );

IPXListenForPacket( IPXTaskID, &svrECB[currPacket] );

start_time = wait_secs = time( &start_secs );
while ( ( svrECB[currPacket].inUseFlag != OK ) && ( (
   wait_secs-start_secs ) < WAITMAX ) )
{
      IPXRelinquishControl();
      Yield();
      time( &wait_secs );
      if ( difftime( wait_secs, start_time ) > 1 )
            start_time = time( NULL );
}

if ( ( wait_secs - start_secs ) >= WAITMAX )
{
      wsprintf( message, "FileServer:Server did not respond Aborting.");
```

```
            MessageBox( hWnd, message, NULL, MB_OK );
            DownSide( hWnd );
        }

        if ( svrECB[currPacket].completionCode != OK )
        {
            wsprintf( message, "FindServer:Bad reception, status =
              %x\nAborting.", svrECB[currPacket].completionCode );
            MessageBox( hWnd, message, NULL, MB_OK );
            DownSide( hWnd );
        }

        movmem( svrIPX.source.node, targetNode, 6 );
        movmem( svrIPX.source.network, targetNetwork, 4 );
        movmem( svrIPX.source.socket, targetSocket, 2 );

    ConnectServer( hWnd );
    MessageBox( hWnd, "Executing last line in FindServer()", NULL, MB_OK );
}

void FAR PASCAL ConnectServer( HANDLE hWnd )
{
    int i, retVal;

    // First, post up a couple of listen ECB's to establish the
    // connection with
    for ( i = 1; i < MAX_PACKETS; i++ )
    {
        SPXSetupRcvPacket( &svrECB[i], &svrSPX[i], talkSocket,
          buff2[i], sizeof( buff ), NULL );
        SPXListenForSequencedPacket( IPXTaskID, &svrECB[i] );
    }
    currPacket = 0;

    // Then setup a Connection Establish ECB
    SPXSetupEstConnPacket( &svrECB[currPacket], &svrSPX[currPacket],
      targetNetwork, targetNode, targetSocket,
            talkSocket, NULL );

    retVal = SPXEstablishConnection( IPXTaskID, RETRY_COUNT,
      DISABLE_WATCHDOG, &connectionID, &svrECB[currPacket] );
    if ( retVal )
    {
        wsprintf( message, "Error in SPXEstablishConnection, return
          value = %X\n", retVal );
        MessageBox( hWnd, message, NULL, MB_OK );
        DownSide( hWnd );
    }

    start_time = time( NULL );
    while ( svrECB[currPacket].inUseFlag != OK )
    {
        if ( difftime( time( NULL ), start_time ) > 1 )
            start_time = time( NULL );
        IPXRelinquishControl();
        Yield();
    }

    if ( svrECB[currPacket].completionCode != OK )
```

```
        {
            wsprintf( message, "ConnectServer:Error establishing SPX
              connection, status = %x Aborting.",
                svrECB[currPacket].completionCode );
            MessageBox( hWnd, message, NULL, MB_OK );
            DownSide( hWnd );
        }
        else
        {
            wsprintf( message, "Connection to Server successful!
              Connection ID = %X", connectionID );
            MessageBox( hWnd, message, "Info", MB_OK );
        }
}

void FAR PASCAL AbortConnection( HANDLE hWnd )
{
    int currPacket;
    time_t start_time;

    // Terminate SPX connection
    MessageBox( hWnd, "Terminating SPX connection", "Status", MB_OK );

    currPacket = MAX_PACKETS - 1;
    IPXCancelEvent( IPXTaskID, &svrECB[currPacket] );

    SPXSetupEstConnPacket( &svrECB[currPacket], &svrSPX[currPacket],
      targetNetwork, targetNode, targetSocket,
        talkSocket, NULL );
    SPXTerminateConnection( IPXTaskID, connectionID,
      &svrECB[currPacket] );

    start_time = time( NULL );
    while ( svrECB[currPacket].inUseFlag != OK )
    {
        IPXRelinquishControl();
        Yield();
        if ( difftime( time( NULL ), start_time ) > 1 )
        {
            start_time = time( NULL );
        }
    }

    if ( svrECB[currPacket].completionCode != OK )
        if ( svrECB[currPacket].completionCode == 0xEE )
            MessageBox( hWnd, "Other side terminated connection",
                "Info", MB_OK );
        else
        {
            wsprintf( message, "AbortConnection:Send error in
              Server ECB, status = %x ",
                svrECB[currPacket].completionCode );
            MessageBox( hWnd, message, NULL, MB_OK );
        }
    else
        MessageBox( hWnd, "SPX Connection Terminated", "Status",
          MB_OK );

    for ( currPacket = 0; currPacket < MAX_PACKETS; currPacket++ )
```

```
                    IPXCancelEvent( IPXTaskID, &svrECB[currPacket] );
}

void FAR PASCAL DownSide( HANDLE hWnd )
{
    // Close sockets and exit
    IPXCloseSocket( IPXTaskID, INVITE_SOCKET );
    IPXCloseSocket( IPXTaskID, RPC_SOCKET );
    IPXSPXDeinit( IPXTaskID );
    MessageBox( hWnd, "This side terminated", "Info", MB_OK );
}

void FAR PASCAL IPXSetupRcvPacket( ECB *ECBptr, IPXHeader *IPXptr,
BYTE Socket[2], char *Buffer,
    WORD Buffsize, void *(ESR)() )
{
    if ( ESR )
        ECBptr->ESRAddress = ( void far * ) ESR;
    else
        ECBptr->ESRAddress = ( void far * ) NULL;

    ECBptr->socketNumber = MK_SOCKET( Socket );
    ECBptr->fragmentCount = 2;

    ECBptr->fragmentDescriptor[0].address = ( void far * ) IPXptr;
    ECBptr->fragmentDescriptor[0].size = sizeof( *IPXptr );

    ECBptr->fragmentDescriptor[1].address = ( void far * ) Buffer;
    ECBptr->fragmentDescriptor[1].size = Buffsize;
}

void FAR PASCAL IPXSetupSendPacket( ECB *ECBptr, IPXHeader *IPXptr,
BYTE Network[4], BYTE Node[6],
    BYTE destSocket[2], BYTE sourceSocket[2], char *Buffer, WORD
Buffsize, void *(ESR)() )
{
    int ttime;
    IPXAddress IPXaddr;

    if ( ESR )
        ECBptr->ESRAddress = ( void far * ) ESR;
    else
        ECBptr->ESRAddress = ( void far *) NULL;

    ECBptr->inUseFlag = 0;
    ECBptr->socketNumber = MK_SOCKET( sourceSocket );
    ECBptr->fragmentCount = 2;

    ECBptr->fragmentDescriptor[0].address = ( void far * ) IPXptr;
    ECBptr->fragmentDescriptor[0].size = sizeof( *IPXptr );

    ECBptr->fragmentDescriptor[1].address = ( void far * ) Buffer;
    ECBptr->fragmentDescriptor[1].size = Buffsize;

    // Setup for call to Get Local Target which gets immediate
    // address
    // and setup the IPX header's destination address
    movmem( Network, IPXaddr.network, 4 );
    movmem( Node, IPXaddr.node, 6 );
    movmem( destSocket, IPXaddr.socket, 2 );
```

```
        IPXGetLocalTarget( IPXTaskID, ( BYTE * )&IPXaddr, ( BYTE *
          )ECBptr->immediateAddress, &ttime );
        movmem( &IPXaddr, &IPXptr->destination, 12 );
}

void FAR PASCAL SPXSetupRcvPacket( ECB *ECBptr, SPXHeader *SPXptr,
BYTE Socket[2], char *Buffer,
    WORD Buffsize, void *(ESR)() )
{
    if ( ESR )
        ECBptr->ESRAddress = ( void far * ) ESR;
    else
        ECBptr->ESRAddress = ( void far * ) NULL;

    ECBptr->socketNumber = MK_SOCKET( Socket );
    ECBptr->fragmentCount = 2;

    ECBptr->fragmentDescriptor[0].address = ( void far * ) SPXptr;
    ECBptr->fragmentDescriptor[0].size = sizeof( *SPXptr );

    ECBptr->fragmentDescriptor[1].address = ( void far * ) Buffer;
    ECBptr->fragmentDescriptor[1].size = Buffsize;
}

void FAR PASCAL SPXSetupSendPacket( ECB *ECBptr, SPXHeader *SPXptr,
BYTE Network[4], BYTE Node[6],
    BYTE destSocket[2], BYTE sourceSocket[2], char *Buffer, WORD
Buffsize, void *(ESR)() )
{
    int ttime;
    IPXAddress IPXaddr;

    if ( ESR )
        ECBptr->ESRAddress = ( void far * ) ESR;
    else
        ECBptr->ESRAddress = ( void far *) NULL;

    ECBptr->inUseFlag = 0;
    ECBptr->socketNumber = MK_SOCKET( sourceSocket );
    ECBptr->fragmentCount = 2;

    ECBptr->fragmentDescriptor[0].address = ( void far * ) SPXptr;
    ECBptr->fragmentDescriptor[0].size = sizeof( *SPXptr );

    ECBptr->fragmentDescriptor[1].address = ( void far * ) Buffer;
    ECBptr->fragmentDescriptor[1].size = Buffsize;

    SPXptr->dataStreamType = 0;
    SPXptr->connectionControl = 0;

    // Setup for call to Get Local Target which gets immediate
    // address
    // and setup the IPX header's destination address
    movmem( Network, IPXaddr.network, 4 );
    movmem( Node, IPXaddr.node, 6 );
    movmem( destSocket, IPXaddr.socket, 2 );
    IPXGetLocalTarget( IPXTaskID, ( BYTE * )&IPXaddr, ( BYTE *
      )ECBptr->immediateAddress, &ttime );
    movmem( &IPXaddr, &SPXptr>destination, 12 );
}
```

```
void FAR PASCAL SPXSetupEstConnPacket( ECB *ECBptr, SPXHeader
*SPXptr, BYTE Network[4], BYTE Node[6],
    BYTE destSocket[2], BYTE sourceSocket[2], void *(ESR)() )
{
    int ttime;
    IPXAddress IPXaddr;

    if ( ESR )
        ECBptr->ESRAddress = ( void far * ) ESR;
    else
        ECBptr->ESRAddress = ( void far *) NULL;

    ECBptr->inUseFlag = 0;
    ECBptr->socketNumber = MK_SOCKET( sourceSocket );
    ECBptr->fragmentCount = 1;

    ECBptr->fragmentDescriptor[0].address = ( void far * ) SPXptr;
    ECBptr->fragmentDescriptor[0].size = sizeof( *SPXptr );

    SPXptr->dataStreamType = 0;
    SPXptr->connectionControl = 0;

    // Setup for call to Get Local Target which gets immediate
    // address
    // and setup the IPX header's destination address
    movmem( Network, IPXaddr.network, 4 );
    movmem( Node, IPXaddr.node, 6 );
    movmem( destSocket, IPXaddr.socket, 2 );
    IPXGetLocalTarget( IPXTaskID, ( BYTE * )&IPXaddr, ( BYTE *
      )ECBptr->immediateAddress, &ttime );
    movmem( &IPXaddr, &SPXptr>destination, 12 );
}

void FAR PASCAL SPXSetupListenConnPacket( ECB *ECBptr, SPXHeader
*SPXptr, BYTE Socket[2], void *(ESR)() )
{
    int ttime;
    IPXAddress IPXaddr;

    if ( ESR )
        ECBptr->ESRAddress = ( void far * ) ESR;
    else
        ECBptr->ESRAddress = ( void far * ) NULL;
    ECBptr->socketNumber = MK_SOCKET( Socket );

    ECBptr->fragmentCount = 1;
    ECBptr->fragmentDescriptor[0].address = ( void far * ) SPXptr;
    ECBptr->fragmentDescriptor[0].size = sizeof( *SPXptr );
}
```

First, we include the appropriate header files and make several definitions that we'll use in the course of the program. Also, here's the C definition of the Pend record—notice that it's identical to the one defined in the Visual Basic code above.

```
#include <windows.h>
#include <ctype.h>
#include <time.h>

#include <nxt.h>
#include <nit.h>
```

```
// Defines
#define WAITMAX              20
#define MAX_PACKETS          10
#define MAX_RECEIVE_ECBS     10
#define RETRY_COUNT          100
#define TEMPORARY_SOCKET     (BYTE)0
#define PERMANENT_SOCKET     (BYTE)0xFF
#define INVITE_SOCKET        0x0350
#define RPC_SOCKET           0X0450
#define OK                   0
#define ENABLE_WATCHDOG      0xFF
#define DISABLE_WATCHDOG     0
#define MK_SOCKET(a)         ( ( a[1] << 8 ) + a[0] )

// Types
typedef long int SSN;

typedef struct
{
    SSN     ssn;
    char    name[40];
    int     dollar;
} PARTINF1;

typedef struct
{
    SSN     ssn;
    char    name[40];
    int     dollar;
} PEND;
```

Next we include the local function call prototypes, and define our global data.

```
// Prototypes
void FAR PASCAL InitializeSPX( HWND hWnd );

int FAR PASCAL CliPlanOpen( HANDLE hWnd, char *planname );
int FAR PASCAL CliPlanClose( HANDLE hWnd );
int FAR PASCAL CliPlanAdd( HANDLE hWnd, PARTINF1 *plan );
int FAR PASCAL CliPlanInfo( HANDLE hWnd, SSN ssn, PARTINF1 *plan );
int FAR PASCAL CliPlanMod( HANDLE hWnd, SSN ssn, char *newName );

void FAR PASCAL SendClientPacket( HANDLE hWnd );
void FAR PASCAL FindServer( HANDLE hWnd );
void FAR PASCAL ConnectServer( HANDLE hWnd );
void FAR PASCAL AbortConnection( HANDLE hWnd );
void FAR PASCAL DownSide( HANDLE hWnd );

void FAR PASCAL IPXSetupRcvPacket( ECB *ECBptr, IPXHeader *IPXptr,
BYTE Socket[2], char *Buffer,
    WORD Buffsize, void *(ESR)() );

void FAR PASCAL IPXSetupSendPacket( ECB *ECBptr, IPXHeader *IPXptr,
BYTE Network[4], BYTE Node[6],
    BYTE destSocket[2], BYTE sourceSocket[2], char *Buffer, WORD
Buffsize, void *(ESR)() );
void FAR PASCAL SPXSetupRcvPacket( ECB *ECBptr, SPXHeader *SPXptr,
BYTE Socket[2], char *Buffer,
```

```
       WORD Buffsize, void *(ESR)() );

void FAR PASCAL SPXSetupSendPacket( ECB *ECBptr, SPXHeader *SPXptr,
BYTE Network[4], BYTE Node[6],
     BYTE destSocket[2], BYTE sourceSocket[2], char *Buffer, WORD
Buffsize, void *(ESR)() );

void FAR PASCAL SPXSetupEstConnPacket( ECB *ECBptr, SPXHeader
*SPXptr, BYTE Network[4], BYTE Node[6],
     BYTE destSocket[2], BYTE sourceSocket[2], void *(ESR)() );

void FAR PASCAL SPXSetupListenConnPacket( ECB *ECBptr, SPXHeader
*SPXptr, BYTE Socket[2], void *(ESR)() );

//Global Data
WORD            connectionID;
ECB             svrECB[MAX_PACKETS];
IPXHeader       svrIPX;
SPXHeader       svrSPX[MAX_PACKETS];
char            buff[100];
char            buff2[MAX_PACKETS][100];
BYTE            targetNetwork[4] = { 0, 0, 0, 0 };
BYTE            targetNode[6] = { 0xFF, 0xFF, 0xFF, 0xFF, 0xFF, 0xFF };
BYTE            targetSocket[2] = { 0, 0 };
BYTE            askSocket[2] = { 0, 0 };
BYTE            talkSocket[2] = { 0, 0 };
time_t          wait_secs, start_secs, start_time;
int             currPacket;

char            message[78];        /*-- Buffer to hold messages.    --*/
int             socketNumber;       /*-- Socket number to talk on.   --*/
WORD            fSocket;                /*-- File server socket number. This
                         is a place holder and not used.  --*/
DWORD           IPXTaskID = 0; // Needs to be 0 so that we allocate
resources separately
```

This function is necessary for the DLL.

```
#pragma argsused
int FAR PASCAL LibMain( HANDLE hInstance, WORD wDataSeg, WORD
wHeapSize,
               LPSTR lpszCmdLine)
{
   if (wHeapSize > 0)
      UnlockData(0);
   return TRUE;
}
```

This following function initializes SPX and opens the sockets we'll be using. If there are any errors, it reports them to the user. Otherwise, it gives a brief status message at the end of the routine.

```
void FAR PASCAL InitializeSPX( HWND hWnd )
{
   HANDLE   hMem;
   int      installed;
   BYTE     major, minor;
   WORD     maxConnections, availConnections;
   WORD     maxNumECBs, maxSizeECB;
```

```
int       ccode;
char      message[75];
```

/*-- The way SPXInitialize is now, you need to pass in the maximum number of ECBs that will be used along with the maximum size of the largest ECB to be used. The other parameters are the same as the C Interface. --*/

```
maxNumECBs = MAX_RECEIVE_ECBS + 3;
maxSizeECB = 576;

installed = SPXInitialize( &IPXTaskID, maxNumECBs, maxSizeECB,
    &major, &minor,
                  &maxConnections, &availConnections );

if( !installed )
   {
   MessageBox( hWnd, "Error -- SPX is NOT installed!", NULL, MB_OK );
   PostQuitMessage( 0 );
   }
```

/*-- There are no short lived sockets under Windows, so a NULL is passed in for the socket type. --*/
```
ccode = IPXOpenSocket( IPXTaskID, (WORD FAR *)talkSocket, NULL );
if ( ( ccode ) && ( ccode != 0xFF ) ) {
   wsprintf( message, "ccode from IPXOpenSocket... %02X", ccode );
   MessageBox( hWnd, message, "Status", MB_OK );
   PostQuitMessage( 0 );
   }

ccode = IPXOpenSocket( IPXTaskID, (WORD FAR *)askSocket, NULL );
if ( ( ccode ) && ( ccode != 0xFF ) ) {
   wsprintf( message, "ccode from IPXOpenSocket... %02X", ccode );
   MessageBox( hWnd, message, "Status", MB_OK );
   PostQuitMessage( 0 );
   }

wsprintf( message, "Sockets open ok. talkSocket is %X askSocket is %X",
    IntSwap( *((WORD *)talkSocket) ),
    IntSwap( *((WORD *)askSocket) ) );
MessageBox( hWnd, message, "Status", MB_OK );

}
```

SendClientPacket is used by other routines to do the work of sending a packet to the application server. It handles all of the logic for the send (and the subsequent reception of a reply from the server) and reports any errors as necessary.

```
void FAR PASCAL SendClientPacket( HANDLE hWnd )
{
   int checkPacket;

   currPacket = 1;

   // Currently, svrECB[1] is listening, so cancel the event & use
   // it to send
   IPXCancelEvent( IPXTaskID, &svrECB[currPacket] );

   SPXSetupSendPacket( &svrECB[currPacket], &svrSPX[currPacket],
      targetNetwork, targetNode,
            targetSocket, talkSocket, buff, sizeof( buff ), NULL );
```

```
SPXSendSequencedPacket( IPXTaskID, connectionID,
  &svrECB[currPacket] );

start_time = time( NULL );
while ( svrECB[currPacket].inUseFlag != OK )
{
    IPXRelinquishControl();
    Yield();
    if ( difftime( time( NULL ), start_time ) > 1 )
    {
        start_time = time( NULL );
    }
}

if ( svrECB[currPacket].completionCode != OK )
{
    wsprintf( message, "SendClientPacket:Send error in svr ECB,
      status = %x ",
        svrECB[currPacket].completionCode );
    MessageBox( hWnd, message, NULL, MB_OK );
    MessageBox( hWnd, "Shutting client down...", NULL, MB_OK );
    AbortConnection( hWnd );
    DownSide( hWnd );
}

// Post svrECB[1] back to listen and check svrECB[1..MAX] for reply

SPXSetupRcvPacket( &svrECB[currPacket], &svrSPX[currPacket],
  talkSocket, buff2[currPacket], sizeof( buff ), NULL );

SPXListenForSequencedPacket( IPXTaskID, &svrECB[currPacket] );

start_time = wait_secs = time( &start_secs );
checkPacket = 1;
while ( ( wait_secs-start_secs ) < WAITMAX )
{
    IPXRelinquishControl();
    Yield();
    time( &wait_secs );
    if ( difftime( wait_secs, start_time ) > 1 )
    {
        start_time = time( NULL );
    }

    if ( svrECB[checkPacket].inUseFlag == OK )
    {
        if ( svrECB[checkPacket].completionCode != OK )
        {
            if ( ( svrECB[checkPacket].completionCode == 0xED ) ||
                ( svrSPX[checkPacket].dataStreamType == 0xFE ) )
                MessageBox( hWnd, "Other side terminated
                  connection", NULL, MB_OK );
            else
            {
                wsprintf( message, "SendClientPacket: Bad
                reception, status = %X\nShutting down...",
                    svrECB[checkPacket].completionCode );
                MessageBox( hWnd, message, "Status", MB_OK );
```

```
                              }
                              AbortConnection( hWnd );
                              DownSide( hWnd );
                         }
                         else
                         {
                              movmem( buff2[checkPacket], buff, sizeof( buff ) );
                              SPXSetupRcvPacket( &svrECB[checkPacket],
                                   &svrSPX[checkPacket], talkSocket,
                                        buff2[checkPacket], sizeof( buff ), NULL );
                              SPXListenForSequencedPacket( IPXTaskID,
                                   &svrECB[checkPacket] );
                              break;
                         }
                    }
                    checkPacket++;
                    if ( checkPacket == MAX_PACKETS )
                         checkPacket = 1;
               }

               if ( ( wait_secs  start_secs ) >= WAITMAX )
               {
                    MessageBox( hWnd, "Server did not respond...shutting down",
                         NULL, MB_OK );
                    AbortConnection( hWnd );
                    DownSide( hWnd );
               }
          }
```

The next five calls (they all start with Cli) simulate the remote procedure call model. Remote procedure calls are like local calls, except the work is done on a different machine. This is exactly what happens in a client-server model.

In the case of our application, if the Visual Basic front-end wants to open the client plan file, it calls CliPlanOpen(). The VB front-end doesn't care who does the work; it simply prints the results to the screen when they are returned. Here in the DLL we set up for the call to SendClientPacket.

For each of the next five calls, we first clear the buffer, buff, that is passed to the server. The first byte in buff (buff[0]) contains a number that indicates the call being made (0 for Open, 1 for Close, 2 for add, 3 for info, 4 for modify). The next byte (buff[1]) is the return code generated by the remote function (0 for success; otherwise, an error). The remaining bytes will be interpreted by the server depending on which call is being made. For instance, the Open function on the server side will look at offset 2 of buff to read the name of the file to open.

```
// Structure for buff now is:
//    buff[0]    = Function number
//    buff[1]    = Return code
//    buff[2n]   = Passed Structure

int FAR PASCAL CliPlanOpen( HANDLE hWnd, char *planname )
{
     memset( buff, NULL, sizeof( buff ) );
     buff[0] = 0;
     strcpy( &buff[2], planname );
```

```
        SendClientPacket( hWnd );
        return buff[1];
}

int FAR PASCAL CliPlanClose( HANDLE hWnd )
{
        memset( buff, NULL, sizeof( buff ) );
        buff[0] = 1;
        SendClientPacket( hWnd );
        return buff[1];
}

int FAR PASCAL CliPlanAdd( HANDLE hWnd, PARTINF1 *plan )
{
        memset( buff, NULL, sizeof( buff ) );
        buff[0] = 2;
        movmem( plan, &buff[2], sizeof( PARTINF1 ) );
        SendClientPacket( hWnd );
        return buff[1];
}

int FAR PASCAL CliPlanInfo( HANDLE hWnd, SSN ssn, PARTINF1 *plan )
{
        memset( buff, NULL, sizeof( buff ) );
        buff[0] = 3;
        movmem( &ssn, &buff[2], sizeof( SSN ) );
        SendClientPacket( hWnd );
        movmem( &buff[2], plan, sizeof( PARTINF1 ) );
        return buff[1];
}

int FAR PASCAL CliPlanMod( HANDLE hWnd, SSN ssn, char *newName )
{
        memset( buff, NULL, sizeof( buff ) );
        buff[0] = 4;
        movmem( &ssn, &buff[2], sizeof( SSN ) );
        strcpy( &buff[2+sizeof(SSN)], newName );
        SendClientPacket( hWnd );
        return buff[1];
}
```

If you remember, we called FindServer in the Visual Basic front-end (after SPXInitialize) in response to the user pressing the first button. FindServer scans the bindery for the application server; the application server "advertises" itself and places its address in the NetWare bindery. FindServer then communicates with the server. If it is successful, it calls ConnectServer, below, to establish an SPX connection.

```
void FAR PASCAL FindServer( HANDLE hWnd )
{
        int status, segmentNumber = 1;
        char objectName[48], propertyName[16];
        char propertySecurity, propertyHasValue, moreProperties;
        BYTE objectHasProperties, objectFlag, objectSecurity;
        long sequenceNumber;
        BYTE moreSegments, propertyFlags;
        WORD objectType;
```

```
IPXAddress serverAddress;
char value[128];
DWORD objectID = 0xFFFFFFFF;

// Scan the bindery for the server we want...
MessageBox( hWnd, "About to call ScanBinderyObject", NULL, MB_OK );
status = ScanBinderyObject( "*", (WORD) OT_JOB_SERVER,
  &objectID, objectName,
          &objectType, &objectHasProperties, &objectFlag,
             &objectSecurity );
if ( status )
{
    wsprintf( message, "Error in ScanBinderyObject, error code = %X\n",
      status );
    MessageBox( hWnd, "Shutting client down...", NULL, MB_OK );
    DownSide( hWnd );
    return;
}
else
{
    MessageBox( hWnd, "ScanBinderyObject successful, calling
      ReadPropertyValue", NULL, MB_OK );
    status = ReadPropertyValue( objectName, objectType,
      "NET_ADDRESS", segmentNumber, value, &moreSegments,
                                 &propertyFlags );
    if ( status )
    {
        wsprintf( message, "Error in ReadPropertyValue, error
          code = %X\n", status );
        MessageBox( hWnd, "Shutting client down...", NULL,
          MB_OK );
        DownSide( hWnd );
        return;
    }
    else
    {
        movmem( value, &serverAddress, sizeof( serverAddress ) );
        MessageBox( hWnd, "ReadPropertyValue ok, doing our
          movmem's and message print", NULL, MB_OK );
        movmem( serverAddress.network, targetNetwork, 4 );
        movmem( serverAddress.node, targetNode, 6 );
        movmem( serverAddress.socket, targetSocket, 2 );
        //*( (int *)targetSocket ) = IntSwap( *( (int
        // *)targetSocket ) );
        wsprintf( message, "Job server is listening on socket %X.\n",
                IntSwap( *( (WORD *)serverAddress.socket ) ) );
        MessageBox( hWnd, message, "Status", MB_OK );
    }
}

MessageBox( hWnd, "Calling application server...", "Info", MB_OK );

strcpy( buff, "Test Server #1" );
IPXSetupSendPacket( &svrECB[currPacket], &svrIPX, targetNetwork,
  targetNode, targetSocket, askSocket, buff, sizeof( buff ),
    NULL );
```

```
IPXSendPacket( IPXTaskID, &svrECB[currPacket] );

start_time = time( NULL );
while ( svrECB[currPacket].inUseFlag != OK )
{
    IPXRelinquishControl();
    Yield();
    if ( difftime( time( NULL ), start_time ) > 1 )
        start_time = time( NULL );
}

if ( svrECB[currPacket].completionCode != OK )
{
    wsprintf( message, "FindServer:Send error in svr ECB,
      status = %x Aborting.",
            svrECB[currPacket].completionCode );
    MessageBox( hWnd, message, NULL, MB_OK );
    DownSide( hWnd );
}

// Setup again and listen for response

IPXSetupRcvPacket( &svrECB[currPacket], &svrIPX, askSocket,
  buff, sizeof( buff ), NULL );

IPXListenForPacket( IPXTaskID, &svrECB[currPacket] );

start_time = wait_secs = time( &start_secs );
while ( ( svrECB[currPacket].inUseFlag != OK ) && ( (
  wait_secs-start_secs ) < WAITMAX ) )
{
    IPXRelinquishControl();
    Yield();
    time( &wait_secs );
    if ( difftime( wait_secs, start_time ) > 1 )
        start_time = time( NULL );
}

if (  ( wait_secs - start_secs ) >= WAITMAX )
{
    wsprintf( message, "FileServer:Server did not respond
      Aborting." );
    MessageBox( hWnd, message, NULL, MB_OK );
    DownSide( hWnd );
}

if ( svrECB[currPacket].completionCode != OK )
{
    wsprintf( message, "FindServer:Bad reception, status =
      %x\nAborting.", svrECB[currPacket].completionCode );
    MessageBox( hWnd, message, NULL, MB_OK );
    DownSide( hWnd );
}

movmem( svrIPX.source.node, targetNode, 6 );
movmem( svrIPX.source.network, targetNetwork, 4 );
movmem( svrIPX.source.socket, targetSocket, 2 );

ConnectServer( hWnd );
```

```
        MessageBox( hWnd, "Executing last line in FindServer()", NULL,
          MB_OK );
}

void FAR PASCAL ConnectServer( HANDLE hWnd )
{
    int i, retVal;
    // First, post up a couple of listen ECB's to establish the
    // connection with
    for ( i = 1; i < MAX_PACKETS; i++ )
    {
        SPXSetupRcvPacket( &svrECB[i], &svrSPX[i], talkSocket,
          buff2[i], sizeof( buff ), NULL );
        SPXListenForSequencedPacket( IPXTaskID, &svrECB[i] );
    }
    currPacket = 0;

    // Then setup a Connection Establish ECB
    SPXSetupEstConnPacket( &svrECB[currPacket], &svrSPX[currPacket],
      targetNetwork, targetNode, targetSocket,
            talkSocket, NULL );

    retVal = SPXEstablishConnection( IPXTaskID, RETRY_COUNT,
      DISABLE_WATCHDOG, &connectionID, &svrECB[currPacket] );
    if ( retVal )
    {
        wsprintf( message, "Error in SPXEstablishConnection, return
          value = %X\n", retVal );
        MessageBox( hWnd, message, NULL, MB_OK );
        DownSide( hWnd );
    }

    start_time = time( NULL );
    while ( svrECB[currPacket].inUseFlag != OK )
    {
        if ( difftime( time( NULL ), start_time ) > 1 )
            start_time = time( NULL );
        IPXRelinquishControl();
        Yield();
    }

    if ( svrECB[currPacket].completionCode != OK )
    {
        wsprintf( message, "ConnectServer:Error establishing SPX
          connection, status = %x Aborting.",
            svrECB[currPacket].completionCode );
        MessageBox( hWnd, message, NULL, MB_OK );
        DownSide( hWnd );
    }
    else
    {
        wsprintf( message, "Connection to Server successful!
          Connection ID = %X", connectionID );
        MessageBox( hWnd, message, "Info", MB_OK );
    }
}
```

The AbortConnection routine breaks the SPX connection with the server, cancelling all of the listening Event Control Blocks.

```
void FAR PASCAL AbortConnection( HANDLE hWnd )
{
    int currPacket;
    time_t start_time;

    // Terminate SPX connection
    MessageBox( hWnd, "Terminating SPX connection", "Status", MB_OK );

    currPacket = MAX_PACKETS - 1;
    IPXCancelEvent( IPXTaskID, &svrECB[currPacket] );

    SPXSetupEstConnPacket( &svrECB[currPacket], &svrSPX[currPacket],
        targetNetwork, targetNode, targetSocket,
            talkSocket, NULL );
    SPXTerminateConnection( IPXTaskID, connectionID,
        &svrECB[currPacket] );

    start_time = time( NULL );
    while ( svrECB[currPacket].inUseFlag != OK )
    {
        IPXRelinquishControl();
        Yield();
        if ( difftime( time( NULL ), start_time ) > 1 )
        {
            start_time = time( NULL );
        }
    }

    if ( svrECB[currPacket].completionCode != OK )
        if ( svrECB[currPacket].completionCode == 0xEE )
            MessageBox( hWnd, "Other side terminated connection",
                "Info", MB_OK );
        else
        {
            wsprintf( message, "AbortConnection:Send error in
                Server ECB, status = %x ",
                    svrECB[currPacket].completionCode );
            MessageBox( hWnd, message, NULL, MB_OK );
        }
    else
        MessageBox( hWnd, "SPX Connection Terminated", "Status", MB_OK );

    for ( currPacket = 0; currPacket < MAX_PACKETS; currPacket++ )
        IPXCancelEvent( IPXTaskID, &svrECB[currPacket] );

}
```

The DownSide routine is called by the client side when it is closing down. It closes all of the open sockets, de-initializes IPX/SPX, and gives a message to the user to that effect.

```
void FAR PASCAL DownSide( HANDLE hWnd )
{
    // Close sockets and exit
    IPXCloseSocket( IPXTaskID, INVITE_SOCKET );
    IPXCloseSocket( IPXTaskID, RPC_SOCKET );
```

```
        IPXSPXDeinit( IPXTaskID );
        MessageBox( hWnd, "This side terminated", "Info", MB_OK );
}
```

The remaining routines are used to setup IPX and SPX header structures and Event Control Blocks. They are used to reduce the repetitive initializations that are done when using the IPX/SPX functions.

```
void FAR PASCAL IPXSetupRcvPacket( ECB *ECBptr, IPXHeader *IPXptr,
BYTE Socket[2], char *Buffer,
    WORD Buffsize, void *(ESR)() )
{
    if ( ESR )
        ECBptr->ESRAddress = ( void far * ) ESR;
    else
        ECBptr->ESRAddress = ( void far * ) NULL;

    ECBptr->socketNumber = MK_SOCKET( Socket );
    ECBptr->fragmentCount = 2;

    ECBptr->fragmentDescriptor[0].address = ( void far * ) IPXptr;
    ECBptr->fragmentDescriptor[0].size = sizeof( *IPXptr );

    ECBptr->fragmentDescriptor[1].address = ( void far * ) Buffer;
    ECBptr->fragmentDescriptor[1].size = Buffsize;
}

void FAR PASCAL IPXSetupSendPacket( ECB *ECBptr, IPXHeader *IPXptr,
BYTE Network[4], BYTE Node[6],
    BYTE destSocket[2], BYTE sourceSocket[2], char *Buffer, WORD
Buffsize, void *(ESR)() )
{
    int ttime;
    IPXAddress IPXaddr;

    if ( ESR )
        ECBptr>ESRAddress = ( void far * ) ESR;
    else
        ECBptr->ESRAddress = ( void far *) NULL;

    ECBptr->inUseFlag = 0;
    ECBptr->socketNumber = MK_SOCKET( sourceSocket );
    ECBptr->fragmentCount = 2;

    ECBptr->fragmentDescriptor[0].address = ( void far * ) IPXptr;
    ECBptr->fragmentDescriptor[0].size = sizeof( *IPXptr );

    ECBptr->fragmentDescriptor[1].address = ( void far * ) Buffer;
    ECBptr->fragmentDescriptor[1].size = Buffsize;

    // Setup for call to Get Local Target which gets immediate
    // address
    // and setup the IPX header's destination address
    movmem( Network, IPXaddr.network, 4 );
    movmem( Node, IPXaddr.node, 6 );
    movmem( destSocket, IPXaddr.socket, 2 );
    IPXGetLocalTarget( IPXTaskID, ( BYTE * )&IPXaddr, ( BYTE *
     )ECBptr->immediateAddress, &ttime );
    movmem( &IPXaddr, &IPXptr->destination, 12 );
}
```

```
void FAR PASCAL SPXSetupRcvPacket( ECB *ECBptr, SPXHeader *SPXptr,
BYTE Socket[2], char *Buffer,
      WORD Buffsize, void *(ESR)() )
{
      if ( ESR )
            ECBptr->ESRAddress = ( void far * ) ESR;
      else
            ECBptr->ESRAddress = ( void far * ) NULL;

      ECBptr->socketNumber = MK_SOCKET( Socket );
      ECBptr->fragmentCount = 2;

      ECBptr->fragmentDescriptor[0].address = ( void far * ) SPXptr;
      ECBptr->fragmentDescriptor[0].size = sizeof( *SPXptr );

      ECBptr->fragmentDescriptor[1].address = ( void far * ) Buffer;
      ECBptr->fragmentDescriptor[1].size = Buffsize;
}

void FAR PASCAL SPXSetupSendPacket( ECB *ECBptr, SPXHeader *SPXptr,
BYTE Network[4], BYTE Node[6],
      BYTE destSocket[2], BYTE sourceSocket[2], char *Buffer, WORD
        Buffsize, void *(ESR)() )
{
      int ttime;
      IPXAddress IPXaddr;

      if ( ESR )
            ECBptr->ESRAddress = ( void far * ) ESR;
      else
            ECBptr->ESRAddress = ( void far *) NULL;

      ECBptr->inUseFlag = 0;
      ECBptr->socketNumber = MK_SOCKET( sourceSocket );
      ECBptr->fragmentCount = 2;

      ECBptr->fragmentDescriptor[0].address = ( void far * ) SPXptr;
      ECBptr->fragmentDescriptor[0].size = sizeof( *SPXptr );

      ECBptr->fragmentDescriptor[1].address = ( void far * ) Buffer;
      ECBptr->fragmentDescriptor[1].size = Buffsize;

      SPXptr->dataStreamType = 0;
      SPXptr->connectionControl = 0;

      // Setup for call to Get Local Target which gets immediate
      // address
      // and setup the IPX header's destination address
      movmem( Network, IPXaddr.network, 4 );
      movmem( Node, IPXaddr.node, 6 );
      movmem( destSocket, IPXaddr.socket, 2 );
      IPXGetLocalTarget( IPXTaskID, ( BYTE * )&IPXaddr, ( BYTE *
        )ECBptr->immediateAddress, &ttime );
      movmem( &IPXaddr, &SPXptr->destination, 12 );
}

void FAR PASCAL SPXSetupEstConnPacket( ECB *ECBptr, SPXHeader
*SPXptr, BYTE Network[4], BYTE Node[6],
      BYTE destSocket[2], BYTE sourceSocket[2], void *(ESR)() )
{
```

```
    int ttime;
    IPXAddress IPXaddr;

    if ( ESR )
         ECBptr->ESRAddress = ( void far * ) ESR;
    else
         ECBptr->ESRAddress = ( void far *) NULL;

    ECBptr->inUseFlag = 0;
    ECBptr->socketNumber = MK_SOCKET( sourceSocket );
    ECBptr->fragmentCount = 1;

    ECBptr->fragmentDescriptor[0].address = ( void far * ) SPXptr;
    ECBptr->fragmentDescriptor[0].size = sizeof( *SPXptr );

    SPXptr->dataStreamType = 0;
    SPXptr->connectionControl = 0;

    // Setup for call to Get Local Target which gets immediate
    // address
    // and setup the IPX header's destination address
    movmem( Network, IPXaddr.network, 4 );
    movmem( Node, IPXaddr.node, 6 );
    movmem( destSocket, IPXaddr.socket, 2 );
    IPXGetLocalTarget( IPXTaskID, ( BYTE * )&IPXaddr, ( BYTE *
      )ECBptr->immediateAddress, &ttime );
    movmem( &IPXaddr, &SPXptr->destination, 12 );
}

void FAR PASCAL SPXSetupListenConnPacket( ECB *ECBptr, SPXHeader
*SPXptr, BYTE Socket[2], void *(ESR)() )
{
    int ttime;
    IPXAddress IPXaddr;

    if ( ESR )
         ECBptr->ESRAddress = ( void far * ) ESR;
    else
         ECBptr->ESRAddress = ( void far * ) NULL;

    ECBptr->socketNumber = MK_SOCKET( Socket );

    ECBptr->fragmentCount = 1;
    ECBptr->fragmentDescriptor[0].address = ( void far * ) SPXptr;
    ECBptr->fragmentDescriptor[0].size = sizeof( *SPXptr );
}
```

Below is the Windows DEFinition file for our DLL. Note the NWIPXSPX and NWNETAPI functions that are imported from the NetWare C Interface for Windows. Note also the functions we export to Windows (and to Visual Basic).

DEF file for CLIDLL.DLL:

```
NAME          CLIDLL
EXETYPE       WINDOWS
DESCRIPTION   'Windows Client Prototype DLL version 1.0'
STUB          'WINSTUB.EXE'
CODE          FIXED
DATA          FIXED SINGLE
HEAPSIZE      8192
```

```
        STACKSIZE      8192
        IMPORTS
                    NWIPXSPX.IPXListenForPacket
                    NWIPXSPX.IPXSendPacket
                    NWIPXSPX.IPXCancelEvent
                    NWIPXSPX.IPXGetLocalTarget
                    NWIPXSPX.IPXCloseSocket
                    NWIPXSPX.IPXInitialize
                    NWIPXSPX.IPXOpenSocket
                    NWIPXSPX.IPXRelinquishControl
                    NWIPXSPX.IPXSPXDeinit
                    NWIPXSPX.SPXEstablishConnection
                    NWIPXSPX.SPXInitialize
                    NWIPXSPX.SPXListenForConnection
                    NWIPXSPX.SPXListenForSequencedPacket
                    NWIPXSPX.SPXSendSequencedPacket
                    NWIPXSPX.SPXTerminateConnection
                    NWNETAPI.ReadPropertyValue
                    NWNETAPI.ScanBinderyObject
                    NWNETAPI.IntSwap
        EXPORTS
                    LibMain

                    InitializeSPX
                    FindServer
                    AbortConnection
                    DownSide

                    CliPlanOpen
                    CliPlanClose
                    CliPlanAdd
                    CliPlanInfo
                    CliPlanMod
```

Client-Server Application, Part II: The Server

Now that you've seen the code to the client, let's review the source code for the application server. The server is an SPX prototype of a server, so it's named SPXPROTO. It is composed of several modules:

main.c	Startup and initialization code. This module parses the command line and calls a function in either client.c or server.c.
server.c	Contains all of the code for the application server.
client.c	Contains code so the application can be a client under DOS.
clisvr.c	Contains code used by both server.c and client.c.

The server operates by typing SPXPROTO followed by /R which tells it to "receive" requests. If you don't have Windows running or just want to test SPXPROTO out, start SPXPROTO on one PC with the /R parameter; then start SPXPROTO (as a client) on another PC using the /S "send" parameter. You can

then press Enter to step through the same sequence of events previously outlined
for CLIENT.EXE.

C SOURCE FOR SPXPROTO: MAIN.C

The main function of this module, shown in Listing 5 below, is to parse the
command line and run either the Advertise() function or the FindServer()
function. If the user typed in "/S" as the command-line parameter then the
application would think you wanted to send a request to the server, so the
FindServer() function in client would be called. If you typed in "/R", the code in
main.c would call Advertise() to announce its availability as an application server
to potential clients.

```c
#define DEBUG

#include <stdio.h>
#include <time.h>
#include <nxt.h>
#include <nit.h>

#include "clisvr.h"
#include "server.h"
#include "client.h"

// Prototypes
void main( int argc, char *argv[] );

// Globals
extern int      errno;
WORD            connectionID;
ECB             svrECB[MAX_PACKETS];
IPXHeader       svrIPX;
SPXHeader       svrSPX[MAX_PACKETS];
char            buff[100];
char            buff2[MAX_PACKETS][100];
BYTE            targetNetwork[4] = { 0, 0, 0, 0 };
BYTE            targetNode[6] = { 0xFF, 0xFF, 0xFF, 0xFF, 0xFF, 0xFF };
BYTE            targetSocket[2] = { 0, 0 };
time_t          wait_secs, start_secs, start_time;
BYTE            askSocket[2]  = { 0, 0 };
BYTE            talkSocket[2] = { 0, 0 };
BYTE            advertising = FALSE;

void main( int argc, char *argv[] )
{
    BYTE majorRev, minorRev;
    WORD maxConn, availConn, status;
    void (*passedFunction)();

    if ( ( argc !=2 ) )
    {
        printf( "Usage: SPXTEST /s - to send a request to
          Application Server\n");
        printf( "                    /r - to wait to receive a
          request\n" );
        exit( 1 );
```

```
        }
        if ( !stricmp( argv[1], "/r" ) )
            passedFunction = Advertise;
        else
            if  ( !stricmp( argv[1], "/s" ) && argc < 4 )
                passedFunction = FindServer;
            else
            {
                printf( "Invalid command-line parameter\n" );
                printf( "Usage: SPXTEST /s - to send a request to
                    Application Server\n");
                printf( "                     /r - to wait to receive a
                    request\n" );
                exit( 1 );
            }
        if ( !IPXInitialize() )
            printf( "IPX ok.\n" );
        else
        {
            printf( "IPX could not be initialized.\n" );
            exit( 1 );
        }
        if ( SPXInitialize( &majorRev, &minorRev, &maxConn, &availConn ) )
            printf( "SPX ok. SPX rev = V%1d.%02d  Max Connections " \
                    "= %-4d  Available Connections = %-4d\n\n",
                    majorRev, minorRev, maxConn, availConn );

        else
        {
            printf( "SPX could not be initialized.\n" );
            exit( 1 );
        }
        status = IPXOpenSocket( talkSocket, TEMPORARY_SOCKET );
        if ( status != OK )
        {
            printf( "Error # %X opening invite socket", status );
            exit( 1 );
        }
        while ( 1 )
            (*passedFunction)();

}
```

C SOURCE FOR SPXPROTO: CLIENT.C

The code in client.c, shown in Listing 6 below, is quite similar to the CLIDLL.DLL code, except it's run under DOS instead of Windows. The printf statement, rather than the Windows MessageBox call, is used to communicate with the user.

```
#define DEBUG

//
// Client.C
//
```

```
#include <time.h>
#include <nxt.h>
#include <nit.h>
#include <sap.h>
#include "clisvr.h"
#include "client.h"

extern WORD          connectionID;
extern ECB           svrECB[MAX_PACKETS];
extern IPXHeader       svrIPX;
extern SPXHeader     svrSPX[MAX_PACKETS];
extern char           buff[100];
extern char          buff2[MAX_PACKETS][100];
extern BYTE          targetNetwork[4];
extern BYTE          targetNode[6];
extern BYTE          targetSocket[2];
extern time_t            wait_secs, start_secs, start_time;
extern BYTE          askSocket[2];
extern BYTE           talkSocket[2];

static int           currPacket = 0;

// Structure for buff now is:
//   buff[0]   = Function number
//   buff[1]   = Return code
//   buff[2-n] = Passed Structure

int CliPlanOpen( char *planname )
{
#ifdef DEBUG
    printf( "Client executing PlanOpen( %s )\n", planname );
#endif

    buff[0] = 0;
    strcpy( &buff[2], planname );
    SendClientPacket();

#ifdef DEBUG
    printf( "Server returned a result code of %2X for PlanOpen\n",
        buff[1] );
#endif
    return buff[1];
}

int CliPlanClose( void )
{
#ifdef DEBUG
    printf( "Client executing PlanClose()\n" );
#endif
    buff[0] = 1;
    SendClientPacket();
#ifdef DEBUG
    printf( "Server returned a result code of %2X for PlanClose()\n",
        buff[1] );
#endif
    return buff[1];
}

int CliPlanAdd( PARTINF1 *plan )
```

```
{
#ifdef DEBUG
     printf( "Client executing PlanAdd( %31d %15s $%3d )\n",
          plan->ssn, plan->name, plan->dollar );
#endif
     buff[0] = 2;
     movmem( plan, &buff[2], sizeof( PARTINF1 ) );
     SendClientPacket();
#ifdef DEBUG
     printf( "Server returned a result code of %2X for PlanAdd()\n",
          buff[1] );
#endif
     return buff[1];
}

int CliPlanInfo( SSN ssn, PARTINF1 *plan )
{
#ifdef DEBUG
     printf( "Client executing PlanInfo( %31d )\n", ssn );
#endif
     buff[0] = 3;
     movmem( &ssn, &buff[2], sizeof( SSN ) );
     SendClientPacket();
     movmem( &buff[2], plan, sizeof( PARTINF1 ) );
#ifdef DEBUG
     printf( "Server returned a result code of %2X for PlanInfo()\n",
          buff[1] );
     printf( "Server returned ( %31d %15s $%3d )\n", plan->ssn,
        plan->name, plan->dollar );
#endif
     return buff[1];
}

int CliPlanMod( SSN ssn, char *newName )
{
#ifdef DEBUG
     printf( "Client executing PlanMod( %31d %15s)\n", ssn, newName );
#endif
     buff[0] = 4;
     movmem( &ssn, &buff[2], sizeof( SSN ) );
     strcpy( &buff[2+sizeof(SSN)], newName );
     SendClientPacket();
#ifdef DEBUG
     printf( "Server returned a result code of %2X for PlanMod()\n",
          buff[1] );
#endif
     return buff[1];
}

void SendClientPacket( void )
{
     int checkPacket;

     currPacket = 1;

     // Currently, svrECB[1] is listening, so cancel the event & use
     // it to send
```

```
IPXCancelEvent( &svrECB[currPacket] );

SPXSetupSendPacket( &svrECB[currPacket], &svrSPX[currPacket],
  targetNetwork, targetNode, targetSocket,
    talkSocket, buff, sizeof( buff ), NULL );

SPXSendSequencedPacket( connectionID, &svrECB[currPacket] );

start_time = time( NULL );
while ( svrECB[currPacket].inUseFlag != OK )
{
    IPXRelinquishControl();
    if ( difftime( time( NULL ), start_time ) > 1 )
    {
        putchar('.');
        start_time = time( NULL );
    }
}
putchar( '\n' );
if ( svrECB[currPacket].completionCode != OK )
{
    printf( "SendClientPacket:Send error in svr ECB, status = %x ",
        svrECB[currPacket].completionCode );
    printf( "Shutting client down...\n" );
    AbortConnection();
    DownSide();
}

// Post our ECB back and check svrECB[1..MAX] for response

SPXSetupRcvPacket( &svrECB[currPacket], &svrSPX[currPacket],
  talkSocket, buff2[currPacket], sizeof( buff ), NULL );

SPXListenForSequencedPacket( &svrECB[currPacket] );

start_time = wait_secs = time( &start_secs );
printf("\n\nWaiting for Application Server to respond to our
  Client-Server call...\n " );
checkPacket = 1;
while ( ( wait_secsstart_secs ) < WAITMAX )
{
    IPXRelinquishControl();
    time( &wait_secs );
    if ( difftime( wait_secs, start_time ) > 1 )
    {
        putchar('.');
        start_time = time( NULL );
    }

    printf( "Checking packet %d\n", checkPacket );

    if ( svrECB[checkPacket].inUseFlag == OK )
    {
        if ( svrECB[checkPacket].completionCode != OK )
        {
            if ( ( svrECB[checkPacket].completionCode == 0xED ) ||
                ( svrSPX[checkPacket].dataStreamType == 0xFE ) )
                printf( "Other side terminated
                    connection.\n" );
            else
```

```
                              printf( "SendClientPacket: Bad reception,
                                  status = %X\nShutting down...",
                                     svrECB[checkPacket].completionCode );
                        AbortConnection();
                        DownSide();
                    }
                    else
                    {
                        movmem( buff2[checkPacket], buff, sizeof( buff ) );
                        SPXSetupRcvPacket( &svrECB[checkPacket],
                          &svrSPX[checkPacket], talkSocket,
                             buff2[checkPacket], sizeof( buff ), NULL );
                        SPXListenForSequencedPacket( &svrECB[checkPacket] );
                        break;
                    }
                }
                checkPacket++;
                if ( checkPacket == MAX_PACKETS )
                    checkPacket = 1;
        }
        putchar( '\n' );

        if (  ( wait_secs - start_secs ) >= WAITMAX )
        {
            printf( "Server did not respond \nShutting down...\n");
            AbortConnection();
            DownSide();
        }
}

void FindServer( void )
{
        int status, segmentNumber = 1;
        char objectName[48], propertyName[16];
        char propertySecurity, propertyHasValue, moreProperties;
        char objectHasProperties, objectFlag, objectSecurity;
        long sequenceNumber, objectID = 0xFFFFFFFF;
        BYTE moreSegments, propertyFlags;
        WORD objectType;
        IPXAddress serverAddress;

        // Scan the bindery for the server we want...
        status = ScanBinderyObject( "*", OT_JOB_SERVER, &objectID,
          objectName,
                  &objectType, &objectHasProperties, &objectFlag,
                  &objectSecurity );
        if ( status )
        {
            printf( "Error in ScanBinderyObject, error code = %X\n",
              status );
            exit( 1 );
        }
        else
        {
            printf( "Found job server %s.\n", objectName );

            status = ReadPropertyValue( objectName, objectType,
              "NET_ADDRESS",
```

```
                    segmentNumber, (BYTE *)&serverAddress,
                    &moreSegments, &propertyFlags );
        if ( status )
        {
            printf( "Error in ReadPropertyValue, error code =
                %X\n", status );
            exit( 1 );
        }
        else
        {
            movmem( serverAddress.network, targetNetwork, 4 );
            movmem( serverAddress.node, targetNode, 6 );
            movmem( serverAddress.socket, targetSocket, 2 );
            //*( (int *)targetSocket ) = IntSwap( *( (int *)targetSocket ) );
            printf( "Job server is listening on socket %X.\n",
                IntSwap( *( (WORD *)serverAddress.socket ) ) );
        }
    }

    status = IPXOpenSocket( askSocket, TEMPORARY_SOCKET );
    if ( status != OK )
    {
        printf( "Error # %X opening invite socket", status );
        exit( 1 );
    }

    printf( "Calling application server on socket %X...\n", IntSwap(
        *( (WORD *)askSocket ) ) );

    strcpy( buff, "Test Server #1" );
    IPXSetupSendPacket( &svrECB[currPacket], &svrIPX, targetNetwork,
      targetNode, targetSocket,
        askSocket, buff, sizeof( buff ), NULL );

    IPXSendPacket( &svrECB[currPacket] );

    start_time = time( NULL );
    while ( svrECB[currPacket].inUseFlag != OK )
    {
        IPXRelinquishControl();
        if ( difftime( time( NULL ), start_time ) > 1 )
        {
            putchar('.');
            start_time = time( NULL );
        }
    }
    putchar( '\n' );

    if ( svrECB[currPacket].completionCode != OK )
    {
        printf( "FindServer:Send error in svr ECB, status =
            %x\nAborting.\n",
            svrECB[currPacket].completionCode );
        DownSide();
    }

    // Setup again and listen for response
```

```
    IPXSetupRcvPacket( &svrECB[currPacket], &svrIPX, askSocket,
      buff, sizeof( buff ), NULL );

    IPXListenForPacket( &svrECB[currPacket] );

    start_time = wait_secs = time( &start_secs );
    printf("\n\nWaiting for Application Server to respond...\n " );
    while ( ( svrECB[currPacket].inUseFlag != OK ) && ( (
      wait_secs-start_secs ) < WAITMAX ) )
    {
        IPXRelinquishControl();
        time( &wait_secs );
        if ( difftime( wait_secs, start_time ) > 1 )
        {
            putchar('.');
            start_time = time( NULL );
        }
    }
    putchar( '\n' );

    if (  ( wait_secs - start_secs ) >= WAITMAX )
    {
        printf( "FindServer:Server did not respond \nAborting.\n");
        DownSide();
    }

    if ( svrECB[currPacket].completionCode != OK )
    {
        printf( "FindServer:Bad reception, status = %x\nAborting.\n",
          svrECB[currPacket].completionCode );
        DownSide();
    }

    printf("\nResult:%s\n", buff);

    movmem( svrIPX.source.node, targetNode, 6 );
    movmem( svrIPX.source.network, targetNetwork, 4 );
    movmem( svrIPX.source.socket, targetSocket, 2 );

    ConnectServer();
}

void ConnectServer( void )
{
    int i, retVal;

    printf( "Received response from app server, establishing
      connection...\n" );

    // First, post up a couple of listen ECB's to establish the
    // connection with
    for ( i = 1; i < MAX_PACKETS; i++ )
    {
        SPXSetupRcvPacket( &svrECB[i], &svrSPX[i], talkSocket,
          buff2[i], sizeof( buff ), NULL );
        SPXListenForSequencedPacket( &svrECB[i] );
    }
    currPacket = 0;

    // Then setup a Connection Establish ECB
```

```
        SPXSetupEstConnPacket( &svrECB[currPacket], &svrSPX[currPacket],
          targetNetwork, targetNode, targetSocket,
                talkSocket, NULL );

      retVal = SPXEstablishConnection( RETRY_COUNT, DISABLE_WATCHDOG,
        &connectionID, &svrECB[currPacket] );
      if ( retVal )
      {
            printf( "Error in SPXEstablishConnection, return value =
              %X\n", retVal );
            exit( 1 );
      }

      start_time = time( NULL );
      while ( ( svrECB[currPacket].inUseFlag != OK ) && ( !kbhit() ) )
      {
            if ( difftime( time( NULL ), start_time ) > 1 )
            {
                  putchar('.');
                  start_time = time( NULL );
            }
            IPXRelinquishControl();
      }
      putchar( '\n' );

      if ( svrECB[currPacket].completionCode != OK )
      {
            printf( "ConnectServer:Error establishing SPX connection,
              status = %x\nAborting.\n",
                  svrECB[currPacket].completionCode );
            DownSide();
      }
      else
            printf( "Connection to Application Server successful! " \
                  "\nConnection ID = %X\n", connectionID );

      QueryServer();
}

void QueryServer( void )
{
      int i, result;
      PARTINF1 sample = { 1, "Server Smith", 100 };
      char searchString[20];

      printf( "Pausing for open. Press any key...\n" );
      bioskey( 0 );
      if ( ( result = CliPlanOpen( "PLAN_A" ) ) )
      {
            printf( "CliPlanOpen: Error %X\n", result );
            exit( 1 );
      }
      else
            printf( "Plan opened successfully\n" );

      printf( "Pausing before adding 30 records. Press any key...\n" );
      bioskey( 0 );

      for ( i = 0; i < 30; i++, sample.ssn++, sample.dollar += 5 )
```

```
        if ( ( result = CliPlanAdd( &sample ) ) )
        {
             printf( "CliPlanAdd: Error %X\n", result );
             exit( 1 );
        }
        else
             printf( "Record %2d added successfully\n", i );
    printf( "Pausing before changing record 15. Press any key...\n" );
    bioskey( 0 );

    strcpy( searchString, "newGuy" );

    if ( ( result = CliPlanMod( 15L, "newGuy" ) ) == -1 )
        printf( "Search string [%s] not found\n" );
    else if ( result )
        {
             printf( "CliPlanMod: Error %X\n", result );
             exit( 1 );
        }
        else
             printf( "Record 15 successfully modded to 'newGuy'\n" );

    printf( "Pausing before listing 30 records. Press any key...\n" );
    bioskey( 0 );

    for ( i = 1; i <= 30; i++ )
    {
        if ( ( result = CliPlanInfo( (SSN)i, &sample ) ) == -1 )
        {
             printf( "CliPlanInfo: SSN %d not found\n", i );
             exit( 1 );
        }
        else if ( result )
             {
                 printf( "CliPlanInfo: Error %X\n", result );
                 exit( 1 );
             }

        printf( "[%2d]: %10ld %40s $%10d\n", i, sample.ssn,
           sample.name,
             sample.dollar );
    }

    printf( "Pausing for close. Press any key...\n" );
    bioskey( 0 );

    if ( ( result = CliPlanClose() ) )
    {
        printf( "CliPlanClose: Error %X\n", result );
        exit( 1 );
    }
    else
    {
        printf( "Plan successfully closed. Terminating...\n" );
        AbortConnection();
        DownSide();
    }
}
```

C SOURCE FOR SPXPROTO: SERVER.C

The following listing shows the source code for the server.c module of
SPXPROTO. Brief explanations of important sections are then provided.

```c
#define DEBUG
//
//   SPX Prototype Application
//      Server Side
//

#include <stdio.h>
#include <io.h>
#include <errno.h>
#include <fcntl.h>
#include <time.h>

#include <nxt.h>
#include <nit.h>
#include <sap.h>

#include "clisvr.h"
#include "server.h"

// Global Definitions
extern int errno;               // C error number
extern int _fmode;               // C default file translation mode
int planHandle;                     // Handle to the plan file

extern ECB          svrECB[MAX_PACKETS];
extern WORD         connectionID;
extern IPXHeader    svrIPX;
extern SPXHeader    svrSPX[MAX_PACKETS];
extern char         buff[100];
extern char         buff2[MAX_PACKETS][100];
extern BYTE         targetNetwork[4];
extern BYTE         targetNode[6];
extern BYTE         targetSocket[2];
extern time_t       wait_secs, start_secs, start_time;
extern BYTE         askSocket[2];
extern BYTE         talkSocket[2];
extern BYTE         advertising;

static int          currPacket;

#ifdef DEBUG2
main( int argc, char *argv[] )
{
    PARTINF1 sample = { 1, "John Smith", 100 };
    int i, result;
    char searchString[20];

    if ( argc < 2 )
    {
        printf( "Usage: SPXPROTO planname" );
        exit( 1 );
    }

    if ( SvrPlanOpen( argv[1] ) )
    {
```

```
                perror( "SvrPlanOpen" );
                exit( 1 );
        }
/*      for ( i = 0; i < 30; i++, sample.ssn++, sample.dollar += 5 )
            if ( SvrPlanAdd( &sample ) )
            {
                    perror( "SvrPlanAdd" )
                    exit( 1 );
            }
*/
        strcpy( searchString, "newGuy" );

        if ( ( result = SvrPlanMod( 15L, "newGuy" ) ) == -1 )
            printf( "Search string [%s] not found\n" );
        else if ( result )
        {
            perror( "SvrPlanMod" );
            exit( 1 );
        }

        for ( i = 1; i <= 30; i++ )
        {
            if ( ( result = SvrPlanInfo( (SSN)i, &sample ) ) == -1 )
            {
                printf( "SvrPlanInfo: SSN %d not found\n", i );
                exit( 1 );
            }
            else if ( result )
            {
                perror( "SvrPlanInfo" );
                exit( 1 );
            }
            printf( "[%2d]: %10ld %40s $%10d\n", i, sample.ssn,
              sample.name,
                sample.dollar );
        }

        if ( SvrPlanClose() )
        {
            perror( "SvrPlanClose" );
            exit( 1 );
        }
}
#endif

int SvrPlanOpen( char *planname )
{
    long numRecords;
    // This will eventually use SPX code to call out to the back end which
    // will open the file and set the global plan file handle planHandle

    if ( ( planHandle = _open( planname, O_RDWR | O_BINARY ) ) == -1 )
        if ( errno == ENOFILE )
        {
            // Create and initialize the plan file
            _fmode = O_BINARY;
```

```
                    planHandle = _creat( planname, NULL );

                    numRecords = 0;

                    if ( lseek( planHandle, 0L, SEEK_SET ) == -1 )
                        return errno;

                    if ( write( planHandle, &numRecords, sizeof(
                      numRecords ) ) == -1 ) return errno;

             }
         else
             return errno;
     return 0;
}

int SvrPlanClose( void )
{
    return close( planHandle );
}

int SvrPlanAdd( PARTINF1 *plan )
{
    long numRecords;

    // Rewind file, get the number of recs
    if ( lseek( planHandle, 0L, SEEK_SET ) == -1 )
        return errno;

    if ( read( planHandle, &numRecords, sizeof( numRecords ) ) == -1 )
        return errno;

    // Seek out 1 record past the last one
    if ( lseek( planHandle, ( numRecords * sizeof( PARTINF1 ) ) +
      sizeof( numRecords ), SEEK_SET ) == -1 )
        return errno;

    // And add the passed record
    if ( write( planHandle, plan, sizeof( PARTINF1 ) ) == -1 )
        return errno;

    // Finally, update the number of records and write it to the header
    // of the plan file
    numRecords++;

    if ( lseek( planHandle, 0L, SEEK_SET ) == -1 )
        return errno;

    if ( write( planHandle, &numRecords, sizeof( numRecords ) ) == -1 )
        return errno;

    return 0;
}

int SvrPlanInfo( SSN ssn, PARTINF1 *plan )
{
    // Tries to match ssn in the plan file. If it's successful, plan
    // is set, otherwise -1 is returned. If a hard error occurred,
    // errno is returned

    long numRecords, i;
```

```
        PARTINF1 readSvrPlan;

            // Rewind file, get the number of recs
            if ( lseek( planHandle, 0L, SEEK_SET ) == -1 )
                return errno;

            if ( read( planHandle, &numRecords, sizeof( numRecords ) ) == -1 )
                return errno;
            // Span file, search for match on passed 'ssn'
            for ( i = 0; i < numRecords; i++ )
            {
                // Read each record and test against passed 'ssn'
                if ( lseek( planHandle, ( i * sizeof( PARTINF1 ) ) +
                   sizeof( numRecords ), SEEK_SET ) == -1 )

                    return errno;

                if ( read( planHandle, &readSvrPlan, sizeof( PARTINF1 ) ) == -1 )
                    return errno;

                if ( ssn == readSvrPlan.ssn )
                {
                    movmem( &readSvrPlan, plan, sizeof( PARTINF1 ) );
                    return 0;
                }

            }

            return -1;
        }

    int SvrPlanMod( SSN ssn, char *newName )
    {
        // Tries to modify ssn in the plan file. If it's successful, newName
        // will be replaced in ssn's record. If ssn was not found, -1 is
        // returned. If a hard error occurred, errno is returned.

        long numRecords, i;
        PARTINF1 readSvrPlan;

        // Rewind file, get the number of recs
        if ( lseek( planHandle, 0L, SEEK_SET ) == -1 )
            return errno;

        if ( read( planHandle, &numRecords, sizeof( numRecords ) ) == -1 )
            return errno;

        // Span file, search for match on passed 'ssn'
        for ( i = 0; i < numRecords; i++ )
        {
            // Read each record and test against passed 'ssn'
            if ( lseek( planHandle, ( i * sizeof( PARTINF1 ) ) +
               sizeof( numRecords ), SEEK_SET ) == -1 )
                    return errno;

            if ( read( planHandle, &readSvrPlan, sizeof( PARTINF1 ) )
                == -1 )
                    return errno;

            if ( ssn == readSvrPlan.ssn )
```

```
        {
                        // Record found, so replace name and write back
                        strcpy( readSvrPlan.name, newName );

                        if ( lseek( planHandle, ( i * sizeof( PARTINF1 ) ) +
                            sizeof( numRecords ), SEEK_SET ) == -1 )

                                return errno;

                        if ( write( planHandle, &readSvrPlan, sizeof( PARTINF1
                            ) ) == -1 )
                                return errno;

                        return 0;
                }
        }

        return -1;
}

void Advertise( void )
{
        int returnVal;

        if ( !advertising )
        {
                printf( "Advertising...\n" );
                returnVal = AdvertiseService( OT_JOB_SERVER, "MASTER",
                    (WORD *)askSocket );
                if ( returnVal )
                {
                        printf( "Error advertising server. Code = %X.\n",
                            returnVal );
                        DownSide();
                }
                else
                {
                        advertising = TRUE;
                        printf( "Advertising on socket %X\n", IntSwap( *(
                            (WORD *)askSocket ) ) );
                }
        }

        currPacket = 0;

        IPXSetupRcvPacket( &svrECB[currPacket], &svrIPX, askSocket,
            buff, sizeof( buff ), NULL );
        IPXListenForPacket( &svrECB[currPacket] );

        printf( "Press any key to exit.\n" );
        printf( "Now waiting for PROCESSING request...\n" );

        while ( 1 )
        {
                if ( bioskey( 1 ) )
                {
                        bioskey(0);
                        printf( "Key pressed, shutting down server...\n" );
                        DownSide();
```

```
            }
            if ( !svrECB[currPacket].inUseFlag )
            {
                if ( !svrECB[currPacket].completionCode )
                {
                    printf( "Received invitation from %s on socket
                      %X\n", buff,
                      IntSwap( *( (WORD *)svrIPX.source.socket ) ) );
                    strcpy( buff, "OK" );

                    /* Place the immediate address returned into
                       our new target node */
                    movmem( svrIPX.source.node,    targetNode, 6 );
                    movmem( svrIPX.source.network, targetNetwork, 4 );
                    movmem( svrIPX.source.socket, targetSocket, 2 );

                    /* Setup to send the reply */
                    IPXSetupSendPacket( &svrECB[currPacket],
                      &svrIPX, targetNetwork, targetNode,
                      targetSocket, talkSocket, buff, sizeof
                        ( buff ), NULL );

                    /* Send the reply about whether we want to chat
                       or not */
                    IPXSendPacket( &svrECB[currPacket] );
                    start_time = time( NULL );
                    while ( ( svrECB[currPacket].inUseFlag != OK )
                      && ( !kbhit() ) )
                    {
                        IPXRelinquishControl();
                        if ( difftime( time( NULL ), start_time ) > 1 )
                        {
                            putchar('.');
                            start_time = time( NULL );
                        }
                    }
                putchar( '\n' );

                    if ( svrECB[currPacket].completionCode != OK )
                    {
                        printf( "Advertise:Send error in Server ECB,
                          status = %x\n",
                            svrECB[currPacket].completionCode );
                        printf( "Shutting down server...\n" );
                        DownSide();
                    }

                    EstablishConnection();
                    return;
                }
            }
        }
    }
}

void EstablishConnection( void )
{
    int i;
```

```
      printf( "Received invitation from client, listening to establish
        connection...\n" );

      // First, post up a couple of listen ECB's to establish the
      // connection with
      for ( i = 1; i < MAX_PACKETS; i++ )
      {
           SPXSetupRcvPacket( &svrECB[i], &svrSPX[i], talkSocket,
             buff2[i], sizeof( buff ), NULL );
           SPXListenForSequencedPacket( &svrECB[i] );
      }
      currPacket = 0;
      // Then setup a Connection Establish ECB
      SPXSetupListenConnPacket( &svrECB[currPacket],
        &svrSPX[currPacket], talkSocket, NULL );

      SPXListenForConnection( RETRY_COUNT, DISABLE_WATCHDOG,
        &svrECB[currPacket] );

      start_time = time( NULL );
      while ( ( svrECB[currPacket].inUseFlag != OK ) && ( !kbhit() ) )
      {
           IPXRelinquishControl();
           if ( difftime( time( NULL ), start_time ) > 1 )
           {
                putchar('.');
                start_time = time( NULL );
           }
      }
      putchar( '\n' );

      if ( svrECB[currPacket].completionCode != OK )
      {
           printf( "EstablishConnection:Error establishing SPX
             connection, status = %x\n",
                svrECB[currPacket].completionCode );
           printf( "Re-starting server...\n" );
           AbortConnection();
           return;
      }
      else
      {
           // Tried to setup targetNode, net, socket here, but you don't
           // get a source in the SPX packet from the Establish Conn ECB...

           connectionID = *( ( WORD *) svrECB[currPacket].IPXWorkspace );
           printf( "Connection to client successful!  Connection ID =
             %X   Socket = %X\n",
                connectionID, IntSwap( * ( (WORD *)targetSocket ) ) );
      }

      AppServer();
}

void AppServer( void )
{
      int returnVal, i, lowPacket;

      currPacket = lowPacket = 1;
```

```
printf( "Connection has been established. Waiting for
  request(s)...\n" );
printf( "Press any key to exit.\n" );

while ( 1 )
{
    IPXRelinquishControl();
    if ( bioskey( 1 ) )
    {
        bioskey(0);
        printf( "Key pressed, shutting down server...\n" );
        DownSide();
    }

    if ( !svrECB[currPacket].inUseFlag )
    {
        if ( !svrECB[currPacket].completionCode )
        {
            if ( svrSPX[currPacket].dataStreamType == 0xFE )
            {
                printf( "Other side terminated
                  connection.\n" );
                printf( "Closing server side & resetting
                  server...\n" );
                AbortConnection();
                return;
            }

            movmem( buff2[currPacket], buff, sizeof( buff ) );

            returnVal = ProcessReceiveBuffer();

            buff[1] = returnVal;
            movmem( buff, buff2[currPacket], sizeof( buff ) );

            /* Place the immediate address returned into
               our new target node */
            movmem( svrSPX[currPacket].source.node,
                targetNode, 6 );
            movmem( svrSPX[currPacket].source.network,
                targetNetwork, 4 );
            movmem(svrSPX[currPacket].source.socket,
                targetSocket, 2 );

            SPXSetupSendPacket( &svrECB[currPacket],
                    &svrSPX[currPacket], targetNetwork,
                    targetNode,
                targetSocket, talkSocket, buff2[currPacket],
                    sizeof( buff ), NULL );

            // Send the reply with the info we just got
            SPXSendSequencedPacket( connectionID,
                &svrECB[currPacket] );
            start_time = time( NULL );
            while ( ( svrECB[currPacket].inUseFlag != OK )
              && ( !kbhit() ) )
            {
                IPXRelinquishControl();
                if ( difftime( time( NULL ), start_time ) > 1 )
```

```
                        {
                                putchar('.');
                                start_time = time( NULL );
                        }
                }
                putchar( '\n' );

                if ( svrECB[currPacket].completionCode != OK )
                {
                    if ( svrECB[currPacket].completionCode == 0xED )
                        printf( "AppServer: Other side
                            terminated connection.\n" );
                    else
                        printf( "AppServer:Send error in Server
                            ECB, status = %X\n",
                                svrECB[currPacket].completionCode );

                    printf( "Aborting connection & resetting
                        server...\n" );
                    AbortConnection();
                    return;
                }

                // Re-post the ECB back to a listening state
                IPXCancelEvent( &svrECB[currPacket] );
                SPXSetupRcvPacket( &svrECB[currPacket],
                    &svrSPX[currPacket], talkSocket, buff2[currPacket],
                    sizeof( buff ), NULL );
                SPXListenForSequencedPacket(
                    &svrECB[currPacket] );
            }
            else
            {

                if ( svrECB[currPacket].completionCode == 0xED )
                    printf( "AppServer:Other side terminated
                        connection\n" );
                else
                    printf( "AppServer:Error receiving server
                        ECB, retcode = %X\n",
                            svrECB[currPacket].completionCode );
                AbortConnection();
                return;
            }
        }

        // Check each packet in our list ( lowPacket to MAX_PACKETS )
        currPacket++;
        if ( currPacket == MAX_PACKETS )
            currPacket = lowPacket;

    }
}

int ProcessReceiveBuffer( void )
{
    PARTINF1 tempPart;
    SSN tempSSN;
    int returnVal;
```

```
            // Structure for buff now is:
            //    buff[0]   = Function number
            //    buff[1]   = Return code
            //    buff[2n]  = Passed Structure

            switch( buff[0] )
            {
                  // PlanOpen
                  case 0:
#ifdef DEBUG
                        printf( "Received PlanOpen( %s ) request\n", &buff[2] );
#endif
                        returnVal = SvrPlanOpen( &buff[2] );
#ifdef DEBUG
                        printf( "Returning %2X for PlanOpen()\n", returnVal );
#endif
                        break;

                  // PlanClose
                  case 1:
#ifdef DEBUG
                        printf( "Received PlanClose() request\n" );
#endif
                        returnVal = SvrPlanClose();
#ifdef DEBUG
                        printf( "Returning %2X for PlanClose()\n", returnVal );
#endif
                        break;

                  // PlanAdd
                  case 2:
                        movmem( &buff[2], &tempPart, sizeof( PARTINF1 ) );
#ifdef DEBUG
                        printf( "ReceivedPlanAdd( %31d %15s $%3d ) request\n",
                              tempPart.ssn, tempPart.name, tempPart.dollar );
#endif
                        returnVal = SvrPlanAdd( &tempPart );
#ifdef DEBUG
                        printf( "Returning %2X for PlanAdd()\n", returnVal );
#endif
                        break;

                  // PlanInfo
                  case 3:
                        movmem( &buff[2], &tempSSN, sizeof( SSN ) );
#ifdef DEBUG
                        printf( "Received PlanInfo( %31d ) request\n", tempSSN );
#endif
                        returnVal = SvrPlanInfo( tempSSN, &tempPart );
                        memset( buff, NULL, 100 );
                        movmem( &tempPart, &buff[2], sizeof( PARTINF1 ) );
#ifdef DEBUG
                        printf( "Returning %2X for PlanInfo()\n", returnVal );
#endif
                        break;

                  // PlanMod
                  case 4:
```

```
                             movmem( &buff[2], &tempSSN, sizeof( SSN ) );
        #ifdef DEBUG
                             printf( "Client executing PlanMod( %3ld %15s)\n",
                                 tempSSN, &buff[2+sizeof(SSN)] );
        #endif
                             returnVal = SvrPlanMod( tempSSN, &buff[2+sizeof(SSN)] );
        #ifdef DEBUG
                             printf( "Returning %2X for PlanMod()\n", returnVal );
        #endif
                             break;

                    default:
                             printf( "Invalid request from client, shutting
                               down...\n" );
                             DownSide();
            }

            return returnVal;
    }
```

The code in server.c is the heart of the application server: It receives the requests, performs the work, and replies to the client.

```
#define DEBUG

//
//  SPX Prototype Application
//      Server Side
//

#include <stdio.h>
#include <io.h>
#include <errno.h>
#include <fcntl.h>
#include <time.h>

#include <nxt.h>
#include <nit.h>
#include <sap.h>

#include "clisvr.h"
#include "server.h"

// Global Definitions
extern int errno;                // C error number
extern int _fmode;                 // C default file translation mode
int planHandle;                     // Handle to the plan file

extern ECB          svrECB[MAX_PACKETS];
extern WORD         connectionID;
extern IPXHeader    svrIPX;
extern SPXHeader    svrSPX[MAX_PACKETS];
extern char         buff[100];
extern char         buff2[MAX_PACKETS][100];
extern BYTE         targetNetwork[4];
extern BYTE         targetNode[6];
extern BYTE         targetSocket[2];
extern time_t       wait_secs, start_secs, start_time;
extern BYTE         askSocket[2];
```

```
extern BYTE        talkSocket[2];
extern BYTE        advertising;

static int         currPacket;
```

The debug statement below is used for testing the local file manipulation functions. The code was left in to illustrate how local testing can be done—it's always best to get the local functions working properly before they are called remotely.

```
#ifdef DEBUG2
// This is code to test the internal SvrPlanXXX functions
main( int argc, char *argv[] )
{
    PARTINF1 sample = { 1, "John Smith", 100 };
    int i, result;
    char searchString[20];

    if ( argc < 2 )
    {
        printf( "Usage: SPXPROTO planname" );
        exit( 1 );
    }

    if ( SvrPlanOpen( argv[1] ) )
    {
        perror( "SvrPlanOpen" );
        exit( 1 );
    }

/*  for ( i = 0; i < 30; i++, sample.ssn++, sample.dollar += 5 )
        if ( SvrPlanAdd( &sample ) )
        {
            perror( "SvrPlanAdd" )
            exit( 1 );
        }
*/

    strcpy( searchString, "newGuy" );

    if ( ( result = SvrPlanMod( 15L, "newGuy" ) ) == -1 )
        printf( "Search string [%s] not found\n" );
    else if ( result )
    {
        perror( "SvrPlanMod" );
        exit( 1 );
    }

    for ( i = 1; i <= 30; i++ )
    {
        if ( ( result = SvrPlanInfo( (SSN)i, &sample ) ) == -1 )
        {
            printf( "SvrPlanInfo: SSN %d not found\n", i );
            exit( 1 );
        }
        else if ( result )
        {
            perror( "SvrPlanInfo" );
            exit( 1 );
```

```
            }
            printf( "[%2d]: %10ld %40s $%10d\n", i, sample.ssn,
                sample.name,
                    sample.dollar );
        }

        if ( SvrPlanClose() )
        {
            perror( "SvrPlanClose" );
            exit( 1 );
        }
    }
    #endif
```

Starting with SvrPlanOpen, the next five functions comprise the actual code that runs on the server in response to the CliPlanOpen and other calls. When you call CliPlanOpen in Visual Basic, the CLIDLL.DLL is called. It creates a request packet and sends it to the application server. Here the server breaks out the request (you will see that part soon) and calls SvrPlanOpen. SvrPlanOpen processes the request and returns. Then the code in SERVER.C packs up a reply and sends it back to CLIDLL.DLL which then returns to Visual Basic (and presents the results to the user). Here's the chain of events:

1. User presses Open in the Visual Basic program, CLIENT.EXE.

2. CLIENT.EXE calls CliPlanOpen in CLIDLL.DLL.

3. CLIDLL.DLL uses the SendPacket function to send a packet to SPXPROTO where it's received in the AppServer function and processed in the ProcessReceiveBuffer function.

4. ProcessReceiveBuffer then calls SvrPlanOpen.

5. SvrPlanOpen attempts to open the file. It passes the result back to ProcessReceiveBuffer.

6. ProcessReceiveBuffer sends the result (via SPX) to the client where SendPacket in CLIDLL.DLL receives the reply and passes it back to CliPlanOpen in CLIDLL.DLL.

7. CliPlanOpen in CLIDLL.DLL returns the result and the Visual Basic program displays the result to the user.

Scan the functions below to see what the actual code is doing when you open a file or read/write records. It's simply using the local C functions _open, read, write, and so on. You might actually be using Btrieve calls here, or an SQL engine, or something more robust.

```
int SvrPlanOpen( char *planname )
{
    long numRecords;

    // This will eventually use SPX code to call out to the back end
    // which
```

```
            // will open the file and set the global plan file handle
            // planHandle

            if ( ( planHandle = _open( planname, O_RDWR | O_BINARY ) ) == -1
        )
                if ( errno == ENOFILE )
                {
                    // Create and initialize the plan file
                    _fmode = O_BINARY;
                    planHandle = _creat( planname, NULL );

                    numRecords = 0;

                    if ( lseek( planHandle, 0L, SEEK_SET ) == -1 )
                        return errno;

                    if ( write( planHandle, &numRecords, sizeof(
                        numRecords ) ) == -1 )
                        return errno;
                }
            else
                    return errno;
        return 0;
    }

int SvrPlanClose( void )
{
    return close( planHandle );
}

int SvrPlanAdd( PARTINF1 *plan )
{
    long numRecords;

    // Rewind file, get the number of recs
    if ( lseek( planHandle, 0L, SEEK_SET ) == -1 )
        return errno;

    if ( read( planHandle, &numRecords, sizeof( numRecords ) ) == -1 )
        return errno;

    // Seek out 1 record past the last one
    if ( lseek( planHandle, ( numRecords * sizeof( PARTINF1 ) ) +
        sizeof( numRecords ), SEEK_SET ) == -1 )

            return errno;

    // And add the passed record
    if ( write( planHandle, plan, sizeof( PARTINF1 ) ) == -1 )
        return errno;

    // Finally, update the number of records and write it to the
    // header
    // of the plan file
    numRecords++;

    if ( lseek( planHandle, 0L, SEEK_SET ) == -1 )
        return errno;

    if ( write( planHandle, &numRecords, sizeof( numRecords ) ) == -1 )
```

```
        return errno;

    return 0;
}

int SvrPlanInfo( SSN ssn, PARTINF1 *plan )
{
    // Tries to match ssn in the plan file. If it's successful, plan
    // is set, otherwise -1 is returned. If a hard error occurred,
    // errno is returned

    long numRecords, i;
    PARTINF1 readSvrPlan;

    // Rewind file, get the number of recs
    if ( lseek( planHandle, 0L, SEEK_SET ) == -1 )
        return errno;

    if ( read( planHandle, &numRecords, sizeof( numRecords ) ) == -1 )
        return errno;

    // Span file, search for match on passed 'ssn'
    for ( i = 0; i < numRecords; i++ )
    {
        // Read each record and test against passed 'ssn'
        if ( lseek( planHandle, ( i * sizeof( PARTINF1 ) ) +
            sizeof( numRecords ), SEEK_SET ) == -1 )
                return errno;

        if ( read( planHandle, &readSvrPlan, sizeof( PARTINF1 ) ) == -1 )
                return errno;

        if ( ssn == readSvrPlan.ssn )
            {
                movmem( &readSvrPlan, plan, sizeof( PARTINF1 ) );
                return 0;
            }
    }

    return -1;
}

int SvrPlanMod( SSN ssn, char *newName )
{
    // Tries to modify ssn in the plan file. If it's successful, newName
    // will be replaced in ssn's record. If ssn was not found, -1 is
    // returned. If a hard error occurred, errno is returned.

    long numRecords, i;
    PARTINF1 readSvrPlan;

    // Rewind file, get the number of recs
    if ( lseek( planHandle, 0L, SEEK_SET ) == -1 )
        return errno;

    if ( read( planHandle, &numRecords, sizeof( numRecords ) ) == -1 )
        return errno;

    // Span file, search for match on passed 'ssn'
    for ( i = 0; i < numRecords; i++ )
```

```
        {
            // Read each record and test against passed 'ssn'
            if ( lseek( planHandle, ( i * sizeof( PARTINF1 ) ) +
              sizeof( numRecords ), SEEK_SET ) == -1 )
                return errno;

          if ( read( planHandle, &readSvrPlan, sizeof( PARTINF1 ) ) == -1 )
                return errno;

          if ( ssn == readSvrPlan.ssn )
            {
                // Record found, so replace name and write back
                strcpy( readSvrPlan.name, newName );

                if ( lseek( planHandle, ( i * sizeof( PARTINF1 ) ) +
                  sizeof( numRecords ), SEEK_SET ) == -1 )
                    return errno;

                if ( write( planHandle, &readSvrPlan, sizeof( PARTINF1
                  ) ) == -1 )
                    return errno;

                return 0;
            }
        }

    return -1;
}

void Advertise( void )
{
    int returnVal;

    if ( !advertising )
    {
        printf( "Advertising...\n" );
        returnVal = AdvertiseService( OT_JOB_SERVER, "MASTER",
          (WORD *)askSocket );
        if ( returnVal )
        {
            printf( "Error advertising server. Code = %X.\n",
              returnVal );
            DownSide();
        }
        else
        {
            advertising = TRUE;
            printf( "Advertising on socket %X\n", IntSwap( *(
              (WORD *)askSocket ) ) );
        }
    }

    currPacket = 0;

    IPXSetupRcvPacket( &svrECB[currPacket], &svrIPX, askSocket,
      buff, sizeof( buff ), NULL );
    IPXListenForPacket( &svrECB[currPacket] );
```

```
printf( "Press any key to exit.\n" );
printf( "Now waiting for PROCESSING request...\n" );

while ( 1 )
{
    if ( bioskey( 1 ) )
    {
        bioskey(0);
        printf( "Key pressed, shutting down server...\n" );
        DownSide();
    }

    if ( !svrECB[currPacket].inUseFlag )
    {
        if ( !svrECB[currPacket].completionCode )
        {
            printf( "Received invitation from %s on socket
              %X\n", buff,
                IntSwap( *( (WORD *)svrIPX.source.socket ) ) );
            strcpy( buff, "OK" );

            /* Place the immediate address returned into
               our new target node */
            movmem( svrIPX.source.node,   targetNode, 6 );
            movmem( svrIPX.source.network, targetNetwork, 4 );
            movmem( svrIPX.source.socket, targetSocket, 2 );

            /* Setup to send the reply */
            IPXSetupSendPacket( &svrECB[currPacket],
              &svrIPX, targetNetwork, targetNode,
                targetSocket, talkSocket, buff, sizeof( buff
                  ), NULL );

            /* Send the reply about whether we want to chat
               or not */
            IPXSendPacket( &svrECB[currPacket] );
            start_time = time( NULL );
            while ( ( svrECB[currPacket].inUseFlag != OK )
              && ( !kbhit() ) )
            {
                IPXRelinquishControl();
                if ( difftime( time( NULL ), start_time ) > 1 )
                {
                    putchar('.');
                    start_time = time( NULL );
                }
            }
        }
        putchar( '\n' );

        if ( svrECB[currPacket].completionCode != OK )
        {
            printf( "Advertise:Send error in Server ECB,
              status = %x\n",
                  svrECB[currPacket].completionCode );
            printf( "Shutting down server...\n" );
            DownSide();
        }
```

```
                              EstablishConnection();
                              return;
                          }
                      }
                  }
              }
```

The Advertise function in the preceding code is called first when you run the application server. Advertise starts the NetWare shell's Asynchronous Event Scheduler to broadcast an advertisement about our little application server every minute (using a protocol called the Service Advertising Protocol). File servers that "hear" this advertisement place the address of our application server in their binderies. Then, when clients go to look for application servers, they just scan the local bindery for objects of type "server." That's how CLIDLL.DLL finds our application server (in the FindServer() function).

```
void EstablishConnection( void )
{
    int i;

    printf( "Received invitation from client, listening to establish
      connection...\n" );

    // First, post up a couple of listen ECB's to establish the
    // connection with
    for ( i = 1; i < MAX_PACKETS; i++ )
    {
        SPXSetupRcvPacket( &svrECB[i], &svrSPX[i], talkSocket,
          buff2[i], sizeof( buff ), NULL );
        SPXListenForSequencedPacket( &svrECB[i] );
    }
    currPacket = 0;

    // Then setup a Connection Establish ECB
    SPXSetupListenConnPacket( &svrECB[currPacket],
      &svrSPX[currPacket], talkSocket, NULL );

    SPXListenForConnection( RETRY_COUNT, DISABLE_WATCHDOG,
      &svrECB[currPacket] );

    start_time = time( NULL );
    while ( ( svrECB[currPacket].inUseFlag != OK ) && ( !kbhit() ) )
    {
        IPXRelinquishControl();
        if ( difftime( time( NULL ), start_time ) > 1 )
        {
            putchar('.');
            start_time = time( NULL );
        }
    }
    putchar( '\n' );

    if ( svrECB[currPacket].completionCode != OK )
    {
        printf( "EstablishConnection:Error establishing SPX
          connection, status = %x\n",
            svrECB[currPacket].completionCode );
        printf( "Restarting server...\n" );
```

```
                AbortConnection();
                return;
        }
        else
        {
            // Tried to setup targetNode, net, socket here, but you don't
            // get a source in the SPX packet from the Establish Conn ECB...

            connectionID = *( ( WORD *) svrECB[currPacket].IPXWorkspace );
            printf( "Connection to client successful!  Connection ID =
                %X  Socket = %X\n",
                    connectionID, IntSwap( * ( (WORD *)targetSocket ) ) );
        }

        AppServer();
}
```

In the preceding code, EstablishConnection is called when the server is being invited to connect to a client. It's essentially a handshake maneuver. Once this is completed, EstablishConnection calls AppServer.

```
void AppServer( void )
{
    int returnVal, i, lowPacket;
    currPacket = lowPacket = 1;

    printf( "Connection has been established. Waiting for
        request(s)...\n" );
    printf( "Press any key to exit.\n" );

    while ( 1 )
    {
        IPXRelinquishControl();
        if ( bioskey( 1 ) )
        {
            bioskey(0);
            printf( "Key pressed, shutting down server...\n" );
            DownSide();
        }

        if ( !svrECB[currPacket].inUseFlag )
        {
            if ( !svrECB[currPacket].completionCode )
            {
                if ( svrSPX[currPacket].dataStreamType == 0xFE )
                {
                    printf( "Other side terminated
                        connection.\n" );
                    printf( "Closing server side & resetting
                        server...\n" );
                    AbortConnection();
                    return;
                }

                movmem( buff2[currPacket], buff, sizeof( buff ) );

                returnVal = ProcessReceiveBuffer();

                buff[1] = returnVal;
```

```
            movmem( buff, buff2[currPacket], sizeof( buff ) );

              /* Place the immediate address returned into
                 our new target node */
              movmem( svrSPX[currPacket].source.node,
                targetNode, 6 );
              movmem( svrSPX[currPacket].source.network,
                targetNetwork, 4 );
              movmem( svrSPX[currPacket].source.socket,
                targetSocket, 2 );

              SPXSetupSendPacket( &svrECB[currPacket],
                &svrSPX[currPacket], targetNetwork, targetNode,
                targetSocket, talkSocket, buff2[currPacket],
                  sizeof( buff ), NULL );

              // Send the reply with the info we just got
              SPXSendSequencedPacket( connectionID,
                &svrECB[currPacket] );
              start_time = time( NULL );
              while ( ( svrECB[currPacket].inUseFlag != OK )
                && ( !kbhit() ) )
              {
                  IPXRelinquishControl();
                  if ( difftime( time( NULL ), start_time ) > 1 )
                  {
                      putchar('.');
                      start_time = time( NULL );
                  }
            }
            putchar( '\n' );

              if ( svrECB[currPacket].completionCode != OK )
              {
                  if ( svrECB[currPacket].completionCode == 0xED )
                      printf( "AppServer: Other side
                          terminated connection.\n" );
                  else
                      printf( "AppServer:Send error in Server
                          ECB, status = %X\n",
                            svrECB[currPacket].completionCode );

                  printf( "Aborting connection & resetting
                    server...\n" );
                  AbortConnection();
                  return;
              }

              // Repost the ECB back to a listening state
              IPXCancelEvent( &svrECB[currPacket] );
              SPXSetupRcvPacket( &svrECB[currPacket],
                &svrSPX[currPacket], talkSocket,
                buff2[currPacket], sizeof( buff ), NULL );
              SPXListenForSequencedPacket(
                &svrECB[currPacket] );
        }
        else
        {
```

```
                              if ( svrECB[currPacket].completionCode == 0xED )
                                 printf( "AppServer:Other side terminated
                                    connection\n" );
                              else
                                 printf( "AppServer:Error receiving server
                                    ECB, retcode = %X\n",
                                       svrECB[currPacket].completionCode );
                              AbortConnection();
                              return;
                         }
                    }

               // Check each packet in our list ( lowPacket to MAX_PACKETS )
               currPacket++;
               if ( currPacket == MAX_PACKETS )

                    currPacket = lowPacket;
          }
     }
```

In the preceding code, the AppServer function is called by EstablishConnection—the application server now stays in a loop waiting for new requests and processing those that come in. This is done until either a "terminate connection" request comes from the client or the user at the server presses a key at the application server.

```
int ProcessReceiveBuffer( void )
{
     PARTINF1 tempPart;
     SSN tempSSN;
     int returnVal;

     // Structure for buff now is:
     //   buff[0]    = Function number
     //   buff[1]    = Return code
     //   buff[2n]   = Passed Structure

     switch( buff[0] )
     {
          // PlanOpen
          case 0:
#ifdef DEBUG
               printf( "Received PlanOpen( %s ) request\n", &buff[2] );
#endif
               returnVal = SvrPlanOpen( &buff[2] );
#ifdef DEBUG
               printf( "Returning %2X for PlanOpen()\n", returnVal );
#endif
               break;

          // PlanClose
          case 1:
#ifdef DEBUG
               printf( "Received PlanClose() request\n" );
#endif
               returnVal = SvrPlanClose();
#ifdef DEBUG
```

```
                                printf( "Returning %2X for PlanClose()\n", returnVal );
#endif
                        break;

                // PlanAdd
                case 2:
                        movmem( &buff[2], &tempPart, sizeof( PARTINF1 ) );
#ifdef DEBUG
                        printf( "ReceivedPlanAdd( %3ld %15s $%3d ) request\n",
                                tempPart.ssn, tempPart.name, tempPart.dollar );
#endif
                        returnVal = SvrPlanAdd( &tempPart );
#ifdef DEBUG
                        printf( "Returning %2X for PlanAdd()\n", returnVal );
#endif
                        break;

                // PlanInfo
                case 3:
                        movmem( &buff[2], &tempSSN, sizeof( SSN ) );
#ifdef DEBUG
                        printf( "Received PlanInfo( %3ld ) request\n", tempSSN );
#endif
                        returnVal = SvrPlanInfo( tempSSN, &tempPart );
                        memset( buff, NULL, 100 );
                        movmem( &tempPart, &buff[2], sizeof( PARTINF1 ) );
#ifdef DEBUG
                        printf( "Returning %2X for PlanInfo()\n", returnVal );
#endif
                        break;

                // PlanMod
                case 4:
                        movmem( &buff[2], &tempSSN, sizeof( SSN ) );
#ifdef DEBUG
                        printf( "Client executing PlanMod( %3ld %15s)\n",
                                tempSSN, &buff[2+sizeof(SSN)] );
#endif
                        returnVal = SvrPlanMod( tempSSN, &buff[2+sizeof(SSN)] );
#ifdef DEBUG
                        printf( "Returning %2X for PlanMod()\n", returnVal );
#endif
                        break;

                default:
                        printf( "Invalid request from client, shutting
                          down...\n" );
                        DownSide();
        }

        return returnVal;
}
```

In the preceding block of code, ProcessReceiveBuffer uses a case statement to check what kind of request is coming in and calls the appropriate function to handle the incoming data. Note that the data in the buffer is interpreted according to the type of request.

C SOURCE FOR SPXPROTO: CLISVR.C

The functions in clisvr.c are mostly used to set up buffers and structures and for initialization tasks. The abort and downside functions are similar to those in CLIDLL.DLL—they cancel the listening Event Control Blocks, stop advertising the server, and close the associated sockets.

```c
#include <time.h>
#include <nxt.h>
#include "clisvr.h"

#define MK_SOCKET(a) ( ( a[1] << 8 ) + a[0] )

extern ECB          svrECB[MAX_PACKETS];
extern WORD         connectionID;
extern IPXHeader    svrIPX;
extern SPXHeader    svrSPX[MAX_PACKETS];
extern char         buff[100];
extern char         buff2[MAX_PACKETS][100];
extern BYTE         targetNetwork[4];
extern BYTE         targetNode[6];
extern BYTE         targetSocket[2];
extern BYTE         askSocket[2];
extern BYTE         talkSocket[2];
extern BYTE         advertising;

void IPXSetupRcvPacket( ECB *ECBptr, IPXHeader *IPXptr, BYTE
Socket[2], char *Buffer,
    WORD Buffsize, void *(ESR)() )
{
    if ( ESR )
        ECBptr->ESRAddress = ( void far * ) ESR;
    else
        ECBptr->ESRAddress = NULL;

    ECBptr->socketNumber = MK_SOCKET( Socket );
    ECBptr->fragmentCount = 2;

    ECBptr->fragmentDescriptor[0].address = ( void far * ) IPXptr;
    ECBptr->fragmentDescriptor[0].size = sizeof( *IPXptr );

    ECBptr->fragmentDescriptor[1].address = ( void far * ) Buffer;
    ECBptr->fragmentDescriptor[1].size = Buffsize;
}

void IPXSetupSendPacket( ECB *ECBptr, IPXHeader *IPXptr, BYTE
Network[4], BYTE Node[6],
    BYTE destSocket[2], BYTE sourceSocket[2], char *Buffer, WORD
      Buffsize, void *(ESR)() )
{
    int ttime;
    IPXAddress IPXaddr;

    if ( ESR )
        ECBptr->ESRAddress = ( void far * ) ESR;
    else
        ECBptr->ESRAddress = NULL;
    ECBptr->inUseFlag = 0;
    ECBptr->socketNumber = MK_SOCKET( sourceSocket );
```

```
        ECBptr->fragmentCount = 2;

        ECBptr->fragmentDescriptor[0].address = ( void far * ) IPXptr;
        ECBptr->fragmentDescriptor[0].size = sizeof( *IPXptr );

        ECBptr->fragmentDescriptor[1].address = ( void far * ) Buffer;
        ECBptr->fragmentDescriptor[1].size = Buffsize;

        // Setup for call to Get Local Target which gets immediate
        // address
        // and setup the IPX header's destination address
        movmem( Network, IPXaddr.network, 4 );
        movmem( Node, IPXaddr.node, 6 );
        movmem( destSocket, IPXaddr.socket, 2 );
        IPXGetLocalTarget( ( BYTE * )&IPXaddr, ( BYTE *
          )ECBptr->immediateAddress, &ttime );
        movmem( &IPXaddr, &IPXptr->destination, 12 );
}

void SPXSetupRcvPacket( ECB *ECBptr, SPXHeader *SPXptr, BYTE
Socket[2], char *Buffer,
     WORD Buffsize, void *(ESR)() )
{
        if ( ESR )
            ECBptr->ESRAddress = ( void far * ) ESR;
        else
            ECBptr->ESRAddress = NULL;

        ECBptr->socketNumber = MK_SOCKET( Socket );
        ECBptr->fragmentCount = 2;

        ECBptr->fragmentDescriptor[0].address = ( void far * ) SPXptr;
        ECBptr->fragmentDescriptor[0].size = sizeof( *SPXptr );

        ECBptr->fragmentDescriptor[1].address = ( void far * ) Buffer;
        ECBptr->fragmentDescriptor[1].size = Buffsize;
}

void SPXSetupSendPacket( ECB *ECBptr, SPXHeader *SPXptr, BYTE
Network[4], BYTE Node[6],
     BYTE destSocket[2], BYTE sourceSocket[2], char *Buffer, WORD
       Buffsize, void *(ESR)() )
{
        int ttime;
        IPXAddress IPXaddr;

        if ( ESR )
            ECBptr->ESRAddress = ( void far * ) ESR;
        else
            ECBptr->ESRAddress = NULL;

        ECBptr->inUseFlag = 0;
        ECBptr->socketNumber = MK_SOCKET( sourceSocket );
        ECBptr->fragmentCount = 2;

        ECBptr->fragmentDescriptor[0].address = ( void far * ) SPXptr;
        ECBptr->fragmentDescriptor[0].size = sizeof( *SPXptr );

        ECBptr->fragmentDescriptor[1].address = ( void far * ) Buffer;
        ECBptr->fragmentDescriptor[1].size = Buffsize;
```

```c
    SPXptr->dataStreamType = 0;
    SPXptr->connectionControl = 0;

    // Setup for call to Get Local Target which gets immediate
    // address
    // and setup the IPX header's destination address
    movmem( Network, IPXaddr.network, 4 );
    movmem( Node, IPXaddr.node, 6 );
    movmem( destSocket, IPXaddr.socket, 2 );
    IPXGetLocalTarget( ( BYTE * )&IPXaddr, ( BYTE *
       )ECBptr->immediateAddress, &ttime );
    movmem( &IPXaddr, &SPXptr->destination, 12 );
}

void SPXSetupEstConnPacket( ECB *ECBptr, SPXHeader *SPXptr, BYTE
Network[4], BYTE Node[6],
    BYTE destSocket[2], BYTE sourceSocket[2], void *(ESR)() )
{
    int ttime;
    IPXAddress IPXaddr;

    if ( ESR )
        ECBptr->ESRAddress = ( void far * ) ESR;
    else
        ECBptr->ESRAddress = NULL;

    ECBptr->inUseFlag = 0;
    ECBptr->socketNumber = MK_SOCKET( sourceSocket );
    ECBptr->fragmentCount = 1;

    ECBptr->fragmentDescriptor[0].address = ( void far * ) SPXptr;
    ECBptr->fragmentDescriptor[0].size = sizeof( *SPXptr );

    SPXptr->dataStreamType = 0;
    SPXptr->connectionControl = 0;

    // Setup for call to Get Local Target which gets immediate
    // address
    // and setup the IPX header's destination address
    movmem( Network, IPXaddr.network, 4 );
    movmem( Node, IPXaddr.node, 6 );
    movmem( destSocket, IPXaddr.socket, 2 );
    IPXGetLocalTarget( ( BYTE * )&IPXaddr, ( BYTE *
         )ECBptr->immediateAddress, &ttime );
    movmem( &IPXaddr, &SPXptr->destination, 12 );
}

void SPXSetupListenConnPacket( ECB *ECBptr, SPXHeader *SPXptr, BYTE
Socket[2], void *(ESR)() )
{
    int ttime;
    IPXAddress IPXaddr;

    if ( ESR )
        ECBptr->ESRAddress = ( void far * ) ESR;
    else
        ECBptr->ESRAddress = NULL;

    ECBptr->socketNumber = MK_SOCKET( Socket );
```

```
        ECBptr->fragmentCount = 1;
        ECBptr->fragmentDescriptor[0].address = ( void far * ) SPXptr;
        ECBptr->fragmentDescriptor[0].size = sizeof( *SPXptr );
}

void AbortConnection( void )
{
    int currPacket;
    time_t start_time;

    // Terminate SPX connection
    printf( "Terminating SPX connection...\n" );

    currPacket = MAX_PACKETS  -1;
    IPXCancelEvent( &svrECB[currPacket] );

    SPXSetupEstConnPacket( &svrECB[currPacket], &svrSPX[currPacket],
      targetNetwork, targetNode, targetSocket, talkSocket, NULL );
    SPXTerminateConnection( connectionID, &svrECB[currPacket] );

    start_time = time( NULL );
    while ( ( svrECB[currPacket].inUseFlag != OK ) && ( !kbhit() ) )
    {
        IPXRelinquishControl();
        if ( difftime( time( NULL ), start_time ) > 1 )
        {
            putchar('.');
            start_time = time( NULL );
        }
    }
    putchar( '\n' );

    if ( svrECB[currPacket].completionCode != OK )
        if ( svrECB[currPacket].completionCode == 0xEE )
            printf( "Other side terminated connection.\n" );
        else
            printf( "AbortConnection:Send error in Server ECB,
              status = %x ",
                svrECB[currPacket].completionCode );
    else
        printf( "SPX Connection Terminated...\n" );

    for ( currPacket = 0; currPacket < MAX_PACKETS; currPacket++ )
        IPXCancelEvent( &svrECB[currPacket] );

}

void DownSide( void )
{
    int returnVal;

    // Shut down advertising, if we were
    if ( advertising )
    {
        returnVal = ShutdownSAP();
        if ( returnVal )
            printf( "Error shutting down SAP.\n" );
    }
```

```
    // Close sockets and exit
    IPXCloseSocket( *( (WORD *)talkSocket ) );
    IPXCloseSocket( *( (WORD *)askSocket ) );
    printf( "This side down.\n" );
    exit( 1 );
}
```

A Installing the NetWare Power Tools for Windows Software

Included with this book, you will find two diskettes. One disk contains the Net Tools software from Automated Design, Inc. The other disk contains Windows applications and utilities written specifically for NetWare. Directions for installation of the software on the Net Tools disk can be found in Chapter 11. This section will explain how to install the software on the other diskette.

To make installation easier, we have included a Windows scripting environment called Oriel, which was developed by the LeBlond Group, authors of *Windows Power Tools 3.1; it is a graphics-based batch language for Windows. Oriel makes installing the software easier for several reasons.*

- It copies several .DLL files that are common to many of the applications on the disk (such as VBRUN100.DLL and BWCC.DLL) to your \WINDOWS\SYSTEM directory.

- It provides a convenient front-end menu that runs in Windows. This front-end shows you how much disk space each application uses and lets you decide which you want to copy from the floppy disk.

- It extracts the files for you, relieving you of the burden of extracting each archive manually, one-by-one.

For many of the applications included on the disk, using Oriel is all you will need to do for installation. For others, however, you will need to perform additional steps to complete the installation. See Chapter 10 for full details on the installation requirements for each application.

Please keep in mind as you browse through the software that it is provided on a "trial" basis. These software vendors have provided fully-functional software—this gives you the opportunity to examine the software at your leisure and test out all of the features of each application. If you decide you like a certain application and want to use it, you are expected to register the product by contacting the vendor and paying the registration fee. Vendor addresses and phone numbers are available in Chapter 10.

Oriel Installation Walk-Through

This section shows you how to install the software on the disk provided.

1. If you are not already running Windows, start Windows.

2. Place the NetWare Power Tools disk in the A: drive.

3. Choose File Run from the Program Manager and type **a:\install.exe.** A window will appear, as shown in Figure A.1.

4. By default, all applications will be installed. If you do not want certain applications installed, click on the check boxes next to the names of the unwanted applications (to unhighlight the box), or choose the Select menu (ALT+S) and pick those items you do (or do not) want installed.

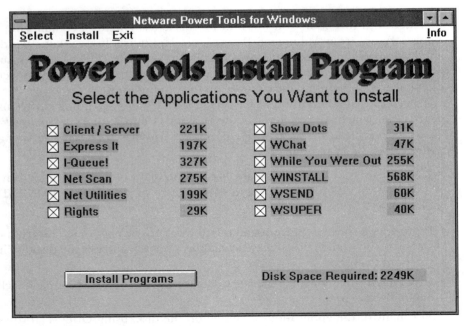

Figure A.1 Power Tools Installation window.

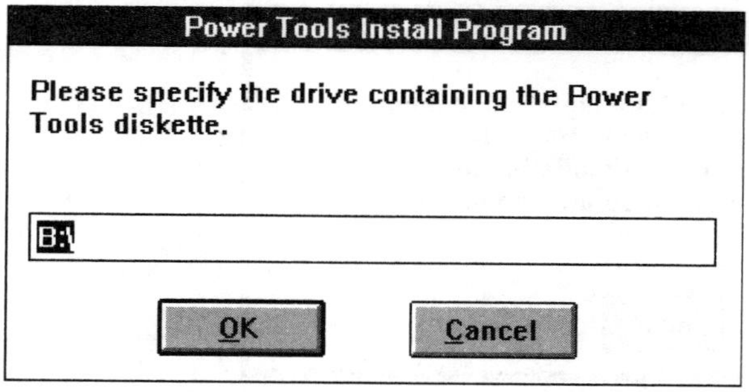

Power Tools Install Program

Please specify the drive containing the Power Tools diskette.

B:\

OK   Cancel

Figure A.2 Source drive prompt.

5. When you've decided on the applications to install, Click on the Install Programs button, or choose the Install menu item (ALT+I). You will then see a window prompting you to specify the source for the files, as shown in Figure A.2.

6. Next, you will be prompted for the target directory, as shown in Figure A.3. The default is C:\PWRTOOLS. You can accept the default, which places the files in directories below the \PWRTOOLS directory on the C drive, or you can specify your own target path.

7. An LHA window which extracts your files to the appropriate directory will start. When Oriel has finished installing files, you will see a window similar to Figure A.4.

The text inside the window in Figure A.4 tells you to refer to this appendix for information on setting up an icon for each application.

> **Note:** Some of the applications included with this disk (such as IQueue! and WChat) require DLLs from Novell. You can contact Novell directly or you can download the WINUPx.ZIP file (where x is the latest revision; WINUP7.ZIP is the most recent, as of this writing) from CompuServe or other on-line services such as RoseNet (see Appendix D for further information).

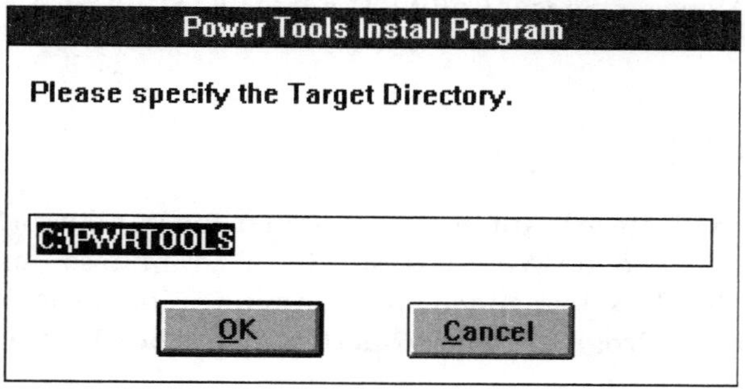

Power Tools Install Program

Please specify the Target Directory.

C:\PWRTOOLS

OK   Cancel

Figure A.3 Target drive/path prompt.

Figure A.4 Installation Complete window.

Setting Up Icons

After you have completed the installation process described above, you will have to perform a few extra steps. In most cases, this simply amounts to assigning icons to each application. In a few instances, you will have to run an application-specific installation program. The following section will describe what must be done for each application.

NetScan

NetScan runs in DOS, so it must run either from the DOS command line outside of Windows or in a DOS box while running Windows. The executable is NETSCAN.EXE. See the discussion in Chapter 10 for assigning a PIF file to NetScan. To set up an icon for this application, provide the following information in the Program Item Properties dialog box in Program Manager:

- Description: NetScan.
- Command Line:

  ```
  C:\PWRTOOLS\NETSCAN\NETSCAN.EXE
  ```

- Icon: Use the SCAN.ICN file included with the archive as an icon. You can use this icon by selecting the Change Icon button from the Program Item Properties dialog box in Program Manager. Specify C:\PWRTOOLS\NETSCAN\SCAN.ICN as the icon file.

Network Application Installer for Windows

The executable file for the Network Application Installer for Windows (NAI) is WINSTALL.EXE. You can use the WINSTADM.EXE program to set up NAI (see Chapter 10 for details). To set up an icon for this application, provide the following information in the Program Item Properties dialog box in Program Manager:

- Description: Network Application Installer for Windows (NAI).
- Command Line:

```
C:\PWRTOOLS\WINSTALL\WINSTALL.EXE
```

- Icon: NAI comes with its own icon.

While You Were Out

The executable file for While You Were Out (WYWO) is WYWO.EXE. You can use the INSTALL.EXE program to set up While You Were Out (see Chapter 10 for details). WYWO creates its own group containing three icons in Program Manager. To set up an icon for this application, provide the following information in the Program Item Properties dialog box in Program Manager:

- Description: While You Were Out (WYWO).
- Command Line:

```
C:\PWRTOOLS\WHILEOUT\WYWO.EXE
```

- Icon: WYWO comes with its own icon.

Show Dots

The executable file for Show Dots is SHOWDOTS.EXE (see Chapter 10 for details). To set up an icon for this application, provide the following information in the Program Item Properties dialog box in Program Manager:

- Description: Show Dots
- Command Line:

```
C:\PWRTOOLS\SHOWDOTS\SHOWDOTS.EXE
```

- Icon: Show Dots comes with its own icon.

WSuper

The executable file for WSuper is WSUPER.EXE (see Chapter 10 for details). To set up an icon for this application, provide the following information in the Program Item Properties dialog box in Program Manager:

- Description: WSuper.
- Command Line:

```
C:\PWRTOOLS\WSUPER\WSUPER.EXE
```

- Icon: WSuper comes with its own icon.

WSend

The executable file for WSend is WSEND.EXE (see Chapter 10 for details). To set up an icon for this application, provide the following information in the Program Item Properties dialog box in Program Manager:

- Description: WSend.
- Command Line:

    C:\PWRTOOLS\WSEND\WSEND.EXE

- Icon: WSend comes with its own icon.

ExpressIt! for Windows

The executable file for ExpressIt! for Windows is EXPWINM.EXE. You will need to run EXINSTAL.EXE and other .EXE files to install ExpressIt! for Windows (see Chapter 10 for details). To set up an icon for this application, provide the following information in the Program Item Properties dialog box in Program Manager:

- Description: ExpressIt! for Windows.
- Command Line:

    C:\PWRTOOLS\EXPWIN\EXPWINM.EXE

- Icon: ExpressIt! for Windows comes with its own icon.

IQueue!

The executable file for IQueue! is IQW.EXE. You will need to run IQINSTAL.EXE and other .EXE files to install IQueue! (see Chapter 10 for details). To set up an icon for this application, provide the following information in the Program Item Properties dialog box in Program Manager:

- Description: IQueue!
- Command Line:

    C:\PWRTOOLS\IQUEUE\IQW.EXE

- Icon: IQueue! comes with its own icon.

Client

The client side of the client-server example, discussed in Chapter 14, is CLI-ENT.EXE, and runs under Windows. The server side, SPXPROTO.EXE, runs under DOS, and can also be run in a DOS window. To set up an icon for the client side of the application, provide the following information in the Program Item Properties dialog box in Program Manager:

- Description: Windows Client.
- Command Line:

  C:\PWRTOOLS\CLISRV\CLIENT.EXE

- Icon: Client comes with its own icon.

If you want to set up an icon for the server side of the application, provide the following information in the Program Item Properties dialog box in Program Manager:

- Description: DOS Server.
- Command Line:

  C:\PWRTOOLS\CLISRV\SPXPROTO.EXE /R

- Icon: There is no icon provided with SPXPROTO.EXE, so you can use an icon in PROGMAN.EXE, if you would like to, by selecting the Change Icon button from the Program Item Properties dialog box in Program Manager.

WChat

The executable file for WChat is WCHAT.EXE. To set up an icon for this application, provide the following information in the Program Item Properties dialog box in Program Manager:

- Description: WChat.
- Command Line:

  C:\PWRTOOLS\WCHAT\WCHAT.EXE

- Icon: WChat comes with its own icon.

RRights

The executable file for RRights is RRIGHTS.EXE. To set up an icon for this application, provide the following information in the Program Item Properties dialog box in Program Manager:

- Description: RRights.
- Command Line:

  C:\PWRTOOLS\RIGHTS\RRIGHTS.EXE

- Icon: RRights comes with its own icon.

About LHA

All of the software included on this disk is compressed using the LHA file compression utility. LHA.EXE was developed by Haruyasu Yoshizaki (Copyright 1988-1991) and uses a compression algorithm developed by Haruhiko Okumura. LHA is "freeware," which means you don't have to register it or pay for it. It can be freely copied and distributed, providing it is not modified or sold without the author's consent. Although it is freeware, it compresses files better than most.

You must run LHA from the DOS command line or in a DOS window (as you see from the software installation described earlier in this Appendix). The command-line syntax for LHA takes the following form:

```
[d:][path] LHA command [/option] filename[.LZH]
[path][filename]
```

where [d:][path]LHA is the path to LHA.EXE, command is one of twelve command parameters, [/option] is one or more of the 34 command switches, filename[.LZH] is the name of the archive file you are working with (the .LZH is assumed as an extension if you don't supply one), and [path][filename] describes the files you want to compress (including wildcards) or the directory to which you want to extract the files.

Acceptable commands are shown below:

Command	Description
A	Add files
D	Delete files
E	Extract files
F	Freshen files
L	List files
M	Move files
P	Display files
S	Make a self-extracting archive
T	Test integrity of an archive
U	Update files
V	View list of file with paths
W	Extract files with paths

B Windows versus NetWare Troubleshooting Tips

Compiled by Brett Warthen (Infinite Technologies)
December 7, 1992 (2nd Edition)

The most important troubleshooting tip for solving conflicts between Windows and NetWare is to remember to use logical deduction and the process of elimination to isolate conflicts.

For example, if you are using a third-party memory manager like QEMM or 386-to-the-MAX, de-install it and try your configuration running Microsoft's HIMEM.SYS that ships with Windows 3.1 instead (try without EMM386). Then, if the problem is related to your memory manager, you should contact that vendor for technical support suggestions.

If you are loading any additional TSRs or device drivers, try your configuration without them loaded; then add them back into your system one by one to determine which is causing the conflict.

If you are using EMSNETX or XMSNETX, try using regular old NETX instead.

While far from being a comprehensive guide to all possible Windows and NetWare conflicts, this document contains some troubleshooting tips for common problems arising while running Windows in the NetWare environment. (Thanks to everyone in NOVB Section 15, the Windows section of the Novell NetWire forums on CompuServe, for helping to compile this list. Acknowledgements are presented at the end of this document.)

The following are recommendations for ALL Systems:

1. In the Windows SYSTEM.INI file, verify the following settings:

   Under the [boot] section header:

   ```
   network.drv=netware.drv
   ```

   Under the [386Enh] section header:

   ```
   network=*vnetbios,vnetware.386,vipx.386
   ```

   > **Note:** *vnetbios can cause some problems with the current IBM LAN Support drivers.

2. Update to the latest NetWare drivers, a minimum level of IPX v3.10 (or IPXODI v1.20) and NETX v3.26 for proper support of the Windows 3.1 environment.

3. Check for duplicate copies of the NWPOPUP.EXE, VNETWARE.386, VIPX.386, and NETWARE.DRV files. (You may find one version in the Windows directory and another in Windows\SYSTEM.) Make sure that the only versions remaining on your system are 1992 dated versions. (The latest versions are on the Windows 3.1 diskettes, but you may have to manually expand them. Or you can download WINUP*.ZIP from NOVLIB Library 5 on CompuServe/NetWire. Additionally, the "security enhancement" updates include new versions of LSL, IPXODI, NETX, VNETWARE.386, VIPX.386, and NETWARE.DRV, and can be found in the NOVFILES area on CompuServe, or requested from Novell at 1-800-NETWARE.)

4. Verify that the NETWARE.DRV file is approximately 125,000 bytes in size. We've seen plenty of problems because installation routines did not properly expand this file.

   The NetWare DOS/Windows Workstation Kit NWSETUP installation procedure is particularly notorious for this type of problem.

5. Use WINSTART.BAT with care. There is a bug with WINSTART.BAT processing under Windows 3.1 on some PCs, which can cause Windows to hang-up when exiting.

   The NetWare DOS/Windows Workstation Kit NWSETUP installation procedure creates a dummy WINSTART.BAT which can trigger this problem.

6. If you want to receive broadcast messages while in Windows, then make sure that NWPOPUP.EXE is included in the "load=" statement in your WIN.INI file.

7. In your NET.CFG (or SHELL.CFG) file, be sure to allocate plenty of file handles. FILE HANDLES=80 is a recommended minimum.

8. In your NET.CFG (or SHELL.CFG) file, allocate additional stacks for IPX/SPX usage by specifying GET LOCAL TARGET STACKS = 5.

    The default setting is 1 stack, which can lead to system lockup problems when receiving NetWare broadcast messages.

    If you plan on making use of IPX/SPX applications on a regular basis, then you should increase this value to GET LOCAL TARGET STACKS = 10.

    (The GET LOCAL TARGET STACKS setting works around a bug in NETX v3.26, and is not necessary if you are running NETX v3.31 or later, which fixes this bug.)

9. If you are running DR-DOS 6, make sure that you have the April Business update installed for Windows 3.1 compatibility.

    This file can be downloaded from the Novell Library forum (NOVLIB) on CompuServe, DR6UP2.EXE in Library 12.

10. If you are attempting to use the Burst Mode shell (BNETX) with Windows 3.1, BNETX v3.31 or later is required for Windows compatibility.

Consider the following if Windows hangs while loading:

1. For Windows 3.0, is your network card set to IRQ 2 or 9, 10, or higher? If it is, then you will need to install the VPICDA.386 patch (included in WINUP*.ZIP in NOVLIB on CompuServe). Copy VPICDA.386 into your Windows\SYSTEM directory, and edit your SYSTEM.INI, replacing the line "device=*vpicd" with "device=vpicda.386."

Note: VPICDA.386 is not required for Windows 3.1; you should specify "device=*vpicd" instead.

---

2. Try loading Windows with a command-line parameter of /D:XSV (e.g., WIN /D:XSV).

    Each of the letters following the /D: are equivalent to placing the following statements under the [386Enh] section header in SYSTEM.INI, one time only:

    ```
    X -> EMMExclude=A000-EFFF
    S -> SystemRomBreakpoint=OFF
    V -> VirtualHDIrq=OFF
    ```

    If Windows now works, use a process of elimination to determine which of the parameters was the key to your success.

    WIN /D:X is most often the solution to these types of problems, which indicates that the shared RAM area used by your network adapter is not properly excluded from your memory manager or the Windows internal memory manager.

For Windows internal memory manager, you exclude this memory range with an EMMExclude=xxxx-xxxx statement under the [386Enh] section header of your SYSTEM.INI. If you are unsure of this range, use EMMExclude=A000-FFFF while troubleshooting. As an example, to exclude a 16KB range of memory at segment D000h, you would specify EMMExclude=D000-D3FF.

For the Microsoft EMM386.EXE memory manager, use a /X=xxxx-xxxx parameter to tell it what range of memory to exclude for your network card.

For the DR-DOS EMM386.SYS memory manager, use a /E=xxxx-xxxx parameter to tell it what range of memory to exclude for your network card.

3. Are you loading MS-DOS 5 SHARE or running MSDOS 4 (DOS 4 automatically loads SHARE if you have a hard disk larger than 32MB)?

   If you can avoid loading SHARE, do so.

   If you cannot, load SHARE before IPX and NETX. Place the statement "FILES=XXX" in your CONFIG.SYS file. XXX is 255 minus 2 (reserved handles) minus the number of file handles defined in your NET.CFG (or SHELL.CFG) file. The default is 40. Therefore, if you are using the default, you would set FILES=213 in your CONFIG.SYS.

   Windows for Workgroups includes a version of SHARE that runs as a Windows enhanced-mode virtual device driver, VSHARE.386. This version reportedly addresses the conflicts between the NetWare shells, SHARE and Windows; however, at the time of this writing, this driver is not available on CompuServe. To install VSHARE.386, specify "device=VSHARE.386" in the [386Enh] section of SYSTEM.INI instead of loading the DOS SHARE.EXE program.

4. There are known conflicts between the IBM LAN Support drivers for Token Ring and the "*vnetbios" driver supplied with Windows.

   If you can use the NetWare drivers that talk directly to the Token Ring adapter, this should work. Otherwise, do not include "*vnetbios" on the "network=" line under the [386Enh] section header of your SYSTEM.INI file, and avoid running any applications that use NETBIOS under Windows.

5. Are you loading SuperStor 2.0, a disk compression device driver? There is a deadlock problem between NETX v3.26 and SuperStor 2.0 under Windows. As a temporary workaround, use the NETX v3.22 shell and contact the software manufacturer for other possible workarounds.

6. There could be an interrupt or I/O conflict between your network card, and Windows searching your COM ports for a mouse. These are the default COM port interrupt (IRQ) and I/O assignments:

```
COM1 = IRQ 4, I/O 3F8h
COM2 = IRQ 3, I/O 2F8h
COM3 = IRQ 4, I/O 2E8h
COM4 = IRQ 3, I/O 2E0h
```

> **Note:** On IBM PS/2s, the settings for COM3 or COM4 are different.

Windows looks for a serial mouse starting at the highest numbered COM port in your system. If a serial mouse is attached to COM1 (IRQ 4) and your network adapter is configured for IRQ 3, this may disrupt the network connection when Windows searches for a mouse on COM2, using IRQ 3.

In the [386Enh] section header of SYSTEM.INI, you can specify COM#Irq=–1 to disable a particular port. For example, specify COM2Irq= –1 to disable COM2.

You could also specify MaxCOMPort=2 under the [386Enh] section header to ensure that COM3 and COM4 are not being used. COM4 may sometimes conflict with Arcnet boards configured for I/O address 2E0h.

If you have system hang-ups running RCONSOLE or other IPX/SPX applications under Windows, try the following:

1. Verify that you have all of the latest drivers for running IPX/SPX under Windows. A minimum version level of IPX v3.10 or IPXODI v1.20 is required.

   For Windows in 386 Enhanced Mode, make sure that you have VIPX.386 v1.10 or v1.11. (Use the NetWare VERSION utility to run against VIPX.386 to determine the version.) Make sure that you do not have duplicate copies of VIPX.386 elsewhere in your path. In particular, check both the Windows and Windows\SYSTEM directories for duplicates. Furthermore, ensure that VIPX.386 is included in the "network=" statement under the [386Enh] section header of your SYSTEM.INI.

   For Windows in Standard Mode, make sure that TBMI2 is loaded before going into Windows; however, this will not be sufficient for many IPX/SPX applications.

2. If you are running NETX v3.26 or lower, place the statement GET LOCAL TARGET STACKS = 10 in your NET.CFG (or SHELL.CFG) file to allocate additional stacks for IPX/SPX multitasking.

3. For RCONSOLE, if all servers do not show up in the display, you need RCONSOLE v2.9 or higher, which is currently available for download from CompuServe/NetWire as RCNSLE.ZIP in NOVLIB Library 4.

For system hang-ups running NETBIOS applications under Windows, try the following:

1. Follow the same guidelines as described for running IPX/SPX applications under Windows above.

2. Include a statement "TimerCriticalSection=10000" under the [386Enh] section header of SYSTEM.INI. This statement will help prevent deadlocks

and re-entry problems when network activity is generated from a timer interrupt.

If you got a "Cannot locate NETWARE.DLL" error when loading NetWare Tools or another application, try the following:

1. See the "Recommendations for ALL Systems" section. There is no NETWARE.DLL; it is actually NETWARE.DRV, which is either not specified as "network.drv=netware.drv" under the [boot] section of SYSTEM.INI, or the NETWARE.DRV file is corrupt.

If the remote boot PCs cannot find WINA20.386, consider:

1. WINA20.386 is a DOS 5 file that is required for running Windows 3.0 in enhanced mode with DOS=HIGH in the CONFIG.SYS. (It is supposedly no longer used by Windows 3.1.)

   Windows looks for WINA20.386 when it is loading in the root of the boot drive *UNLESS* you include SWITCHES=/W in your CONFIG.SYS file, and specify "device=d:\path\WINA20.386" under the [386Enh] section header of SYSTEM.INI to tell Windows where to find this driver.

If the remote boot PCs cannot find EMM386.EXE, consider:

1. If you are using the Microsoft EMM386.EXE device driver to provide expanded memory emulation, then be aware that Windows needs to reload EMM386.EXE when Windows is started to load a virtual device driver for upper memory management in 386 enhanced mode.

   Windows looks for EMM386.EXE in the drive/directory that it was loaded from in CONFIG.SYS. If you need to specify an alternate path, include a /y=d:\path\EMM386.EXE parameter when loading EMM386.EXE in CONFIG.SYS. This path should be one that will be valid when Windows is later started.

If the remote boot PCs running QEMM v6.0x will not run Windows in enhanced mode, consider:

1. Similar to the EMM386 issue above, if you are running QEMM v6.0x, certain files—WINHIRAM.VXD and WINSTLTH.VXD—need to be reloaded when Windows v3.x is being initialized. Windows looks for these files in the drive/directory from which QEMM was loaded in CONFIG.SYS. If you need to specify an alternate path, include a VXDDIR=d:\path parameter when loading QEMM in CONFIG.SYS. This path should be one that will be valid when Windows is later started.

If broadcast messages do not display when in Windows applications, try the following:

1. Verify that NWPOPUP.EXE is included in the "load=" statement of your WIN.INI file.

2. In the Windows Control Panel, Network Options, ensure that the "Messages Enabled" button is clicked.

3. See the "Recommendations for ALL Systems" section.

If broadcast messages lock up Windows, do the following:

1. See the "Recommendations for ALL Systems" section. In particular, focus on the GET LOCAL TARGET STACKS statement that should be placed in your NET.CFG (or SHELL.CFG) file. It is recommended that you upgrade to NETX v3.31 or higher to avoid this problem.

   Ensure that this statement is echoed to the screen when IPX or IPXODI is loaded.

If the DOS DIR command shows no files when used on Network Drives, do the following:

1. See the "Recommendations for ALL Systems" section. In particular, focus on the GET LOCAL TARGET STACKS statement that should be placed in your NET.CFG (or SHELL.CFG) file. It is recommended that you upgrade to NETX v3.31 or higher to avoid this problem.

   Ensure that this statement is echoed to the screen when IPX or IPXODI is loaded.

How do I update to IPX.COM v3.10?

1. If you installed Windows 3.1 for a Novell network, it should have copied an IPX.OBJ file to your Windows\SYSTEM directory.

   Copy this file to your WSGEN or SHGEN diskette, and re-run the WSGEN or SHGEN procedure to create an updated IPX.

   Now might be a good time to consider migrating to the IPX ODI drivers, which do not require this generating process, and are generally more up-to-date, as Novell is no longer certifying new drivers for the linkable IPX.COM.

   The IPX ODI drivers are included in the DOSUP*.ZIP file in NOVLIB Library 5 on CompuServe/NetWire, and documentation is included in ODIDOC.ZIP in this same library.

Control Windows Swap Files as follows:

1. The following statements under the [386Enh] section header of SYS-TEM.INI control the creation and placement of Windows temporary swap files in 386 enhanced mode:

   Paging=Off (disables paging)

   MaxPagingFileSize=xxxx (max size of temporary swap file in KB)

PagingDrive=d (paging files will be placed in the root of this drive)

PagingFile=d:\path\SWAPFILE (Windows 3.1 only; name to use for swap file, overrides PagingDrive entry)

2. The following statement under the [NonWindowsApp] section of SYS-TEM.INI controls the placement of swap files created when switching between DOS applications in Windows Standard mode:

```
SwapDisk=c:\path
```

If this path is not specified, then Windows will default to the directory pointed to by the TEMP DOS environmental variable (which many Windows applications also use for controlling where they create temporary files), or the root directory of your first hard disk if the TEMP variable is not defined.

3. The following statements under the [386Enh] section header of SYS-TEM.INI control the location of permanent swap files (Windows 3.1 Only):

PermSwapDOSDrive=c (drive letter)

PermSwapSizeK=xxxx (desired size of permanent swap file)

If Windows is very slow while loading, consider:

1. This is probably due to Windows creating a temporary swap file when loading, possibly to a network drive.

Under NetWare 2.x, this process is much slower than with NetWare 3.x. See "Controlling Windows Swap Files" above for more information.

If printing to a NetWare print queue results in 65,535 copies requested, consider:

1. This is a problem with the NE3200 EISA network adapterdriver. In the NET.CFG file, under the "LINK DRIVER NE32001" section, include a "Double Buffer1" statement.Note that there are a number of 32-bit EISA adapters that are OEM versions of the NE3200, including theIntel EtherExpress/32.

If you are loading NetWare Windows drivers when not attached to a network and a warning message that the network is not present is displayed, try the following:

1. Specify "NetWarn=0" under the [windows] section of your WIN.INI file, which tells Windows not to warn you about loading network drivers when no network is present.

If you receive garbage when printing from Windows to a network printer, try the following:

1. Are you running PSERVER? If you are, then you need to be running PSERVER v1.22 or later. PSERV1.ZIP can be downloaded from NOVLIB

Library 6 on CompuServe/NetWire. (Browse on PSERV*.ZIP to find the latest version.)

2. What is the CAPTURE statement that you execute before going into Windows? You need to specify the NT (no tabexpansion) flag, and I recommend a timeout of at least 60 seconds (TI=60). For PostScript printers, NB (no banner) and NFF (no form feed) are also necessary. NA (no autoendcap) is also required in some Windows configurations.

   The NA flag will cause you some problems if you are printing to LPTx.OS2 (or LPTx.DOS in Windows 3.1) instead of LPTx. While previous recommendations were to print to LPTx.OS2, these recommendations have been superseded because of updated Novell drivers.

   If you are using all Windows applications, you should be able to set TI=0 to disable the timeout feature, as it is not necessary if applications print through the standard Windows APIs.

   NETX v3.26 has a bug in handling CAPTURE timeout values under some configurations when running with the IPX ODI drivers. Instead of the timeout occurring after an xx second pause in printing, the timeout occurs xx seconds after printing begins, which can cause considerable printing problems for large print jobs. NETX v3.31 addresses this problem.

3. In the Windows Control Panel/Printers/Configure menu, disable the Print Manager if it is not already disabled. (Since NetWare print jobs are spooled to disk anyway, using the Print Manager when spooling to a network printer is redundant and can slow things down.)

4. Make sure that you have the latest NetWare drivers for Windows. For Windows 3.1, the drivers that ship with the product are satisfactory. For Windows 3.0, you need VNETWARE.386 v2.0, the version that is included in the WINUP*.ZIP file in NOVLIB Library 5 on CompuServe/NetWire.

5. Type CAPTURE SHOW in a DOS Window after going into Windows, and make sure that these settings are the same as those set before going into Windows. A Windows "permanent list" setting can override the CAPTURE that you set before going into Windows. Check the [network] section of your WIN.INI and delete any statements that reference print captures to avoid confusion.

6. When all else fails, try connecting the printer directly to the workstation to verify that this is indeed a network problem.

7. Are you running RPRINTER on a workstation running Windows in enhanced mode? If so, see the "RPRINTER and Windows" section of this document.

If Windows hangs when opening a DOS Window or DOS application, try the following:

1. Make sure that you have the NetWare drivers for Windows loaded: "network.drv=netware.drv" under the [boot] section of SYSTEM.INI, and for

386 enhanced mode, "network.drv=vnetware.386" (*vnetbios and vipx.386 may also be specified in this command) under the [386Enh] section of SYSTEM.INI.

2. For Windows 3.0, is your network card set to IRQ 2 or 9, 10, or higher? If it is, then you will need to install the VPICDA.386 patch (included in WINUP*.ZIP in NOVLIB on CompuServe). Copy VPICDA.386 into your Windows\SYSTEM directory, and edit your SYSTEM.INI, replacing the line "device=*vpicd" with "device=vpicda.386."

> **Note:** VPICDA.386 is not required for Windows 3.1; you should specify "device=*vpicd" instead.

3. You may be running out of file handles. Increase the value specified in the FILE HANDLES statement in your NET.CFG (or SHELL.CFG) file.

4. You may be experiencing swap file corruption. Refer to the section entitled "Controlling Windows Swap Files" to ensure that swap files are being created in the correct locations. (If you are swapping to the network, swap files must be stored in unique directories.)

5. A TSR that you are running may require that you specify "TimerCriticalSection=10000" under the [386Enh] section header of your SYSTEM.INI.

If you get the message "DOS Environment Missing or Corrupt" in DOS windows, do the following:

1. Make sure that you have the NetWare drivers for Windows loaded: "network.drv=netware.drv" under the [boot] section of SYSTEM.INI, and for 386 enhanced mode, "network.drv=vnetware.386" (*vnetbios & vipx.386 may also be specified in this command) under the [386Enh] section of SYSTEM.INI.

2. Verify that your NetWare drivers are up to date. Review "Recommendations for ALL systems" in this document.

Changing directories on a network drive in one window affects all windows:

1. If you have NWShareHandles=TRUE in the [NetWare] section of your WIN.INI file, then this is what is causing the problem.

2. If you have a TASK MODE = statement in your NET.CFG (or SHELL.CFG) file, then this is what is causing the problem.

If the NetWare MENU program freezes or performs erratically after executing Windows from a menu option, consider:

1. This is a known incompatibility; there is not a fix at this time.

There are RPRINTER and Windows problems:

1. These don't peacefully coexist at this time; the best solution is to purchase a third-party alternative. Alternatives include hardware-based solutions such as network cards installed in laser printers, as well as the Castelle LanPress and Intel NetPort. Software solutions like Fresh Technologies Printer Assist, BrightWork's PSPrint, and Intel's LanSpool are also reported to work.

   I-Queue! Server (IQS) from Infinite Technologies is an additional software-based print server solution that is compatible with Windows. In addition to providing Windows compatibility, IQS has also been shown to prevent hair loss, primarily the type that occurs when you're pulling your hair out trying to make RPRINTER work. A 30-day trial version of I-Queue! Server can be downloaded under the filename IQS.ZIP in Library 4 of the NOVVEN forum on CompuServe. Or call Infinite Technologies at 410-363-1097 for additional information. (A subtle plug for my own company.)

   If you want to try RPRINTER, you can also experiment with the following suggestions.

2. Run Windows in Standard Mode (WIN /S) on PCs that are running RPRINTER.

3. Disable the Windows print manager.

4. Try increasing the SPX timeout values specified in your NET.CFG (or SHELL.CFG). For example:

```
SPX ABORT TIMEOUT = 4000
SPX LISTEN TIMEOUT = 2500
```

5. Try installing Microsoft's VPD.386 driver as "device=vpd.386" under the [386Enh] section header of SYSTEM.INI. This driver can be downloaded from the Microsoft Software Library on CompuServe (GO MSL) under the filename VPD386.EXE.

6. Review "Recommendations for ALL Systems" to ensure that you have the latest drivers and proper configuration support.

Running Windows 3.1 on a non-dedicated NetWare 2.x File Server:

1. This is NOT possible. The NetWare 2.x operating system requires all available extended memory and exclusive control of protected mode operations.

If you have problems retrieving files from network drives with Microsoft Word for Windows,

1. Include the statement "NovellNet=Yes" in the [Microsoft Word] section of your WIN.INI file.

Problems running Windows in Enhanced Mode with Thomas Conrad Token Ring Cards require the following:

1. When using the TCTOKSH ODI driver, in the NET.CFG file, include a "NON_VDS" statement under the "LINK DRIVER TCTOKSH" section.

If a Windows application no longer runs after flagging the executable file Execute Only, note the following:

1. The execute-only attribute will not work with any executable file that uses internal overlays, which is the inherent design of all Windows applications. You CANNOT use the execute-only attribute with Windows applications.

For the undocumented option of changing drives and printers built into NetWare Drivers, note the following:

There is an undocumented option built into NETWARE.DRV that gives you hotkey access to a dialog that allows you to change drive mappings, print queue assignments, and attach/detach to other servers in your network.

Under the [options] section of your NETWARE.INI file, include a statement "NetWareHotKey=123."

Restart Windows and press F12. Any time you press F12, it will pop up a selection menu that gives you access to a menu of NetWare functions. Do not minimize this window or switch away from it while active, or the application that you popped this window up over will no longer be able to receive keystrokes.

Where to Go for More Information

Running Windows on NetWare by Stephen Saxon from M&T Books

Networking Windows: NetWare Edition by Howard Marks, Kristin Marks and Rick Segal from Sams Books

Microsoft Windows Resource Kit from Microsoft

Windows 3.1 Secrets by Brian Livingston

NetWare Power Tools for Windows by Charles Rose from Bantam Books

NOVB Section 15 in the NetWire Family of Forums on CompuServe

---

Compiled by Brett Warthen (Infinite Technologies).
Address comments via e-mail...
MHS: Brett @ Infinite (via CSERVE or NHUB)
CompuServe: >MHS:Brett@Infinite
(or 76704,63 in NOVVEN Sec 4 or NOVB Sec 15)
Internet: Brett@Infinite.mhs.compuserve.com
FAX: +1-410-363-3779
Others: > NUL

Special thanks to all of those who participate and contribute in NOVB Section 15 on the NetWire forums on CompuServe, including:

Jimmy Wright, Novell

Rich Adams, volunteer NetWire Sysop

Dennis Beach, volunteer NetWire Sysop

Sandra Duncan, Novell

Jon Hunt, Novell

Mickey, Dave, Andy and Deb on NetWire

Charles Rose, Author *NetWare Power Tools for Windows* on Bantam Books

Stephen Saxon, Author *Running Windows on NetWare* on M and T Books (1-800-533-4372 to order)

Howard Marks, CoAuthor *Networking Windows: NetWare Edition* on Sams Books

Rick Smith, Synergy Computing

Tom Berdan

Greg McGovern

David Chamberlain

Alan Woolfson

Barry St. John

Peter O'Rourke

Peter Hauptmanns

Michael Hader

Jim Reese

. . . and the original cast and crew of Gilligan's Island, for their inspiration.

C PC Memory Architecture Overview

by Brett Warthen (Infinite Technologies)

DOS users are faced with a confusing array of memory configurations today. There are conventional memory, upper memory, expanded memory, extended memory, and the high memory area to name a few. Plus there are acronyms like UMB (Upper Memory Block), EMS (Expanded Memory Specification), XMS (eXtended Memory Specification), HMA (High Memory Area), VCPI (Virtual Control Program Interface), and DPMI (DOS Protected Mode Interface), which confuse matters even further.

In this document, we'll try to explain the PC Memory Architecture, as well as popular memory management techniques and standards.

The reason for all of these different types of memory has to do with the evolution of the Intel 80x86 family of microprocessors over the years. Since the 8086 and 8088 microprocessors, used in the original IBM PC and "XT-class" machines, we've seen tremendous growth in the speed and capabilities of PC microprocessors; yet limitations of the original 8086 design still hold us back. The primary limitation is that the 8086 and 8088 processors can only address a 1MB range of memory—this seemed like a lot for their time, when 64KB was the extent of the addressing capability of competing non-Intel microprocessors.

When IBM designed the original PC, they reserved the upper 384KB of this 1MB for the PC BIOS (Basic Input/Output System), the video memory, and the adapter boards to install additional RAM, allowing applications to write directly to added RAM in order to communicate with the adapter. This left us with 640KB for DOS and application programs.

The 80286 microprocessor supports a full 16MB address space; however, this additional memory is only accessible when the 80286 operates in what is termed as its protected mode. The default mode of operation for the 80286 is real mode, which is 8086 compatible. In real mode, the 80286 is little more than a fast 8086.

At the time that the 80286 was being designed by Intel, they had no idea that the PC and the 8086 would enjoy widespread popularity; hence, the design of 80286 protected mode is very incompatible with real mode. Intel anticipated that since protected mode offered so many advantages over real mode, that real mode would just "go away."

While there is a processor instruction to put the processor into protected mode, there is no way to return! Applications like nondedicated NetWare 2.x, OS/2 v1.x, and the various DOS extenders, have to play some real feats of magic in order to switch between real and protected modes.

Mostly, the switch from protected mode back to real mode is done by performing a hard reset on the microprocessor (CTRL-ALT-DEL like). Before the processor is reset, a command is sent out to the keyboard controller. The response from the keyboard controller is what wakes the processor up from its reset, now in real mode. This is the reason why people often report sluggish keyboard problems with non-dedicated NetWare. Not all keyboard controllers are designed to support this operation.

The 80386 added some exciting new features. In addition to supporting 8086 real mode and 80286 protected mode, the 80386 supports even more than 16MB, 4GB of physical memory, and 1TB of virtual memory. Thanks to a flat 32-bit address space, all physical memory is accessible in one flat address space (programmers are often hampered by 64KB at a time addressing limits on the 8086 and 80286).

One of the really exciting enhancements of the 80386 is its virtual 8086 mode. Through the 80386's hardware features, it is able to emulate multiple 8086 microprocessors! This is how DesqView, Windows enhanced mode, and OS/2 v2 perform their magic multitasking DOS applications (with varying degrees of success).

The 80386 also supports memory paging in its hardware. Applications only see a logical view of memory. When an application makes a memory request, the processor redirects the access to the actual physical location. The 80286 also provided a limited subset of memory paging support in protected mode only (on the 80286, paging is on a per 64KB segment basis; the 80386 pages on 4KB boundaries), but the 80386 makes this available in virtual 8086 mode as well, so that memory management products like QEMM, 386-to-the-MAX, and MS-DOS 5/DR-DOS 6 EMM386 can perform memory management magic for DOS applications.

Since we're talking about microprocessors for a background, I'll also mention the 80486. Effectively, the 80486 is a highly-tuned, highly-optimized 80386, which doesn't add many new capabilities, mostly just FASTER execution than past designs of this family. The 486 also includes an integrated math coprocessor (there is no need for an 80487) that really speeds up number crunching. The 486SX is essentially a crippled 486 without the built-in math coprocessor.

For the sake of completeness, I'll also mention the 386SX. The 386SX is software compatible with the 80386, except that all its external accesses to the outside world are made 16 bits at a time instead of 32 bits; this makes it a tad slower than a full-blown 386 when it comes to accessing memory and devices. Similarly, the 8088 is an 8086 compatible processor, except that it makes its external accesses 8 bits at a time instead of 16 bits at a time. While this type of design makes the system a little slower, it allows for lower priced components to be used in building the system, making enhanced processor capabilities available in machines at lower price points.

With a history of the Intel family of processors in mind, let's move on to the different types of memory.

Conventional Memory is the memory range between 0 and 640KB, which is directly accessible to DOS applications. DOS and TSRs begin loading at the bottom area of memory and work their way up.

Upper Memory (UMB for upper memory blocks) is memory between 640KB and 1MB. This memory begins at segment A000h, and is directly accessible from real mode, just "reserved" by the original PC design.

Video buffers comprise the first 128KB of memory. The first 64KB (A000-AFFF) is typically used by EGA/VGA graphics modes. The next 32KB is the monochrome video text buffer (B000-B7FF), followed by 32KB for the color text video buffer (B800-BFFF). (The different buffer addresses were intended to allow color and monochrome systems to both reside in the same system.)

Other ranges of upper memory are used by other adapters (like network cards), and the PC's BIOS. The BIOS area is normally the top 64KB (F000-FFFF), although some systems use a 128KB BIOS (like PS/2s) (E000-FFFF).

The leftover memory can be used for various purposes. On a 386 system, the 386 processor's paging techniques are used to map extended memory (memory beyond the 1MB limit; we'll get to it shortly) into the upper memory area, so that it can be addressed by the processor in real mode (or really virtual 8086 mode). On a 286 system, an expanded memory board can be installed, which, in turn, installs physically addressable memory into this range of upper memory.

Upper Memory blocks, or UMBs, are used for loading TSR programs "high," such as with the MS-DOS 5 LOADHIGH and DR-DOS 6 HILOAD commands. Memory managers for the 80386 can map memory into the upper memory area so that TSRs can be loaded outside of the standard 640KB. It is interesting to note that LOADHIGH and HILOAD load programs into upper memory, and not the actual area of memory known as the High Memory Area (HMA), which we will cover shortly.

The memory manager remaps exTENded memory for use as upper memory. On a 286 or 8086 with exPANded memory hardware supporting the LIM EMS 4.0 specification, Quarterdeck's (the QEMM developers) QRAM product can convert exPANded memory into upper memory.

ExPANded memory itself is actually addressed out of upper memory. In most implementations, 64KB of the upper memory area is set aside as the expanded memory page frame. Applications can then map in 64KB of expanded memory at a time, requesting different "pages" of expanded memory. (The LIM EMS 4.0 specification can get a little more flexible than this.) Usually, the expanded memory (EMS) page frame is located at segment D000h.

ExTENded memory is memory that is not addressable by an 80x86 processor in real mode. It is memory above the 1MB boundary—accessible only from protected mode (or made accessible to other applications in virtual 8086 mode on a 386 through paging), which means it is only of real use to protected mode applications such as those built with a DOS extender (Lotus Release 3.x), non-dedicated NetWare, OS/2, and others.

A memory manager like QEMM or 386-to-the-MAX or MS-DOS 5/DR-DOS 6 EMM386 can convert extended memory into expanded memory and/or upper memory through 80836 memory paging techniques.

Ironically, the VCPI (Virtual Control Program Interface) is used by memory managers and DOS Extenders to convert this exPANded memory back to exTENded memory, for programs like Lotus 3.x, which require exTENded memory instead of exPANded memory. Essentially, VCPI (supported by QEMM and 386-to-the-MAX, and available only on 80386 and above processors), is intended to give the application the type of memory that it wants—exPANded memory or exTENded memory. Rather than setting aside a pre-allocated amount of each type of memory, both exPANded and exTENded memory are allocated from the same pool.

DPMI (DOS Protected Mode Interface), is similar to VCPI in concept, but different in implementation. DPMI, supported by Windows 3.x, updated versions of QEMM and 386-to-the-MAX, and several popular DOS extenders, is designed to allow applications running in protected mode access to DOS and BIOS services. As DOS is a real mode operating system, it requires extensions to allow protected mode applications access to DOS services.

Real mode DOS applications can also access extended memory by transferring data in and out of extended memory (which involves toggling the processor between real and protected modes with a little help from the BIOS). These days, most applications that do this use the XMS specification. QEMM and 386-to-theMAX provide this support, as does Microsoft HIMEM.SYS. The XMS specification provides some sort of memory management over extended memory.

There is a special area of exTENded memory, called the High Memory Area (HMA), which is the first 64KB of extended memory; it can be directly accessed from DOS without the processor being in protected mode.

The HMA is used by MS-DOS 5 when DOS=HIGH is specified in the CONFIG.SYS file to load part of DOS into the HMA, making more conventional memory available to applications. Similar support is provided in DR-DOS by HIDOS.SYS and/or the EMM386.SYS /B=FFFF command-line option and HIDOS=ON in the CONFIG.SYS.

For versions of DOS prior to MS-DOS 5, Novell's XMSNETX shell also makes use of the XMS HMA to load part of the NetWare shell outside of conventional memory. With MS-DOS 5 or DR-DOS 6, it is typically better to let DOS use the HMA as it will give you better performance and more memory.

Here's a memory chart to help you out:

	16MB and beyond
EXTENDED MEMORY	Addressable in protected mode, not real mode
	1MB + 64KB (16 bytes if you're picky)
EXTENDED MEMORY	first 64KB of exTENded memory
HMA	used by MS-DOS DOS=HIGH or XMSNETX shell
	1MB
UPPER MEMORY	(LOADHIGH into unused blocks)
PC BIOS	(usually F000h-FFFFh, sometimes E000h-FFFFh)
Expanded Memory Page Frame	(usually D000h-DFFFh)
Network Cards & other RAM/ROM	(Varies)
Video Buffer	(A000h-BFFFh)
	640KB (segment A000h)
CONVENTIONAL MEMORY	
Applications	
TSRs DOS BIOS data area	
	0KB (bottom of memory)

Confused? Well, the PC memory architecture is confusing.

In real terms, what all of this means is that there are reasons, other than processing speed, why the 80386 and 80486 architectures are important. 80286 and below machines are dead-end products for the future, as they lack the extendibility and flexibility of the 386/486 architecture.

386 and 486 computers can turn exTENded memory into exPANded memory and Upper memory for applications that use those types of memory, yet still support applications that use exTENded memory, making memory configuration issues far simpler.

Of course, chances are that you won't have to understand how your system memory is being used. Instead, you'll have the joy of watching Windows and OS/2 use larger amounts of RAM than our hard disk capacities just 10 years ago.

PC Memory Management Conflicts

The most common conflict in configuring PCs with memory managers has to do with not properly excluding shared adapter RAM areas in upper memory from your memory manager.

Most memory managers go out of their way to attempt to identify shared RAM areas on installed adapters. However, particularly in the case of network cards, it can be difficult to detect if a shared memory area is present, so the area must be explicitly excluded from being remapped by the memory manager.

The most common symptom of such a problem is when a machine will function correctly after a warm boot (the adapter RAM has been initialized so it can be detected by the memory manager), but not after a cold boot.

Most memory managers use command-line parameters that can tell them to exclude certain areas of memory from being remapped. These memory ranges are specified in hexidecimal segment addresses. For example, many popular Arcnet cards default to a 16KB range of shared memory beginning at segment D000h. The proper range to exclude in this case is D000-D3FF.

For MS-DOS 5, this is specified with a /X=D000-D3FF option on the DE-VICE=EMM386.EXE statement in CONFIG.SYS. DRDOS 6 users instead specify /E=D000-D3FF on the DEVICE=EMM386.SYS statement in CONFIG.SYS.

D NetWare/Windows Resources

Once you've been through the book, you may want to look to other sources for further information, such as on-line services, books, and publications. This appendix provides a list of places you can look for further information. Besides these, you should investigate the Windows Resource Toolkit from Microsoft, which, as of this writing, sells for $19.95. Microsoft can be reached at (206) 882-8080.

On-Line Services

CompuServe Information Service

CompuServe Information Service is one of the largest on-line services in the world. Novell hosts **NetWire**, a collection of on-line forums that provide a daily assortment of messages and files relevant to NetWare. Microsoft also hosts a collection of forums. Between the two, you should be able to get almost any NetWare or Windows question answered. Also, the Novell third-party vendor (NOVVEN) forum is now on-line; companies like Brett Warthen's Infinite Technologies host sections on NOVVEN. WINVENA, WINVENB, and WINVENC are the Windows third-party software forums.

PHONE

To subscribe to CompuServe call their customer service line at 1-800-848-8990. To get the access number nearest you, call 1-800-635-6225.

RoseNet On-line

RoseNet is an on-line information service for the local area network community and provides files and message bases geared specifically to those involved with networking. You will find a wide variety of network software, utilities, drivers, and information on RoseNet. There's even a NetWare/Windows file area where you can get more Windows applications that take advantage of NetWare resources. You can also receive the latest version of any shareware in this book.

PHONE

Call (703) 799-25036 (V.32bis/HST) with your modem for a brochure and free trial account. Access speeds range from 300 to 16,800 bps.

ADDRESS

P.O. Box 257
Mount Vernon, VA 22121-0257

Magazines

Windows Magazine

CMP Publications
600 Community Drive
Manhasset, NY 11030
(516) 562-5000

InfoWorld

155 Bovet Road, Suite 800
San Mateo, CA 94402
(800) 457-7866 for subscription info

PC Week

Ziff Communications Company
One Park Avenue
New York, NY 10016
(609) 461-2100 for subscription info

NetWare Solutions

10711 Burnet Road, Suite 305
Austin, TX 78758
(512) 873-7761

LAN Times

> 1900 O'Farrell St., Suite 200
> San Mateo, CA 94403.
> (415) 513-6800

LAN Magazine

> 600 Harrison Street
> San Francisco, CA 94107
> (216) 206-6660

Newsletters

Inside Windows/Inside NetWare

> The Cobb Group
> P.O. Box 35160
> Louisville, KY 40232
> (800) 223-8720

The Cobb Group publishes many newsletters. *Inside Microsoft Windows* is a monthly newsletter providing Windows tips and information. *Inside NetWare* is another monthly newsletter providing NetWare information.

Network Developer Resource

> RoseWare
> P.O. Box 257
> Mount Vernon, VA 22121-0257
> (703) 799-2509

The NDR is a monthly journal devoted to the technical side of NetWare. It is intended to provide power users, software developers, network administrators, and consultants a hands-on look at the more developer-related aspects of the network. Included are discussions of network management, API programming, and methods for overcoming the technical hurdles the manuals and sales literature never mention. See offer at the back of the book for more information.

WUGNET Journal

> WUGNET
> P.O Box 1967
> 107 S. Monroe St., 2nd floor
> Media, PA 19063
> (215) 565-1861

WUGNET (the Windows Users Group NETwork) publishes a monthly newsletter and manages the WINADV forum on CompuServe.

Computhink Windows Watcher

P.O. Box 99
Quakertown, PA 18951

This is a good newsletter for product releases and Windows gossip in general.

Trade Shows

NetWorld

Bruno Blenheim, Inc.
Fort Lee Executive Park
One Executive Drive
Fort Lee, NJ 07024

Windows and OS/2 Conference

Boston, August
CM Ventures, Inc.
5720 Hollis St.
Emeryville, CA 94608

Comdex Spring/Fall

Chicago/Las Vegas
The Interface Group
300 First Avenue
Needham, MA 02194
(617) 449-6600

Books

There are countless books on NetWare and Windows as individual topics, so we won't list those here. However, there are a few specifically about NetWare and Windows together.

Networking Windows	Howard Marks, Kristin Marks, and Rick Segal, SAMS Publishing, 1992.
Running Windows on NetWare	Steve Saxon, M&T Publishing, 1992.
Windows 3.1 Networking	Jeffrey Sloman, Jim Boyce, and Kimberly Maxwell, New Riders Publishing, 1992.

E NetWare Shell History File

The following listing shows the history of the NetWare shell file through the most recent version as of this writing (3.31). This list may be useful in determining what version of the shell fixes which problems, and which shell versions add new features. The following was provided by Novell and is used with permission.

Shell v3.01 Rev A
The initial release of the v3.01 shell files forms the beginning of the DOS shell history file. The files included were:

NETx.COM	3.01 Rev. A	5-8-90
EMSNETx.COM	3.01 Rev. A	5-8-90
XMSNETx.COM	3.01 Rev. A	5-8-90

Shell v3.01 Rev B
The second release of the v3.01 shell corrected a problem with the Rev A shell in which loading SiteLock by Brightworks would fail, thus causing the DOS workstation to hang.

NETx.COM	3.01 Rev. B	6-6-90
EMSNETx.COM	3.01 Rev. B	6-6-90
XMSNETx.COM	3.01 Rev. B	6-6-90

Shell v3.01 Rev C
The NetWare DOS Shell v3.01 Rev C was made available only to NetWare developers. It corrected a number of problems with the Rev B shell, as detailed below. (These changes were all incorporated into the Rev D release dated 9-7-90.)

NETx.COM	3.01 Rev. C	Not released
EMSNETx.COM	3.01 Rev. C	Not released

```
XMSNETx.COM          3.01 Rev. C          Not released
```

- Using the "Preferred Server" option with the Rev B shell caused the network response time to be functionally slower than if the user did not use this option.

- When using DOS 4.0 with the EMSNETx and XMSNETx shells, the DOS directories would not display correctly under Windows.

- The enhanced memory shells were not sending header information when using print job configurations that included escape codes. For example, a print job that should print landscape would print using the default mode (portrait).

- When printing to a captured LPT device, a "Device not ready" error message would appear. A retry would allow the job to continue.

- Fake roots were being deleted on paths with volume names before the path was determined valid; for example, CD PRN: would delete the fake root.

- On NetWare v2.x-based servers, memory in Dynamic Memory Pool 1 (DMP 1) was not being released properly with the XMSNETx and EMSNETx shells, eventually causing the server to hang. With the v3.01 Rev C shell, the memory is released when the user exits the Windows DOS prompt.

Shell v3.01 Rev D

The NetWare DOS shell v3.01 Rev D, dated 9-7-90, was released to users and contains all of the changes listed above for the Rev C shell.

Another release of the Rev D shell occurred on 9-18-90.

```
NETx.COM             3.01 Rev. D          9-18-90
EMSNETx.COM          3.01 Rev. D          9-18-90
XMSNETx.COM          3.01 Rev. D          9-18-90
```

This release contained the following changes:

- When running the v3.01 Rev D shell with a NetWare v2.15 or previous OS, external program execution from the login script (using the # command) does not work unless the user has Open privileges at the volume root. This was corrected in the shells dated 9-18-90 and later.

- The NVER command returns Rev C instead of Rev D. This was corrected in the shells dated 9-18-90 and later.

Shell v3.01 Rev E

This revision of the shell included the files listed below.

```
NETx.COM             3.01 Rev. E          11-27-90
EMSNETx.COM          3.01 Rev. E          11-27-90
XMSNETx.COM          3.01 Rev. E          11-27-90
```

This revision corrected the following problems and also incorporated several enhancements:

- When using the DOS 4.0 "TrueName" command (an undocumented DOS command), invalid data was returned to the shell. This invalid data causes Emerald's System's backup to not function properly.

- Microsoft Link was reporting a scratched file error when linking a large number of files.

- The rename function returned the wrong error code to applications such as Platinum Accounting by Advanced Business Microsystems. This error was also exhibited with the NETGEN message "Cannot find DRVRDATA.DAT."

- The shell was not correctly maintaining the default server after logout when an X.25 bridge was used.

- On ELS NetWare servers, you would get one less connection than the maximum when using remote boot. The v3.01 Rev E shell allows the maximum number of server connections.

- Rev E enabled file caching in EMSNETx and XMSNETx shells, which was not enabled in earlier releases of the enhanced memory shells.

- Rev E added support for the VERSION.EXE utility, which was not present in earlier releases of the shell.

- Rev E added the "/?" option to the command line, to display version and usage information.

- Rev E added a feature that informs the user if a terminate-and-stay-resident (TSR) program is loaded above the shell when the user is trying to unload the shell.

Shell v3.02
Version 3.02 of the NetWare DOS shell included the files listed below.

NETx.COM	3.02	2-06-91
EMSNETx.COM	3.02	2-06-91
XMSNETx.COM	3.02	2-06-91

This release contained the following fixes and enhancements:

- Corrected a problem that caused some applications that use EMS or XMS (such as DESQview, NetRemote, and such) to occasionally hang when using the enhanced memory shells.

- Corrected a problem where capturing to a file would result in truncated print files. These files are now created and printed correctly.

- Unloading the shell now relinquishes all connections (previously it retained one connection).

- Corrected a problem with the file caching introduced with the NetWare shell v3.01 Rev E. Users were experiencing problems when running Paradox, Quattro, and Lotus 1-2-3 with the extended memory shells.

- Enhanced the speed of file caching, which improves the speed of file read and writes.

- Setting the parameter "CACHE BUFFERS = 0" in the NET.CFG file now turns off the shell's file caching.

- Added two new NET.CFG parameters—DOS NAME and ENVIRONMENT PAD:

  DOS NAME=name

  This option specifies the name of the DOS version used by the workstation. This name could be something like "MSDOS," "PCDOS," "DRDOS," and should correspond to the %OS name in the login script and the name of the DOS directory. The maximum length of the DOS NAME is five characters.

  ENVIRONMENT PAD=number

  This option specifies the number of bytes that can be added to the DOS environment space for storing search drive path names. If you are specifying many long path names for search drives with the MAP command, you may need to add extra environment space to hold those names. The number of bytes can be any number from 17 to 512 (17 is the default). Novell recommends that you leave this option at the default value unless you are encountering environment space problems.

Shell v3.10

Version 3.10 of the NetWare DOS shell included the new NET5.COM, XMSNET5.EXE, and EMSNET5.EXE files that work with DOS 5.0.

NETx.COM	3.10	3-07-91
EMSNETx.COM	3.10	3-07-91
XMSNETx.COM	3.10	3-07-91

Shell v3.21

Starting with this release of the NetWare DOS shell, the same three files—NETX.COM, XMSNETX.EXE, and EMSNETX.EXE—work with DOS 3.x, 4.x, and 5.x. This is the so-called "generic" shell.

NETX.COM	3.21	7-18-91
EMSNETX.COM	3.21	7-18-91
XMSNETX.COM	3.21	7-18-91

In addition, the v3.21 shell contained the following corrections and enhancements:

- Fixed a problem with the "Preferred Server" function that caused some machines to hang randomly.

- Fixed a problem with being denied simultaneous access to a shared file.

- Corrected "call 5" functions for programs ported from CP/M to DOS.

- Resolved a problem where Btrieve files were being corrupted when the server was downed improperly.

- Fixed a cache problem that was causing a WordPerfect disk full error.

- Fixed the DOS NAME parameter problem that was causing the EMS and XMS shells to hang when loading.

- Fixed the problem with the "P_STATION" variable returning bad information in the login script. (This problem occurred only with the v3.2 shell.)

- Fixed a problem that was causing DOS 5.0 "Load High" not to work properly with NET5.COM. (DOS "Load High" works with NETX.COM v3.21 and later.)

- Fixed a problem that caused the DOS 5.0 MEM program to display program names improperly after the shell was loaded.

- Fixed a problem that made the DOS ATTRIB command unable to find hidden directories on network drives.

- Fixed a problem with remote boot on workstations with hard drives.

- Added the "/C = filename" option to allow flexible naming of the shell configuration file (for instance, /C=NET.CFG).

- Added the "/F" option to allow the shell to be unloaded after it has been loaded high.

- Added a date code to the shell. The command "NETX i" will now display the shell's date of creation along with the version and copyright information.

- Added a feature to display the version of DOS that is currently running when the shell is loaded.

- Enhanced the shell to be able to locate the master environment regardless of its location.

- Added support for EMS memory handle names.

- Added support for international date and time formats.

Shell v3.22
This release of the NetWare DOS shell corrected a problem with remote boot and DOS 5.0. Previously, the shell would look to the F drive rather than the A (virtual) drive.

NETX.COM	3.22	7-31-91
EMSNETX.EXE	3.22	7-31-91
XMSNETX.EXE	3.22	7-31-91

Shell v3.26
This release of the NetWare DOS shell included the new Burst Mode (Packet Burst) shell, BNETX.COM.

NETX.COM	3.26	2-11-92
BNETX.COM	3.26	2-11-92
EMSNETX.EXE	3.26	2-11-92
XMSNETX.EXE	3.26	2-11-92

It incorporated the following corrections and enhancements:

- Corrected a problem where CAPTURE would return "garbage" characters to the screen when capturing without a specified queue name.

- Corrected a problem in which COMSPEC was not being reset to the local drive when the shell was unloaded with COMSPEC set to a network drive.

- Corrected a problem with the MS-DOS DOSNAME function not working properly with EMSNETX.EXE and XMSNETX.EXE.

- Corrected a problem with certain database applications which issue the commit file command. (The file is now properly updated on the file server disk.)

- Corrected network errors due to a packet size negotiation problem. This problem occurred when using the "Preferred Server" option on a workstation with a packet size greater than that of the preferred server, and the initial server also had a packet size greater than the preferred server.

- Enhanced the shell so that memory display applications such as the MSDOS MEM program display the name of the shell as well as its size and location.

- Added a procedure to check if the total of "FILE HANDLES=" in NET.CFG and "FILES=" in CONFIG.SYS exceeds 254. If so, an error is returned and the shell is not loaded.

- Added two new NET.CFG parameters—SEARCH DIR FIRST and NCP TIMEOUT FLAG:

SEARCH DIR FIRST=ON/OFF

This option determines the order in which the shell searches files and directories on a NetWare file server. If SEARCH DIR FIRST=ON, the shell searches for directories first. If SEARCH DIR FIRST=OFF, the shell searches for files first. The default is OFF.

SEARCH DIR FIRST applies only to handle-oriented directory searches, as from within Windows' File Manager, not to FCB directory searches, as in DOS's DIR command.

NCP TIMEOUT Options

These options add the ability to change the default timeout value of the shell. Three options need to be set:

```
NCP TIMEOUT FLAG=ON    (default is OFF)
NCP TIMEOUT BASE=n     (default is 10; range 1-255)
NCP TIMEOUT MULTIPLIER=n   (default is 4; range 1-255)
```

If only "NCP TIMEOUT FLAG=ON" is set, the shell uses the default values for the NCP timeout base and multiplier. Setting the base and multiplier lower than these default values reduces the shell's timeout. Setting the values too low will cause an excessive number of network errors.

Increasing the base by increments of 1 increases the NCP timeout by 1 tick. The shell multiplies the NCP TIMEOUT BASE number by the value set for NCP TIMEOUT MULTI-PLIER. The result should not exceed 255.

NOTE: This option was added for unusual circumstances and may cause unpredictable results when used incorrectly! Novell recommends that these values not be changed from the defaults except in special circumstances.

Shell v3.30

This revision of the NetWare DOS client software was not released. The changes and enhancements detailed below were all incorporated into the v3.31 release dated 11-12-92.

```
NETX.EXE            3.30              Not released
BNETX.EXE           3.30              Not released
EMSNETX.EXE         3.30              Not released
XMSNETX.EXE         3.30              Not released
```

This revision of the shell incorporates some significant enhancements that enable it to work with upcoming products such as SFT Level III and NetWare v4.0. (A v3.30 client can attach to a NetWare v4.0 server, but the shell does not support any Directory Services functionality.)

- The v3.30 shell has been language enabled so that all initialization and run-time messages are accessed from the NETX.MSG file. This file must be located in the same directory as NETX.EXE.

- NETX and BNETX are now .EXE files. This makes it easier to load them high, since the message file is appended and doesn't affect the load image size. It now takes a 60KB contiguous upper memory block (UMB) to load NETX.EXE high.

NOTE: If *NETX.COM files reside in the same directory as *NETX.EXE files, users must rename or remove the *.COM files to be able to run the *.EXE files.

- Fixed the shell to allow it to be unloaded when it has been loaded into a UMB.

- Modified the shell so it can correctly handle doublebyte and foreign characters in path and file names. Removed support for the SPECIAL UPPERCASE keyword in NET.CFG.

- Enhanced the shell to handle broadcast messages that, when translated, are longer than the current maximum 22-character clear text message. When the user presses <Ctrl>+<Enter>, the remainder of the message will be displayed.

- Enhanced the shell so that broadcast messages are always displayed at the bottom of the screen. The shell now reads the number of active display rows before displaying the broadcast message.

- Enhanced the shell's ability to adapt to network changes by re-negotiating packet size when a router or an SFT III mirrored server goes down.

- Added Large Internet Packet (LIP) capability for routers that are enabled for large packets. Refer to the documentation that accompanies the LIP software.

- In light of Novell's change of the default Ethernet frame type from 802.3 to 802.2, support was added for IPX checksumming on 802.2 frames.

- Changed how the shell looks for its configuration file:

  1. It first looks for a NET.CFG file in the current working directory.

  2. If not found, it looks for a NET.CFG file in the directory the LSL was loaded from, or in the current working directory at the time the LSL was loaded, in that order.

  3. If still not found, it looks for a SHELL.CFG file in the current working directory.

- Fixed a memory allocation error caused when the ENVIRONMENT PAD variable in NET.CFG was set below the minimum of 11 decimal.

- Fixed a problem where the shell was printing out the "Pipe not found in transient portion of COMMAND.COM" warning when the shell had already patched the pipe string. It now only prints the warning if the shell couldn't find a pipe string, either modified or not.

- Fixed a bug that was causing the shell, when used with IPXODI, to hang after receiving a broadcast.

- Fixed a problem where the shell was changing the value of the stack pointer without disabling interrupts first, which caused occasional lockups.

Shell v3.31

The latest release of the NetWare DOS client software supports the "NCP Packet Signature" security enhancement for NetWare v3.11.

NETX.EXE	3.31	11-12-92
BNETX.EXE	3.31	11-12-92
EMSNETX.EXE	3.31	11-12-92
XMSNETX.EXE	3.31	11-12-92

It incorporates the following corrections and enhancements:

- Enhanced all shell files to perform NCP packet signing. This feature is enabled through the following NET.CFG setting:

SIGNATURE LEVEL = n

The default value for n is 1, which means the client signs packets only if the server requests it. Other valid values are:

0 Client does not sign packet

2 Client signs packets if the server is capable of signing

3 Client signs packets and requires the server to sign packets (or logging in will fail)

Refer to the documentation file that comes with the security enhancement for more information.

- Added two new NET.CFG parameters to limit packet sizes:

LI FRAME MAX=n

Sets the maximum frame size when using Large Internet Packet (LIP). The default is 8192 bytes (8KB). Valid range for n is 512 to 16,384 bytes.

PB FRAME MAX=n

Sets the maximum frame size when using Burst Mode (Packet Burst).

The default is 2112 bytes. Valid range for n is 576 to 8256 bytes.

In almost all cases, the default values are the best ones to use. These parameters should be changed only by a qualified NetWare technician.

- Fixed a problem where the shell would not unload properly under DR DOS v6.0.

- Fixed several problems with the Burst Mode shell: a memory allocation bug, an incomplete write problem, and a timing problem that was manifest in various ways, including hanging under Windows.

INDEX

F

M

RoseWare
A RoseWare Publication

Special Bantam Offer

Announcing the Network Developer's Resource!

The *Network Developer's Resource (NDR)* is a technical newsletter that addresses the complex topics facing you, the networking professional, today. Now that you have purchased *NetWare Power Tools for Windows* you have the opportunity to receive a monthly journal that provides you with up-to-date technical information about NetWare.

Every month you will receive information on the latest NetWare API's, bug fixes, NetWare products, and new technologies. You'll see complete code samples explaining in detail how to perform a particular function. You will be able to download these code samples from our support section within the Novell Vendor Forum on CompuServe (type GO ROSEWARE while on CompuServe®).

Who are we?

The *Network Developer's Resource* is edited and published by Charles Rose, author of the *Programmer's Guide to NetWare* and *NetWare Power Tools for Windows*. Rose works daily as a sysop on the NOVDEV forum on CompuServe, Novell's private forum for

GO ROSE-WARE

Visit our section on the Novell Vendor Forum on CompuServe! Just type GO ROSEWARE. Subscribers get a FREE CompuServe Introductory Membership.

YES! Send my FREE issue of the *Network Developer's Resource* and start my one year subscription (12 issues in all) for $95 (25% off the regular rate!). I will start receiving other issues and my FREE CompuServe Starter Kit when I have paid the invoice.

(Cut-out and mail this form TODAY! or contact us via e-mail, phone, BBS, or fax)

Name _____

Company _____

Address _____

City _____ State __ Zip Code _____

Phone _____ Fax _____

Address:	RoseWare
	P.O. Box 257
	Mount Vernon, VA 22121-0257
Phone:	(703) 799-2509
Fax:	(703) 799-8041
BBS:	(703) 799-2536 (V.32bis)
CompuServe:	76711,110
InterNet:	76711.110@compuserve.com

Novell Professional Developers' Program members, and stays on top of the questions you have about developing for NetWare. In the spirit of *Programmer's Guide to NetWare*, Rose will ensure that you receive the most in-depth and hands-on discussions of topics you want to read about.

What's in it?

Many issues face networking professionals in 1993 and the *NDR* will be covering them in-depth and hands-on. You won't want to miss coverage of topics like NetWare 4.0, Windows for Workgroups, OS/2, UnixWare, and Windows/NT. Here is just a small sample of articles upcoming this year:

- Configuring and Developing on the Workstation Client. Virtual Loadable Modules (VLMs), new utilities, and changes that you should be aware of.

- NetWare 4.0, Migrating to the New APIs. A continuing series of articles covering the new and changing APIs in NetWare 4.0, and how to convert your applications.

- Making Windows for Workgroups work in the NetWare Environment. Microsoft may have gone too far in their claims of NetWare compatibility for Windows for Workgroups, but the *NDR* will pull it together and sort out the issues surrounding NDIS, ODI, and configuring Windows for Workgroups to work with NetWare.

- An Intimate Look at the NetWare APIs. While many of the NetWare APIs are documented, you often need a deeper level of understanding to make them truly useful. In this series, we will probe the NetWare APIs and discuss the often hidden workings of them. Expect to see lots of examples and source code.

- Getting the Message with NetWare MHS and NetWare Global Messaging. Whether you're a developer interested in writing applications for MHS, or just want to know how to better troubleshoot your e-mail systems, we'll help put the pieces into perspective.

End-User License Agreement
Limited Warranty and Damage Disclaimer

PLEASE READ THIS NOTICE BEFORE OPENING THE PACKAGE CONTAINING THE SOFTWARE PROGRAM AND RELATED MATERIALS, IF ANY (COLLECTIVELY, THE "PRODUCT"). OPENING THE PACKAGE OR USING ITS CONTENTS CONSTITUTES YOUR COMPLETE AND UNCONDITIONAL ACCEPTANCE OF THE TERMS AND CONDITIONS OF THIS END-USER LICENSE AGREEMENT ("AGREEMENT"). IF YOU DO NOT AGREE WITH THESE TERMS AND CONDITIONS, PROMPTLY RETURN THE UNOPENED PACKAGE TO THE POINT OF PURCHASE FOR FULL REFUND. SHOULD YOU HAVE ANY QUESTIONS CONCERNING THIS AGREEMENT, YOU MAY CONTACT AUTOMATED DESIGN SYSTEMS, INC., BY WRITING AUTOMATED DESIGN SYSTEMS, INC., 375 NORTHRIDGE ROAD, SUITE 270, ATLANTA, GA 30350.

License: Automated Design Systems, Inc. ("Licensor") hereby grants to you a non-exclusive, non-transferable, and non-assignable license to use the computer software programs in object code form ("Software") on a single processing unit ("file server"). You agree that you will not sublicense, rent, lease, sell, assign, or transfer the Product or share your rights under this license with a third party. You may make one (1) copy of the Software for backup purposes and agree to affix Licensor's copyright and other proprietary rights notices to such copy.

Ownership: You acknowledge and agree that all right, title, and interest in and to the Product are and shall remain with Licensor. This Agreement conveys to you only a limited right of use revocable in accordance with the terms of this Agreement.

Limited Warranty: Licensor warrants to you that for a period of ninety (90) days from the date you receive this Product the magnetic media contains an accurate reproduction of the Software. This limited warranty covers only the original user of the Product. Licensor does not warrant that the Product will be free from error or will meet your specific requirements. Except for the warranties set forth above, the Product is licensed "as is," and LICENSOR DISCLAIMS ANY AND ALL

OTHER WARRANTIES, WHETHER EXPRESS OR IMPLIED, INCLUDING WITHOUT LIMITATION, ANY IMPLIED WARRANTIES OF MERCHANT ABILITY AND FITNESS FOR A PARTICULAR PURPOSE. Some states do not allow limitations on how long implied warranty lasts, so the above limitations may not apply to you. This warranty gives you specific legal rights, and you may also have other rights which may vary from state to state.

Limitation of Liability: You acknowledge and agree that in no event will Licensor, its affiliates, or any officers, directors, employees, or agents thereof be liable to you or any third party for injury or damage caused directly or indirectly by the Product, including but not limited to, incidental, special, consequential, indirect, or exemplary damages, and legal expenses or loss of good will, whether based on contract, tort, or otherwise arising out of or resulting from or in connection with the use of or inability to use or performance of the Product, even if Licensor has been advised of the possibility of such damages or costs. Some states do not allow the exclusion or limitation of incidental or consequential damages so the above limitation or exclusion may not apply to you.

U.S. Government Restricted Rights: The product is provided with RESTRICTED AND LIMITED RIGHTS. Use, duplication, or disclosure by the U.S. Government is subject to restriction as set forth in FAR S52.227-14 (June 1987) Alternate III (8) (3) (June 1987), FAR S52.227-19 (June 1987), or DFARS S52.227-7013 (c) (1) (iii) (June 1987) as applicable. Contractor/manufacturer is Automated Design Systems, Inc., 375 Northridge Road, Suite 270, Atlanta, GA 30350.

Term & Termination: The limited license granted to you is effective from the date you open this package and shall continue until terminated. You may terminate it at any time by returning the Product to Licensor. The license will also terminate automatically if you fail to comply with any term or condition of this Agreement. You agree upon termination for any reason to return the Product together with any copies to Licensor.

Severability: Should any term of this Agreement be declared void or unenforceable by any court of competent jurisdiction, such declaration shall have no effect on the remaining terms hereof.

Governing Law: This agreement is governed by and construed in accordance with the laws of the State of Georgia.

IBM Compatible 5.25" Diskettes

This Bantam software product is also available in an IBM compatible 5.25"/1.2M format. If you'd like to exchange this software for the 5.25" format, please:

- Package your original 3.5" diskettes in a mailer.
- Include a check or money order for US $7.95 ($9.95 Canadian) to cover media, postage and handling (California and Massachusetts residents add sales tax). Foreign orders: Please send international money orders; no foreign checks accepted.
- Include your completed warranty card.

Upon receipt Bantam will immediately send your replacement disks via first class mail.

Mail to: Bantam Electronic Publishing
1540 Broadway
New York, NY 10036
Attn: NWPTW/5.25 Disk